Albert SCHWEITZER

An International Bibliography

Photograph by Erica Anderson.

Albert SCHWEITZER

An International Bibliography

NANCY SNELL GRIFFITH
LAURA PERSON

G.K.HALL &CO.

70 LINCOLN STREET, BOSTON, MASS.

Library of Congress Cataloging in Publication Data

Griffith, Nancy Snell.
　Albert Schweitzer　:　an international bibliography.

　Includes index.
　1.　Schweitzer, Albert, 1875-1965--Bibliography.
I.　Person,　Laura.　II.　Title.
Z8797.75.G74　[CT1018.S45]　016.610'92'4　81-747
ISBN 0-8161-8531-X　　　　　　　　　AACR2

This publication is printed on permanent/durable acid-free paper
MANUFACTURED IN THE UNITED STATES OF AMERICA

To

John, Matthew,

and

Christopher

Contents

Contents

Contents

The Authors

The late Laura Person was a librarian by profession. She initiated
the research into the writings of and about Albert Schweitzer that is
contained in this volume. Mrs. Person, a native of Pennsylvania,
sought to gather the voluminous materials concerning Dr. Schweitzer
from many countries, and traveled to Europe to supplement the information she had already collected in the United States. Her ability to
speak and write in German and in French helped greatly in her work.

Nancy Snell Griffith was graduated summa cum laude, Phi Beta
Kappa in 1968 from Dickinson College, Carlisle, Pennsylvania, with
majors in English and German literature. She did graduate work in
German at Johns Hopkins University and in 1978 received a Master of
Library Science degree from the School of Information Studies,
Syracuse University. In the autumn of 1978, under the auspices of
the Albert Schweitzer Fellowship, she undertook to complete the international bibliography of writings both by and about Albert
Schweitzer. Hers was the enormous task not only to update and
augment the existing material but also to verify titles and organize
and prepare the manuscript for publication.

Forewords

The greatness of Schweitzer--indeed the essence of Schweitzer--is the man as symbol. It is not so much what he has done for others, but what others have done because of him and the power of his example. This is the measure of the man. What has come out of his life and thought is the kind of inspiration that can animate a generation. He has supplied a working demonstration of reverence for life. He represents enduring proof that we need not torment ourselves about the nature of human purpose. The scholar, he once wrote, must not live for science alone, nor the businessman for his business, nor the artist for his art. If affirmation for life is genuine, it will "demand from all that they should sacrifice a portion of their own lives for others."

Thus, Schweitzer's main achievement was a simple one. He was willing to make the ultimate sacrifice for a moral principle. And because he was able to feel a supreme identification with other human beings he exerted a greater force than millions of armed men on the march. It is unimportant whether we call Schweitzer a great religious figure or a great moral figure or a great philosopher. It suffices that his words and works are known and that he is loved and had influence because he enabled men to discover mercy in themselves.

Schweitzer's aim was not to dazzle an age but to awaken it, to make it comprehend that moral splendor is part of the gift of life, and that each man has unlimited strength to feel human oneness and to act upon it. He proved that although a man may have no jurisdiction over the fact of his existence, he can hold supreme command over the meaning of existence for him. Thus, no man need fear death; he need fear only that he may die without having known his greatest power--the power of his free will to give his life for others.

Norman Cousins
Honorary President
Albert Schweitzer Fellowship
and
Chairman, Board of Directors
Albert Schweitzer Center

Albert Schweitzer was truly one who, by deed, gave meaningful expression to his philosophy. In his ninety-year span he touched many lives, and we can see today from the wide range of writings by and about him, the extent of his influence. Albert Schweitzer's message was a simple one: to respect oneself, one must respect others. Whether by delivering sermons, treating the sick, or speaking out for disarmament and on the awesome consequences of an atomic war, he gave witness to his ethic of "Reverence for Life."

In 1939, American friends and colleagues formed the Albert Schweitzer Fellowship to help him continue his mission of medical aid to the people of Lambarene. This major purpose of the Fellowship continues, and has been expanded to include a second major function: to inform and educate people about the philosophy and ethic of Albert Schweitzer.

The initial efforts of Laura Person to amass a bibliography of writings by and about Dr. Schweitzer has been a considerable part of the Fellowship's information and education purpose. Mrs. Person's dedication to this task over a span of twenty years was invaluable. In more recent years, the work directed by Antje B. Lemke and carried out by Nancy Griffith have brought this bibliography to fruition. The Fellowship is grateful to them, and to G. K. Hall, publishers of this volume, for making this publication available to a wide audience.

Lawrence Gussman
President
Albert Schweitzer Fellowship

Preface

Purpose

This bibliography has been prepared to provide Schweitzer scholars
and others interested in the work of Albert Schweitzer with a comprehensive record of publications by and about Albert Schweitzer. The
last extensive Schweitzer bibliography was compiled by Robert Amadou
(see no. 4794) in 1952. There have been selective lists in connection
with books, dissertations, and exhibitions, but none of these has attempted comprehensiveness.

The arrangement and documentation given for each title are de-
signed to meet the needs of those with a general interest in Albert
Schweitzer, as well as those who want to pursue specific aspects,
e.g., musicians, theologians, or ecologists.

Scope

Included in this bibliography are books, articles, dissertations,
pamphlets, major journals, films, and recordings by and about Albert
Schweitzer from 1875-1979. An effort has been made to list the publications of Albert Schweitzer as completely as possible. This effort
has not been made concerning the materials about Albert Schweitzer.
Even when known to the compiler, some items had to be excluded because
of redundancy and the impossibility of tracing every brief statement
in publications like regional religious papers or pharmaceutical ad-
vertisements. Such materials as birthday tributes and obituaries have
been included only if they have significant subject content.

Materials that could be examined or traced in bibliographies and
indexes have been verified. Others have been included on the basis
of secondary references that were provided by reliable sources. The
coverage of materials from North America and Western Europe did not
present any problems; other areas were more difficult to research,
and omissions there are possible.

Preface

Subject Arrangement

The actual bibliography is preceded by a chronology of Schweitzer's life, a chronological list of his major works, and a list of title abbreviations; frequently cited works have been abbreviated in the text; these abbreviations are listed in alphabetical order, with full entries for the works to which they refer. The material in the bib-liography itself is arranged by subject first, and is then divided into works by and about Schweitzer within each subject. In each of the sections, works by and about Schweitzer are divided into books and articles.

This subject classification posed two major difficulties. The first arose from the fact that this is a two-person bibliography. Laura Person had classified hundreds of entries; those added later were classified by me. In some cases there may be inconsistencies in our ideas of what should go into the various subject areas. The sec-ond difficulty arises from the impossibility of examining some of the more recent materials, especially those in non-English sources. Where the items were not available, I attempted to verify their subject con-tent from other sources or to classify them from external evidence such as the title. Where this was impossible, they were omitted.

Each section devoted to a book of Schweitzer's, or each major subject section, such as those on Goethe or peace, is preceded by a brief background sketch. Laura Person had written some of these; others were added later. In a letter to Arthur Denues in December 1972, Laura Person stated her rationale for this:

> I should explain that when I first started the bibliography,
> I thought it might be of interest to those who did not have
> the background of A.S.'s books, or to students, to know
> something of the circumstances, or reasons, for the writing
> of his various works. So it was that I undertook to add an
> introductory paragraph, or introduction, under the title of
> each of his books, taking my facts generally from prefaces
> or from Aus meinem Leben und Denken. . . .

This practice was continued, using the same sources, for the more recent works and for sections which she had not completed.

The general subject arrangement of the bibliography is as follows:

Collected and Selected Works. Lists the collected (but not complete) edition of Schweitzer's works which appeared in Japan, and the edi-tion of selected works published in Germany, which includes most of Schweitzer's books and shorter works but excludes his works on Bach.

Anthologies, Collections, Festschriften, and Other Writings. Includes collections of works by and about Schweitzer. Anthologies on spe-cific subjects (such as Reverence for Life, sermons, etc.) have been included in the appropriate subject sections, with cross-references here. Selections from Schweitzer's works which include all or a major part of the original work have been indexed in the title index of works by Schweitzer.

Life and Work. Includes materials of a general biographical nature covering several phases of Schweitzer's life. This excludes biographies specifically for youth, which are in the separate youth section, and films, which are included under drama and films. The section is divided into several parts:

1. General.
2. Works about Helene Schweitzer-Bresslau.
3. Works about other family, friends and coworkers, including tributes written by Schweitzer and those written by others. Tributes written by Schweitzer about musicians are found in the general music section. The section of materials written about Schweitzer's friends and coworkers is not comprehensive.
4. Accounts of visits and meetings with Schweitzer. Where possible, this section includes only visits to Schweitzer other than at Lambarene. The latter are included in the next section on Africa and Lambarene.

Africa and Lambarene. Includes general materials on Schweitzer's work in Africa, except those of a technical medical nature. The materials by Schweitzer in this section are divided into:

1. Books and articles of general description.
2. Report letters and bulletins sent to Schweitzer supporters and periodicals. These are arranged chronologically.

The various Schweitzer periodicals and newsletters contain reports by workers and administrators at the hospital; not all of these have been included. Rather, a representative sample of the more significant has been provided. For a complete record the individual issues of the periodicals can be consulted.

Medicine. Includes works by and about Schweitzer related to his work as a doctor. The Psychological Study of Jesus is included here because, although it is also theological in nature, it was written in completion of his medical degree. The other materials concern the professional medical aspects of Schweitzer's work at Lambarene.

Philosophy. Contains two sections:

1. A general section with books and articles by and about Schweitzer on philosophy in general. Some of these include theology, and, where necessary, cross-references have been made.
2. Materials which deal primarily with Schweitzer's ethic of Reverence for Life. There are also, of course, works in the more general section which touch on this topic.

Preface

Theology and Religion. Contains two sections:
1. A general section of titles dealing with theology in general. Some of these cover philosophy also; again, appropriate cross-references have been made.
2. Anthologies and reprints of Schweitzer's sermons, as well as articles written specifically about them, or about Schweitzer as preacher.

Music. Contains four sections:
1. General, including tributes written by Schweitzer to other musicians.
2. Works on Bach and Schweitzer's relationship to him, including his treatise on the round violin bow.
3. Works on organs and organ building, including articles dealing with Schweitzer's organ concerts.
4. A discography, including a representative list of reviews of Schweitzer's various recordings.

Albert Schweitzer and Johann Wolfgang von Goethe. Includes the four speeches and one essay which Schweitzer wrote on Goethe, and commentaries on each. Contains two parts:
1. Includes these five items as they were published either monographically or in periodicals or parts of books.
2. Includes books and articles by others about Schweitzer and Goethe.

Albert Schweitzer and World Peace. Contains four parts:
1. General works on peace both by and about Schweitzer.
2. Works by and about Schweitzer in relationship to the German peace prize.
3. Schweitzer's Nobel Peace Prize address and works about it.
4. Materials by and about Schweitzer on the subject of the nuclear test ban.

Each section is subdivided into monographs and articles by Albert Schweitzer, and monographs and articles about him.

Miscellaneous Works by Albert Schweitzer. Includes works of various types which could not be categorized under the various subject areas: letters (not dealing with one of the subject areas); speeches, addresses, and lectures (excluding sermons and speeches on Goethe, peace, the nuclear test ban, and other specific subjects); prefaces in books by others; and miscellaneous items.

Miscellaneous Works about Albert Schweitzer. Includes twelve different areas of material about Schweitzer:
1. Honors and awards, including prizes (except the peace and Goethe prizes), honorary degrees, stamps, and other honors.
2. Schweitzer's influence around the world, including education, hospitals, villages, supporting committees, periodicals, and miscellaneous.

xviii

3. Works for youth, including books and articles on various aspects of Schweitzer's life and work intended especially for children. Where available, intended age ranges of materials have been given.
4. Dissertations. Complete entries for dissertations have been given here, with cross-references included in the various subject sections.
5. Drama and films, including a list of films and slide series, and reviews of them. The lists of slide series and reviews are not comprehensive, and constitute primarily samples.
6. Book reviews. This is a representative, but not exhaustive, list of reviews of Schweitzer's works in various languages. Entries are classified alphabetically by the English title of the work reviewed, and then arranged alphabetically by author or title of review within each section.
7. Meetings and symposia, listing large-scale meetings held to honor Albert Schweitzer. If proceedings are available, this is indicated, as are articles relating to the event. Individual papers presented at each meeting are included in the appropriate subject sections.
8. Bibliographies. Lists entire books, exhibition catalogs, and bibliographies in articles or books. Those in books were included only if they were five or more pages in length. The general scope of those bibliographies that could be examined is indicated.
9. Poetry. Includes poems, available to the compiler, written about Schweitzer and his work. This is a sample only.
10. Fiction.
11. Complete journal issues. Includes the names of journals which devoted complete issues or significant parts of issues to Albert Schweitzer. Separate articles are included in the appropriate subject areas.
12. Miscellaneous works about Albert Schweitzer.

Indexes
There are two indexes:
1. Personal name index. Includes, in alphabetical order, the names of authors, editors, compilers, photographers, correspondents, and subjects of works.
2. Title index. Includes sections for titles of works by Albert Schweitzer and titles of works about him. If one of Schweitzer's works is the subject of an item, and its title serves as the entire title of the item, it is not listed in the index of works about Schweitzer, but in the index of works by Schweitzer as a subject.

For further information on the indexes and their use, please refer to the instructions preceding each index.

An addendum, covering materials published or discovered during publication has been included preceding the indexes. These entries have not been indexed.

Preface

Arrangement within each Subject Section

1. Articles by Schweitzer are arranged alphabetically by title; articles and books about Schweitzer have been arranged alphabetically by author, or by title where the author is not known. Where possible, translations or reprints of articles are all included under the entry for the original publication of the piece.

2. Books by Schweitzer are listed chronologically within each subject area. Under each subject work, the language of original publication is listed first, with the languages of the various translations following in alphabetical order. Where possible, new editions or reprints have been noted, as far as this information has been available.

Format of Entries

1. Books

       author   title

NOSSIK, BORIS. Albert Schweitzer; ein Leben für die Menschlichkeit.

                       city of
      translator   publ.   publisher

Tr. Lothar Pickenhain. Leipzig: S. Hirzel Verlag,

date of
publ.   pages   series (if any)

1977. 372 pp. (Series: Humanisten der Tat).

Also included here might be ed. (editor), comp. (compiler), illus. (illustrations), etc.

2. Articles

       author   title of article

GELL, CHRISTOPHER W. M. "Dr. Schweitzer--a Reassessment."

                  city of vol. date of
    name of journal   publ.   no.   publ.

The Hibbert Journal (London) 55:4 (July 1957),

pages.

pp. 330-34.

3. Parts of Books

        author of   title of
        selection   selection   title of book

COUSINS, NORMAN.   "Albert Schweitzer." In: <u>Heroes for our</u>
                                             <u>Times.</u>

      authors and/or editors of book if different from author

      Edited for the Overseas Press Club of America by Will

                               city of
        of selection   publ.   publ.

      Yolen and Kenneth S. Giniger. New York: Giniger,

      date of pages on which
      publ.   selection appears

      1968, pp. 150-69.

All journal entries have been Anglicized--they are cited under the
original title of the article, followed by volume, number, page, etc.,
rather than Jahrgang, Heft, Seite, etc. Dates have also been Angli-
cized. Where the same author has written several works which appear
in sequence in the bibliography, the author's full name will be given
in the first entry of the sequence, and a line (_____) will be used
in place of the author's name in the remaining entries. Parentheses
around a title indicate that it has been translated or supplied by
the compilers; those around the name of an author mean that the name
was not printed with the piece but has been supplied by the compilers.
Letters to the editor have generally been included with the article
to which they refer. Frequently used titles have been abbreviated
in the text; these abbreviations appear in capital letters, and are
explained in the list of abbreviations at the front of the text.

Acknowledgments

I too would like to acknowledge the help of all those people men-
tioned by Antje Lemke in her introduction. I would also like to
thank Antje herself, whose sponsorship and advice have sustained me
throughout this long project. In addition, I would like to thank
Harriet Kessler, who reviewed the Spanish titles in the bibliography
for accuracy.

Introduction

This long-anticipated bibliography is the first international and comprehensive record of publications by and about Dr. Albert Schweitzer. Covering the years 1898 to 1979, it includes 5003 items.

Anyone familiar with the life and work of Schweitzer realizes the magnitude of such a project, due not only to the worldwide recognition of the Nobel Laureate as one of the great humans of this century, but also to the unusual range of his writings, which encompass philosophy, theology, medicine, and music, and to his long life span. In addition, his publications have been translated into over twenty languages and include many genres, from scholarly works to popular magazines and spoken and music recordings.

With the growing recognition of the significance of Schweitzer's philosophy and lifestyle in recent years, especially in the areas of ethics and ecology, the demand for this bibliography has increased beyond the initial purpose of documentation of Schweitzer's work for scholars in his subject fields. Browsing through the titles in this volume, one can quickly see the close relationship between Schweitzer's concerns and those of today, from human rights and Third World issues to music interpretation and medical ethics.

The compilers, Laura Person and Nancy Griffith, have made every effort to gather information about published materials by and about Schweitzer. Over twenty years ago, Laura Person, librarian at the Mission Research Library of Union Theological Seminary in New York, began this bibliography, which she called her "Lebenswerk," and it indeed became the legacy of her life. After canvassing North American libraries, she visited Schweitzer collections in Europe, supported by the Albert Schweitzer Fellowship in New York. She had hoped to complete a bibliography of all titles in all languages, a goal beyond any compiler's reach. Even in the age of electronic information technology, and with unlimited resources, it would be neither possible nor desirable to produce a record of all materials associated with Albert Schweitzer because of the great amount of duplication and ephemera.

Introduction

When Laura Person died in 1976, she left an immense amount of
files and drafts, including material up to and including 1965, the
year of Schweitzer's death. The major task of verification, updating,
organizing, and editing remained to be done when the Albert Schweitzer
Fellowship became the recipient of Laura Person's papers. It was our
good fortune that Nancy Griffith, a librarian with a background in
theology and foreign languages then at the University of Michigan at
Ann Arbor, was interested in undertaking the gigantic task. In the
course of the three years which she has devoted to it, she has become
much more than an editor, but the coauthor of this bibliography of
Albert Schweitzer.

Among those who have been especially helpful to Laura Person are
Rhena Schweitzer Miller, the daughter of Albert Schweitzer, and Erica
Anderson, documentary filmmaker and close associate of Albert
Schweitzer, as well as many librarians at the universities of
Princeton, Yale, Strasbourg, and other European academic institu-
tions. When Nancy Griffith undertook the project under my guidance,
it could never have succeeded without the constant, knowledgeable
assistance of Estelle Linzer, executive director of the Albert
Schweitzer Fellowship, and the financial support of the Fellowship
Board under the leadership of its president, Larry Gussman. Among
other Schweitzer specialists who have given invaluable advice and
information we would like to thank especially Ali Silver of the
Maison Albert Schweitzer at Günsbach, France; Harold Robles of the
Albert Schweitzer Center at Deventer, Holland; Ardelle Gile of the
Albert Schweitzer Friendship House in Great Barrington, Mass.; the
late Erwin Jacobi of Zürich, Switzerland, who supplied information
on Schweitzer's music writings and recordings; Josef Bogusz and
Henryk Gaertner of Krakow, Poland; Wu Fu Chen of Taipei, Republic
of China; and Robert S. Fraser and Stephen Ferguson of Princeton
University. We are also indebted to the editorial staff at G. K.
Hall, especially to Janice Meagher, Meghan Wander, and Linda Smith
for their skillful assistance in the final, important stages of this
publication.

We are confident that this bibliography will be useful both to
those already interested in Albert Schweitzer and to those who look
for an introduction to his life and thought. Author and publisher
will be grateful for any ideas, suggestions, and additional materials.
With the increase of Schweitzer studies over recent years, the publication of supplements or a new edition is anticipated.

Antje Bultmann Lemke
Professor
School of Information
    Studies
Syracuse University

Chronology

1875	January 14, born in Kaysersberg, Alsace. During the year, family moved to Günsbach.
1880	First music instruction.
1880–1884	Attended village school in Günsbach.
1883	First played the organ.
Autumn 1884–Autumn 1885	Attended Realschule in Münster/Alsace in preparation for the Gymnasium.
Autumn 1885–August 1893	Attended gymnasium in Mülhausen/Alsace.
1893	October, first sojourn in Paris. Studied organ with Widor.
1893–Spring 1898	Studied theology, philosophy, and musical theory at University of Strasbourg.
April 1894–April 1895	Military service.
1896	Decided to devote life to service of humanity beginning at age thirty.
1898	May 6, passed first theology examination before faculty. First publication: Eugene Munch, 1857-1898.
October 1898–March 1899	Second sojourn in Paris. Again studied under Widor.
1899	April–July, studied philosophy and organ in Berlin. July, received Ph.D. at Strasbourg. December, The Religious Philosophy of Kant

published. Appointed to staff of St. Nicolai's
Church in Strasbourg.

1900   "Die Philosophie und die Allgemeine Bildung"
published. July 21, obtained licentiate degree
in theology, Strasbourg. September 23, ordained
as a regular curate, St. Nicolai, Strasbourg.

1901   Publication of The Mystery of the Kingdom of God.
May-September, provisional appointment at St.
Thomas Theological School in Strasbourg.

1903   October, appointed principal of the theological
school in Strasbourg.

1904   Sees article about missionary work in Gabon.
Decides to serve as missionary there himself.

1905   J. S. Bach le musicien-poète published in Paris.
October 13, informed friends of decision to study
medicine, serve in Africa. October, resigned his
post at the theological seminary.

1905-
1912   Medical studies, University of Strasbourg.

1906   The Art of Organ-Building and Organ-Playing in
Germany and France and The Quest of the Historical
Jesus published.

1908   J. S. Bach published.

1909   Third Congress of the International Music Society
in Vienna. Schweitzer responsible for formula-
tion of Internationales Regulativ für Orgelbau.

1911   Published Paul and His Interpreters. December,
passed his medical examinations.

1912   Spring, resigned his post at St. Nicolai.
June 18, married Hélène Bresslau. First two
volumes of Bach's Complete Organ Works published
with Widor.

1913   February, granted Dr. Med. Psychiatric Study of
Jesus published. Second edition of The Quest of
the Historical Jesus published. Volumes 3-5 of
Bach's Complete Organ Works published. March 26,
departed for Lambarene with his wife. Arrived
April 16.

Chronology

1913–1917	First sojourn in Lambarene.
1914	August–November, interned as enemy alien at Lambarene.
1915	September, concept of Reverence for Life came to him during Ogowe River journey.
Fall 1917–Summer 1918	Internment in Bordeaux, Garaison, and St. Remy.
1918	July, returned to Günsbach. Illness.
1919–April 1921	Again served at St. Nicolai, and as a doctor in the Strasbourg city hospital.
1919	January 14, daughter Rhena born.
1920	In Sweden for lectures at the University of Uppsala. Also lectures and concerts to raise money for Lambarene. Awarded honorary doctorate in divinity by the theological faculty of the University of Zürich.
1921	On the Edge of the Primeval Forest published.
1921–1922	Lectures and concerts in Switzerland, England, Sweden, and Denmark.
1923	The Philosophy of Civilization published. Christianity and the Religions of the World published in English; German translation in 1924.
1924	Memoirs of Childhood and Youth published.
April 1924–July 1927	Second sojourn in Lambarene, this time without his wife.
1925	More from the Primeval Forest, Part I, published.
1926	More from the Primeval Forest, Part II, published.
1927	January 21, moved hospital to new site near Lambarene.
July 1927–December 1929	Lectures in Sweden, Denmark, Holland, Great Britain, Czechoslovakia, and Switzerland. Concerts in Germany. Presented Universal Order of Human Merit at Geneva for services to civilization and humanity. Presented honorary degree of doctor of philosophy from the University of Prague.

Chronology

1928	August 28, received Goethe Prize from the city of Frankfurt. <u>More from the Primeval Forest</u>, Part III, published.
December 1929–February 1932	Third sojourn in Africa. His wife joined him until Easter 1930.
1929	<u>Selbstdarstellung</u> published. Awarded honorary doctorates in theology and philosophy, University of Edinburgh.
1930	<u>The Mysticism of Paul the Apostle</u> published.
1931	<u>Out of My Life and Thought</u> published. Awarded honorary doctorate in music, University of Edinburgh.
February 1932–April 1933	In Europe for lectures and concerts.
1932	March 22, Goethe Gedenkrede, Frankfurt. June, awarded honorary doctorate in theology from Oxford and honorary LL.D. from St. Andrews. July, "Goethe als Denker und Mensch," Ulm.
April 1933–January 1934	Fourth sojourn in Africa, again without his wife.
February 1934–February 1935	In Europe.
1934	October, Hibbert Lectures, Manchester College, Oxford: "Religion in Modern Civilization." November, Gifford Lectures in Edinburgh, resulting in separate book on <u>Indian Thought and Its Development</u>, published in same year.
1935	February-August, fifth sojourn in Lambarene, again without his wife.
September 1935–February 1937	In Europe. Second series of Gifford Lectures. Lectures and concerts in England. Recorded Bach organ music for Columbia.
1936	<u>African Hunting Stories</u> published in book form.
February 1937–January 1939	Sixth sojourn in Lambarene, without Hélène.
1938	<u>From My African Notebook</u> published.

Chronology

1939	February, arrived in Europe; returned immediately to Lambarene because of danger of war.
March 1939– October 1949	Seventh sojourn in Lambarene. His wife joined him from 1941–1946.
1948	The Jungle Hospital and Goethe: Two Addresses published.
October 1948– October 1949	Mostly in Europe.
1949	June 11, awarded honorary LL.D. by the University of Chicago. July, Goethe Bicentennial Convocation in Aspen, Colorado. Goethe: Drei Reden published.
October 1949– June 1951	Eighth sojourn in Lambarene. His wife joined him until June 1950.
1950	Goethe: Vier Reden published. A Pelican Tells About His Life published in book form.
1951	July, returned to Europe. Made further recordings for Columbia. September 16, Peace Prize of the West German Book Publishers. December 3, elected to the French Academy.
December 1951– July 1952	Ninth sojourn in Lambarene.
July– December 1952	In Europe for lectures and recitals. September, awarded Paracelsus Medal by the German Medical Society. October, speech before the French Academy. Received Prince Carl Medal, grand medal of the Swedish Red Cross. Installed as a member of the Swedish Royal Academy of Music and awarded an honorary doctorate of theology by the University of Marburg.
December 1952– June 1954	Tenth sojourn in Lambarene.
1953	October, awarded the Nobel Peace Prize for 1952. Awarded honorary degree by University of Kapstadt.
June– December 1954	In Europe. Volume 6 of Bach's Complete Organ Works published with Edouard Nies-Berger. April, letter to the London Daily Herald concerning the H-bomb. November 4, Nobel Peace Prize speech, "The Problem of Peace in the World of Today," in Oslo.

Chronology

December 1954– July 1955	Eleventh sojourn in Lambarene. January 14, 1955, 80th birthday celebrated in Lambarene.
July– December 1955	In Europe. Received Order of Merit in London; Order Pour le Merite, Germany; and honorary Dr. Jur., Cambridge University.
December 1955– June 1957	Twelfth sojourn in Lambarene. Hélène with him until May 22, 1957.
1957	April 23, first nuclear test ban broadcast. June 1, Hélène Schweitzer-Bresslau died in Zürich. June 21–December 4, in Europe. Visited Switzerland and Germany.
December 1957– August 1959	Thirteenth sojourn in Lambarene.
1958	April 28, 29, 30, three addresses over Norwegian radio about nuclear war. Published as Peace or Atomic War. Awarded honorary Dr. Med., University of Münster. Awarded Dr. Theol. h.c., Tübingen.
1959	March 23, awarded Sonning Prize in Copenhagen for "work to the benefit of European culture." August–December, in Europe. September 29, accepted Sonning Prize in Copenhagen. November 18, awarded Joseph Lemaire Prize in Brussels. December, final departure for Lambarene.
1960	January 14, 85th birthday celebrated in Lambarene.
1963	Die Lehre der Ehrfurcht vor dem Leben published.
1965	January 14, 90th birthday celebrated in Lambarene. September 4, died in Lambarene.
1966	Reverence for Life (Strassburger Predigten) published posthumously.
1967	The Kingdom of God and Primitive Christianity published. Volumes 7 and 8 of Bach's Complete Organ Works published.
1974	Was sollen wir tun? published.

Chronological List
of Albert Schweitzer's Major Works

1898   Eugene Munch, 1857–1898

1899   The Religious Philosophy of Kant (Die Religionsphilosophie
        Kants)

1901   The Mystery of the Kingdom of God (Das Messianitäts und
        Leidensgeheimnis)

1905   J. S. Bach le musicien-poète

1906   The Art of Organ-Building and Organ-Playing in Germany and
        France (Deutsche und Französische Orgelbaukunst und
        Orgelkunst)

        The Quest of the Historical Jesus (Von Reimarus zu Wrede:
        eine Geschichte der Leben-Jesu-Forschung)

1908   J. S. Bach

1909   Internationales Regulativ für Orgelbau

1911   Paul and his Interpreters (Geschichte der Paulinischen
        Forschung)

1912   First two volumes of J. S. Bach's Complete Organ Works
        (with C. M. Widor)

1913   Psychiatric Study of Jesus (Die Psychiatrische Beurteilung
        Jesu)

        Second edition of The Quest of the Historical Jesus
        (Geschichte der Leben-Jesu-Forschung)

        Volumes 3–5 of Complete Organ Works (again with C. M. Widor)

1921   On the Edge of the Primeval Forest (Zwischen Wasser und
        Urwald)

1923   The Philosophy of Civilization (Kulturphilosophie)

            Christianity and the Religions of the World (Das Christentum und die Weltreligionen)

1924   Memoirs of Childhood and Youth (Aus meiner Kindheit und Jugendzeit)

1925   More from the Primeval Forest (Mitteilungen aus Lambarene), Part I

1926   More from the Primeval Forest (Mitteilungen aus Lambarene), Part II

1928   More from the Primeval Forest (Mitteilungen aus Lambarene), Part III

1929   Selbstdarstellung

1930   The Mysticism of Paul the Apostle (Die Mystik des Apostels Paulus)

1931   Out of My Life and Thought (Aus meinem Leben und Denken)

1934   Indian Thought and Its Development (Die Weltanschauung der Indischen Denker)

1936   African Hunting Stories (Afrikanische Jagdgeschichten)

1938   From My African Notebook (Afrikanische Geschichten)

1948   The Jungle Hospital (Das Spital im Urwald)

1950   A Pelican Tells About His Life (Ein Pelikan erzählt aus seinem Leben)

1954   Vol. 6 of Bach's Complete Organ Works (with Eduard Nies-Berger)

            The Problem of Peace in the World of Today (Le Probleme de la Paix)

1958   Second nuclear test ban broadcasts published as Peace or Atomic War? (Friede oder Atomkrieg?)

1963   The Teaching of Reverence for Life (Die Lehre der Ehrfurcht vor dem Leben)

1966   Reverence for Life (Strassburger Predigten)

1967   The Kingdom of God and Primitive Christianity (Reich Gottes und Christentum)

         Vols. 7 and 8 of Bach's Complete Organ Works (again with Nies-Berger)

1974   Was sollen wir tun?

List of Abbreviations

ACADEMIE   Academie des sciences morales et politiques.
Paris. Celebration du centenaire de la naissance
d'Albert Schweitzer: séance du lundi 27 Janvier
1975/Institut de France, Academie des Sciences
Morales et Politiques. Paris: Institut de
France, 1975. 39 pp.

ALBUM   Anderson, Erica. The Schweitzer Album, a Portrait
in Words and Pictures. Additional text by Albert
Schweitzer. New York: Harper and Row; London:
Adam and Charles Black, 1965. 176 pp.

BEGEGNUNG   Bähr, Hans Walter, and Robert Minder, eds.
Begegnung mit Albert Schweitzer. Berichte und
Aufzeichnungen. Munich: C. H. Beck, 1965.
336 pp.

BEITRÄGE   Götting, Gerald, ed. Albert Schweitzer. Beiträge
zu Leben und Werk. Berlin: Union Verlag, 1966.
183 pp.

BERICHTE   Berichte aus Lambarene. Published by the Schweizer
Hilfsverein für das Albert Schweitzer Spital in
Lambarene, Basel.

BERY   Oswald, Suzanne. Mein Onkel Bery. Erinnerungen
an Albert Schweitzer. Zürich, Stuttgart: Rotapfel
Verlag, 1971. 211 pp. Second edition, 1972;
third edition, 1973, 311 pp.

BRABAZON   Brabazon, James. Albert Schweitzer, a Biography.
New York: G. P. Putnam, 1975. 509 pp. London:
Gollancz, 1976.

BRIEFE   Briefe aus den Lambarene Spital. 23 letters
covering the period 1924-46.

BRITISH BULLETIN	Dr. Schweitzer's Hospital Fund. British Bulletin. Published in London since 1925.
CAHIERS	Cahiers Albert Schweitzer (prior to 1976 entitled Cahiers de l'Association Francaise des Amis d'Albert Schweitzer).
CAHIERS/BELGE	Cahiers de l'Association Belge des Amis d'Albert Schweitzer. Published since 1960 in Seraing, Belgium.
CENTENNIAL	The Albert Schweitzer Centennial Week in St. Louis, Missouri, 1975. Records. Mimeographed, unpaged.
CHARISMATISCHE DIAKONIE	Heipp, Günther, ed. Charismatische Diakonie; in memoriam Albert Schweitzer. 4.9.1965. Dankesgabe der deutschsprachigen Theologen. Hamburg: H. Reich, 1967. 93 pp. (Evangelische Zeitstimmen 27-II).
CONVOCATION RECORD	Albert Schweitzer International Convocation, Aspen, Colorado, 1966. The Convocation Record. Aspen, Colorado, 1966.
COURIER	The Courier. Published by the Albert Schweitzer Fellowship in New York City.
DEBRECEN	Albert Schweitzer; conférences du Congrès international de écrevains-médecins, Debrecen, 1966. Debrecen: Orvostudomanyi Egyetem, 1966. 209 pp. Proceedings of the Conference of the International Federation of Medical Writers, August 26-30, 1966.
DENKEN UND WEG	Bähr, Hans Walter, ed. Albert Schweitzer. Sein Denken und sein Weg. Tübingen: J. C. B. Mohr, 1962. 578 pp.
DEVENTER	International Albert Schweitzer Symposium. 28 September-1 Oktober 1978 Deventer-Holland. 120 pp.
DOKUMENTE	Kik, Richard, ed. Dokumente. Aus den Rundbriefen 1 bis 11, 1930-57. (Zum 90. Geburtstag von Albert Schweitzer). Für den Freundeskreis als Sammelband hrsg. von Richard Kik. Heidenheim (Brenz): R. Kik (Selbstverlag), 1965. 384 pp.
EERBIED	Eerbied voor het Leven en Nieuws uit Lambarene. Published in Deventer, Holland by the Netherlands Albert Schweitzer Fonds. (Formerly Nieuws uit Lambarene.)

List of Abbreviations

EHRFURCHT   Buri, Fritz, ed. Ehrfurcht vor dem Leben Albert Schweitzer, eine Freundesgabe zu seinem 80. Geburtstag. Bern: P. Haupt, 1955. 268 pp.

ETUDES   Amadou, Robert. Albert Schweitzer; études et témoignages. Publiés sous la direction de Robert Amadou par André Siegfried et al. Brussels, Paris: Editions de la Main Jetee, 1951. 299 pp. Second edition Paris: L'Arche, 1952.

FACKELTRÄGER   Wech, Leopold, ed. Albert Schweitzer, Fackelträger der Menschlichkeit. Vienna: Österreichischen Albert Schweitzer Gemeinde, 1959.

FAMILIEN-KALENDAR   Elsass-Lothringischer Familien-Kalendar, Strassburg.

FESTGABE   Albert Schweitzer, Mensch und Werk; eine kleine Festgabe zu seinem 85. Geburtstag von Willy Bremi et al. Bern: P. Haupt, 1959. 143 pp.

FESTSCHRIFT   Jack, Homer A., ed. To Albert Schweitzer; a Festschrift commemorating his 80th birthday from a few of his friends. Evanston, Ill.: 1955. 178 pp.

FYRBÅKEN   Lagerfelt, Greta, ed. Fyrbåken i Urskogen. Albert Schweitzer in Lambarene 1925-1950. Uppsala: Lindblad, 1950.

GESTERN-HEUTE   Wenzel, Lene, ed. Albert Schweitzer Gestern-Heute, eine Anthologie der Begegnungen. Hamburg: Herbert Reich Evangelischer Verlag, 1972. 78 pp.

HALFEN   Wir halfen dem Doktor in Lambarene. Festgabe zum 85. Geburtstag von Albert Schweitzer dargeboten von den schweizerischen Mitarbeitern. Zürich: Schweizer Druck- und Verlagshaus, 1960. 237 pp.

HEIPP   Heipp, Günther, ed. Es geht ums Leben: der Kampf gegen die Bombe, 1945-1965. Hamburg: Herbert Reich Evangelischer Verlag, 1965.

HOMMAGE   Les Amis d'Albert Schweitzer. Hommage à Albert Schweitzer. Paris: Diffusion le Guide, 1955. 141 pp.

JUBILEE   Roback, A. A., ed. The Albert Schweitzer Jubilee Book. Cambridge, Mass.: Sci-Art Publishers, 1945. 508 pp.

List of Abbreviations

KIRCHENBOTE — Evangelisch-Protestantischer Kirchenbote für Elsass und Lothringen (Strasbourg).

LETTRES — Lettres de l'hôpital du docteur Schweitzer à Lambaréné. Published by Imprimerie Alsacienne, Strasbourg.

MANNEN — Lagerfelt, Greta Elizabeth, ed. Albert Schweitzer, mannen och hans gärning; vanners hylling till Lambarenes jukhusets 25-åriga tillvaro. . . . Uppsala: Lindblad, 1938. 252 pp.

MARSHALL & POLING — Marshall, George N., and David Poling. Schweitzer, a Biography. Garden City, N.Y.: Doubleday and Co., 1971. 342 pp.

MEDDELANDEN — Meddelanden från professor Albert Schweitzers verksamhet. Published in Stockholm by the Svenska Förbundet til stöd för Albert Schweitzers Verksamhet.

MISÉRICORDE — Goettmann, Alphonse, ed. L'Evangile de la miséricorde, hommage au Dr. Schweitzer par D. Pire et al. Paris: Editions du Cerf, 1965. 445 pp.

NEUES — Neues von Albert Schweitzer (Basel).

NIEUWS — Nieuws uit Lambarene; mededilingenblad van en over Prof. Dr. Albert Schweitzer (Assen).

NOUVELLES — Nouvelles de Lambarene et de l'oeuvre d'Albert Schweitzer dans le monde. Published by the Association Suisse de l'aide a l'hopital, section de la Suisse romande, Montreux.

PROPHET — Albert Schweitzer, Prophet of Survival. Berkeley, Calif: Uniquest Foundation, 1975. 44 pp.

RAYONNEMENT — Minder, Robert, ed. Rayonnement d'Albert Schweitzer. 34 etudes et 100 temoignagnes. Colmar: Editions Alsatia, 1975.

REALMS — Roback, A. A., ed. In Albert Schweitzer's Realms: a Symposium. Cambridge, Mass.: Sci-Art Publishers, 1962. 441 pp.

REVUE — Revue d'Histoire et de Philosophie Religieuses (Strasbourg).

List of Abbreviations

RUNDBRIEF

Rundbrief für den Freundeskreis von Albert Schweitzer und den deutschen Hilfsverein e V (Rottenburg a.N.). Formerly Rundbrief für den Freundeskreis von Albert Schweitzer (Heidenheim/Brenz).

RUNDBRIEFE/DDR

Rundbriefe der Albert Schweitzer Komitee in der Deutschen Demokratischen Republik, Dresden.

SCHWEITZER

Bähr, Hans Walter, ed. Albert Schweitzer. Freiburg, Basel, Wien: Herder Bücherei, 1966. 159 pp.

SELECTION

Friends of Albert Schweitzer, Boston, Mass. A Selection of Writings of and about Albert Schweitzer. Boston: Friends of Albert Schweitzer, 1958. 83 pp.

TIERE

Albert Schweitzer und die Tiere. Vevey: Schweizer Hilfsverein für das Albert Schweitzer Spital in Lambarene, 1979. 30 pp.

TRIBUTE

Booth, Edwin Prince, et al., eds. A Tribute on the Ninetieth Birthday of Albert Schweitzer. Presented by the Friends of Albert Schweitzer, Boston, Mass. Boston: Henry N. Sawyer, 1964.

VERMÄCHTNIS

Vermächtnis und Wirklichkeit; zum 100. Geburtstag Albert Schweitzers. Berlin: Union Verlag, 1974.

WÜRDIGUNG

Schneider, Camille, comp. Albert Schweitzer, eine Würdigung. Strassburg: Heitz et Cie, 1934. 46 pp.

I. Collected and Selected Works

A. Collected Works

Japan is the only country in which the collected works of Albert
Schweitzer have appeared. They were published by Hakusuisha in
Tokyo, by arrangement with Dr. Schweitzer through Dr. Minoru Nomura.
They appeared between 1956 and 1961 in 19 volumes under the general
title Chosakushū (Collected works). A supplement was added in 1962.

The title-page in each volume is bilingual, recto verso, Japanese
and German, and the text, in Japanese characters, is translated from
the original German, French, or English. Portraits of Albert
Schweitzer and illustrations are included. The contents of each
volume are here listed, with titles and the translations, and names
of the translators.

1   Volume I. 1956. 308 pp., front., illus., map.
        Mizu to Genshirin no aidani (Zwischen Wasser und Urwald).
            Translated by Masao Asai.
        Oitachi no Ki (Aus meiner Kindheit und Jugendzeit).
            Translated by Kōji Kunimatsu.
        Mukashi no Colmar no Omoide ("Souvenirs du vieux Colmar").
            Translated by Kōji Kunimatsu.

2   Volume II. 1956. 298 pp., front. (port.), illus.
        Waga Shōgai to Shisō yori (Aus meinem Leben und Denken).
            Translated by Michio Takeyama.

3   Volume III. 1957. 279 pp., front. (port.), illus.
        Lambarene Tsūshin, 1 (Mitteilungen aus Lambarene).
            Translated by Minoru Nomura.

4   Volume IV. 1957. 300 pp.
        Lambarene Tsūshin, 2 (Mitteilungen aus Lambarene).
            Translated by Minoru Nomura.
        Shokuminchi Afurika ni okeru Watashitachi no Shigoto
            ("Our Task in Colonial Africa"). Translated by
            Minoru Nomura.

1

Collected and Selected Works

5   Volume V. 1957. 289 pp., front. (port.), illus.
    Pelikan no Seikatsu to Iken (Ein Pelikan erzählt aus
        seinem Leben). Translated by Kōji Kunimatsu.
    Genshirin no Byōin (Das Spital im Urwald). Translated
        by Kōji Kunimatsu.
    Afurikamonogatari (Afrikanische Geschichten). Translated
        by Masao Asai.
    Iesu (Die psychiatrische Beurteilung Jesu). Translated
        by Minoru Nomura.

6   Volume VI. 1957. 361 pp.
    Goethe (Goethe. Vier Reden). Translated by Tomio Tezuka.
    Ningen no Shisō no Hatten to Rinri no Mondai ("Le problème
        de l'éthique dans l'évolution de la pensée humaine").
        Translated by Kōji Kunimatsu.
    Gendai ni okeru Heiwa no Mondai (Das Problem des Friedens
        in der heutigen Welt). Translated by Tomio Tezuka.
    Bunka no Taihai to Saiken (Verfall und Wiederaufbau der
        Kultur. Kulturphilosophie, I). Translated by Kōji
        Kunimatsu.
    Mizu to Genshirin no aidano Interview ("Interview zwischen
        Wasser und Urwald"). Translated by Tomio Tezuka.
    Schweitzer-Nenpu (Index). Compiled by Masao Asai. Com-
        mentary by Tomio Tezuka.

7   Volume VII. 1957. 364 pp., front. (port.), illus.
    Bunka to Rinri (Kultur und Ethik. Kulturphilosophie, II).
        Translated by Hidehiro Higami.

8   Volume VIII. 1957. 362 pp., front. (port).
    Kirisutokyō to Sekai no Shūkyō (Das Christentum und die
        Weltreligionen). Translated by Yasumasa Ōshima.
    Gendai Bunmei ni okeru Shūkyō ("Religion in Modern
        Civilization"). Translated by Yasumasa Ōshima.
    Iesu-Shōden (Das Messianitäts- und Leidensgeheimnis).
        Translated by Bansetsu Kishida.
    Shūmatsuron no Hensen ni Okeru Kami no Kuni no Rinen
        ("Die Idee des Reiches Gottes im Verlaufe der Umbildung
        des eschatologischen Glaubens in den
        uneschatologischen"). Translated by Yasumasa Ōshima.
    Kaisetsu (Commentary). By Yasumasa Ōshima.

9   Volume IX. 1957. 316 pp., illus.
    Indo Shisōka no Sekaikan. Shimpi-shugi to Rinri (Die
        Weltanschauung der indischen Denker). Translated by
        Hajime Nakamura and Kōshirō Tamaki.
    Schweitzer ni taisuru Radhakrishnan no Hihan ("Mysticism
        and Ethics in Hindu Thought." S. Radhakrishnan's
        critique of Schweitzer's view on Hindu philosophy).

2

Collected and Selected Works

Translated by Hajime Nakamura.
Kaisetsu (Commentary). By Hajime Nakamura.

10   Volume X. 1957. 388 pp.
          Shito Paulo no Shinpishugi, 1 (Die Mystik des Apostels
              Paulus). Translated by Kazuo Muto and Bansetsu
              Kishida.
          Kaisetsu (Commentary). By Kazuo Muto.

11   Volume XI. 1958. 374 pp.
          Shito Paulo no Shinpishugi, 2 (Die Mystik des Apostels
              Paulus). Translated by Kazuo Muto and Bansetsu
              Kishida.
          Atogaki (Postscript). By Bansetsu Kishida.

12   Volume XII. 1957. 427 pp.
          Bach, 1 (J.S. Bach. 1908). Translated by Masao Asai,
              Keiichi Uchigaki, and Yoshimu Sugiyama.
          Kaisetsu (Commentary). By Masao Asai.

13   Volume XIII. 1958. 418 pp.
          Bach, 2 (J.S. Bach. 1908). Translated by Masao Asai,
              Keiichi Uchigaki, and Yoshimu Sugiyama.
          Atogaki (Postscript). By Keiichi Uchigaki.

14   Volume XIV. 1958. 358 pp.
          Bach, 3 (J.S. Bach. 1908). Translated by Masao Asai,
              Keiichi Uchigaki, and Yoshimu Sugiyama.
          Atogaki (Postscript). By Yoshimu Sugiyama.

15   Volume XV. 1959. 306 pp.
          Kanto no Shukyo-tetsugaku, 1 (Die Religionsphilosophie
              Kants von der Kritik der reinen Vernunft bis zur
              Religion innerhalb der Grenzen der blossen Vernunft).
              Translated by Giichi Saito and Shizuteru Ueda.
          Atogaki (Postscript). By the translators.

16   Volume XVI. 1959. 295 pp.
          Kanto no Shukyo-Tetsugaku, 2 (Die Religionsphilosophie
              Kants . . .). Translated by Giichi Saito and
              Shizuteru Ueda.
          Atogaki (Postscript). By Giichi Saito.

17   Volume XVII. 1960. 404 pp.
          Iesuden-kenkyushi, 1 (Geschichte der Leben-Jesu-
              Forschung, Chaps. 1-14). Translated by Akira Endo
              and Yuzaburo Morita.
          Atogaki (Postscript). By the translators.

3

Collected and Selected Works

18   Volume XVIII. 1960. 370 pp.
         Iesuden-kenkyūshi, 2 (Geschichte der Leben-Jesu-Forschung,
            Chaps. 15-21). Translated by Akira Endō and Yūzaburo
            Morita.

19   Volume XIX. 1961. 321 pp.
         Iesuden-kenkyūshi, 3 (Geschichte der Leben-Jesu-Forschung,
            Chaps. 22 to end). Translated by Akira Endō and
            Yūzaburo Morita.

20   Supplement. 1962. 171 pp.
         Genshi jidai no seiji to seron. (Politik ohne öffentliche
            Meinung im Atomzeitalter; Krieg und Völkerrecht).
            Translated by Minoru Nomura.

                    B. Selected Works

This selection of Schweitzer's writings, the first such collection
to appear in German, was conceived by Rudolf Grabs. His intent was
to give friends of Schweitzer in the German Democratic Republic an
insight into Schweitzer's personality and activities, and to honor
Schweitzer as a humanitarian, theologian, philosopher, musician, and
advocate for peace.

    Included in the edition are the complete unabridged texts of the
majority of Albert Schweitzer's books and many of his important addresses, articles, and shorter works. Not included, as explained by
the editor in Volume 5, are the books written by Schweitzer on the
music of Johann Sebastian Bach. Each of the volumes contains not
only an index for the volume itself, but the forewords or prefaces
and indexes as they appear in the original works. A comprehensive
introduction by the editor precedes the text of each volume. Below
are listed the contents of the five volumes.

         SCHWEITZER, ALBERT. Ausgewählte Werke in Fünf Bände.
            Herausgegeben von Rudolf Grabs. Berlin: Union Verlag,
            1971.

21   Volume 1. 700 pp.
         Geleitwort (Gerald Götting), p. 5; Einleitung (Rudolf
         Grabs), p. 9; Aus meinem Leben und Denken, p. 19; Aus
         meiner Kindheit und Jugendzeit, p. 253; Zwischen Wasser
         und Urwald, p. 315; Briefe aus Lambarene, 1924-1927,
         p. 477.

22   Volume 2. 739 pp.
         Einleitung, p. 5; Verfall und Wiederaufbau der Kultur,
         Kulturphilosophie, Erster Teil. Olaus Petri Vorlesungen

an der Universität Upsala, p. 17; Kultur und Ethik,
Kulturphilosophie, Zweiter Teil. Olaus Petri Vorlesungen
an der Universität Upsala, p. 95; Die Weltanschauung der
indischen Denker. Mystik and Ethik, p. 421; Das
Christentum und die Weltreligionen, p. 665.

23   Volume 3. 932 pp.
        Einleitung, p. 5; Geschichte der Leben-Jesu-Forschung
        (includes Albert Schweitzer's Vorwort to the first edition,
        1906, the Vorwort to the second edition, 1913, and the
        "Vorrede" for the sixth edition, 1950), p. 15.

24   Volume 4. 773 pp.
        Einleitung, p. 5; Die Mystik des Apostels Paulus, p. 15;
        Reich Gottes und Christentum, p. 511.

25   Volume 5. 653 pp.
        Einleitung, p. 5; Aus Afrika: Vom Regen und schön Wetter
        auf dem Äquator, p. 19; Afrikanische Jagdgeschichten,
        p. 27; Ojembo der Urwaldschulmeister, p. 40. Berichte
        aus Lambarene: Fünfundzwanzig Jahre Spitalarbeit, p. 49;
        Afrikanisches Tagebuch 1939-1945, p. 52; Das Lambarenespital
        vom Herbst 1945 bis Frühjahr 1954, p. 75; Der Alltag in
        Lambarene, p. 103; Ansprache in Andende, p. 112.
        Kulturphilosophie und Ethik: Strassburger Predigten
        über die Ehrfurcht vor dem Leben, p. 117; Philosophie und
        Tierschützbewegung, p. 135; Das Problem der Ethik in der
        Höherentwicklung des menschlichen Denkens, p. 143;
        Ansprache bei Entgegennahme des belgischen Joseph-
        Lemaire-preises, p. 160; Humanität, p. 167; Die Entstehung
        der Lehre der Ehrfurcht vor dem Leben und ihre Bedeutung
        für unsere Kultur, p. 172.
           Religion and Theologie: Das Messianitäts und
        Leidensgeheimnis. Eine Skizze des Lebens Jesu, p. 195;
        Ansprache auf der Tagung der Schopenhauer-Gesellschaft,
        p. 375; Botschaft an die Teilnehmer der Tagung des
        Weltbundes für freies Christentum, p. 378; Spitalandachten
        zu Lambarene, p. 380.
           Deutsche und französische Orgelbaukunst und Orgelkunst,
        p. 389; Nachwort von 1927, p. 441.
           Goethe: Vier Reden. Ansprache bei der Verleihung des
        Goethepreises der Stadt Frankfurt (am 28. August 1928),
        p. 469; Gedenkrede (Frankfurt a.M., am 22. März 1932),
        p. 478; Goethe als Denker und Mensch (Ulm im Juli 1932),
        p. 509; Goethe der Mensch und das Werk (Aspen, Colorado,
        U.S.A., am 8. Juli 1949), p. 523.
           Ethik und Völkerfrieden: Interview im Urwald, p. 557;
        Appell an die Menschheit, p. 564; Friede oder Atomkrieg,
        p. 578; Der Weg des Friedens heute, p. 612; Nachwort
        (Gerhard Fischer), p. 631.

5

Collected and Selected Works

26   SCHWEITZER, ALBERT.   Gesammelte Werke.   Verantwortlich für
        die Betreuung der Originaltexte, für die Einleitung und
        für den Anhang, Dr. Rudolf Grabs.   München: C. H. Beck,
        1973.   5 vols., 700 p., 739 p., 932 p., 773 p., 640 p.
        Identical to the 1971 edition, above, except that Götting's
        foreword has been replaced by one by Grabs, and Fischer's
        afterword has been deleted.

27   Same.   Zürich: Ex Libris Verlag, 1974.

II. Anthologies, Collections, *Festschriften,* and Other Writings

A. Works by Albert Schweitzer

28   Albert Schweitzer: An Anthology. Edited by Charles R. Joy.
     Presentation edition. Boston: Beacon Press, 1947.
     xxviii, 323 pp. (limited edition).
     (Trade edition). New York: Harper and Brothers; Boston:
          The Beacon Press, 1947. xxviii, 323 pp. Enlarged
          edition, 1960, 355 pp.
     (First paperback edition). Boston: The Beacon Press,
          1955. xxviii, 323 pp. Enlarged editions 1956, 1957,
          1960. xv, 355 pp. (Bound in cloth by Peter Smith,
          Gloucester, Mass., 1961.)
     (First British edition). Revised and enlarged. London:
          A. and C. Black, 1952. xix, 303 pp. Reprinted 1955.
     (Revised and enlarged edition in honor of Albert
          Schweitzer's ninetieth birthday.) Boston: Beacon
          Press; New York: Harper and Row, 1965. 367 pp.
          Reissued, 1977.

     TRANSLATIONS

     Albert Schweitzer, une anthologie. Publiée par Charles R. Joy,
          avec une introduction biographique. Paris: Payot, 1950.
          186 pp. Reprinted, 1952. Second edition, 1956.[1]

     Anthologia tōn ergōn tou Alvertou Svaitzer. Hypo Charles R.
          Joy. Metaphrasis: Agnēs N. Diamantopoulou. Athens:
          1963. 174 pp.

---

[1]This edition differs from the original American edition. The French
translations were made from the original texts, and were then revised
by Albert Schweitzer. The compiler is indebted to Professor Gustave
Woytt of the University of Strasbourg, who collaborated with
Dr. Schweitzer on this edition, for this information.

Anthologies, Collections . . .

Rispetto per la vita. A cura di C. R. Joy. Traduzione di
Constanza Walter. Milano: Edizioni di Comunità, 1957.
403 pp. Second edition, 1965. 376 pp. Third edition,
1977. 220 pp. Illus.

29   Albert Schweitzer. Bilder und Worte aus seinem Leben und
Wirken. Hamburg: R. Meiner; Stuttgart: Kreuz-Verlag,
1961. 27 pp. Illus.

30   Albert Schweitzer. Denken und Tat. Zusammengetragen und
dargestellt von Rudolf Grabs. Hamburg: Richard Meiner,
1950. xxiv, 320 pp. Second edition, 1952. Third edition, unrevised, 1954.

TRANSLATIONS

Elämän Kunnioitus. Koonnut ja esittänyt Rudolf Grabs.
Suomentanut Juho Tervonen. Porvoo, Helsinki: Werner
Soderström, 1956. 359 pp. Second and third editions,
1957. Fourth edition, 1959, 363 pp. Fifth edition,
1964, 362 pp. Sixth edition, 1966, 362 pp.

Aerefrykt for livit. Et Utvalg av Schweitzers verker.
Redigert av Rudolf Grabs. Med forord av Max Tau.
Oversatt av Oddvar Bjørklund. Oslo: Johan Grundt Tanum,
1951. 310 pp. Reprinted 1951, 1952, 1955.

Vördnad för Livet. Urval ur Albert Schweitzers Skrifter,
redigerat av Rudolf Grabs. Stockholm: Svenska Kyrkans
Diakonistyrelses Bogförlag, 1950. 326 pp. Port. Second
revised edition, 1959, 247 pp., illus. (Includes "Albert
Schweitzers Kamp mit atombomben," edited by Bengt Andreas,
pp. 225-36). Third revised edition, 1961. 247 pp.

31   Albert Schweitzer, életem és gondolataim. Budapest:
Gondolat, 1974. 524 pp.

32   Albert Schweitzer en Africa. Extracts from the African
writings of Albert Schweitzer. Edited by Jan Eigenhuis.
Haarlem: Tjeenk Willink, 1928. 261 pp.

33   Albert Schweitzer erzählt. Eine Auswahl. Herausgegeben von
Karl O. Nordstrand. Lund: Gleerup Bokförlag, 1961.
72 pp. (Deutsche Lesehefte, 2.)

34   Albert Schweitzer. Ein Leben im Dienste der Menschheit.
Abschnitte aus den Werken Albert Schweitzers. Verbindende
Texte von Heinrich Geffert. Für den Gebrauch an Schuler.
Hamburg: Gesellschaft der Freunde des vaterländischen
Schul- und Erziehungswesens zu Hamburg; Braunschweig,

Anthologies, Collections . . .

Berlin, Hamburg, u.a.: Georg Westermann, 1953. 52 pp.
Illus. (Deutsche Lesewerk, Nr. 32.) Second edition,
1954. Reprinted, 1960.

35   Albert Schweitzer. The Man and his Thought. Edited by Yil
Sun Rhee. In celebration of Albert Schweitzer on the 40th
year of his work in Africa. Seoul: Sasangesa Publishing
Co., 1954. 355 pp. Illus., port., cover port. Collec-
tion of works by Albert Schweitzer and other writers.
Second edition, revised and enlarged. Seoul: Sungnohakaa
Publishing Co., 1958. 552 pp.

36   Albert Schweitzer. Por qué Premio Nóbel de la Paz. Una
antologia seleccionada, traducida y prologada por Alberto
Colao. Cartagena, Spain: Athenas-Ediciones, 1958.
132 pp. (Lectio Philosophica, 1).

37   Albert Schweitzer: Reverence for Life. The inspiring words
of a great humanitarian. With a foreword by Norman
Cousins. Selected by Peter Seymour. Illustrated by
Walter Scott. Kansas City, Mo.: Hallmark Cards, Inc.,
1971. 62 pp. Illus.

38   Albert Schweitzer. Selections. Edited by R. H. Dahl and
S. H. Steinberg. London: Macmillan and Co., 1953.
xviii, 114 pp. (Text in German, introduction and notes
in English. For school use.)

39   Albert Schweitzer spricht zu uns (recording). Ed. Harold
Robles. Includes 4 speeches: Aus meinem Leben: Vortrag
am Kölner Rundfunk 20.4.1932; Vortrag im Holländischen
Rundfunk vom 16.11.1952; Gedenkrede für Henri Dunant;
Ansprache an Schulkinder und Lehrer in der Schweiz, 1954;
and a Bach chorale prelude. Available from the Internationales Albert Schweitzer Sekretariat, P.O. Box 15,
7400 N.A., Deventer, Holland.

40   Albert Schweitzer: Thoughts for our Times. Edited by Erica
Anderson. Illustrated by Vee Guthrie. Mount Vernon,
N.Y.: Peter Pauper Press, 1975. 61 pp. Reprinted,
Pilgrim Press, 1980.

41   Albert Schweitzer. Veien til deg selv. Ved Max Tau og Lotte
Gerhold. Oversatt fra tysk, fransk, engelsk av Bjørn
Braaten. Oslo: H. Aschehoug & Co. (W. Nygaard), 1956.
265 pp. (Fredsbiblioteket 2). Reprinted 1956, 1957.
A compilation of writings by Albert Schweitzer and
selections from essays and articles about him by other
authors.

Anthologies, Collections . . .

TRANSLATIONS

Albert Schweitzer. Vejen til dig selv. En bog om og of
    Albert Schweitzer. Ved Max Tau og Lotte Gerhold. Oversat
    af Karl Hornelund. Copenhagen: Jespersen and Pio, 1957.
    250 pp. (Fredsbiblioteket).

Albert Schweitzer. El camino hacia ti mismo. Selección
    de Max Tau y Lotte Gerhold. Versión castellana de J. R.
    Wilcock. Buenos Aires: Sur, 1958. 222 pp. Second
    edition, 1960, 240 pp.

42 Albert Schweitzer. Vom Licht in uns. Ausgewählte Worte.
    Vorwort, Richard Kik. Stuttgart-Degerloch: Vita Nuova
    Verlag, 1947. 40 pp. (Ausgewählte Worte, 7.) Reprinted
    Tübingen: Vita Nuova (Kurt Jetsche), 1948.
    (Second edition). Stuttgart: J. F. Steinkopf, 1954. 86 pp.
        (Steinkopfs Haus-Bücherei 37). Third edition 1955;
        fourth edition, 1956; fifth edition, 1957; sixth
        edition, 1958; seventh edition, 1959; eighth edition,
        1961, 95 pp.; ninth edition, 1967.

    TRANSLATIONS

    Het licht in ons. Woorden van Albert Schweitzer. Rotterdam:
        A. Kapsenberg & Zonen, 1950. 42 pp. Port.

    The Light Within Us. New York: Philosophical Library;
        London: John Calder, 1959. 58 pp. Reprinted Westport,
        Conn.: Greenwood Press, 1971.

    (Paperback edition). London and New York: Wisdom Library,
        1959. 58 pp. (Wisdom Library, 45.)

43 Albert Schweitzer. Weg zur Humanität. Eine Auswahl aus
    seinen Werken zusammengestellt von Rudolf Grabs.
    Stuttgart: Reclam-Verlag, 1957. 85 pp. (Reclams
    Universal-Bibliothek, 7880). Reprinted 1958.

    TRANSLATIONS

    Pilgrimage to Humanity. Edited by Rudolf Grabs. Translated
        by Walter E. Stuermann. New York: Philosophical Library,
        1961. 107 pp.

44 Albert Schweitzer, Werk, Leven en Humor. Deventer: Kluwer,
        1941. 28 pp.

45   Albert Schweitzer. Zeitliches und Überzeitliches. Eine
        Auswahl aus seinen Werken von August Heisler. Hamburg:
        Johann Trautmann, 1947. 42 pp.

46   Albert Schweitzers Leben und Denken. Selections chosen from
        the autobiographical writings of the author and edited by
        Kurt Bergel. New York: Henry Holt and Co., 1949. xviii,
        103, lxvii pp. Port. Edition for students, with vocabu-
        lary. Reprinted 1951, 1956.
     (Leben und Denken.) Selections (chosen and edited by Kurt
        Bergel) from the autobiographical writings of Albert
        Schweitzer, with an introduction by J. Bronowski and
        grammatical notes by H. C. Howlett Jones. Melbourne,
        London, Toronto: William Heinemann, 1951. xii, 106,
        lxvii pp. (The Heinemann Creative Language Series.)
        (Same.) Fragen und Übungen by Ian G. Ferguson. 2 parts
           in one. Toronto: Irwin Clarke and Co., 1956. 104,
           lxvii, 31 pp.

47   Anekdoten um Albert Schweitzer. Gesammelt und erzählt von
        Roland Schütz. Munich and Esslingen: Bechtle, 1966.
        83 pp. Includes selections by and about Albert Schweitzer.

48   The Animal World of Albert Schweitzer: Jungle Insights into
        Reverence for Life. Translated and edited, with an intro-
        duction, by Charles R. Joy. Boston: The Beacon Press,
        1950. 207 pp. Illus., ports. (The Beacon Press
        Schweitzer Series.) Reprinted 1951, 1956.
        (Beacon Paperback Edition.) Boston: The Beacon Press,
           1958. 209 pp. Illus.

49   Aus dem Leben und Denken Albert Schweitzers. Ein Leseheft
        für Unterricht. Zusammengestellt von R. Brüllmann. Hrsg.
        von Schweizer Hilfsverein für das Albert Schweitzer Spital
        in Lambarene. Vevey, 1974. 32 pp. Illus.

50   Briefe. Hrsg. von Hans W. Bähr. Heidelberg: Lambert
        Schneider. IN PREPARATION.

51   Dem Dasein einen Sinn setzen. Worte von Albert Schweitzer.
        Hrsg. von Bernhard Funck. Munich: Funck, 1966. 64 pp.
        (Die Aphorismen-Reihe, Bd. 17.)

52   Denken. (Aus meinen Leben und Denken.) Ausgewählte Worte
        Albert Schweitzers. Kulturkreis Junges Europa.
        Heidelberg: Schneider, 1948. 10 pp. (Europäischer
        Lesebogen.) Not available in bookstores.

Anthologies, Collections . . .

53   Durch's Jahr mit Albert Schweitzer. Hrsg. von William Debus.
      Uslar (Solling): Albert Schweitzer Familienwerk E.V.

54   For all that Lives. Edited by Ann Atwood and Erica Anderson.
      New York: Scribner, 1975. 32 pp. Includes brief selec-
      tions from Schweitzer's works. Illus.
      (Filmstrip.) For all that Lives. The Words of Albert
         Schweitzer. Edited by Ann Atwood and Erica Anderson.
      Lyceum Productions, 1974.

55   Gelebter Glaube. Eine Lesebuch. Ausgewählt und dargestellt
      von Rudolf Grabs. Berlin: Evangelische Verlagsanstalt,
      1957. 256 pp. Port., illus. Reprinted 1957, 1959, 1960.

56   Glauben, Lieben, Handeln. Ausgewählte Schriften. Sonderausgabe
      Europäischer Buchklub. Stuttgart, Zürich, Salzburg:
      Europäische Buchklub, 1957. 429 pp. (Lizenzausgabe,
      C. H. Beck, München; Paul Haupt, Bern. Nur für
      Mitglieder.)
      (Same.) Zürich: Buchklub Ex Libris, 1957. 430 pp.
         Nur für Mitglieder.

57   Im Banne der Musik. Worte Albert Schweitzers. Herausgegeben
      und zusammengestellt von Richard Kik. Freiburg im
      Breisgau: Hyperion-Verlag, 1959. 155 pp. (Hyperion-
      Bücherei).

58   Kein Sonnenstrahl geht verloren. Worte Albert Schweitzers.
      Eingeleitet und zusammengestellt von Richard Kik.
      Freiburg im Breisgau: Hyperion-Verlag, 1955. 114 pp.
      Port. (Hyperion-Bücherei). Reprinted 1960.

59   Lambarene, mijn Werk aan de Zoour van het Oerwoud. Haarlem:
      Tjeenk Willink, 1950. 282 pp. Selections from
      Schweitzer's writings about Africa.

Die Lehre der Ehrfurcht vor dem Leben. See Philosophy--
      Reverence for Life, nos. 2697-2701 below.

Die Lehre von der Ehrfurcht vor dem Leben: Grundtexte aus
      fünf Jahrzehnten. See Philosophy--Reverence for Life,
      no. 2702 below.

Music in the Life of Albert Schweitzer, with selections from
      his Writings. See Music, no. 3210 below.

60   Reverence for Life. An Anthology of Selected Writings.
      Edited by Thomas Kiernan. New York: Philosophical
      Library, 1965. 74 pp.

Anthologies, Collections . . .

61 Schriften aus dem Nachlass. Hrsg. von Ulrich Neuenschwander
        und Johann Zürcher. Heidelberg: Lambert Schneider.
        5 vols. IN PREPARATION. I. Kultur und Weltreligionen;
        II. Natürliche Religion und natürliche Ethik; III. Die
        Weltanschauung der Chinesischen Denker; IV. Die
        Weltanschauung der Ehrfurcht vor dem Leben; V. Kleinere
        Arbeiten. Persönliches. Fragmente.

62 Schweitzer no kotoba to Shisô; Heiwa e no Susume. Tr. Isao
        Takahashi. Tokyo: Kodansha, 1966. 211 pp.

63 Selbstzeugnisse. (Sonderausgabe). Munich: C. H. Beck. 1959.
        397 pp. (Die Bücher der Neunzehn, Bd. 60). Reprinted
        1967, 1975, 1980.

64 A Selection of Writings of and about Albert Schweitzer.
        Presented by the Friends of Albert Schweitzer, Boston,
        Massachusetts, 1958. vi, 83 pp. Illus.

    Strassburger Predigten. See Theology and Religion--Sermons,
        nos. 3162-69 below.

65 The Theology of Albert Schweitzer for Christian Inquirers.
        By E. N. Mozley. With an epilogue by Albert Schweitzer.
        London: Adam and Charles Black, 1950. vii, 108 pp.
        New York: The Macmillan Company, 1950. vii, 117 pp.
        Reprinted, 1951. Epilogue: "The Conception of the
        Kingdom of God in the Transformation of Eschatology."
        For German version, see no. 2860 below.
        (Same.) New York: Gordon Press, 1977. (Modern Religion
            Series.)

66 A Treasury of Albert Schweitzer. Edited by Thomas Kiernan.
        New York: Distributed by Citadel Press by arrangement
        with Philosophical Library, 1965. This work is a com-
        posite of Pilgramage to Humanity (no. 43 above), and
        parts of Light within us (no. 42 above), Reverence for
        Life (no. 60) and The Philosophy of Religion (no. 2232
        below).

67 Uit een werold van licht. Gedachten van Albert Schweitzer.
        Verzameld end vertaald door A. J. Werner. Deventer:
        A. E. Kluwer, 1941. 32 pp.

68 Unter den Negern Äquatorialafrikas. Auszüge aus den Werken
        von Albert Schweitzer. Eingeleitet und zusammenstellt
        von Wilhelm Schlipköter. Bielefeld u. Leipzig: Velhagen
        und Klasing, 1926. 82 pp. (Velhagen und Klasings
        Jugendbücherei, Bd. 7.)

Anthologies, Collections . . .

69 Der Urwalddoktor von Lambarene. Schulerleseheft. Stuttgart:
    Deutsche Sparkassenverlag, 1960. 45 pp. Illus. (Not
    available in book trade.)

70 Vom Sinn des Lebens. Ein Gespräch zu fünft. Aus den Werken
    und dem Leben Albert Schweitzers. Gestaltet von Peter
    Lotar. Munich: C. H. Beck, 1951. 66 pp. Reprinted
    1952. Bern: P. Haupt, 1953. 71 pp. Reissued 1954,
    58 pp. Second revised edition, 1961, 63 pp. "Dieses
    Gespräch wurde gestaltet mit den worten Albert
    Schweitzers selbst . . . und nach den Monographien von
    Oskar Kraus und Marie Woytt-Secretan."
    (Same.) Ein Gespräch. Aus Werk und Leben Albert
        Schweitzers. Mit fünf obligaten Stimmen. Gestaltet
        von Peter Lotar. Strasbourg: Editions Oberlin, 1951.
        66 pp. Reprinted, 1952.

71 Waffen des Lichts. Worte aus den Werken von Albert
    Schweitzer. Ausgewählt von Fritz Pfäfflin. Heilbronn,
    Stuttgart: Eugen Salzer, 1940. 78 pp. (Salzers
    Volksbücher, Bd. 81). 2nd edition, 1949; 3rd edition,
    1953; 4th edition, 1962, 85 pp.; 5th edition, 1966, iv,
    80 pp.

    Was sollen wir tun? 12 Predigten über ethische Probleme.
        See Theology and Religion--Sermons, nos. 3170-73 below.

72 Wijsheid uit het oerwoud. (Citaten). Samengest, door H.
    Icke. Met voorwoord van C. B. Burger. Assen: De
    Torenlaan, 1955. Unpaged (249 pp.) Port. Illus. (A
    diary, with selections from Albert Schweitzer's writings
    for each day of the year.

73 The Wit and Wisdom of Albert Schweitzer. Edited, with an
    introduction, by Charles R. Joy. Boston: The Beacon
    Press, 1949. vii, 104 pp. (The Beacon Press Schweitzer
    Series). A collection of aphorisms taken from various
    works by Albert Schweitzer.

        B. Works by Others About Schweitzer

NOTE: Individual contributions to these volumes are listed by author
under the appropriate subject headings.

74 About Albert Schweitzer. Pleasantville, N.Y.: Reader's
    Digest Association, 1956. 9 pp. Illus.

75   Albert Schweitzer, Prophet of Survival. Berkeley, Calif.:
        Uniquest Foundation, 1975. 44 pp. Illus.

76   Albert Schweitzer und die Tiere. Vevey: Schweizer Hilfsverein
        für das Albert Schweitzer Spital in Lambarene, 1979.
        30 pp.

77   AMADOU, ROBERT. Albert Schweitzer; études et témoignages.
        Publiés sous la direction de Robert Amadou par André
        Siegfried et al. Brussels, Paris: Editions de la Main
        jetee, 1951. 299 pp. Illus., ports. Second edition:
        Paris: L'Arche, 1952.

78   LES AMIS D'ALBERT SCHWEITZER. Hommage à Albert Schweitzer.
        Paris: Diffusion le Guide, 1955. 141 pp. "Au docteur
        Albert Schweitzer pour son quatre-vingtième anniversaire
        le 14 janvier 1955."

79   BÄHR, HANS WALTER, ed. Albert Schweitzer. Sein Denken und
        sein Weg. Tübingen: J. C. B. Mohr, 1962. xiv, 578 pp.
        Port. (This collection contains many of the selections
        from the Schweitzer number of Universitas, see no. 4885
        below.)

        TRANSLATIONS

     Albert Schweitzer. Eenheid van denken en leven. Tr.
        E. Franken-Liefrinck. Haarlem: H. D. Tjeenk Willink,
        1963. ix, 325 pp. Illus.

80   BÄHR, HANS WALTER, ed. Albert Schweitzer. Freiburg, Basel,
        Wien: Herder-Bücherei, 1966. 159 pp. (Herder-Bücherei,
        Bd. 247.)

81   _____ and ROBERT MINDER, eds. Begegnung mit Albert Schweitzer.
        Berichte und Aufzeichnungen. Munich: C. H. Beck, 1965.
        336 pp.

82   BOOTH, EDWIN PRINCE, et al, eds. A Tribute on the Ninetieth
        Birthday of Albert Schweitzer, presented by the Friends of
        Albert Schweitzer, Boston, Massachusetts. Boston:
        Henry N. Sawyer, 1964. Illus.

83   BREMI, WILLI, ed. Albert Schweitzer Mensch und Werk. Eine
        kleine Festgabe zu seinem 85. Bern: P. Haupt, 1959.
        143 pp. "Hrsg. im Auftrag des Hilfsvereins für das
        Albert Schweitzer-Spital in Lambarene."

Anthologies, Collections . . .

84   BURI, FRITZ, ed. Ehrfurcht vor dem Leben Albert Schweitzer,
     eine Freundesgabe zu seinem 80. Geburtstag. Bern:
     P. Haupt, 1955. 268 pp. Illus.

     FRIENDS OF ALBERT SCHWEITZER, BOSTON, MASS. A Selection of
     Writings of and about Albert Schweitzer. See no. 64
     above.

85   GODDARD, MICKEY. The Thoughts of Albert Schweitzer (cartoons).
     Taiwan: Evergreen Cultural Enterprise Co., 1978. 62 pp.
     Chinese-English edition.

86   GÖTTING, GERALD, ed. Albert Schweitzer. Beiträge zu Leben
     und Werk. Berlin: Union Verlag, 1966. 183 pp.

87   GOETTMANN, ALPHONSE. L'Evangile de la miséricorde, hommage au
     Dr. Schweitzer, par D. Pire et al. Présenté par Alphonse
     Goettmann. Paris: Editions du Cerf, 1965. 445 pp.
     (L'Évangile au xxe siècle, 13.)

88   HEIPP, GÜNTHER, ed. Charismatische Diakonie; in memoriam
     Albert Schweitzer 4.9.1965. Dankesgabe der
     deutschsprachigen Theologen. Hamburg: H. Reich, 1967.
     93 pp. Illus. (Evangelische Zeitstimmen, 27-II.)

89   I-SHENG, SHIH, ed. [This book is a memorial to Dr. Albert
     Schweitzer.] Taiwan: Evergreen Cultural Enterprise Co.,
     1974. 120 pp. Collection of lectures.
     (Same). Taiwan: Evergreen Cultural Enterprise, 1975.
        150 pp.

90   JACK, HOMER A., ed. To Albert Schweitzer: a Festschrift com-
     memorating his 80th birthday from a few of his friends.
     Evanston, Ill.: 1955. 178 pp.

91   KIK, RICHARD, ed. Dokumente. Aus den Rundbriefen 1 bis 11,
     1930-57. (Zum 90.Geburtstag von Albert Schweitzer.) Für
     den Freundeskreis als Sammelband hrsg. von Richard Kik.
     Heidenheim (Brenz): R. Kik (Selbstverlag), 1965.
     384 pp. Illus., ports.

92   LAGERFELT, GRETA ELIZABETH, ed. Albert Schweitzer, mannen
     och hans gärning; vänners hyllning till Lambarenes jukhusets
     25-åriga tillvaro. . . . Uppsala: Lindblad, 1938.
     252 pp. Illus.

93   MINDER, ROBERT, ed. Rayonnement d'Albert Schweitzer. 34
     Études et 100 témoignagnes. Publiés sous la direction
     de Robert Minder. Colmar: Editions Alsatia, 1975. Préf.
     du Alfred Kastler.

RHEE, YIL SUN, ed. Albert Schweitzer, the Man and his Thought. See no. 35 above.

94   ROBACK, A. A., ed. The Albert Schweitzer Jubilee Book. "Edited by A. A. Roback . . . with the co-operation of J. S. Bixler . . . and George Sarton." Cambridge, Mass.: Sci-Art Publishers, 1945. 508 pp. Illus.

95   _____, ed. In Albert Schweitzer's Realms: a symposium. Cambridge, Mass.: Sci-Art Publishers, 1962. 441 pp. Illus.

96   SCHNEIDER, CAMILLE, comp. Albert Schweitzer, eine Würdigung. Strassburg: Heitz and Co., 1934. 46 pp. "Dieses Heft gilt als letzte nummer der ersten Reihe der Elsässer und Lothringer Hefte . . . hrsg. vom Elsass-Lothringischen Schriftsteller-Verband."

TRANSLATIONS

Albert Schweitzer naar zijn waarde geschat, vertaald door mevr A. D. W.-Br. . . . Deventer: A. E. Kluwer, 1934. 56 pp.

SCHÜTZ, ROLAND. Anekdoten um Albert Schweitzer. See no. 47 above.

97   SZAPIRO, W. J. Albert Szwejcer--Wielikij gumanist XX Wieka. Wospominanija i Statji. Moscow: 1970. 238 pp.

TAU, MAX and LOTTE GERHOLD, eds. Albert Schweitzer. Veien til deg Selv. See no. 41 above.

98   WECH, LEOPOLD, ed. Albert Schweitzer, Fackelträger der Menschlichkeit. Vienna: Österreichischen Albert Schweitzer Gemeinde, 1959.

99   WENZEL, LENE, ed. Albert Schweitzer gestern-heute, eine Anthologie der Begegnungen. Hamburg: Herbert Reich Evangelischer Verlag, 1972. 78 pp. (Evangelische Zeitstimmen 63/64.)

100   Wir halfen dem Doktor in Lambarene. Festgabe zum 85. Geburtstag von Albert Schweitzer dargeboten von den schweizerischen Mitarbeitern. Zürich: Schweizer Druck- und Verlagshaus, 1960. 237 pp. Illus.

Anthologies, Collections . . .

101 ZWEIG, STEFAN, et al. <u>Albert Schweitzer, Genie der</u>
       <u>Menschlichkeit</u>. Dargestellt von Stefan Zweig, Jacques
       Feschotte und Rudolf Grabs. Frankfurt a.M.: Fischer,
       1955. 239 pp.

III. Life and Work

A. General

1. Books by Schweitzer

AUS MEINER KINDHEIT UND JUGENDZEIT
(Memoirs of Childhood and Youth)

The published record of Albert Schweitzer's childhood and youth is
connected, he relates, "with a visit to my friend Dr. O. Pfister, the
well-known Zürich psychoanalyst. In the early summer of 1923, while
traveling across Switzerland from West to East, I had to wait two
hours in Zürich, and went to visit him. He relieved my thirst and
gave me an opportunity to stretch out and rest my weary body. But
he at the same time made me narrate to him, much as they came into
my mind, some incidents of my childhood, that he might make use of
them in a young people's magazine. Soon afterwards he sent me a
copy of what he had taken down in shorthand during those two hours.
I asked him not to publish it, but to leave it to me to complete.
Then, shortly before my departure to Africa, one Sunday afternoon
when it was pelting with rain and snow alternately, I wrote down as
an epilogue to what I had narrated, thoughts that used to stir me
when I looked back upon my youth."[1]

This description of Albert Schweitzer's youthful years was first
published in 1924 in two family magazines--Die Garbe (Basel) and
Elsass-Lothringischer Familien-Kalender (Strasbourg)--with the title
"Aus meiner Kindheit und Jugendzeit" (nos. 199 and 200 below). Later
in the same year, the text was published as a book, with the same
title, appearing in Strasbourg, Bern, and Munich.

102   Aus meiner Kindheit und Jugendzeit. Strasbourg: Librarie
       Evangélique; Bern: Paul Haupt Akademische Buchhandlung
       vorm Max Drechsel; Munich: C. H. Beck (Imprimerie

---

[1]Out of My Life and Thought. New York: Holt, Rinehart and Winston,
1961, pp. 202-03.

Life and Work

Alsacienne), 1924. 73 pp. Certain variations occur in this early edition after its first printing, especially in the front matter, and in type faces, imprints, omission or inclusion of a frontispiece, and in format and decorations.

103   Same. 2. unveränderte Auflage. Bern: Paul Haupt; Munich: C. H. Beck, 1925. 63 pp. Reprinted by C. H. Beck, 1926, 1928, 1929, 1932, 1940, 1941, 1946, 1947, 1949 (Biederstein), 1950, 1951, 1952, 1953, 1954, 1955, 1956, 1957. Reprintings were also issued in certain of these years by Paul Haupt, Bern; in the earlier years by Heitz et Cie and Fischbacher, Strasbourg (Elsässische Ausgabe); and, later, during the Second World War, by Biederstein Verlag, Munich, an affiliate of C. H. Beck. Additional editions appeared as follows:

104   Same. Herausgegeben von F. Westra. Zutphen, Netherlands: W. J. Thieme & Cie, 1936. iv, 82 pp.

105   Same. Olten (Schweiz: Veröffentlichung auf Veranlassung von William Matheson für die Vereinigung Oltner Bücherfreunde), 1952. 95 pp. (Vereinigung Oltner Bücherfreunde, Olten, Schweiz, Nr. 53). Limited edition.

106   Same. [Lizenzausgabe für die Deutsche Demokratische Republik, C. H. Beck, München.] Berlin: Evangelische Verlagsanstalt, 1953. 63 pp. Illus.

107   Same. Bern: Gute Schriften, 1959. 64 pp. Port. (Issued in both boards and paper cover, Gute Schriften, no. 201.)

108   Same. Mit 2 Abbildungen. Munich: C. H. Beck, 1967. 57 pp. Reprinted 1972. Neuausgabe 1978.

109   (Phonodisc). Die Problem des Friedens in der heutigen Welt [und] Aus meiner Kindheit und Jugendzeit. Stimme der Wissenschaft 21/1. 1966. 2 sides. 12 in. 33-1/3 rpm.

Afrikaans

110   Uit my jong dae. Vertaal deur Hymne en Detlev Weiss. Cape Town, South Africa: Balkema, 1957. 57 pp.

Chinese

111   [Aus meiner Kindheit und Jugendzeit.] Tr. Yang Guo Ming. Taiwan: Evergreen Cultural Enterprises, 1975. 86 pp.

General

Life and Work

Czech

112   Z Mého Dětsví a Mládi. Tr. Otakar Kurz. Nákladem vlastnim.
V gen. komisi naklad. Prague: Plamja, 1931. 58 pp.
Port.

113   Z Môjho Dětstva a Mladosti. Přeložila Masta Repásová.
Mikuláši: Tranoscius v Liptovskom, 1943. 68 pp.
(Knižnica Vnutornomisijná Sväzok, 26).

Danish

114   Fra min Barndom og Ungdom. [Autoriseret Oversaettelse for
Danmark og Norge.] Copenhagen: V. Pios Boghandel, Povl
Branner, 1927. 85 pp. Cover port. Second edition Askov
(Kolding): Askov Boghandel, 1940. 82 pp. Cover port.

115   Same. Oversat . . . af Johs. Novrup. Copenhagen: Det danske
Forlag, 1948. 90 pp. Port. Third edition, 1952; Fourth
edition, 1954.

116   "Albert Schweitzer: Fra min Barndom og Ungdom" udkom i 1948
paa Det danske Forlag i oversaettelse ved Magister Johs.
Novrup. Med forfatterens Tilladolse udsendes mermed to
Afsnit af Bogen som Nytaarshilsen 1951-52. Omslag af
Keld Helmer-Petersen. Bogtryk af J. H. Schultz
(Copenhagen, 1951). 16 unnumbered pages.
   Two of the final chapters of Aus meiner Kindheit und
Jugendzeit, reproduced as a New Year's greeting to Albert
Schweitzer, in 1951, by the printer, J. H. Schultz,
Copenhagen.

117   "Albert Schweitzer. Fra min Barndom og Ungdom" udkom 1948 paa
Det danske Forlag i oversaettelse ved Magister Johs.
Novrup. To Kapitler af Bogen bringes her som Nytaarshilson.
Skriften er engelsk Antikva of Trykningen er udført af
Bianco Luno: Omslag af Keld Helmer-Petersen. Typografi
ved Viggo Naae. [Copenhagen: 1952]. xvii pp.
   Two of the final chapters in Aus meiner Kindheit und
Jugendzeit, reproduced as a New Year's greeting to Albert
Schweitzer, in 1952, by the printer Bianco Luno,
Copenhagen.

Dutch

118   Uit mijn jeugd. Vertaald door H. Bervoets. Haarlem:
H. D. Tjeenk Willink & Zoon, 1925. 108 pp.. Reprinted
1927, 1928, 1952 (vii, 99 pp., port.).

Life and Work

English

119   Memoirs of Childhood and Youth. Translated by C. T. Campion.
        London: George Allen & Unwin, 1924. 103 pp. Illus.
        Second printing, 1926.

120   Same. New York: The Macmillan Co., 1925. 103 pp. Illus.
        (Printed in Great Britain.) Reprinted 1931. First
        American edition, The Macmillan Co., 1949. 78 pp.
        Reprinted 1950, 1958.

121   (Paperback edition). New York: The Macmillan Co., 1963.
        124 pp.

122   My Childhood and Youth. Translated from the German by
        C. T. Campion. London: Allen & Unwin, 1960. 96 pp.
        (Unwin Books, no. 4.)

French

123   Souvenirs de mon enfance. Avec un portrait. Lausanne:
        Editions la Concorde, 1926. 84 pp. Port. Reprinted
        1927, 1930.

124   Same. Paris-Strasbourg: Istra, 1950. 100 pp. Port., illus.
        Reprinted 1951, 1952, 1956.

125   Same. Paris: Albin Michel, 1951. Reprinted 1960.

126   Souvenires de mon Enfance. Suivi de les Titteuls de Gunsbach,
        par Gilbert Chesbron. Paris: Brodard et Taupin, 1975.
        124 pp. (Editions j'ai lu, 596.)

127   (Braille edition). Transcription of the edition by Istra,
        1950. Transcrit en Braille par Mme. Julien Kubler.
        Menton (A.M.), 1952. 3 vols. 89, 73, 64 pp.

Greek

128   Ta Paidika mou Hronia. Tr. Agnē Diamantopoulou. Athens:
        Phēxes, 1964. 124 pp.

Icelandic

129   AEskuminningar. Tr. Baldur Palmason. Reykjavik: Setberg,
        1965. 108 pp.

Italian

130   Infanzia e giovinezza. Traduzione dal tedesco di Edgardo
        Pfeifer. Milan: Ugo Mursia-A. P. E. Corticelli, 1959.
        93 pp. Illus. (Le occasioni dello Spirito, 6). Second
        edition, 1965, 96 pp.; Revised edition, 1966, 142 pp;
        Seventh edition, 1969, 144 pp.

Japanese

       Oitachi no Ki. Tokyo: Hakusuisha, 1956. See Collected
        Works, no. 1 above.

131   Waga Yonenjidai to Shonenjidai. Tr. Keizo Saigo. Tokyo:
        Nagasake Shoten, 1942. 215 pp.

132   Waga Yoshonen Jidai. Tr. Seiji Hagii. Tokyo: Shinkyo
        Shuppansha, 1961. 117 pp. Illus.

133   Watashi no Yoshonenjidai. Tr. Seiji Hagii. (Title page
        bilingual, recto-verso in Japanese and German; text in
        Japanese characters.) Tokyo: Shinkyo Shuppansha, 1950.
        126 pp. Port., illus.

Norwegian

134   Fra min Barndom og ungdom. Oversatt etter en ny utgave fra
        1949 av Stephan Tschudi. Oslo: Land og Kirke, 1952.
        95 pp. Cover port. 2 opp., 1953.

Portuguese

135   Minha infancia e mocidade. Traducāo de Otto Schneider.
        São Paulo: Melhoramentos, n.d. (1959), pp. 9-70.
        Port., illus. (Caminhos da Vida, 16). (Included in
        the volume is Histórias Africanas, no. 1329 below.)

Spanish

136   De mi infancia y juventud. Traducción de A.W. Buenos Aires:
        La Aurora; Mexico, D.F.: Case Unida de Publicaciones,
        1945. 86 pp. Illus. Second edition, 1954.

137   Same. Traducción por Ana María Gathmann (y otras). Caracas:
        Universidad Central de Venezuela, 1962. 57 pp. Port.,
        illus.

Life and Work

138   Minnen från min barndoms- och ungdomstid. Tr. Greta
         Lagerfelt. Stockholm: Svenska Krykans Diakonistyrelses
         Bokförlag, 1925. 84 pp. Illus. 2. uppl., 1926.

Welsh

139   Atgofion bore oes. Troswyd i'r Gymraeg gan T. Glyn Thomas.
         Llandybie (Carmathen, Wales): Llyfrau'r Dryw, 1960.
         85 pp.

SELBSTDARSTELLUNG

In the preface of his autobiography, Aus meinem Leben und Denken,
Albert Schweitzer states that in 1929 he published "a concise report
concerning the origin of and the matter contained in my scientific
works" to serve as a chapter in a larger work for a "professional
group of readers." This autobiographical sketch was republished in
the same year as a separate volume with the title Selbstdarstellung.
Two years later it was rewritten and enlarged by the author and was
published with the title Aus meinem Leben und Denken.

140   "Albert Schweitzer" (Selbstdarstellung). In: Die Philosophie
         der Gegenwart in Selbstdarstellungen, Vol. VII. Hrsg. von
         Dr. Raymond Schmidt. Leipzig: Felix Meiner, 1929,
         pp. 205-48. Port.

141   Selbstdarstellung. Leipzig: Felix Meiner; Bern: Paul Haupt;
         Strassburg: Heitz & Cie and Fischbacher, 1929. 44 pp.
         Port. (Sonderdruck aus Die Philosophie der Gegenwart in
         Selbstdarstellungen.) Reprinted 1930, 1931.

AUS MEINEM LEBEN UND DENKEN
(Out of My Life and Thought)

In the preface of this volume, Albert Schweitzer wrote that after
the publication of his earlier biographical sketch, Selbstdarstellung
(1929), "in order to avoid confusion and misunderstanding" he would
write an enlarged and complete biography of his life and work. This
new book, published in 1931 and containing a record of his life, activities, thought, and ethical philosophy, bore the title Aus meinem
Leben und Denken.

142   Aus meinem Leben und Denken. Leipzig: Felix Meiner; Bern:
         Paul Haupt, 1931. 211 pp. Port., illus. Reprinted 1932,
         1933, 1935, 1937, 1940, 1947, 1954, 1971.

General

143   Same. London: Kriegsgefangenenhilfe des Weltbundes der
          Christlichen Vereins Junger Männer in England, n.d.
          (1948). 271 pp. Port. (Zaunkönig Bücher, 510).
          (Ausschliesslich für deutsche Kriegsgefangene gedruckt.
          Made and printed in England by the Dragon Press for the
          World's Alliance of the Young Men's Christian Association's
          War Prisoner's Aid, Geneva, Switzerland.)

144   Same. (Mit Genehmigung der Verlages Felix Meiner in Leipzig.)
          Hamburg: Richard Meiner, 1949. 291 pp. Port., illus.
          Reprinted 1950, 1951, 1952.

145   Same. (Volkesausgabe, ungekürzte Ausgabe). Hamburg: Richard
          Meiner; Bern: Paul Haupt, 1954. 201 pp. Port., illus.
          Reprinted 1955, 1956, 1959.

146   (Paperback edition). (Ungekürzte, Lizenzausgabe des Felix
          Meiner Verlages). Frankfurt a.M., Hamburg: Fischer
          Bücherei, 1952. 201 pp. Cover port. (Fischer Bücherei,
          18). Reprinted 1953, 1954, 1958.

147   Same. Gekürzt und erläutert von Akihiro Tanaka. Tokyo:
          Ikubundo Verlag. I. Teil, 1952. 56 pp. Illus.
          (Anmerkungen und Erläuterung in Japanisch, 14 pp.)
          II. Teil, 1953. 58 pp. (Anmerkungen und Erläuterung in
          Japanisch, 8 pp.) Text in German.

148   Same. Eingeleitet von Max Tau. Munich: Siebenstern
          Taschenbuch, 1955.

149   (Book club edition). Stuttgart: Stuttgarter Hausbücherei,
          1956. Reprinted 1957, 1958.

150   Same. Ausgewählt und erläutert von Henrik Lange. Copenhagen:
          H. Hirschsprung, 1956. 99 pp. (Deutsche Texte für das
          dänische Gymnasium, 8).

151   Same. (Ungekürzte Lizenzausgabe des Felix Meiner Verlages.)
          Leipzig: Koehler & Amelang, 1957. 235 pp. Port.
          Reprinted 1960.

152   Same. Mit einem abschliessenden Kapitel "Die weiteren Jahre"
          (1931-1965) von Rudolf Grabs. Hamburg: F. Meiner, 1975.
          235 pp. Includes three appendices: Lebensdaten; Die
          Werke Albert Schweitzer; Personenregister.

General

Life and Work

Chinese

153   Man huang ch'ang yeh chih. Translated by Shen Szu-chuang.
        (Title page bilingual, Chinese and English; text in Chinese
        characters.) Shanghai: Association Press of China, 1934.
        176 pp. Port. (Youth Library, 18.) Literature Promotion
        Fund Projects, vol. 8.

154   Shih wei Che Tzu Ch'uan. Tr. Hwang Shao-Tzu, et al. Taipei:
        Chang Chung Book Co., 1955.

155   Tzu Chuan. Tr. Ta-tsun Ch'en. Taipei: Hsieh Chih Industrial
        Publishing Co., 1958. vii, 277 pp. 9th edition, 1974.

156   [Out of my Life and Thought.] Tr. Chung-Yee Chen. Taiwan:
        Taiwan Shih Dai Book Co., 1976. 306 pp.

Czech

157   Z Meho Života a Díla. Přeložila Jiřina Lány. Prague: Orbis,
        1938. 196 pp. (Knihy Usudů a Práce, Svazek XXII).

158   Same. Prague: Vysehrad, 1974. 230 pp. Includes Die Lehre
        von der Ehrfurcht vor dem Leben.

Danish

159   Fra mit liv og min Taenkning. Oversat af Olga Bartholdy og
        Johannes Novrup. Askov: Askov Boghandel, n.d. (1941).
        227 pp. Port. 2. ugd. Copenhagen: Det Danske Forlag,
        n.d. (1952). 243 pp. 3 opl., 1953; 4 opl., 1954
        (247 pp.); 5 opl., 1956 (Slight variation in number of
        pages).

Dutch

160   Uit mijn leven en denken. Geautoriseerde vertaling van
        H. M. Eigenhuis-van Gendt en J. Eigenhuis. Haarlem:
        H. D. Tjeenk Willink & Zoon, 1932. vii, 245 pp.
        Port., illus. Reprinted 1949, 1950, 1953, 1955 (223 pp.).

English

161   My Life and Thought: An Autobiography. Tr. C. T. Campion.
        London: George Allen and Unwin, 1933. 288 pp. Illus.,
        port. Reissued 1934 and 1966 (paperback edition).

162   Out of my Life and Thought: An Autobiography. Tr. C. T.
        Campion. New York: Henry Holt and Co., 1933. 288 pp.
        Port., illus. Reprinted 1937.

163   Same. Postscript by Everett Skillings. New York: Henry Holt
        and Co., 1949. 274 pp. (This edition has been redesigned
        and re-set, and the translation has been partially revised.)
        Reprinted 1950, 1955, 1957, and 1961.

164   (Paperback edition). Postscript 1932-1949 by Everett
        Skillings. New York: The New American Library of World
        Literature, 1953. 213 pp. (A Mentor Book, M83.) Re-
        printed 1953, 1957, 1958, 1959, 1960, 1972.

165   Same. Toronto: New American Library of Canada, 1963.
        213 pp.

166   (Paperback edition). London: Frederick Muller, 1958.
        280 pp. (Mentor and Signet Key, 83.)

167   (Paperback edition). New York: Holt, Rinehart and Winston,
        1972. 274 pp. (Holt Paperback 34).

168   (Braille edition). Transcription into Braille of the 1933
        Henry Holt edition. 2 vols.

169   (Talking book for the blind). Edition of Henry Holt and Co.,
        1949. Read by Kermit Murdock, 1950. American Foundation
        for the Blind. 18 records.

Finnish

170   Piirteitä Elämästant ja Ajattelustani. Suomentanut E. Hagfors
        ja A. J. Palmen. Porvoo-Helsinki: Werner Söderström,
        1950. 202 pp. (Humanitas-Sarja, 16). Second edition,
        1963, 214 pp.; Third edition, 1965, 215 pp.

French

171   Ma vie et ma pensée. Paris: Albin Michel, 1959. 286 pp.
        Port. "Notice bibliographique" par Robert Minder,
        pp. 279-85.

172   Same. Paris: Club des Editeurs, 1960. 251 pp. Port.
        (Club des Editeurs, 121).

Greek

173   Hē zōē kai hē skepsis mou. Tr. Agnēs Diamantopoulou. Athens:
        Galaxia, 1965. 274 pp.

General

Life and Work

Italian

174   <u>La mia Vita e il mio Pensiero</u>. Tr. A. Guadagnin. Milan:
Edizioni di Communita, 1965. 218 pp. 2nd ed., 1977.
220 pp. Illus.

Japanese

175   <u>Waga Seikatsu to Shisō Yori</u>. Translated from the German by
Michio Takeyama. (Title page bilingual, recto verso,
Japanese and German. Text in Japanese characters.)
Tokyo: Hakusuisha, 1939. 321 pp.

176   (Second edition). Tokyo: Hakusuisha, 1953. 253 pp.
Reprinted 1958, 1959.

<u>Waga Shogai to Shisō Yori</u>. Tr. Michio Takeyama. Tokyo:
Hakusuisha, 1956. See Collected Works, no. 2 above.

177   <u>Genshirin no Henkyô Nite</u>. Tr. Toshiharu Haneda. Tokyo:
Naniun-Dô, 1963. 172 pp. Bound with <u>Zwischen Wasser und
Urwald</u>, see no. 1270 below.

Korean

178   <u>Na ui sarang kwa saengmyongul tahayo</u>. Tr. Sa-mok Kim.
Seoul: Hwimun Publishing Co., 1962. 308 pp. Reprinted
1970.

179   <u>Na ui Saenghwal Kwa Sasang Eso</u>. Tr. Myong-Gwan Chi. Seoul:
Gyeongjisa, 1962. 308 pp.

Malaysian

180   <u>Ente jīvitavum cintayam</u>. Tr. from the English by M. C.
Nampūtirippatu. Trichur: Mangalodayam, 1957. xiv,
191 pp.

Norwegian

181   <u>Liv og tanker</u>. Fra tysk ved Carl Fredrik Engelstad. Oslo:
Johan Grundt Tanum, 1953. 248 pp. 7th edition, 1954;
8th edition, 1955; 9th edition Oslo: Aschehoug, 1966,
184 pp.

Oriyan

182   <u>Mojībana o Sādhanā</u>. Tr. from the English by Cittaranjan Dās.
Cuttack (Orissa): Prafulla Chandra Das, 1959. lx,
300 pp. Illus. (Introductory notes in Western

General

languages, including preface-letters from Hermann Hesse,
Albert Schweitzer, Rene Maran, and Pere Dominique Pire.)

Portuguese

183 Minha vide e minhas ideias. Traducāo de Otto Schneider.
     São Paulo: Melhoramentos, n.d. (1959). 252 pp. Port.,
     illus. (Serie Albert Schweitzer.)

Spanish

184 Mi vida y mi pensamiento. Buenos Aires: La Aurora.

185 Same. Versión castellana de Horacio A. Maniglia. Buenos
     Aires: Hachette, 1961. 248 pp. Illus. (Colleción
     Nuevo Mirador.) Translation of the French edition.
     Reprinted 1962.

186 De me Vida y mi Pensamiento. Trad. de Concha Aguirre.
     Barcelona: Ayma, 1965. 191 pp.

Swedish

187 Ur mitt liv och tänkande. Bemyndigad översättning från tyskan
     av Greta Lagerfelt. Med förord av Anton Fridrichsen.
     Uppsala: J. A. Lindblad, 1936. 241 pp. Port., illus.
     Reprinted 1936. New edition, 1953, 241 pp. Reprinted
     1954, 1959.

Tamil

188 Alpart Svaitsarin ouyacaritem. Tr. from the English by
     K. N. Subrahmanyam. Madras: Orient Longmans for Southern
     Languages Book Trust, 1958. xii, 196 pp.

Telugu

189 Atmakatha. Tr. from the English by Srinivasa Chakravarti.
     Vijayavada: Adarsa Granthamandali (under the auspices
     of the Southern Languages Book Trust, Madras), 1960.
     xii, 223 pp. Cover port.

2. Shorter Writings by Schweitzer

190 "Albert Schweitzer." In: Schouten, Jan Hendrik, ed.
     Lebensdienst: Robert Koch, Fridtjof Nansen, Albert
     Schweitzer. Biographische Fragmente gesammelt und
     erläutert von J. H. Schouten. Amsterdam: J. M. Melenhoff,
     1943, pp. 65-99.

Life and Work

191   "Albert Schweitzer: a Self-Portrait" (phonodisc). Recorded
       at Lambarene by Erica Anderson. Notes on slipcase by
       Norman Cousins. Caedmon TC 1335. 1972.

192   "Albert Schweitzer--sa vie et sa pensée." CAHIERS/BELGE
       1 (November 1960), pp. 6-7.

193   "Albert Schweitzer über sich selbst" (extracts from Aus meiner
       Kindheit und Jugendzeit, etc.). Die Christengemeinschaft
       (Stuttgart) 27:1 (January 1955), pp. 22-24.

194   "Aus Albert Schweitzers Leben." Die Evangelischen Missionen
       (Berlin-Steglitz) 36:4 (1930), pp. 73-78.

195   "Aus der Jugenderinnerungen." In: SCHWEITZER, pp. 70-75.
       Extracts from Aus meiner Kindheit und Jugendzeit.

196   "Aus meinem Leben." EERBIED 23:2 (December 1974), pp. 32-34.

197   "Aus meinem Leben. Ein unveröffentlichen Vortrag."
       Mitgeleitet von Erwin R. Jacobi. Schweizer Monatshefte
       (Zürich) 50:3 (June 1970), pp. 224-31. Text of a presen-
       tation on Radio Köln, April 20, 1932. Reprinted in
       BERICHTE 32 (September 1970), pp. 19-26; also in Der
       Samariter (January 17, 1971), pp. 1-2; RUNDBRIEFE/DDR
       17 (1971), pp. 1-9; RUNDBRIEF 34 (Dec. 1, 1971), pp. 5-8
       and 42 (October 1976), pp. 29-32, including only
       Schweitzer's address. Translated as "Albert Schweitzer
       Speaks. Radio Cologne 1932." In: PROPHET, pp. 3-6;
       Also in Cahiers Europeens/Europäische Hefte/Notes from
       Europe (Munich) 2:1 (Jan. 1975), pp. 12-19, including
       only Schweitzer's address; in Sonderdruck aus Europäische
       Hefte, Heft 1/75 (Basel, 1975), pp. 5-13; as "Allocution
       radiophonique sur sa vie" in CAHIERS 29 (Summer 1973),
       pp. 10-14; also in NOUVELLES 37 (January 1976), pp. 20-21;
       in A Study of Schweitzer, I. Tokyo: Albert Schweitzer
       Fellowship of Japan, 1971, pp. 61-69.

198   "Aus meinem Leben und Denken." Das Werk (Gelsenkirchen) 2
       (1953), pp. 201-05.

199   "Aus meiner Kindheit und Jugendzeit." FAMILIEN-KALENDAR 21
       (1924), pp. 55-63. Extracts from book of the same title.

200   "Aus meiner Kindheit und Jugendzeit." Die Garbe,
       Schweizerischen Familienblatt (Basel) 7:9 (Feb. 1, 1924),
       pp. 273-78; 7:10 (Feb. 15, 1924), pp. 306-11; 7:11
       (March 1, 1924), pp. 341-46; 7:12 (March 15, 1924),
       pp. 374-79; 7:13 (April 1, 1924), pp. 400-05.

201   "Christmas Thank-you Letters--When Albert Schweitzer was a
         Boy." Journal of the American Medical Association
         (Chicago) 194:12 (December 20, 1965), p. 99. (Excerpt
         from Memoirs of Childhood and Youth.)

202   "Education of Albert Schweitzer." In: Morgan, Stewart S.,
         John Q. Hays and Fred E. Ekfelt, eds. Readings for
         Thought and Expression. New York: Macmillan, 1955,
         pp. 52-65. (Excerpt from Memoirs of Childhood and Youth.)

203   [Excerpts from Memoirs of Childhood and Youth and On the Edge
         of the Primeval Forest.] In: Campion, Charles T.,
         compiler. Albert Schweitzer, Philosopher, Theologian
         Musician, Doctor. Some Biographical Notes. London:
         A. and C. Black, 1928.

204   "De Fiets." NIEUWS 3:3 (October 1954), pp. 93-94.

205   "I quietly began my work, my search was over." In: Dunaway,
         Philip and George DeKay, eds. Turning Point: Fateful
         Moments that revealed men and made history. New York:
         Random House, 1958, pp. 145-48. (Excerpt from Out of
         my Life and Thought.)

206   "Ik heb de roepstem gehoord." Vertaling van de toespraak op
         Zondagmiddag 16 November om 17.00 uur gehouden voor de
         microfoon van de V.P.R.O. NIEUWS 1:4 (December 1952),
         pp. 55-57. Reprinted as: Dr. Albert Schweitzer in
         Holland. Radiorede van Dr. Albert Schweitzer op 16
         November 1952 uitgesproken voor de V.P.R.O.-microfoon en
         op 15. November gepubliceerd in Vrije geluiden met een
         woord ter inleiding van Dr. E. D. Spelberg. Delft:
         Gaade, 1953. 30 pp.

207   "Kreigsausbruch 1914." Epoca 2:8 (August 1964). Reprinted
         in the A.I.S.L. Bulletin 3 (February 1977), p. 15.

208   "Les Gendarmes." In: RAYONNEMENT, pp. 206-08.

209   "Mes souvenirs du Vieux Colmar." Journal d'Alsace et de
         Lorraine (March 1949), pp. 16-17. Text of a speech
         given by Dr. Schweitzer at a reception in Colmar,
         February 23, 1949. Reprinted as "Retour à Colmar."
         Réforme (Paris) 5:234 (Sept. 10, 1949), p. 4; "Mes
         Souvenirs du Vieux-Colmar." Annuaire de la société
         historique et litteraire de Colmar (1950), pp. 97-104;
         "Souvenirs du vieux Colmar." In: Feschotte, Jacques.
         Albert Schweitzer. Paris: Editions Universitaires,
         1952. Extracts only. Also as "Souvenirs du Vieux Colmar."

Life and Work

In: RAYONNEMENT, pp. 21-25. Also in CAHIERS 29
(Summer 1973), pp. 17-21. Translated as "Return to
Colmar." World Review (London) (June 1949), pp. 11-14;
"Return to Colmar." The Daily Mail (London), September 25,
1950; "Childhood Recollections of Old Colmar." In
Feschotte, Jacques. Albert Schweitzer, an Introduction.
Tr. John Russell. London: A. and C. Black, 1954, ex-
cerpts only; "Meine Erinnerungen an das alte Colmar . . . ."
Les Dernières Nouvelles du Haut-Rhin (Colmar) 29:63
(March 16, 1949), p. 4; 29:64 (March 17, 1949), p. 3;
29:65 (March 18, 1949), p. 7.

210   "My Childhood and Youth." In: Rosen, George and Beate
       Caspari-Rosen, eds. 400 Years of a Doctor's Life.
       Schuman, 1947, pp. 44-50 and 119-22. (Excerpts from
       Memoirs of Childhood and Youth.)

211   "Out of my Life and Thought." In: Burnett, Whit, ed. The
       World's Best. New York: The Dial Press, 1950, pp. 810-23.

212   "Playboy Interview: Albert Schweitzer, a candid interview
       with Africa's enigmatic doctor of the body and soul."
       Playboy (Chicago) 10:12 (Dec. 1963), pp. 89-92.

213   "Ungdomsidealismen." Svenska Dagbladet (Stockholm),
       June 14, 1925.

214   "Von Danken und Dienen." Neubau (Munich) 5:7 (July 1950),
       pp. 298-99. (Excerpts from Aus meiner Kindheit und
       Jugendzeit.)

215   "Der Weg." In: SCHWEITZER, pp. 15-38. (Contains portions
       of Aus meinem Leben und Denken and Zwischen Wasser und
       Urwald.)

216   "Wie ich Urwaldarzt wurden." Die Kirche (Berlin-Dahlem) 2:25
       (1927), p. 2. Also "Der Entschluss Urwaldarzt zu werden."
       The American-German Review (Philadelphia) 21:2 (Dec. 1954-
       Jan. 1955), pp. 10-12. Excerpt from Aus meinem Leben und
       Denken. Also in Kneipp-Blätter (Bad-Wörishofen) 60 (1957),
       pp. 333-36; RUNDBRIEF 14 (July 1, 1959), pp. 11-18. Trans-
       lated as "Why I became a doctor." Coronet (Chicago) 42:2
       (June 1957), pp. 42-43; "Comment je suis devenu médecin."
       Semaine de France (Paris), May 8, 1952.

3. Works by Others

    a. Books

217   ACHTERBERG, EBERHARD. Albert Schweitzer. Ein Leben in der
        Zeitwende. Hameln: H. Soltsien, 1968. 88 pp.
        (Leitbilder, Bd. 2).

218   Albert Schweitzer. Deventer: Ned. Albert Schweitzer Centrum.
        17 pp. Illus.

219   Albert Schweitzer. Actuele Onderwerpen, 1965. 16 pp.
        (A. O. Series No. 1077.)

220   Albert Schweitzer, der Urwalddoktor von Lambarene. Bonn:
        Deutscher Sparkassen- und-Giroverband, 1959. 46 pp.

221   ALLINGES, JEAN D'. Le Docteur et Madame Schweitzer. Paris:
        Fernand Lanore, 1962. 125 pp.

222   AMADOU, ROBERT. Albert Schweitzer. Éléments de Biographie et
        de Bibliographie. Paris: L'Arche, 1952. 142 pp.

223   ANDERSON, ERICA. Albert Schweitzer's Gift of Friendship.
        New York and Evanston: Harper and Row, 1964. vii,
        152 pp. Illus., ports. London: Robert Hale, 1966.
        142 pp. Illus. Paperback edition, 1976.

        TRANSLATIONS

        Ystävyyden lahja--Albert Schweitzer. 1965. 172 pp.
           (Finnish).

        Albert Schweitzer--ett vänporträtt. 1965. 151 pp.
           (Swedish).

224   _____. The Schweitzer Album, a portrait in works and
        pictures. Additional text by Albert Schweitzer. New
        York: Harper and Row; London: Adam and Charles Black,
        1965. xii, 176 pp. Ports., illus.

225   _____ and EUGENE EXMAN. The World of Albert Schweitzer. A
        Book of Photographs . . . with text and captions by
        Eugene Exman. New York: Harper and Brothers; London:
        A. and C. Black, 1955. 144 pp. Illus., ports.

        TRANSLATIONS

        Albert Schweitzers värld. Inledning, Stefan Zweig. Tr. Anna
           Bohlin. Uppsala: Lindblad, 1955. 131 pp. Illus.

Life and Work

Albert Schweitzers Werden. Foreword by Stefan Zweig.
Copenhagen: Branner og Korch, 1955.

Le Monde d'Albert Schweitzer. Avant-Propos de Daniel Halévy.
Paris: Albin Michel, 1955. 134 pp. Illus.

Die Welt Albert Schweitzers. Einleitung von Stefan Zweig.
S. Fischer Verlag. 134 pp. (German).

Die Wereld van Albert Schweitzer. The Hague: M. C. Stok, n.d.

(Japanese). Tokyo: Hakusuisha, 1957.

(Chinese). Taiwan: Evergreen Cultural Enterprise Co.,
1975. 57 pp.

226 ANTAL, MAREK. Igy élt Albert Schweitzer. Budapest: Mora
Könyvkadi, 1976.

227 AUGUSTINY, WALDEMAR. Albert Schweitzer und Du. Witten/Ruhr:
Luther Verlag, 1955, 1957, 1959. 224 pp. Port.
(Ausgabe für die DDR). Berlin: Union Verlag, 1957.
306 pp.
(Nur für die Mitglieder). Gütersloh: Bertelsmann
Lesering, 1958. 187 pp. Illus.
(Paperback edition). Gütersloh: Gütersloher Verlagshaus
Gerd Mohn, 1960. 190 pp.

TRANSLATIONS

Albert Schweitzer en wij. Voorwoord van Albert Schweitzer.
Vertaald door Lidy van Rijnsselsteijn. Delft: W. Gaade,
1955. 221 pp.

The Road to Lambarene. A Biography of Albert Schweitzer.
Tr. William J. Blake. London: Frederick Muller, 1956.
228 pp.

Albert Schweitzer. Suomentanut Mani Malm. Helsinki:
Kirjayhtymäoy, 1959. 195 pp.

228 AVILÉS FABILA, RENÉ. Albert Schweitzer: O, el Respeto por
la Vida. Mexico: Secretaría de educación publica,
Subsecretaría de Asuntos Culturales, 1967. 45 pp.
(Cuadernos de Lectura Popular, 62. Serie la Honda del
Espirita).

229 AYASSOT, ERNESTO. Il Medico della Giungla. Vita e opere del
dottore Alberto Schweitzer, premio Nobel 1953 per la pace.

Torino: Editrice Claudiana, 1954. 136 pp. Illus.
Second edition, 1962, 125 pp. Illus.

230   BABEL, HENRY ADALBERT. Schweitzer tel qu'il fut. Neuchatel:
La Baconniere, 1966. 160 pp. Illus. Second enlarged
edition, 1970. 198 pp., illus.

231   BALCAR, JOSEF. Albert Schweitzer. Lékař, Misionář, evorpan
v pralese. Prague: Kalich, 1948. 62 pp. Port.

232   BALORY, LOUISE. Docteur Schweitzer. Paris: Editions du
Scorpion, 1960. 256 pp. (Collection Alternance.)

233   BAUR, HERMANN. Für oder gegen Albert Schweitzer. Stuttgart:
Hippokrates Verlag, 1962. 16 pp. Reprinted from
Hippokrates 33:23 (1962), pp. 982-89.

TRANSLATIONS

Albert Schweitzer, a Clarification. Tr. Alisa Jaffa. Issued
by the British Council for Dr. Schweitzer's Hospital Fund.

Pour ou contre Albert Schweitzer. Basel: Assoc. Suisse d'Aide
à l'Hôpital Albert Schweitzer à Lambarene, 1962. 15 pp.

234   BIEZAIS, H. Alberts Sveicers. Lielais Zinatnieks un Arsts
Afrikas mūža mezos. Riga: Ev.-Luth. Baznicas Virsvalde,
1940. 53 pp. (Bopgrafisku Ratstu Serija, 6.)

BOURDIER, ROLAND. La Vie et la Pensée d'Albert Schweitzer.
See Dissertations, no. 4312 below.

235   BRABAZON, JAMES. Albert Schweitzer: a Biography. New York:
G. P. Putnam, 1975. 509 pp. Illus. London: Gollancz,
1976.

236   BRAUN, REINHOLD (Pseud. for Reinhold Braun-Echelsbach).
Albert Schweitzer. Konstanz: Christliche Verlagsanstalt,
1956. 31 pp. Illus. Reprinted 1958. (Christliche
Lebensbilder, H. 17.)

237   CESBRON, GILBERT. Albert Schweitzer. Begegnungen. Berlin:
Union Verlag, 1957. 60 pp. Heidelberg: Drei Brücken
Verlag, 1958. 66 pp. (German translation of "Sur Albert
Schweitzer" from Unser Jahrhundert ruft um Hilfe, see
no. 460 below).

238   CHASSÉ, CHARLES. Docteur Schweitzer. Illus. de André Bacon.
Paris: Librairie Charpentier, 1959. 182 pp. Illus.
(Lecture et Loisir, no. 7.)

Life and Work

239 CHRISTALLER, HELENE. Albert Schweitzer; ein Leben für andere.
     Mit einem Nachwort von Richard Kik. Stuttgart: J. F.
     Steinkopf, 1954. 88 pp. Ports. "Erschien in Berlin.
     Vorliegende neue Auflage wurde von Richard Kik . . . bis
     in unsere Tage fortgeführt."

240 CHRISTEN, ERNEST. Schweitzer l'Africain. Quelques traits
     d'une belle vie. Ill. de Fernand Gilbert et portr.
     d'Alexandre Matthey. Geneva: Ed. Labor et Fides, 1948.
     200 pp. (Les vainqueurs 18.) Fourth edition, 1952,
     199 pp.; sixth edition, 1954, 194 pp. Also Lausanne:
     Plaisir de Lire, 1961. 199 pp. Ill. (Plaisir de lire
     112.)

     TRANSLATIONS

     Albert Schweitzer: Leben und Werk. Einzig berechtige
        Übertragung aus dem Französischen von Alexandra Brun.
        Bern: Alfred Scherz, 1955. 219 pp.

     Albert Schweitzer, Negrernas vän. Översätting fran 6:e
        franska upplagen av Anna Bohlin. Uppsala: Lindblad,
        1955. 159 pp. Illus.

     Albert Schweitzer, Zijn Leven en Werk. Vertaling uit het
        Frans door J. B. van Houten. Zwolle: La Riviere &
        Voorhoeve, 1957. 187 pp.

     Schweitzer. Tr. Mark Clement. London: Parrish, 1962.
        viii, 148 pp. Illus.

241 CORUH, HAKKI SINASI. Aborra Oganga, Tesekkur Ederiz Beyaz
        Sihirbaz. Dr. Albert Schweitzer in Hayati. Istanbul:
     Kitapclic Ticaret Ltd., SRT, 1967. 122 pp. (Aksam Kitap
     Külübü Serisi, no. 38.)

242 COUSINS, NORMAN. Dr. Schweitzer of Lambarene. With photos
     by Clara Urquhart. New York: Harper, 1960. 254 pp.
     Illus. Reprinted Westport, Conn.: Greenwood Press, 1973.

     TRANSLATIONS

     Albert Schweitzer und sein Lambarene. Stuttgart: Gunther,
        132 pp. Illus. (Shorter German version of above.)

     Skyer over Lambarene. Copenhagen: Branner og Korch, 1961.
        257 pp. Illus.

Life and Work

DOTY, JAMES EDWARD. Reverence for Life in the Career of
Albert Schweitzer. See Dissertations, no. 4315 below.

243 DUINO, MICHEL. Albert Schweitzer, le Grand Sorcier Blanc.
Paris: Ed. Inter. 1959. 152 pp. Illus.

244 EIGENHUIS, JAN. Albert Schweitzer. Haarlem: Tjeenk Willink,
1929. 260 pp.

245 EINARSSON, SIGURBJÖRN. Albert Schweitzer. Reykjavik, 1955.

246 ENGELSTAD, CARL FREDRIK. Albert Schweitzer Erobrer Norge;
en liten bok om en stor opplevelse. Redigert av Carl
Fredrik Engelstad and Max Tau. Oslo: J. G. Tanum, 1954.
64 pp. Mostly illustrations.

247 FABRICIUS, JOHS. Albert Schweitzer, Kaetter og Helgen.
Copenhagen: Forlaget Credo, 1959. 192 pp. Illus.

248 FESCHOTTE, JACQUES. Albert Schweitzer (avec des textes
inédits). Paris: Éditions Universitaires, 1952. 129 pp.
Port. (Classiques du XXe siècle).

TRANSLATIONS

Albert Schweitzer, an Introduction. With two unpublished
addresses by Albert Schweitzer. London: Adam and Charles
Black, 1954. 130 pp. Boston: Beacon Press, 1955.
130 pp.

Same. London: Collins, 1956. 128 pp. (Comet Books.)

Albert Schweitzer. Tr. A. Braga. Milan: Curci, 1954.
138 pp.

Albert Schweitzer. Tr. Av. Boch M. Stolpe. Stockholm:
Svenska kyrkans diakonistyrelses Bokförlag, 1954. 157 pp.

249 FIERZOVA, OLGA. Albert Schweitzer, Doktor Pralesa. Prague:
Czech. Cervenho Krize, 1933. 60 pp.

250 FISCHER, GERHARD, ed. Albert Schweitzer. Leben, Werk und
Wirkung. Eine Bilddokumentation. Berlin: Union Verlag,
1977. 123 pp. Illus.

251 FREYER, PAUL HERBERT. Albert Schweitzer: ein Lebensbild.
Berlin: Union Verlag, 1978.

Life and Work

252   FRIIS, BØRGE. Hjemme hos Albert Schweitzer. Copenhagen:
        Branner og Korch, 1953. 48 pp. Illus.

253   GAERTNER, HENRYK. Albert Schweitzer. Krakow: Polska
        Akademia Nauk, 1978. 33 pp. (Nauka Ala Wszystkich,
        Nr. 283.)

254   GÖTTING, GERALD. Albert Schweitzer--Pionier der
        Menschlichkeit. Berlin: Union Verlag, 1970. 174 pp.
        Illus. Reprinted 1979. 190 pp. Illus.

255   GOLLOMB, JOSEPH. Albert Schweitzer: Genius in the Jungle.
        New York: Vanguard Press; Toronto: Copp Clark Co., Ltd.
        1949. 249 pp.

        TRANSLATIONS

        Albert Schweitzer. Milan: Giunti-Martello. 204 pp.

        Albert Schweitzer, genius in der Wildnis. Übers. und bearb.
            von Christian und Otto Albrecht Isbert. Stuttgart:
            H. E. Günther, 1957. 241 pp. Illus., ports.

        Schweitzer. Trad. par Mina Zografau et K. Meranaios.
            Athens: Ed. Galaxis, 1954. 154 pp.

        La Vie ardente d'Albert Schweitzer. Tr. Michel Deon. Paris:
            Editions Sun, 1950. 177 pp. Illus.

256   GRABS, RUDOLF. Albert Schweitzer. Berlin: Steuben-Verlag,
        Paul G. Esser, 1949. 428 pp. Port.
        (Second edition). Albert Schweitzer, gehorsam und Wagnis.
            Hamburg: Meiner, 1952. 428 pp.
        (Neu bearb. aufl.). Hamburg: R. Meiner, 1958. 428 pp.

257   _____. Albert Schweitzer. Dienst am Menschen. Ein
        Lebensbild. Halle/Saale: Max Niemeyer, 1961. 267 pp.
        Enlarged edition, 1964, 288 pp.; further enlarged edition,
        1964, 298 pp. 6th edition, 1969, 270 pp.

258   _____. Albert Schweitzer; ein Leben im Dienste der
        sittlichen Tat. Berlin: Evangelische Verlagsanstalt,
        1952. 71 pp. Port.
        (Second edition). Albert Schweitzer. Tat und Gedanke.
            Eine Hinführung zu Weg u. Lebenslehre Albert Schweitzers.
            Hrsg. v. der Pressestelle der Evangelisch-Lutherische
            Kirche in Thüringen. Berlin: Ev. Verlagsanstalt, 1967.
            79 pp.

(Third edition). Hrsg. von der Pressestelle der
Evangelisch-Lutherische Kirche in Thüringen. Berlin:
Evangelische Verlagsanstalt (In Verb. mit der Wartburg-
Verlags Kessler, Jena, 1968), 102 pp.

259 _____. Albert Schweitzer. Weg und Werk eines Menschenfreundes.
Stuttgart: Reclam, 1954. 95 pp. (Reclams Universal-
Bibliothek, Nr. 7754).

260 _____. Albert Schweitzer. Wegbereiter der ethischen
Erneuerung. 2nd ed. Berlin: Union Verlag, 1965. 31 pp.
Illus. (Reihe Christ in der Welt, Heft 3).

261 _____. Albert Schweitzer: Wirklichkeit und Auftrag. Hrsg.
v.d. Pressestelle d. Ev.-Luth. Kirche in Thüringen.
Berlin: Evangelische Verlagsanstalt, 1975. 77 pp.
Illus. 2nd edition, 1977.

262 HAGEDORN, HERMANN. Prophet in the Wilderness; the Story of
Albert Schweitzer. New York: Macmillan, 1947. 221 pp.
Illus. Revised edition, 1955, 240 pp.
(New revised edition). Albert Schweitzer; prophet in the
Wilderness. New York: Collier Books, 1962. 224 pp.
(Collier Books, AS150).
(Condensed version). In: Reader's Digest Family Treasury
of Great Biographies, vol. X. Pleasantville, N.Y.:
Reader's Digest Association, 1971, pp. 169-250.

TRANSLATIONS

Albert Schweitzer. Korskaran, musician, tropical doctor.
Tr. Margareta Astrand. Stockholm: Svenska Kyrkhans
Diakonistyrelsens, 1950. 228 pp.

[The Biography of Dr. Albert Schweitzer.] Tr. Chung Chao-
Cheng. Taiwan: Chih Wen Publ. Co., 1977. 289 pp.

Menschenfreund in Urwald; das leben Albert Schweitzers.
Tr. Otto von Czernicki. Hamburg: Meiner, 1954. 224 pp.
Illus.

O Profeta das Selvas: a História de Albert Schweitzer.
Tr. Ilydio Burgos Lopes. São Paulo: União Cultural,
1955.

Vredesapostel in het Oerwoud. 240 pp. (Dutch).

263 HALLEN, G. Albert Schweitzer. Stockholm: Modin-Tryck,
1970. 32 pp.

General

Life and Work

264   HAUTERRE, HENRI.   Albert Schweitzer.   Nürnberg; Verlag die
      Egge, 1948.

265   ITALIAANDER, ROLF.   Gedanken über Albert Schweitzer.
      Dortmunder Rede.   Hamburg: Freie Akademie der Künste,
      1968.   24 pp.

266   KALFUS, RADIM.   Vzpominky na Dr. Alberta Schweitzera a na
      Lambaréné: 1875-1975.   Prague: Prace, 1975.   92 pp.
      Illus.   (Editions Kniznice Zare).

267   KANTZENBACH, FRIEDRICH WILHELM.   Albert Schweitzer.
      Wirklichkeit und Legende.   Göttingen: Musterschmidt-
      Verlag, 1969.   114 pp.   Illus.   (Persönlichkeit und
      Geschichte, Bd. 50).

      TRANSLATIONS

      Albert Schweitzer.   Realtà et Leggenda.   Tr. A. Frioli.
        Rome: Edizioni Paoline, 1971.   162 pp.

268   KARCZOCH, JAN.   Zycie i Mysli Alberta Schweitzera.   Warsaw:
      Wydawnictwo, 1977.

269   KLEINE, H. O.   Albert Schweitzer, der Baumeister einer neuen
      Ordnung.

270   KUMARAN, (pseud).   Taktar Alpart Svaitsar.   1963.   156 pp.
      Ports.   (In Tamil).

271   LAMM-NATANNSEN, M.   Albert Schweitzer; kurzer Überblick
      über sein Leben und seine Arbeit.   1960.   69 pp.

272   LAZARI-PAWLOWSKA, IJA.   Schweitzer.   Warsaw: Wiedza
      Powzechna, 1976.   248 pp.

273   LIND, EMIL.   Albert Schweitzer, aus seinem Leben und Werk.
      Bern: P. Haupt, 1948.   216 pp.
      (Autorisierte jubiläumsausgabe zum 80. Geburtstag
        Dr. Schweitzers).   Wiesbaden: Necessitas-Verlag,
        1955.   388 pp.   Illus.   (Die weissen Hefte, 5).

      TRANSLATIONS

      Albert Schweitzer, zijn Leven en Werk.   Naarden: Uitgeverij
        "in den Toren," 1949.   224 pp.   2nd edition, 1950.

274   MARSHALL, GEORGE N.   An Understanding of Albert Schweitzer.
      New York: Philosophical Library; London: Vision Press,
      1966.   180 pp.   Illus., ports.

General

Life and Work

275 _____ and DAVID POLING. Schweitzer, a Biography. Garden
    City, N.Y.: Doubleday and Co., 1971. viii, 342 pp.
    Illus., ports.

276 MAZARIN, ROBERT. Un homme de pensée et d'action au service
    du prochain: Albert Schweitzer, Discours. . . . Colmar:
    Alsatia, 1968. 48 pp. Illus. (Cour d'appel de Colmar.
    Audience solonnelle de rentrée du 16 septembre 1966).

277 MC KNIGHT, GERALD. Verdict on Schweitzer, the man behind the
    legend of Lambarene. London: F. Muller; New York: John
    Day, 1964. 254 pp. Illus.

278 MONESTIER, MARIANNE. Le grand docteur blanc. Avant-propos
    de Gilbert Cesbron. Paris: La Table ronde, 1954.
    240 pp. Illus.

    TRANSLATIONS

    Alberto Schweitzer, el gran doctor blanco. Tr. Pilar
    Guibelalde, prólogo de Gilbert Cesbron. Barcelona;
    Iberia, 1954. 204 pp. Illus.

    Der grosse weisse Doktor: Albert Schweitzer. Mit einem
    Vorwort von Gilbert Cesbron. Tr. Gertrud Stucki-Sahli.
    Bern: A. Scherz, 1953. 255 pp.

279 MONTAGUE, JOSEPH FRANKLIN. The Why of Albert Schweitzer.
    An appraisal in depth of the career of an extraordinary
    man of medicine. New York: Hawthorne Books, 1965.
    312 pp. Illus. Also Ulverscroft, Leicester, Eng.:
    Thorpe, 1967. 241 pp. (The Ulverscroft Large Print
    Series. Non Fiction).

280 NOMURA, MINORU. [Grandes Vies: Albert Schweitzer,
    Livingston, Uchimura.] Tokyo, 1950.

281 _____. Ningen Schweitzer. Tokyo: Iwanami Shoten, 1955.
    204 pp.

282 _____. Shubaitsuā Hakushi o Kataru. 1961. 292 pp.
    Illus.

283 NOSSIK, BORIS MICHAILOWITSCH. Shveitser. Moscow: La Jeune
    Garde, 1971. 412 pp.

    TRANSLATIONS

    Schweitzer. Tallinn: Kirjastus "Eesti Raamat," 1976.
    (Estonian)

41

Life and Work

Schweitzer. Kossuth Konyvkaido, 1975. (Hungarian)

Albert Schweitzer: ein Leben für die Menschlichkeit. Tr.
Lothar Pickenhain. Leipzig: S. Hirzel Verlag, 1977.
372 pp. (Series: Humanisten der Tat).

284 OBERMAN-OBERMAN, H. Albert Schweitzer, een blik in zijn leven
en arbeid. The Hague: J. N. Voorhoeve, 1949. 23 pp.
Illus. (Lichtstralen op de akker der wereld, 50. jaarg.,
1949, nr. 4).

285 _____. Albert Schweitzer, een blik in zijn leven en Werken.
The Hague: Voorhoeve, 1950. 95 pp. Illus. (Lichtstralen
op de akker der wereld, no. 1).

286 OSWALD, SUZANNE. Geist der Humanität: Beitrag zu einem
Lebensbild Albert Schweitzers. Mit einem Auszug aus
der Frankfurter Rede vom 16. September 1951 von Albert
Schweitzer. St. Gallen: Tschudy, 1954. 28 pp. (Der
Bogen, Heft 35).

287 _____. Mein Onkel Bery. Erinnerungen an Albert Schweitzer.
Zürich, Stuttgart: Rotapfel Verlag, 1971. 211 pp.
Illus. Second edition, 1972; Third edition, 1973. 311 pp.

TRANSLATIONS

[Dutch.] Tr. Foppe Oberman. Baarn: Edition Ten Have, 1977.

Mon oncle Albert Schweitzer. Souvenirs. Tr. Madeleine Horst.
Colmar: Editions Alsatia, 1974.

PAYNE, PIERRE STEPHEN ROBERT. The Three Worlds of Albert
Schweitzer. See Youth, no. 4240 below.

PETRIZKI, WILLI. Light in the Jungle. See Youth, no. 4241
below.

288 PFEIFFER, HERMANN. Albert Schweitzer. Werden und Wirken.
Kreiztal: Jung-Stilling-Verlag, 1946, 1948. 69 pp.
(Kleine Biographen). 3. enlarged edition, 1954, 103 pp.

289 PHILLIPS, HERBERT M. Safari of Discovery: the Universe of
Albert Schweitzer. New York: Twayne Publishers, 1958.
271 pp. Illus.

290 PICHT, WERNER ROBERT VALENTIN. Albert Schweitzer; Wesen und
Bedeutung. Hamburg: R. Meiner, 1960. 320 pp. Illus.

TRANSLATIONS

Albert Schweitzer, the Man and his Work. Tr. Edward
   Fitzgerald. London: Allen, 1964. 288 pp. Illus.

The Life and Thought of Albert Schweitzer. Tr. Edward
   Fitzgerald. New York: Harper and Row, 1964. 288 pp.
   Ports.

291 PIERHAL, JEAN. Albert Schweitzer, das Leben eines guten
     Menschen. Mit einer Einführung von Robert Jungk und
     einem Epilog von Niko Kazantzakis. Munich: Kindler,
     1955. 350 pp. Illus.

     TRANSLATIONS

     Albert Schweitzer dit was zijn Leven. Tr. J. F. Kliphuis.
        Amsterdam: Scheltens & Giltay. 268 pp.

     (Second edition). Albert Schweitzer; het Leven van een goed
        Mens. Foreword by E. D. Spelberg. 271 pp.

     Albert Schweitzer, the Life of a Great Man. London:
        Lutterworth Press, 1956. 160 pp. Illus. (Shorter
        version of German original).

     Albert Schweitzer; the story of his life. New York:
        Philosophical Library, 1957. 160 pp. Illus., ports.

292 POORTENAR, JAN. Albert Schweitzer een man van de daad.
     Amsterdam: Ditmar, 1952. 38 pp. Illus. (Avontuur
     en Techniekreeks, no. 33).

     RAAB, KARL. Albert Schweitzer. Persönlichkeit und Denken.
     See Dissertations, no. 4337 below.

293 RATTER, MAGNUS. Albert Schweitzer, a Biography and Analysis.
     London: Allenson and Co., 1935.
     (Revised and much enlarged). Albert Schweitzer. London:
        Lindsey Press, 1949. 214 pp. Port.
     (American Edition). Albert Schweitzer, Life and Message.
        Boston: Beacon Press, 1950. 214 pp.

293a _____. Schweitzer: Ninety Years Wise. Wallington, Surrey,
      Eng.: Religious Education Press, 1964. 192 pp.

294 REGESTER, JOHN DICKINSON. Albert Schweitzer, the Man and his
     Work. New York, Cincinnati, etc.: The Abingdon Press,
     1931. 145 pp.

Life and Work

295   REHM, MAX. Erinnerungen an Albert Schweitzer in Heimat und
        Fremde. Studien der Erwin von Steinbuch-Stiftung, Band
        4, 1975.

296   RODE, EBBE. Møde med Albert Schweitzer; streger til et
        portraet. Copenhagen: J. H. Schultz, 1959. 63 pp.
        Illus.

297   SALMON, DOROTHEA. Jungle Doctor: The Story of Albert
        Schweitzer. London: SCM Press, 1948. 47 pp.

298   SATO, MITSURU. Albert Schweitzer. Tokyo: Sekiya-Shoto,
        1936. 260 pp.

299   SCHULTZ, HANS J. Albert Schweitzer. Reinbek: Rowohlt
        Taschenbuch Verlag, 1978. (Rowohlts Monogr. 263).

300   SEAVER, GEORGE. Albert Schweitzer, the Man and his Mind.
        With 30 Illustrations from Photographs. New York,
        London: Harper and Brothers, 1947. 346 pp. Revised
        edition, 1955, 370 pp. Sixth, definitive edition,
        London: A. and C. Black, 1969. xiii, 365 pp. Illus.

        TRANSLATIONS

        Albert Schweitzer als Mensch und als Denker. Göttingen:
            Vandenhoeck & Ruprecht, 1949. 10. ergänzte Auflage,
            1959. 373 pp.

        Albert Schweitzer. Tr. Borge Friis. Copenhagen: Forlag
            Branner og Korell, 1950.

        (Second edition). Mennesket Albert Schweitzer. 1951.
            204 pp. Illus.

        Albert Schweitzer, Mannen og Verket. Tr. Jan Berggrav.
            Oslo: Arne Giurnes Forlag, 1950.

        Albert Schweitzer, zijn Leven en Denken. Baarn: 1950.
            314 pp.

        Schweitzer: so no ningen to Seishin. Tr. Shin Aizu.
            Tokyo: Misuzushobo, 1952. 261 pp.

        Schweitzer, sono shisō no ayumi. Tr. Shin Aizu. Tokyo:
            Misuzu shobo, 1953. 327 pp.

        Schweitzer ningen to Seishin. Tr. Shin Aizu. Tokyo:
            Misuzu-Shobo, 1959. 573 pp. Illus.

General

SHARP, WILLIAM JAMES. A Sociological Interpretation of the
Life and Work of Albert Schweitzer. See Dissertations,
no. 4341 below.

301 SIMONSEN, SEVALD. Legen i Urskogen. Albert Schweitzer.
3rd edition. Oslo: Misjonsselskapets Forlag, 1950.
214 pp. Illus. (Pionerserien 1.)

302 SNETHLAGE, HENDRIK ANN CONSTANTIJN. Albert Schweitzer, de
man de tot allen spreekt. Amsterdam: Lankamp and
Brinkman, 1935. 100 pp.

303 SPYROPOULOS, N. Albert Schweitzer. Athens, 1967. 117 pp.
Illus.

304 STEFFAHN, HARALD, ed. Albert Schweitzer in Selbstzeugnissen
und Bilddokumenten. Reinbek bei Hamburg: Rowohlt
Taschenbuch Verlag, 1979.

305 _____. Du aber folge mir nach. Albert Schweitzers Werk und
Wirkung. Bern und Stuttgart: P. Haupt, 1974. 262 pp.

306 STRICKER, NOÉMI. Pèlerins du Monde. Avignon: Aubanel, 1957.
43 pp. Illus.

TRANSLATIONS

Weltpilger. Tr. M. Herling. Freiburg i. B.: Hyperion,
1961. 104 pp.

307 SUZUKI, TOSHIRO et al, eds. Seiki no Hito. Tokyo: Shinkyo
Shuppansha, 1948. 257 pp.

308 TAKAHASHI, ISAO. Arberuto Shuwaitsua.
Tamagawadaigakushuppanbu, 1963. 208 pp. Illus., ports.

309 _____. Shubaitsa Hakushi to Tomo ni. Tokyo: Hakusuisha,
1961. 280 pp.

310 _____. Shuwaitsuā Hakushi to no Hachinenkan.
Asahishinbunsha, 1966. 294 pp.

311 _____. Shuwaitsā to no Schichinenkan. 1967. 254 pp. Illus.

312 _____. Seimi e no Ikei. 1975. 244 pp. Illus.

313 TAKEYAMA, MICHIO. Hikari to ai no Senshi. Tokyo:
Shincho-Sha, 1942. 347 pp.

Life and Work

314   VASWANI, THANWARDAS LILARAM. <u>Albert Schweitzer</u>. Poona:
      Gita Publishing House, 1962. 32 pp. (East and West
      Series, no. 76).

315   VEEN, JAN MARIE VAN. <u>Albert Schweitzer</u>. Baarn: Bosch and
      Keuning, 1975. 103 pp.

316   VENNIYURI, E. M. J. <u>Svaittsar: oru visvamanavante caritram</u>.
      Kozhikode: K. R. Bros., 1957. 344 pp.

317   WEGMANN, HANS. <u>Albert Schweitzer als Führer, mit einem
      Lebensbild</u>. Zürich: Beer and Co., 1928. 80 pp.

      <u>TRANSLATIONS</u>

      <u>Albert Schweitzer als Leidsman, met een Levensbeschrijving</u>.
         Tr. H. Van Lunzen. Utrecht: De Wachttoren, 1929.
         103 pp.

318   WEISS, ROBERT. <u>Albert Schweitzer als Arzt und als Mensch</u>.
      Kehl: A. Morstadt, 1976. 85 pp. Illus.

319   WERNER, A. J. <u>Van en over Albert Schweitzer; persoonlijkheid
      en humor</u>. 1946. 20 pp.

320   WERNER, D[IRK] A[DRIANUS]. <u>Albert Schweitzer, een strijder
      voor de ware menselijkheid</u>. Assen: De Torenlaan,
      1953. 40 pp., Illus.

321   WIESNER, KURT. <u>Albert Schweitzer zum 85. Geburtstag</u>.
      (Festvortrag . . . 14 Januar 1960 in Berlin.) Hrsg. von
      der Zentralen Schulungsstätte der CDU "Otto Nuschke" in
      Verbindung mit der Parteileitung der Christliche-
      Demokratischen-Union. 38 pp.

322   WOYTT-SECRETAN, MARIE. <u>Albert Schweitzer, un Médecin dans la
      Forêt Vierge</u>. Lausanne: F. Rouge et Cie, S.A., 1948.
      176 pp. Illus.
      (Second edition). Strasbourg: Oberlin, 1953. 183 pp.
         Illus.

      <u>TRANSLATIONS</u>

      <u>Albert Schweitzer, der Urwalddoktor von Lambarene</u>. Bern:
         P. Haupt; Strasbourg: Oberlin, 1947. 188 pp. Illus.

      (Second edition). Munich: Beck, 1949. 191 pp.

      (Third edition). Munich: Beck, 1953. 182 pp.

Life and Work

Albert Schweitzer; die Oerwouddokter van Lambarene. Vertaald
door A.D. Werner-Brinkerink. 2. Druk. Assen: De Torenlaan,
1954. 177 pp. Illus.

323 YOKOYAMA, YOSHIKAZU. Albert Schweitzer. Tokyo: Tatesina
Shobo, 1950. 174 pp.

b. Articles, Parts of Books

324 "AP (Associated Press) über Schweitzer erbost." Neue Zeit
(East Berlin) 220 (Sept. 20, 1961), p. 2.

325 "A.S.--A Biographical Sketch." COURIER, May 1974, n.p.
(8-10).

326 AIZU, NOBORU. "Schweitzer: sono hito to chosaku." Shuppan
News (Tokyo) 233 (May 1953), p. 7.

327 AIZU, SHIN. "Schweitzer no Tsuite." Kirisutokyō Bunka
(Tokyo), October 1950, pp. 52-61.

328 ALBERS, AUGUST. "Albert Schweitzer--wie ich ihn sehe."
Münchner Neueste Nachrichten (Munich) 12 (January 14, 1925),
pp. 1-2. Reprinted in: BEGEGNUNG, pp. 172-75.

329 "Albert Schweitzer." Christ und Welt (Stuttgart) 1:1
(June 6, 1948), p. 7. Port.

330 "Albert Schweitzer." International Echo (London) 5:9
(July 1950), pp. 49-58.

331 "Albert Schweitzer." The Lancet (London), Sept. 11, 1965,
pp. 547-48.

332 "Albert Schweitzer." Hokke (Tokyo) 35:2 (Oct. 1949).

333 ["Albert Schweitzer."] In: Anna Söderblom, en Minnesbok.
Uppsala: J. A. Lindblad, 1956, pp. 132-33. Illus., port.

334 "Albert Schweitzer." Current Biography. New York: H. W.
Wilson, 1948, pp. 564-67. Port.

335 "Albert Schweitzer." Der Spiegel (Hamburg) 19:38
(Sept. 15, 1965), p. 124. Port.

336 "Albert Schweitzer." Das Fenster (Jugendheim Wulfsdorf),
June 1955, pp. 2-5.

Life and Work

337 "Albert Schweitzer" (editorial). New York Times, Sept. 6,
1965, p. 14.

338 "Albert Schweitzer" (editorial). The Washington Post,
Sept. 6, 1965, p. A22.

339 "Albert Schweitzer." Europäische Aktion (Ulm/Donau) 1:21/22
(1951), p. 13.

340 "Albert Schweitzer." Norsk Sang (Bergen) 4:7 (September 1949),
pp. 3-5.

341 "Albert Schweitzer." Arbor (Madrid) 3:112 (April 1955),
pp. 600-02.

342 "Albert Schweitzer." Der Aufstieg (Wiesbaden) 15
(Aug. 15, 1949), pp. 643-44.

343 "Albert Schweitzer à l'école." Les Derniéres Nouvelles
d'Alsace (Strasbourg) 54 (March 4, 1955), p. 13.
Reprinted from l'Education Nationale.

344 "Albert Schweitzer--a way-shower, 1875-1965." New Age
Interpreter (Santa Monica, Calif.) 26:4 (1965), pp. 3-14 f.
Cover port.

345 "Albert Schweitzer--an Evaluation at Ninety." The Register
Leader (Boston) 147:1 (Jan. 1965), pp. 2-13f.

346 "Albert Schweitzer arbeidt eenzaam voort aan volbracht werk."
Algemeen Handelsblad (Amsterdam), March 28, 1963.

347 "Albert Schweitzer, de moderne Franciscus van Assissi."
Algemeen Handelsblad (Amsterdam), January 7, 1950.
Reprinted in Tijdschrift voor Ziekenverpleging
(Amsterdam) 3:8 (April 15, 1950), pp. 184-85. Port.

348 "Albert Schweitzer, doctor." Journal of the American Medical
Association (Chicago) 156-17 (Dec. 25, 1954), p. 1586.
Illus. Accompanied by an editorial, pp. 1547-49.

349 "Albert Schweitzer, doctor of medicine, music, and theology."
The Living Age (New York) 335 (January 1929), pp. 352-53.

350 "Albert Schweitzer, een dag in Holland, vertelt ons over
zijn werk." Het Parool (Amsterdam), September 15, 1949,
pp. 3, 5.

351   "Albert Schweitzer; ein Theologe und Philosoph wird noch
        Arzt." Der Aufstieg (Wiesbaden) 15 (August 15, 1949),
        pp. 643-44. Port.

352   "Albert Schweitzer esta ficando/cego. O Ilustre Filantropo
        não deseja ser operado." O Estado de São Paulo,
        July 15, 1955.

353   "Albert Schweitzer in Europe." RUNDBRIEF 15 (January 14, 1960),
        pp. 37-45.

354   "Albert Schweitzer is moe." NIEUWS 3:3 (Oct. 1954), pp. 90-91.

355   "Albert Schweitzer, medicus, filosof, theologen, musicus."
        Uitkijk (Haarlem) 14 (April 4, 1953), pp. 10-11. Port.

356   "Albert Schweitzer. Mythos des 20. Jahrhunderts." Der
        Spiegel (Hamburg) 14:52 (Dec. 21, 1960), pp. 50-61.
        Illus., cover port.

357   "Albert Schweitzer, 1875-1965" (editorial). The Christian
        Century (Chicago) 82:37 (Sept. 15, 1965), pp. 1116-17.

358   "Albert Schweitzer, 90, dies at his hospital." New York
        Times, Sept. 6, 1965, pp. 1, 16. Port., illus.

359   "Albert Schweitzer, O.M., D. Phil., M.D., D.D., LL.D."
        British Medical Journal 5462 (Sept. 11, 1965),
        pp. 651-52. Port.

360   "Albert Schweitzer, RIP." National Review (New York) 17:38
        (Sept. 21, 1965), pp. 807-08.

361   "Albert Schweitzer se sentui na verdade e na justica com a
        manifestacão da solidariedade de um menino." A Gazeta,
        Sept. 8, 1959.

362   "Albert Schweitzer. Sonnenstrahl in finsterer Zeit." Voix
        d'Alsace (Geudertheim) 6:21 (1958), pp. 1-2.

363   "Albert Schweitzers Irrtum" (editorial). Christ und Welt
        (Stuttgart) 14:36 (Sept. 8, 1961), p. 2.

364   "Albert Schweitzers letzter Europa-Aufenhalt." Deutsches
        Pfarrerblatt (Essen) 50:1 (Jan. 1, 1950), pp. 16-17.

365   ALLARY, JEAN. "Albert Schweitzer." La Revue de Paris
        (Paris) 58:5 (May 1951), pp. 88-95.

General

Life and Work

366   ALLSPACH, W. "Albert Schweitzer, der weltbekannte
           Urwalddoktor." Form und Geist (Zürich) 5 (May 1948),
           pp. 73-76.

367   _____. "Analyse des Bildes von Albert Schweitzer."
           Der Hochwart (Berlin) 11:1 (Jan. 1941).

368   AMADOU, ROBERT. "Introduction à Ma Vie et ma pensée d'Albert
           Schweitzer." CAHIERS 4 (Dec. 1960), pp. 3-5.

369   _____. "La légende et l'histoire d'Albert Schweitzer."
           France-Asie (Saigon) 70 (March 1952), pp. 957-62.

370   _____. "L'oeuvre inconnue d'Albert Schweitzer." Arts
           (Paris) 275 (Sept. 1, 1950), pp. 1-2.

371   "America in tribute to Dr. Schweitzer." The Diapason
           (Chicago) 40:9 (Aug. 1, 1949), pp. 1-2. Illus.

372   ANDERSON, ERICA, photographer. "Albert Schweitzer. A picture
           story of the genius in the jungle." Illustrated (London),
           Sept. 11, 1954, pp. 19-24.

373   _____. "A glimpse of greatness." The Christian Register
           (Boston) 133:3 (March 1954), pp. 16-17.

374   _____. "Albert Schweitzer: The African Years." The Saturday
           Review (New York) 48:39 (Sept. 25, 1965), pp. 19-20f.

375   _____. Introduction to the film: 'Schweitzer and Bach.'
           In: THE CONVOCATION RECORD, III/3-4.

376   _____. "Meeting at the Summit." The American Weekly/Journal
           American (New York), Dec. 25, 1960, pp. 2-5. Illus.

377   _____. "Personal glimpses during an extensive trip." In:
           REALMS, pp. 42-51.

378   _____. "A world-wide miracle! How Albert Schweitzer,
           'greatest man alive,' inspired the men of Medico." The
           American Weekly/Journal American (New York), March 29,
           1959, pp. 10f. Port. Also issued as a one-page reprint
           by Medico, New York, N.Y.

379   ANDEREGG-GURTNER, E. "Der grosse, weisse Doktor--Albert
           Schweitzer. Ein Nachfahre aus Toggenburgischem
           Geschlecht." Toggenburger Heimat-Jahrbuch (Bazenheid)
           16 (1956), pp. 129-32. Illus.

380   ANDREWS, C. F. "Albrecht Schweitzer and the Visva-Bharati
        Ideal." The Visva-Bharati Quarterly (Calcutta) 4:3
        (October 1926), pp. 248-61.

381   ARMATTOE, RAPHAEL E. G. "Homage to three great men
        (Schweitzer, Schroedinger, de Gennaro)." The Londonderry
        Sentinel (Londonderry, N.I.), January 30, Feb. 1, and
        Feb. 3, 1945. Also issued as an 11-page offprint.

382   ARNOLD, MELVIN. "The greatest soul in Christendom." The
        Christian Register (Boston) 126:8 (September 1947),
        pp. 324-27. Illus.

383   ARNOULD, THÉRÈSE P. "Un héros d'humanité: Albert Schweitzer."
        Harmonie (Paris) 14:8 (April-June 1951), pp. 24-27.

384   "Der Arzt in der Kunst. Albert Schweitzer: Arzt, Musiker,
        und Philosophe." Berliner Ärzteblatt (Berlin) 65:4
        (Feb. 16, 1952), pp. 77-78.

385   AUGUSTINY, WALDEMAR. "Kräfte praktischer Lebenshilfe."
        In: GESTERN-HEUTE, pp. 17-18. Reprinted from Albert
        Schweitzer und Du, no. 227 above.

386   BACHMANN, ELSE. "Ein deutscher Arzt in Africa." Daheim
        (Leipzig) 68:15 (Jan. 7, 1932), pp. 13-14.

387   BÄHR, H. W. "Albert Schweitzer et l'Allemagne." Communautés
        et Continents (Paris) 67:37 (Jan.-March 1975), pp. 15-18.

388   BÄHR, HANS WALTER. Einleitung. In: BEGEGNUNG, pp. ix-xv.

389   BALBAUD, RENÉ. "Albert Schweitzer: deuemos carregar uma
        parte da miséria que assoberba o mundo." Folha da Tarde,
        Aug. 21, 1959.

390   BALCAR, JOSEF. "Die Fackelträger Jan Amos Comenious--Albert
        Schweitzer." In: BEITRÄGE, pp. 17-22.

391   _____. [Tribute without title.] In: DENKEN UND WEG,
        pp. 400-04.

392   BARBER, B. AQUILA. "Dr. Schweitzer's autobiography." The
        London Quarterly and Holborn Review (London) 158
        (July 1933), pp. 395-401.

393   BARKER, W. P. "Albert Schweitzer." In: Who's Who in Church
        History. Old Tappan, N.J.: Revell, 1969, pp. 248-49.

Life and Work

394   BARTHEL, ERNST. "Albert Schweitzer." Geisteskultur
       (Berlin) 37 (1928), pp. 39-44.

395   BARTLETT, ROBERT MERRILL. "Albert Schweitzer: Christian
       superman." World Unity Magazine (New York) 13:2
       (November 1933), pp. 89-97.

396   _____. [Albert Schweitzer.] In: Builders of a New World.
       New York: Friendship Press, 1933, pp. 148-57.

397   BAUR, HERMANN. "Albert Schweitzers Persönlichkeit."
       RUNDBRIEF 19 (January 14, 1962), pp. 23-36. Excerpted
       from his "Albert Schweitzer als Arzt," no. 2907 below.
       Reprinted in: SCHWEITZER, pp. 81-97 and in DENKEN UND
       WEG, pp. 216-30.

398   _____. "Für oder gegen Albert Schweitzer." Hippokrates
       (Stuttgart) 33:23 (1962), pp. 982-86. Also issued as a
       reprint, see no. 233 above. Translated as "Pour ou
       contre Albert Schweitzer." CAHIERS/BELGE 5 (April 1965),
       pp. 22-30.

399   _____. "Ein vergessener Warner?" In: GESTERN-HEUTE,
       pp. 20-23.

400   BELZNER, EMIL. "Puritaner verleumden Albert Schweitzer."
       Rhein-Neckar Zeitung (Heidelberg), Sept. 5, 1956.

401   BERGIUS, YNGVE. I. "Albert Schweitzer, Jesu-Livsforskaren,
       musikern och lakaremissionäre." II. "Från Albert
       Schweitzers missionsarbete." Svenska Dagbladet
       (Stockholm), September 20 and 21, 1925.

402   BERGMANN, HILDA. "Albert Schweitzer. Sein Weg und sein
       Werk." Reclams Universum (Leipzig) 47:6 (Nov. 6, 1930),
       pp. 121-23.

403   BERNARD, ALBERT. "Europäische Sonntage bei Dr. Albert
       Schweitzer in Günsbach." Les Dernières Nouvelles du
       Haut-Rhin (Colmar) October 13, 1955, p. 8.

404   _____. "Sonntagsgaste aus aller Herren Länder bei Dr. Albert
       Schweitzer." Les Dernières Nouvelles du Haut-Rhin
       (Colmar) 229 (Oct. 1, 1952), p. 8.

405   BERNSTORF, OTTO. "Ein Hauch von Chloroform. Strassburger
       Erinnerungen an den Stud. med. Albert Schweitzer."
       Münchner Merkur (Munich) 307/308 (Dec. 24, 1965), p. vi.

406   BESSESEN, CAMILLA WING. "His brother's keeper" (a series of
         eighteen articles about Albert Schweitzer). The
         Minneapolis Star (Minneapolis, Minn.), March 24-April 13,
         1955.

407   BICKERS, WILLIAM M. "Dr. Albert Schweitzer." The Journal of
         the American Medical Association (Chicago) 193:11
         (Sept. 13, 1965), pp. 184-85.

408   BILLY, ANDRÉ. "En Alsace: De Requewihr, capitale du vin, à
         Günsbach, lieu de péleringe des innombrales admirateurs
         du Dr. Schweitzer." Le Figaro Littéraire (Paris) 7:328
         (Aug. 2, 1952), pp. 1-2.

409   BINDER, THEODOR. "Ein Dank an Albert Schweitzer." RUNDBRIEF
         17 (Jan. 14, 1961), pp. 80-81.

410   BIRNEBURG, KURT. "Albert Schweitzer, der Urwalddoktor."
         Die Neue Schau (Kassel) 10 (March 1949), pp. 64-66.

411   BISKAROP, DR. "Was hat Albert Schweitzer uns heute zu sagen?"
         Hessische Nachrichten (Kassel) 10 (Jan. 12, 1950).

412   BIXLER, J. S. "Albert Schweitzer." The Christian Register
         (Boston) 121:4 (April 1942), p. 111.

413   BIXLER, JULIUS SEELYE. "Contemporary thought around the
         world: Albert Schweitzer." The Christian Register
         (Boston) 113:1 (Jan. 4, 1934), pp. 3-4.

414   _____. "Interpreter of Jesus and of Bach." The Christian
         Century (Chicago) 45:46 (Nov. 15, 1928), pp. 1395-96.

415   _____. "Letters from Dr. Albert Schweitzer in the Colby
         Library." Colby Library Quarterly (Waterville, Me.)
         6:9 (March 1964), pp. 373-82.

416   _____. "More than Miracles." The Christian Register
         (Boston) 126:8 (Sept. 1947), p. 317.

417   _____. "Portrait of an Internationalist." Christendom
         (Chicago) 9:1 (Winter 1944), pp. 35-39.

418   BJÖRKQUIST, MANFRED. [Tribute without Title.] In: DENKEN
         UND WEG, p. 87.

419   BLYTH, JEFFREY. "Schweitzer awaits the great in a tea shop."
         The Daily Mail (London), October 18, 1955.

Life and Work

420 BOEGNER, MARC. "Notes sur la miséricorde." In: MISÉRICORDE,
     p. 393.

421 _____. "Le plus grand homme vivent dans le monde
     d'aujourd'hui à 90 ans." Les Nouvelles Littéraires
     (Paris) 43:1950 (Jan. 14, 1965), p. 3.

422 BÖHRINGER, H. "Erinnerungen." Basler Nachrichten (Basel)
     Sonntagsblatt, 49:2 (Jan. 16, 1955), pp. 1-2.

423 BOGARDUS, EMORY S. "Albert Schweitzer as a leader."
     Sociology and Social Research (Los Angeles) 42:1
     (Sept./Oct. 1957), pp. 46-53.

424 BOISDEFFRE, PIERRE DE. "Albert Schweitzer à Paris. Études
     (Paris) 271 (Nov. 1951), pp. 251-54.

425 BOOTH, EDWIN PRINCE. "An Appreciation of Albert Schweitzer."
     In: TRIBUTE, pp. 37-43.

426 BORCHARD, ADOLPHE. "Albert Schweitzer, organiste" (radio
     address). L'Alsace Francaise (Strasbourg) Annee 18,
     no. 2, tome 33, no. 789 (February 10, 1938), p. 38.

427 BOYD, CHARLES N. "Albert Schweitzer, the man who gives organ
     recitals and writes books to provide funds for his work
     as African medical missionary." The American Organist
     (Staten Island, NY) 18:11 (Nov. 1935), pp. 415-18.

428 BOYLE, HAL. "Albert Schweitzer. He lives by three words."
     Chicago Sunday Tribune Magazine, April 28, 1957,
     pp. 10-11. Illus.

429 BRABAZON, JAMES. "Albert Schweitzer and the art of living."
     COURIER (Winter 1978), pp. 28-35. Also in: DEVENTER,
     pp. 105-112. Summaries in French, German and Dutch.

430 BRAND-VON SELTEI, ERNA. "Albert Schweitzer--der grosse
     Helfer der Menschheit." Deutsche Schwesternzeitung
     (Marburg/Lahn) 1:7 (April 1949), pp. 7-9.

431 BREIT, HARVEY. "Talk with Albert Schweitzer." The New York
     Times Book Review, July 17, 1949, p. 15.

432 BREMI, WILLI. "Albert Schweitzer--Erinnerungen 1921-1922."
     BERICHTE 32 (Sept. 1970), pp. 27-29.

433 _____. "Albert Schweitzer, Theolog, Arzt u. Künstler."
     Glaube und Gewissen (Halle) 12:1 (Jan. 1966), p. 8.

434   BRESSLAU-HOFF, LOUISE. "Albert Schweitzer." I. "Segue-me
        tu. . . ?" Fé e Vida (São Paulo), June 1944, pp. 39-43;
        II. "Um aventureiro da dedicacão." Aug. 1944, pp. 52-54;
        III. "Um aventureiro da dedicacão," Sept. 1944, pp. 38-40;
        IV. "A revêrencia pela vida," October 1944, pp. 48-50.

435   BROMAGE, BERNARD. "Albert Schweitzer; the seer as practical
        healer." Tomorrow (London) 10:4 (Autumn 1962), pp. 51-57.

436   BRUNNER-TRAUT, EMMA. "Begegnung und Erkenntnis." In:
        DENKEN UND WEG, pp. 268-71.

437   BUCKE, EMORY STEVENS. "With reverence for life" (editorial).
        Zions Herald (Boston) 127:30 (July 27, 1949), pp. 702-03.

438   BUCKLEY, WILLIAM F., JR. "The fall of Dr. Schweitzer."
        The Plain Dealer (Cleveland), August 4, 1964, p. 10.

439   BURCKHARDT, CARL J. "Albert Schweitzer--Geist und Tat."
        Universitas (Stuttgart) 21:8 (Aug. 1966), pp. 827-35.
        (Gedankrede auf Albert Schweitzer auf der Sitzung der
        Friedensklasse des Ordens Pour le Merite gesprochen.)

440   _____. [Tribute without title.] In: DENKEN UND WEG,
        p. 399. Translated as "Thanks to Dr. Schweitzer."
        Universitas (English language edition) 7:1 (1964),
        pp. 37-38.

441   BURGER, C. B. "Albert Schweitzer 90 Jaar." NIEUWS
        (Jan. 1965) pp. 3-5.

442   BURI, FRITZ. "Albert Schweitzer." In: Denker und Deuter im
        heutigen Europa. Hrsg. von Hans Schwerte und Wilhelm
        Spengler. Oldenburg: Gerhard Stalling, 1954, Vol. 1,
        pp. 52-64. Port.

443   _____. "Albert Schweitzer als Christ. Ansprache, gehalten
        an der Gedenkfeier im Basler Münster am 14. Januar 1955."
        Basler Kirchenbote (Basel) 1 (February 1955).

444   _____. "Wiedersehen mit Albert Schweitzer." Schweizerisches
        Reformiertes Volksblatt (Basel) 83:1 (Jan. 1949), pp. 5-7.

445   BURNS, OLIVE A. "My father Albert Schweitzer." Biography
        News (Detroit) 1:11 (November 1974), pp. 1322-25. Repro-
        duction of an interview with Rhena Schweitzer Miller in
        the Atlanta Journal and Constitution (Atlanta, Ga.) on
        Sept. 15, 1974.

Life and Work

446   C., E. "Musicien et philosophe, Albert Schweitzer s'est fait
      médecin au Gabon pour agir." La Vie Catholique Illustrée
      (Paris), May 28, 1950, pp. 10-11.

447   CABALLERO, FRANCISCO DE A. "Albert Schweitzer ha cumplido
      ochenta y cinco años." Arbor (Madrid) 45:171 (March 1960),
      pp. 369-73.

448   CACHERA, ANDRÉ. "Le docteur Schweitzer à Gunsbach." In:
      DEBRECEN, pp. 123-30.

449   CAMERON, JAMES. [Chapter ten.] In: Point of Departure:
      Experiment in Biography. London: Arthur Barker Ltd.,
      1967, pp. 152-74.

450   _____. "Albert Schweitzer und seine Legende. Heiliger oder
      Snob?" Die Weltwoche (Zürich) 1661 (Sept. 10, 1965),
      p. 25. Port.

451   _____. "Albert Schweitzer at ninety." The Listener
      (London) 73:1869 (Jan. 21, 1965), pp. 95f. Port.

452   CANNEGIETER, HENDRIK GERRIT. "Bij Schweitzer's Afschied."
      Nieuwe Rotterdamsche Courant (Rotterdam) 127 (May 7, 1928),
      Avondblad B, p. 1.

453   CANTO, GILBERTO DE ULHÔA. "Albert Schweitzer, o homen do
      século." Brazil Rotario (Rio de Janeiro) 29:334
      (Dec. 1956), pp. 8-12. Port.

454   CARPEAUX, OTTO MARIA. "Albert Schweitzer: dados biográficos."
      O Estado de São Paulo, July 13, 1941.

455   _____. "A árvore de Schweitzer: personalidade e obra."
      Diário de Notícias (Rio de Janeiro), March 13, 1953.

456   _____. "Schweitzer em Estrasburgo." Correio de Manhã
      (Rio de Janeiro), July 1, 1953.

457   CARY, MARY. "He also bore witness, an appreciation of Albert
      Schweitzer." The American-German Review (Philadelphia)
      14:1 (Oct. 1947), pp. 3-4f.

458   CESBRON, GILBERT. "D'une prétendu 'démystification' d'Albert
      Schweitzer." CAHIERS 11 (July 1964), pp. 11-13.

459   _____. "Une image d'Albert Schweitzer." In: HOMMAGE,
      pp. 33-34.

460 _____. "Sur Albert Schweitzer." In: Ce siècle appelle au secours. Paris: Robert Laffont, 1955, pp. 221-66. Translated in Unser Jahrhundert ruft um Hilfe. Heidelberg: Dreibrücken, 1956. German translation reprinted as "Ein überholtes Vorbild?" in: GESTERN-HEUTE, pp. 29-30.

461 _____. "Les tilleuls de Gunsbach." La Table Ronde (Paris) 24 (Dec. 1949), pp. 1975-86. Reprinted in: ETUDES, pp. 17-20.

462 _____. "Tu est mort, mon ami." Le Figaro Littéraire (Paris) 20:1012 (Sept. 9-15, 1965), pp. 1f.

463 CHAIX-RUY, J. "Albert Schweitzer: sein Leben und sein Denken." Antares (Baden-Baden) 2:5 (July 1954), pp. 10-18; 2:7 (September 1954), pp. 21-30.

464 CHAKRAVARTY, AMIYA. [Tribute without title.] In: DENKEN UND WEG, pp. 83-84.

465 CHAUCHARD, P. "Teilhard, le miséricordieux." In: MISÉRICORDE, p. 219.

466 CHOI, KI-SIK. [Tribute without title.] In: DENKEN UND WEG, pp. 404-05. Reprinted in: BEGEGNUNG, pp. 310-11.

467 CHRISTEN, ERNEST. "La vocation d'Albert Schweitzer." NOUVELLES 27 (July 1961), pp. 16-17.

468 CLAUSEN, BERNARD C. "Baffled Kindness." The Christian Century (Chicago) 56:30 (Sept. 27, 1939), pp. 1166-67.

469 COHN, JONAS. "Albert Schweitzers Botschaft." Frankfurter Zeitung, August 9, 1924.

470 COLLIER, PAULETTE. "Dr. Schweitzer." The Central African Journal of Medicine (Salisbury, Southern Rhodesia) 9:12 (Dec. 1963), pp. 483-86; 10:1 (Jan. 1964), pp. 20-23; 10:2 (Feb. 1964), pp. 58-62.

471 "Come and follow me" (editorial). Time (New York) 50:24 (Dec. 15, 1947), pp. 53-56.

472 COUSINS, NORMAN. "Albert Schweitzer." In: Heroes for our Times. Edited for the Overseas Press Club of America by Will Yolen and Kenneth S. Giniger. New York: Giniger, 1968, pp. 150-69.

Life and Work

473 _____. "Education for world freedom." The American Association of Colleges for Teacher Education, Tenth Yearbook
(1957), pp. 26-40. (Albert Schweitzer, pp. 33-36.) His
address at their annual meeting, Chicago, 1957.

474 _____. "Günsbach and London." The Saturday Review (New York)
40:43 (Oct. 26, 1957), pp. 24-25. Cover port. Reprinted
in: SELECTION, pp. 55-60.

475 _____. "How Schweitzer exerted his influence." Washington
University Magazine (St. Louis, Mo.) (Spring 1975),
pp. 31-34. Condensed version of his keynote address at
the St. Louis Albert Schweitzer Centenary Week. Reprinted
in COURIER (Summer 1975), pp. 12-19.

476 _____. "The Point about Schweitzer." The Saturday Review
(New York) 37:40 (Oct. 2, 1954), pp. 22-23. Also issued
as a 2-page offprint by the Saturday Review, 1954, and
as a 1-page offprint by the Albert Schweitzer Fellowship,
New York. Reprinted in SELECTION, pp. 12-14; also in
FESTSCHRIFT, pp. 32-36. For replies to this article by
Emory Ross, Henry A. Sosland, Hans A. Illing, Robert Wilson
Hays, Henry S. M. Uhl, and George W. Phinney, see Saturday
Review 37:43 (Nov. 20, 1954), p. 25. An additional reply
by Patricia McManus is in Saturday Review 37:44
(Oct. 30, 1954), p. 26.

477 _____. "Schweitzer--symbol of the human spirit." Saturday
Review (New York) 2 (Feb. 22, 1975), p. 6.

478 _____. "What matters about Schweitzer" (editorial).
Saturday Review (New York) 48:39 (Sept. 25, 1965),
pp. 30-32. Illus. For a letter to the editor in
reply by L. A. Campbell, see Saturday Review 48:42
(Oct. 16, 1965), p. 41.

479 CRUCY, FRANCOIS. "Albert Schweitzer, médecin-musicien-
philosophe." France-Asie (Saigon) 70 (March 1952),
pp. 963-65. Translated as "O médico, músico, e
filósofo." Diário de Notícias (Rio de Janeiro),
March 2, 1952.

480 D., F. "Apôtre de Lambaréné et de Gunsbach: le Dr. Schweitzer
est feté par ses contemporains." Magazin Ringier
(St. Louis, France) 43 (Oct. 25, 1952), p. 34.

481 D., J.-M. "De L'Alsace au Gabon." Le Monde (Paris) 6422
(Sept. 7, 1965), p. 6.

482   D., M. "Albert Schweitzer--der Mensch." Allgemeine Missions-
           Nachrichten (Hamburg) 30:3 (June 1950), pp. 2-3.

483   D'AVILA, CARLOS. "Quem é Albert Schweitzer." Correio
           Paulistano (São Paulo), March 29, 1949.

484   "Een Dag uit het leven van de gevangene van Lambarene." Het
           Parool (Amsterdam), Nov. 12, 1949, p. 3.

485   DAHL, HARALD. "Ett celebert Sverigebesok, Albert Schweitzer
           på blixtvisit i Gammalkill." Vår Kyrka (Stockholm)
           90:46 (Nov. 15, 1951), pp. 6-8. Ports.

486   _____. "Från Älvadalen till Landskrona. Glimtar från resor
           som tolk och registreringsbiträde åt Albert Schweitzer."
           In: MANNEN, pp. 173-83.

487   DANIEL, ANITA. "Schweitzer at 77--no isms but humanism."
           The New York Times Magazine, Jan. 13, 1952, p. 17. Illus.

488   _____. "Schweitzer, man of many parts; a glimpse of
           Dr. Schweitzer, Nobel Peace Prize winner, organist, and
           humanitarian. Christian Science Monitor (Boston),
           Dec. 29, 1955, p. 7.

489   "Dank an Albert Schweitzer." Archiv (Göttingen) 8, Kommentare
           45 (Nov. 11, 1954), mimeographed, unpaged.

490   DE VAERE, ULRIC. "Schweitzer's reverence for life." Music
           Journal (New York) 32:10 (Dec. 1974), pp. 22-24.

491   "The death of Albert Schweitzer: theologian, musician and
           man of action." Illustrated London News 247:6580
           (Sept. 11, 1965), pp. 12-13. Illus.

492   DECRAENE, PHILIPPE. "Depassé par sa gloire." Le Monde
           (Paris) 6422 (Sept. 7, 1965), p. 6.

493   DENTAN, YVES. "Albert Schweitzer à Gunsbach." In: HOMMAGE,
           pp. 39-45.

494   DENU, ALFRED. "La vie et l'oeuvre d'Albert Schweitzer."
           La Vie en Alsace (Strasbourg) 8 (1930), pp. 207-12.
           Illus., port.

495   DEREU, CHARLES. "Albert Schweitzer, homme, et médecin
           généreux." In: DEBRECEN, pp. 25-32.

Life and Work

496   DIECKERT, FREDERICK. "'L'Albert du Presbytère,' un Schweitzer
       familier." L'Illustré Protestant (Lyon) 13
       (Jan./Feb. 1954), pp. 8-9f.

497   _____. "A Statement" (the author's relations with
       Dr. Schweitzer in Gunsbach). In: THE CONVOCATION
       RECORD, pp. VI/9-11.

498   "Dienaar van het leven. De jonge Albert Schweitzer." De
       Groene Amsterdammer (Amsterdam) 60:3091 (Aug. 29, 1936),
       pp. 11-13.

499   DINNER, FRITZ and CHARLES MICHEL. "Die letzten Wochen und
       Tage von Dr. Albert Schweitzer in seinen Spital zu
       Lambarene." RUNDBRIEF 27 (Nov. 21, 1965), pp. 39-41.
       Translated as "Dr. Schweitzer's last weeks and days."
       BRITISH BULLETIN 28 (Nov. 1965), pp. 3-6; Translation
       reprinted in COURIER, (April-May 1966), pp. 4-6; Trans-
       lated as "De laatste weken en dagen van Dr. Albert
       Schweitzer in Lambarene." NIEUWS 14:2 (Dec. 1965),
       pp. 6-9. Illus.; Translated as "Derniers jours et
       dernières semaines d'Albert Schweitzer." CAHIERS 14
       (Dec. 1965), pp. 7-8; "Les dernières semaines et les
       derniers jours du docteur Albert Schweitzer dans son
       Hôpital de Lambaréné." CAHIERS/BELGE 6 (Dec. 1965),
       pp. 7-9; Reprinted as "Die Abschied. . . ." BERICHTE
       29 (April 1966), pp. 3-6. Illus.

500   DIRKS, WALTER. "Das Porträt: Albert Schweitzer."
       Frankfurter Hefte 3:3 (March 1948), pp. 257-62.

501   "A doctor and theology." Newsweek (New York) 30:13
       (Sept. 29, 1947), p. 78.

502   DODD, E. M. "Kierkegaard and Schweitzer, an essay in com-
       parison and contrast." The London Quarterly and Holborn
       Review (London), 170 (April 1945), pp. 148-53.

503   "Dr. Albert Schweitzer." The Canon (Sydney, Australia)
       7:5-6 (Dec./Jan. 1953-54), pp. 244-46.

504   "Dr. Albert Schweitzer. Dates de sa vie; fragments de son
       oeuvre." Quadrige (Nice) 15 (Dec. 1950), pp. 118-20.
       Port.

505   "Dr. Albert Schweitzer hat die Rückreise nach Afrika
       angetreten." Les Dèrnieres Nouvelles du Haut-Rhin
       (Colmar), December 8, 1959, p. 20.

506   "Dr. Albert Schweitzer--humanitarian" (editorial). Journal
           of the American Medical Association (Chicago) 140:12
           (July 23, 1949), p. 1032.

507   "Dr. Albert Schweitzer in England" (from a correspondent).
           The Musical Standard (London) 30:523 (Oct. 8, 1927),
           p. 126.

508   "Dr. Albert Schweitzer, O.M." The Lancet (London) 269:6896
           (Oct. 29, 1955), p. 916.

509   "Dr. Albert Schweitzer, a reverence for life." New York
           Herald Tribune (New York), Sept. 6, 1965, p. 4. Illus.

510   "Dr. Albert Schweitzer, O.M., medical missionary, philosopher,
           theologian, and musician. The Times (London), Sept. 6,
           1965, p. 10. Illus.

511   "Dr. Schweitzer in London, October 1951." BRITISH BULLETIN
           20 (Sept. 1952), pp. 6-7.

512   "Dr. Schweitzer, 90, is buried in jungle." New York Herald
           Tribune, Sept. 6, 1965, pp. 1, 5. Port.

513   "Dr. Schweitzer over medische Zending." Mededeelingen
           Tijdschrift voor Zendings-Wetenschap (Oegstgeest) 72
           (1928), p. 279.

514   DUARTE, G. "Schweitzer de Lambarene" (editorial). Revista
           Chilena de Pediatria (Santiago) 36:7 (July 1965),
           pp. 407-08.

515   DUNGAN, DAVID L. "Reconsidering Albert Schweitzer." The
           Christian Century (Chicago) 92:32 (Oct. 8, 1975),
           pp. 874-80. Originally presented as part of the Albert
           Schweitzer Centenary in Atlanta, at a meeting of the
           Society of Biblical Literature and the American Academy
           of Religion.

516   DURAND-REVILLE, LUC. "Albert Schweitzer, le Grand Docteur
           Blanc." Revue Littérature, Histoire, Arts et Sciences
           des Deux Mondes (Paris) 22 (Nov. 15, 1965), pp. 230-41.

517   ECKERT-SCHWEITZER, RHENA. "Erinnerungen an meinem Vater."
           Sonntagspost (Winterthur) 65:2 (Jan. 13, 1945), pp. 9-10.
           For other remembrances by Schweitzer's daughter, see
           Burns, Olive A. (no. 445 above) and Kupferberg and
           Michaels (nos. 680 and 730 below).

Life and Work

518   EDDY, GEORGE S. "The modern discovery of God." In: <u>Man</u>
        <u>Discovers God</u>. New York: Harper, 1942, pp. 230-41.
        Reprinted in 1968 by Books for Libraries Press as part
        of their Essay Index Reprint Series. Quoted and adapted
        as "Albert Schweitzer." In: <u>Pathfinders of the World</u>
        <u>Missionary Crusade</u>. New York: Abingdon-Cokesbury, 1945,
        pp. 251-58.

519   EDSCHMID, KASIMIR. "Abschnitt aus dem Leben Albert
        Schweitzers." <u>Rhein-Neckar Zeitung</u> (Heidelberg),
        Sept. 17, 1949.

520   EHLERS, ALICE. "Thoughts on revisiting Gunsbach." In:
        REALMS, pp. 171-75.

521   EHRETSMANN, LÉON. "Schweitzer." <u>Le Rotarien Français</u> (Lyon)
        105 (March 1961), pp. 26-31. Illus., ports.

522   "Ehrfurcht vor dem Leben. Die DDR verehrt den grossen
        Humanisten Albert Schweitzer in seinem Kampf für Frieden"
        (letters exchanged between Walter Ulbricht, Chairman of
        the East German government, and Albert Schweitzer). <u>Neue</u>
        <u>Zeit</u> (East Berlin) 197 (Aug. 25, 1961), pp. 1-2.[1] For
        articles, comments and criticism related to this corre-
        spondence, see the following entries: 324, 944, 951,
        953, 1664, 1665.

523   EIGENHUIS, JAN. "In het 'atelier' van Albert Schweitzer."
        <u>Algemeen Handelsblad</u> (Amsterdam) 33302 (Nov. 7, 1929),
        Avondblad, p. 9; 33303 (Nov. 8, 1929), Avondblad, p. 9.
        Illus.

524   EINWECK. "Albert Schweitzer, der Goethepreisträger dieses
        Jahres" (mit biographischer Einführung und Teilabdruck
        "Aus meiner Kindheit und Jugendzeit"). <u>Graphische</u>
        <u>Berufsschule</u> (Munich) 14:3 (Dec. 1928), pp. 37-41.

525   EINSTEIN, ALBERT. "Albert Schweitzer at eighty." In:
        FESTSCHRIFT. Reprinted in <u>The Christian Century</u>

---

[1]In 1961, Walter Ulbricht wrote to congratulate Albert Schweitzer on
an honorary degree presented to him by Humboldt University.
Schweitzer replied courteously. Unfortunately, it was the time of
the Berlin Wall crisis, and when Ulbricht published the letter
Schweitzer was accused of sympathy with East Germany. The controversy which followed is indicated by the many articles and letters
written concerning this issue.

(Chicago) 72:2 (Jan. 12, 1955), p. 42; translated as
"Schlichte Grosse" in: EHRFURCHT, p. 232; Translation
reprinted in Neue Zürcher Zeitung, Jan. 9, 1955, p. 4;
reprinted in Neue Schweizer Rundschau, Jan. 9, 1955, p. 4;
reprinted in: BEGEGNUNG, pp. 322-23; also in: GESTERN-
HEUTE, p. 31.

526 EKMAN, HENRIK. "Med Albert Schweitzer på Konsert--och
     Foredragaresa." In: MANNEN, pp. 157-71.

527 E., F. M. [ELIOT, FREDERICK M.] "Salute to Albert
     Schweitzer." The Christian Register (Boston) 126:8
     (Sept. 1947), p. 319.

528 _____. "Schweitzer in America." The Christian Register
     (Boston) 128:6 (June 1949), p. 13.

529 ESCANDE, JEAN. "La triple signification de la personnalité
     d'Albert Schweitzer." CAHIERS 24 (Winter 1970/71),
     pp. 11-13.

530 ESENKOVA, PERVIN. [Brief tribute without title.] In:
     DENKEN UND WEG, p. 99.

531 FANGUINOVENY, J. R. "Hommage d'un Gabonais au 'Grand Docteur'
     de Lambaréné." Communautés et Continents (Paris) 67:37
     (Jan.-March 1975), pp. 31-32.

532 FARNSWORTH, DANA L. "Doctors afield: Albert Schweitzer,
     physician, philosopher, theologian, musician." The New
     England Journal of Medicine (Boston) 247:2 (July 10, 1952),
     pp. 62-64.

533 FELLOWES-GORDON, IAN. Heroes of the Twentieth Century.
     New York: Hawthorn Books, 1966, pp. 99-106.

534 FELS, ANDREE. "Albert Schweitzer." In: Le Grand Messager
     Boiteux de Strasbourg Almanach. Strasbourg: F.-X. le
     Roux and Co., 1953, pp. 80-83.

535 FESCHOTTE, JACQUES. "Albert Schweitzer m'a dit. . . ."
     Les Nouvelles Littéraires/Artistiques et Scientifiques
     (Paris) 30 (1951), pp. 1f.

536 _____. "Albert Schweitzer resuscite au XXe siècle la haute
     figure de Goethe." Rivarol (Paris), May 1, 1951, p. 5.
     Port., illus.

Life and Work

537 _____. "D'Alsace au Gabon." Les Nouvelles Littéraires
(Paris) 29:1195 (July 27, 1950), p. 5. Port.

538 _____. "Un grand homme de chez nous; Albert Schweitzer."
Départs (Strasbourg) 1:4 (March 1950), p. 15. Port.

539 _____. "Das Leben Albert Schweitzers." In: Albert
Schweitzer, Genie der Menschlichkeit. Dargestellt von
Stefan Zweig, Jacques Feschotte und Rudolf Grabs.
Frankfurt, Hamburg: Fischer Bücherei, 1955, pp. 21-104.
Translation by Ilse Wildekampf of Feschotte's book Albert
Schweitzer, see no. 248 above. Excerpts reprinted in:
BEGEGNUNG, pp. 219-28.

540 _____. "Rayonnement universel d'Albert Schweitzer."
Cahiers d'Information et de Culture Musicale Populaire
(Paris) 10 (April 1952), pp. 1-2.

541 _____. "Le vrai visage d'Albert Schweitzer." L'Automobile
de France (Paris) 33 (April 1952), unnumbered pp. Illus.

542 FISCHER, EDITH. "Albert Schweitzer, der Mann des Denkens und
der Tat." Die Agnes-Karll-Schwester (Frankfurt a.M.) 14
(1960), pp. 4-7. Reprinted in RUNDBRIEF 15 (Jan. 14, 1960),
pp. 45-51.

543 FISCHER, W. F. J. "Herdenkingswoord." EERBIED 23:2
(Dec. 1974), pp. 26-27.

544 FLETCHER, A. H. S. "Albert Schweitzer: a review from
1875-1957." The Central African Journal of Medicine
(Salisbury, Southern Rhodesia) 5:12 (Dec. 1959),
pp. 570-76.

545 FLETCHER, JOHN P. "Dr. Schweitzer in Great Britain."
BRITISH BULLETIN 8 (Winter 1933-34), p. 10.

546 FLETCHER, MARIE. "Schweitzer no saint, quite human."
Syracuse Herald-Journal (Syracuse, N.Y.) Feb. 27, 1975,
p. 29.

547 FOLLEREAU, RAOUL. "Le frère de tous les hommes." Les
Nouvelles Littéraires (Paris) 43:1984 (Sept. 9, 1965),
p. 9. Illus.

548 FOOTE, ARTHUR. "A little lower than the angels. The story
of the incredible Albert Schweitzer." Motive (Nashville,
Tenn.) 5:1 (Oct. 1944), pp. 19-20ff. Also issued as an
11-page pamphlet.

549   FORBECH, RAGNAR. "Albert Schweitzer erobert Norwegen." In:
          BEITRÄGE, pp. 52-53.

550   "Un Français inconnu rentre d'Afrique. Pour les Américains,
          c'est le plus grand homme du monde, Albert Schweitzer."
          Samedi-Soir, January 17, 1948.

551   FRANCK, FREDERICK. "Schweitzer 85 Thursday: man behind the
          myth." New York Herald-Tribune, Sunday, Jan. 10, 1960,
          Section 2, pp. 1ff. Translated as "Das Licht von
          Lambarene. Der Mythos Albert Schweitzer." Der Spiegel
          (Hamburg) 14:4 (Jan. 20, 1960), p. 45. Port. For a
          letter to the editor in reply by Ernst Häckermann, see
          Der Spiegel 14:7 (Feb. 10, 1960), p. 5.

552   FRIIS, BØRGE. "Albert Schweitzer. Vor Tids Frans af Assissi."
          Våbenhuset (Copenhagen) 3:6 (1951), pp. 190-97. Other
          articles of this title were published in: Berlingske
          Tidende (Copenhagen), Nov. 21, 1951; Fyens Stiftstidende
          (Odense), Nov. 3, 1953, p. 6; Aarhus Stiftstidende
          (Aarhus, Denmark) Nov. 9, 1953; and Landet (Copenhagen)
          Dec. 10, 1953.

553   _____. "Et naerbillede af Albert Schweitzer." Aarhus
          Stifstidende (Aarhus, Denmark), May 14, 1959.

554   FUCHS, EMIL. "Das Leben zweier Pfarrerssöhne von 1874/75 bis
          heute." In: BEITRÄGE, pp. 54-61.

555   FUERSTNER, C. "Albert Schweitzer: a Recollection." Your
          Musical Cue 2:3 (1965-66), pp. 11-14. Port.

556   FULTON, WILLIAM. "The life and work of Albert Schweitzer."
          The Expository Times (Edinburgh) 43:8 (May 1932),
          pp. 354-58.

557   G., F. "Arzt, Denker, Musiker." The Spectator (London)
          154:5561 (Jan. 25, 1935), p. 119. Text in German.

558   G., M. R. "A legend in his lifetime." Illustrated Weekly of
          India (Bombay), Oct. 3, 1965, pp. 35-38.

559   GAERTNER, HENRYK. "Albert Schweitzer jako teolog i folozof."
          Ruch Mucyczny (Warsaw) 20:6 (1976), pp. 6-7. Illus.

560   _____. "Albert Schweitzer 1875-1965." Zycie i Mysl 9
          (1975), pp. 25, 30-40.

Life and Work

561 _____ (interview with). [Albert Schweitzer's work.]
Kierunki 22 (1977), pp. 8-9.

562 GALVÁN, ENRIQUE TIERNO. "Perfil de Albert Schweitzer y de
su obra." Arbor (Madrid) 26:95 (Nov. 1953), pp. 263-79.
An article with similar content but different wording
appeared under the title "Albert Schweitzer und sein
Werk." Schweizer Rundschau 54:6 (Sept. 1954), pp. 301-08.

563 GARDNER, HY. "Dr. Schweitzer writes." New York Herald
Tribune, June 13, 1959, p. 13.

564 GARDNER, NELLIE. "Organ recital here will aid Dr. Schweitzer's
work in Africa." New York Herald Tribune, Jan. 12, 1947.

565 GARDNER, PERCY. "Albert Schweitzer." The Modern Churchman
(Oxford) 23:2 (May 1933), pp. 74-78.

566 GELL, CHRISTOPHER W. M. "Dr. Schweitzer--a reassessment."
The Hibbert Journal (London) 55:4 (July 1957), pp. 330-34.
Reprinted in The Forum (Johannesburg, South Africa) 6:4
(July 1957), pp. 38-41.

567 _____. "Albert Schweitzer at eighty." The Contemporary
Review (London) 187:1069 (Jan. 1955), pp. 18-22.

568 _____. "Tribute to Albert Schweitzer." The Forum
(Johannesburg, South Africa) 3:10 (Jan. 1955), pp. 34-36.

569 "Genius in the Jungle" (editorial). The Living Church
(Milwaukee, Wis.) 130:3 (Jan. 16, 1955), p. 7. Cover
port.

570 "Gentle giant of the jungle." Wilmington, Magazine of Lower
Cape Fear, May 1975, pp. 7f.

571 GEORGE, MANFRED. "Mann aus dem Urwald." Aufbau (New York)
15:27 (July 8, 1949), pp. 1-2. Port.

572 GEYER, CARL. "Albert Schweitzer-Sebastian Kneipp." Kneipp-
Blätter (Stuttgart) 58:3 (March 1955), p. 71.

573 GIVEN-WILSON, F. G. "Albert Schweitzer." The Modern Churchman (Oxford) 12:8 (Nov. 1922), pp. 461-66.

574 GODMAN, STANLEY. "Albert Schweitzer, 'Grand Old Man Europas'.
Bericht über eine Englische Würdigung." Die Wandlung
(Heidelberg) 4 (1949), pp. 268-78.

575 GOETTMANN, ALPHONSE. Introduction. In: MISÉRICORDE,
         pp. 9-11.

576 GOLDSCHMID, LADISLAS. "Memories and Meditations: 1935-55."
         In: FESTSCHRIFT, pp. 43-47.

577 GOLDSCHMIDT, HELMUT. "'Wie gerne käm' ich noch einmal nach
         Wien.' Albert Schweitzer--das Gewissen der Menschheit--
         feiert seinen 83. Geburtstag." Neue Illustrierte
         Wochenschau (Vienna) 49:3 (Jan. 19, 1958), p. 6.

578 "The good man at 80." Newsweek (New York) 45:3 (Jan. 17, 1955),
         p. 82.

579 GOODALL, NORMAN. "Schweitzer has an appointment." The
         Congregational Quarterly (London) 32:3 (July 1954),
         pp. 230-34.

580 _____ and others. "Albert Schweitzer: Man of many Aspects."
         The Listener (London) 53:1351 (Jan. 20, 1955), pp. 103-04.

581 GOTTSTEIN, WERNER. "Albert Schweitzer and America." The
         American-German Review (Philadelphia) 16:4 (April 1950),
         pp. 6-8f.

582 GRABS, RUDOLF. "Ein Rufer zu wahren Menschentum. Begegnung
         mit Albert Schweitzer in seinem Briefen." Neue Zeit
         (East Berlin) 11 (Jan. 14, 1960), p. 3.

583 _____. "Sinngebung des Lebens." In: Albert Schweitzer,
         Genie der Menschlichkeit. Dargestellt von Stefan Zweig,
         Jacques Feschotte und Rudolf Grabs. Frankfurt, Hamburg:
         Fischer Bücherei, 1955, pp. 105-222. Reprint of his book
         of the same name, see no. 2356 below.

584 GRAY, TONY. "1952--Albert Schweitzer." In: Champions of
         Peace: The Story of Alfred Nobel, the Peace Prize, and
         the Laureates. The Paddington Press, 1976, pp. 227-32.

585 "A great human being" (editorial). New York Herald Tribune,
         Sept. 6, 1965, p. 12.

586 "Great man in the jungle." Time (New York) 47 (April 1, 1946),
         pp. 66f.

587 "The greatest Christian." Newsweek (New York) 34:2
         (July 11, 1949), pp. 58f.

Life and Work

588   "The greatest man in the world." Life (New York) 23:14
        (Oct. 6, 1947), pp. 95-96f.

589   GUIMARÃES, NEY. "Un homen, no superlative." A Tribuna de
        Santos (São Paulo), Jan. 14, 1960.

590   HAANTJES, JOHANNES. "Albert Schweitzer." Stemmen des Tijds
        (Utrecht) 23:2 (Nov. 1934), pp. 401-37. Also issued as
        a reprint: Zutphen: Ruys, 1934. 36 pp.

591   HABERMAN, FREDERICK W., ed. "Peace 1952 (Prize awarded in
        1953): Albert Schweitzer." In: Peace 1951-1970: Nobel
        Lectures, including presentation speeches and laureates'
        biographies, Vol. III. Amsterdam, London, New York:
        Elsevier Publishing Company, 1972, pp. 37-61. Schweitzer's
        address, pp. 37-57; biography and bibliography, pp. 58-61.

592   HABRAN, J. "Qui est le Docteur Schweitzer?" No tre Lieu
        (Papeete) 21:250 (June 1958), pp. 5-7.

593   HAGEDORN, HERMANN. Selection without title. In: BEGEGNUNG,
        pp. 200-07. Reprinted from Prophet in the Wilderness,
        no. 262 above.

594   HAINISCH-MARCHET, LUDOVICA. "'Ich bin den Wienern so
        Dankbar.' Gespräch mit dem Nobelpreisträger Dr. Albert
        Schweitzer." Neue Illustrierte Wochenschau (Vienna)
        45:29 (July 18, 1954), p. 3.

595   _____. "Persönliche Aussprache mit Albert Schweitzer."
        Wissen und Gewissen (Vienna) 26 (July 1954), pp. 394-96.
        Port. Reprinted in RUNDBRIEF 6 (Dec. 1, 1954), pp. 17-20.

596   HALÉVY, DANIEL. "Albert Schweitzer." In: Courrier d'Europe.
        Paris: Grasset, 1933, pp. 307-12.

597   _____. "Un Grand Alsacien, Albert Schweitzer." La Revue
        Littérature, Histoire, Arts et Sciences des Deux Mondes
        (Paris), Oct. 15, 1950, pp. 677-89; Nov. 1, 1950,
        pp. 101-13. Reprinted as "Connaissance d'Albert
        Schweitzer." In: ÉTUDES, pp. 219-52.

598   _____. "Dès Octobre Schweitzer rejoindra l'Afrique."
        Réforme (Paris) 5:234 (Sept. 10, 1949), pp. 4-5. Port.,
        illus.

599   HAMANO, O. "Albert Schweitzer no Sekai." Shuppan News
        (Tokyo), Jan. 1956, p. 10.

600   HARPER, HOWARD V. "Albert Schweitzer." In: Profiles of
        Protestant Saints. New York: Fleet Press, 1968,
        pp. 224-31.

601   HARRINGTON, DONALD SZANTHO. "Debunking Howe." Africa Today
        12:8 (Oct. 1965), pp. 12-13.

602   HAUTER, CHARLES. "Albert Schweitzer, professeur de théologie
        à Strasbourg." In: HOMMAGE, pp. 53-58.

603   HAYES, PAUL G. "Schweitzer--lover of God and man." The
        Chinese Recorder (Shanghai) 64:2 (Feb. 1933), pp. 85-89.

       HEARD, GERALD. "The Pattern of Prestige." See Philosophy,
        no. 2502 below.

604   HEBESTREIT, WILHELM. "Albert Schweitzer, guter Geist unserer
        Zeit." Münchner Mittag (Munich) 2:42 (May 9, 1947), p. 3.

605   HEISLER, AUGUST. "Albert Schweitzer, der Arzt." Hippokrates
        (Stuttgart) 9:12 (March 24, 1935), pp. 309-10.

606   _____. "Albert Schweitzer, der Menschenfreund und
        Weltbürger aus der Nähe gesehen." Aerztliche Mitteilungen
        (Cologne) 2 (Jan. 10, 1951).

607   HELGASON, JÓN. "Albert Schweitzer, laekningatrúboöi."
        Prestafelagsritid (Iceland) 15 (1933), pp. 16-43.

608   HELLPACH, WILLY. "Albertus Universus." In: EHRFURCHT,
        pp. 220-27. Reprinted in: BEGEGNUNG, pp. 229-32.

609   HELLSTERN, HEINRICH. "Im Dienst am Menschen." Standpunkt:
        Evangelische Monatsschrift (Berlin) 3:1 (Jan. 1975),
        pp. 8-9.

610   HENDERSON, A. M. "Albert Schweitzer as man and musician.
        Personal memories." Musical Opinion and Music Trade
        Review (London) 79:939 (Dec. 1955), p. 169.

611   HEUCH, I. C. "Albert Schweitzer." I Dag (Copenhagen) 3:12
        (1948), pp. 8-11. Port.

612   HEUSCHELE, OTTO. "Albert Schweitzer." Das Werk (Düsseldorf)
        13 (Aug. 1933), p. 343. Translated by F. Eppling Reinartz
        in The Lutheran Church Quarterly (Gettysburg) 8
        (Jan. 1935), pp. 29-34.

Life and Work

613 HEUSS-KNAPP, ELLY. [Begegnung mit Helene Bresslau, Albert
     Schweitzer, und seine Eltern.] In: Ausblick vom
     Münsterturm. Erinnerungen. Berlin-Tempelhof: Hans
     Bott, 1934, pp. 61-62. Second edition Strassburg:
     Hünenburg-Verlag, 1941, pp. 60-61. Reprinted in:
     BEGEGNUNG, pp. 119-23.

614 HIDDING, K. A. "Spannung und Leben in Schweitzers
     Persönlichkeit." In: DENKEN UND WEG, pp. 231-35.
     Also issued as a reprint: Tübingen: Mohr, 1962. 4 pp.

615 HIGHET, G. "Albert Schweitzer." In: The Immortal Profession:
     The Joys of Teaching and Learning. New York: Weybright
     and Talley, 1976, pp. 175-97.

616 HITCHEN, HERBERT. "A prophet of freedom." The Christian
     Register (Boston) 126:8 (Sept. 1947), pp. 317-18.

617 HODGKIN, THOMAS. "Albert Schweitzer." The Spectator
     (London) 191:6541 (Nov. 6, 1953), p. 505.

618 HOFFET, MARIELEINE. [Albert Schweitzer.] L'Illustré
     Protestant (Lyon) 13 (Jan./Feb. 1954), p. 8.

619 HOFFMEYER, SKAT. I. "Filantrop, taenker og kunstner." II.
     "Det rige menneske Albert Schweitzer." Aarhus
     Stiftstidende (Aarhus, Denmark), Jan. 13, 1950. Port.

620 HOLDT, JENS. "Echo Schweitzers in Dänemark." In: BEITRÄGE,
     pp. 78-82.

621 HOWE, RUSSELL WARREN. "Albert Schweitzer, facts and fancies."
     Africa Today 12:8 (Oct. 1965), pp. 11-12.

622 HUARD, P. "Albert Schweitzer l'Africain." Le Concours
     Medical (Paris) 85:1 (Jan. 1, 1966), pp. 113-23.

623 HÜBSCHER, ARTHUR. "Albert Schweitzer." In: Denker unserer
     Zeit. Munich: R. Piper, 1956, pp. 132-36.

624 HUNTER, ALLAN A. "Schweitzer at eighty." Advance (New York)
     147:1 (Jan. 12, 1955), pp. 5-6f.

625 _____. "The lion who laughs--and weeps." In: FESTSCHRIFT,
     pp. 59-63. Reprinted in Friends Intelligencer
     (Philadelphia) 112:3 (Jan. 15, 1955) pp. 32-33.

626 _____. "Schweitzer." In: Three Trumpets Sound: Kagawa,
     Ghandi, Schweitzer. New York: Association Press, 1939,
     pp. 107-50.

627   _____. "Schweitzer at Aspen." The Christian Century
         (Chicago) 66:30 (July 27, 1949), pp. 890-91.

628   ICE, JACKSON LEE. "Dr. Schweitzer at ninety." The Hibbert
         Journal (London) 63:249 (Winter 1965), pp. 72-77.

629   ILLINGWORTH, FRANK. "Spabio, heroi ou santo?" O Jornal
         (Rio de Janeiro), April 13, 1956.

630   IMAZ, EUGENIO. "Albert Schweitzer. El hombre del siglo."
         Cuadernos Americanos (Mexico) Vol. 43, Anno. 8, No. 1
         (Jan./Feb. 1949), pp. 133-36.

631   "In eerbied voor het leven. Gesprek met een nicht van
         Dr. Albert Schweitzer." NIEUWS 2:5 (July 1954),
         pp. 68-69.

632   INGERMAN, K. J. JUNIUS. "Albert Schweitzer." NIEUWS 5:1
         (April 1956), pp. 12-13.

633   _____. "Het is mijn schuld." NIEUWS 5:3 (Dec. 1956),
         pp. 5-7.

634   "Invloed van Albert Schweitzer verrassend groot in Amerika."
         NIEUWS 1:1 (Dec. 1951), p. 9.

635   ISOM, JOHN B. "Religious and ethical evolution" (letter to
         the editor). Saturday Review (New York) 37 (Oct. 2, 1954),
         pp. 22-23.

636   IVERSEN, FELIX. "Kraft und Zuversicht gehen von Schweitzer
         aus." In: BEITRÄGE, pp. 83-84.

637   JACK, HOMER A. "Dr. Albert Schweitzer: a profile." Chicago
         Daily News, Jan. 14, 1959, p. 14.

638   _____. "The popularity of Albert Schweitzer." In: REALMS,
         pp. 80-92.

639   _____. "20 questions about Albert Schweitzer." The
         Christian Century (Chicago) 75:44 (Oct. 29, 1958),
         pp. 1243-44. Also issued as a reprint by the Albert
         Schweitzer Fellowship.

640   JACOBI, ERWIN. "Albert Schweitzer: Unveröffentliche Briefe
         an Margit Jacobi." Librarium: Zeitschrift der
         Schweizerischen Bibliophilen 19:1 (May 1976), pp. 2-21.

General

Life and Work

641 _____. "Albert Schweitzer als Feriengast in unser Bergen."
Der Bund (Bern) Feuilleton, Feb. 13, 1975, p. 37.
Reprinted in BERICHTE 39 (March 1975), pp. 13-18;
condensed as "Wo Albert Schweitzer früher Ferien machte."
RUNDBRIEFE/DDR 28 (1976), pp. 14-20.

642 JACOBI, HUGO. "Das Profil" (Albert Schweitzer). Die
Weltwoche (Zürich) 992 (Nov. 14, 1952), p. 5.

643 JOHANNES, ANT. "De man uit Lambarene: Albert Schweitzer
verjaart." Haagse Post (The Hague) 1991 (Feb. 7, 1953),
p. 7.

644 JOHNSON, G. E. HICKMAN. "Albert Schweitzer the missionary."
Peace News (London) 968 (Jan. 14, 1955), p. 4.

645 JONZON, BENGT. "Några intryck av Albert Schweitzer." In:
MANNEN, pp. 153-56.

646 JOUBERT, SYLVIA. "Mon oncle le docteur Schweitzer." Noveau
Femina (Paris) 8 (Nov. 1954), pp. 107-11.

647 JOY, CHARLES R. "Introduction." In: Albert Schweitzer, an
Anthology. Boston: Beacon Press, 1956, pp. xiii-xxii.
Reprinted in part as "A modern man's quest for the holy
grail." In: SELECTION, pp. 2-7.

648 _____. "Muzykant v 84 goda." Sovetskaya Muzyka (Moscow)
39:1 (Jan. 1975), pp. 135-37.

649 _____. "With Schweitzer in Oslo." The Christian Register
(Boston) 134:1 (Jan. 1955), pp. 16-18. Illus., cover
port.

650 JUNGHEINRICH, HANSJÖRG. "Landessynode (Westfalen) grüsst
Albert Schweitzer." Freies Christentum (Frankfurt a.M.)
12:2 (Feb. 1, 1960), col. 26.

651 JUNGK, ROBERT. "Albert Schweitzer." Welt und Wort
(Tübingen) 10:1 (Jan. 1955), pp. 6-9.

652 _____. "Albert Schweitzer." Haagse Post (The Hague)
January 8, 1955.

653 _____. "Der unbekannte Albert Schweitzer." Die Weltwoche
(Zürich) 1103 (Dec. 31, 1954), p. 3. Port.

654 KABIR, HUMAYNUN. "Pionier der Weltkultur." In: BEITRÄGE,
pp. 85-87.

655   KALFUS, RADIM. "A statement" (love of his fellow men as
         exemplified by Albert Schweitzer). In: THE CONVOCATION
         RECORD, pp. VI/31-32.

656   KAPF, RUDOLF. "Albert Schweitzer und wir." Der Convent
         (Mannheim-Sandhofen, Germany) 2:6 (June 1951), pp. 129-30.

657   KARSH, YOUSUF. "The camera's eye: Albert Schweitzer." The
         Atlantic Monthly (Boston) 200:6 (Dec. 1957), pp. 93-94.
         Reprinted from the author's book The Faces of Destiny.
         Condensed as "Albert Schweitzer." The Reader's Digest
         (Pleasantville, NY) 73:435 (July 1958), pp. 151-53;
         Translated as "Das Auge der Kamera." Zeitwende 29:7
         (July 1958), pp. 479-80; Translated in Seleções do
         Reader's Digest (Brazil), Sept. 1958.

658   _____. In Search of Greatness. Reflections of Yousuf Karsh.
         London: Cassell, 1963, pp. 101-02, 149-55, and other
         single pages.

659   KELLER, ADOLF. Von Geist und Liebe: ein Bilderbuch aus dem
         Leben. Gotha: Leopold Klotz, 1934, pp. 192-93. Port.

660   KELLER, HERMANN. "Albert Schweitzer." Jahrbuch der Musikwelt/
         Annuaire du Monde Musicale (Bayreuth) 1 (1949/1950),
         pp. 5-6. Port.

661   KELLOGG, GEORGE A. "Albert Schweitzer, administrator,
         humanitarian, musician." Hospital Management (Chicago)
         68 (Aug. 1949), pp. 29-31. Illus., port.

662   KENDON, FRANK. "Albert Schweitzer." The Fortnightly
         (London) 163 (Jan. 1948), pp. 59-64.

663   KENT, ROGER. "Albert Schweitzer," In: Canning, John, ed.
         100 Great Modern Lives. New York: Hawthorn Books, 1965,
         pp. 395-400.

664   KIEBER, H. "Erinnerungen an Albert Schweitzer." In:
         WÜRDIGUNG, pp. 41-43.

665   KIK, RICHARD. "Dank und Gruss." RUNDBRIEF 18 (July 15, 1961),
         pp. 51-52.

666   _____. [Letter from the editor to readers of the Rundbrief
         about the campaign by the press and others against Albert
         Schweitzer.] RUNDBRIEF 11 (Aug. 1, 1957), pp. 42-46.

General

Life and Work

667   KIK, RICHARD. "Der Theologe, Musiker, Arzt, und Philosophe
      Albert Schweitzer." Aussaat (Lorch-Stuttgart) 1:6/7
      (1946), pp. 14-16.

668   KLOTZ, H. "Albert Schweitzer in memoriam." Acta Musicologica
      (Basel) 37:3/4 (1965), pp. 91-94.

669   KNITTEL, JEAN. "Elsass hedrar doktor Albert Schweitzer och
      hans verk." MEDDELANDEN (1949), pp. 4-6. Reprinted in:
      FYRBÅKEN, pp. 246-48.

670   KOLLBRUNNER, F. "Albert Schweitzer und die Mission."
      Neue Zeitschrift für Missionswissenschaft (Immensee,
      Switz.) 31:4 (1975), pp. 288-93.

671   KOROLEC, JERZY B. "Albert Schweitzer." Wiez (Warsaw) 12
      (1965), pp. 59-63. Illus.

672   KRAATZ, PROF. DR. H. "Erinnerungen an Albert Schweitzer."
      Standpunkt: Evangelische Monatsschrift (Berlin) 3:1
      (Jan. 1975), pp. 12-13.

673   KRESS, HANS. "Albert Schweitzer und die Jugend." Colloquium
      (Berlin) 9:1 (1955), pp. 6-7. Illus.

674   KRISTJÁNSSON, BENJAMÍN. "Albert Schweitzer, líf hans og
      starf." Kirkjuritinu (Iceland) 16 (1950), pp. 158-82.

675   KUEHN-LEITZ, ELSIE. "The practical Christianity of Albert
      Schweitzer." The Cresset (Valparaiso, Ind.) 30:6
      (April 1967), pp. 8-13.

676   KUNZE, OTTO. "Albert Schweitzer." Allgemeine Rundschau
      (Munich) 25:36 (Sept. 8, 1929), pp. 574-75.

677   KUPFERBERG, HERBERT. "Albert Schweitzer--a legend in his
      time." New York Herald Tribune, Jan. 14, 1960, p. 16.
      Illus.

678   _____. "Albert Schweitzer, here, denies 36 African years
      are 'sacrifice.'" New York Herald Tribune, June 29,
      1949, p. 1. Port.

679   _____. "An all-around authority. Dr. Schweitzer noted as
      expert in many fields." New York Herald Tribune,
      July 3, 1949.

680   _____. "A daughter remembers her famous father." Parade
      Magazine, Washington Post, Jan. 12, 1975, p. 12.

681   KURZ, GERTRUD. "Müde werden? Nein, die Arbeit drängt."
         In: BEITRÄGE, pp. 91-92.

682   KYPRIANOS, ARCHBISHOP. "Rayonnement d'Albert Schweitzer en
         Grèce." CAHIERS 13 (June 1965), pp. 20-21.

683   LAMBIRI, IO. "Albert Schweitzer et son oeuvre." In:
         DEBRECEN, pp. 69-80.

684   LAMM, GRETA. "Albert Schweitzer." Studiekamraten
         (Stockholm) 36:6 (1954), pp. 119-25. Port.

685   LANCZKOWSKI, GÜNTER. "Albert Schweitzer in Europe."
         Hessische Nachrichten (Kassel), Jan. 15, 1949.

686   LARTER, LAURENCE. "Schweitzer: Musician, missionary and
         mystic." The Methodist Magazine (London) (Feb. 1949),
         pp. 77-79.

687   LEAKE, CHAUNCEY D. "Albert Schweitzer: physician balances
         the biad." In: THE CONVOCATION RECORD, pp. II/4.

688   _____. "Appraisal of Albert Schweitzer (1875-1965)."
         Geriatrics (Minneapolis, Minn.) 21:10 (Oct. 1966),
         pp. 117-18.

689   "The legacy of Albert Schweitzer." Journal of Church Music
         (Philadelphia) 8:10 (Nov. 1966), pp. 2-4, 32.

690   "Lepers weep at Schweitzer funeral." The Times (London),
         Sept. 6, 1965, p. 8.

691   "Leuchtturm der Humanität. Albert Schweitzer-Ausstellung in
         Weimar." Neue Zeit (East Berlin) 11 (Jan. 14, 1960),
         p. 2.

692   LEVAILLANT, PIERRE. "Philosophe, médecin, et musicien,
         Albert Schweitzer applique le nouvel humanisme dont il
         est l'apôtre." Le Figaro (Paris) 2122 (July 5, 1954),
         p. 8.

693   LEWIS, LEO RICH. "Albert Schweitzer." Unity (Chicago)
         60:17 (Jan. 9, 1933), pp. 264-65.

694   LIND, EMIL. "Albert Schweitzer in Amerika: in de
         Californische zephir." NIEUWS 1:1 (Dec. 1951), p. 7.

695   _____. "Der 'alte Doktor' von Lambarene und die Jugend."
         RUNDBRIEF 8 (Nov. 1, 1955), pp. 48-50.

Life and Work

696 ____. "Dr. Schweitzer in Aspen." NIEUWS 1:1 (Dec. 1951),
pp. 8-9. Illus.

697 ____. "Wie ich Albert Schweitzer kennen lernte." Freies
Christentum (Frankfurt a.M.) 12:1 (Jan. 1, 1960),
cols. 9-10.

698 LINHARDT, STEPHAN. "Uma vida dedicada ao próximo." Correio
de Manhā (Rio de Janeiro), Jan. 21, 1960.

699 LINSI, ERNST. "Sie brauchen mich in Afrika. Das Hilfswerk
Albert Schweitzers." St. Galler Tagblatt (St. Gall,
Switz.) 22 (Jan. 14, 1955).

700 LIPSCHÜTZ, ALEJANDRO. Prólogo. In: Entre el Agua y la Selva
Virgen. Madrid: Javier Morata, 1932, pp. 11-24. Reprinted in Atenea (Santiago) Ano IX, Tomo XXII, nos. 91
and 92 (Sept. and Oct. 1932), pp. 42-52. Also issued as
a reprint.

701 LIPSKY, MORTIMER. Quest for Peace: the Story of the Nobel
Award. South Brunswick and New York: A. S. Barnes;
London: Thomas Yoseloff, 1966, pp. 176-80.

702 "Living with a verity." Time (New York) 86:12
(Sept. 17, 1965), p. 108. Illus.

703 LÖHLEIN, HERBERT A. "Horoskope Albert Schweitzers."
Kristall (Hamburg) 21:1 (1966), pp. 58-59. Port., illus.

704 LOT, FERNAND. "Albert Schweitzer. Prix Nobel de la Paix."
L'Education Nationale (Paris) 9:32 (Dec. 3, 1953), p. 8.

705 "The manifold life of Albert Schweitzer." The Literary
Digest (New York) 116 (Aug. 26, 1933), p. 19.

706 MANZ, GUSTAV. "Ein Prediger der Ehrfurcht: Dr. Albert
Schweitzer, Theologe, Musiker und Arzt." Die Gartenlaube
(Leipzig) 39 (Sept. 30, 1926), pp. 771-72.

707 MARÁN, R. "Una gran figura francesca Albert Schweitzer."
Vida Nueva (Havana) 65 (June 6, 1950), pp. 201-02.

708 MARCHAL, GEORGES. "Albert Schweitzer a-t-il des opposants?"
CAHIERS 5 (Sept. 1961), pp. 7-8.

709 ____. "Le fait Schweitzer." Communautés et Continents
(Paris) 67:37 (Jan.-March 1975), pp. 4-7.

710   MARGOLIUS, HANS. "Albert Schweitzer's philosophy of life."
      The Standard (New York) 41:6 (Nov./Dec. 1955), pp. 193-96.

711   MARHOLD, HERMANN. "Albert Schweitzer im engeren Kreise der
      Freunde des freien Christentums in Frankfurt am Main."
      Freies Christentum (Frankfurt a.M.) 7:10 (Oct. 1, 1955),
      col. 131.

712   MARLEY, HAROLD P. "Reflections on Schweitzer's departure."
      The Christian Register (Boston) 128:8 (Sept. 1949), p. 20.

713   MARTÍN, ALONSO. "O desengano do Dr. Schweitzer." Jornal
      do Brasil (Rio de Janeiro), Jan. 23, 1963.

714   MARTIN, EMMY. "Les derniers jours du Docteur." In:
      RAYONNEMENT, pp. 245-48.

715   "A master in darkest Africa." Etude (Philadelphia) 62
      (Jan. 1944), p. 10. Port.

716   MAURON, MARIE. "Albert Schweitzer prissonier à Saint-Remy-
      de-Provence." Réforme (Paris) 10:501 (Oct. 23, 1954),
      p. 5.

717   _____. "Quand le gouvernement français internait le
      Dr. Schweitzer." Revue Générale Belge (Brussels) 91
      (Feb. 15, 1955), pp. 551-59.

718   MAYER, LOUIS. "Lieber Brüder Albert." In: FESTSCHRIFT,
      pp. 64-71.

719   _____. "With Schweitzer in Europe." The Christian Register
      (Boston) 131:9 (Nov. 1952), pp. 16-17.

720   MAYS, VERNA. "The Schweitzer legacy." International Wild-
      life (Washington, D.C.) 4:6 (Nov./Dec. 1974), pp. 48-55.
      Illus.

721   MEHL, ROGER. "Albert Schweitzer, théologien et bâtisseur."
      Le Monde, Jan. 15, 1975. Reprinted in CAHIERS 33
      (Winter 1975), pp. 8-10.

722   MERANT, PIERRE. "Der Urwalddoktor. Das Leben des grossen
      Menschenfreundes Albert Schweitzer." Munchberg-
      Helmbrechts Zeitung (Munchberg), Jan. 11-Feb. 8, 1955.

723   MERAUT, PIERRE. "Ein Leben für Lambarene. Tatsachenbericht."
      Kölner Stadt-Anzeiger 139-65 (June 20/21-July 21, 1959),
      p. 5 in almost every issue.

Life and Work

724 MERKEL, GEORG. "Der Urwalddoktor." In: Die Mission auf der
     Kanzel: ein Missionshomiletisches Hilfsbuch, par J. Hesse.
     Stuttgart: Celwer Vereinbuchhandlung, 1930, pp. 303-406.

725 MERTZ, RICHARD. "Albert Schweitzer--ein beispielhaftes Leben."
     Rheinische Post (Düsseldorf) 97 (Aug. 17, 1949).

726 METZGER, LUDWIG. "Albert Schweitzer, lauchtendes Vorbild
     unserer Zeit." Kommunalpolitische Rundschau für das
     Land Hessen (Frankfurt a.M.) 8 (1955), p. 17.

727 MEYER, ARNOLD. "Albert Schweitzers Lebenslehre."
     Der Lesezirkel (Zürich) 15:5 (Feb. 1928), pp. 52-54.

728 MEYER, ERICH. "Albert Schweitzer in Europa." Freies
     Christentum (Frankfurt a.M.) 3:8 (Aug. 1, 1951), cols. 4-5.

729 MICHAELIS, OTTO. "Albert Schweitzer." In Elsässische
     Gestalten, Begegnungen in zwölf Jahrhunderten.
     Strassburg i. Els.: Evangelische Buchhandlung, 1942,
     pp. 133-37.

730 MICHAELS, JULIE. "Albert Schweitzer--a Berkshire Connection."
     Berkshire Sampler (Pittsfield, Mass.), Sunday, March 26,
     1978, pp. 4-5. Illus. (Interview with Rhena Schweitzer
     Miller.)

731 MICKLEM, NATHANIEL. "'Pity for all living things.' Albert
     Schweitzer at seventy." The Listener (London) 333:836
     (Jan. 18, 1945), pp. 74-75. Illus. Reprinted in the
     New Zealand Listener (Wellington) 12:304 (April 20, 1945),
     pp. 14-15. Port.; Reprinted with title "Work of Mercy
     to the Suffering." London Calling 281 (1945), p. 13f.
     This is a text of a talk over the BBC in honor of
     Schweitzer's 70th birthday.

732 MILLER, RHENA SCHWEITZER. "My father Albert Schweitzer."
     In: PROPHET, pp. 37-39.

733 MINDER, ROBERT. "Albert Schweitzer." Europe 6:22
     (Aug. 15, 1924), pp. 240-42.

734 _____ (under pseudonym "Max Gilmore"). "Albert Schweitzer."
     Europe 15 (Sept. 15, 1927), pp. 56-59.

735 _____. "Albert Schweitzer, humaniste alsacien et citoyen du
     monde." Saisons d'Alsace (Strasbourg) 11:18 (Spring 1966),
     pp. 141-64. Also issued as a reprint: Strasbourg:
     Istra, n.d., 22 pp. Address delivered at conference

of Semaine Nordique, Palais Universitaire, Strasbourg,
March 26, 1966.

736 _____. "Albert Schweitzer u. das Elsass." Les Dernières
Nouvelles du Haut-Rhin (Colmar), Jan. 14, 1960. Translated as "Albert Schweitzer et l'Alsace." CAHIERS 3
(June 1960), pp. 11-13; reprinted in: DENKEN UND WEG,
pp. 210-15; reprinted without title in: BEGEGNUNG,
pp. 25-30.

737 _____. "Albert Schweitzer et Romain Rolland." Europe
(Paris) 43:439/40 (Nov./Dec. 1965), pp. 136-47.

738 _____. "Un berceau de la famille: Pfaffenhoffen. Le
grand-père contestatiare et son journal politique." In:
RAYONNEMENT, pp. 37-49.

739 _____. "Brazza, Peguy et Schweitzer." CAHIERS 3 (June 1960),
pp. 27-28.

740 _____. "Emmy Martin." In: Emmy Martin, die Mitarbeitern
Albert Schweitzers. Tübingen: Katzmann-Verlag, 1964,
pp. 12-83. Contains copious and unusual data about
Dr. Schweitzer's earlier years.

741 _____. "Internement et retour en Alsace." In: RAYONNEMENT,
pp. 189-202.

742 _____. "Introduction et plan de l'ouvrage." In:
RAYONNEMENT, pp. 11-20.

743 _____. "De Kaysersberg au Presbytère de Gunsbach et à
Mulhouse." In: RAYONNEMENT, pp. 49-59.

744 _____. "Premiers contacts avec Paris et Berlin et retour à
Strasbourg." In: RAYONNEMENT, pp. 59-75.

745 _____. "Le Prix Goethe de 1928--Albert Schweitzer."
Revue d'Allemagne (Paris) 13-14 (Nov./Dec. 1928),
pp. 538-42.

746 _____. "Les Raisons du départ pour Lambarene." In:
RAYONNEMENT, pp. 75-91. Reprinted in CAHIERS 32
(Spring 1975), pp. 15-19; Translated as "Warum Schweitzer
nach Lambarene Ging." SZ am Wochenende, Süddeutsche
Zeitung (Munich), Jan. 24/25, 1976, pp. 107-08.

747 _____. "Respect de la vie--enracinement dans le passé,
perspective sur l'avenir." In: DEVENTER, pp. 59-70.
Summaries in German, English and Dutch.

Life and Work

748 _____. "Schweitzer l'Alsacien." Saisons d'Alsace
(Strasbourg) 3:1 (Winter 1951), pp. 3-10. Reprinted in:
ETUDES, second edition, pp. 33-48.

749 _____. "Schweitzer, Sartre und der Grossvater."
Süddeutsche Zeitung (Munich) 14 (Jan. 16/17, 1965),
Feuilleton, pp. 1-2.

750 _____. "Über das Alemannische bei Albert Schweitzer." In:
Festgabe für Wilhelm Hausenstern zum 70. Geburtstag.
Hrsg. von W. E. Süskind. Munich, 1952, pp. 149-58.

751 MIZOGUCHI, Y. "Albert Schweitzer." In: Shinkō Ijin Gunzō:
Kinseihen. Tokyo: 1954, pp. 387-402.

752 MOEHLMANN, CONRAD HENRY. "Why a genius went to the jungle."
The World Tomorrow (New York) 13:10 (Oct. 30, 1930),
pp. 418-19.

753 MONNIER, MAGDALENE. [Albert Schweitzer als Gast bei seinem
Zwischenaufenthalt in Douala, Weihnachten 1956.]
RUNDBRIEF 10 (Dec. 1, 1956), pp. 14-17.

754 MONTGOMERY, W. "Albert Schweitzer." The Expositor (London)
39th year, series 8, volume 6, no. 32 (Aug. 1913),
pp. 165-72.

755 _____. "Dr. Albert Schweitzer." St. Martin's Review
(London) 416 (Oct. 1925), pp. 496-99. Reprinted with
alterations and additions in: Albert Schweitzer, Philosopher, Theologian, Musician, Doctor. Compiled by C. T.
Campion. London: A. and C. Black, 1928.

756 MÜLLER, HERMANN VON. "Albert Schweitzer, seine Persönlichkeit
und sein Werk." Westermanns Monatshefte (Braunschweig)
70:140 (May 1926), pp. 309-13.

757 MULKEY, FLOYD. "Albert Schweitzer, wartime's greatest hero."
The Christian Advocate (Chicago) 122:43 (Oct. 23, 1947),
pp. 8-9ff.

758 MULLER, P. H. "Albert Schweitzer." In: Gedenkt uwen
Voorgangers. Amsterdam: Bigot und Van Rossum,
pp. 293-321.

759 MUNCH, CHARLES. "Albert Schweitzer and the Munch family."
Concert Bulletin of the Boston Symphony Orchestra No. 24
(April 27, 1951), pp. 1243-44.

760 _____. "A tribute to Albert Schweitzer" (preface). In:
Joy, Charles R., ed. Music in the Life of Albert
Schweitzer. New York: Harper and Bros., 1951, pp. ix-xi.
London: A. and C. Black, 1953, pp. viii-x. Reprinted
in Concert Bulletin of the Boston Symphony Orchestra
no. 24 (April 27, 1951), pp. 1244-51.

761 N., L. "Albert-Schweitzer-Jubiläum: Nachträgliches und
Nachdenkliches." Der Bund (Bern) 133 (March 20, 1955).

762 NATVIG, HAAKON. "Albert Schweitzer. En stor mann hog hans
syn på livet." Urd (Oslo) 38:5 (Feb. 3, 1934), pp. 138-40.
Port., illus.

763 NEUMANN, SIGMUND. "Albert Schweitzer. Der Mann und sein
Werk." New Yorker Staats-Zeitung und Herold, July 3,
1940, p. 30.

764 NIELSEN, WALDEMAR A. "The meaning and the future of Albert
Schweitzer's thought and work." In: THE CONVOCATION
RECORD, pp. VII/7-17.

765 NIES-BERGER, EDOUARD. "Strasbourg recollection of Albert
Schweitzer." Musical America (New York) 68:5
(April 1948), p. 23. Illus.

766 NOEL, PAUL. "Albert Schweitzer, humaniste." In: DEBRECEN,
pp. 45-52.

767 NOMURA, MINORU. "Albert Schweitzer und Japan." Universitas
(Stuttgart) 15:1 (Jan. 1960), pp. 122-24. Reprinted
without title in: DENKEN UND WEG, pp. 412-14 and in:
BEGEGNUNG, pp. 282-85; translated, without title, in
Universitas (English language edition) 7:1 (1964),
pp. 103-06.

768 _____. "Schweitzer no kinkyō." Dokuritsu (Tokyo) 18,
pp. 39-40.

769 _____. "Seiki no Hito Albert Schweitzer." Denki Shuppansha
(Tokyo) 3:2 (Feb. 1949), pp. 10-17.

770 _____. "Taisen-chū no Schweitzer." Dokuritsu (Tokyo) 1:4
(Sept. 1948), pp. 45-50.

771 NOORDHOFF, W. R. M. "Albert Schweitzer in Amerika." Het
Remonstrantse Weekblad (Scheveningen) 38 (Oct. 7, 1949),
p. 5.

General

Life and Work

772   NORTHCOTT, CECIL. "Albert Schweitzer--spiritual adventurer."
       The Christian Century (Chicago) 72:2 (Jan. 12, 1955),
       pp. 42-43.

773   _____. "Schweitzer returns." The Spectator (London)
       182:6295 (Feb. 8, 1949), pp. 213-14. Translated as
       "Albert Schweitzers Rückkehr." Die Brücke (Essen) 121
       (Feb. 23, 1949), pp. 13-14.

774   "Notice, bio-bibliographique d'Albert Schweitzer." Aesculape
       43 (Feb. 1960), pp. 39-61. Illus.

775   O., F. E. "Jubiläum in Lambarene. Vor 40 Jahren ging Albert
       Schweitzer nach Afrika." Schwäbische Landeszeitung
       (Augsburg) 72 (March 27, 1953), p. 2.

776   O'BRIEN, JOHN A. "God's eager fool." The Reader's Digest
       (Pleasantville, N.Y.) 48:287 (March 1946), pp. 43-47.
       Reprinted in: About Albert Schweitzer. Three articles
       from the Reader's Digest. 1956. 9 pp.; also in Native
       Teacher's Journal (Pietermoritzburg, So. Africa) 26
       (Oct. 1946), pp. 1-3; in SELECTION, pp. 19-20; in 30th
       Anniversary Reader's Digest Reader. New York: Doubleday,
       1951, pp. 99-103; translated as "Albert Schweitzer--ein
       Leben der Nächstenliebe." Der Allgäur (Kempton/Allgau)
       44 (June 5, 1948), p. 2; translated as "Moderno apóstolo
       dos Negros." Seleções do Reader's Digest (Brazil),
       July 1946.

777   O'CONNOR, JOHN J. "Albert Schweitzer." The Magnificat
       (Manchester, NH) 94 (Jan. 1955), pp. 110-14.

778   OCHS, SIEGFRIED. "Albert Schweitzer." Vossische Zeitung
       60 (March 12, 1927), p. 1.

779   "Octogenarians--three abundant lives--Kreisler, Monteux,
       Schweitzer." Musical America (New York) 75 (Feb. 1, 1955),
       pp. 3-4.

780   OLÁH, VILMOS. "Ein Leben im Dienste der Menschheit.
       Gedanken über das Leben Albert Schweitzers." In:
       DEBRECEN, pp. 99-105.

781   "Onlooker." "Commentary" (editorial). African World
       (London) Oct. 1965, p. 3.

782   OSWALD, SUZANNE. "Daheim in Günsbach. Erinnerungen an Albert
       Schweitzer und seine elsässische Heimat." Atlantis
       (Zürich) 17 (May 1945).

783 _____. "Die Persönlichkeit Albert Schweitzers." Basler
Nachrichten, Sonntagsblatt (Basel) 2 (Jan. 16, 1955),
p. 1. (From the author's book Geist der Humanität,
no. 286 above.)

784 OXENSTIERNA, BENGT. "Albert Schweitzer. Ett Kristet
människoliv." För Hemmets Kalender (Stockholm), 1924,
pp. 30-57.

785 _____. "Mina personliga minnen av Albert Schweitzer."
In: MANNEN, pp. 194-203.

786 P., W. "Arzt im Urwald--Arzt an der Menschheit. Morgen wird
Albert Schweitzer 80 Jahre alt." Schwarzwälder Bote
(Oberndorf am Neckar) 9 (Jan. 13, 1955), p. 3.

787 PAEPCKE, ELIZABETH. "In the eye of the beholder lies the
virtue of that which he sees." In: THE CONVOCATION
RECORD, pp. I/11-18.

788 PALAISEUL, JEAN. "Respectez tout ce qui vit. Tel est
l'admirable message du Dr. Schweitzer." Noir et Blanc
(Paris) 7:342 (Sept. 12, 1951), p. 619. Illus.

789 PAQUET, ALFONS. "Albert Schweitzer." The Living Age (New
York) 348:4422 (March 1935), pp. 43-46. Translated from
the Frankfurter Zeitung.

790 PARKER, ROBERT ALLERTON. "Albert Schweitzer . . . famous
unknown." Vogue (New York) 114 (July 1949), pp. 76 ff.
Port.

791 PATON, A. "Planned life." Times Literary Supplement
(London) 3902 (Dec. 24, 1976), p. 1603.

792 PAULI, AUGUST. "Albert Schweitzer." Die Christengemeinschaft
(Stuttgart) 6:7 (Oct. 1929), pp. 193-95.

793 PEET, HUBERT W. "One of the world's greatest men." The
Christian Herald (New York) 54:4 (March 1931), pp. 10-11ff.
Illus.

794 "PEN-ULTIMATE." "The quest of the historical Schweitzer."
The Christian Century (Chicago) 80:5 (Jan. 30, 1963),
p. 159.

795 PENOFF, DIMITAR. "Sohn und Bürger der Menschheit." In:
BEITRÄGE, pp. 123-30.

Life and Work

796   PETRICKIJ, V. ["Le grand docteur blanc."] Azija i Afrika
         Segodnja 3 (1967), pp. 52-53.

797   _____. ["Histoire du Docteur."] Le Globe (Leningrad) 1964,
         pp. 228-34.

798   PFISTER, MAX. "Albert Schweitzers Botschaft an unsere Zeit."
         Schweizerisches Kaufmännisches Zentralblatt (Zürich) 58:8
         (Feb. 19, 1954), pp. 81-82.

799   PFISTER, OSKAR. "Albert Schweitzers Persönlichkeit und
         Mission in Lichte seiner Jugenderinnerungen." Neue
         Zürcher Zeitung (Zürich) 570 (April 17, 1924), pp. 1-2;
         577 (April 18, 1924), pp. 1-2. Translated as "Albert
         Schweitzer--missionary, musician, physician." The Living
         Age (New York) 320:4178 (Aug. 2, 1924), pp. 229-33.

800   PHILLIPS, MC CANDLISH. "Casals dedicates Schweitzer library."
         The New York Times, June 28, 1971, p. 36.

801   PIASECKI, BOLESLAW. "Der Mann, der sich selbst gab." In:
         BEITRÄGE, pp. 137-41.

802   PICHT, WERNER. "Albert Schweitzer; ich kreise um Jesus."
         Wort und Wahrheit (Freiburg i. Br.) 8:8 (1953), pp. 565-77.

803   _____. "Albert Schweitzer, geb. 1875. Der 'Urwalddoktor'
         und Verkünder der Ehrfurcht vor dem Leben." In: Via
         Humana; Wohltäter der Menschheit. Hrsg. von Dr. Rudolf
         Erckmann. Munich, Vienna: Wilhelm Andermann Verlag,
         1958, pp. 271-86. Port.

804   PICK, ROBERT. "The thirteenth disciple." The Saturday
         Review (New York) 30:50 (Dec. 13, 1947), pp. 11-13.

805   PIERHAL, JEAN. "Arzt eines kranken Jahrhunderts: Albert
         Schweitzer. Das Leben eines guten Menschen." Revue
         (Munich) numbers 46-52 (Nov. 13-Dec. 25, 1954); numbers
         1-6 (Jan. 1-Feb. 5, 1955). Serial publication of
         author's book Albert Schweitzer, das Leben eines guten
         Menschen, see no. 291 above.

806   PIRE, DOMINIQUE. [Extract d'une discours, prononcé an
         février 1963.] CAHIERS 11 (July 1964), p. 14.

807   _____. "Préface. Pour les 90 ans du docteur Albert
         Schweitzer." In: MISÉRICORDE, pp. 13-21. Reprinted in:
         Pire, D. Vivre ou mourir ensemble. Brussels: Presses
         Académiques Europeens S.C., 1969, pp. 417f.

808   PLACE, JOSEPH. "Albert Schweitzer." Bulletin du Bibliophine
           et du Bibliothécaire (Paris) 1951, pp. 153-55.

809   PLENDER, JAMES. "The Enigma of Albert Schweitzer."
           Humanist (London) 77:4 (April 1962), pp. 111-13.

810   PLOJHAR, JOSEF. "Albert Schweitzer weihte sein Leben den
           Menschen." In: BEITRÄGE, pp. 142-46.

811   POCAR, ERVINO. [Tribute without title.] In: DENKEN UND WEG,
           pp. 416-17.

812   PREMINGER, MARION MILL. "I have found a living saint."
           New York World Telegram (Saturday Feature Magazine),
           Oct. 9, 1954.

813   [_____.] "von einer Amerikanerin." "Mein Lehrer-Albert
           Schweitzer." RUNDBRIEF 13 (Dec. 15, 1958), pp. 53-55.

814   _____. "Twentieth century's greatest philanthropist."
           Philanthropy (New York) 3:4 (Summer 1955), pp. 78-81.
           Illus.

815   _____. "When you are doing good, you are not making a
           sacrifice." Seventeen (New York) 21:12 (Dec. 1962),
           pp. 98-99.

816   PRIESTLY, PETER. "Grossangriff auf Dr. Schweitzer. Englands
           Fleetstreet fällt ein vernichtendes Urteil über den alten
           Mann von Lambarene." Abendpost (Frankfurt a.M.),
           April 30, 1964, pp. 4f.

817   "Prof. Albert Schweitzer in Aspen--Bach-Bicentennial in
           Jahre 1950?" New Yorker Staats-Zeitung und Herold,
           July 13, 1949, p. 8.

818   "Prof. Albert Schweitzer. Zijn medische Zending." Algemeen
           Handelsblad (Amsterdam) 100:32330 (March 3, 1927), p. 2.

819   "Profile--Albert Schweitzer." London Observer (London)
           Dec. 24, 1944.

820   QUENZER, W. "Autobiographische Schriften. . . ." Universitas
           (Stuttgart) 15:1 (Jan. 1960), pp. 119-20. Reprinted as
           "Zu Schweitzers autobiographischen Schriften." In:
           DENKEN UND WEG, pp. 236-39.

821   RATTER, MAGNUS. "Our member in the spiritual parliament of
           mankind." The Christian Register (Boston) 134:1

Life and Work

(Jan. 1955), pp. 19-20f. Reprinted as "Albert Schweitzer."
In: FESTSCHRIFT, pp. 78-85.

822   RAUCH, KARL. "Albert Schweitzer, Arzt und Helfer." Die
Aussprache (Düsseldorf) 3:4 (Sept. 1951), pp. 308-12.
Port.

823   _____. "Arzt und Helfer: Albert Schweitzer." In: Das
grosse Vorbild: Gestalt und Bild deutscher Menschen aus
unseren Tagen. Berlin: Holle & Co., 1934, pp. 60-91.
Port.

824   _____. "Denker, Arzt und Helfer. Zu Albert Schweitzers 60.
Geburtstag." Westermanns Monatshefte (Braunschweig)
79:941 (Jan. 1935), pp. 482-84. Port.

825   REDMOND, BERNARD S. "Schweitzer at Günsbach." The Christian
Register (Boston) 130:10 (Nov. 1951), pp. 13-16.

826   REDSLOB, ROBERT. [Tribute without title.] In: DENKEN UND
WEG, pp. 115-17. Reprinted with title "Aus der Frühzeit
Schweitzers." In: SCHWEITZER, pp. 115-16.

827   "Renaissance Man" (editorial). The Washington Post,
Jan. 14, 1955, p. 20.

828   [Report of Albert Schweitzer on his 70th birthday.] BRITISH
BULLETIN 17 (Jan. 1945), pp. 1-2.

829   "Le retour d'Albert Schweitzer en Elsace et Réunion amicale
à Colmar." CAHIERS 2 (Dec. 1959), pp. 25-26.

830   "Reverence for life." MD (New York) 19:10 (Oct. 1975),
pp. 113-20. Illus.

831   "Reverence for life." Time (New York) 54:2 (July 11, 1949),
pp. 68-74. Cover port., illus.

832   "Revue de la presse hebdomadaire--Albert Schweitzer." La Vie
Catholique Illustrée (Paris) 254 (May 28, 1950), pp. 10-
11. Reprinted in Le Figaro (Paris) 1778 (May 29, 1950),
p. 6.

833   RICE, HOWARD C. "Albert Schweitzer; some bibliographical
digressions." (Victor Robinson Lecture IV.) Transactions
and Studies of the College of Physicians of Philadelphia
31:3 (4th series) (Jan. 1964), pp. 216-26. Issued also
as a reprint.

834 RICHTER, ERNST. "Albert Schweitzer. Ein Genie der
        Menschlichkeit. Seine Forderung an unsere Zeit:
        Ehrfurcht vor dem Leben." Frankfurter Illustrierte
        40:38 (Sept. 21, 1952), pp. 18-21. Illus., cover port.

835 ROBACK, A. A. "Albert Schweitzer the man." In: JUBILEE,
        pp. 23-68.

836 _____. "Albert Schweitzer's impact on America." In: REALMS,
        pp. 415-23. Translated without title in: DENKEN UND WEG,
        pp. 417-23.

837 _____. "In the presence of Albert Schweitzer." In:
        REALMS, pp. 95-110.

838 RODGER, GEORGE (photographer). "Urwalddoktor von Lambarene--
        Albert Schweitzer schreibt die Geschichte seines Lebens."
        Münchner Illustrierte (Munich) 31 (Aug. 4, 1951),
        pp. 3-5. Illus.

839 ROLLAND, ROMAIN. [extracts from diary and letters, contrib-
        uted by his widow.] In: HOMAGE, pp. 101-04. Reprinted,
        with title "Schweitzer, ein Ausnahmemensch" in GESTERN-
        HEUTE, p. 59.

840 ROMBACH, K. A. "Albert Schweitzer 1875--14 January 1935 van
        een musicus, prediker, philosoof, medicus." Eigen Haard
        (Baarn, Netherlands) 61:3 (Jan. 19, 1935), pp. 42-45.
        Illus.

841 ROOVERS, HENRI. "Albert Schweitzer weer in Europe." De Linie
        (Amsterdam) April 18, 1949. Port.

842 ROSENBERG, SAM. "Who writes to Dr. Schweitzer." Collier's
        Magazine (New York) 135:3 (Feb. 4, 1955), pp. 68-69.

843 ROSS, EMORY. "Albert Schweitzer, the man and his mind."
        International Review of Missions (London) 37 (July 1948),
        pp. 330-33. Also issued as a 4-page reprint by the
        Albert Schweitzer Fellowship, New York.

844 _____. "Portrait--Albert Schweitzer." The American Scholar
        (New York) 19:1 (Winter 1949/50), pp. 83-88. Issued also
        as a reprint by the Albert Schweitzer Fellowship, New
        York.

845 _____. "Schweitzer in America." The Saturday Review
        (New York) 48:39 (Sept. 25, 1965), pp. 25-26.

Life and Work

846 _____. "Schweitzer: man of action." The Christian Century
(Chicago) 65:1 (Jan. 7, 1948), pp. 9-11.

847 _____. "Schweitzer--man of God." The Christian Century
(Chicago) 66:31 (Aug. 3, 1949), p. 916.

848 _____ and MYRTA ROSS. "Ross on Schweitzer." COURIER,
May 1974, n.p. (pp. 11-12).

849 ROSS, MRS. G. A. JOHNSTON. "Lecture notes on Dr. Albert
Schweitzer." The Friend (Honolulu) 103 (Dec. 1933),
pp. 232-34.

850 ROUSSEL, JEAN. "Albert Schweitzer." Larousse Mensuel
(Paris) 451 (March 1952), p. 46. Port.

851 ROYDEN, MAUDE. "Dr. Albert Schweitzer." In: Men of Turmoil.
Biographies by leading authorities of the dominating
personalities of our day. New York: Minton, 1935,
pp. 258-66. Reprinted Freeport, N.Y.: Books for
Libraries Press, 1969. (Essay Index Reprint Series).
Published in England with the title: Great Contemporaries.
London: Cassell, 1935, pp. 371-81.

852 RUBENS, FRANCISCO. "A figura da Semana: Albert Schweitzer."
A Tribuna de Santos (São Paulo), Nov. 24, 1959.

853 RÜF, E. "Heiliger--und doch kein Christ?" Offenes Wort
(Graz, Vienna) 7:7 (Feb. 14, 1953).

854 RÜHLE, JÜRGEN. "Der gute Mensch von Lambarene. Eine
marxistische Stimme im Chor der Schweitzer-Würdigungen."
Neue Zeit (East Berlin) 9 (Jan. 12, 1955), p. 3.

855 RUSK, HOWARD A. "A global birthday fête--review of the life
of Dr. Schweitzer as he approaches his 80th milestone."
The New York Times, Jan. 9, 1955, Sect. 1, p. 55.

856 RUSSELL, JOHN. "Man of compassion: a portrait of Albert
Schweitzer." The Sunday Times (London), Oct. 17, 1954.
Illus.

857 _____. "Schweitzer centennial today: a legacy eclipsed?"
The New York Times, Jan. 14, 1975, pp. 35, 41. Illus.

858 S., J. "Albert Schweitzer, le plus grand homme du monde."
Le Figaro (Paris) 124:1840 (Aug. 9, 1950), p. 7.

859 S., M. "Albert Schweitzer, der Urwalddoktor von Lambarene."
     Das Reich der Landfrau (Frankfurt a.M.) 69:11
     (March 18, 1954), pp. 81-82. Port.

860 S., M. "Albert Schweitzer." Chroniques Badoises
     (Freiburg i.B.) 2:38 (June 1955), pp. 1-5. Cover port.

861 S., W. E. "Albert Schweitzer und der Urwald." Velhagen &
     Klasings Monatshefte (Berlin, Bielefeld, Leipzig, Vienna)
     47, 2: Heft 9 (May 1933), pp. 292-97.

862 SAGINJAN, M. [Portrait d'un homme.] Literaturna ja Gazeta
     (June 20, 1957), p. 4.

863 SARGEANT, WINTHROP. "Albert Schweitzer." Life (New York)
     27:4 (July 25, 1949), pp. 74-82. Illus. Also issued
     as a 4-page reprint by the Albert Schweitzer Education
     Foundation. Reprinted as "Close-up--Albert Schweitzer."
     Life (International edition) 7:4 (Aug. 15, 1949),
     pp. 50-54.

864 SCHIMANSKI, STEFAN. "Albert Schweitzer at home." Manchester
     Guardian, April 27, 1949. Port.

865 _____. "A great man of our day." Picture Post (London)
     45:4 (Oct. 22, 1949), pp. 34-37.

866 SCHLEMMER, ANDRÉ. "Un musicien Alsacien; médecin au Gabon."
     Le Ménestrel (Paris) 87:20 (May 15, 1925), pp. 217-19.

867 SCHMID-AMMANN, P. "Albert Schweitzer. Aus seinem Leben."
     Volksrecht (Zürich), Jan. 14, 1955. Illus.

868 SCHMID-HERZOG, ELSE. "Albert Schweitzer in Zürich."
     Schweizerisches Protestantenblatt (Basel) 51:11
     (March 17, 1928), pp. 83-84.

869 SCHMIDT, K. O. "Albert Schweitzer und das innere Licht."
     Die Weisse Fahne (Pfullingen, Württemberg) 32:1
     (Jan. 1959), pp. 4-15. Port.

870 SCHMIDT, WERNER. "Albert Schweitzer. Ein Leben für die
     Menschheit." Alt-Katholisches Volksblatt (Bonn) 2:5
     (May 1950), pp. 52-53; 2:6 (June 1950), pp. 66-68;
     2:7 (July 1950), pp. 76-78; 2:9 (Sept. 1950), pp. 114-15;
     2:11 (Nov. 1950), pp. 124-25.

871 SCHMITT, BERNARD. "L'évolution d'Albert Schweitzer dans le
     miroir du drame Alsacien." In: DEBRECEN, pp. 167-74.

Life and Work

872 SCHMOECKEL, REINHARD. "'Ehrfurcht vor dem Leben,' Albert
        Schweitzer." In: <u>Stärker als Waffen</u>. Düsseldorf:
        Hoch-Verlag, 1957, pp. 147-66.

873 SCHNEIDER, CAMILLE (under pseudonym A. Müller). "Albert
        Schweitzer als Gesamterscheinung." In: WÜRDIGUNG,
        pp. 1-10.

874 _____. "Une leçon de morale autour de la vie d'Albert
        Schweitzer." <u>L'Education Nationale</u> (Paris) 11:2
        (Jan. 13, 1955), pp. 22f.

875 SCHOENBERNER, FRANZ. "Albert Schweitzer und Amerika." <u>Die
        Amerikanische Rundschau</u> (Munich) 5:23 (Feb. 1949),
        pp. 124-26.

876 SCHOLDER, KLAUS. "Albert Schweitzer im Tübinger Stift, 1959."
        <u>Universitas</u> (Stuttgart) 15:1 (Jan. 1960), pp. 124-25.

877 SCHOMERUS, HANS. "Der Heilige im Tropenheim." <u>Christ und
        Welt</u> (Stuttgart) 15:32 (Aug. 10, 1962), p. 10.

878 SCHOU, AUGUST. "The Peace Prize." In: <u>Nobel: The Man and
        his Prizes</u>, edited by the Nobel Foundation. Amsterdam,
        London, New York: Elsevier Publishing Co., 1962, pp. 620-
        22. 2nd ed. Third revised and enlarged edition, 1972,
        pp. 596-98.

879 SCHULENBURG, WERNER VON DER. "Albert Schweitzer." <u>Die Eiche</u>
        (Pretoria, Minerva) Beilage, No. 11 (1952), 10 pp. Port.

880 SCHULTZ, HANS JÜRGEN. "Albert Schweitzer oder eine Nussschale
        voll Frieden." In: <u>Liebhaber des Lebens: Biographische
        Erzählungen für meine Mutter</u>. Stuttgart, Berlin: Kreuz
        Verlag, 1975, pp. 53-92.

881 SCHWEITZER-MILLER, RHENA. "My father: Albert Schweitzer."
        In: DEVENTER, pp. 115-20. Summaries in German, French,
        Dutch.

882 _____. "Mein Vater." RUNDBRIEF 47 (May 1979), pp. 46-50.

883 "Schweitzer enlarges hospital." <u>The Presbyterian Outlook</u>
        (Richmond, Va.) 135:46 (Nov. 23, 1953), pp. 6-7.

884 "Schweitzer--his black brother's keeper." <u>The Literary Digest</u>
        (New York) 108:12 (March 21, 1931), pp. 18-19.
        Illus., port.

885   "Schweitzer monogatari." Ongaku no Tomo (Tokyo), March 1953,
          pp. 92-96.

886   "Schweitzer, o medico missionario--um pouco da historia do
          benfeitor que acaba de receber o premio Nobel da paz."
          Fôlha da Manhã, Nov. 15, 1953.

887   "Schweitzer: 'Reverence for Life.'" Newsweek (New York)
          66:11 (Sept. 13, 1965), p. 62. Port.

888   "Schweitzer to visit America this summer." Musical America
          (New York) 69 (March 1949), p. 27.

889   "Schweitzer visits Sweden." The American Organist (Staten
          Island, N.Y.) 43:3 (March 1960), p. 22. Illus.

890   SEAVER, GEORGE. "Albert Schweitzer." The Spectator (London)
          174:6080 (Jan. 12, 1945), p. 31. Also issued as an
          offprint.

891   _____. "Saint of our century." Wisdom (Beverly Hills,
          Calif.) 1:2 (Feb. 1956), p. 27. Port.

892   SEIDENSPINNER, CLARENCE. "Goethe and Schweitzer." The
          Christian Advocate (Chicago) 124:25 (June 23, 1949),
          pp. 4-5.

893   "Sejour d'Albert Schweitzer en Europe." CAHIERS 2
          (Dec. 1959), p. 26.

894   SELBIE, W. B. "Leaders of theological thought--Albert
          Schweitzer." The Expository Times (Edinburgh) 39:6
          (March 1928), pp. 256-59.

895   SEYMOUR, DAVID M. "A sketch of Albert Schweitzer--his life
          and works." Christian Medical Society Journal (Chicago)
          2:5 (Nov./Dec. 1950), pp. 1-4.

896   SHEPHERD, R. H. W. "Four men in one: a sketch of the life
          of Dr. Albert Schweitzer." South Africa Outlook
          (Lovedale, C.P., South Africa) 83 (Jan. 1953), pp. 12-14.

897   SHIMAZAKI, T. "Schweitzer to Gendai." Nippon Hijōron
          (Tokyo) Oct. 1950, pp. 36-40.

898   SIEBECK, RICHARD. "Lebensbild Albert Schweitzer zu seinem
          80. Geburtstag am 14. Januar 1955." Münchener Medizinische
          Wochenschrift 97:2 (Jan. 14, 1955), pp. 54-55.

Life and Work

899 SIEGFRIED, ANDRÉ. "Preface." In: ÉTUDES, pp. 11-15; second
      edition, pp. 11-16.

900 SILCOX, CLARIS EDWIN. "Albert Schweitzer comes to America:
      great soul of Africa." Saturday Night (Toronto) 64:40
      (July 12, 1949), pp. 6-7. Port.

901 SIMON, SACHA. "Albert Schweitzer cet alsacien têtu qui
      combattait pour l'homme." Le Figaro Litteraire (Paris)
      20:1012 (Sept. 9-15, 1965), p. 7. Illus.

902 SIMSA, JAROSLAV. "Begegnung und Erkenntnis." In: DENKEN
      UND WEG, pp. 120-21.

903 SINGH, RAHUL. "Albert Schweitzer: universal man." Times of
      India (Bombay) 127:251 (Sept. 12, 1965), p. 8.

904 SITTLER, LUCIEN. "Ein Grosser unter uns." Almanach du
      Paysan du Haut-Rhin (Colmar) 1951, pp. 121-24. Port.,
      illus.

905 SIWA, REMY-ANDRE. "Albert Schweitzer." Envol (Leopoldville,
      Belgian Congo) 20 (July 1956), pp. 10-11.

906 SKELTON, HUMPHREY. "The saint in the forest." The Literary
      Guide (London) 70:10 (Oct. 1955), pp. 9-11.

907 SKILLINGS, EVERETT. "Experiencing Albert Schweitzer."
      Religion in Life (New York) 17:3 (Summer 1948), pp. 423-33.

      SLOAN, RAYMOND P. "Albert Schweitzer--Humanitarian." See
      Lambarene, no. 1984 below.

908 SMITH, ASBURY. "Albert Schweitzer." The Methodist Review
      (New York) 114 (Jan./Feb. 1931), pp. 24-29.

909 SOUPAULT, PHILIPPE. "Albert Schweitzer." Réalités (Paris)
      66 (July 1951), pp. 60-65ff. Ports., illus.

910 SPELBERG, E. D. "Schweitzer: lastig, beminnelijk, geleerd
      en universeel." Vrij Nederland (Amsterdam) 19
      (Jan. 8, 1955), p. 1.

911 STADE, FRANS. I. "Levnaden ach Verket." II. "Livaskadningen
      och Personligheten." In: MANNEN, pp. 27-59.

912 _____. "Människan Albert Schweitzer. Minnen och intryck."
      In: MANNEN, pp. 184-93.

913   STAHLER, ROBERT. "Das Universale, das Menschliche, das
          Christliche im Wesen Albert Schweitzers." Freies
          Christentum (Frankfurt a.M.) 9:1 (Jan. 1, 1957), cols. 4-6.

914   STALDER, HANS. "Lebensauffassung und Werk." In: HALFEN,
          pp. 218-27. Excerpted from "Albert Schweitzer und sein
          Afrikanisches Werk," see Lambarene, no. 1995 below.

915   STAMM, FREDERICK K. "I know ten true Christians." The North
          American Review (New York) 228:6 (Dec. 1929), pp. 674-81.

916   STASSEN, HAROLD E. "Schweitzer vs. Stalin." Ladies' Home
          Journal (Philadelphia) 68:7 (July 1951), pp. 36-37ff.
          Port.

917   STEELE, ROBERT. "Albert Schweitzer: a nonagenarian estimate."
          Ghandi Marg (New Delhi) 9 (2) (April 1965), pp. 133-42.

918   STEERE, DOUGLAS V. "Don't forget those leather gloves."
          Friends Journal (Philadelphia) 21:3 (Feb. 1, 1975),
          pp. 72-73.

919   STEFFAHN, HARALD. "'Mein Leben ist mir ein Rätsel.' Der
          Alltag des 87 jährigen Albert Schweitzer." Christ und
          Welt (Stuttgart) 16:1 (Jan. 4, 1963), pp. 8-9.

920   STEIGER, EDUARD. "Zum Persönlichkeitsbild Albert Schweitzers."
          Standpunkt: Evangelische Monatsschrift (Berlin) 3:1
          (Jan. 1975), pp. 11-12.

921   STEINBERG, GELSON. "A significacão de Albert Schweitzer."
          A Gazeta, June 24, 1958.

922   STEVENSON, ADLAI E. "An emissary of Western civilization."
          In: FESTSCHRIFT, pp. 102-03. Translated as "Der
          Weltbürger." In: EHRFURCHT, p. 231.

923   STINZI, MARIE-PAULE and ROBERT MINDER. "Origines de la
          famille." In: RAYONNEMENT, pp. 33-37. (Le texte complet
          de l'étude de M. P. Stinzi figure dans la Revue d'Allemagne
          5:3 (1973). Edited, abridged, and augmented at certain
          points by Robert Minder.)

924   STOPPELMANN, JOSEPH W. F. "'Man van Lambarene' komt orgels
          bespelen. Albert Schweitzer besoekt Amerika." Het
          Vrije Volk (Amsterdam), July 23, 1949.

925   STRANSKY, EUGENE. "Albert Schweitzer." Philippine Medical
          Association Journal (Manila) 37:1 (Jan. 1961), pp. 39-43.

Life and Work

> Port. Delivered at Medical History Club monthly meeting,
> May 9, 1956.

926 STUBBE, HEINRICH. "Ein Weltverführer war er niemals. Albert
Schweitzers 100. Geburtstag." Deutsche Zeitung 4
(Jan. 1, 1975), p. 22. Port.

927 SUHRKAMP, PETER. "Albert Schweitzer. Zu seinem sechzigsten
Geburtstag." Die Neue Rundschau (Berlin and Leipzig)
46:1 (Feb. 1935), pp. 223-24.

928 SY., F. "Le Dr. Schweitzer a retrouvé son pays natal."
Magazin Ringier Alsace et Moselle (St. Louis/Haut Rhin)
38 (Sept. 17, 1955), pp. 2-3. Illus.

929 SZUMOWSKI, WLADYSLAW. "Filozofia Alberta Schweitzera
Alzatezyka, doctora filozofii, doktora teologii, doktora
medycyny, wirtuoza na organach, lekarza-misjonarza
Afrykanskiego." In: O Eunuchach i Kastracji W. Rozaych
krajach i Czasach Oraz kilka Drobnych Artykulow z
ilustracjanii. Krakow: Sebethner i Wolff, 1946,
pp. 50-60.

930 TAKAHASHI, ISAO. "Albert Schweitzer ni tsuite." Gakutō
(Tokyo) 49:7 (July 1952), pp. 23-27.

931 _____. "Schweitzer hakase no kinkyo." Gakutō (Tokyo)
50:2 (Feb. 1953), pp. 27-29.

932 _____. "Schweitzer no hito to ongaku." Ongaku Gejutsu
(Tokyo) 10:2 (Feb. 1952), pp. 62-72.

933 _____. "Schweitzer to Dōbutsutachi." Gakutō (Tokyo)
(Jan. 1954), pp. 16-24.

934 TAU, MAX. "Albert Schweitzer." Vinduet (Oslo) 5:6
(Summer 1951), pp. 409-21. Illus.

935 _____. "Albert Schweitzer." Der Speicher (Gütersloh)
5 (1951), pp. 6-23.

936 _____. "Im dienstndes Friedens für alle Menschen. Albert
Schweitzer und unsere Zeit." Hannoversche Allgemeine
Zeitung (Hannover) 11 (Jan. 14, 1960), p. 6.

937 _____. "Wegbereiter des Friedens." In: GESTERN-HEUTE,
pp. 60-62. Excerpted from Albert Schweitzer und der
Friede, see no. 3621 below.

938   TAUSCHINSKI, O. I. "Der Samariter, Albert Schweitzer." In:
       Jugend der Welt. Biographische Erzählungen aus den
       Jugendjahren berühmter Männer und Frauen. Bearbeitung:
       Hans F. Muller. Murnau, Munich, Innsbruck, Basel:
       Sebastian Lux, 1963, pp. 441-43.

939   TERRY, ANNA. "Albert Schweitzer, the man of the world."
       In: DEBRECEN, pp. 53-64.

940   THEOPHRASTUS. "Über die Fronten hinweg. Von Tageslärm zur
       Humanität." Berliner Ärzteblatt 61:1 (Jan. 2, 1952),
       pp. 1-2.

941   THIOUT, MICHEL. "Transforma-se o maior interprete de Bach
       no melhor missionario dos brejos africanos." O Tempo
       (São Paulo), Nov. 14, 1953.

942   THOMAS, DANA (Pseudonym for Dana A. Schnittkind). "Healer in
       the Tropics, Albert Schweitzer." In: Crusaders for God.
       New York: A. A. Wyn, 1952, pp. 222-45. Translated in
       Taten der Liebe. Vienna, Munich: Verlag Herold, 1955.

943   THOMPSON, EILEEN J. "Albert Schweitzer, man of the century."
       Presbyterian Record (Toronto) 81:2 (Feb. 1956), pp. 18-21.
       Illus., cover port.

944   TILL. "Albert Schweitzer vor Ulbrichts Karren." Abendpost
       (Frankfurt a.M.) 197 (August 26/27, 1961), p. 2.

945   TILLMANN, FRIEDRICH. "Albert Schweitzer. A portrait drawn
       for his seventy-fifth birthday, January 14, 1950." The
       Ecumenical Review (Geneva) 2:2 (Winter 1950), pp. 170-75.

946   TJØNN, INGEBJØRG. "Albert Schweitzer. Mannen som er et
       forbilde for mennesker verden over." Samtidekunnskap
       (Oslo) 8:1 (1954), pp. 22-31. Illus.

947   TREBS, HERBERT. "Der gute Mensch von Lambarene." Neue Zeit
       (East Berlin) 11 (Jan. 14, 1960), pp. 1-2. Port.

948   TSANOFF, RADOSLAV A. "Albert Schweitzer." In: Autobiogra-
       phies of Ten Religious Leaders: Alternatives in Christian
       Experience. San Antonio, Texas: Trinity University
       Press, 1968, pp. 231-66.

949   TSUCHIDA, S. "Albert Schweitzer." Ongaku Geijutsu (Tokyo)
       3:8 (Aug. 1945), pp. 58-61.

Life and Work

950   TSUGAWA, SHUICHI. "Saikin no Schweitzer Hakase." Ongaku no
          Tomo (Tokyo), July 1950.

951   TUNGEL, RICHARD. "Geschäft mit Schweitzer. Ein grosser Name
          missbraucht--Propaganda für Ulbricht." Welt am Sonntag
          (Hamburg) 36 (Sept. 3, 1961), p. 4.

952   UCHIMURA, YÛSHI. [Tribute without title--Albert Schweitzer
          in Japan.] Universitas (Stuttgart) 15:1 (Jan. 1960),
          pp. 19-22. Reprinted with title "Der ärztliche Weg
          der Humanität." In: DENKEN UND WEG, pp. 336-39.

953   "Ein übler Propagandatrick." Telegraf (Berlin) 198/16
          (Aug. 26, 1961), p. 2.

954   ULDALL, STEN. "En gerning mellem oversete blev hans
          livsbekraeftelse." Den Indre Missions Tidende (Haslev,
          Denmark) 97:3 (Jan. 15, 1950), pp. 30-32. Port.

955   UNSINGER, EDM. "An die Leser und Mitarbeiter des Kirchenbote."
          KIRCHENBOTE 50:15 (April 9, 1921).

956   UNTERMEYER, LOUIS. "Albert Schweitzer." In: Makers of the
          Modern World. New York: Simon and Schuster, 1955,
          pp. 500-05.

957   URMATT, FRÉDÉRIC. "La vie étonnante d'Albert Schweitzer."
          La Revue Hebdomadaire (Paris) 46:5 (May 1937), pp. 409-23.

958   URQUHART, CLARA. "Albert Schweitzer. Behind the legend."
          The Saturday Review (New York) 48:39 (Sept. 25, 1965),
          pp. 26-27.

959   UTZINGER, RUDOLF. "Albert Schweitzer." Annalen (Horgen-
          Zürich) 1:7 (June 1927), pp. 550-52.

960   UYS, P. H. DE V. "Albert Schweitzer." Lantern (Praetoria,
          South Africa) 9:3 (March 1960), pp. 228-33. Illus.
          Afrikaans, with a brief summary in English.

961   VAN DER LEEUW, G. "Albert Schweitzer." Wending
          ('s-Gravenhage) 2:4 (June 1947), pp. 253-61.

962   VAN HOEK, KEES. "Albert Schweitzer. The great men's greatest
          man." Rotarian (Evanston, Ill.) 80:3 (March 1952),
          pp. 6-8ff. Based on an interview with Albert Schweitzer.

963   VAN PAASSEN, PIERRE. "Albert Schweitzer." In: That Day
          Alone. New York: The Dial Press, 1941, pp. 372-77.
          Reprinted 1946.

964   VENGROVA, I. V. ["Un remarquable humaniste de notre temps:
           Albert Schweitzer."] Klinicnaja Medicina 44:12 (1966),
           pp. 133-37.

965   VEPA, RAM K. "Salute to Schweitzer." Yojana (New Delhi)
           9:19 (Sept. 26, 1965), pp. 27f. Reprinted in Bhavan's
           Journal (Bombay) 12:6 (Oct. 10, 1965), pp. 47-53. On
           page 51 is included an excerpt from "Schweitzer's testa-
           ment" entitled "The violence that can master all other
           violence."

966   VERNIER, JEAN FRÉDÉRIC. "Schweitzer cet inconnu."
           Communautés et Continents (Paris) 67:37 (Jan.-March 1975),
           pp. 10-13.

967   "14 Januari 1875-1965." NIEUWS (Jan. 1965), pp. 6-18.
           Photographic essay.

968   "Visionary, thinker, philosopher . . . and Alsatian peasant
           who is Albert Schweitzer." Picture Post (London),
           Oct. 22, 1949, pp. 35-36. Illus.

969   VOSS, CARL HERMANN. "Schweitzer's birthplace revisited."
           United Church Herald (St. Louis) 2:1 (Jan. 1, 1956),
           pp. 4-6. Illus., cover port.

970   VOYENNE, BERNARD. "La découverte d'Albert Schweitzer."
           Revue de la Pensée Française (Paris, New York, Montreal)
           10:6 (June 1951), pp. 57-61. Cover port.

971   W. "Dr. Schweitzer." Nieuwe Rotterdamsche Courant 85:102
           (April 13, 1928), Avondblad Feuilleton, p. 2.

972   W. "Het geheim van Schweitzers eenvoud." NIEUWS 4:3
           (Oct. 1955), p. 8.

973   "Waarheen gaat gij, mensheid? Albert Schweitzers werk der
           naastenliefde." NIEUWS 5:1 (April 1956), pp. 14-15.

974   WALD, RODERICH. "Moderne Dichterärzte. IX: Albert
           Schweitzer." Fortschritte der Medizin (Würzburg) 50:14
           (July 8, 1932), pp. 553-60.

975   _____. "Deutsche Ärzte, wie sie denken und dichten. VIII:
           Albert Schweitzer." Zeitschrift für Ärztliche Fortbildung
           (Jena) 34:20 (Oct. 15, 1937), pp. 603-06.

976   WALKER, KENNETH. "The man in the small back room." Picture
           Post (London) 69:7 (Nov. 12, 1955), pp. 37-39. Illus.

Life and Work

977   WANNER, J.   "Albert Schweitzer.   Seine Botschaft an unsere
       Zeit."   Volksrecht (Zürich) 11 (Jan. 14, 1955).

978   WANTZ, ANDRÉE.   "Albert Schweitzer."   La Revue du Christianisme
       Social (St. Etienne) 43:3 (April 1930), pp. 352-57.

979   WASHBURN, RICHARD KIRK.   "Albert Schweitzer, saint and
       scholar."   Approach (Rosemont, Pa.) 16 (1955), pp. 15-21.

980   WASSER, CHRISTIAN.   "'Es begann vor 50 Jahren. . . .'"
       Ringiers Unterhaltungs-Blätter (Zofingen) 79:13
       (March 30, 1963), p. 725.   Port.

981   WECH, LEOPOLD.   "Das Leben Albert Schweitzers."   In:
       FACKELTRÄGER, pp. 35-44.

982   WEHRUNG, G.   "Albert Schweitzer."   Elsass-Lothringen
       Heimatstimmen (Berlin) 3:2 (Feb. 15, 1925), pp. 100-02.

983   WEISSINGER, FRIEDRICH.   "Albert Schweitzer und sein Werk."
       Der Hochwart (Berlin) 5:2 (Feb. 1935), pp. 74-76.

984   WELCH, HERBERT.   "Albert Schweitzer."   In: Men of the Out-
       posts.   The Romance of the Modern Christian Movement.
       Abingdon, 1937, pp. 169-86.   (Drew Lectures in Christian
       Biography).   Reprinted Freeport, N.Y.:   Books for Librar-
       ies Press, 1969, pp. 169-86.   (Essay Index Reprint Series.)

985   WELLE, IVAR.   "Albert Schweitzer."   Fast Grun (Bergen,
       Norway) 6:5 (1953), pp. 298-303f.   Illus.

986   _____.   "Albert Schweitzer."   Luthersk Kirketidende (Oslo)
       69:5 (March 5, 1932), pp. 112-19.

987   WERNER, A. J.   "Albert Schweitzer en zijn beteekenis voor
       onzen tijd."   Leven en Werken (Rotterdam) 3:3
       (March 1939) pp. 1-19.   Illus., port.

988   WERNER, D. A.   "Albert Schweitzer."   Malgranda Revuo (Hagge,
       Sveduj.) 8:2 (1950), pp. 2-5.   In Esperanto.

989   _____.   "Portret van Albert Schweitzer" (Uitgesproken voor
       de V.P.R.O.-microfoon op 10 mei 1958).   NIEUWS 7:1
       (July 1958), pp. 29-32.

990   _____.   "Portrait of Albert Schweitzer."   News Digest of the
       International Association for Liberal Christianity and
       Religious Freedom (The Hague) 55 (Feb. 1965), pp. 6-10.

991   _____. "Schweitzerverering?" NIEUWS 1:2 (March 1952),
          pp. 30-31.

992   _____. "A Statement" (Schweitzer's humor). In: THE
          CONVOCATION RECORD, pp. VI/35-36.

993   WERSINGER-LILLER, ANNA. "Albert Schweitzer à Saint-Rémy--
          récit d'un témoin." In: RAYONNEMENT, pp. 203-06.

994   WEST, RICHARD. Brazza of the Congo: European Exploration and
          Exploitation in French Equatorial Africa. London:
          Jonathan Cape, 1972, pp. 227-50. Published in the United
          States with the title Congo. New York: Holt, Rinehart
          and Winston, 1972, pp. 227-50.

995   WHARTON, DON. "Albert Schweitzer: the man behind the genius."
          Reader's Digest (Pleasantville, N.Y.) 109 (Sept. 1976),
          pp. 39-42f. Quotes from Schweitzer and others, inter-
          spersed with a biographical sketch.

996   WHITMAN, ALDEN. "Albert Schweitzer." In: The Obituary Book.
          New York: Stein and Day, 1971, pp. 53-63.

997   "Wie es Dr. Schweitzer in Weltkrieg erging." Der Speyerer
          Protestant (1934), pp. 5, 21, 45, 62.

998   WIESER, E. "Universalgenies." Schweizer Illustrierte Zeitung
          (Zofingen) 19:31 (July 1930), pp. 1258f.

999   WILLE, BRUNO. "Ein Held der Güte. Münchner Neuste
          Nachrichten (Munich) 226 (Aug. 20, 1924), p. 1.

1000   WINJE, TROND. "Albert Schweitzer." Morgenbladet (Oslo) 214
          (Sept. 15, 1951), p. 3.

1001   WINTTERLE, JOHN and R. S. CRAMER. Portraits of Nobel Laureates
          in Peace. Abelard-Schman, 1971, pp. 180-86.

1002   "Wir fanden die Menschen des Friedens. Die Wahl
          der 'Ungefragten' Albert Schweitzer." Abendpost
          (Frankfurt a.M.) 299 (Christmas, 1954), p. 1.

1003   WIRTH, JUAN CARLOS. "Schweitzer." In: Inquietudes
          Argentinas: Docencia y Predica. Buenos Aires:
          Methopress, 1967, pp. 71-83. "Conferencia pronunciada
          el 11 de setiembre de 1966 en el Teatro 3 de Febrero en
          el acto de homenaje Alberto Schweitzer en el primer
          aniversario de su muerte. . . ."

General

Life and Work

1004   WOLFSKEHL, KARL. "Albert Schweitzer, der Arzt und Missionar,
        der Musiker und Forscher." Münchner Illustrierte Presse
        (Munich) 7:6 (Feb. 9, 1930), pp. 187-88, 192. Port.

1005   WOODS, BRENDA. "Memories of a truly memorable father." Daily
        News, Jan. 7, 1975, p. 9c. Reprinted in The Detroit News,
        Jan. 10, 1975, p. 1-C.

1006   WOYTT, G[USTAVE]. "Wir wären ärmer ohne Albert Schweitzer.
        Zu seinem 90 Geburtstag." Evangelisches Gemeindeblatt
        für Württemberg (Stuttgart) 60:2 (Jan. 10, 1965), p. 8.
        Illus.

1007   WYBIERALSKI, ANDRZEJ. "Albert Schweitzer (1875-1965)."
        Archiwum Historii Medycyny (Warsaw) 29:1-2 (1966),
        pp. 161-66.

1008   "ROBERT R." (YACHSAW, ROBERT R.). "A note on Albert
        Schweitzer." The Catholic Messenger (Davenport, Iowa),
        Nov. 19, 1953, p. 5. Reprinted in The Catholic Mind
        (New York) 52 (June 1954), pp. 334-37.

1009   YAST, HELEN. "The settlement of 45 roofs." Hospitals
        (Chicago) 28 (May 1954), pp. 80-82. Illus.

1010   YSUNDER, TORSTEN. Förord. In: FYRBÅKEN, pp. 7-10.

1011   ZAVARSKY, E. "Albert Schweitzer, 12.1.1875-4-IX-1965."
        Slovenska Hudba (Bratislava) 9:8 (1965), pp. 399-400.

1012   ZBINDEN, HANS. "Über die Machte persönlichen Helfens." In:
        EHRFURCHT, pp. 170-73.

1013   ZWEIG, STEFAN. "Un portrait d'Albert Schweitzer." CAHIERS/
        BELGE 2 (Nov. 1961), pp. 32-33.

1014   ZYCHIEWICZ, TADEUSZ. "Albert Schweitzer." Tygodnik
        Powszechny (Krakow) 20:32 (7 Sierpnia 1966), pp. 1, 5.
        Illus.

                    B.   Helene Schweitzer-Bresslau

1. Works by Schweitzer

1015   SCHWEITZER, ALBERT. "Todesanzeige und Danksagung für
        Helene Schweitzer-Bresslau." RUNDBRIEF 11 (Aug. 1, 1957),
        pp. 3f.

2. Works by Others

    a. Books

1016   FLEISCHHACK, MARIANNE. Helene Schweitzer: Stationen ihres
          Lebens. Konstanz: Christliche Verlagsanstalt, 1968.
          134 pp.

       ALLINGES, JEAN D'. Le Docteur et Madame Schweitzer. See
          Life and work, no. 221 above.

    b. Articles, Parts of Books

1017   "Abschied von Helene Schweitzer." Neue Zürcher Zeitung,
          June 8, 1957.

1018   [Death of Madame Schweitzer.] BRITISH BULLETIN 23
          (July 1957), p. 2.

1019   "Frau Helene Schweitzer sprach in Freiburg." Badische Zeitung
          (Freiburg), June 14-15, 1952.

1020   GOLDSCHMIDT, HELMUT. "Die Frau des Urwalddoktors--zum Tode
          Helene Schweitzer." Neue Illustrierte Wochenschau
          (Vienna) 48:23 (June 9, 1957), p. 6.

1021   "Helene, Albert Schweitzer's Gefährtin." Rheinische Post
          (Düsseldorf) 122 (May 27, 1950).

1022   "Hélène Marianne Bresslau Schweitzer." Time (New York)
          69:23 (June 10, 1957), p. 96.

1023   [Helene Schweitzer's visit to England in September 1950.]
          BRITISH BULLETIN 19 (June 1951), p. 7.

1024   H., A. [HENRY, ANDRÉ]. "Madame Albert Schweitzer."
          NOUVELLES 4 (June 1958), p. 2.

       HEUSS-KNAPP, ELLY. [Begegnung mit Helene Bresslau, Albert
          Schweitzer, und seine Eltern.] See Life and Work,
          no. 613 above.

1025   KIK, LOTTE. [Zum Tode von Helene Schweitzer.] RUNDBRIEF 11
          (Aug. 1, 1957), pp. 12-13.

1026   "Die Lebensarbeit Helene Schweitzers." Basler Nachrichten
          (Basel) 251 (June 18, 1957), p. 2.

Life and Work

1027   MILLER, RHENA SCHWEITZER. "My mother: a remembrance."
           COURIER, Summer 1977, pp. 3-5.

1028   "Mme. Albert Schweitzer." The Times (London), June 3, 1957,
           p. 3.

1029   [Mrs. Helene Bresslau Schweitzer.] Newsweek (New York) 49:23
           (June 10, 1957), p. 76.

1030   O., S. [OSWALD, SUZANNE]. "Zum Hinschied von Hélène
           Schweitzer-Bresslau." Schweizer Frauenblatt (Zürich),
           June 21, 1957. Illus.

1031   Pressestimmen zum Tode Frau Helene Schweitzers. Reports taken
           from Christ und Welt, Tagesspiegel, Neue Zürcher Zeitung,
           Colmarer Zeitung, Tagesanzeiger für Stadt und Kanton
           Zürich. RUNDBRIEF 11 (Aug. 1, 1957), pp. 26-29.

1032   RINDERKNECHT, PETER. "Hélène Schweitzer. Die Frau eines
           grossen Mannes." Zürichsee-Zeitung (Zürich) 135
           (June 12, 1957). Reprinted in RUNDBRIEF 11 (Aug. 1, 1957),
           pp. 14-18; also in: DOKUMENTE, pp. 366-69.

1033   ROGERS, MIRIAM. "Madame Schweitzer." In: SELECTION,
           pp. 9-10. Illus.

1034   _____. "Madame Schweitzer." In: TRIBUTE, pp. 35-36.

1035   S. "Helene Schweitzer zum Gedächtnis." Deutsches
           Pfarrerblatt (Essen) 57:13 (July 1957), pp. 290-92.

1036   SCHEMPP, O. "Helene Schweitzer: am liebsten Inkognite."
           Christ und Welt (Stuttgart) 9:42 (Oct. 18, 1956), p. 3.
           Reprinted with title "Helene Schweitzer." Kirchliches
           Monatsblatt for Evangelisch-Lutherische Gemeinden in
           Amerika (Philadelphia) 14:5 (May 1957), pp. 145-47.

1037   SCHÜTZ, ROLAND. "Die Lebensgefährtin Albert Schweitzers."
           Evangelischer Digest (1960), pp. 24-29.

1038   _____. "Zu Besuch bei Helene Schweitzer-Bresslau in
           Königsfeld im Schwarzwald." RUNDBRIEF 8 (Nov. 1, 1955),
           pp. 34-36. Reprinted in: DOKUMENTE, pp. 262-64;
           translated as "Op bezoek bij Helene Schweitzer-Bresslau."
           NIEUWS 5:1 (April 1956), pp. 9-11. Port.

1039   _____. "Dem Gedächtnis an Helene Schweitzer-Bresslau."
           Freies Christentum (Frankfurt a.M.) 9:8 (Aug. 1, 1957),
           cols. 105-06.

1040   [SCHWEITZER, HELENE.] "Ein Leben im Schatten eines grossen
         Mannes. Helene Schweitzer--Selbstlos und voller
         Aufopferung." Der Deutsche Eisenbahner (Frankfurt a.M.)
         4:5 (1951), p. 5.

1041   SCHWEITZER-MILLER, RHENA. "Helene Bresslau-Schweitzer."
         A.I.S.L. Bulletin 4 (July 1977), pp. 2-4 (English);
         6-8 (German).

1042   "Schweitzer's wife honored with him." The New York Times,
         July 19, 1949, p. 19.

1043   SIEBER, ELFRIEDE. "Helene Schweitzer--Frau eines grossen
         Mannes." Frau und Frieden (Hannover) 11 (1957), p. 8.

1044   SPEAR, OTTO. "Helene Bresslau: Fürsorgarbeit in Strassburg."
         RUNDBRIEF 46 (Nov. 1978), pp. 30-32.

1045   TIGERSTRÖM, HARALD. "Till minnet av Professorskan Helene
         Schweitzer." MEDDELANDEN 25 (1957), pp. 12-16.

1046   [Tour of lectures by Helene Schweitzer in the United States.]
         BRITISH BULLETIN 16 (Summer 1939), p. 12.

1047   "'Treue Gehilfen' ihres Mannes; in Zürich starb Frau Helene
         Schweitzer." Hannoversche Allgemeine Zeitung (Hannover)
         9:127 (June 3, 1957), p. 8.

1048   W., D. A. [WERNER, D. A.]. "In memoriam Helene Schweitzer-
         Bresslau." NIEUWS 6:2 (Dec. 1957), pp. 3-4. Port.

1049   WIRCKAU, WINNIFRIED. [Brief zum Tode Helene Schweitzers an
         Richard Kik.] RUNDBRIEF 11 (Aug. 1, 1957), pp. 13-14.

1050   WOYTT, GUSTAV. "Helene Bresslau." RUNDBRIEF 11
         (Aug. 1, 1957), pp. 22-25. Reprinted in: DOKUMENTE,
         pp. 370-72.

1051   ZIMMERMAN, KARL. [Ansprache bei der 'Gedenkfeier anlasslich
         der Bestattung von Helene Schweitzer-Bresslau, 5. Juni
         1957 im Krematorium in Zurich.'] RUNDBRIEF 11
         (Aug. 1, 1957), pp. 4-11. Reprinted in: DOKUMENTE,
         pp. 362-65.

Life and Work

C. Other Family, Friends, Coworkers

1. Writings by Schweitzer (Tributes, Remembrances, Etc.)

1052   "Brief über Rudolf Virchow" (dated January 20, 1960,
        Lambarene). In: Jubilee Volume--100th Anniversary
        Festschrift zur 100-Jahr-Feier, November 7, 1860-1960.
        Rudolf Virchow Medical Society in the City of New York.
        Basel: S. Karger, 1960, pp. 8-11. Letter in German
        (facsimile), followed by English translation.

1053   "Cousin Stoskopf." Saisons d'Alsace (Strasbourg) 6:4
        (Autumn 1954), pp. 263-64.

1054   Emil Mettler, 1895-1959. Some Recollections by Dr. Albert
        Schweitzer and Other Friends. London: A. Ehretsmann,
        1960. 8 pp.

1055   "Emil Mettler" (memoir on the death of Albert Schweitzer's
        oldest friend in London). BRITISH BULLETIN 25 (May 1962),
        pp. 9-10.

1056   "Emma Haussknecht" (interment of her ashes). BRITISH BULLETIN
        23 (July 1957), pp. 5-7. Illus.

1057   "Erinnerungen an Simmel von Albert Schweitzer." In: Gassen,
        Kurt and Michael Landmann, eds. Buch des Dankes an Georg
        Simmel: Briefe, Erinnerungen, Bibliographie. Berlin:
        Duncker u. Humbolt, 1958, pp. 292-94.

1058   "Ferdinand Bastian." Elsass-Lothringen Heimatstimmen
        (Berlin) 5:1 (Jan. 15, 1927), pp. 59-60.

1059   "Gruss an Emil Fuchs." Ruf und Antwort. Festgabe für Emil
        Fuchs zum 90. Geburtstag. Leipzig: Koehler und Amelang,
        1964, p. 13.

1060   "Meine Begegnung mit Rudolf Steiner." RUNDBRIEF 37
        (Sept. 4, 1973), pp. 33-34.

1061   "Mrs. Alice Williams" (memorial tribute). BRITISH BULLETIN
        23 (July 1957), pp. 7-8.

1062   "Pensées sur la Croix-Rouge." Written for the 125th anniver-
        sary of the birth of Henri Dunant, founder of the Red
        Cross. Ligue des Sociétés de la Croix-Rouge. Document
        no. 5 (Feb. 12, 1958), p. 6.

1063   "Tolstoi, der Erzieher der Menschheit." RUNDBRIEF 42
          (Oct. 1976), p. 50.

1064   "Tribute to Pablo Casals." In: Corredor, J-Ma. Conversations
          avec Pablo Casals. Paris: Albin Michel, 1955. Trans-
          lated as Conversations with Pablo Casals. London:
          Hutchinson, 1956; New York: Dutton, 1957, p. 11.

1065   "Tribute to Theodor Heuss." In: Bott, Hans and Herman Leins,
          compilers. Begegnungen mit Theodor Heuss. Tübingen:
          Rainer Wunderlich Verlag, 1954, pp. 439-43.

1066   "Utöver mattet av sina krafter." In: Anna Söderblom: en
          minnesbok. Uppsala: J. A. Lindblad, 1956, pp. 132-33.

1067   "En Välgörare for de Primitiva invanarna Ogowe's Urskogar."
          In: Thulen, Sven, ed. Hågkomster och Livsintryck. Till
          Minnet au Nathan Söderblom. Uppsala: J. A. Lindblad,
          1933.

1068   "Viktor Hugo." KIRCHENBOTE 31:9 (March 1, 1902), pp. 69-70.

2. Works by Others

    a. Books

1069   Discours prononcés aux obsèques de Charles-Albert
          Schillinger . . . le 21 juin 1872. Strasbourg:
          Treuttel et Wurtz, 1872. 27 pp. Schillinger was
          Schweitzer's mother's half-brother, after whom Schweitzer
          was named.

1070   GEISER, SAMUEL. Albert Schweitzer im Emmenthal: vier
          Jahrzehnte Zusammenarbeit zwischen dem Urwalddoktor von
          Lambarene und der Lehrerin Anna Joss in Kröschenbrunner.
          Zürich and Stuttgart: Rotapfel Verlag, 1974.

1071   MINDER, ROBERT and HANS WALTER BÄHR. Emmy Martin; die
          Mitarbeiterin Albert Schweitzers. Zum 80. Geburtstag
          Emmy Martins. Tübingen: Katzmann Verlag; Bern:
          P. Haupt, 1964. 175 pp.

1072   WOLFF, CHRISTIAN. Les Ancêtres d'Albert Schweitzer. Liste
          établie par le Cercle Généalogique d'Alsace. . . .
          Strassburg: CGA, 1978. 93 pp.

Life and Work

   b. Articles, Parts of Books

1073   "An der Seite Dr. Schweitzers" (Hermann Mai). RUNDBRIEF 46
          (Nov. 1978), pp. 21-22.

1074   BÄHR, H. W. "75. Geburtstag von Professor Dr. Robert Minder."
          RUNDBRIEF 44 (Nov. 1977), pp. 34-36. Illus.

1075   BAUR, H. "Vater Ludwig Schweitzer. Ein Pfarrergrab im
          Elsass." Schweizerisches Protestantenblatt (Basel) 48
          (Aug. 1925). Reprinted in NEUES V (Ende August 1925),
          p. 1.

1076   BERNARD, ALBERT. "Zum Heimgang von Mlle. Emma Haussknecht.
          Eine Würdigung." Les Dernières Nouvelles du Haut-Rhin
          (Colmar), June 6, 1956, p. 8. Port.

1077   "Bij de dood van Emma Haussknecht." NIEUWS 5:2 (Oct. 1956),
          pp. 3-5. Illus.

1078   BURI, FRITZ. [Essay without title--about Emma Haussknecht.]
          In: BEGEGNUNG, pp. 257-59.

1079   _____. "Eine Mitarbeiterin Albert Schweitzers gestorben"
          (Emma Haussknecht). Basler Nachrichten (Basel) 234
          (June 6, 1956).

1080   CHAKRAVARTY, AMIYA. "Emmy Martin: a memory of friendly
          visits." In: TRIBUTE, pp. 75-80.

1081   CHEVALLAZ, MADELINE. "Die Familie von Albert Schweitzer."
          Annabelle (Zürich) 22:259 (July 1959), pp. 34-36. Port.,
          illus.

1082   COLLIN, ROBERT. "La milliardaire malheureuse" (Olga
          Deterding). Paris Match (Paris) 413 (March 9, 1957),
          pp. 78-79ff. Illus.

1083   CONNAUGHT, VERE and RICHARD BOYD. "The women around
          Dr. Schweitzer." The American Weekly/Journal American
          (New York), Oct. 16, 1960, pp. 4-5f. Illus. Translated
          as "Vroue om Albert Schweitzer." Sarie Marais
          (Capetown, South Africa) 13:8 (Oct. 25, 1961), pp. 26-27;
          also as "Elas São Atraídas irrestivelmente para o seu
          servico." Folha de São Paulo, Sept. 17, 1963.

1084   "Emil Mettler, London." RUNDBRIEF 20 (Sept. 1, 1962),
          pp. 40-41.

1085   ENNIS, THOMAS W. "Erica Anderson, 62, a film maker and
        Schweitzer associate is dead." The New York Times,
        Sept. 25, 1976, p. 22.

1086   "Erica Anderson, 62, filmed Schweitzer." A.I.S.L. Bulletin
        2 (Nov. 1976), p. 6.

1087   F., G. "'Ich fahre nach Lambarene.' Die Milliardärin Olga
        Deterding arbeitet im Urwald-Hospital von Albert
        Schweitzer." Rheinische Post (Düsseldorf) 13
        (Jan. 16, 1957).

1088   "The Fergus Pope family." COURIER, April–May 1966, p. 22.

1089   FESCHOTTE, JACQUES. Pour l'anniversaire de Madame Emmy
        Martin." CAHIERS 8 (Dec. 1962), pp. 11–13.

1090   FISCHER, EDITH. "Zum gedenken an Dr. René Kopp." RUNDBRIEFE/
        DDR 26 (1975), pp. 25–27.

1091   FREYER, PAUL HERBERT. "Ein Tag im Urwaldspital" (Emmy Martin
        zum Gedenken). RUNDBRIEFE/DDR 20 (1972), pp. 14–16.

1092   GOLDSCHMIDT, HELMUT. "Die Lockungen der Welt. Olga Deterding
        verliess Albert Schweitzer." Neue Illustrierte
        Wochenschau (Vienna) 49:11 (March 16, 1958), p. 16.

1093   _____. "Mich nennen hier alle Olga! Bei Dr. Schweitzer,
        der Olga Deterding Friede und Ruhe bietet." Neue
        Illustrierte Wochenschau (Vienna) 48:19 (May 12, 1957),
        pp. 1–2.

1094   "A good servant dies at Lambarene" (Chaplain Andre Vigné).
        BRITISH BULLETIN 27 (Jan. 14, 1965), pp. 11–12.

1095   HAUSSKNECHT, EMMA. "Mlle. Emma Haussknecht." In: SELECTION,
        pp. 31–32. Port.

1096   KIK, RICHARD. "Die Beisetzung der Asche von Frl. Haussknecht
        am 17.8.56." RUNDBRIEF 10 (Dec. 1, 1956), pp. 11–14.
        Illus.

1097   LIND, EMIL. "Im Dienste das 'Haussknechts Gottes.'" Pfalz
        und Pfalzer 7 (July 1952). Reprinted in RUNDBRIEF 3
        (Jan. 14, 1953), pp. 14–15; also in: DOKUMENTE,
        pp. 177–78.

1098   LOCHER, GOTTFRIED W. "Zum Gedenken an Ulrich Neuenschwander."
        Der Bund (Bern), July 4, 1977. Reprinted in A.I.S.L.
        Bulletin 5 (Nov. 1977), p. 6.

Life and Work

1099   MARTIN, EMMY. "Un bon serviteur de l'hôpital: André Vigne."
        CAHIERS/BELGE 5 (April 1965), pp. 31-32.

1100   MILLER, RHENA SCHWEITZER. "Erica Anderson." A.I.S.L.
        Bulletin 2 (Nov. 1976), pp. 7-8 (German) and 9-10
        (English).

1101   MINDER, ROBERT. "M. et Mme. F. Dinner-Obrist ou 34 ans au
        service de Lambarene." CAHIERS 19 (June 1968), pp. 20-23.

1102   _____. "Un precurseur d'Albert Schweitzer: Albert
        Schillinger (1839-1872)." CAHIERS 6 (Dec. 1961), pp. 6-10.

1103   _____ and LUC DURAND-REVILLE. "Hommage à Madame Emmy Martin
        (1883-1971)." CAHIERS 26 (Winter 1971/72), pp. 14-16.

1104   "Missionary from Lambarene" (Emma Haussknecht). Time (New
        York) 63 (Jan. 25, 1954), pp. 82ff. Port.

1105   MUNZ, WALTER. "Mirielle Caulet, 1927-1976." A.I.S.L.
        Bulletin 3 (Feb. 1977), p. 21.

1106   _____. "Pierre Fanguinoveny 1926-1978." A.I.S.L. Bulletin
        8 (Nov. 1978), pp. 13-14.

1107   "Nachruf für Emma Haussknecht mit den Ansprachen von Pfarrer
        Mary. Messager Évangelique (Strasbourg), June 17, 1956.
        German and French. Reprinted in RUNDBRIEF 10
        (Dec. 1, 1956), pp. 3-8.

1108   "Der neue Arzt von Lambarene." Welt am Sonntag, Dec. 24, 1974.
        Reprinted RUNDBRIEF 40 (1975), pp. 121-22.

1109   "Neue Helferinnen." NEUES 9 (Whitsunday 1927), pp. 7-8.
        Translated as "Nya medhjalpare." MEDDELANDEN 2
        (Sept. 1927), pp. 5-6.

1110   OSWALD, SUZANNE. "En Souvenir de Adele Woytt-Schweitzer."
        CAHIERS 22 (Dec. 1969), pp. 20-21.

1111   PIEPENHORN, CHARLOTTE. "Ein Leben in Freundschaft und im
        Dienste für Albert Schweitzer" (Herr und Frau Kik).
        A.I.S.L. Bulletin 5 (Nov. 1977), pp. 4-5. Also
        RUNDBRIEF 44 (Nov. 1977), pp. 7-8.

1112   RZ., CL. "Le visage de la semaine." La Vie Protestant
        20:4 (Jan. 24, 1958), p. 10. Port. (Offer of 100
        million dollars to Dr. Schweitzer by Olga Deterding.)
        Translated as "Pourquoi de Dr. Schweitzer a-t-il refusé

6 millions de dollars?" Paix et Liberté (Gilly, Belgium) 58:14 (April 6, 1958), pp. 1f.

1113   S., R.   "Pfarrer Louis Schweitzer."   FAMILIEN-KALENDAR 33 (1926), pp. 53-54.   Obituary.

1114   SCHWARZ, WILLY.   "Prof. Dr. Ulrich Neuenschwander."   RUNDBRIEF 44 (Nov. 1977), pp. 37-38.

1115   SITTLER, LUCIEN.   "Eugen Debs, aus Colmarer Familie, Gründer des Sozialismus in den Vereinigten Staaten von Nordamerika."   In: Annuaire de la Société historique et littéraire de Colmar V (1955), pp. 121-25.   About Debs and Schweitzer.

1116   "Das Spital war ihr Leben--Nachruf für Mathilde Kottman." RUNDBRIEF 40 (Jan. 14, 1975), pp. 114-16.

1117   STEFFAHN, HARALD.   "'Das Spital für uns noch einmal gebaut.' Ein Rückblick auf die 'Ära Kik.'"   RUNDBRIEF 44 (Nov. 1977), pp. 8-21.   Illus.

1118   TAURIAC-DALMAS, MICHEL.   "Olga Deterding, die Milliarden-Erbin der 'Shell' als Krankenpflegerin bei Dr. Albert Schweitzer."   L'Alsace Illustrée (Mulhouse) 14:13 (July 1, 1959), pp. 5-9.   Illus.

1119   THOMMEN-WEISSENBERGER, Med. Dr.   "Ein englischer Heiler in Afrika."   Schweizerisches Protestantenblatt (Basel) 56:28 (July 15, 1933), pp. 221-23; 56:29 (July 22, 1933), pp. 228-30.

1120   "Vater Ludwig Schweitzer gestorben.   Ein Pfarrergrab im Elsass."   RUNDBRIEF 21 (Jan. 14, 1963), pp. 26-27.   Port.

1121   "Walter Munz, M.D., medical director, Albert Schweitzer Hospital, Lambarene."   COURIER, Autumn 1968, pp. 8-9.

1122   WERNER, D. A.   "In memoriam Mevrouw Hanna Oberman-Oberman." EERBIED 27:3 (Dec. 1978), pp. 28-29.   Illus.

1123   WIJNEN, ARY VAN.   "In memoriam Dr. Kopp."   EERBIED 23:2 (Aug. 1974), p. 37.

1124   WOYTT, G.   "Leon Morel, 1883-1976."   A.I.S.L. Bulletin 3 (Feb. 1977), pp. 18-19.

1125   WOYTT-SECRÉTAN, MARIE.   "Le Docteur Victor Nessman (1900-1944)." CAHIERS 2 (Dec. 1959), pp. 17-20.   Reprinted RUNDBRIEF 15 (Jan. 1960), pp. 13-20.

Life and Work

1126 _____. "Mrs. C. E. B. Russell." RUNDBRIEF 14 (July 1, 1959),
        pp. 3-10. Revised version in CAHIERS 6 (Dec. 1961),
        pp. 16-18.

1127 _____. "Olga Deterdings Aufenhalt in Lambarene." RUNDBRIEF
        12 (June 15, 1958), p. 64.

1128 "Zum Gedanken: Dr. Paul Fischer--ein Freund Albert
        Schweitzers." RUNDBRIEF 46 (Nov. 1978), pp. 24-30.

                    D. Visits and Meetings
                 (Other Than Those at Lambarene)

    a. Books

1129 DORYAN, MME. MIREIO. En Alsace chez le docteur Albert
        Schweitzer. Paris: La Riveraine, 1956. 107 pp.

     WENZEL, LENE, ed. Albert Schweitzer gestern-heute, eine
        Anthologie der Begegnungen. See Collections, no. 99
        above.

    b. Articles, Parts of Books

1130 "Als Gast bei Albert Schweitzer. Der Hebelpreisträger empfing
        das Prasidium des Hebelbundes." Badische Zeitung
        (Freiburg) 154a (Oct. 5, 1951), p. 6.

1131 ANDERSON, ERICA. "Father Pire meets Dr. Schweitzer."
        Catholic Digest (St. Paul, Minn.) 25:8 (June 1961),
        pp. 97-102.

1132 ARONS, HANNS. "Strassburg Speichergasse 2. Begegnung und
        Gespräch mit Albert Schweitzer." Rhein-Neckar Zeitung
        (Heidelberg) 2 (Jan. 4, 1960), p. 2; 3 (Jan. 5/6, 1960),
        p. 2.

1133 "Begegnung mit Albert Schweitzer. Der Doktor aus Lambarene
        in Europa." Christ und Welt (Stuttgart) 2:4
        (Jan. 27, 1949), p. 12.

1134 "Begegnung mit Albert Schweitzer in Gunsbach." Strassburger
        Nachrichten, Nov. 3, 1952. Reprinted in RUNDBRIEF 3
        (Jan. 14, 1953), pp. 19-20.

1135 BRICO, ANTONIA. [Brieflicher Bericht über Besuch bei
        Schweitzer in Günsbach und bei seiner Tochter in der
        Schweiz.] RUNDBRIEF 3 (Jan. 14, 1953), pp. 18-19.

1136   BRZYGODA, URSULA. "Begegnung mit Albert Schweitzer."
        Politische Rundschau (Lübeck) 2:12 (1950), p. 5.

1137   BUNK, GERARD. "Ontmoeting met Albert Schweitzer." Nieuwe
        Rotterdamsche Courant, Aug. 22, 1953, p. 5.

1138   CASALS, PABLO. "Begegnung in Edinburgh." In: GESTERN-HEUTE,
        p. 28.

1139   DANIEL, ANITA. "A visit with Albert Schweitzer." Glamour
        (New York) 28 (Dec. 1952), pp. 83ff.

1140   DOLENS, VIKTOR. "Eine Stunde mit Albert Schweitzer."
        Schweizerisches Protestantenblatt (Basel) 51:42
        (Oct. 20, 1928), pp. 350-52; 43 (Oct. 27, 1928),
        pp. 357-59.

1141   DURAND, LIONEL. "A talk with Albert Schweitzer." New Era
        (Paris) 1:11 (1952), pp. 5-8.

1142   DURAND-REVILLE, LUC. "Remembering le Grand Docteur" (excerpt
        from a speech before l'Academie des Sciences Morales et
        Politiques, Jan. 1975). COURIER, Summer 1975, pp. 22-24.

1143   FEHR, GÖTZ. "Gespräch mit Albert Schweitzer." Deutsches
        Rotes Kreuz (Lübeck) 1 (Jan. 1956), p. 8. Reprinted in
        same with title "Prof. Albert Schweitzer wird am 14.
        Januar 90 Jahre. Ausgabe A, Heft 1 (Jan. 1965), pp. 30-
        31; reprinted in Jugendrotkreuz und Erzieher 1 (Jan. 1956),
        p. 8.

1144   FESCHOTTE, JACQUES. "Entretien à Gunsbach." Réforme (Paris)
        5:234 (Sept. 10, 1949), p. 5.

1145   _____. "Gunsbach, été 1954." Réforme (Paris) 10:501
        (Oct. 23, 1954), pp. 4-5.

1146   _____. "Im Haus über der Strasse nach Munster." In:
        GESTERN-HEUTE, pp. 32-33.

1147   FLACHS, CHARLOTTE. "Besuch bei Albert Schweitzer." Isar-Post
        (Landshut/Bayern) 4:59, p. 6.

1148   FRANCK, FREDERICK. "Schweitzer ohne Heiligenschein." In:
        GESTERN-HEUTE, pp. 34-35. Translated from Days with
        Albert Schweitzer, no. 1459 below.

1149   FRIIS, BØRGE. "Besøg hos Albert Schweitzer." Fyens
        Stiftstidende (Odense), Nov. 13, 1953.

Life and Work

1150   _____. "Besøg hos Albert Schweitzer." Berlingske Tidende
         (Copenhagen), Nov. 23, 1951, p. 6.

1151   _____. "Besøg hos Albert Schweitzer." Berlingske Aftenavis
         (Copenhagen), Jan. 11, 1950.

1152   GEORGE, MANFRED. "Begegnung mit Albert Schweitzer." Die Neue
         Zeitung (Munich) 8:264 (Nov. 8/9, 1952), p. 10.

1153   GRABS, RUDOLF. "Zeugnis und Begegnung." In: GESTERN-HEUTE,
         pp. 36-38.

1154   GRASHEY-STRAUB, IRMINGARD. "Briefauszug vom 16.7.1954 an
         Richard Kik über die Begegnung mit Albert Schweitzer in
         Lindau." RUNDBRIEF 6 (Dec. 1, 1954), pp. 20-21.

1155   HAINISCH-MARCHET, LUDOVICA. "Treffen mit Albert Schweitzer."
         Die Ungefarbte Brille (Göttingen) 1:1 (1955-56), pp. 62-64.

1156   HAINMÜLLER, WILHELM. "Begegnung (In Gunsbach) mit Albert
         Schweitzer." RUNDBRIEF 8 (Nov. 1, 1955), pp. 25-31.
         Reprinted in: DOKUMENTE, pp. 259-61.

1157   HARSHBERGER, GARTH. "A 1-W meets Dr. Schweitzer." The
         Mennonite (Berne, Indiana) 73:31 (Aug. 12, 1958), p. 490.

1158   HARTMANN, CARL. "Wiedersehen mit Albert Schweitzer."
         Hessische Nachrichten (Kassel) 212 (Sept. 12, 1951).

1159   HAUPT, PAUL. "Erste Begegnung mit Albert Schweitzer." In:
         EHRFURCHT, pp. 266-68.

1160   HAUTERRE, HENRY. "Besuch bei Albert Schweitzer." Die Neue
         Zeitung (Munich) 50:4 (April 5, 1949), p. 3.

1161   HEINRICH, HELMUT. "Begegnung mit Albert Schweitzer."
         Deutsches Rotes Kreuz (Lübeck) 1 (Jan. 1955), p. 13.
         Illus.

1162   HENNING, OTTO. "Bei Albert Schweitzer in Günsbach."
         RUNDBRIEF 8 (Nov. 1, 1955), pp. 33-34.

1163   HEUSCHELE, OTTO. "Begegnung mit Albert Schweitzer" (am 11.
         Oktober in Tübingen). RUNDBRIEF 23 (Jan. 14, 1964),
         pp. 58-61.

1164   HIRSCH, FELIX EDWARD. "Bei Albert Schweitzer in Günsbach."
         Rhein-Neckar Zeitung (Heidelberg) 243 (Oct. 16/17, 1954),
         p. 17.

1165   _____. "My visit with Albert Schweitzer." The Christian
              Advocate (Chicago) 130 (Oct. 20, 1955), pp. 6ff.

1166   HUME, EDWARD. "We visited Albert Schweitzer." Advance
              (New York) 146:2 (Jan. 25, 1954), p. 10.

1167   JACOBI, ERWIN. "Begegnungen mit Albert Schweitzer (1875–1965).
              Vortrag, gehalten im Rahmen der Veranstaltungen der
              Jüdischen Liberalen Gemeinde Zürich am 3. Nov. 1978."
              Luchot (Zürich) 8 (Dec. 15, 1978), pp. 7–26.

1168   KIRKPATRICK, PAULINE. Selection without title. In:
              BEGEGNUNG, pp. 196–99. Reprinted from George Seaver's
              Albert Schweitzer, the Man and his Mind, no. 300 above.

1169   KRÄMER. [Begegnung mit Albert Schweitzer in Frankfurt,
              anlässlich der Einweihung des Goethe-Museums. Auszug
              aus einem Brief an Richard Kik von 28.8.54.] RUNDBRIEF
              6 (Dec. 1, 1954), pp. 23–25.

1170   KÜHN-LEITZ, ELSIE. "Begegnung mit Albert Schweitzer."
              RUNDBRIEF 8 (Nov. 1, 1955), pp. 31–32.

1171   LIND, EMIL. "Der 28. August 1949." In: GESTERN-HEUTE,
              pp. 48–49.

1172   _____. "Wir besuchen Dr. Schweitzer in seiner Heimat.
              Eindrücke von einer Sommerfahrt der Albert-Schweitzer-
              Kameradschaft Speyer nach Günsbach am 5. August 1954."
              RUNDBRIEF 6 (Dec. 1, 1954), pp. 33–36.

1173   LONICER, HEINZ. "Besuch bei Albert Schweitzer in Günsbach."
              Freies Christentum (Frankfurt a.M.) 10:1 (Jan. 1, 1958),
              cols. 7–8.

1174   LORENZ, HEINZ. "Eine Wallfahrt zu Albert Schweitzer" (in
              Gunsbach). Pro Musica (Trossingen, Wolfenbüttel) 4
              (Oct./Dec. 1959), pp. 148–51. Reprinted in RUNDBRIEF 16
              (Oct. 1, 1960), pp. 40–43.

1175   MEYER, ERICH. "Besuch bei Albert Schweitzer." Freies
              Christentum (Frankfurt a.M.) 3:11 (Nov. 1, 1951), col. 6.

1176   MINDER, ROBERT. "Klavierunterricht bei Albert Schweitzer."
              RUNDBRIEF 24 (June 1964). Reprinted in: GESTERN-HEUTE,
              pp. 50–52.

1177   MÜLLER, HELMUT. "Ontmoeting met Albert Schweitzer."
              Deventer Kerkbode 35:19 (May 10, 1935), pp. 1–2.

Life and Work

1178   MÜLLER, K. "Unerwartete Begegnung in Günsbach." <u>Kirche und Mann</u> (Gütersloh) 5:11 (Nov. 1952), p. 5. Port., illus.

1179   NEUFFER, PROF. DR. "Albert Schweitzer 80 Jahre alt." <u>Deutsche Medizinische Wochenschrift</u> (Stuttgart) 80:2 (Jan. 14, 1955), pp. 92-93.

1180   NEY, ELLY. "Eine Besuch bei Albert Schweitzer in seinem Heimatort Günsbach." RUNDBRIEF 12 (June 15, 1958), pp. 49-51.

1181   NOMURA, M. "Schweitzer Hakase to tomoni." <u>Bungei Shunjū</u> (Tokyo) 11 (Nov. 1954), pp. 200-01.

1182   PETERS, SARAH. "She was Schweitzer's guest." <u>Christian Advocate</u> (Chicago) 128:31 (July 30, 1953), pp. 5f. Illus.

1183   PITSCH, F. W. "Ein Besuch bei Albert Schweitzer." <u>Das Evangelische Deutschland</u> (Berlin) 6:37 (Sept. 15, 1929), pp. 313-15.

1184   PREMINGER, MARION MILL. "Schweitzer is eighty." <u>Journal of the American Geriatrics Society</u> (Baltimore) 2:12 (Dec. 1954), pp. 769-71.

1185   PRÉVOT, RENÉ. "Der Doktor spielt die Orgel--hören sie, ein Besuch bei Albert Schweitzer in seiner Elsässischen Heimat." <u>Münchner Merkur</u> (Munich) 74 (March 27, 1953), p. 7.

1186   REYMANN, M. "Besuch bei Albert Schweitzer." RUNDBRIEF 16 (Oct. 1, 1960), pp. 23-27.

1187   RHODE, H. O. "Auch eine Begegnung mit Albert Schweitzer. Eine Erinnerung aus dem Kriegsjahr 1918." <u>Kirchliches Monatsblatt für Evangelisch-Lutherische Gemeinden</u> (Philadelphia) 6:5 (June 1949), pp. 4-6.

1188   RINDERKNECHT, PETER. "Begegnungen mit Albert Schweitzer. Zum 80. Geburtstag des Urwalddoktors am 14. Januar 1955." <u>Volksrecht</u> (Zürich), Jan. 14, 1955. Also in <u>Der Landschäftler</u> (Liesthal) 11 (Jan. 14, 1955). Port.

1189   _____. "Begegnung mit Albert Schweitzer." <u>Die Weltwoche</u> (Zürich) 792 (Jan. 14, 1949), p. 2. Port.

1190   ROGERS, FRED B. "Memoir of Albert Schweitzer." <u>Transactions and Studies of the College of Physicians of Philadelphia</u> 33:3 (Jan. 1966), pp. 209-12. Also issued as a reprint.

1191   ROSENBERG, SAMUEL. "Albert Schweitzer: the man from
         Strasbourg." In: The Come as you are Masquerade Party.
         Englewood Cliffs, N.J.: Prentice-Hall, 1970, pp. 117-52.

1192   ROSENKRANTZ, GERHARD. "Begegnung mit Albert Schweitzer,
         1957-1964. Zum 90. Geburtstag." Universitas (Stuttgart)
         20:1 (Jan. 1965), pp. 17-21. Enlarged version, without
         title, printed in BEGEGNUNG, pp. 36-42.

1193   RUSSELL, JOHN. "Mein Besuch bei Albert Schweitzer." Welt am
         Sonntag (Hamburg), June 19, 1955, p. 12.

1194   SCHAEFFER, LOUIS EDOUARD. "Begegnungen mit Albert Schweitzer."
         Cigognes: Grande Revue Illustrée d'Alsace (Strassburg)
         4:9 (Feb. 27, 1949), pp. 1-2. Reprinted in: Schaeffer,
         Louis Edouard. Weltbürger. Porträts von Meistern und
         Freunden. Strasbourg: Schaeffer, 1950, pp. 47-61.

1195   SCHIMANSKI, STEFAN. "'God's eager fool.' A note on a meeting
         with Albert Schweitzer." World Review (London), New
         Series, no. 4 (June 1949), pp. 15-17. Port.

1196   SCHNEIDER, REINHOLD. Selection without title. In: BEGEGNUNG,
         pp. 254-56.

1197   SCHÜLKE, HORST. "Noch ein Besuch bei Albert Schweitzer."
         Freies Christentum (Frankfurt a.M.) 4:1 (Jan. 1, 1952),
         cols. 7-10.

1198   SCHÜTZ, ROLAND. "Mein Besuch bei Albert Schweitzer in
         Günsbach vom 31. August bis 3. September." RUNDBRIEF 3
         (1953), pp. 15-18.

1199   SCHWEITZER, WALDEMAR. "Begegnung mit Prof. Albert
         Schweitzer. . . ." Hessische Nachrichten (Kassel) 156
         (July 7, 1954).

1200   SIEBERT, HANS EBERHARD. "Besuch bei Albert Schweitzer." Die
         Schwarzburg (Hamburg) 60:7 (Dec. 1951), pp. 141-42.
         Reprinted in Der Convent (Mannheim-Sandhofen) 3:1
         (Jan. 1952), pp. 8-9.

1201   SIEBERT, THEODOR. "Unerwartete Begegnung im Elsass."
         RUNDBRIEF 9 (Jan. 1, 1956), pp. 46-53. Reprinted from
         Evangelisches Gemeindeblatt.

1202   SKILLINGS, MILDRED DAVIS. "A Day with Albert Schweitzer."
         The American-German Review (Philadelphia) 2:1
         (Sept. 1935), pp. 33-35f.

Life and Work

1203   STEINER, HANS, photographer. "A Visit with Albert
       Schweitzer and friends in Günsbach and Colmar." The
       Rotarian (Evanston) 92:3 (March 1958), pp. 18-23.

1204   TAU, MAX. "Botschaft des Guten. Besuch bei Albert
       Schweitzer." Velhagen und Klasings Monatshefte
       (Bielefeld, Berlin, Darmstadt) 61:6 (June 1953),
       pp. 468-70.

1205   VILLINGER-ZIPPERLING, IRMGARD. "Meine Begegnung mit Albert
       Schweitzer." Die Agnes-Karll-Schwester (Frankfurt a.M.),
       Feb. 1955.

1206   WALTHER, DANIEL. "Albert Schweitzer." L'Illustré (Lausanne)
       15:7 (Feb. 14, 1935), pp. 165-66. Illus.

1207   _____. "A visit to Albert Schweitzer." The Contemporary
       Review (London) 170 (Sept. 1946), pp. 160-66.

1208   WESTRA, P. "Mijn ontmoeting met Albert Schweitzer." NIEUWS
       1:1 (Dec. 1951), pp. 14-16.

1209   WIKSTRÖM, JAN-ERIK. "Visit hos Albert Schweitzer."
       Ansgarius 60 (1965), pp. 65-70.

1210   "Wir traffen Albert Schweitzer." Die Farben-Post (Hoechst,
       Germany) 2:1 (Jan. 28, 1955).

1211   YI, IL SUN. "A visit to Dr. Schweitzer." Sae Kah Jung
       (Seoul) 6:12 (Dec. 1959), pp. 107-11.

1212   ZURLINDEN, HANS. "Von einem Besuch bei Albert Schweitzer."
       Der Bund (Bern) 165 (April 8, 1955), p. 7.

1213   _____. "Von einem Besuch bei Albert Schweitzer." In:
       Zurlinden, Hans. Erinnerungen an Richard Straus, Carl
       Spitteler, Albert Schweitzer, Max Huber, Cuno Amiet,
       Arthur Honegger. St. Gallen: Tschudy, 1962, pp. 51-62.

1214   ZWEIG, STEFAN. "Albert Schweitzer. Dieser Name hat für
       viele Menschen starken Klang, aber fast für jeden unter
       diesen verschiedenen, besonderen Sinn." Die
       Friedensrundschau 8 (Feb. 1954), p. 10.

1215   _____. "Begegnung zweier Europäer. Stefan Zweig mit Albert
       Schweitzer." Deutsche Blätter 1:5 (May 1943), pp. 19-22.

1216   _____. "Bei Albert Schweitzer." Das Inselschiff (Leipzig)
       14:2 (Spring 1933), pp. 73-83.

1217   _____. "Unvergessliches Erlebnis. Ein Tag bei Albert Schweitzer." Annuaire de la Société Historique et Littéraire de Colmar V (1955), pp. 131-33. Reprinted in: Woytt-Secretan, Marie. Souvenir de Lambarene. Stefan Zweig: Ein Tag bei Albert Schweitzer. Pub. à l'occasion du 80e anniversaire du dr. Albert Schweitzer. Colmar, 1955. 8 pp.; Reprinted in: Albert Schweitzer, Genie der Menschlichkeit, see no. 101 above, pp. 7-20; Reprinted with title "Albert Schweitzer, dieser Name hat für viele Menschen schon einen starken Klang." Universitas (Stuttgart) 15:1 (Jan. 1960), p. 82; Reprinted in Die Welt Albert Schweitzers; ein Photobuch von Erica Anderson und Eugene Exman; Reprinted in: BEGEGNUNG, pp. 185-91; Reprinted in: Begegnungen mit Menschen, Büchern, Städten. Vienna, Leipzig, Zürich: Reichner, 1937, pp. 118-27. Also Berlin and Frankfurt a.M.: S. Fischer, 1955, pp. 113-22; Excerpted with title "Ein vollkommener Tag ist selten." In: GESTERN-HEUTE, pp. 72-76; translated, without title, in Universitas (English language edition) 7:1 (1964), pp. 41-42; translated as "Dzien z Albertem Schweitzerem." Kierunki. Pismo Spoleczno-Kulturalne Katolikow 38:5 (1965), pp. 26-27.

IV. Africa and Lambarene

A.   Books by Schweitzer

Schweitzer's activities in Africa were described in a series of reports and letters sent to his friends and supporters in Europe and
America. The earlier reports, covering the period from 1913-1927,
were collected by Schweitzer into two books, Zwischen Wasser und
Urwald (On the Edge of the Primeval Forest) and Mitteilungen aus
Lambarene (More from the Primeval Forest). The reports covering
the later period have not been collected into book form, but appear
as letters and reports in various periodicals (see Section IV-2
below). Schweitzer did, however, publish several other books describing his experiences in Africa which are not in the tradition of
his chronological reports. These are also described below.

ZWISCHEN WASSER UND URWALD
(On the Edge of the Primeval Forest)

The first series of Mitteilungen (News Reports) von Prof. Dr. Albert
Schweitzer was based on letters and reports sent by Schweitzer to
friends in Europe after his arrival in Africa in 1913 and was published in 1913 and 1914 in Strasbourg. They appeared as small pamphlets, in French- and German-language editions, for distribution to
friends and supporters of his work. In 1920, following a journey to
Sweden for concerts and lectures, Schweitzer collected and revised
these reports under the title Zwischen Wasser und Urwald. While this
account, covering the period 1913-1917, is based on his earlier reports and letters, much information found in the earlier reports is
omitted, due to space limitations imposed by the publisher.

The book first appeared in Swedish in 1921 and later in the same
year was published in German in Switzerland. In the following year
it was translated into Danish, Dutch, English, and Finnish.

First Series

1218   Mitteilungen von Prof. Dr. Albert Schweitzer aus Lambarene
(Ogowe-Gabun, Afrika). (1. Bericht). Strassburg i.E.:
Druck von M. DuMont Schauberg, 1913. 36 pp. (Signed
at end "Juli 1913, Albert Schweitzer.")

119

Africa and Lambarene

1219   Same. Zweiter Bericht. (Juli 1913 bis Januar 1914).
        Strassburg i.E.: Druck von M. DuMont Schauberg, 1914.
        38 pp. (Signed at end "Januar 1914, Albert Schweitzer.")

1220   Same. Dritter Bericht. (Januar bis Mai 1914). Strassburg
        i.E.: Druck von M. DuMont Schauberg, 1914. 29 pp.
        (Signed at end "Mai 1914, Albert Schweitzer.")

First Series in French

1221   Notes et nouvelles de la part du Prof. Dr. Albert Schweitzer.
        Lambaréné (S. Ogooué, Gabon). Strasbourg: Imprimerie
        M. DuMont Schauberg, 1913. 21 pp. (Signed at end,
        "Juillet 1913, Albert Schweitzer.")

1222   Same. Dieuxième Rapport. Strasbourg: Imprimerie M. DuMont
        Schauberg, 1914. 43 pp. (Signed at end, "Janvier 1914,
        Albert Schweitzer.")

1223   Same. Troisième Rapport (de janvier à mai 1914). Chambery:
        Imprimerie Chamberienne, 1914. 33 pp. (Signed at end,
        "Mai 1914, Albert Schweitzer.")

1224   Zwischen Wasser und Urwald. Erlebnisse und Beobachtungen
        eines Arztes im Urwalde Äquatorialafrikas. Bern: Paul
        Haupt, 1921. 165 pp., 16 pls., map, illus. cover.
        Reprinted 1922, 1923.

1225   Same. München: C. H. Beck'sche Verlagsbuchhandlung, 1922.
        165 pp., pls., map, illus. cover. Reprinted 1923
        (153 pp.).

1226   Same. Bern: Paul Haupt; München: C. H. Beck'sche
        Verlagsbuchhandlung, 1925. 154 pp., pls., map.

1227   Same. Bern: Paul Haupt (149 pp.); München: C. H. Beck'sche
        Verlagsbuchhandlung, 1926. vii, 169 pp., 14 pls., map.
        Reprinted 1927, 1928, 1931, 1940, 1942.

1228   (Transcription into Braille). From edition of C. H. Beck,
        1928.

1229   Same. Genf, Paris. Sonderdruck für die deutschen
        Kriegsgefangenen . . . Verlag dargeboten vom Weltkomitee
        der Christlichen Vereine Jünger Männer (YMCA), 1945.
        165 pp., map. Reprinted, 1947.

1230   Same. München: Biederstein Verlag, 1949. 149 pp., pls.,
        map.

Africa and Lambarene

1231   Same. Bern: Paul Haupt, 1926; München: C. H. Beck, 1950.
           149 pp., 16 pls., map. Reprinted, 1951, 1952, 1953, 1954,
           1955, 1957, 1963.

1232   Same. In: Selbstzeugnisse, pp. 65-209 (See no. 63 above).

1233   Same. Gekürzte, für den Schulgebrauch mit Erläuterung
           versehene Ausgabe von H. Groeneweg. Groningen: J. B.
           Wolters, 1935. 125 pp., port. (Von deutschen Art und
           Kunst, 14.) Reprinted 1937, 1940, 1946, 1948, 1950,
           1955, 1957, 1961.

1234   Same. Gekürzt und erläutert von Shin Aizu. (Lizenzausgabe
           von Prof. A. Schweitzer--Zum Doktors 79. Geburtstags.)
           Tokyo: Ikubundo Verlag, 1954. 78 pp. Illus., map.
           Text in German.

1235   Same. Aus dem Buch "Zwischen Wasser und Urwald." Husum:
           Matthiesen. 16 pp. (Leserunde 16.)

Chinese

1236   [Zwischen Wasser und Urwald.] Tr. Yü Ah-Hsün. Taiwan:
           Chih Wen Publishing Co., 1976. 202 pp.

Czech

1237   Lidé v pralesích. S 8 přilohami. V. Praze: Nakladatelství
           "Orbis," 1935. 270 pp., front. (port.), illus., illus.
           cover. (Ěvrope a za Oceánem, Svazek, VI.) Reprinted
           1936, 1937 (266 pp.), 1946. Contains Lékařem y Pralese
           (Zwischen Wasser und Urwald, C. H. Beck, 1926) přeložila
           Maria Skrachová and Co Isem Zazil y Lambarene
           (Mitteilungen aus Lambarene, C. H. Beck, 1929) přeložila
           Pavla Stuchlikavá.

1238   Same. 4. Aufl. (Obálku navrhl Josef Ficenec.) Praze:
           "Orbis," 1948. 319 pp., 13 pls., map. (Knihy Osudü a
           Práce, Svazek, 43.) 7th edition, 1968, 288 pp.

1239   Same. Doslov: Eduard Wondrák. Kresby: Podle
           Dokumtárních Snímků Zprac Jaroslava Běhounková. 8. vyd.
           (V. Orbisu 4 vyd). Praha: Orbis, 1971. 286 pp.

Danish

1240   Mellem Floder og Urskov. En Laeges Oplevelser og Iagttagelser
           i AEkvatorial-Afrikas Urskove. Tr. Ellen Thejll.

Africa and Lambarene

>Copenhagen: V. Pios Boghandel, Povl Branner, 1922.
>153 pp., illus., illus. cover. 2 opl., 1922; 3. opl,
>1928 (155 pp.).

1241   Same. (4. opl.) Copenhagen: Branner og Korch, 1951.
>158 pp., map, illus. cover. 5. opl., 1953; 6. opl.,
>1955 (155 pp.); 7. opl., 1956.

Dutch

1242   Aan den zoom van het oerwoud. Ervaringen en opmerkingen van
>een arts in het oerwoud van Aequatoriaal Afrika. Tr.
>J. Eigenhuis. Haarlem: H. D. Tjeenk Willink & Zoon,
>1922. 183 pp., 16 illus.

1243   Same. 2^e herziene druk. Haarlem: H. D. Tjeenk Willink,
>1925. 232 pp., front., illus., map. 3^e druk, 1926;
>4^e-5^e druk, 1928.

1244   Same. 6^e herziene druk. Haarlem: H. D. Tjeenk Willink,
>1939. 211 pp., front., illus., map.

1245   Lambarene. Mijn Werk aan de zoom van het oerwoud. Tr.
>J. Eigenhuis e.a. Haarlem: H. D. Tjeenk Willink & Zoon,
>1950. vii, 232 pp., front. (port.), illus. Fragmenten
>uit diverse vroeger verschenen uitgaven. 2^e druk, 1953.
>3^e druk, 1955 (viii, 223 pp.). Contains translations of
>Zwischen Wasser und Urwald, Mitteilungen aus Lambarene
>3rd part, and reports for later years, including the 1945
>report.

English

1246   On the Edge of the Primeval Forest. The Experiences and Obser-
>vations of a Doctor in Equatorial Africa. Tr. by Ch. Th.
>Campion, containing 16 illustrations from photographs, and
>a sketch map. London: A. and C. Black, 1922. 180 pp.,
>front., 16 pls., map. Reprinted 1922, 1923, 1924, 1926,
>1928, 1929, 1931, 1934, 1935, 1937, 1944, 1949, 1950.
>(The impressions of 1922 and 1931 appeared also with the
>imprint of the Macmillan Co., New York.)

1247   (Popular edition). London: A. and C. Black, 1953. 127 pp.,
>front. (Paper edition). Reissued, 1954, 1955.

1248   Same. London: Hodder and Stoughton, 1938. 255 pp. (Black
>Jacket Series.) Reprinted, 1943.

Africa and Lambarene

1249   (Paperback edition). London, Glasgow: William Collins Sons,
          Fontana Books, 1956. 126 pp., cover port. (Fontana Books,
          148.) Reprinted 1957, 1958, 1961.

1250   (Paperback Edition). Cleveland, O.: Collins-World, 1976.
          (Fount Religious Paperback Series.)

1251   On the Edge of the Primeval Forest and More from the Primeval
          Forest. Experiences and Observations of a Doctor in
          Equatorial Africa. Tr. C. T. Campion. With 35 photo-
          graphs. London: A. and C. Black; New York: The Macmillan
          Co., 1948. vii, 222 pp., front. (port.), pls., map.
          (Combined edition. More from the Primeval Forest was
          previously published in the United States with the title
          The Forest Hospital at Lambarene, no. 1299 below.) Re-
          printed (London), 1949, 1951, 1956, (New York) 1952.

1252   Same. New York: AMS Press, 1976. vii, 222 pp. (Reprint of
          the 1948 Macmillan edition.)

1253   Same. London: Readers' Union, A. and C. Black, n.d. xii,
          244 pp., illus., map.

1254   The Primeval Forest (includes On the Edge of the Primeval
          Forest and More from the Primeval Forest). New York:
          Pyramid Books, 1963. 239 pp. (Pyramid Books, R856.)
          Paperback edition.

Finnish

1255   Aarnio metsän Lääkärinä. Lääkärin kokemuksia ja Havaintoja
          Keski-Afrikan aarniometsässä. Suomentanut Armas Holmio.
          Porvoosa: Werner Söderström, 1922. 180 pp., illus., map.
          (Suomen Kristillisen Ylioppilasliton Julkaisuja, 21.)

French

1256   A l'orée de la forêt vierge. Récits et réflexions d'un
          médecin en Afrique équatoriale française. Lausanne:
          Edition la Concorde; Strasbourg: Librarie Evangélique,
          1923. ix, 192 pp., front. (map), illus., illus. cover.
          Reprinted, 1925.

1257   Same. Avec seize planches hors texte. Paris: F. Rieder,
          1929. 231 pp., 16 pls., map. (Collection d'études, de
          documents, et de témoignages pour servir à l'histoire de
          notre temps.) Reprinted, 1935 (236 pp.).

Africa and Lambarene

1258 Same. Nouvelle édition. Paris: Albin Michel, 1952. 221 pp.,
     16 pls., map, illus. cover. (The text of this edition
     has been revised and, in some instances, brought up to
     date by Dr. Schweitzer; also, a new "Preface," dated
     "le 15 décembre 1951," has been added by him (pp. 9-13).
     Reprinted 1954 (218 pp.), 1956, 1958 (216 pp.), 1965
     (221 pp.).

1259 Same. Paris: Albin Michel, 1952. Selection des Amis du
     Livre, n.d. 218 pp., illus., map. (Limited edition,
     "hors commerce.")

1260 Same. Paris: Le Club francais du Livre, 1953. vi. 232 pp.,
     illus., port., couv. en couleur. (L'édition en tirage
     limité hors commerce, et reservée exclusivement aux
     membres du Club français du Livre.)

1261 A l'orée de la fôret vierge. (Récits et réflexions d'un
     médecin en Afrique équatoriale française.) Amsterdam:
     Drukkerij "Holland" . . . Collection "Le Meilleur Livre
     du Mois" . . . "reservé aux adhérents du Club du Livre
     du Mois . . .), 1955. 196 pp. (L'authorisation des
     Editions Albin Michel, Paris.)

1262 Same. Paris: Club de la Femme (Imprim. Brodard et Taupin),
     1964. 256 pp. (Bibliothéque du Club de la Femme.)

1263 Same. Levallois-Perret (Hts-de-Seine): Circle du Bibliophile
     (Impr. Brodard et Taupin), 1965. 256 pp., illus.

Hungarian

1264 Orvos az Öserdöben. Fordította Gizella Klopstock. As
     elöszót írta László Györkovacs. 17 képmellekléttal és
     1 térképpel. Budapest: Franklin-Társulat (1935).
     165 pp. Map.

Italian

1265 Dove comincia la foresta vergine. Vicende e riflessioni di un
     medico nell'Africa Equatoriale Francese. Tr. Giovanna
     Zorzli. Milan: Edizioni di Comunità, 1959. 156 pp.
     16 illus.

Japanese

1266 Mizu to Genseirin no Hazama nite. Tr. Minoru Nomura. Text
     in Japanese characters. Tokyo: Kōzandō Shoten, 1932.
     174 pp., illus. Reprinted, 1934.

Africa and Lambarene

1267   Same.   Tokyo: Nagasaki Shoten, 1941.   201 pp.

1268   Same.   Tokyo: Shinkyo Shuppansha, 1954.   214 pp., front.

Mizu to Genshirin no Aidani.   Tr. Masao Asai.   Tokyo:
       Hakusuisha, 1956.   See collected works, no. 1 above.

1269   Mizu to Genseirin no Kazama de.   Tr. Minoru Nomura.   Tokyo:
       Iwanami Shoten, 1957.   188 pp.

1270   Genshirin no Henkyô Nite.   Tr. Toshiharu Haneda.   Tokyo:
       Nan'un-Dô, 1963.   172 pp.   (Combined edition with Aus
       Meinem Leben und Denken.)

Norwegian

1271   Mellom elver og urskog.   En leges opplevelser og iakttagelser
       i urskogen i Ekvatorial-Afrika.   Oversatt av Ragnvald
       Skrede.   Oslo: Johan Grundt Tanum, 1952.   199 pp.,
       front. (port.).   2. oppl, 1953; 5. oppl., 1954.

Polish

1272   Wśród Czarnych na Równiku.   Tr. Zofji Petersowej.   Warsaw:
       Premje Powieściowe "Swiata," 1935.   262 pp., Illus., map.

1273   Same.   Warsaw: Biblioteka Prenumeratorów "Kurjera Porannego,"
       1938.   262 pp.

Portuguese

1274   Entre á agua e a selva.   Narrativas e reflexões dum médico na
       selva da Africa Equatorial.   Traducão de José Geraldo
       Vieira.   São Paulo: Melhoramentos, 1953.   155 pp.,
       front. (port.), illus., illus. cover.   (Caminhos da Vida,
       No. 2.)   Second ed., 1956; Third edition, 1961 (172 pp.).

Serbo-Croatian

1275   Na ivici prašumē.   Písma iz Lambarenes.   Uspomene i
       Razmišljanja jednog lekara.   Ed. Dragan Jeremíc.
       Beograd: "Kultura," 1958.   273 pp.   (Srpska Knjizevna
       Zadruga, Kdo 51, Knjiga 347).   In Cyrillic characters.
       Selections from Zwischen Wasser und Urwald, tr. Vera
       Naumov and Mitteilungen aus Lambarene, tr. Zdenka Brkíc.

Africa and Lambarene

Spanish

1276   Entre el agua y la selva virgen. Relatos y reflexiones de un
       médico en la selva del Africa Ecuatorial. Prólogo de
       Alejandro Lipschütz. Madrid: Javier Morata, 1932.
       240 pp., front. (port.), illus.

1277   Same. Versión castellana de Juan Alvedo. Buenos Aires:
       Hachette, 1955. 164 pp., front. (port.), illus., illus.
       cover. (Colleción el Mirador.) (This new edition has
       been revised in accordance with the new French edition of
       1952.) Reprinted, 1956.

Swedish

1278   Mellan urskog och vatten. En läkares upplevelser och
       iakttagelser i Ekvatorialafrikas urskogar. Bemyndigad
       översättning fran tyskan av Greta Lagerfelt. Uppsala:
       J. A. Lindblad, 1921. 168 pp., illus., map. illus. cover.
       2.-3. uppl., 1922; 4. uppl. (new edition, 185 pp.), 1934.

1279   Same. 5 uppl. med efterskrift av Harald Dahl. Uppsala:
       J. A. Lindblad, 1954. 189 pp., illus., map, illus.
       cover. New edition.

                    MITTEILUNGEN AUS LAMBARENE
                 (More from the Primeval Forest)

Mitteilungen aus Lambarene, reports of Albert Schweitzer's second
period of work in Africa and of the rebuilding of his hospital after
his absence during the First World War, appeared between 1925 and
1929. The three booklets which comprise the series originated in
German and were published simultaneously in Switzerland, Germay, and
Alsace (in French) for supporters of the Lambarene hospital. Translations into Dutch and Swedish immediately followed, and, at later
intervals, translations into Czech, Danish, English, Japanese, and
also, more recently, into Serbo-Croatian. The English translation,
published in London with the title More from the Primeval Forest, and
in New York as The Forest Hospital at Lambarene, appeared as a sequel
to the earlier volume, Zwischen Wasser und Urwald. In 1928 the three
parts of the series were united in one volume and published in Germany
with the title Mitteilungen aus Lambarene. In 1955 they were reprinted in a new edition entitled Briefe aus Lambarene, 1924-1927.

1280   Mitteilungen aus Lambarene. Früjahr bis Herbst 1924. Bern:
       Paul Haupt, Akademische Buchhandlung vorm. Max Drechsel,
       1925. 48 pp.

1281   Same. Munich: C. H. Beck, 1925. 45 pp.

1282   Mitteilungen aus Lambarene. Zweites Heft. Herbst 1924 bis
        Herbst 1925. Bern: Paul Haupt, Akademische Buchhandlung
        vorm. Max Drechsel; Munich: C. H. Beck; Strasbourg:
        Imprimerie Alsacienne, 1926. 73 pp.

1283   Same. Drittes Heft. Herbst 1925 bis Sommer 1927. Bern:
        Paul Haupt, Akademische Buchhandlung vorm. Max Drechsel;
        Munich: C. H. Beck; Strasbourg: Imprimerie Alsacienne,
        1928. 59 pp.

1284   Same. Ernstes und zweites Heft. Früjahr 1924 bis Herbst
        1925 (neue Ausgabe). Munich: C. H. Beck, 1928. 164 pp.
        Cover illus. Contains a new introduction by Albert
        Schweitzer. Reprinted 1929.

1285   Same. Drittes Heft. Herbst 1925 bis Sommer 1927. Munich:
        C. H. Beck, 1928. 74 pp. Illus. Reprinted 1929.

1286   (Braille edition). The first three booklets have been tran-
        scribed into Braille. The names of the transcriber and
        publisher are unknown.

1287   Mitteilungen aus Lambarene. Drei Hefte, 1924-1927. Munich:
        C. H. Beck; Bern: Paul Haupt, 1928. Front., pls.

1288   Briefe aus Lambarene 1924-1927. Mit 14 Abbildungen. Munich:
        C. H. Beck, 1955. 195 pp., illus., ports.

        Same. In: Selbstzeugnisse, 1959, pp. 211-397 (see no. 63
        above).

1289   Die erste Monate in Lambarene (aus Briefe aus Lambarene).
        Tokyo: Ikubundo Verlag, 1961. 59 pp. Anmerkungen in
        Japanisch.

Chinese

1290   [Briefe aus Lambarene.] Tr. Lin Miao-Ling. Taiwan: Chih
        Wen Co., 1977. 196 pp.

Czech

        "Co Isem Zazil v Lambarene." In: Lidé v Pralesich (combined
        edition), see no. 1237 above.

Africa and Lambarene

Danish

1291 I Lambarenes Urskovshospital. Tr. Alette Schou. Copenhagen:
      Povl Branner, 1933. 137 pp., illus., pls., map.

1292 Mit Urskovshospital. Met et forord af Børge Friis. Tr.
      Alette Schou. (2. oplag af I Lambarenes Urskovshospital.)
      Copenhagen: Branner og Korch, 1952. 139 pp. Cover
      illus. 3. opl., 1954; 4. opl., 1955; 5. opl., 1959.

Dutch

1293 Opnieuw naar Lambarene. Nieuwe Ervaringen en opmerkingen van
      een arts in aequatorial Afrika. Tr. H. M. Eigenhuis-Van
      Gendt. Haarlem: H. D. Tjeenk Willink & Zoon, 1927.
      216 pp., 6 pls. 2^e druk, 1928.

1294 Bouwen in het oerwoud. Nieuwste ervaringen en opmerkingen van
      een arts in aequatorial Afrika. Tr. J. Eigenhuis en H. M.
      Eigenhuis-Van Gendt. Haarlem: H. D. Tjeenk Willink &
      Zoon, 1928. 106 pp., illus. (Translation of the author's
      Mitteilungen aus Lambarene, pt. 3.)

      See also Lambarene. Mijn werk aan de zoom van het oerwoud,
      no. 1245 above.

English

1295 More from the Primeval Forest. Tr. C. T. Campion. London:
      A. and C. Black, 1931. xiii, 173 pp., front,, 15 pls.,
      ports., plan. (Sequel to the author's On the Edge of the
      Primeval Forest.)

1296 Same. London: A. and C. Black, 1956. 128 pp., front.

1297 (Paperback edition). London, Glasgow: William Collins and
      Sons, 1958. 128 pp., front. (Fontana Books, No. 221.)

1298 (Paperback edition). Cleveland, O.: Collins-World, 1976.
      (Fount Religious Paperback Series.)

1299 The Forest Hospital at Lambarene. Tr. C. T. Campion. Intro-
      duction by Karl Reiland. New York: Henry Holt and Co.,
      1931. 191 pp., front., 15 pls., map, plan. (Sequel to
      the author's On the Edge of the Primeval Forest.)

      See also On the Edge of the Primeval Forest and More from the
      Primeval Forest (combined edition), no. 1251 above.

128

Africa and Lambarene

French

1300   Nouvelles de Lambaréné du Printemps à l'automne 1924.[1]
         Automne 1924 à automne 1925. Automne 1925 à été 1927.
         Strasbourg: Librarie Evangélique, 1925-1928. 3 vols.

Japanese

1301   Lambarene Tsūchin. Tr. Minoru Nomura and Yosiyuki Yokoyama.
         Tokyo: Shinkyo Shuppansha, 1954. 271 pp., front., illus.

         Same. Tokyo: Hakusuisha, 1957. See Collected Works, no. 3
         above.

Russian

1302   [Mitteilungen aus Lambarene.] Tr. Willy Petritzky.
         Leningrad: Edition la Science, 1978.

Serbo-Croatian

Na ivici prasumé. Písma iz Lambarenea (combined edition).
    See no. 1275 above.

Swedish

1303   Brev från Afrikas urskog. Tr. Greta Lagerfelt. Med förord av
         Oscar Krook. Stockholm: Svenska Krykans Diakonistyrelses
         Bokförlag, 1925. 86 pp., cover illus.

1304   Nya brev från Afrikas urskog. Tr. Greta Lagerfelt.
         Stockholm: Svenska Kyrkans Diakonistyrelses Bokförlag,
         1927. 109 pp., cover illus.

1305   Nya Lambarenebrev. Hösten 1925 till sommaren 1927.
         Översättning av Anna Taube. Stockholm: Svenska
         Kyrkans Diakonstyrelses Bokförlag, 1929. 77 pp.,
         cover illus.

AFRIKANISCHE JAGDGESCHICHTEN
(African Hunting Stories)

Africanische Jagdgeschichten appeared, first, in 1926 in the Elsass-
Lothringischen Familien-Kalender (No. 1347) and, in 1936, in

---

[1]This edition in French was reprinted in the periodical Europe (Paris)
with the title "Premiers mois à Lambaréné," no. 1385 below.

Africa and Lambarene

Strasbourg in book form. A year later, illustrations were added, and a new edition was published in Leipzig. The "stories" also form the first half of a small volume published in Basel in 1943, with the title Afrikanische Tiergeschichten (no. 1308 below).

1306   Afrikanische Jagdgeschichten (followed by) Ojembo, der
        Urwaldschulmeister. Strasbourg: Edition des Sources
        (Imprimerie de la Petite-France), 1936. 16 pp., illus.
        cover.

1307   Same. 2. aufl. Mit 6 Bildern. Leipzig: Felix Meiner, 1937.
        30 pp., illus., illus. cover.

1308   Afrikanische Tiergeschichten (followed by) Ojembo, der
        Urwaldschulmeister. Basel: Basler Missionsbuchhandlung,
        1943. iv, 24 pp., illus. cover. (Von Fernen Ufern,
        Heft 15.) (These two titles comprise the first part of
        the book, pp. 3-14, the latter part containing two African
        stories by George Haessig.)

Dutch

1309   Afrikaansche Jachtverhalen. Uitgave ten bate van het
        ziekenhuis te Lambarene. Deventer: Salland, 1937.
        16 pp., illus. cover.

English

        See The Animal World of Albert Schweitzer, no. 48 above. The
        stories from Afrikanische Jagdgeschichten are not in-
        cluded as a complete unit, but are incorporated into
        various parts of the text, viz.: pp. 74, 75-76, 82-86,
        87-91, 97-101, 104, 108-111. The same pagination will be
        found in the paperback edition (1958).

AFRIKANISCHE GESCHICHTEN
(From My African Notebook)

"The house in which I am writing these stories about Africa stands on a little hill overlooking the Ogowe [River] above Lambaréné, the Adolinanonge—which means 'looking out over the nations.'" With this description, Albert Schweitzer begins his introduction to this volume describing the site of his hospital in Lambaréné in Equatorial French Africa. He continues with a brief historical background of the Ogowe territory, tales from its folklore, taboos, and magic, and anecdotes about the hospital and the lives of its patients. In-cluded in all editions and translations is the story of "Ojembo, the Forest Schoolmaster," first published in 1929 in the Elsass-Lothringischer Familien-Kalender (no. 1377 below).

130

Africa and Lambarene

1310   Afrikanische Geschichten. Mit acht Bildern und einer Karte
        des Ogowe-Gebietes. Leipzig: Felix Meiner; Bern: Paul
        Haupt, 1938. 98 pp., pls., illus., map. Dated at the end
        "Juni 1938." Reprinted, 1939 (107 pp.)

1311   Same. Hamburg: Richard Meiner, 1950 (ᶜ1938). 97 pp., illus.,
        map. Reprinted, 1952, 1953, 1955.

1312   Same. Gekürzter Nachdruck der 1939 im Verlag Paul Haupt
        erschienene Ausgabe. Einleitung von Werner Juker. Bern:
        Gute Schriften, 1951 (and successive reprints through
        1956). 62 pp., illus. cover. (Gute Schriften, 71.) This
        edition has been published in both boards and paper covers,
        and the imprint has slight variations.

1313   Same. Gekürzt und erläutert von Chuzo Nakagome. Tokyo:
        Ikubundo Verlag, 1952. 59 pp., front. (port.), illus.,
        map. Included is "Ojembo. . . ."

1314   Verschiedene Geschichten. Tokyo: Ikubundo Verlag, 1963.
        29 pp.

Chinese

1315   [African Notebook.] Tr. Shih Yuan-Kang. Taiwan: Yao Chih
        Publ. Co., 1971. 138 pp.

1316   [Afrikanische Geschichten, Das Spital im Urwald, Ein Pelikan
        erzählt aus seinem Leben.] Tr. Chao Chen. Taiwan: Chih
        Wen Publ. Co., 1977. 192 pp.

Danish

1317   Mit Afrika. Tr. Børge Friis. Copenhagen: Branner og Korch,
        1955. 93 pp., illus. cover. 2. oplag, 1955.

Dutch

1318   Schweitzer vertelt. Verhalten uit Africa. Tr. J. Eigenhuis.
        Haarlem: H. D. Tjeenk Willink & Zoon, 1938. 153 pp.,
        front., illus., map.

English

1319   From my African Notebook. Tr. Mrs. C. E. B. Russell. London:
        George Allen and Unwin, 1938. 132 pp., front., 13 pls.,
        map. Reprinted 1939, 1951.

Africa and Lambarene

1320   <u>African Notebook</u>. Tr. Mrs. C. E. B. Russell. New York:
           Henry Holt and Co., 1939. 144 pp., front., pls., map.

1321   Same. Bloomington, Ind.: University of Indiana Press, 1958.
           144 pp., Illus. (22 Photographs by Erica Anderson).
           Issued also in a paperback edition. (A Midland Book,
           MB 14).

1322   Same. Toronto: The Copp Clark Co., 1958. 144 pp., illus.
           Issued also in a paperback edition.

1323   Same. Gloucester, Mass.: Peter Smith, 1966. 144 pp. Illus.

French

1324   <u>Histoires de la forêt vierge</u>. Avec une carte. Paris: Payot,
           1941. 174 pp. Illus. (Collection d'études, de documents
           et de témoignages pour servir à l'histoire de notre temps).
           Reprinted 1950, 1952, 1955 (176 pp.)

Italian

1325   <u>Storie africane</u>. Tr. Mira Pia Stacul. Milan: Il Saggiatore,
           1960. 99 pp. (Biblioteca delle Silerchi, 53).

Japanese

1326   <u>Afurikamonogatari</u>. Tr. Toshio Nakahara. Tokyo: Shinkyo
           Shuppansha, 1952. 164 pp. Illus.

1327   <u>Afurika Monogatari</u>. <u>Perikan no Seikatsu to Iken</u>. Tr. Masao
           Asai and Kōji Kunimatsu. Tokyo: Hakusui-Sha, 1963.
           194 pp. Illus. (Bound with <u>Ein Pelikan erzählt aus</u>
           <u>seinem Leben</u>.)

           <u>Afurikamonogatari</u>. Tr. Masao Asai. Tokyo: Hakusuisha,
           1957. See Collected Works, no. 5 above.

Korean

1328   <u>Ap'urika myongsang</u>. Tr. Myong-gwan Chi. Seoul: Tongyang
           Publ. Co., 1960. 203 pp.

Portuguese

1329   <u>Histórias Africanas</u>. Tr. José Geraldo Vieira. São Paulo:
           Melhoramentos, 1959, pp. 71-157. Illus. (Caminhos da
           Vida, 16.) This text is contained in the same volume
           with <u>Minha Infância e Mocidade</u>, no. 135 above.

Africa and Lambarene

<u>Swedish</u>

1330 <u>Berattelser från urskogen</u>. Tr. Ingeborg Wikander. Uppsala:
   J. A. Lindblad, 1940. 127 pp. Illus.

DAS SPITAL IM URWALD
(The Jungle Hospital)

The short text of <u>Das Spital im Urwald</u>, a brief résumé of the history
and work of the Lambaréné hospital, was written by Albert Schweitzer
to accompany the group of full-page photographs of the hospital--its
buildings, patients, and helpers--by Dr. Anna Wildikann. Dr. Wildikann
served as one of the hospital doctors during two periods, from 1937-
1939 and 1940-1946. Her photographs form the first "picture-book"
description of Dr. Schweitzer's work in Africa.

1331 <u>Das Spital im Urwald</u>. Aufnahmen von Anna Wildikann. Bern:
   Paul Haupt, 1948. 52 pp., illus. (32 photos), map.
   (Das Offene Fenster, 1.) Reprinted by Katzmann-Verlag,
   Tübingen, 1952.

1332 Same. Mit 32 Aufnahmen von Anna Wildikann. Munich:
   C. H. Beck, 1950. 52 pp., illus., map.

<u>Chinese</u>

See combined edition, no. 1316 above.

<u>Dutch</u>

1333 <u>Een hospital in het oerwoud</u>. Vertaling door Jan Poortenaar.
   Foto's van Anna Wildikann. Naarden: In den Toren, 1949.
   52 pp., illus. (32 pls.), illus. cover.

<u>Japanese</u>

<u>Genshirin no Byōin</u>. Tr. Kōji Kunimatsu. Tokyo: Hakusuisha,
   1957. See Collected Works, no. 5 above.

<u>Swedish</u>

1334 <u>Sjukhuset i urskogen</u>. Tr. Elisabet Åkesson. Fotografier av
   Anna Wildikann. Uppsala: J. A. Lindblad, 1952. 56 pp.,
   illus. (32 photos), map, illus. cover.

Africa and Lambarene

OJEMBO DER URWALDSCHULMEISTER
(Ojembo, the Jungle Schoolmaster)

The first mention by Albert Schweitzer of Ojembo, the jungle school-master, whose character and attainments he so greatly admired, was in Zwischen Wasser und Urwald, where he wrote: "There are native Christians who are in every respect thoroughly moral personalities; I meet one every day. It is Ojembo, the teacher in our boys' school, whose name means 'a song'; I look upon him as one of the finest men that I know anywhere."[1] In Afrikanische Geschichten he added: "Probably no one has ever borne so beautiful a name more worthily than this black teacher."[2] The story was first published in the Elsass-Lothringischer Familien-Kalender in 1929 (no. 1377 below) and later in Afrikanische Jagdgeschichten and Afrikanische Geschichten in all editions and translations of both texts.

1335 Ojembo der Urwaldschulmeister. Heilbronn, Stuttgart: Eugen
       Salzer, 1948. 15 pp., illus. cover. (Das Samenkorn,
       H. 15.) 2. Aufl. (Heilbronn), 1953.[3]

Dutch

1336 Ojembo, de schoolmeester van het oerwoud. Uitgegeven ten
       voordeele van het ziekenhuis te Lambarene. Deventer:
       AE. E. Kluwer, 1937. 20 pp., front., illus., illus. cover.

1337 Ojembo. Vertaling en inleiding van K. H. R. de Josselin de
       Jong. Delft: W. Gaade, 1955. 61 pp., illus.
       (Preciosa-Reeks.)

Swedish

See Fyrbåken i urskogen, 1950, pp. 83-87 (no. 1400 below).
See also no. 1377 below.

EIN PELIKAN ERZÄHLT AUS SEINEM LEBEN
(A Pelican Tells About His Life)

Previous to its publication in book form, the story of "Monsieur le Pélican," Albert Schweitzer's "night watchman," was published in 1948 in the Swiss periodical Atlantis (no. 1384 below). In the same

---

[1]On the Edge of the Primeval Forest. London: Adam and Charles Black, 1922.

[2]Afrikanische Geschichten. Leipzig: Felix Meiner, 1938, p. 74.

[3]Contains also "Albert Schweitzer" by Friedrich Pfäfflin, pp. 10-15.

134

year, it was reprinted in Germany and Austria in <u>Neue Auslese</u>, a
publication of the British and United States governments (no. 1384
below). More recently it has again been issued in book form both in
France and Germany, in the latter country in a book-club edition.

1338   <u>Ein Pelikan erzählt aus seinem Leben</u>. Text von Albert
        Schweitzer. Mit 48 Bildern von Anna Wildikann. Hamburg:
        Richard Meiner, 1950. 63 pp., illus. 2. Aufl., 1952;
        3. Aufl., 1955.

1339   Same. Mit 48 Bildern von Anna Wildikann. (Lizenzausgabe.
        Gütersloh): Bertelsmann Lesering, 1960. 119 pp., illus.
        (Kleine Lesering Bibliothek, 47.) Nur für Mitglieder.

Afrikaans

1340   <u>'n Pelikaan vertel</u>, met 48 opnamen deur Anna Wildikann, uit
        Duits. Vertaal deur Hymne en Detlev Weiss. Amsterdam,
        Kaapstade: A. A. Balkema, 1956. 64 pp., illus., cover
        port.

Chinese

See combined edition with <u>Afrikanische Geschichten</u>, no. 1316
above.

Danish

1341   <u>En Pelikan fortaeller</u>. Tekst: Albert Schweitzer; Billeder:
        Anna Wildikann. Tr. Børge Friis. Copenhagen: Branner
        og Korch, 1952. 60 pp., illus., illus. cover.

English

1342   <u>The Story of my Pelican</u>. Tr. Martha Wardenburg. London:
        Souvenir Press, 1964. 70 pp.

1343   (Same). New York: Hawthorn Books, 1965. 65 pp.

French

1344   <u>Le pélican du Docteur Schweitzer</u>. Photographies d'Anna
        Wildikann. Paris: Editions Sun, 1952. 64 pp., illus.,
        illus. cover. (Limited edition of 200 copies which were
        sold for the exclusive benefit of the hospital at
        Lambarene.)

1345   <u>L'Histoire de mon pélican</u>. Photographies d'Anna Wildikann.
        Paris: Albin Michel, 1963. 72 pp., illus.

Africa and Lambarene

Japanese

Pelikan no Seikatsu to Iken. Tr. Kojī Kunimatsu. Tokyo:
    Hakusuisha, 1957. See Collected Works, no. 5 above.

Same. Combined edition with Afrikanische Geschichten, see
    no. 1327 above.

Norwegian

1346   En Pelikan forteller fra sitt Liv. Bilder, Anna Wildikann.
       Oslo: Land og Kirke, 1954. 60 pp., illus.

See also no. 1384 below.

B. Shorter Writings by Schweitzer

This section includes general materials written by Albert Schweitzer
about Africa and his work there. His periodic reports and report
letters, disseminated to his supporters through the various bulletins,
will be included in the next section, numbers 1400-1451.

1. General

1347   "Afrikanische Jagdgeschichten." FAMILIEN-KALENDAR 33 (1926),
       pp. 47-53. Reprinted in Hochschulwissen. Monatsschrift
       für das deutsche Volk und seine Schule (Warnsdorf i. Böhm)
       IV (1927), pp. 286-90.

1348   "Albert Schweitzer baute eine Brücke." RUNDBRIEF 19
       (Jan. 14, 1962), p. 20.

1349   "Albert Schweitzer erzählt von seinen Kranken." FAMILIEN-
       KALENDAR 43 (1936), p. 82.

1350   "Albert Schweitzer wieder in Lambarene." Der Christliche
       Welt (Gotha) 44:8 (April 19, 1930), pp. 397-99. Consists
       of two letters from Schweitzer.

1351   "Allocution lors des fêtes du cenquantenaire de son arrivée
       à Lambaréné. Andende 16 Avril 1963." In: RAYONNEMENT,
       pp. 244-45. Translated as "Ansprache von Dr. Schweitzer
       zum 18. April 1963 in Andende." RUNDBRIEF 22
       (April 18, 1963), p. 94; also as "Comments to Gabonese
       on April 18, 1963 on the 50th anniversary of his arrival
       at Lambarene." In: ALBUM, p. 172.

Africa and Lambarene

1352   "Asservissement de l'homme moderne. De bureaucratie en
        Afrique." CAHIERS 21 (June 1969), pp. 3-8.

1353   "Busy days in Lambarene." The Christian Century (Chicago)
        51:11 (March 14, 1934), pp. 355-57.

1354   "Das ist mein Werk in Lambarene." Bunte Deutsche Illustrierte,
        Nov. 7, 1959, pp. 26-29. Illus.

1355   "Dr. Schweitzer and his work." The Spectator (London) 155:
        5593 (Sept. 6, 1935), p. 357. Letter from Schweitzer.

1356   "Dorfleben im Urwald." FAMILIEN-KALENDAR 29 (1922), pp. 36-40.

1357   "De eerste Reis naar Lambarene in 1913 60 jaar geleden."
        NIEUWS 22:1 (May 1973), pp. 4-5.

1358   "Fifty years of Lambarene." BRITISH BULLETIN 27
        (Jan. 14, 1965), pp. 8-11. Illus.

1359   "The hospital jubilee." BRITISH BULLETIN 27 (Jan. 14, 1965),
        pp. 6-8.

1360   "The hospital as it is today." Episcopal Churchnews
        (Richmond, Va.) 120:4 (Feb. 21, 1954), pp. 18-21. Port.,
        illus. Reprinted in COURIER, May 1954.

1361   "Ich achte und schätze die Schwarzen. Der Urwalddoktor von
        Lambarene, der seinen 82. Geburtstag feiert, bericht eine
        Lanze für die Neger." Münchner Merkur 35 (Feb. 9/10, 1957),
        p. 17.

1362   "Ich muss wieder Bauunternehmer sein. Die Schaffung des
        Lepradorfes 1954." Universitas (Stuttgart) 10:4
        (April 1955), pp. 337-53. Includes map and plan of the
        hospital. Reprinted with title "Der Bau des Lepradorfes
        1954." In: SCHWEITZER, pp. 52-69.

1363   "Im Lande der Schlangen." Evangelischer Familien-Kalender
        für Elsass und Lothringen (Strasbourg) 46 (1939),
        pp. 75-80.

1364   [JACOBI, ERWIN R.] "Le Second depart du Dr. Schweitzer pour
        Lambarene (1924)--lettres inédites d'Albert Schweitzer
        et de son compagnon de voyage Noel-A. Gillespie." CAHIERS
        25/26 (Summer 1971/Winter 1971/72), pp. 3-13. Reprinted
        in NOUVELLES, special number (August 1973), pp. 9-27;
        translated as "Albert Schweitzers zweite Ausreise nach
        Lambarene (1924) . . . . RUNDBRIEFE/DDR 19-21 (1972-73),

Africa and Lambarene

> pp. 19-22, 21-28, 8-16 respectively; reprinted in BERICHTE
> 35 (Jan. 1973), pp. 9-30; Japanese translation in A Study
> of Schweitzer II. Tokyo: Albert Schweitzer Fellowship of
> Japan, 1972. Translation reprinted as a separate brochure
> with Japanese commentary by Yoshishige Matsuno. Japan:
> Asahi Verlag, 1974.

1365 "Josephine des zähme Wildschwein." FAMILIEN-KALENDAR 30
(1923), pp. 54-62. Reprinted in Die Ernte, Schweizerisches
Jahrbuch 1923. Basel, 1923, pp. 161-73; excerpted with
title "Josephine" in RUNDBRIEF 40 (Jan. 14, 1975),
pp. 128-31; excerpted with title "Wildschwein Josephine."
The American-German Review (Philadelphia) 5:5 (June 1939),
pp. 24-25.

1366 "Das Krankenhaus in Afrika. Wie mein Lebenswerk entstand."
Rheinischer Merkur (Koblenz) 8:12 (March 20, 1953), p. 16.
Illus.

1367 "Letter from Lambarene." The Living Age (New York) 355
(Sept. 1938), pp. 70-72. Translated from Pariser
Tagezeitung.

1368 "Ein Lichtbild aus Lambarenes Urwaldspital" (Brief Albert
Schweitzers vom 20. März 1926). Schweizerisches
Protestantenblatt (Basel) 49:17 (May 1, 1926), p. 136.

1369 "Ein Marge de l'oeuvre médicale" (extraits de Nouvelles de
Lambaréné). Almanach des Missions (Société des Amis des
Missions, Faculté de Theologie, Montpellier, France),
Dec. 1930, pp. 33-35. Illus.

1370 ["La mariage au Gabon."] Azija i Afrika Segodnja 2 (1969),
pp. 53-54.

1371 [MARTIN, EMMA, ed.] "Aus Briefen Albert Schweitzers."
Schweizerisches Protestantenblatt (Basel) 48:48
(Nov. 28, 1925), pp. 396-97.

1372 "Medicine vs. magic." Photos by Erica Anderson. The American
Weekly/Journal American (New York), Jan. 9, 1955, pp. 10-11.

1373 "Mein Spital im Urwald." Universitas (Stuttgart) 6:3
(March 1951), pp. 269-75.

1374 "La métapsychique au Gabon." Revue Métapsychique (Paris)
New Series 16 (Oct.-Dec. 1951), pp. 162-68. Excerpted in
CAHIERS 1 (April 1959), pp. 11-12; translated as "Old
black magic reborn." Tomorrow (New York) 1:1 (Autumn
1952), pp. 4-9.

1375   "La mission chrétienne et l'oeuvre médicale." CAHIERS 31
         (Summer 1974), pp. 3-7.

1376   "My church in the jungle." The American Weekly/Journal
         American (New York), Oct. 5, 1958, p. 11. Illus.

1377   "Ojembo, der Urwaldschulmeister." FAMILIEN-KALENDAR 36
         (1929), pp. 149-54. Reprinted in: Das Silberweisse Lama.
         Erzählungen aus fernen Ländern. Berlin: Evangelische
         Verlagsanstalt, 1957, pp. 3-9; translated as "Ojembo,
         Maître de école dans la forêt vierge." Départs
         (Strasbourg) 1:4 (March 1950), pp. 30-31; 1:5, p. 28.

1378   "On the edge of the primeval forest." In: Neider, Charles,
         ed. Man against Nature: Tales of Adventure and Explora-
         tion. New York: Harper, 1954, pp. 375-88. Excerpted
         from the 1922 edition of the book of the same name.

1379   "Ontwikkelingshulp in 1931." EERBIED 23:2 (Dec. 1974),
         pp. 35-36.

1380   "Our pets at Lambarene: I. Sakku and Kudeku; II. Tetchen and
         Antelöpeli; III. Antelöpeli, Samba and Josephine: IV.
         Josephine goes to Church--and farther." Everyland. A
         Children's Annual (London) (n.d.--1926?), pp. 150-51.

1381   "Our task in colonial Africa." Concluding essay in: Joy,
         Charles R. and Melvin Arnold. The Africa of Albert
         Schweitzer. Photographs by Charles R. Joy. New York:
         Harper; Boston: Beacon Press, 1948. Translated as Bei
         Albert Schweitzer. Munich: Beck, 1950.

1382   "Panorama de Lambaréné." Saisons d'Alsace (Strasbourg) 3
         (1951), pp. 247-50.

1383   [Part of a talk given by Schweitzer to Swiss and Alsatian
         helpers of his hospital before they went to Lambarene,
         Summer 1959.] In: Anderson, Erica. Albert Schweitzer's
         Gift of Friendship, see no. 223, pp. 144-48. Reprinted
         in: BRABAZON, Appendix B, pp. 481-84.

1384   "Ein Pelikan erzählt aus seinem Leben." Atlantis (Zürich),
         Feb. 1948, pp. 57-62. Reprinted in Neue Auslese. Aus
         der Schrifttum der Gegenwart. Published by the United
         States and British governments in Germany and Austria.
         3:5 (March 1948), pp. 110-21.

1385   "Premiers mois à Lambaréné." Europe. Revue Mensuelle
         (Paris) 15:57 (Sept. 15, 1927), pp. 61-88.

Africa and Lambarene

1386   "The relations of the white and coloured races." The Con-
        temporary Review (London) 133:475 (Jan. 1925), pp. 65-70.
        Reprinted in: Seaver, George. Albert Schweitzer: the
        Man and his Mind. New York and London: Harper, 1947,
        pp. 317-28; revised edition, 1955, pp. 341-52; excerpted
        in: Montague, Joseph F. The Why of Schweitzer. New
        York: Hawthorn Books, 1965, pp. 307-12.

1387   [SKILLINGS, EVERETT, ed.] "Concerning Dr. Schweitzer." The
        Christian Century (Chicago) 64:3 (Jan. 15, 1947), p. 82.
        Excerpts from a letter of Schweitzer's, December 1946.

1388   "Sur les chantiers d'esploitation forestière au Gabon vers
        1930." CAHIERS 7 (Sept. 1962), pp. 3-9; 8 (Dec. 1962),
        pp. 3-7.

1389   "Tiergeschichten aus Lambarene" (with Emmy Martin). BERICHTE
        37 (March 1974), pp. 21-27. Reprinted in: TIERE,
        pp. 13-20.

1390   "Une déclaration d'Albert Schweitzer à La Dernière Heure--
        'Il est incomprehensible qu'il se trouve de nos jours en
        Etat étranger en guerre avec le Katange pour le forcer à
        payer des redevances a l'àutre Etat congolais'" (signed
        at end "Albert Schweitzer"). La Dernière Heure (Brussels)
        57:354 (Dec. 20, 1962), p. 1. "Le Dr. Schweitzer reaffirm
        son point de vue essentiellement juridique," 58:9
        (Jan. 9, 1963), pp. 1, 3.

1391   "Der Urwald Doktor" (excerpt from Afrikanische Geschichten).
        Welt-Stimmen (Stuttgart) 24:3 (1955), pp. 97-99.

1392   "Das Urwaldspital zu Lambarene (nach Mitteilungen von Albert
        Schweitzer)." FAMILIEN-KALENDAR 34 (1927), pp. 135-37.
        Reprinted in Deutsche Evangelischer Missionskalender
        (Berlin) 3 (1928), pp. 56-59.

1393   "Vom Regen und schön Wetter auf dem Äquator." FAMILIEN-
        KALENDAR 39 (1932), pp. 59-62. Reprinted in RUNDBRIEF 8
        (Nov. 1, 1955); reprinted in: DOKUMENTE, pp. 264-68;
        translated as "Van regen en mooi weer." NIEUWS 1:2
        (March 1952), pp. 20-22.

1394   "Von der Mission. Gedanken und Erfahrungen." KIRCHENBOTE 48
        (Jan. 12-Aug. 23, 1919).

1395   "Von unseren Tieren in Lambarene." FAMILIEN-KALENDAR (1923),
        pp. 54-62. Reprinted in Die Ernte, Schweizerisches
        Jahrbuch (Basel) 1923, pp. 161-73. Illus. Includes

Africa and Lambarene

"Wildschwein Josephine." Reprinted in: TIERE, pp. 5-13.
Illus.

1396 "The war on Katanga." Atlas (New York) 5:4 (April 1963),
pp. 226-27. Translated and reprinted from Les Dernières
Nouvelles d'Alsace, Strasbourg.

1397 "Weinachten unter Palmen." KIRCHENBOTE 47:52 (Dec. 29, 1918),
pp. 214-15.

1398 "Wie mein Lebenswerk entstand." In: Erziehung zur
Menschlichkeit. Die Bildung im Umbruch der Zeit.
Festschrift für Eduard Spränger zum 75. Geburtstag
27. June 1957. Tübingen: Max Niemeyer, 1957, pp. 23-29.
Reprinted in RUNDBRIEF 40 (Jan. 1975), pp. 5-10.

1399 "Word from Dr. Schweitzer." Christian Century (Chicago)
62:22 (May 30, 1945), p. 655.

2. Report Letters and Bulletins

Schweitzer's reports on his work in Lambarene have appeared in a
number of forms. His work from 1913-1917 was described in Zwischen
Wasser und Urwald; Mitteilungen aus Lambarene covered the period
1924-1927. Since 1927, however, these materials have not been collected into a single volume. Rather, they have been printed as a
series of reports and letters in various bulletins published for the
benefit of his supporters (see nos. 4131-46 below for a list of these
bulletins).

I have attempted in this section to list the numerous reports and
bulletins written by Schweitzer. The section is divided into two
parts. The first lists materials which cover a period of several
years; the second is a chronological listing of separate letters and
reports.

C. Materials Covering Several Years

a. Books

1400 LAGERFELT, GRETA, ed. Fyrbåken i Urskogen. Albert Schweitzer
i Lambarene 1925-1950. Uppsala: J. A. Lindblad, 1950.
Includes letter-reports and personal correspondence covering the years 1925-1950.

Africa and Lambarene

    b. Articles, Parts of Books

1401   "Afrikanisches Tagebuch 1939-1945." Universitas (Stuttgart)
          1:8 (Nov. 1946), pp. 929-43. Translated into Russian in
          1975 by W. A. Petrizkij.

1402   "Afrikanisches Tagebuch 1944-45." In: SCHWEITZER, pp. 39-51.
          This is excerpted from the preceding item.

1403   "Das Spital während der Kriegesjahre." BRIEFE 23 (March 1946).
          Reprinted in: DOKUMENTE, pp. 120-35; translated as "At
          Lambarene in wartime: how the hospital fared 1939-1945."
          BRITISH BULLETIN 18 (Spring 1946), pp. 2-20. Illus.;
          "The hospital at Lambarene during the war years, 1939-
          1945." Special bulletin issued on the occasion of Dr.
          Schweitzer's 72nd birthday. COURIER, Jan. 1947, 19 pp.
          Illus.; also translated as "L'hôpital de Lambaréné pendant
          les années de guerre." LETTRES 13 (March 1946), 21 pp.;
          also as "Het ziekenhuis te Lambarene in de oorlogsjaren."
          NIEUWS 13 (March 1946), 15 pp.

1404   "Das Lambarenespital vom Herbst 1945 bis Frühjahr 1954.
          Bericht von Dr. Albert Schweitzer." BRIEFE 24 (Oct. 1954),
          pp. 1-20. Reprinted in: DOKUMENTE, pp. 136-50. Trans-
          lated as "L'Hôpital de Lambaréné de 1945 à 1954. . . ."
          LETTRES 14 (May 1954), pp. 1-21.

1405   "Lambarene 1946-1954." BRITISH BULLETIN 22 (Jan. 14, 1955),
          pp. 2-17. Translated as "Van 1946 tot 1954." NIEUWS
          4:1 (Jan. 1955), pp. 99-111; "Eight year report on
          Lambarene Hospital . . . to friends of the hospital in
          all lands, from 1946-1954." COURIER, Jan. 1955, 22 pp.

Chronological Listing

1406   "Journal du Dr. Schweitzer. I. L'arrivée . . .; II. Premières
          impressions . . .; III. Réglement . . .; IV. Premières
          observations. . . ." Journal de Société des Missions
          Évangeliques (Paris) (Sept. 1913), pp. 204-16; (Jun. 1913
          a Janvier 1914, April 1914), pp. 301-18; (May 1914),
          pp. 373-80.

1407   "Aus Briefen Albert Schweitzers: 'Am Abend der Himmelfahrt
          1924' und 'Lambarene, 15. September 1924.'" NEUES 3
          (Oct. 1924), pp. 2-3.

1408   "Aus Briefen Albert Schweitzers" (to Pfarrer H. Baur, Basel,
          1925). NEUES 5 (Aug. 1925), pp. 2-3.

Africa and Lambarene

1409　"Erzählender Teil.　Ein älterer, aber nicht veralteter Brief
　　　　Albert Schweitzers.　Lambarene, August 20, 1925."　NEUES
　　　　7 (Feb. 1926).

1410　"The doctor as builder."　BRITISH BULLETIN 2 (Summer 1926),
　　　　pp. 3-4.

1411　"Das Spital.　Letter 18. Mai 1927."　NEUES 10 (July 1927),
　　　　pp. 4-6.

1412　"From the old hospital to the new."　BRITISH BULLETIN 3
　　　　(Spring 1928), pp. 3-11.

1413　"Brief von Dr. Albert Schweitzer."　BRIEFE 11 (March 1930),
　　　　pp. 1-5.　Leter dated January 8, 1930.　Reprinted in:
　　　　DOKUMENTE, pp. 25-27; translated as "Letter from Dr.
　　　　Schweitzer."　BRITISH BULLETIN 4 (Spring 1930), pp. 3-11;
　　　　also as "Lettre du Dr. Schweitzer."　LETTRES I
　　　　(Jan.-March 1930).

1414　"Brief von Dr. Albert Schweitzer" (Jan. 9, 1930).　BRIEFE 11
　　　　(March 1930).　Reprinted in: DOKUMENTE, pp. 27-28.

1415　"Aus Lambarene.　Brief von 6. Februar 1930."　Der Speyerer
　　　　Protestant (Speyer, Germany) 1 (April 1930), pp. 59-60.

1416　"Brief von Dr. Albert Schweitzer" (Sonntag vor Palmsonntag
　　　　1931).　BRIEFE 12 (Pfingsten 1931), pp. 1-10.　Illus.
　　　　Reprinted in: DOKUMENTE, pp. 34-40; reprinted as
　　　　"Lambarene am Sonntag vor Palmsonntag 1931. . . ."
　　　　Der Speyerer Protestant (Speyer, Germany), 2 (July 1931),
　　　　pp. 100-06.

1417　"L'Hôpital en 1930.　Lettre du docteur A. Schweitzer
　　　　(22. mars 1931)."　LETTRES 2 (Pentecôte 1931), 12 pp.

1418　"Letters from Lambarene."　BRITISH BULLETIN 6 (Summer 1931),
　　　　pp. 1-5.

1419　"Brief Dr. Schweitzers aus Lambarene."　Der Speyerer
　　　　Protestant (Speyer, Germany) 3 (1932), pp. 148, 172.

1420　"Brief von Dr. Albert Schweitzer (Freitag 28. April 1933)."
　　　　BRIEFE 14 (July 1933), pp. 1-10.　Illus.　Reprinted in:
　　　　DOKUMENTE, pp. 62-65; reprinted with title "Aus einem
　　　　Brief . . . aus Lambarene geschrieben am Freitag, den 28.
　　　　April 1933."　Speyerer Protestant (Speyer, Germany) 4
　　　　(Sept. 1933), pp. 148-52; translated as "Lettre du
　　　　Dr. Schweitzer (28 avril 1933)."　LETTRES 4 (May 1933),
　　　　12 pp.

Africa and Lambarene

1421   "Brief von Dr. Albert Schweitzer, Dienstag, May 2, 1933."
        BRIEFE 14 (July 1933). Reprinted in: DOKUMENTE,
        pp. 65-69; reprinted with title "Aus einem Brief vom 2.
        Mai 1933. Über das Leben im Spital." Der Speyerer
        Protestant (Speyer, Germany) 4 (Oct. 1933), pp. 172-76.

1422   "Letters from Lambarene." BRITISH BULLETIN 8 (Winter 1933-34),
        pp. 1-6.

1423   "Brief von Dr. Albert Schweitzer" (den dritten Adventssonntag
        1933). BRIEFE 15 (Feb. 1934). Reprinted in: DOKUMENTE,
        pp. 70-76; reprinted with title "Brief vom dritten
        Adventssonntag 1933 aus Lambarene." Der Speyerer Protestant
        (Speyer, Germany) 5 (June 1934), pp. 96-98; (July 1934),
        pp. 109-11; (August 1934), pp. 125-28; (September 1934),
        pp. 142-44.

1424   "Lettre du docteur Schweitzer (17 décembre 1933)." LETTRES
        5 (Feb. 1, 1934), 10 pp.

1425   "A letter from Lambarene." BRITISH BULLETIN 9 (Spring 1934),
        pp. 1-8. Illus.

1426   "Brief vom 12. Dezember 1934 aus Strassburg." Der Speyerer
        Protestant (Speyer, Germany) 6 (August 1935), pp. 126-30.

1427   "Brief von Dr. Albert Schweitzer (13. Dezember 1934)."
        BRIEFE 16 (Jan. 1935), pp. 1-5. Illus. Reprinted in:
        DOKUMENTE, pp. 77-79.

1428   "Lettre du docteur Schweitzer (décembre 1934)." LETTRES 6
        (Jan. 1935), 7 pp.

1429   "Brief von Dr. Albert Schweitzer" (March 5, 1935). BRIEFE
        17 (June 1935), pp. 1-11. Illus. Reprinted in:
        DOKUMENTE, pp. 80-84.

1430   "Dr. Schweitzer's report." BRITISH BULLETIN 10 (Spring 1935),
        pp. 1-5. Illus.

1431   "Brief von Dr. Albert Schweitzer" (May 5, 1935). BRIEFE 17
        (June 1935). Reprinted in: DOKUMENTE, pp. 84-88.

1432   "Dr. Schweitzer's report." (Lambarene, March 5, April 7 and
        May 5, 1935). BRITISH BULLETIN 11 (Autumn 1935),
        pp. 1-10. Illus.

1433   "Brief von Dr. Albert Schweitzer (11-19 August 1935)."
        BRIEFE 19 (November 1935), pp. 1-17. Illus. Reprinted
        in: DOKUMENTE, pp. 89-105.

1434   "Lettre du Docteur Schweitzer (11 août 1935)." LETTRES 8
         (Nov. 1935), 15 pp.

1435   "A day at the hospital." BRITISH BULLETIN 12 (Spring 1936),
         pp. 1ff. Reprinted in BRABAZON, pp. 473-80.

1436   "Lettre du docteur Schweitzer (Septembre 1936)." LETTRES 9
         (Oct. 1936), 6 pp.

1437   "Brief von Dr. Albert Schweitzer (Günsbach, Sept. 1936)."
         BRIEFE 19 (Oct. 1936), pp. 1-4. Illus. Reprinted in:
         DOKUMENTE, pp. 106-07; translated as "Brieven uit
         Lambarene." NIEUWS 9 (Nov. 1936), pp. 1-4.

1438   "Dr. Schweitzer's report." BRITISH BULLETIN 13 (Autumn 1936),
         pp. 1-4. Illus.

1439   "Brief von Dr. Albert Schweitzer (28. Februar 1937)." BRIEFE
         20 (May 1937), pp. 1-7. Illus. Reprinted in: DOKUMENTE,
         pp. 108-112; translated as "Lettre du docteur Schweitzer
         (28 fevrier 1937)." LETTRES 10 (April 1937), 8 pp.

1440   "Dr. Schweitzer's report." BRITISH BULLETIN 14 (Spring 1937),
         pp. 2-7. Illus.

1441   "Brief von Dr. Albert Schweitzer (19. September, 26. September
         1937)." BRIEFE 21 (March 1938), pp. 1-8. Illus. Re-
         printed in: DOKUMENTE, pp. 113-17.

1442   "Dr. Schweitzer's report" (contains letters dated September 19
         and December 26, 1937). BRITISH BULLETIN 15 (Spring
         1938), pp. 2-11. Illus. Excerpted in translation with
         title "Lettre du docteur Schweitzer (19 septembre 1937)."
         LETTRES 11 (March 1938), 14 pp.

1443   "Brief von Dr. Albert Schweitzer (4. dezember 1938)." BRIEFE
         22 (Feb. 1939), pp. 1-11. Illus. Reprinted in part in:
         DOKUMENTE, pp. 118-19; translated as "Lettre du docteur
         Schweitzer (4 decembre 1938)." LETTRES 12 (Feb. 1939),
         13 pp.

1444   "Letter from Dr. Schweitzer." BRITISH BULLETIN 16 (Summer
         1939), pp. 2-11.

1445   "Letters from Lambarene (extracts)." Parts of letters from
         May 24, April 30, Sept. 21 and Oct. 25, 1944. BRITISH
         BULLETIN 17 (Jan. 1945), pp. 3-5.

Africa and Lambarene

1446   "Letters from Lambarene." BRITISH BULLETIN 18 (Spring 1946),
        pp. 3-18.

1447   "Excerpts from letters, 1947-1951." RUNDBRIEF 2 (Dec. 1951).
        Reprinted in: DOKUMENTE, pp. 154-69.

1448   "Der Alltag in Lambarene" (dated 21. Dezember 1958).
        RUNDBRIEF 15 (Jan. 14, 1960), pp. 7-12. Translated as
        "Albert Schweitzer over de huidige stand van zaken in
        zijn Ziekenhuis." NIEUWS 7:1 (July 1958), pp. 4-8.
        Illus.; also as "Daily life in Lambarene in 1958."
        BRITISH BULLETIN 24 (Sept. 1959), pp. 2-9. Illus.;
        "La vie quotidienne à Lambaréné en 1958." CAHIERS 1
        (April 1959), pp. 6-10.

1449   "Aus einem Brief Albert Schweitzers vom 23. Februar 1960 und
        vom 14. Oktober 1960." BERICHTE 27 (July 1961), pp. 3-6.

1450   "From Dr. Schweitzer." Excerpts of a letter, October 1961.
        BRITISH BULLETIN 25 (May 1962), pp. 1-2.

1451   Notes of recent news from Lambarene, including excerpts of
        letters from Albert Schweitzer and Emmy Martin. BRITISH
        BULLETIN 27 (Jan. 14, 1965), pp. 1-4. Illus.

D. Writings by Others About Schweitzer

a. Books

1452   ANSTEIN, HANS. Mein Besuch bei Dr. Albert Schweitzer in
        Lambarene. Sonderdruck aus dem Buch "Ruf und Dienst der
        ärztlichen Mission." [n.p., 192-], 11 pp., illus.

1453   BARTHÉLEMY, GUY et GREET. Au coeur du Gabon. Recontre avec
        Albert Schweitzer. Photographies A.I.D. Paris:
        Editions A.I.D. (Association d'Information pour le
        Developpement) and P.F.A.H., 1962. 117 pp., illus.
        (Peuples du Monde, vol. 2.)

1454   BESSUGES, JACQUES. Lambaréné à l'ombre de Schweitzer.
        Limoges: Dessagne, 1968. 148 pp.

1455   DEGREEF, J. D. Die Wonderdokter van Lambarene. 88 pp.

1456   DOTY, JAMES EDWARD. Postmark Lambarene: a Visit with
        Albert Schweitzer. Indianapolis: John Woolman Press,
        1965. 99 pp.

Africa and Lambarene

1457   EDSMYR, FOLKE. Albert Schweitzer, Människan vetenskapsmannen
        konstnären. Vällingby, Sweden: Verlag Harriers, 1976.

        FANONI, ROY H. Peter Parker and Albert Schweitzer. See
            Dissertations, no. 4316 below.

1458   FEDOROWSKI, GRZEGORZ. Oganga, Wielki Czarodziej. Il. J.
            Kirylenko. Warsaw: Nasza Ksiegarnia, 1967. 39 pp.

1459   FRANCK, FREDERICK S. Days with Albert Schweitzer: a Lambarene
            Landscape. Illustrated by the author. New York: Holt;
            Canada: George McLeod Ltd., 1959. xii, 178 pp. Re-
            printed Westport, Conn.: Greenwood Press, 1974.

            TRANSLATIONS

        Tage mit Albert Schweitzer. Leben und Wirken des grossen
            weissen Doktors. Mit 41 illus. des autors. Tr. Inge
            Marten. Bern, Stuttgart, Vienna: Scherz, 1960. 200 pp.

        (Same). Lizenzausg. Zürich: Büchergilde Gutenberg, 1964.
            200 pp.

        (Dutch). Het Landschap van Lambarene. 199 pp.

1460   GÖTTING, GERALD. Zu Gast in Lambarene. Begegnung mit Albert
            Schweitzer. Berlin: Union Verlag, 1964. 206 pp. Illus.

            TRANSLATIONS

        Na Navsteve v Lambarene. Tr. Vera Fedorova. (Czech).

1461   ITALIAANDER, ROLF. Im Lande Albert Schweitzers, ein Besuch in
            Lambarene. Hamburg: Broschek, 1954. 40 pp. Illus.

            (Same). Zum 100. Geburtstag des Urwaldarztes. Munich:
                Claudius Verlag, 1974. 68 pp. Illus. "Gekürzte
                Ausgabe für die Claudius-Bücherei."

            See also no. 1716 below.

            TRANSLATIONS

        In het lande van Albert Schweitzer; een bezoek aan Lambarene.
            Rotterdam: A. Donker, 1955. 38 pp. Illus.

1462   JENSEN, JANS MARINUS. Albert Schweitzer, Laegen i Urskoven.
            Copenhagen: Woels Forlag, 1929.

147

Africa and Lambarene

1463   JOY, CHARLES RHIND and MELVIN ARNOLD. The Africa of Albert
        Schweitzer. With a concluding essay by Albert
        Schweitzer. New York: Harper; Boston: Beacon Press,
        1948. 160 pp. Illus.
        (Second edition, revised). London: A. and C. Black;
            New York: Harper, 1958. 159 pp. Illus.

        TRANSLATIONS

        Het Afrika van Albert Schweitzer. Amsterdam: Het
            Vereldvenster, 1949. 159 pp.

        Bei Albert Schweitzer in Afrika. Munich: Beck, 1948.
            158 pp. Illus.

        LAGERFELT, GRETA. Fyrbåken i urskogen. See no. 1400 above.

1464   LAUTERBURG-BONJOUR, ELSA. Lambarene: Erlebnisse einer
            Bernerin im Afrikanischen Urwald. Leipzig: Felix Meiner,
            1931.

1465   MARTIN, E. Tiergeschichten um Albert Schweitzer. Dettingen:
            Freundeskreis Albert Schweitzer, 1974. 26 pp.

1466   MERCIER, ANNE-MARIE. Lambaréné. Paris: Editions des
            Horizons de France, 1958. 33 pp. Illus.

1467   MONFRINI, HENRI. Schweitzer demain. Lausanne: Payot, 1966.
            119 pp.

1468   MOVSESSIAN, SUZANNE. Départ du Bourget pour Lambaréné
            (Gabon), 1971. Vaulx-en-Vexin (Rhône), l'auteur, 99,
            Rue Anatole, France.

1469   ØSTERGARRD-CHRISTENSEN, LAVRIDS. Dansk laege hos Albert
            Schweitzer. Copenhagen: Munksgaard, 1959. 156 pp.
            Illus.

        TRANSLATIONS

        At Work with Albert Schweitzer. Tr. F. H. Lyon. Boston:
            Beacon Press, 1962. 117 pp. Illus.

1470   PATEL, M. S. Albarta Svaitjhara. 1964. 110 pp. Illus.
            (Gujarat Vidyapith. Gujarata Vidyapith Granthavali 140.)
            In Gujarati.

1471   PEET, HUBERT WILLIAM. Schweitzer of the African Forest.
            London: The Religious Tract Society, 1933. 31 pp.
            (The Little Library of Biography.)

Africa and Lambarene

1472   PFENNINGER, URSULA. Tiergeschichten aus Lambarene. Bern: P. Haupt, 1965. 85 pp. Illus.

1473   PIERSON, ANTOINE. Le Clair regard de Schweitzer; ou la leçon de Lambaréné. Casablanca: Maroc-Médical, 1956. Ill.

1474   RIBERAUER, RICHARD. A Lambarenei Doktor. Budapest, 1932.

1475   RYSSEL, EDITH. Hos Albert Schweitzer i Urskoven. Copenhagen: Berlingske Forlag, 1954. 193 pp. Illus.

1476   _____. Albert Schweitzer den store laege i urskoven. Odense: Normann, 1958. 44 pp. Illus. (Normanns Laeseserie.)

1477   SERMONTI, ENRICO. Schweitzer e la Coscienza del Terzo Mondo. Rome: Cermonese, 1974. 126 pp. (Series Uomini e Problemi, 22.)

1478   SHYR, YEE TSEUR. [Albert Schweitzer in Lambarene.] Tr. Lin Maio-Ling. Taiwan: Chih-Wen Co., 1975. 150 pp.

1479   STALDER, HANS. Albert Schweitzer und sein Afrikanisches Werk. Zürich: Beer, 1933.

1480   STEFFAHN, HARALD. Abend am Ogowe. Heidenheim (Brenz): Hergenheimer Zeitung Verlagsanstalt, n.d. 40 pp.

1481   SUNIOUSEN, SEVALD. Legen i Urskogen. Albert Schweitzer. Oslo, 1950.

1482   SWIRIDOFF, PAUL. Lambarene. Pfullingen: Günther Neske, 1966. 102 pp. Illus. (Swiridoff-Bildbande, no. 17.)

1483   TAAP, ERIKA. Lambarene Tagebuch. Berlin: Evangelische Verlagsanstalt, 1964. 124 pp. Sixth edition, 1967; Seventh edition, 1968; Tenth edition, 1974, 143 pp.

1484   TAKAHASHI, ISAO. Omoide no Rambarene. 1971. 158 pp.

1485   _____. Shuwaitsā Byōin. 1964. 174 pp. Illus., ports.

1486   TANNO, S. Afurika no Ijin. Tokyo: Hada Haneda Shoten, 1950. 72 pp.

1487   TERNING, OSKAR. Den store doktorn, Albert Schweitzer. 2nd edition. Stockholm: Gummesson, 1954. 158 pp. Illus.

Africa and Lambarene

1488　URQUHART, CLARA.　With Dr. Schweitzer in Lambarene.　Text and
　　　　photographs.　London:　Harrap, 1957.　63 pp.　Illus.

　　　　WENZEL, LENE and FERDINAND BECHTLE.　Albert Schweitzer--
　　　　Lambarene einst und jetzt.　See Books for Youth, no. 4257
　　　　below.

1489　WINKLER, JOHAN.　Naar het Land van Brazza en Albert
　　　　Schweitzer.　's-Gravenhage:　D. A. Daamen, 1951.　189 pp.
　　　　Illus.

　　　　WORBOYS, LAWRENCE W.　The Missionary Principles and Methods
　　　　of Albert Schweitzer.　See Dissertations, no. 4346 below.

1490　WOYTT-SECRETAN, MARIE.　Albert Schweitzer baut Lambarene.
　　　　Königstein im Taunus:　Langewiesche, 1957.　112 pp.　Illus.

　　　　TRANSLATIONS

　　　　Albert Schweitzer construit l'hôpital de Lambaréné.
　　　　Paris, Strasbourg:　Oberlin, 1959. 112 pp.

　　　　(Second edition).　Strasbourg:　Editions des Dernieres
　　　　Nouvelles de Strasbourg, 1975.

1491　_____.　Albert Schweitzer.　26 pp.　(Excerpts from the above
　　　　and from Albert Schweitzer, un médecin dans la fôret
　　　　vierge, no. 322 above.)

1492　_____.　Albert Schweitzers Lambarene lebt.　Königstein im
　　　　Taunus:　Karl R. Langewiesche Nachfolger Hans Köster
　　　　(Das Blauebuch), 1979.　Photo album with commentary
　　　　covering 1931-1979.

　　b.　Articles, Parts of Books

1493　ADLER, ROLF.　"Brief aus Lambarene" (August 1960).　BERICHTE
　　　　27 (July 1961), pp. 7-8.　Reprinted in RUNDBRIEF 19
　　　　(Jan. 14, 1962), pp. 21-22.

1494　"Albert Schweitzer binnenkort 90. jaar.　Toekomst van
　　　　'Lambarene' not onduidelijk.　Binnenkort overleg op int.
　　　　conferentie."　Nieuwe Apeldoorns Courant (Apeldoorn),
　　　　Nov. 18, 1964, p. 7.　Port.

1495　"Albert Schweitzer geht in den Urwald."　Der Speyerer
　　　　Protestant (Speyer, Germany) 3 (1932), p. 68.

Africa and Lambarene

1496   "Albert Schweitzer in den Augen von Afrikanern." In:
        CHARISMATISCHE DIAKONIE, pp. 58-60.

1497   "Albert Schweitzer, le grand docteur. Zum erstenmal
        Lambarene-bericht im Fernsehen--Max Sefrin würdigt
        Rufer zum Frieden." Neue Zeit (East Berlin) 14
        (Jan. 16, 1960), p. 10.

1498   "Albert Schweitzer. Opvatting van 90-jarige botst tegen
        onbesuisde nationalistische staat. Toekomst van het
        ziekenhuis onzeker na Schweitzers dood." Het Vaderland
        (The Hague), Nov. 19, 1964, p. 13.

1499   "Albert Schweitzer trouva en Walter Munz le disciple apte à
        reprendre le flambeau." Le Figaro (Paris), ed. de Paris
        6539 (Sept. 7, 1965), p. 24.

1500   "Albert Schweitzer und sein Hospital in Lambarene . . ."
        (recording). Credo, best. nr. GK-B 510/8. Quotes from
        Schweitzer and his helpers.

1501   "Albert Schweitzer's hospital in Gabon to be modernized."
        The New York Times, Feb. 15, 1966, p. 10.

1502   "Als Pflegerin bei Dr. Albert Schweitzer im Urwaldspital zu
        Lambarene. Ein interessanter Bericht einer Elsässerin."
        RUNDBRIEF 3 (Jan. 14, 1953), pp. 7-9.

1503   "Among the human leopards." The Literary Digest (New York)
        110 (Sept. 26, 1931), pp. 18-19.

1504   "An African missionary." Tablet (London) 204:5970
        (Oct. 23, 1954), p. 397.

1505   ANDERSON, ERICA. "À 80 ans, Schweitzer retourne pour le 21^e
        fois chez les lépreux." Paris Match (Paris) 304
        (Jan. 22/29, 1955), pp. 44-47. Illus.

1506   _____. "God bless all living things." Ladies' Home Journal
        (Philadelphia) 80:10 (Dec. 1963), pp. 26-28. Illus.

1507   _____, photographer. "He dedicated his life." Episcopal
        Churchnews (Richmond, Va.) 119:40 (Nov. 8/15, 1953),
        pp. 22-25. Cover port., illus. (Picture story).

1508   _____. "Schweitzer and Lambarene." The Saturday Review
        (New York) 48:39 (Sept. 25, 1965), pp. 19-20f.

151

Africa and Lambarene

1509 ANSTEIN, HANS. "Bei Dr. Schweitzer in Lambarene." In:
Afrika wie ich es erlebte. Stuttgart, Basel:
Evangelischer Missionsverlag, 1933, pp. 69-75. Illus.

1510 "Arbeit und Plannung der 'Association de l'Hôpital du
Dr. Albert Schweitzer.'" BERICHTE 29 (April 1966),
pp. 27-29. Reprinted in RUNDBRIEF 29:2 (Dec. 1, 1966),
pp. 12-15.

1511 ARNOLD, MELVILLE. "In the African night the voice of Bach."
The Christian Register (Boston) 126:8 (Sept. 1947),
p. 527.

1512 ARNOLD, TRAUTE. "Begegnung mit Menschen aus Lambarene."
Neue Zeit (East Berlin) 13 (Jan. 15, 1961), p. 4.

1513 ASHFORD, NICHOLAS. "Schweitzer philosophy lives on as his
hospital is rebuilt." The Times (London), Aug. 30, 1977,
p. 12. Illus. Reprinted in the A.I.S.L. Bulletin 5
(Nov. 1977), p. 42.

1514 AURELIUS, BENGT. "Kristus läkaren. Ein skisse, tillägnad
Albert Schweitzer." In: MANNEN, pp. 137-49.

1515 "Aus Professor Albert Schweitzers ärztlicher Missione." Die
Evangelischen Missionen (Berlin-Steglitz) 33:4 (1927),
pp. 78-81.

1516 "L'avenir de l'Hôpital de Lambaréné." CAHIERS 15 (June 1966),
pp. 19-20. Translated as "Die Zukunft des Spitals von
Dr. Albert Schweitzer in Lambarene." In: CHARISMATISCHE
DIAKONIE, pp. 60-62.

1517 BAKER, RICHARD. "A South African visits Lambarene."
Personality (Bloemfontein, South Africa), Jan. 5, 1967,
pp. 60-65. Port., illus.

1518 BALSIGER, GRETI. "Ein helles Band und ein Sonntag." In:
HALFEN, pp. 139-50.

1519 BARTHÉLEMY, GUY. "Albert Schweitzer et les bêtes." La Vie
des Bêtes (Paris) 4 (Nov. 1958), pp. 26-28. Illus.

1520 _____. "Un homme et son oeuvre. Le Dr. Schweitzer et
Lambaréné." La Revue Française de L'Elite Européenne
(Paris) 6:60 (Sept. 1954), pp. 5-8.

1521 _____. "Quelques précisions sur l'oeuvre du Dr. Schweitzer en
Afrique." Les Amis d'Albert Schweitzer (Jan. 14, 1954),
pp. 8-10. Illus.

Africa and Lambarene

1522   _____. "Séjour à Lambaréné." CAHIERS 4 (Dec. 1960), pp. 6-8.

1523   _____ et GREET BARTHÉLEMY. "Une soirée à Lambaréné."
         CAHIERS 5 (Sept. 1961), pp. 3-4.

1524   "Basic human standards." Time (New York) 54 (July 18, 1949),
         pp. 58ff.

1525   BAUMANN, HANS. "Tecknik im Urwaldspital." BERICHTE 30
         (Sept. 1967), pp. 26-27. Illus.

1526   BAUR, HANS. "Albert Schweitzers neue Sorgen und Pläne."
         Schweizerisches Protestantenblatt (Basel) 49:27
         (July 3, 1926), pp. 224-25; 29 (July 17, 1926), pp. 241-43;
         30 (July 24, 1926), pp. 249-50.

1527   _____. "Die Hungersnot in Lambarene." NEUES 7, p. 1.

1528   _____. "Neues von Albert Schweitzer." Schweizerisches
         Protestantenblatt (Basel) 47:13 (March 29, 1924), p. 103;
         40 (Oct. 4, 1924), pp. 318-19.

1529   _____. "Von Andende nach Adoli-Nanongo. Aus Briefen."
         NEUES 9 (Whitsuntide 1927), pp. 1-5. Includes portion
         of a letter from Albert Schweitzer.

1530   _____. "Ein Zimmerman für Lambarene." Schweizerisches
         Protestantenblatt (Basel) 49:9 (Feb. 27, 1926), p. 71.

1531   BAUR, HERMANN. Selection without title. In: BEGEGNUNG,
         pp. 162-65. Excerpted from FESTGABE.

1532   _____. "Die Zukunft von Lambarene." BERICHTE 31
         (June 1969), pp. 15-17.

1533_____. "Zukunft Lambarene." RUNDBRIEF 33 (Oct. 10, 1970),
         pp. 31-32.

1534   BEAUFORT, JOHN. "Missionary from Lambarene translates his
         mission." Christian Science Monitor (Boston), June 29,
         1949. Port.

1535   BEERLI, MADELEINE. "Hilaires Huhn." In: HALFEN, pp. 201-04.

1536   BEIJER, ERIK. "Albert Schweitzer. Människovännen i tropiska
         urskogen." Julhälsningar till Församlingarna i Visby
         Stift (Visby, Sweden) 32 (1954), pp. 121-38. Illus.,
         ports.

153

Africa and Lambarene

1537 BERGGRAV, EIVIND. "Kjaerlighet till Kannibaler." Kirke og
      Kultur (Kristiania) 29 (July 1922), pp. 307-17; reprinted
      in 58 (1953), pp. 236-48.

1538 BERNARD, ALBERT. "Neues aus dem Urwaldspital von Lambarene."
      Les Dernières Nouvelles de Colmar, Jan. 13, 1959.

1539 BJERHAGEN, JAKOB. "Intryck från ett besök: Lambarene." In:
      FYRBÅKEN, pp. 161-64.

1540 BLANDFORD, LINDA. "Schweitzer hospital may have to close."
      The Sunday Times (London), Dec. 10, 1967 (air edition),
      p. 4. Photos.

1541 BLOMBERG, HARRY. "Kampen i Kongo." Svenska Morgonbladet
      (Stockholm), Aug. 30, 1946.

1542 _____. "Orgeltoner i urskogen." Jönköping-Posten
      (Jönköping, Sweden), May 15, 1936. Reprinted in Västgöta
      Demokraten (Shövde), June 4, 1936.

1543 BÖHMER, GÜNTER. "Lambarene--das Heiligtum des Urwalddoktors.
      Ein Reisebericht." Münchner Merkur (Munich) 306
      (Dec. 21/22, 1957), p. 25. Illus.

1544 BÖHRINGER, MARIANNE. "Tiere in Lambarene." BERICHTE 25
      (Nov. 1953), pp. 4-6. Reprinted in RUNDBRIEF 5
      (June 1, 1954), pp. 23-25; also in DOKUMENTE, pp. 210-13.
      Translated as "Dieren in Lambarene." NIEUWS 2:4
      (March 1954), pp. 55-56.

1545 BOIS-REYMOND, LILI DU. "Weshalb ein Genius in den Urwald
      ging." Die Christliche Welt (Gotha) 44:24 (Dec. 13, 1924),
      p. 1218.

1546 BOWSER, HALLOWELL. "Lambarene since Schweitzer." The
      Saturday Review (New York) 50:47 (Nov. 25, 1967), p. 30.

1547 BREIT, HARVEY. "Albert Schweitzer." In: Writer Observed.
      Cleveland: World Publishing, 1956, pp. 61-65.

1548 BROCK, GEORGE. "Weisser Mann, go home." Bunte/Münchner/
      Frankfurter Illustrierte (Offenburg/Baden) 3
      (Jan. 20, 1963), pp. 28-37. Illus. Letters to the
      editor in reply by H. J. Klinger, Paul Dämmig and Klaus
      Heine can be found in 8 (Feb. 24, 1963), p. 74 and 10
      (March 10, 1963), p. 80.

1549   BRODMANN, ROMAN. "Die Wahrheit über Lambarene." Zürcher
           Woche (Zürich), Jan. 10, 1964, pp. 1f. Reprinted in:
           Albert Schweitzer zum 90sten Geburtstag. Soziale Schriften
           no. 41. Schriftenreihe des Landesverbandes freier
           Schweizer Arbeiter. St. Gallen: Fehr'sche Buchhandlung,
           1964, pp. 9-32; reprinted with title "Begegnung mit Albert
           Schweitzer." Universitas (Stuttgart) 20:1 (Jan. 1965),
           pp. 24-28; reprinted without title in: BEGEGNUNG, pp. 67-
           70; translated as "La vérité sur Lambaréné." Illus. de
           Wilhelm Kaufmann. Saisons d'Alsace (Strasbourg) 10:14
           (Spring 1965), pp. 120-52. Illus., port. Offprint pub-
           lished by l'Association Francaise des Amis d'Albert
           Schweitzer with title "Albert Schweitzer dans sa vérité."

1550   BRUWER, T. "Hond en hoender kom saam hospitael toe." Sarie
           Marais (Capetown, South Africa) 14:6--15:1 (July 3-
           July 7, 1963). Illus.

1551   BUDDE, KARL. "Nachrichten von Albert Schweitzer." Die
           Christliche Welt (Gotha) 39:46/7 (Nov. 19, 1925),
           pp. 1049-50.

1552   _____. "Das Neueste von Albert Schweitzer." Die Christliche
           Welt (Gotha) 39:27/28 (July 2, 1925), pp. 615-16.

1553   BUNGENER, PIERRE. "Le docteur Schweitzer. Il a donné 50
           ans à l'Afrique." L'Illustré Protestant (Lyon) 12:109
           (June 1963), pp. 16-17. Illus.

1554   CAMERON, ALAN. "A visit to Lambarene." COURIER, Winter 1976,
           pp. 19-22.

1555   CAMERON, JAMES. ["Visit to Lambarene."] News Chronicle
           (London) Dec. 8, 1953. Translated as "Besuch in
           Lambarene." Series of three articles. Stuttgarter
           Zeitung 10:5-7 (Jan. 7-9, 1954), pp. 9, 30. Port.,
           illus.; also in Englische Rundschau (Bonn) 4:1
           (Jan. 8, 1954), pp. 10-11; 4:2 (Jan. 15, 1954), pp. 22-
           23; 4:3 (Jan. 22, 1954), pp. 38-39; reprinted with
           titles "Bei Albert Schweitzer im Urwaldhospital. Besuch
           in Lambarene," "Spaziergang mit Albert Schweitzer," and
           "Abschied von Lambarene" in Katholischer Digest
           (Aschaffenburg) 8:6-8 (June-August 1954), pp. 501-06,
           672-76 and 98-104.

1556   "Le carrière Africaine du docteur Schweitzer." L'Entraineur
           (Vigner, Switz.) 25:2 (Jan. 2, 1954), 31 pp. Short
           essays by various authors, and other contents.

Africa and Lambarene

1557   CAULET, MAX. "Bericht des Verwalters." BERICHTE 34
       (Aug. 1972), pp. 6-7.

1558   _____. "Bericht des Verwalters." RUNDBRIEF 40 (1975),
       p. 119.

1559   _____. "Bericht des Verwalters." BERICHTE 42 (Oct. 1976),
       pp. 7-10. Illus.

1560   _____. "Max Caulet über seine Spitalsorgen." RUNDBRIEF 46
       (Nov. 1978), pp. 13-14. From an interview with Dernières
       Nouvelles d'Alsace, end of May 1978. For two additional
       interviews with Max Caulet, see nos. 1816 and 1948 below.

1561   "Un centre écologique dans la ligne Schweitzer." A.I.S.L.
       Bulletin 3 (Feb. 1977), p. 11.

1562   CHELMINSKI, RUDOLPH. "Goodbye at Lambarene. Albert
       Schweitzer is buried at his jungle mission." Life
       (New York) 59:12 (Sept. 17, 1965), pp. 90-92f. Port.,
       illus.

1563   CHESTERMAN, CLEMENT C. C. "Dr. Schweitzer's hospital"
       (letter to the editor). The Times (London), Oct. 25, 1976,
       p. 13.

1564   _____. "The strange case of Dives and Lazarus." In:
       JUBILEE, pp. 375-83. Translated as "Die besonderen Fälle
       des reichen Mannes und des armen." In: DENKEN UND WEG,
       pp. 358-63.

1565   COOLIDGE, GLORIA. "Return to the forest hospital." The
       Christian Register (Boston) 129-10 (Nov. 1950), pp. 17-19.

1566   _____. "Schweitzer's jungle hospital." The Christian
       Register (Boston) 128:6 (June 1949), pp. 17-18ff.

1567   CORSON, J.-P. "Weekend à Lambarene." Aesculape 43
       (Feb. 1960), pp. 3-38. Illus., ports.

1568   C., N. [COUSINS, NORMAN.] "Jungle doctor go home." The
       Saturday Review (New York) 46:11 (March 16, 1963), p. 30.
       Reprinted in Science Digest (New York) 54:1 (July 1963),
       pp. 50-52.

1569   _____. "Lambarene." In: BEGEGNUNG, pp. 3-14. Excerpts
       from the author's book Albert Schweitzer und sein
       Lambarene, no. 242 above.

1570 _____. "Lambarene and the image of Schweitzer" (editorial).
The Saturday Review (New York) 40:52 (Dec. 28, 1957),
pp. 18–20.

1571 _____. "Lambarene revisited." The Saturday Review (New
York) 52 (Oct. 4, 1969), pp. 28–32. Illus. Reprinted in
The Enquirer and News (Battle Creek, Mich.), Sunday,
Jan. 18, 1970, pp. A12f.

1572 D., A. "Wolken übern Urwaldkrankenhaus. Lambarenes Zukunft
ist ungewiss-Sorgen um Schweitzers Werk." Telegraf
(West Berlin) 164 (July 18, 1957), p. 3.

1573 d'A., A. "Der Urwalddoktor kehrt zurück." Schweizerische
Allgemeine Volks-Zeitung (Zofingen) 31 (July 30, 1955),
p. 24.

1574 DANAN, ALEXIS. "Visite à Albert Schweitzer, providence des
lépreux." Franc-Tireur (Paris), June 20 and 21, 1951.

1575 DARLING, ANNE. "The Schweitzer hospital after Schweitzer."
Saturday Review World (New York) 1 (March 23, 1974),
pp. 62–63.

1576 DAUCOURT. W. "En mission à l'hôpital Albert Schweitzer
Lambaréné du 7 août au 1er septembre 1969." NOUVELLES
31 (May 1970), pp. 15–19.

1577 DAUR, RUDOLF. "Warum nach Afrika?" RUNDBRIEF 8 (Nov. 1, 1955),
pp. 43–44. Reprinted in: DOKUMENTE, pp. 269–70.

1578 DAVENPORT, MANUEL M. "The moral paternalism of Albert
Schweitzer." Ethics (Chicago) 84:2 (Jan. 1974),
pp. 116–27.

1579 DE PURY, ROLAND. "Visite au Gabon." Journal de Société des
Missions Évangéliques de Paris 133:5 (June/July 1958),
pp. 135–36.

1580 "Les déclarations d'Albert Schweitzer sur la décolonisation
politique de l'Afrique noire." Aux Ecoutes (Paris),
Sept. 9, 1965.

1581 DEFAYE, CHRISTIAN. "L'hôpital Albert Schweitzer à Lambaréné
continue. . . ." Tribune de Lausanne, Dec. 25–29, 1965.
Issued also as a brochure by l'Association suisse d'Aide
à l'Hôpital Albert Schweitzer à Lambaréné, section de la
Suisse romande. Numero Special (April 1966), 32 pp.

Africa and Lambarene

1582 DELAGE, EDMOND. "Un après-midi dans la brousse chez Albert
        Schweitzer. Nouvel Pris Nobel de la Paix." Le Figaro
        (Paris) 2845 (Nov. 2, 1953), p. 7.

1583 DENEKE, MARGARET. "Albert Schweitzer, physician, philosopher
        and musician." The Christian Advocate (New York) 108
        (April 27, 1933), pp. 390-91.

1584 DENSFORD, KATHERINE J. "A visit to Dr. Albert Schweitzer's
        hospital at Lambarene, French Equatorial Africa."
        Nursing Mirror (London) Supplement 15 (March 1, 1957).
        Illus.

        DESAI, RAM, ed. Albert Schweitzer--an African Image. See
        Sithole, Ndabaningi, no. 1981 below.

1585 DIAZ, ALBERTO FRANCO. "Oganga: Capitulo XI, El Viejo
        Doctor." Arco Iris (Montivideo) 8:85 (n.d.), pp. 14-15.

1586 DINNER-OBRIST, ANITA and FRITZ. "Im Albert-Schweitzer-Spital
        in Lambarene, 28. Juni bis 12. Juli 1958." BERICHTE 26
        (May 1959), pp. 2-10. Translated as "Visite à l'Hôpital
        de Lambaréné, 28 Juin au 12 juillet 1958." Rapports sur
        Lambarene (Bâle) 26 (May 1959), pp. 2-10.

        "DIOGENES." "Albert Schweitzer." See Philosophy, no. 2451
        below.

1587 DOTY, JAMES EDWARD. "My visit with Albert Schweitzer."
        Together (Chicago) 1:10 (July 15, 1957), pp. 34-42.
        Illus., port.

1588 "Dr. Albert Schweitzer im Strassburger 'Centre de transfusion
        sanguine.' Zweihundert Blutspender aus dem Elsass und
        aus Lothringen gaben Blut für das Spital von Lambarene."
        Les Dernières Nouvelles d'Alsace (Strasbourg) 274
        (Nov. 22, 1955), p. 13.

1589 "Dr. Schweitzer." The Christian Register (Boston) 122:4
        (April 1943), p. 139.

1590 "Dr. Schweitzer described." The Baptist (Chicago) 14:1
        (Jan. 14, 1933), p. 2.

1591 "Dr. Schweitzer explains plans for leprosy work on eve of
        departure." Voice of Missions (New York) 50:8 (Aug. 1949),
        p. 5.

Africa and Lambarene

1592   "Dr. Schweitzer: misery in paradise." <u>Africa Today</u> 1:1
            (Feb. 1960), p. 1.

1593   "Dr. Schweitzer: the jungle is home." <u>Philippines Herald</u>
            <u>Magazine</u> (Manila), May 4, 1963, p. 36.

1594   DU BOIS, W. E. B. "The Black man and Albert Schweitzer."
            In: JUBILEE, pp. 119-30.

1595   DUNSTAN, J. LESLIE. "Modern spiritual frontiersmen--Africa's
            greatest friend." <u>The Friend</u> (Honolulu) 106:3 (March 1936),
            p. 46.

1596   DURAND-REVILLE, LUC. "L'affrontement des complexes dans
            l'assistance au Tiers-Monde." CAHIERS 7 (Sept. 1962),
            pp. 10-12.

1597   _____. "Lambaréné 1957." NOUVELLES 4 (June 1958), pp. 1-2.

1598   _____. "Nouvelles confessions de Lambaréné." CAHIERS 9
            (May 1963), pp. 8-12.

1599   _____. "Présence d'Albert Schweitzer." <u>Resonances</u> (Paris)
            2e trimestre 1954, pp. 41-47. Illus.

1600   EASTVOLD, S. C. "Albert Schweitzer, PLC's newest alumnus."
            In: <u>Around the World in 180 Days</u>. Minneapolis:
            Augsburg Publishing House, n.d., pp. 55-65.

1601   ECKERT-SCHWEITZER, RHENA. "The Albert Schweitzer Hospital."
            In: THE CONVOCATION RECORD, pp. IV/5-8.

1602   _____. "Bericht der Administrativen Leiterin." BERICHTE 30
            (Sept. 1967), pp. 16-17.

1603   _____. "Fifty years at Lambaréné." COURIER, May 1964,
            pp. 149-51. Port.

1604   _____. "Fonctionnement de l'hôpital et projets d'avenir."
            CAHIERS 21 (June 1969), pp. 9-11.

1605   _____. "Lambarene 1966." RUNDBRIEF 30 (1967).

1606   _____. "Lambarene en 1964." CAHIERS/BELGE 5 (April 1965),
            pp. 16-20.

1607   _____. "Lambarene et l'aide aux enfants Biafra." CAHIERS
            20 (Dec. 1968), pp. 14-16.

Africa and Lambarene

1608   _____. "Lambarene und die Zukunft." RUNDBRIEF 31 (1968).

1609   _____. "Mme. Rhena Eckert-Schweitzer reports." COURIER,
        April-May 1966, pp. 19-21.

1610   _____. "Pläne für heute und morgen." RUNDBRIEFE/DDR 11
        (1967), pp. 1-5.

1611   _____. "Schweitzer; fé inabalável na vida humana." Díario
        de São Paulo, October 11, 1964.

1612   _____. "Das Spital arbeitet weiter." RUNDBRIEF 27
        (Nov. 21, 1965), pp. 42-44.

1613   EHRBAR, K. "Ein Gespräch am Ogowe." BERICHTE 42 (Oct. 1976),
        pp. 21-23.

1614   EIGENHUIS, JAN. "Albert Schweitzer en zijn negers."
        Amsterdamer Weekblad, April 19, 1930.

1615   ELLERBROCK, LEE. "Berichte aus Lambarene." RUNDBRIEFE/DDR
        23 (1973), pp. 20-27.

1616   _____. "Lambarene--Bericht nr. 4, März 1973." RUNDBRIEF 37
        (Sept. 4, 1973), pp. 2-7.

1617   _____. "Lambarene--Bericht nr. 5, Juni 1973." RUNDBRIEF 37
        (Sept. 4, 1973), pp. 8-11.

1618   _____. "Rapport de Lambaréné, Septembre 1972." CAHIERS 28
        (Spring 1973), pp. 18-19.

1619   _____. "Rapports sur Lambarene, Decembre 1972 et mars 1973."
        CAHIERS 29 (Summer 1973), pp. 22-27.

1620   _____. "'Rundbriefe' aus dem Spital." RUNDBRIEFE/DDR 22
        (1973), pp. 15-21.

1621   ELST, P. R. VAN DER. "Bij Prof. Albert Schweitzer te
        Lambarene." Buiten (Amsterdam) 26:11 (March 12, 1932),
        pp. 128-31. Illus.

1622   "Die Emanzipation der Kolonialvölker--Albert Schweitzer; ein
        schwieriger Prozess." Frankfurter Allgemeine Zeitung
        (Frankfurt a.M.) 257 (Nov. 4, 1954), p. 5.

1623   EPARVIER, JEAN. "La prodigieuse destinée du Docteur
        Schweitzer." France-Soir (Paris) 2176-2178
        (July 29-31, 1951), p. 8.

1624   "Ernstige kritiek op Albert Schweitzer." Trouw (Amsterdam),
        Nov. 21, 1964.

1625   EVOLOGA, J. F. "A l'intention de l'hôpital Dr. Albert
        Schweitzer. Regard sur le travail et sa discipline."
        A.I.S.L. Bulletin 8 (Nov. 1978), pp. 48-49.

1626   EXMAN, EUGENE. "God's own man." United Nations World
        (New York) 6:12 (Dec. 1952), pp. 29-34. Illus.,
        cover port.

1627   _____. "A visit with Albert Schweitzer." Presbyterian Life
        (Philadelphia) 4:23 (Nov. 24, 1951), pp. 14-21. Illus.,
        port.

1628   FAHRENKRUG, ARTUR. "Desde 1913 Albert Schweitzer vive
        auxiliando os selvagens africanos." Folha da Tarde,
        July 10, 1957.

1629   FEHR-WELTER, A. "Op Bezoek bij Prof. Albert Schweitzer in
        Afrikas Oerwoud." Algemeen Handelsblad (Amsterdam),
        Nov. 7 and 8, 1929.

1630   FEICHTINGER, GEORG. "Albert Schweitzer, der Negerdoktor."
        Biochemische Monatsblätter (Leipzig) 9:1 (Jan. 1932),
        pp. 18-21.

1631   FERNANDEZ, JAMES W. "The sound of bells in a Christian
        country--in quest of the historical Schweitzer."
        Massachusetts Review (Amherst, Mass.) 5:3 (Spring 1964),
        pp. 537-62.

1632   FINK, ROBERT. "Ein Besuch bei Dr. Albert Schweitzer in
        Lambarene." Schweizerische Ärztezeitung (Bern) 34
        (Dec. 11, 1953), pp. 453-58.

1633   _____. "Lambarene heute: 1974/75." RUNDBRIEF 40
        (Jan. 14, 1975), pp. 25-29.

1634   _____. "Lambarene--Sommer 1978." RUNDBRIEF 46 (Nov. 1978),
        pp. 6-9.

1635   FISCHER, EDITH. "Appell zum Glauben an das Gute." RUNDBRIEF
        18 (July 15, 1961), pp. 44-48.

1636   _____. "Lambarene heute." RUNDBRIEFE/DDR 21 (1973), pp. 3-7.

1637   _____. "Lebensbereicherung durch Albert Schweitzer."
        RUNDBRIEF 45 (May 1978), pp. 50-54.

Africa and Lambarene

1638   _____. "Meine dritte Lambarene-Reise." RUNDBRIEFE/DDR 7
         (1966), pp. 4-6.

1639   FISCHER, GERHARD. "Lambarene--gestern, heute, morgen." In:
         VERMÄCHTNIS UND WIRKLICHKEIT, pp. 91-97.

1640   _____. "Spital setzt Tätigkeit fort." RUNDBRIEFE/DDR 28
         (1976), pp. 7-9.

1641   FISCHER, R. "Im Schussfeld der Reporter." BERICHTE 42
         (Oct. 1976), pp. 23-24.

1642   FLIFLET, ALBERT LANGE. "Hos Albert Schweitzer." Aftenposten
         (Oslo) 502-04 (Oct. 30-Nov. 2, 1954), p. 3 in each issue.
         Illus.

1643   _____. "En vår hos Albert Schweitzer." Samtid och Framtid
         (Stockholm) 12:3 (March 1955), pp. 126-28.

1644   FLUCK, DAVID A. "Trenton doctor in the Congo. Finds
         Schweitzer healthy and a very busy man." Trenton Evening
         Times (Trenton, N.J.), Sept. 5, 1961.

1645   FORREST, A. C. "An editor's visit to Schweitzer's Lambarene."
         United Church Observer (Toronto) Old Series 128:10, New
         Series 20:3 (April 1, 1958), pp. 7ff.

1646   "46 anos de medicina no corcão da Africa." Folha da Manha,
         Aug. 30, 1959.

1647   FRANCK, FREDERICK S. "Schweitzer and the new Africa." The
         Atlantic Monthly (Boston) 208:5 (Nov. 1961), pp. 53-56.
         Excerpted from African Sketchbook, no. 1459 above.

1648   _____. [Text without title.] In: BEGEGNUNG, pp. 15-24.
         Excerpted from Tage mit Albert Schweitzer, no. 1459 above.

1649   FREYER, PAUL-HERBERT. "Gespräch in Lambarene." RUNDBRIEFE/
         DDR 2 (Nov. 30, 1963), pp. 9-12.

1650   _____. "Letzter Besuch in Lambarene." RUNDBRIEFE/DDR 6
         (1965), pp. 17-21.

1651   FRIEDRICH, LOTTE. "Das Herz befiehlt es." RUNDBRIEFE/DDR
         2 (Nov. 30, 1963), pp. 16-18.

1652   _____. "In gemeinsamen Dienst verbunden." RUNDBRIEFE/DDR
         11 (1967), pp. 14-16.

1653   "50 Jahre in Lambarene." <u>Schweizer Illustrierte Zeitung</u>
        (Zofingen) 52:16 (April 15, 1963), pp. 52-53. Illus.

1654   FÜLLEMANN, EMMY. "Aus jüngster Zeit." In: HALFEN,
        pp. 160-64.

1655   FÜSSLI, O. "Prof. Dr. Albert Schweitzer und seine Tätigkeit
        in Urwald Aequatorialafrikas." <u>Illustrierte
        Wochenschrift</u>, April 18, 1925.

1656   GAERTNER, HENRYK. "Schweitzer jako lekarz." <u>Ruch Muzyczny</u>
        (Warsaw) 20:13 (1976), pp. 17-19. Illus.

1657   _____. "Szpital Alberta Schweitzera w Lambaréné."
        <u>Szpitalnictwo Polskie</u> (Warsaw) 5 (1976), pp. 219-25.

1658   GAGNEBIN, EDMONDE. "Die Schulschwester, Edmonde Gagnebin,
        berichtet." RUNDBRIEF 46 (Nov. 1978), pp. 9-10.

1659   "Eine Geburtstagfeier im Urwald." <u>Schweizerisches
        Protestantenblatt</u> (Basel) 48:2 (Jan. 10, 1925), pp. 15-16.

1660   GERHOLD, LOTTE. "Lambaréné 1961." BRITISH BULLETIN 25
        (May 1962), pp. 2-6. Illus.

1661   GILLESPIE, NOEL A. "Letters" (dated February 29, March 22
        and April 21, 1924). NEUES 2 (Pfingsten 1924), pp. 1-5.

1662   _____. [Letter dated July 20, 1924.] NEUES 3 (Oct. 1924),
        pp. 5-6.

1663   [_____.] "With Schweitzer in Lambarene. Noel Gillespie's
        letters from Africa." <u>Wisconsin Magazine of History</u>
        (Madison) 54:3 (Spring 1971), pp. 167-204. For other
        letters by Gillespie, see Jacobi, Erwin R., no. 1364
        above.

1664   GÖTTING, GERALD. "Licht über dem schwarzen Kontinent.
        Gespräch Gerald Göttings . . . über seine Afrika-Reise
        und den Besuch in Lambarene." <u>Neue Zeit</u> (East Berlin)
        43 (Feb. 20, 1960), pp. 1, 3.

1665   _____. "Zwölf Tage in Lambarene. Besuch bei Albert
        Schweitzer." <u>Neue Zeit</u> (East Berlin) 49 (Feb. 27, 1960),
        p. 7. Illus.

1666   GOLDSCHMIDT, HELMUT. ". . .die Erlösung bringen wollen . . .
        Im Urwaldspital Dr. Albert Schweitzer." <u>Neue Illustrierte
        Wochenschau</u> (Vienna) 48:20 (May 19, 1957), pp. 5-6.

Africa and Lambarene

1667   _____. "In der Leprastation Dr. Schweitzers." Neue
         Illustrierte Wochenschau (Vienna) 48:21 (May 26, 1957),
         p. 6.

1668   GOLETTY-BRAZZAVILLE, MAX. "Die Klinik im Urwald. Besuch bei
         Albert Schweitzer." Heute und Morgen (Düsseldorf) 1:5
         (May 1951), pp. 190-91.

1669   GONGGRIJP, FRITZ. "Max Caulet beheert Albert Schweitzers
         Erfenis: 'Lambarene is nieuw leven begonnen.'" EERBIED
         27:2 (Aug. 1978), pp. 11-12.

1670   GONSER, SOFIE. "Besuch in Lambarene." RUNDBRIEF 18
         (July 15, 1961), pp. 37-43. Illus.

1671   GOSSETT, PIERRE et RENÉE. L'Afrique, les Africains. 3 vols.
         Paris: René Juilliard, 1958-59. Albert Schweitzer:
         Vol. 1: France-Afrique, le mythe qui prend corps,
         pp. 160-64.

1672   GOUZY, RENÉ. "Du côté de Lambaréné." L'Illustré (Lausanne)
         15:7 (Feb. 14, 1935), pp. 164-65.

1673   "Gov. Williams, wife critical of Schweitzer." Chicago
         Tribune, Dec. 14, 1965, p. 22. For a letter to the
         editor in reply by Alice G. Winters entitled "Schweitzer
         in Africa," see the Chicago Tribune, Dec. 22, 1965, p. 20.

1674   GRAF, C. "Lambarene--Februari 1978." RUNDBRIEF 45 (May 1978),
         pp. 6-9. Also in EERBIED 27:2 (Aug. 1978), pp. 4-7.

1675   "Der grosse Doktor. Albert Schweitzer 40 Jahre später."
         Frankfurter Illustrierte 41:45 (Nov. 7, 1953), pp. 10-11.
         Illus.

1676   "Grossvater Albert Schweitzer . . . Enkelkinder beim
         Urwalddoktor in Lambarene." Revue (Munich) 21
         (May 23, 1959), pp. 5-7. Illus.

1677   GUGGISBURG, KURT. "Lambarene in den Briefe Albert
         Schweitzers an Martin Werner." BERICHTE 31 (June 1969),
         pp. 22-26.

1678   GUNTHER, JOHN. "A visit to Albert Schweitzer." The Reader's
         Digest (Pleasantville, N.Y.) 65:388 (Aug. 1954), pp. 43-
         49. Reprinted in: Inside Africa. New York: Harper,
         1955, pp. 712-34; Reprinted in: Procession. New York:
         Harper and Row, 1965, pp. 417-36; Reprinted in: Meet the
         Congo and its Neighbors. New York: Harper and Row, 1959,

Africa and Lambarene

pp. 194-219; translated as "Besuch bei Dr. Albert
Schweitzer." In: Afrika von Innen, 1957; translation
abridged as "Der alte Mann und seine Schwächen, Besuch
bei Albert Schweitzer." Der Spiegel (Hamburg) 11:27
(July 3, 1957), p. 42. For replies to this article, see
Der Spiegel 29 (July 17, 1957), p. 9 and RUNDBRIEF 11
(Aug. 1, 1957), pp. 46-50. Also translated as "Ein Tyran
mit goldenem Herzen. Ein Amerikaner schildert seinen
Besuch bei Albert Schweitzer." Passauer Neue Presse 43
(Feb. 21, 1957), p. 4; also as "Uma visita a Albert
Schweitzer." Seleções do Reader's Digest (Brazil),
Oct. 1954.

1679   GUSSMAN, LAWRENCE. "Introductory remarks" (Lambarene). In:
THE CONVOCATION RECORD, pp. IV/1-3.

1680   _____. "Meeting in Strasbourg, France." COURIER, April-
May 1966, p. 18.

1681   _____. "To friends of the Fellowship." COURIER, Spring 1976,
pp. 1-3. On the state of the hospital.

1682   HACKER, W. "Albert Schweitzer und der Pelikan." Die Vogelpost
(Munich) 6:5 (May 1956), p. 99.

1683   HARRINGTON, DONALD S. "Three days with Schweitzer at
Lambarene." Ghandi Marg (New Delhi) 9:2 (April 1965),
pp. 143-53.

1684   HARRIS, GEORGE B. "A visit to Albert Schweitzer."
Cosmopolitan (New York) 151:1 (July 1961), pp. 80-87.
Illus.

1685   HAUSER-WIEDMER, HELENE. "Ein Morgen im Urwaldspital." In:
HALFEN, pp. 44-46.

1686   HAUSSKNECHT, EMMA. "Un tournée médicale à travers la steppe
et la fôret. Lettre de Mlle. Emma Haussknecht." LETTRES
3 (Aug. 1931), pp. 1-12. Reprinted in CAHIERS 3
(June 1960), pp. 14-23; Translated as "Auf ärztlicher
Wanderung in Urwald und Steppe. Brief von Frl. Emma
Haussknecht. . . ." BRIEFE 13 (Nov. 1931), pp. 1-14.
Illus.; Reprinted in: DOKUMENTE, pp. 50-61; reprinted
with title "Zum Gedenken an Emma Haussknecht . . . aus
ärztlicher Wanderung in Urwald und Steppe." RUNDBRIEF
16 (Oct. 1, 1960), pp. 6-20. Port.; Same was privately
printed, 16 pp., illus.; Also reprinted as "Durch Urwald
und Steppe. Bericht from frl. Haussknecht." Der Speyerer
Protestant (Speyer, Germany) 2 (1931), pp. 12 and 24.

Africa and Lambarene

Translated as "On Trek: a letter from Lambarene."
BRITISH BULLETIN 7 (Spring 1932), pp. 1-12. Illus.; also
as "Een medische expeditie door de steppen en de wildernis.
Uit een brief van mej. Emma Haussknecht." NIEUWS 2:2/3
(Sept., Dec. 1953), pp. 21-25, 45-47; nos. 4/5 (March,
July 1954), pp. 61-62, 77-78. Illus.

1687   _____. "Brief von Fräulein Emma Haussknecht" (dated Lambarene,
Palmsonntag 1931). BRIEFE 12 (Whitsuntide 1931), pp. 11-
14. Illus. Reprinted in: DOKUMENTE, pp. 40-44; Extracts
translated as "From a letter from Mlle. Emma Haussknecht."
BRITISH BULLETIN 6 (Summer 1931), pp. 6-7.

1688   _____. "Briefe von Emma Haussknecht." RUNDBRIEF 6
(Dec. 1, 1954). Reprinted in: DOKUMENTE, pp. 220-22.

1689   _____. "Christmas at the hospital." BRITISH BULLETIN 19
(June 1951), pp. 4-5. Illus. Excerpts translated as
"Kerstmis in het Ziekenhuis." NIEUWS 1:1 (Dec. 1951),
pp. 3-4; translated as "Noël à l'hôpital du Dr. Albert
Schweitzer à Lambaréné." Almanach de l'Eglise Reformée
de France 44 (1952), pp. 98-102. Illus.

1690   _____. "Emma Haussknecht vertelt over Albert Schweitzer. Een
ideale arbeidsgemeenschap in het oerwoud." NIEUWS 2:4
(March 1954), pp. 51-52.

1691   _____. [Excerpts of letters written during 1927 and 1931.]
In: FYRBÅKEN, pp. 59-60, 90-91, 124-27, 139-40.

1692   _____. "Fräulein Emma Haussknecht erzählt von ihrer Arbeit,
aus Briefen und Berichten." RUNDBRIEF 10 (Dec. 1, 1956),
pp. 8-11.

1693   [_____.] "Frl. Haussknecht spricht zu uns." Der Speyerer
Protestant (Speyer, Germany) 1 (1930), p. 104.

1694   _____. "Der Haushalt" (letter dated May 18, 1927). NEUES 7,
pp. 1-4.

1695   _____. "The Leper Village." BRITISH BULLETIN 21 (Feb. 1954),
pp. 6-8. Illus. Translated as "Das Dorf der Aussätzigen."
RUNDBRIEF 5 (June 1, 1954), pp. 34-36; reprinted in:
DOKUMENTE, pp. 213-14; translated as "Het Leprozendorp."
NIEUWS 5:1 (April 1956), pp. 3-4. Illus.

1696   [_____.] "Vortrag von Frl. Haussknecht im Missionskranz in
Speyer an 18. Juni 1930 über Lambarene." Der Speyerer
Protestant (Speyer, Germany) 1 (July 1930), supplement,
following p. 104.

1697   HEINZERLING, LARRY. "Schweitzer's character pervades hospital
          he left behind." Herald Statesman (Yonkers, N.Y.),
          Nov. 1, 1968, p. 23.

1698   HEIPP, GÜNTHER. "Respekt vor Lambarene." Evangelisches
          Gemeindeblatt für München (Munich) 68:2 (Jan. 10, 1965),
          p. 24.

1699   HELFFERICH, REGINALD H. "I visited Albert Schweitzer in
          Africa." The Messenger (St. Louis) 21:12 (June 12, 1956),
          pp. 20-21. Port. Translated as "Ich habe Albert
          Schweitzer in Afrika besucht." Der Friedensbote
          (St. Louis), July 15, 1956, pp. 7-8ff.

1700   HELLSTERN, HEINRICH. "Es geht um die Zukunft von Lambarene."
          BERICHTE 35 (Jan. 1973), pp. 3-5.

1701   _____. "Um die Zukunft von Lambarene." RUNDBRIEFE/DDR 22
          (1973), pp. 12-14.

1702   HENRY, ANDRÉ. "Nous avons besoin de lui. . . ." NOUVELLES 4
          (June 1958), p. 1.

1703   H., A. [HENRY, ANDRÉ]. "Optimisme." NOUVELLES 4 (June 1958),
          p. 7.

1704   HERZOG, WILHELM. "Albert Schweitzer." In: Menschen denen
          ich begegnete. Bern und Munich: Francke Verlag, 1959,
          pp. 107-59. Reprinted in part as "Acht Tage bei Albert
          Schweitzer." Süddetusche Zeitung (Munich) 13:213
          (Sept. 5, 1957), p. 3.

1705   HILLENBRANDT, LUDWIG. "Eine Christnacht Dr. Schweitzers."
          Silva (Zürich), Deutsche Ausgabe Nr. 69, Dec. 4, 1963.

1706   HOENTZSCH, A. "Lambarene--Albert Schweitzers Hospital
          zwischen Wasser und Urwald." Der Allgäuer (Füssen) 7:158
          (Aug. 17, 1951), p. 4.

1707   "Hommage à Albert Schweitzer pour le cinquantenaire de la
          Fondation de Lambaréné." CAHIERS 9 (May 1963), pp. 3-7.

1708   "Hospital receives Lions Award." COURIER, Autumn 1968,
          pp. 2-6. Includes Walter Munz's speech on the history
          of the hospital.

1709   "Hospital to be modernized, Schweitzer's daughter says."
          The New York Times, May 20, 1966, p. 22.

Africa and Lambarene

1710   HUME, EDWARD H.   "Disciple in action."   In: Doctors Coura-
          geous. New York: Harper and Brothers, 1950, pp. 114-22.

1711   HUNTER, GENE.   "People counted for more" (interview with
          Dr. David Miller, heart specialist to Dr. Schweitzer and
          consultant to the Lambarene hospital.) The Sunday Star-
          Bulletin and Advertiser (Honolulu), June 25, 1967, p. A-4.
          Illus.

1712   "Insel der Menschlichkeit; mit Albert Schweitzer im Lepra-dorf
          von Lambarene." Revue (Munich) 22 (May 30, 1959),
          pp. 10-11. Illus.

1713   ITALIAANDER, ROLF.   "Albert Schweitzer als tuinman." NIEUWS
          3:3 (Oct. 1954), p. 83. Reprinted from In het land van
          Albert Schweitzer, no. 1461 above.

1714   _____. "Hexenkessel Westafrika--im höchster Lebensgefahr."
          Frankfurter Illustrierte (Frankfurt a.M.) 48:6
          (Feb. 6, 1960), pp. 40-42.

1715   _____. "Ich besuchte den Menschenfreund Albert Schweitzer."
          Frankfurter Nachtausgabe 224 (Sept. 27, 1954), p. 3.

1716   _____. "Ich komme von Albert Schweitzer." Frankfurter
          Illustrierte (Frankfurt a.M.) 42:13 (March 27, 1954),
          pp. 2-3ff. Illus.; 42:14 (April 3, 1954), pp. 18-22,
          illus. Enlarged and published as a book, Im Lande Albert
          Schweitzers, no. 1461 above.

1717   _____. "Im Lande Albert Schweitzers." In: Brüder der
          Verdammten. Gütersloh: Signum Verlag, 1963, pp. 8-100.
          Illus., port. (Signum Taschenbücher 233). Reprinted as
          Neue Hoffnung für Aussätzige. Stuttgart: Evang.
          Missionsverlag, 1971. (Weltweite Reihe, 25.)

1718   _____. "Een Nederlander in de Afrikaanse rimboe."
          Amerfoortse Courante (Amsterdam), March 12, 1957, p. 5.
          Illus.

1719   _____. "Was wird aus Lambarene?" Frankfurter Illustrierte
          (Frankfurt a.M.) 43:46 (Nov. 12, 1955), pp. 34-39. Illus.

1720   JACK, HOMER A.   "Changes at Lambarene." The Christian Century
          (Chicago) 79:34 (Aug. 22, 1962), pp. 1006-07.

1721   _____. "With Schweitzer in Africa." The Christian Century
          (Chicago) 69:29 (July 16, 1952), pp. 823-25. Reprinted
          in The Progressive (Madison, Wis.) 16:8 (Aug. 1952),

pp. 13-14; translated as "Bei Albert Schweitzer zu Besuch."
Kirchliches Monatsblatt für Evangelisch-Lutherische
Gemeinden in Amerika (Philadelphia) 10:1 (Jan. 1953),
pp. 17-20; also as "Med Schweitzer i Afrika." Svenska
Journalen (Stockholm) 28:36 (Sept. 7, 1952), pp. 16-17ff.
Illus.; "Mit Dr. Schweitzer in Afrika." NIEUWS 1:4
(Dec. 1952), pp. 58-60.

1722   _____. "With Schweitzer in Lambarene." The Saturday Review
(New York) 36:18 (May 2, 1953), pp. 16-17.

1723   JACOBI, CLAUS. "Schweitzers Uhr geht anders." Der Spiegel
(Hamburg) 14:52 (Dec. 21, 1960), pp. 62-67.

1724   JAGER, BERND (as told by Bill Chambless). "My two years with
Albert Schweitzer." Minutes (Columbus, Ohio), June 1955,
pp. 5-7.

1725   JAQUET-CHAPPUIS, ISABELLE. "Die Nähe des Urwaldes." In:
HALFEN, pp. 47-51.

1726   "Jeszce raz Lambarene." Tworczosc (Warsaw) 4 (1975),
pp. 150-52.

1727   JOHNSON, THOMAS A. "His Gabon hospital is busy and growing."
The New York Times, Jan. 14, 1975, p. 35. Illus.

1728   _____. "Schweitzer hospital at Lambarene aiming to specialize
in rehabilitation." The New York Times, Oct. 9, 1972,
p. 2. Illus.

1729   _____. "Schweitzer unit in Gabon begins $6-million hospital
on founder's centennial." The New York Times, Jan. 19,
1975, p. 12.

1730   JOY, CHARLES R. "The hospital without Schweitzer." The
Register-Leader (Boston) 148:10 (Dec. 1966), pp. 3-6.

1731   _____. "Schweitzer's animal friends." Introduction to The
Animal World of Albert Schweitzer. Boston: Beacon Press,
1951. Third printing, 1956, pp. 11-37. See no. 48 above.

1732   _____. [Selection without title.] In: BEGEGNUNG, pp. 208-18.
Excerpted from Joy and Arnold, Bei Albert Schweitzer in
Afrika, see no. 1463 above.

1733   JÜTTNER, HANS-UDO. "Mein Weg nach Lambarene--mein Weg in
Lambarene. 15 Monate als Medizinalassistent bei Albert
Schweitzer, April 1962-August 1963." RUNDBRIEF 24
(June 1964). Also issued as an 11-page offprint.

Africa and Lambarene

1734　JUNGBLUT, [MICHAEL.] "Das Erbe Albert Schweitzers in alten
　　　　　Baracken." Die Zeit (Hamburg) 11 (March 21, 1972), p. 23.
　　　　　Reprinted in RUNDBRIEF 35 (June 15, 1972), pp. 13-14.

1735　"Jungle medicine. The life and work of Dr. Albert Schweitzer."
　　　　　The Radisian (New York), May-June 1955, pp. 5-6.

1736　JUNN, OOM. "Het was een Paasmorgen in Lambarene." Vrije
　　　　　Geluiden (Hilversum), April 12, 1953. Reprinted in NIEUWS
　　　　　2:1 (May 1953), pp. 5-6.

　　　　　JUNOD, MICHEL. "Schweitzer ou l'anti-progrès." See Philosophy,
　　　　　no. 2521 below.

1737　JUSTITZ, H. "L'hôpital Albert Schweitzer à Lambaréné."
　　　　　NOUVELLES 30 (Jan. 1969), pp. 8-16. Illus.

1738　K. "Albert Schweitzer als Prediker." Algemeen Weekblad voor
　　　　　Christentum en Cultuur 37 (July 15, 1932). Reprinted as
　　　　　"Albert Schweitzer als Prediger." Die Opwekker
　　　　　(Bandeong, Indonesia) 9 (Sept. 1932), pp. 450-51.

1739　KETTLER, L.-H. "Bei Albert Schweitzer zu Gast." RUNDBRIEFE/
　　　　　DDR 2 (1963).

1740　KIEBER, H. L. "Albert Schweitzer am Kongo." Die Christliche
　　　　　Welt (Gotha) 28:23 (June 4, 1914), pp. 544-46.

1741　KIK, RICHARD. "Aus Tagebuchblättern unserer 2monatigen
　　　　　Reise." RUNDBRIEF 22 (April 22, 1963), pp. 46-66.

1742　_____. "Den alle Menschen sind Brüder." Westdeutsche
　　　　　Rundschau (Wuppertal-Barmen) 11 (Jan. 14, 1960), p. 12.

1743　_____. "Eine Reise zu Albert Schweitzer nach Lambarene,
　　　　　Jul-Aug 1956." RUNDBRIEF 10 (Dec. 1, 1956), pp. 20-65.
　　　　　Reprinted in: DOKUMENTE, pp. 32-56; also in Ärzte helfen
　　　　　in aller Welt. Das Buch der ärztlichen Mission. Hrsg.
　　　　　von Samuel Müller. Stuttgart: Evang. Missionsverlag,
　　　　　1957, pp. 69-82; excerpted in: BEGEGNUNG, pp. 260-65.

1744　_____. "Tage mit Albert Schweitzer." RUNDBRIEF 40 (1975),
　　　　　pp. 111-14.

1745　KILGALLEN, JAMES L. "Aos 82 anos, A. Schweitzer trabalha 16
　　　　　horas por dia em seu hospital na Africa." Folha da Noite
　　　　　(São Paulo), March 2, 1957.

Africa and Lambarene

1746   KNIGHTLEY, PHILLIP. "A crisis for leprosy." The Times
        (London), Sunday, Nov. 30, 1975, p. 15.

1747   KNOOP, FRED. "Fresh milk for the jungle." The Farm Journal
        (Cincinnati) 12:3 (Autumn 1957), pp. 64-67ff. Illus.

1748   KOCH, GERTRUD. "Brief von Fräulein Gertrud Koch" (dated
        Lambarene, 30. März 1931). BRIEFE 12 (Pfingsten 1931).
        Reprinted in: DOKUMENTE, pp. 44-46; excerpts translated
        in BRITISH BULLETIN 6 (Summer 1931), pp. 7-8.

1749   _____. "Geburtsfeier im Urwald." Volksrecht (Zürich),
        Jan. 14, 1955. Illus.

1750   KONICHEV, KONSTANTIN IVANOVICH. [La ou l'on brise les fers
        de l'esclavage.] Leningrad: Editions Lenine, 1962,
        pp. 93-108.

1751   KOPP, RENE and MAX CAULET. "Aus der Arbeit des Spitals."
        RUNDBRIEFE/DDR 21 (1973), pp. 17-19.

1752   KOREYWO, MAREK. "Lekarz z Lambarene." Pieleg i Polozna
        (Warsaw) 1 (1966), pp. 28-29. Illus.

1753   KOTTMANN, MATHILDE. [Auszuge aus Briefen aus Lambarene an
        Richard Kik.] RUNDBRIEF 2 (Jan. 15, 1952), pp. 5-9,
        11-13ff; RUNDBRIEF 4 (Jan. 14, 1954), pp. 7-10. Reprinted
        in: DOKUMENTE, pp. 156-68.

1754   _____. "Letter from Mathilde Kottmann" (Lambarene, 14. Mai
        1925). NEUES 5 (Aug. 1925), pp. 4-5.

1755   _____. "Letter" (dated Lambarene, 14. September 1924).
        NEUES 3 (Oct. 1924), pp. 6-8.

1756   _____, EMMY MARTIN and CHARLES MICHEL. "The Ownership,
        direction and future of the hospital." BRITISH BULLETIN
        28 (Nov. 1965), pp. 6f. Reprinted in COURIER, April-May
        1966, pp. 7-8; translated in CAHIERS/BELGE (Dec. 1965),
        p. 17.

1757   KRAMMER, HELENA. "Lambarene als Stätte der Begegnung."
        A.I.S.L. Bulletin 5 (Nov. 1977), p. 7.

1758   "Krankendorf am Ogowe wächst." Neue Zeit (East Berlin)
        Dec. 29, 1976. Reprinted A.I.S.L. Bulletin 3
        (Feb. 1977), p. 4.

Africa and Lambarene

1759   KRASNOGLJADOVA, JU. [À Lambarene sans Schweitzer.] Azija i
       Afrika Segodnja 9 (1968), pp. 12-13.

1760   KROOK, OSCAR. "Förord." In: Brev från Afrikas Urskog av
       Schweitzer. Uitgiven av Greta Lagerfelt. Stockholm:
       Svenska Diakonistyrelses Bokförlag, 1925, pp. 3-15.
       Reprinted with title "Albert Schweitzer och Lambarene."
       In: FYRBÅKEN, pp. 17-27; reprinted with title "Albert
       Schweitzer gärning som missionsläkare." In: MANNEN,
       pp. 101-13.

1761   _____. "Till vännerna av Albert Schweitzers verksamhet."
       MEDDELANDEN 2 (Sept. 1927), pp. 3-4.

1762   KÜHN-LEITZ, ELSIE. "Besuch in Lambarene." RUNDBRIEF 15
       (Jan. 14, 1960), pp. 25-37.

1763   LACK, MAURICE. "Lambarene als ökologisches Zentrum."
       BERICHTE 42 (Oct. 1976), p. 25.

1764   LAFONTAINE, LÉON. "Un haut Lieu." NOUVELLES 4 (June 1958),
       p. 5.

1765   LAGENDIJK, MARIA J. "Zuster Maria Lagendijk vertelt."
       NIEUWS 6:1 (May 1957), pp. 3-5.

1766   "Lambarene Bericht 1." RUNDBRIEF 36 (Jan. 14, 1973), pp. 2-6.

1767   "Lambarene Bericht 2." RUNDBRIEF 36 (Jan. 14, 1973), pp. 7-11.

1768   "Lambarene, das Dorf Albert Schweitzers. Farbbildericht."
       Bunte/Münchner/Frankfurter Illustrierte (Offenburg/Baden)
       11 (1961), pp. 28-37. Illus.

1769   "Lambarene in den oorlog." Hervormd Nederland, Aug. 30, 1945.
       Also issued as a 2-page offprint.

1770   "Lambarene." L'Union (Quotidien Gabonais d'Information),
       March 9, 1977. Reprinted in the A.I.S.L. Bulletin 4
       (July 1977), p. 13.

1771   "Lambarene--mehr Licht." Der Spiegel (Hamburg) 38
       (Sept. 15, 1965), p. 125.

1772   "Lambarene without Schweitzer." World Outlook (New York)
       56:9 (Sept. 1966), pp. 16-19. Illus.

1773   "Lambarene zwischen gestern und morgen." RUNDBRIEF 36
       (Jan. 14, 1973), pp. 27-30.

1774   "Lambarene's Lesson. The critics have missed the point about
        Albert Schweitzer." The Economist (London) 216:6368
        (Sept. 11, 1965), pp. 963-64. Reprinted in The Yomiuri
        (Tokyo), Sept. 18, 1965.

1775   LAUTERBURG, MARK. "Ein Brief des Chirurgin Dr. Lauterburg."
        NEUES 7, pp. 4-6.

1776   _____. "Briefe von Dr. Markus Lauterburg." NEUES 5
        (August 1925), pp. 5-10.

1777   LAUTERBURG-BONJOUR, ELSA. "Negerspital 'Lambarene.' Mit
        Albert Schweitzer in Afrikanischen Urwald." Das Werk
        (Gelsenkirchen) 2, Ausgabe B: 9 (Nov. 1953), pp. 199-200.

1778   LAUTERBURG-BONJOUR, MARC. "Aus Tagebüchern und Erinnerungen."
        In: HALFEN, pp. 18-44. Reprinted, with omissions, in:
        BEGEGNUNG, pp. 166-71.

1779   LE FORRESTIER, R. "À l'hôpital de Lambaréné." Mission
        Médicale (Société des Missions Evangéliques, Paris) 9:17
        (Oct. 1934), pp. 192-94. Illus.

1780   LEEB, JOHANNES (text) and KARL BREYER (photos). "Was ist
        mit Albert Schweitzer los?" Quick (Munich) 17:28
        (July 12, 1964), pp. 12-17, 44-47. Illus.

1781   LEEUWIS, LEO. "Nieuwbouw in Schweitzers stijl." EERBIED
        27:3 (Dec. 1978), pp. 24-26.

1782   "The legacy of Albert Schweitzer." Canadian Medical Associa-
        tion Journal (Toronto) 93 (Oct. 2, 1965), pp. 768-69.

1783   LEROY, ALAIN. "Impressions de Lambaréné." CAHIERS 7
        (Sept. 1962), pp. 18-19.

1784   LEWIS, ANTHONY. "Man of our century." Cosmopolitan
        (New York) 134:2 (Feb. 1953), pp. 64-71. Illus.

1785   LIND, EMIL. "Durch das südliche Gabon. Expeditionsbericht
        nach Aufzeichnungen von Emma Haussknecht." Rhein-Pfalz-
        Monatshefte 4 (March 1953), pp. 17-22.

1786   LINDEMANN, HANNES. "Im Einbaum zu Albert Schweitzer." Die
        Barmer Ersatzkasse (Wuppertal-Barmen) 4 (Dec. 1959),
        pp. 157-61; 1 (March 1960), pp. 17-20. Illus.

1787   LISSNER, IVAR. "Une journée avec Albert Schweitzer." Paris
        Match 858 (Sept. 18, 1965), pp. 60-63.

Africa and Lambarene

1788   LOHFELD, HEINZ and ROBERT LEBECK. "Lambarene--was nun?"
        Kristall (Hamburg) 20:20 (Oct. 1965), pp. 20-25. Illus.

1789   LOUROS, N. ["Le phenomene de Lambarene."] In:
        [Retrospectives.] Athens: Ed. G. Parissianos, 1967.

1790   LUDER, MARIANNE. "Wiedersehen mit Lambarene." BERICHTE 42
        (Oct. 1976), pp. 19-21. Illus.

1791   M., E. [Letter from one of Dr. Schweitzer's helpers in
        Lambarene.] NEUES 6 (Christmas 1925), pp. 5-6.

1792   M., H. "Ein halbes Jahrhundert Urwaldspital Lambarene."
        Schweizerische Allgemeine Volkszeitung (Zofingen) 79:18
        (May 4, 1963), p. 2.

1793   "MAGNUM." "Geniet if Afrikas Urskogen." Aktuell (Oslo) 21
        (Oct. 20, 1951), pp. 3-5. Illus.

1794   MAI, HERMANN. "Aus einem Reisebericht . . . Lambarene
        3.4.1956." RUNDBRIEF 10 (Dec. 1, 1956), pp. 17-19.
        Reprinted in: DOKUMENTE, pp. 322-24.

1795   _____. "Besucher in Lambarene." RUNDBRIEF 46 (Nov. 1978),
        pp. 15-21. Illus.

1796   _____. "Im Geiste Albert Schweitzers." BERICHTE 42
        (Oct. 1976), pp. 14-16.

1797   _____. "Steht Albert Schweitzers Urwald-Hospital in Lambarene
        in einer Krise?" RUNDBRIEF 35 (June 1972), pp. 2-6.

1798   MARKUSSEN, G. W. "Hos den store Doktore i junglen." B.T.
        (Copenhagen), Jan. 14, 1955.

1799   MARSHALL, GEORGE N. "Albert Schweitzer, man and doctor."
        (Series of 13 articles). The Boston Globe, Sept. 12-24,
        1965. Later enlarged and published as An Understanding
        of Albert Schweitzer, see no. 274 above.

1800   _____. "Evening worship service at Lambarene." The Unitarian
        Christian (Boston) 18:4 (July 1963), pp. 7-9. Reprinted
        in Faith and Freedom (Manchester College, Oxford),
        Vol. 16, Part 3, No. 48 (Summer 1963), pp. 117-20;
        translated as "Ein Abend in Lambarene." Eleusis
        (Kulmbach, Germany) 20:4 (July/Aug. 1965), pp. 171-74.

1801   _____. "Lambarene fifty years later." Humanist World Digest
        (Berkeley, Calif.) 36:4 (Fall 1963), pp. 4-11. Also

174

Africa and Lambarene

issued by the author as an 8-page reprint. Reprinted in:
TRIBUTE, pp. 84-90; translated as "Lambarene nach 50
Jahren." Eleusis (Kulmbach, Germany) 19:6 (Nov./Dec. 1964),
pp. 328-35.

1802 _____. "Schweitzer hospital without Schweitzer" (two articles). The Boston Globe, Sept. 4-5, 1966.

1803 _____. "Sweet smell of success in air at Schweitzer's jungle
hospital." The Boston Globe, Sept. 4, 1967, p. 12-A.
Illus.

1804 MARTIN, EMMY. [Auszüge aus Briefen aus Lambarene vom
18.3.1951 and 15.12.1951 an Richard Kik.] RUNDBRIEF 2
(Jan. 15, 1952), pp. 8, 22. Reprinted in: DOKUMENTE,
pp. 159-60.

1805 _____. "Brief von Frau Emmy Martin, Gunsbach" (dated
Lambarene, August 1962). RUNDBRIEF 20 (Sept. 1, 1962),
Beilage. 4 pp. Reprinted in: Emmy Martin, die
Mitarbeiterin Albert Schweitzer. Hrsg. von Robert Minder
und Hans Walter Bähr. Tübingen: Katzmann Verlag, 1964,
pp. 103-107; reprinted in: BEGEGNUNG, pp. 74-77; trans-
lated as "Lettre de Madame Emmy Martin--Gunsbach."
CAHIERS 8 (Dec. 1962), pp. 8-10.

1806 _____ (published anonymously). "Im Urwaldspital." Zeitwende
(Munich) 4 (1928), pp. 248-55. Reprinted with title "Im
Urwaldspital in Lambarene." Universitas (Stuttgart) 13:9
(Sept. 1958), pp. 917-25; also in RUNDBRIEF 13
(Dec. 15, 1958), pp. 30-38; RUNDBRIEF 40 (Jan. 14, 1975),
pp. 36-41; BEGEGNUNG, pp. 176-84; translated by Shin Aizu
in Journal of the Japanese Hospital Association (Tokyo)
2 (Feb. 1960), pp. 134-40; translated with title "Un
séjour à l'hôpital de Lambaréné en 1925." CAHIERS 2
(Dec. 1959), pp. 11-16; reprinted in CAHIERS/BELGE 1
(Nov. 1960), pp. 15-23; translated as "In the jungle
hospital at Lambarene." Universitas (English language
edition) 2:4 (1958/59), pp. 365-73; reprinted in
Universitas 7:1 (1964), pp. 81-89; Reprinted in: TRIBUTE,
pp. 67-74; translated as "U Doktora pralesa v Lambarene."
Přeložil J. Balcar. 1960 Blahoslav, Rodinný Kalendář
círckve československé, Praha, pp. 69-77.

1807 _____. "Lambarene 1951." BRITISH BULLETIN 19 (June 1951),
pp. 2-4. Translated as "Nieuws uit Lambarene." NIEUWS
1:1 (Dec. 1951), pp. 2-3.

175

Africa and Lambarene

1808 _____. "Lettre de Madame Emmy Martin." CAHIERS/BELGE 3
(Feb. 1963), pp. 22-25.

1809 _____. "Séjour à Lambaréné--au cimetiere des aides africains."
CAHIERS 10 (Dec. 1963), pp. 12-14. Illus.

1810 _____. "Weihnachtsabend im Urwaldspital." Schweizerisches
Reformiertes Volksblatt (Basel) 85:3 (Feb. 3, 1951),
p. 23. Translated as "Christmas eve at Lambarene. Pages
out of my diary." In: REALMS, pp. 36-41.

1811 MARTINELLI-STETTLER, IDA. "Colmar weckte Erinnerungen."
In: HALFEN, pp. 120-22.

1812 MARTON, KÁLMÁN. "Magyarországról Jöttünk, Doktor Schweitzer."
In: DEBRECEN, pp. 179-91. Translated as "Nous voici,
arrives de la Hongri, Docteur." In: DEBRECEN,
pp. 192-207.

1813 MATCHET. "Matchet's Diary." West Africa (London), Sept. 11,
1965, p. 1017.

1814 MATHIEN, MICHEL. "Lambarene après le Dr. Schweitzer. La
Réalité de la modernisation." NOUVELLES 35 (Sept. 1974),
pp. 7-8.

1815 MATTHEY, NELLY. "Lambarene--ein unvergessliches Erlebnis."
BERICHTE 42 (Oct. 1976), pp. 16-19. Illus.

1816 MAURER, P. "L'directeur de Lambarene in Alsace: davantage
de concertation pour l'oeuvre" (interview with Max
Caulet). Dernières Nouvelles d'Alsace, May 6, 1979.
Reprinted in the A.I.S.L. Bulletin 10 (Oct. 1979), p. 21.

1817 MC CALL, REGINALD L. "Dr. Schweitzer's pedal piano on its
way to Africa." The Diapason (Chicago) 29:10
(Sept. 1, 1938), p. 1. Illus.

1818 MC GREGOR, ROBERT G. "Schweitzer day by day." The Atlantic
Monthly (Boston) 198:6 (Dec. 1956), pp. 37-40. Also
issued as a reprint by the Albert Schweitzer Fellowship,
New York. Reprinted in Foreign Service Journal
(Washington, D.C.) 34:4 (April 1957), pp. 44f; reprinted
in: SELECTION, pp. 23-28.

1819 _____. "Schweitzer's birthday at Lambarene." The Saturday
Review (New York) 38:15 (April 9, 1955), pp. 13, 44-45.
Illus. Translated as "Schweitzers Geburtstag in
Lambarene." RUNDBRIEF 9 (Jan. 1, 1956), pp. 61-67;
reprinted in: DOKUMENTE, pp. 313-17.

Africa and Lambarene

1820   MC GURN, BARRETT. "A visit with Dr. Schweitzer" (series of
        three articles). New York Herald Tribune, July 26–28,
        1959, pp. 1, 4 and 8 respectively. Illus.

1821   MEES, ELEONORE F. "Letter from Lambarene." NIEUWS 1:3
        (July 1952), pp. 35–37; 1:4 (Dec. 1957), pp. 57–58.

1822   _____. "Nieuws uit Lambarene." NIEUWS 2:1 (May 1953),
        pp. 3–4f. Illus.

1823   MENSCHING, WILHELM. "Der Europäer unter dem fremden Rassen."
        Die Christliche Welt (Gotha) 43:6 (March 16, 1929),
        col. 264.

1824   MERCIER, ANNE-MARIE. "Impressions d'une artiste, retour de
        Lambaréné." CAHIERS 1 (April 1959), p. 14.

1825   METZGER, LUDWIG. "Albert Schweitzer. Abstecker nach
        Lambarene." Darmstädter Echo (Darmstadt), Jan. 14, 1965,
        p. 3.

1826   MIEDEMA, M. "Over Albert Schweitzer." Het Remonstrantse
        Weekblad (Lochem) 23:47 (Dec. 12, 1964), pp. 5f.

1827   MIEJERS, J. A. "Werken met mijn handen. Gesprak met Albert
        Schweitzer." De Groene Amsterdammer (Amsterdam),
        Sept. 24, 1949, pp. 9–10.

1828   MILLER, RHENA SCHWEITZER. "Lambarene 1976." COURIER,
        Winter 1976, pp. 3–11.

1829   _____. "Ma visite à Lambarene." A.I.S.L. Bulletin 8
        (Nov. 1978), pp. 29–30.

1830   MINDER, ROBERT. "Des chiffres et des faits--l'hôpital A.
        Schweitzer à Lambaréné." CAHIERS 11 (July 1964),
        pp. 15–17.

1831   MITTALHOLZER, W. "Neues von Albert Schweitzer." Neue
        Zürcher Zeitung, Jan. 2, 1925.

1832   "Mitteilungen aus Lambarene." RUNDBRIEF 20 (Sept. 1, 1962),
        pp. 3–5.

1833   MOFFETT, HUGH. "The white wizard's 90th. An inquiring visit
        to Dr. Schweitzer. Life (New York) 58:7 (Feb. 19, 1965),
        pp. 82–95. Port., illus.

Africa and Lambarene

1834   MONTGOMERY, W. "Schweitzer as missionary." The Hibbert
        Journal (London) 12:4 (July 1914), pp. 871-85.

1835   MORAES, FRANK. "With Albert Schweitzer." In: The Importance
        of being Black: an Asian looks at Africa. New York:
        Macmillan; London: Collier-Macmillan, 1965, pp. 159-75.

1836   MOREL, LÉON. "Au Gabon avant l'arrivée du Dr. Schweitzer."
        In: HOMMAGE, pp. 81-88. Reprinted in: RAYONNEMENT,
        pp. 185-89; translated as "Im Gabon vor 50 Jahren."
        RUNDBRIEF 22 (April 18, 1963), pp. 7-11; reprinted with
        some omissions with title "1908-1913." In: BEGEGNUNG,
        pp. 139-42.

1837   MORGAN, THOMAS B. and ERICA ANDERSON. "Albert Schweitzer,
        a picture story of the 20th century's greatest man."
        Look Magazine (New York) 18:12 (June 15, 1954), pp. 34-44.
        Illus.

1838   MÜLLER, LYDIA. "Vom Saley: verzellt in Baseltitsch." In:
        HALFEN, pp. 210-17.

1839   MUNCK, FERD. "Albert Schweitzer og hans Gerning i
        aekvatorialafrika." Nordisk Missions-Tidsskrift
        (Viborg, Norway) Bd. 33, Rk. 3, Arg. 11 (1922), pp. 241-50.

1840   MUNDLER, E. "La mort de thecla." In: HALFEN, pp. 205-07.

1841   "El mundo del Doctor Schweitzer." Eva (Santiago) 24:1081
        (Dec. 24, 1965), pp. 32-34. Illus.

1842   MUNZ, WALTER. "Afrikanisches Denken und Glauben im Alltag
        von Lambarene." BERICHTE 32 (Sept. 1970), pp. 7-10.
        Translated as "Pensée et foi africaines dans la vie
        quotidienne de la region de Lambarene." CAHIERS 32
        (Spring 1975), pp. 21-24.

1843   _____. "Bewährung und neues Streben." RUNDBRIEFE/DDR 11
        (1967), pp. 6-11.

1844   _____. "Images et souvenirs de Lambarene." CAHIERS 11
        (July 1964), pp. 8-10.

1845   _____. "Lambarene. Wir wollen uns versehen." A.I.S.L.
        Bulletin 10 (Oct. 1979), pp. 7-9.

1846   _____. "Ein neues Lambarene." BERICHTE 34 (Aug. 1972),
        pp. 9-10.

1847   _____. "Een nieuw Lambarene." NIEUWS 22:1 (May 1973),
           pp. 8-9.

1848   _____. [Selection without title.] BERICHTE 28 (March 1964).
           Reprinted in: BEGEGNUNG, pp. 43-51.

1849   _____. "Das Spital lebt weiter." RUNDBRIEFE/DDR 29 (1976),
           pp. 26-27.

1850   _____. "Der 4. September 1976 in Lambarene." BERICHTE 42
           (Oct. 1976), pp. 3-7. Illus.

1851   _____ and ST.-G. BROWNE. "Projet de construction d'un nouvel
           hôpital." CAHIERS 28 (Spring 1973), pp. 20-22.

1852   "Nachrichten von Albert Schweitzer." Neue Auslese (Munich)
           1:10 (Nov. 1946), pp. 123-24.

1853   "Nachtgang in Lambarene." Die Kirche (Berlin-Dahlem) 13:32
           (Aug. 10, 1958), p. 3.

1854   NAEGELE, P. "Unser Tag--Lambarene 1951." RUNDBRIEF 2
           (Jan. 15, 1952), pp. 16-20.

1855   NAGY, JOZSEF. "Bunte Wegweiser nach Lambarene." RUNDBRIEFE/
           DDR 33 (1978), pp. 6-10.

1856   NAKAMURA, T. "Lambarene Tsushin." Fukuin to Sekai (Tokyo)
           7:5 (Aug. 1952), pp. 43-49.

1857   NESSMAN, VIKTOR. "Ein Brief des 'ambulanten' Arztes
           Dr. Nessman. Auf der Fahrt nach Port-Gentil im August
           1925." NEUES 7, pp. 2-3.

1858   "Neues von Albert Schweitzer." Der Speyerer Protestant
           (Speyer, Germany) 2 (1931), pp. 203-04.

1859   "Neues von Urwaldsdoktor." Der Speyerer Protestant (Speyer,
           Germany) (1936), pp. 10-15.

1860   "Neuigkeiten rund um Lambarene." RUNDBRIEFE/DDR 29 (1976),
           pp. 28-30.

1861   "The new Lambarene hospital." COURIER, May 1974, pp. 2-3.

1862   NICOL, DAVIDSON. Africa--a subjective view. Accra, Ghana:
           Longmans and Ghana Universities Press, 1964, pp. 16-24.
           Reprinted with title "Albert Schweitzer and his view of
           Africa." Transition (Uganda) 5:22 (1965), pp. 33-35.

Africa and Lambarene

1863   NIEMÖLLER, MARTIN. "Der erste Tag im Lambarene."
        Sonntagsgruss (Heusweiler), April 11, 1965. Reprinted
        in: CHARISMATISCHE DIAKONIE, pp. 28-31.

1864   "Nieuws uit Lambarene." NIEUWS 1:2 (March 1952), pp. 19-20;
        1:3 (July 1952), p. 35; 2:2 (Sept. 1953), pp. 19-20; 2:3
        (Dec. 1953), pp. 35-36.

1865   [Notes of recent news from Lambarene, including excerpts of
        letters from Albert Schweitzer and Emmy Martin.] BRITISH
        BULLETIN 27 (Jan. 14, 1965), pp. 1-4. Illus.

1866   NÖTZLI, GERTRUD. "Boumba and Tsinda: Meine Afrikanischen
        Küchengehilfen." In: HALFEN, pp. 192-99.

1867   NÜENSCH-WOHLFENDER, ELISABETH. "Hausfrauliches." In:
        HALFEN, pp. 150-60.

1868   O'BRIAN, HUGH. "Albert Schweitzer gave me a glimpse of the
        impossible dream." Guideposts (Chinese edition), Oct.
        1970, pp. 3-11. In Chinese and English.

1869   _____. "How a week in deepest Africa changed my life forever."
        Family Weekly, Enquirer and News (Battle Creek, Mich.),
        Aug. 11, 1974.

1870   O'BRIEN, CONOR CRUISE. "Africa's answer to Schweitzer."
        The Atlantic Monthly (Boston) 217:3 (March 1966),
        pp. 68-71. For a letter to the editor in reply by Erik
        Olssen, see The Atlantic Monthly 217:6 (June 1966), p. 44.

1871   _____. "Albert Schweitzer and contemporary Africa." Arts
        and Sciences (New York University) 66:24 (June 13, 1966),
        pp. 1-9.

1872   OBERMAN-OBERMAN, H. "Bestrijding van de meiaatsheid."
        NIEUWS 2:5 (July 1954), pp. 67-68.

1873   _____. "Een droevige plechtigheid in Lambarene." NIEUWS
        5:2 (Oct. 1956), p. 6.

1874   _____. "Een spannende dag in Lambarene." NIEUWS 4:3
        (Oct. 1955), pp. 3-4.

1875   _____. "Kerstfeest in Lambarene." NIEUWS 2:3 (Dec. 1953),
        pp. 37-38. Illus.

1876   "Ook hun vacantie is werk." NIEUWS 2:5 (July 1954), pp. 69-70.

1877   OSWALD, SUZANNE. "Bei Albert Schweitzer in Lambarene. Zum
        80. Geburtstag des 'Grand-Docteur.'" Neue Zürcher Zeitung,
        Jan. 15, 1955, pp. 1-2. Reprinted with title "Lambarene
        Diary." Swiss Review of World Affairs (Zürich) 5:1
        (April 1955), pp. 11-16. Illus. Photos by Erica
        Anderson.

1878   OTT, EMMA. "Kleine Steine im grossen Mosaik." In: HALFEN,
        pp. 105-14.

1879   OTTO, BERND. "Das Albert Schweitzer Spital als Urzelle der
        Entwicklungshilfe." BERICHTE 36 (Sept. 1973), pp. 28-30.

1880   _____. "Das Urwald-Hospital Albert Schweitzer in Lambarene--
        ein Modell für Hospitäler in Entwicklungsländern."
        RUNDBRIEF 41 (Feb. 1976), pp. 12-22.

1881   PAAR, JACK. "A visit with Dr. Schweitzer, November, 1963."
        In: Three on a Toothbrush. Garden City, N.Y.: Doubleday,
        1965, pp. 149-72.

1882   "Paradijs der dieren; Lambarene, een moderne ark van Noach."
        NIEUWS 4:3 (Oct. 1955), pp. 5-6. Illus.

1883   PAUL, JOHANNES, ed. Von Grönland bis Lambarene:
        Reisebeschreibungen christlicher Missionäre aus drei
        Jahrhunderten. Berlin: Evangelische Verlags-Anstalt,
        1951, 1953, pp. 183-92.

1884   ["Peace bells in the leper village of Lambarene hospital
        dedicated in honor of Dr. Schweitzer's 80th birthday."]
        RUNDBRIEF 16 (Oct. 1, 1960), p. 55.

1885   [PEPPER, CURTIS G.] "'. . .A grain of sand.'" Newsweek
        (New York) 54:6 (Aug. 10, 1959), p. 86. Port.

1886   PETER, CHARLOTTE. "Diskussion um Doktor Schweitzer." Elle
        (Zürich) 11:6 (March 1963), pp. 58, 9. Port.

1887   PETERSEN, CHRISTIAN. "Der grosse Doktor wirkt in Lambarene
        weiter." Kölnische Rundschau (Cologne) 198a
        (Aug. 28, 1966), illus.

1888   PETRICKIJ, V. "Gabon-Leningrad." Neva 10 (1962), pp. 214-15.

1889   PFENNINGER, URSULA. "Katzenfütterung." In: TIERE, pp. 20-21.

1890   _____. "Peter." In: TIERE, pp. 21-23.

Africa and Lambarene

1891   PFISTER, OSKAR. "Sundar Singh und Albert Schweitzer. Zwei
        Missionare und zwei missionsprogramme." Zeitschrift für
        Missionskunde und Religionswissenschaft (Berlin) 37:1
        (1922), pp. 10-25. Also issued as a 16-page offprint.

1892   PHILLIPS, HERBERT M. "A visit to Dr. Schweitzer." Chicago
        Sunday Tribune Magazine, Dec. 14, 1958, pp. 9ff. Illus.

1893   PIDOUX, EDMOND. "Les deux côtés du fleuve" (Dr. Schweitzer
        et Lambaréné). In: L'Afrique à l' âge ingrat.
        Neuchâtel, Paris: Delachaux and Niestlé, 1956, pp. 63-68.
        Translated as "Die beiden Ufer des Stroms." In: Afrika.
        Ein Kontinent--zwei Welten. Tr. Winfried Theimer. Basel:
        Basler Missionsbuchhandlung; Konstanz: Bahn, 1957,
        pp. 63-71.

1894   PIERSON, C.-A. "Une semaine à Lambaréné chez le Docteur
        Schweitzer. Un voyage--une leçon." Maroc Médical
        (Casablanca) 34:357 (Feb. 1955), pp. 174-87. Later
        enlarged as the author's book Le Clair regard de
        Schweitzer, see no. 1473 above.

1895   PLAUT, WALTER. "Alltag im Urwald. Ein Besuch bei Albert
        Schweitzer in Lambarene." Aufbau (New York) 2
        (Jan. 14, 1955), pp. 1f.

1896   POLIDORI, MAURICE. "Schweitzer l'Africain." In: ETUDES,
        2nd edition, pp. 49-72.

1897   PORTUGALOV, N. S. (Article written at request of Novosti
        Press Agency.) Izvestia, Jan. 4, 1962, p. 6. Short
        English summary appears in The Current Digest of the
        Soviet Press (New York) 14:1 (Jan. 31, 1962), pp. 24-25;
        translated as "Zu Gast beim 'Urwalddoktor.'" Neue Zeit
        (East Berlin) 37 (Feb. 13, 1962), p. 3; also as "Im
        Dschungel von Gabon. Ein Sowjetbürger zu Gast beim
        'Urwalddoktor' Albert Schweitzer." RUNDBRIEF 20
        (Sept. 1, 1962), pp. 36-39; reprinted without title in:
        BEGEGNUNG, pp. 31-33.

1898   PREMINGER, MARION MILL. All I want is Everything. New York:
        Funk and Wagnalls, 1957, pp. 292-303.

1899   PRICE, WILLARD. "Albert Schweitzer." In: Incredible Africa.
        London: William Heinemann, 1961, pp. 66-79. Port.

1900   PUNER, MORTON. "The Kingdom of Schweitzer." The Reporter
        (New York) 24:3 (Feb. 2, 1961), pp. 37-41.

Africa and Lambarene

1901   [RAMSAY, LISLE.] "Schweitzer on race." Newsweek (New York)
        61:14 (April 8, 1963), p. 95. Port.

1902   [RANDAL, JON.] "Albert Schweitzer: an anachronism." Time
        (New York) 81:25 (June 21, 1963), p. 35. Illus. For
        letters to the editor in reply by William E. Ruehling
        and J. Phillipson, see Time 82 (July 5, 1963), pp. 5-6.

1903   RANDIN, WILLY. "Rapport de notre directeur administratif."
        NOUVELLES 32 (Sept. 1971), pp. 7-9.

1904   READING. "Brief eines Negers." NEUES 3 (Oct. 1924), pp. 3-5.
        Reprinted in Schweizerisches Protestantenblatt (Basel)
        47:48 (Nov. 29, 1924), pp. 381-82.

1905   REGESTER, JOHN D. "Christmas at Lambarene." Alumnus of the
        University of Puget Sound 8:4 (Oct./Dec. 1966), pp. 7-8.

1906   REICHARDT, HORST-PETER. "Die Brüderschaft der vom Schmerz
        gezeichneten." In: BEITRÄGE, pp. 151-61.

1907   [Report of Dr. Schweitzer's work.] BRITISH BULLETIN 2
        (Summer 1926), pp. 1-3.

1908   RESCH-MEIER, HEDWIG. "'Mein' Gemüsegarten." In: HALFEN,
        pp. 117-20.

1909   REYER, GEORGES. "Albert Schweitzer, l'homme qui a vécu tous
        vos rêves." Paris Match 123 (July 28, 1951), pp. 25-27;
        125 (August 11, 1951), pp. 24-25. Illus., ports.

1910   [ROBACK, A. A.] "Albert Schweitzer--Pontifex." In: REALMS,
        pp. 424-26.

1911   ROBLES, HAROLD E. "Lambarene im Oktober 1978/Lambarene in
        October 1978/Lambarene en octobre 1978." A.I.S.L.
        Bulletin (Nov. 1978), pp. 15-16, 23-24, 31-32, respectively.
        German/English/French.

1912   _____. "Lambarene 1978." EERBIED 27:3 (Dec. 1978),
        pp. 21-23. Illus.

1913   _____. "Lambarene 4 September 1976." EERBIED 25:2
        (Nov. 1976), pp. 8-9. Illus.

1914   ROHNER, HÉLÈNE. "Doktor Schweitzer als Baumeister." BERICHTE
        25 (Nov. 1953), pp. 10-12. Translated as "Dr. Schweitzer
        som byggmästare." MEDDELANDEN 24 (1954), pp. 12-15.

Africa and Lambarene

1915   ROSS, EMORY. "Albert Schweitzer--on and on!" COURIER,
            May 1964, pp. 131-32.

1916   _____. "Wer wird einst die Nachfolge Albert Schweitzers in
            Lambarene übernehmen?" Basler Nachrichten (Basel) 251
            (June 18, 1957), p. 2.

1917   ROSS, MYRTA. "A letter from Mrs. Emory Ross--on the Ogowe
            River, Gabon, West Africa, August 7, 1946." The Scroll
            (Chicago) 45:9 (Nov. 1948), pp. 266-73.

1918   ROSS, S. G. "Albert Schweitzer, physician." Canadian Medical
            Association Journal (Toronto) 70:4 (April 1954),
            pp. 459-62.

1919   ROTH, LUCIEN. "Albert Schweitzer." Evolution (Paris) 5:54
            (June 1930), pp. 54-64.

1920   RUARK, ROBERT C. "A couple of miracles in one day";
            "Miracles at Dr. Schweitzer's--aides glad to work at no
            pay"; "Schweitzer laments loss of humanism" (series of
            three articles). New York World Telegram and Sun,
            March 9-11, 1960.

1921   RUSSELL, MRS. C. E. B. (LILIAN). "Animals at Dr. Schweitzer's
            African hospital." The Animal's Friend (London) 39:2
            (Feb. 1933), pp. 43-45.

1922   _____. "Der Garten." NEUES 7, pp. 6-9.

1923   _____. "Gorillas I have known." The Animal's Friend
            (London) 38:10 (Oct. 1932), pp. 287-88.

1924   _____. "Mit Albert Schweitzer in Lambarene." In: WÜRDIGUNG,
            pp. 21-24.

1925   _____. "More about the hospital" (letters dated May 2 and
            August 30, 1933). BRITISH BULLETIN 8 (Winter 1933-34),
            pp. 7-9.

1926   _____. "Practical internationalism." The Aryan Path
            (Bombay) 3:6 (June 1932), pp. 429-31.

1927   _____. "Rats as I know them." The Animal's Friend (London)
            42 (March 1936), p. 90.

1928   _____. "The youth of Thekla." Animal Pictoral (London) 3:2
            (March 1940), pp. 86-90.

Africa and Lambarene

1929 RUSSELL, JOHN. "Le docteur Schweitzer chez lui." L'Alsace
        (Mulhouse), June 8-11, 1955, pp. 5f in each issue.

1930 RUTISHAUSER, ARMIN. "Brief des neuen Arztes, Herrn Armin
        Rutishauser" (dated Lambarene, ende August 1937). BRIEFE
        21 (March 1938), pp. 9-12. Illus. Translated as "Van de
        reis naar Lambarene en de aankomst aldaar. Brief van den
        nieuwen arts." NIEUWS 11 (April 1938), pp. 10-13; also as
        "My journey and arrival at Lambarene." BRITISH BULLETIN
        15 (Spring 1938), pp. 11-15; "Le voyage et l'arrivée à
        Lambaréné. Lettre du noveau médecin M. Armin Rutishauser."
        LETTRES 11 (March 1938), pp. 8-11.

1931 _____. "Wie eine Insel." In: HALFEN, pp. 130-33.

1932 RYSSEL, EDITH. "Hos Albert Schweitzer i Urskoven" (a series
        of 15 articles). Berlingske Tidende (Copenhagen) June 6-
        Sept. 12, 1954. Illus., ports. Later published as a
        book, see no. 1475 above.

1933 SAINZ, XAVIER. "Une journée à l'hôpital de Lambaréné." In:
        DEBRECEN, pp. 113-21.

1934 SANDERSON-BOCHSLER, TRUDI. "Leprösendorf." In: HALFEN,
        pp. 187-90.

1935 "Le scandale de Lambaréné." Jeune Afrique (Tunis) 101
        (Sept. 24-30, 1962), pp. 14-15. Illus.

1936 SCHAEFFER, LOUIS-EDOUARD. "Entretien avec Emmy Martin.
        Pourquoi Albert Schweitzer ne viendra pas cette année
        en Europe." CAHIERS 7 (Sept. 1962), pp. 16-17.

1937 SCHNABEL, ILSE. "Albert Schweitzers Urwaldspital in
        Lambarene." Schweizerische Ärztezeitung (Bern) 46:45
        (1965), p. 1042.

1938 _____. "Ango." In: HALFEN, pp. 207-09.

1939 _____. "Journalistischer Beitrag Albert Schweitzers zu den
        Problem von Weiss und Farbig." Schweizer Frauenblatt
        (Zürich) 35:37 (Sept. 11, 1953), p. 1.

1940 _____. "N'Touga, ein indelkind im Spital zu Lambarene."
        In: EHRFURCHT, pp. 167-69.

1941 _____. "Reise im Einbaum." In: HALFEN, pp. 60-77.

Africa and Lambarene

1942   SCHNEIDER, VERENA. "Ein Besuch bei Albert Schweitzer."
        Deutsche Medizinische Wochenscrift (Stuttgart) 79:23
        (June 4, 1954), p. 929.

1943   SCHNEPP, F. "L'avenir de l'hôpital est assuré." CAHIERS 14
        (Dec. 1965), p. 30.

1944   SCHNEPP, MARCEL. "Neues Entappe für das Urwaldspital Albert
        Schweitzers. Die Weiterführung des Werkes des grossen
        Elsässers ist gesichert." Basler Nachrichten (Basel) 24
        (Jan. 17, 1967), p. 2.

1945   SCHOENFELD, EUGENE. "Lambarene without Schweitzer." The
        Journal of the American Medical Association (Chicago)
        200:10 (June 5, 1967), pp. 830-32.

1946   SCHRÖDER, MARGRIT. "On fait ce qu'on pout." In: HALFEN,
        pp. 169-81.

1947   SCHRÖDER, MATHILDE. "Die anhänglichkeit der Neger." BERICHTE
        25 (Nov. 1953), pp. 12-15. Translated as "Negrernas
        tillgivenhet." MEDDELANDEN 24 (1954), pp. 15-18.

1948   SCHUFFENECKER, GERARD. "Zwei Wörte über Lambarene mit Max
        Caulet. . . ." Dernières Nouvelles d'Alsace (Strasbourg)
        254 (Oct. 31, 1976). Reprinted in A.I.S.L. Bulletin 2
        (Nov. 1976), pp. 23-24.

1949   _____. [Selection without title.] In: BEGEGNUNG, pp. 112-18.

1950   SCHULHOFER, KARL. "Zu Besuch in Lambarene." In: FACKELTRÄGER.
        pp. 1-34.

1951   SCHULTE, MARCEL. "Besuch beim Urwalddoktor--Albert
        Schweitzers Werk." Rheinische Post (Düsseldorf) 33
        (Feb. 8, 1958).

1952   SCHUYLER, PHILIPPA DUKE. Adventures in Black and White.
        New York: Robert Speller and Sons, 1960, pp. 241-48, 251.

1953   SCHWEITZER, HELENE. "Brev från Professorkan Schweitzer"
        (dated Lambarene, 5 Juni 1943). MEDDELANDEN 18 (1944),
        pp. 9-11. Reprinted in: FYRBÅKEN, pp. 219-21.

1954   _____. "Brief von Frau Schweitzer" (dated Lambarene, den 10.
        Januar 1930). BRIEFE 11 (March 1930), pp. 6-8. Illus.
        Reprinted in Der Speyerer Protestant (Speyer, Germany) 1
        (May 1930), pp. 72-74; also in: DOKUMENTE, pp. 28-30;
        translated as "Letter from Madame Schweitzer, January 10,

Africa and Lambarene

1930." BRITISH BULLETIN 4 (Spring 1930), pp. 11-14;
"Brev från frü Schweitzer." MEDDELANDEN 6 (May 1930),
pp. 20-24; "Brev från Professorskan Helene Schweitzer."
In: FYRBÅKEN, pp. 104-07; "Lettre de Madame Schweitzer."
LETTRES 1 (Jan.-March 1930), pp. 6-8. Illus.

1955 _____. "Professorskan Schweitzer skriver et par dagar
sevare" (dated Lambarene 12.XI.44). MEDDELANDEN 14
(1945), pp. 5-6. Reprinted in: FYRBÅKEN, pp. 226-27.

1956 H. W. P. [SCHWEITZER, HELENE.] "Madame Schweitzer reports."
British Weekly (London) 128:3335 (Oct. 12, 1950), p. 2;
3336 (Oct. 19, 1950), p. 4. Translated as "Neues aus
Lambarene." Allgemeine Missions-Nachrichten (Hamburg)
30:6 (Dec. 1950), p. 6.

1957 SCHWEITZER, HELENE. "With Schweitzer in Africa." The
Christian Century (Chicago) 65:16 (April 21, 1948),
pp. 345-46. Translated in: Fleischhack, Marianne.
Helene Schweitzer. Berlin: Evangelische Verlagsanstalt,
1967, pp. 127-31.

1958 SCHWEITZER-MILLER, RHENA. "Die Ibo-Kinder in Lambarene und
ihre Rückkehr nach Nigeria." RUNDBRIEFE/DDR 19 (1972),
pp. 9-11.

1959 _____. "Mein Besuch in Lambarene." RUNDBRIEF 47 (May 1979),
pp. 13-15.

1960 _____. "En visite à Lambaréné." CAHIERS 28 (Spring 1973),
pp. 16-17.

1961 "Schweitzer hospital needs funds. May close." San Francisco
Sunday Examiner and Chronicle, Dec. 10, 1967, p. 30.

1962 "Schweitzer method hit." Science News Letter (Washington,
D.C.) 88:12 (Sept. 18, 1965), p. 180.

1963 "Schweitzer plans fight on leprosy." The Christian Century
(Chicago) 66:32 (Aug. 10, 1949), p. 944.

1964 "Schweitzer's hospital imperiled by finances." The New York
Times, Nov. 30, 1975, p. 19.

1965 "Schweitzers preeken voor de negers." Algemeen
Protestantenblad 11:19 (Mari 13, 1931). Reprinted in
De Opwekker (Bandeong, Indonesia) 76:1-2 (Jan.-Dec. 1931),
pp. 224-27.

Africa and Lambarene

1966   "Schweitzer's trial" (photo essay). <u>Science Digest</u>
(New York) 54:1 (July 1953), pp. 45-49.

1967   SECRETÁN, MARIE. "Als technische Assistentin im Urwald."
<u>Monatshefte für die Technische Assistentin</u> (Berlin-
Grünewald) 6:2 (Feb. 1931), pp. 105-07.

1968   _____. "Auf Missionsreise im Urwald." KIRCHENBOTE 60:42
(Oct. 18, 1931), pp. 330-31; 43 (Oct. 25, 1931),
pp. 338-39.

1969   _____. "Aus dem Leben in einem Urwaldspital." (Vortrag in
der Ortsgruppe Berlin des V.T.A.) <u>Monatshefte für die
Technische Assistentin</u> (Berlin-Grünewald) 7:11 (Nov. 1932),
pp. 524-28.

1970   _____. "Brief von Frl. Marie Secretan." <u>Der Speyerer
Protestant</u> (Speyer, Germany) 1 (1930), p. 88.

1971   _____. "Brief von Frl. Marie Secretan. Erste Eindruck von
Afrika und Lambarene." BRIEFE 11 (March 1930). Reprinted
in: DOKUMENTE, pp. 30-33; translated as "Letter from
Fräulein Marie Secretan." BRITISH BULLETIN 4 (Spring
1930), pp. 15-18; "Lettre de Mlle. Marie Secretan."
LETTRES 1 (Jan.-March 1930), pp. 8-10; "Brev från fröken
Marie Secretan." MEDDELANDEN 6 (May 1930), pp. 25-30.

1972   _____. "Brief von Fräulein Marie Secretan" (dated Lambarene,
den 26.3.1931). BRIEFE 12 (Pfingsten 1931). Reprinted
in: DOKUMENTE, pp. 46-49.

1973   _____. "Letter from Mlle. Marie Secretan." BRITISH BULLETIN
6 (Summer 1931), pp. 9-10.

1974   SEYNES, J. DE and J. BIANQUIS. "Une oeuvre médicale au Congo."
<u>Journal de Société des Missions Évangéliques</u> (Paris)
87:2 (Aug. 1912), pp. 93-96.

1975   "Einer sicheren Zukunft entgegen." <u>Westfälische Nachrichten</u>,
Dec. 4, 1976. Reprinted in the <u>A.I.S.L. Bulletin</u> 3
(Feb. 1977), p. 3.

1976   SIEFERT, JEANETTE. "Vingt-cinq ans après. . . ." CAHIERS/
BELGE 1 (Nov. 1960), pp. 26-32. Reprinted, with title
"Lambarene, 25 ans après." NOUVELLES 27 (July 1961),
pp. 9-15.

1977   SIEGFRIED, RUTH. "Lambarene memories." In: <u>Missionary Diary</u>.
London: Salvationist Publishing and Supplies, 1956,
pp. 199-208.

1978   SILVER, ALI. "Lambarene 1963." BRITISH BULLETIN 26
            (April 1963), illus.

1979   _____. "The leper village." BRITISH BULLETIN 20 (Sept. 1952),
            pp. 4-7.

1980   _____. "Oudjaars avond in Lambarene." Het Remonstrantse
            Weekblad (Lochem) 7:5 (Feb. 6, 1948), p. 5.

1981   SITHOLE, NDABANINGI. African Nationalism. Capetown: Oxford
            University Press, 1959, pp. 118-23. Reprinted as "Albert
            Schweitzer--an African image." In: Christianity in
            Africa as seen by Africans. Edited and with an introduc-
            tion by Ram Desai. Denver, Col.: Allan Swallow, 1962,
            pp. 103-08.

1982   SITTE, FRITZ. "Letzter Besuch in Lambarene." Neue Zeit
            (Graz, Austria), Oct. 2, 1965.

1983   "Sleeping sickness" (letter to the editor from the members of
            Dr. Schweitzer's Hospital Fund). The Times (London),
            Aug. 22, 1925, p. 6. Reprinted in BRITISH BULLETIN 1
            (Autumn 1925), laid in; translated in NEUES 5 (Aug. 1925),
            pp. 10-11.

1984   SLOAN, RAYMOND P. "Albert Schweitzer--humanitarian. A
            Modern Hospital interview." The Modern Hospital
            (St. Louis, Mo.) 73:3 (Sept. 1949), pp. 59-64. Illus.

1985   SMITH, ASBURY. "Albert Schweitzer's mission to Africa."
            The Christian Advocate (New York) 106:28 (July 9, 1931),
            pp. 867-68. Port.

1986   SMITH, W. EUGENE, photographer. "A man of mercy." Life
            (New York) 37:20 (Nov. 15, 1954), pp. 161-72. Illus.

1987   SNETHLAGE, H. A. C. "Een ontmoeting met Schweitzer." NIEUWS
            1:1 (Dec. 1951), p. 4.

1988   SONNTAG, WOLFGANG. "Albert Schweitzer und die Entwicklungs-
            länder." Darmstädter Echo (Darmstadt), Jan. 14, 1963,
            p. 3.

1989   SOUBEYRAN, LÉON. "Rapport de la mission du Congo, Août 1912-
            Août 1913--V. Oeuvre médicale." Journal des Missions
            Évangéliques (Paris) 88:2 (Oct. 1913), pp. 296-97.

1990   SPEISER, PETER P. "Urwaldtagebuch (9. April 1950)." CIBA-
            Blätter (Basel) 7:84 (Sept. 1950), pp. 9-12; 8:85
            (Oct. 1950), pp. 12-17. Port., illus.

Africa and Lambarene

1991   SPERISEN-SCHWENK, V. "Un pharmacien à Lambaréné." NOUVELLES
            35 (Sept. 1974), pp. 19-20.

1992   "De Sphinx van Lambarene" and "De opvolger bezorgdheid heerst
            rondom werk van menslievendheid." Algemeen Handelsblad
            (Amsterdam), Nov. 20, 1964, p. 17. Port.

1993   STAATS, WALTER. "Lambarene 1960." RUNDBRIEF 17 (Jan 14, 1961),
            pp. 27-29.

1994   STALDER, ELISE. "Musterchen." In: HALFEN, pp. 77-79.

1995   STALDER, HANS. "Albert Schweitzer und sein Afrikanisches
            Werk." Die Ernte, Schweizerisches Jahrbuch (Basel) 14
            (1933), pp. 113-33. Also issued as an offprint, Günsbach,
            1933.

1996   STEERE, DOUGLAS VAN. "Death at Lambarene." The Saturday
            Review (New York) 36:24 (June 13, 1953), pp. 11-12. Illus.

1997   _____. "Dr. Schweitzer of Lambarene." The Friend
            (Philadelphia) 126:2 (Seventh Month 24, 1952), pp. 22-25.

1998   STEFFAHN, HARALD. "Afrikanisches Tagebuch." RUNDBRIEF 20
            (Sept. 1, 1962), pp. 6-17. Reprinted without title and
            with some omissions in: BEGEGNUNG, pp. 56-64.

1999   _____. "Abend am Ogowe." RUNDBRIEF 25 (Jan. 14, 1965),
            pp. 2-40.

2000   _____. "Albert Schweitzer. Patriarch oder letzter
            Kolonialherr." Darmstädter Echo, Dec. 29, 1964, Jan. 2,
            1965, p. 3. Reprinted as "Patriarch oder Kolonialherr?
            . . . die Wahrheit über der Urwalddoktor von Lambarene."
            Nürnberger Nachrichten, Jan. 9/10, 1965.

2001   [STEINER, ANDREAS.] "Der Chefarzt, Dr. Andreas Steiner,
            bericht." RUNDBRIEF 46 (Nov. 1978), p. 9.

2002   STOLARSKI, TADEUSZ. "Wielki Doktor z Lambarene." Sluzba
            Zdrowia (Warsaw) 35 (1968), p. 6.

2003   STRIFFELER-KIENLI, MARGRIT. "Geburtstag und anderes." In:
            HALFEN, pp. 127-29.

2004   _____. "Der Gouverneur kommt." In: HALFEN, p. 200.

2005   T., J. "Paradoks Alberta Schweitzera." Tygodnik Powszechny
            (Krakow) 29:16 (20 Kwietnia 1975), p. [6].

Africa and Lambarene

2006   T., R. "Forest hospital at Lambarene." The Living Church
       (Milwaukee, Wis.) 86 (Nov. 7, 1931), p. 16.

2007   TAKAHASHI, ISAO. I to Kango no Rinri. 1967. 163 pp. Illus.
       About J. H. Dunant, Clara Barton, Florence Nightingale,
       and Albert Schweitzer.

2008   TAS, S. "Ontmoeting met Albert Schweitzer. Lambarene:
       Europeesfiliaal van menselijke barmhartidheid." Het
       Parool (Amsterdam) 4165 (Aug. 9, 1958), pp. 1, 6-7.

2009   TASKER, J. G. "Dr. Albert Schweitzer's work in Lambarene."
       London Quarterly and Holborn Review 151, fifth series,
       no. 37 (Jan. 1929), pp. 98-101.

2010   _____. "Dr. Albert Schweitzer." London Quarterly and Holborn
       Review 148, fifth series, no. 34 (July 1927), pp. 106-09.

2011   TELTSCH, KATHLEEN. "Schweitzer hospital opened to Biafran
       children." New York Times, Nov. 1, 1968, p. 4. Reprinted
       in COURIER, Autumn 1968, p. 18.

2012   TÉTAZ-NIEDERHAUSER, ERNA. "Lambarene überlebt." Neue Zürcher
       Zeitung, Dec. 16, 1976. Reprinted in A.I.S.L. Bulletin
       3 (Feb. 1977), p. 11.

2013   TILTMAN, MARJORIE H. "Lone doctor of Lambarene; Albert
       Schweitzer's great work in Africa." In: God's Adventures.
       London: G. G. Harrap, 1933; reprinted Freeport, N.Y.:
       Essay Index Reprint Series, 1968, pp. 246-54.

2014   TOKARCZYK, ANDRZEJ. "Testament z Lambarene." Argumenty
       (Warsaw) 31 (1975), pp. 1, 4-5.

2015   TOMBE, M. DES. "Verpleegster in Lambarene. Tussen Water en
       Oerwoud." De Waagschaal (Amsterdam) 1:37/38 (June 1946),
       pp. 9-10. Port.

2016   TOWNSEND, PETER. "Ik sprak met doktor Schweitzer."
       Telegraaf (Amsterdam), March 15, 1958.

2017   "Les travaux du nouvel hôpital Albert Schweitzer à Lambaréné."
       Courrier du Vignoble, Jan. 14, 1977. Reprinted in the
       A.I.S.L. Bulletin 3 (Feb. 1977), p. 6.

2018   TRENSZ, F[REDERIC]. "Neue Verhältnisse--neue Aufgaben."
       BERICHTE 31 (June 1969), pp. 11-14.

Africa and Lambarene

2019   _____. "Vom alten zum neuen Spital in Lambarene." NEUES 9
        (Whitsunday 1927), pp. 5-7. Translated as "Brev från
        doktor Trensz våren 1927." MEDDELANDEN 2 (Sept. 1927),
        pp. 6-10.

2020   TUGGENER-ZINSER, IRMGARD. "Arbeit-Geburt-Leben-Tod." In:
        HALFEN, pp. 114-17.

2021   "Unermüdlicher 'Urwalddoktor.'" Kirchliches Monatsblatt für
        Evangelisch-Lutherische Gemeinden in Amerika
        (Philadelphia) 12:6 (June 1955), p. 183.

2022   U., E. [EDM. UNSINGER]. "Albert Schweitzer im afrikanischer
        Urwald." FAMILIEN-KALENDAR 32 (1925), pp. 34-35.

2023   URQUHART, CLARA. "The Africa of Albert Schweitzer." The
        Forum (Johannesburg, South Africa) 1:12 (March 1953),
        pp. 24-28.

2024   _____. "Ein Besuch in Dr. Albert Schweitzers Afrika."
        Neue Schweizer Rundschau (Zürich) 20:11 (March 1953),
        pp. 653-62.

2025   _____. "Dr. Schweitzer at 82." BRITISH BULLETIN 23
        (July 1957), pp. 2-5.

2026   _____. "Durch eines Mannes Ideal und Persönlichkeit
        vereint." In: GESTERN-HEUTE, pp. 63-64. Reprinted
        from With Dr. Schweitzer in Lambarene, see no. 1488 above.

2027   _____. "Rückkehr nach Lambarene." Neue Schweizer Rundschau
        (Zürich) 22:6 (Oct. 1954), pp. 371-78.

2028   _____. "A visit to the Africa of Dr. Albert Schweitzer."
        Phylon (Atlanta) 14:3 (Sept. 1953), pp. 295-301.

2029   V., H. "O apóstolo das selvas." Diário da noite (São Paulo),
        Jan. 14, 1965.

2030   V., T. "Besuch in Lambarene (Horst und Helga Krüger)."
        Nürnberger Nachrichten, Ausgabe A, no. 41 (Feb. 19, 1964),
        p. 13. Illus.

2031   VACCA, GAETNO. "Albert Schweitzer médico apóstolo a
        Lambaréné." In: DEBRECEN, pp. 107-11.

2032   VAN HICHTUM, N. "Albert Schweitzer." Karakter-Kennis-Kunst
        voor de Lagere School (Groningen) 10 (1928), pp. 142-63.
        Illus., port.

Africa and Lambarene

2033   VAN LEER, TONY. "Brieven uit Lambarene." NIEUWS 5:2
         (Oct. 1956), pp. 10-12.

2034   _____. "Kerstfeest in Lambarene." NIEUWS 2:3 (Dec. 1953),
         p. 39.

2035   _____. "Kinderen in het Ziekenhuis." NIEUWS 2:3 (Dec. 1953),
         pp. 40-42. Translated as "Children and Animals at
         Lambarene." BRITISH BULLETIN 21 (Feb. 1954), pp. 9-10;
         translated as "Kinder und Tiere in Lambarene." RUNDBRIEF
         5 (June 1, 1954); reprinted in: DOKUMENTE, pp. 214-16.

2036   VAN ROYEN, C. J. "Onrust om Albert Schweitzer." Kerk en
         Wereld (Assen) 56:24 (Dec. 4, 1964), p. 6.

2037   "La vie à Lambaréné." NOUVELLES 35 (Sept. 1974), pp. 1-2.
         Illus.

2038   VIGUE, FRANK. "La Lámpara arde todavía en Lambarene."
         Photos by Erica Anderson. Revista Rotaria (Evanston,
         Ill.) 81:4 (Oct. 1973), pp. 4-7. Translated as "The
         lamp still burns at Lambarene." The Rotarian (Evanston,
         Ill.), Oct. 1973, pp. 19-21.

2039   "A visit by Mme. Martin." BRITISH BULLETIN 25 (May 1962),
         pp. 8-9.

2040   VISSER, C. CH. G. "Geruchten om Dr. Albert Schweitzer."
         Evangelisch-Luthers Weekblad (Rotterdam) 43 (Dec. 5, 1964),
         p. 277. Port.

2041   "Voici le flambeau symbolique à Lambaréné et le docteur
         Schweitzer." France d'outre-mer (Paris) 30:269
         (March 1952), p. 19.

2042   "Das wachsende Liebeswerk Albert Schweitzers." Deutsches
         Pfarrerblatt (Stuttgart) 52:16 (Aug. 1952), p. 500.

2043   WALDER, ROLF. Afrika-fahrt: Tagebuch einer Studienreise.
         Birkmannsweiler: privately printed, 1954, pp. 15-17.
         Reprinted as "Bei Albert Schweitzer in Lambarene."
         RUNDBRIEF 6 (Dec. 1, 1954); reprinted in: DOKUMENTE,
         pp. 224-25.

2044   WEMAMBU, S. [Brief tribute without title.] In: DENKEN UND
         WEG, p. 427. Reprinted in: BEGEGNUNG, p. 311.

2045   WENZEL, LENE. "Zwei unvergessliche Erlebnisse (in Lambarene)."
         RUNDBRIEF 17 (Jan. 14, 1961), pp. 25-27.

Africa and Lambarene

2046   "Werk in Lambarene in discussie. Gerechtvaardigde kritiek
           op Albert Schweitzer?" Waag (Utrecht) 1:3 (Nov. 1964),
           p. 1.

2047   WERNER, D. A. "Albert Schweitzer binnenkort 90. jaar.
           Toekomst van hospitaal in Lambarene is not onzeker.
           Kritike op Dr. Schweitzer in Utrecht weerlegd."
           Deventer Dagblad, Nov. 17, 1964, p. 9. Reprinted in
           Nieuwe Apeldoornse Courant (Apeldoorn), Nov. 18, 1964,
           p. 7. Port.

2048   WERNER, D. A. "Volgens dominee ut wassenaar. Kritiek op
           Schweitzer neit geheel terecht. Utrechts Nieuwsblad,
           Nov. 17, 1964.

2049   _____. "Lambarene." Weekend Ad, Algemeen Dagblad (Dortenaar)
           283 (April 1, 1966), pp. 11-15. Illus.

2050   _____. "Schweitzer houdt hart vast stormachtige
           ontwikkeling." Gelders Dagblad, Nov. 24, 1964.

2051   _____. "Waarheid en leugen over 'Lambarene.'" Trouw
           (Amsterdam), Nov. 21, 1964.

2052   _____. "Ziekenhuis Dr. Schweitzer. 75gebouwen met 1000
           mensen--moderner en wat uitgebried." Het Vaderland
           (The Hague), March 10, 1966, p. 12.

2053   WEST, RICHARD. In: Brazza of the Congo. London: Jonathan
           Cape, 1972, pp. 259-64; American edition: Congo. New
           York: Holt, Rinehart and Winston, 1972, pp. 259-64.

2054   WESTPHAL, CLARENCE. "The good doctor of Lambarene." In:
           African Heritage; the story of Africa's Contribution to
           the World. Minneapolis, Minn.: T. S. Denison and Co.,
           1960, pp. 199-209.

2055   "What the doctor is doing." BRITISH BULLETIN 1 (Autumn 1925),
           pp. 3-4.

2056   [WICHT, ANDRÉ.] "Der verantwortliche Baufuhrer, André Wicht,
           berichtet." RUNDBRIEF 46 (Nov. 1978), pp. 10-12. Illus.

2057   WIJNEN, ARY VAN. "Nieuws uit Lambarene." NIEUWS 19:1
           (June 1970), pp. 3-5. Illus.

2058   _____. "Nieuws uit Lambarene." EERBIED 23:2 (Aug. 1974),
           pp. 38-39.

2059   WIKSTRÖM, JAN-ERIK. "Visit hos Albert Schweitzer." Ansgarius
       60 (1965), pp. 65-70.

2060   WILDERMUTH, ULRICH. "Afrikanische Melancholie: Christus war
       ein Weisser . . . beim 86jahrigen Albert Schweitzer."
       Münchner Merkur (Munich) 12 (Jan. 14/15, 1961), p. 3.

2061   WILDIKANN, ANNA. "On the hill of Adalinanongo." In:
       FESTSCHRIFT, pp. 114-21. Hebrew translation in Journal
       des Jeunesses Musicales d'Israel (Tel Aviv) 3:3
       (Jan. 1960), pp. 5-6.

2062   _____. "Der Pelikan des Urwalddoktors." Atlantis (Zürich)
       20:2 (Feb. 1948), pp. 54-56.

2063   _____. "A statement" (Lambarene). In: THE CONVOCATION
       RECORD, pp. VI/37-39.

2064   WILKINS, ANNE (as told to Tom Wilkins). "I worked for
       Dr. Albert Schweitzer." The Atlanta Journal and the
       Atlanta Constitution, June 27, 1965, pp. 5Ef. Illus.

2065   WINKLER, JOHAN. "Met een Junkers naar Schweitzer." Vrij
       Nederland (Amsterdam) 36 (May 5, 1951), p. 8.

2066   _____. "Hier werkt Schweitzer." Vrij Nederland (Amsterdam)
       37 (May 12, 1951), p. 8. Illus.

2067   _____. "Bach aan de zoom het oerwoud." Vrij Nederland
       (Amsterdam) 38 (May 19, 1951), p. 8.

2068   _____. "Afschied van Lambarene." Vrij Nederland (Amsterdam)
       39 (May 26, 1951), p. 8. Illus.

2069   _____. "Schweitzer en Lambarene zign niet te schieden."
       De Hervormde Kerk (The Hague) 7:15 (April 14, 1951), p. 1.

2070   WITHERSPOON, JINX. "My visit to Lambarene." United Nations
       World (New York) 6:12 (Dec. 1952), p. 35. Originally
       published in The Outspan, Blomfontein, South Africa.

2071   WOYTT, G. "Schweitzer et le Gabon." Strasbourg-Actualités
       (Strasbourg), June 1961, pp. 37-39.

2072   WOYTT-SECRETAN, MARIE. "À l'hôpital de Lambaréné." In:
       HOMMAGE, pp. 119-25.

2073   _____. "Albert Schweitzer und seine Beziehung zu den
       Gefangenen." Zeitschrift für Strafvollzug (Wiesbaden)
       3:6 (1953), pp. 356-60.

Africa and Lambarene

2074   _____. "Herinnering aan Lambarene." NIEUWS 4:3 (Oct. 1955),
         pp. 9-13. Illus. Translated as "Erinnerungen an
         Lambarene." RUNDBRIEF 8 (Nov. 1, 1955); reprinted in:
         DOKUMENTE, pp. 254-58.

2075   _____. "In der Speichergasse 2." RUNDBRIEF 40 (1975),
         pp. 54-56. Reprinted from Der Urwalddoktor van Lambarene,
         no. 322 above.

2076   _____. "Placide und die weisse Hose. Eine Geschichte aus
         Dr. Schweitzers Urwaldspital." Almanach de L'Église
         Évangélique Lutherienne (Strasbourg) 1952, pp. 49-52.

2077   _____. "Über das Lepradorf." RUNDBRIEF 4 (Jan. 14, 1954).
         Reprinted in: DOKUMENTE, pp. 193-94.

2078   WÜST, MARIE LOUISE. "Impressions de Lambaréné." NOUVELLES
         32 (Sept. 1971), pp. 10-15. Illus.

2079   WYMER, NORMAN. "The hospital in the forest." In: Canning,
         John. 100 Great Adventures. New York: Taplinger, 1960,
         pp. 430-35.

2080   ZBINDEN, HANS. "Lambarene--Sinnbild heilender Menschenliebe."
         In: DENKEN UND WEG, pp. 384-91.

2081   "Zeep voor Lambarene." NIEUWS 2:4 (March 1954), pp. 53-54.

2082   ZELLWEGER, HANS. "Die Macht des Aberglaubens." In: HALFEN,
         pp. 100-05.

2083   _____. "Rückblick." In: HALFEN, pp. 80-84.

2084   _____. "Das Urwaldspital von Albert Schweitzer in Lambarene."
         Atlantis (Zürich), March 1950.

V. Medicine

A.   Books by Schweitzer

DIE PSYCHIATRISCHE BEURTEILUNG JESU
(The Psychiatric Study of Jesus)

This work, which arose out of Schweitzer's thesis for his medical
degree at the University of Strasbourg, was originally printed at
Tübingen in 1913 under the title "Kritik der von Medizinischer Seite
veröffentlichen Pathographien über Jesus." In the same year, it was
published by J. C. B. Mohr under the title Die Psychiatrische
Beurteilung Jesu. Schweitzer describes the origins of the study:
"Now I had to write my thesis for the doctorate. For this I chose
as my subject the collection and examination of all that had been
published from the medical side on the mental derangement of which
the writers supposed Jesus to have been a victim. . . . In my studies in the life of Jesus I had shown that He lived in the thought
world (which seems to us such a fantastic one) of the late Jewish
expectation of the end of the world and the appearance, thereupon,
of a supernatural Messianic Kingdom. I was at once reproached with
making him a visionary, or even a person under the sway of delusions.
My task now was to decide, from the medical standpoint, whether this
peculiar Messianic consciousness of His was in any way bound up with
some psychic disturbance."[1] Among those whose works Schweitzer con-
siders are de Loosten, Benet-Sanglé, and William Hirsch. His conclusion is "That these medical experts . . . succeed in throwing
doubt on the mental soundness of Jesus, is explicable only by the
fact of their not being sufficiently familiar with the historical
side of the question."[2]

2085   Die Psychiatrische Beurteilung Jesu. Darstellung und Kritik.
        Tübingen: J. C. B. Mohr (Paul Siebeck), 1913. 46 pp.

----

[1]Out of My Life and Thought. New York: Holt, Rinehart and Winston,
1961, p. 108.

[2]Ibid, p. 110.

Medicine

2086   Same.   2. photomechanisch gedruckte Auflage.   Tübingen:
        Mohr, 1933.   46 pp.

Chinese

2087   [The Psychiatric Study of Jesus.]   Tr. Chin Ing-Sh.   Taiwan:
        Evergreen Cultural Enterprises, 1975.   60 pp.

English

2088   The Psychiatric Study of Jesus, Exposition and Criticism.
        Translated and with an introduction by Charles R. Joy
        and a foreword by Winfred Overholser.   Boston: Beacon
        Press, 1948.   81 pp.   Paperback edition, 1958.   Reprinted
        Magnolia, Mass.:   Peter Smith.

        "The Sanity of the Eschatological Jesus."   See no. 2091 below.

Japanese

2089   [Die psychiatrische Beurteilung Jesu.]   Tr. Minoru Nomura.
        Tokyo: Misuru-Shobo, 1951.

        B.   Shorter Writings by Schweitzer

2090   "Medicine in the Jungle."   Journal of the American Medical
        Association (Chicago) 156:17 (Dec. 25, 1954), pp. 1547-49.
        Reprinted in Philanthropy (New York) 3:4 (Summer 1955),
        pp. 82-84.

2091   "The Sanity of the Eschatological Jesus."   Tr. William
        Montgomery.   The Expositor (London) 6 (July-Dec. 1913),
        pp. 328-42; 439-55; 554-68.

2092   "Le Secours médical aux colonies."   La Revue des Deux Mondes
        (Paris) 8:5 (Sept. 15, 1931), pp. 390-404.   Reprinted in
        Revue et Bulletin d'Information, publ. mensuelle de la
        Ligue des Sociétés de la Croix-Rouge 12:12 (Dec. 1931),
        pp. 444-50; translated as "El socorro de la cruz Roja."
        Revista y Boletín de Información de la Liga de sociedades
        de la Cruz Roja 12:12 (Dec. 1931), pp. 449-55; translated
        as "Medical aid in the colonies."   Review and Information
        Bulletin of the League of Red Cross Societies 12:12
        (Dec. 1931), pp. 456-62.

C.   Works by Others About Schweitzer

a.   Books

BOURDIER, ROLAND. La vie et la pensée d'Albert Schweitzer. Plaidoyer pour un nouvel humanisme médical. See Dissertations, no. 4312 below.

2093   JOSSELIN DE JONG, R. DE. De Taak van den arts in verband met de person en het werk van Albert Schweitzer. Utrecht: Oosthoek, 1927, 31 pp.

LEWIS, MELVA JEAN. Significance and contribution of Albert Schweitzer's medical work in Africa. See Dissertations, no. 4327 below.

WEISS, ROBERT. Albert Schweitzer als Arzt und als Mensch. See Life and Work, no. 318 above.

b.   Articles, Parts of Books

2094   "An alumna visits Schweitzer." New York University Medical Quarterly (New York) 17:3 (Winter 1962), pp. 4-8.

2095   ANDREWS, GEORGE R. "Psychiatric facilities at the Albert Schweitzer hospital." The American Journal of Psychiatry (Hanover, N.H.) 118:6 (Dec. 1961), pp. 524-28.

2096   AUJOULAT, PIERRE. "Albert Schweitzer, médecin de brousse." CAHIERS 18 (Dec. 1967), pp. 17-20. Reprinted as "Une médecine pour la Brousse: Malades noirs et médecins blancs." Anhang zu Santé et deocloppement en Afrique. Paris: Librarie Armand Colin, 1969, pp. 272-85; shortened version included in: RAYONNEMENT, pp. 220-25.

2097   BAUR, HERMANN. "Albert Schweitzer als Arzt." In: FESTGABE, pp. 91-143. Excerpted in RUNDBRIEF 15 (Jan. 14, 1960), pp. 52-56; reprinted, with omissions, in: DENKEN UND WEG, pp. 343-57; condensed version published with title "50 Jahre Urwaldspital. Albert Schweitzers Werk in Lambarene." National-Zeitung (Basel) 174 (April 17, 1963), p. 3.

2098   BERG, C. VAN DEN. "De betekenis van het werk van Albert Schweitzer voor de internationale gesondheidszoid." NIEUWS 19:1 (June 1970), pp. 8-13.

2099   BRANCO E CASTRO, J. C. "Medecine e música: Albert Schweitzer." Jornal do Médico (Porto, Portugal) 16:391 (July 22, 1950), pp. 131-34.

Medicine

2100   BROWN, ROBERT L. "Albert Schweitzer as a physician." The
        Emory University Quarterly (Atlanta, Ga.) 10:3
        (Oct. 1954), pp. 172-80.

2101   BROWNE, STANLEY G. "Lambarene und die Lepra." RUNDBRIEFE/
        DDR 23 (1973), pp. 16-17.

2102   CATCHPOOL, FRANK. "A statement" (Dr. Schweitzer and the
        Lambarene hospital). THE CONVOCATION RECORD, pp. VI/
        25-28.

2103   CHESTERMAN, CLEMENT C. "Medical care in developing countries,
        the contribution of Dr. Albert Schweitzer." In: THE
        CONVOCATION RECORD, pp. II/11-18.

2104   DARLINGTON, CHARLES F. and ALICE B. DARLINGTON. "Albert
        Schweitzer." In: African Betrayal. New York: David
        McKay Co., 1968, pp. 285-300.

        DAWE, DONALD G. "Schweitzer on the paranoia of Jesus." See
        Theology and Religion, no. 2964 below.

2105   DENUES, A. R. T. and WALTER MUNZ. "Malignancies at the
        Hospital of Doctor Albert Schweitzer, Lambarene, Gabon,
        1950-1965." International Journal of Cancer (Copenhagen)
        2:4 (July 15, 1967), pp. 406-11. Also issued as a 6-page
        reprint.

2106   _____. "Malignancies at Lambaréné." In: Clifford, Peter;
        C. Allen Linsell and Geoffrey L. Timme, eds. Cancer in
        Africa. Nairobi: East Africa Journal and East African
        Publishing House, 1968, pp. 97-103.

2107   _____. "Cancer at Dr. Albert Schweitzer's hospital,
        Lambaréné (equatorial Africa), 1929-1966." World Medical
        Journal (New York) 16:1 (Jan./Feb. 1969), pp. 16-19.

2108   DOUVIGOU, ALAIN. "Les activités du village de lumière."
        NOUVELLES 31 (May 1970), pp. 24-25.

2109   DURAND-REVILLE, LUC. "Albert Schweitzer, médicin colonial."
        In: ACADEMIE.

2110   ECKERT-SCHWEITZER, RHENA. "Le noveau laboratoire d'analyses
        médicales." CAHIERS 9 (May 1963), pp. 14-16. Translated
        as "Het nieuwe medisch-analytische laboratorium." NIEUWS
        12:2 (Nov. 1963), pp. 5-7; also as "Das neue medizinische-
        analytische Laboratorium." RUNDBRIEF 24, pp. 30-32.

2111   _____. "La vie à l'hôpital de Lambaréné, Mars–Août 1964."
        CAHIERS 12 (Dec. 1964), pp. 7–9. Translated as "Lambarene
        März–August 1964." RUNDBRIEF 25 (Jan. 14, 1965), pp. 75–78.

2112   FARNSWORTH, DANA L. "The meaning of Albert Schweitzer's life
        to medicine." In: REALMS, pp. 280–91.

2113   FAUSEL–WIEBER, OLGA. "Lieber grand Docteur." In: HALFEN,
        pp. 123–27.

2114   FIELDS, ALBERT. "Schweitzer and humanity." Health Education
        Journal (London) 22 (Jan. 1959), pp. 18–19. Also issued
        as a 4-page offprint.

2115   FINK, ROBERT. "Im Operationssaal von Lambarene." BERICHTE
        25 (1953), pp. 1–4. Reprinted in RUNDBRIEF 5
        (June 1, 1954), pp. 20–23; reprinted in: DOKUMENTE,
        pp. 208–10; translated as "I operationsalen pa ajukhuset
        i Lambarene." MEDDELANDEN 24 (1954), pp. 9–11.

2116   _____. "Lambarene aus ärztlicher sicht." RUNDBRIEFE/DDR
        27 (1975), pp. 22–25.

2117   FISCHER, EDITH. "Un cas de tétanos à l'hôpital du Dr.
        Schweitzer." CAHIERS 9 (May 1963), pp. 17–18.

2118   FREY, MAURICE. "A dentist at Lambarene." BRITISH BULLETIN
        25 (May 1962), pp. 7–8.

2119   GAERTNER, HENRYK. ["Albert Schweitzer als Arzt."] Ruch
        Muzyczny (Warsaw) 12 (1976), pp. 219, 225.

2120   GAGNEBIN, EDMONDE. "Eseignement et formation du personnel
        para-médical." A.I.S.L. Bulletin 8 (Nov. 1978), p. 47.

2121   GILLESPIE, NOEL. "Philosophical learning and medical science."
        In: FESTSCHRIFT, pp. 39–42.

2122   GOLDSCHMID, LADISLAS. [Letter from the Albert Schweitzer
        Hospital, Lambarene, 1935.] BRIEFE 16 (June 1935),
        pp. 3–5.

2123   GOLDWYN, ROBERT M. "Dr. Schweitzer as a Doctor." In:
        TRIBUTE, pp. 61–63. Reprinted as "Albert Schweitzer as
        doctor." Unitarian Universalist, the Register-Leader
        (Boston) 147:1 (Jan. 1965), pp. 10–11; excerpted in
        Marshall, George N., An Understanding of Albert Schweitzer
        (no. 274 above), pp. 144–46.

Medicine

2124 _____ and RICHARD L. FRIEDMANN. "Surgery at the Albert
Schweitzer Hospital, Lambarene." The New England Journal
of Medicine (Boston) 264:20 (May 18, 1961), pp. 1031-33.

2125 GOTTSTEIN, WERNER K. "Albert Schweitzer." Journal of the
American Medical Association (Chicago) 110:10
(July 9, 1949), p. 909.

2126 GROSS, EMANUEL and WALTER POLLAK. "Albert Schweitzer als
Arzt." Die Medizinische Welt (Berlin) 4:5 (Feb. 1, 1930),
pp. 178-80.

2127 GUIGNARD, J. F. "Rapport de la clinique dentaire." A.I.S.L.
Bulletin 8 (Nov. 1978), pp. 50-53.

2128 _____. "Renouveau de la clinique dentaire de l'hôpital
Albert Schweitzer." A.I.S.L. Bulletin 5 (Nov. 1977),
pp. 33-34.

2129 HABICHT, H. "Bericht des Chefarztes 1975." BERICHTE 42
(Oct. 1976), pp. 11-13. Illus.

2130 "Heart surgery in Africa mapped. Dr. White, back from visit
at Schweitzer mission, to send aid and device." The New
York Times, May 3, 1959, p. 12.

2131 HEIPP, GÜNTHER. "Der Arzt von Lambarene." RUNDBRIEFE/DDR
20 (1972), pp. 11-13; 22 (1973), pp. 6-8.

2132 HILGERS, HANS-GÜNTHER. "Bericht aus Lambarene. Stand der
Projekte am 1.5.1970, neue Pläne für die Zukunft."
RUNDBRIEF 33 (Oct. 10, 1970), pp. 14-16.

2133 _____. "Stand der Zahnärztlichen Projekte zum 1.8.1971."
RUNDBRIEF 34 (Dec. 1, 1971), pp. 27-30.

2134 HOLM, STIG. "Les états de la refraction oculaire chez les
palénégtides au Gabon, Afrique Equatorial Française."
In: Supplement till Acta Opthalmologica. Copenhagen:
Levin och Munksgaard, 1937.

2135 _____. "Tva år som lakare vid sjukhusit i Lambarene." In:
MANNEN, pp. 114-36.

2136 "I Lambarenes urskovshospital." Ugeskrift for Laeger
(Copenhagen) 95 (1937, 1938), p. 596.

2137 ILOWECKI, MACIEJ. "Czarownikj." Polityka (Warsaw) 24
(June 12, 1971).

2138   KOELBING, HULDRYCH M. "Ärztliches Wirken und ärztliche Ethik.
        Das Beispiel Albert Schweitzers." Neue Zürcher Zeitung,
        March 20, 1975, p. 52.

2139   KOPP, RENÉ. "L'activité médicale de l'hôpital Schweitzer en
        1970." NOUVELLES 32 (Sept. 1971), pp. 5-7.

2140   _____. "Bericht des Chefarztes." BERICHTE 34 (Aug. 1972),
        pp. 3-5.

2141   _____. "Bericht des Chefarztes." RUNDBRIEF 40 (1975),
        pp. 120-21.

2142   _____. "Medisch Rapport over het jaar 1972." NIEUWS 22:1
        (May 1973), pp. 6-7.

2143   _____. "Rapport médical." CAHIERS 29 (Summer 1973),
        pp. 28-30.

2144   _____. "Rapport médical de l'année 1973." NOUVELLES 35
        (Sept. 1974), pp. 2-3.

        KRETSCHMER, WOLFGANG. "Albert Schweitzers Lehre von der
        Ehrfurcht vor dem Leben und die Behandlung seelischer
        Krankheiten." See Philosophy--Reverence for Life, no.
        2763 below.

2145   LAGENDIJK, MARIE J. "Nursing at Lambarene." BRITISH
        BULLETIN 20 (Sept. 1952), pp. 2-4.

2146   "Lambarene: a medical report." COURIER, Summer 1977, p. 6.

2147   "Lambarene: then and now." M.D. (New York) 8:9 (Sept. 1965),
        pp. 130-34.

2148   LAUTERBURG-BONJOUR, MARKUS. "Albert Schweitzer als Arzt."
        In: EHRFURCHT, pp. 159-66.

2149   LIPSCHÜTZ, ALEXANDER. Tres Médicos Contemporáneos: Pavlov,
        Freud, Schweitzer. Buenos Aires: Losada, 1958.

2150   MAI, HERMANN. "Albert Schweitzers Denken und Handeln als
        Arzt." Universitas (Stuttgart) 30:12 (Dec. 1975),
        pp. 1285-1300.

2151   _____. "Der Arzt Albert Schweitzer." Jahresschrift 1967 der
        Gesellschaft zur Förderung der Westfälischen Wilhelms-
        Universität zu Münster (Münster/Westf.), 1967. Also
        issued as a 17-page offprint: Münster: Gesellschaft

Medicine

zur Förderung der Westfälischen Wilhelms-Universität, 1967. Reprinted in RUNDBRIEF 31 (1968).

2152 _____. "Der Arzt Albert Schweitzer--Begegnung und Werk." Universitas (Stuttgart) 24:6 (June 1969), pp. 629-40.

2153 _____. "Einige Beobachtungen am Verhalten der Kinder in Lambarene." RUNDBRIEF 40 (Jan. 14, 1975), pp. 30-36. Translated as "Working with children at Lambarene." COURIER, Winter 1976, pp. 12-15.

2154 _____. "Erlebnisse des Kinderarztes in Lambarene." RUNDBRIEF 42 (Oct. 1976), pp. 16-23.

2155 _____. "Expériences récentes d'un Pédiatrie à Lambaréné." CAHIERS 23 (June 1970), pp. 12-15.

2156 _____. "Het spreekour van de kinderarts in Lambarene." NIEUWS 19:2 (Dec. 1970), pp. 26-30.

2157 _____. "Lambarene mit den Augen eines Arztes gesehen." RUNDBRIEF 15 (Jan. 14, 1960), pp. 20-25.

2158 _____. "Das Lepradorf Lambarene. Aus den Urwaldhospital Dr. Albert Schweitzer." Medizinische Klinik (Munich) 58:10 (March 8, 1963), pp. 408-12. Reprinted in RUNDBRIEF 22 (1963), pp. 38-45.

2159 _____. "Masern im Urwald Zentralafrikas. Aus dem Urwald-hospital Albert Schweitzers, Lambarene." Münchener Medizinische Wochenschrift (Munich) 103:26 (June 30, 1961), pp. 1293-95.

2160 _____. "Pädiatrie in Lambaréné." RUNDBRIEF 35 (June 15, 1972), pp. 6-12.

2161 _____. "Über 40 Jahre Urwaldspital Albert Schweitzer in Lambarene." Medizinische Klinik (Munich) 56:38 (Sept. 22, 1961), pp. 1613-21. Reprinted in: DENKEN UND WEG, pp. 364-83; reprinted, with new introduction and enlarged text, in: BEGEGNUNG, pp. 85-107; enlarged text issued as a reprint, Munich: Beck, 1965, 22 pp.

2162 _____. "Un stage médical à Lambaréné en été 1965." CAHIERS 13 (June 1965), pp. 14-15.

2163 _____. "Zum Welt-Lepratag 1978." RUNDBRIEF 45 (May 1978), pp. 25-32.

2164   MARTINI, PAUL. "Albert Schweitzer als Arzt." In: DENKEN
        UND WEG, pp. 313-20. Translated as "Albert Schweitzer--
        physician in Lambarene." Universitas (English Language
        edition) 7:1 (1964), pp. 25-32.

2165   MILLER, DAVID C. "Schweitzer als Arzt und Chirurg."
        RUNDBRIEF 47 (May 1979), pp. 43-45.

2166   _____. "Schweitzer's contribution to medicine." In: THE
        CONVOCATION RECORD, pp. IV/17-19.

2167   _____, STEVEN S. SPENCER and PAUL DUDLEY WHITE. "Survey of
        cardio-vascular disease among Africans in the vicinity
        of the Albert Schweitzer Hospital in 1960." The American
        Journal of Cardiology (New York) 10:3 (Sept. 1962),
        pp. 432-46.

2168   MONTAGUE, JOSEPH FRANKLIN. "Albert Schweitzer as a man of
        medicine." In: DEBRECEN, pp. 33-43.

2169   MULLER, ROLF. "50 Jahre Albert Schweitzer-Spital in
        Lambarene." Münchener Medizinische Wochenschrift
        (Munich) 105:51 (Dec. 20, 1963), pp. 2521-30. Trans-
        lated in Médicine et Hygiene (Geneva) 21 (Dec. 18, 1963);
        22 (Jan. 5, 1964).

2170   MUNZ, WALTER. "Die Arbeit--Bericht über das Jahr 1965 in
        Lambarene. Das medische Jahr." BERICHTE 29 (April 1966),
        pp. 16-22. Translated as "Bilan de l'Année 1965 à
        Lambaréné--dernières initiatives du Doctor." CAHIERS 15
        (June 1966), pp. 10-15.

2171   _____. "Jahresbericht des Chef-Arztes." BERICHTE 31
        (June 1969), pp. 2-6.

2172   _____. "Lambarene 1966--das erste Jahr nach Albert
        Schweitzer." Münchener Medizinische Wochenschrift
        (Munich) 109:44 (1967), pp. 2325-31. Also issued as an
        offprint. Translated as "Lambarene 1966. Premier année
        après la mort d'Albert Schweitzer." CAHIERS 18
        (Dec. 1967), pp. 11-16; Reprinted as "Bericht des
        Chefarztes." BERICHTE 30 (Sept. 1967), pp. 5-15.

2173   NESSMANN, VIKTOR. "Le médecin Albert Schweitzer." In:
        WÜRDIGUNG, pp. 14-20. Reprinted in: RAYONNEMENT,
        pp. 217-20; translated as "Albert Schweitzer als Doktor."
        In: Albert Schweitzer. Naar zijn Waarde geschat.
        Deventer: AE Kluwer, pp. 18-26.

Medicine

2174 _____. "Het ordeel van een Doktor over het ziekenhuis, en het werk in Lambarene." NIEUWS 9 (Nov. 1936), pp. 5-7.

2175 _____ and FREDERIC TRENSZ. "Nouveau cas de bilharzoise intestinale à schistosomo haematobium observé au Gabon" (Laboratoire de l'hôpital du Dr. Schweitzer à Lambaréné, Gabon). In: Annales de Parisitologie Humaine et Comparée (Paris) 6:2 (April 1, 1928), pp. 182-85.

2176 NISSEN, RUDOLF. "Die Konsequenter der Ehrfurcht vor dem Leben für die Medizin." Universitas (Stuttgart) 15:1 (Jan. 1960), pp. 83-88. Reprinted in: DENKEN UND WEG, pp. 321-25.

2177 NOMURA, M. "Shinko no ijin Albert Schweitzer." Igaku to Fukuin (Tokyo) 1:1 (May 1949), pp. 4-12.

2178 OLPP, GOTTLIEB. [Albert Schweitzer.] In: Charakterköpfe der Tropenmedizin. Berlin: Verlag die Brücke zur Heimat, 1936, pp. 91-92. Port.

2179 OTT, EMMA. "Natur, Mensch, und Tier." In: HALFEN, pp. 133-39.

2180 PAULING, LINUS and FRANK CATCHPOOL. "Doktor der Humanität." In: BEITRÄGE, pp. 116-22.

2181 PENN, JACK. "Lambaréné." Medical Proceedings--Mediese Bydraes (Johannesburg, South Africa) 11:24 (Nov. 20, 1965), pp. 578-84.

2182 _____. "A visit to Albert Schweitzer." Plastic and Reconstructive Surgery (Baltimore) 18:3 (Sept. 1956), pp. 161-68. Condensed in Current Medical Digest (Hagerstown, Md.), Jan. 1957, pp. 44-49.

2183 PERCY, EMERIC. "Medical work at Lambarene today." BRITISH BULLETIN 21 (Feb. 1954), pp. 4-6. Translated as "Medizinische Arbeit in Lambarene." RUNDBRIEF 5 (June 1, 1954), pp. 31-34; translated as "Medische arbeid in Lambarene." NIEUWS 3:3 (Oct. 1954), pp. 83-85.

2184 PERIER-DAVILLE, DENIS. "La bronchite fait, en Afrique, plus de victimes que la lépre." Le Figaro (Paris) 2799 (Sept. 9, 1953), p. 5.

2185 POPE, FERGUS and SIMON OBAME BIKORO. "Les soins aux enfants à l'hôpital du Docteur Albert Schweitzer." CAHIERS 15 (June 1966), pp. 16-18.

2186   RANDIN, W.   "Pourquoi y a-t-il encore un village de lépreux
         à Lambaréné?"   NOUVELLES 25 (Sept. 1974), pp. 5-7.

2187   "Resume des activites médicales pour le mois d'Octobre 1978."
         A.I.S.L. Bulletin 8 (Nov. 1978), pp. 44-45.

2188   RÜTTI, WALTER.   "Aus unserer Klinik."   RUNDBRIEF 45 (May 1978),
         pp. 12-13.   Illus.

2189   RUSSELL, MRS. C. E. B. (LILIAN M.).   "For the sick in mind
         and body."   BRITISH BULLETIN 5 (Spring 1931), pp. 2-8.
         Illus.

2190   RUTISHAUSER, ARMIN.   "Beitrag zur Operation der Skrotumele-
         phantiasis.   Erfahrung aus dem Spital von Dr. Albert
         Schweitzer in Lambarene, Gabon."   Deutsche
         Tropenmedizinische Zeitschrift (Leipzig) 45:14 (1941),
         pp. 436-40.   Also issued as an offprint.

2191   _____.   "Erfahrung und Beobachtungen in der Geburtshilfe im
         Gabon (Afrique Equatoriale Francaise)."   Separatdruck
         aus Sozialanthropologie und Rassenhygiene (Zürich) 16:1/2
         (1941), pp. 235-67.

2192   SCHNABEL, ILSE.   "Medizinisches aus Albert Schweitzers
         Urwaldspital (nach einem Vortrag, gehalten in der
         Vereinigung der prakt. Aertze von Zürich und Umgebung)."
         Schweizerische Medizinische Wochenschrift (Basel) 66:16
         (April 18, 1936), pp. 379-81.

2193   _____.   "Von ärztlichen Verrichtungen."   In: HALFEN,
         pp. 52-60.

2194   SCHOENFELD, EUGENE.   "Dr. Schweitzer's hospital."   The New
         Physician (St. Louis, Mo.) 10:3 (March 1961), pp. 81-88.
         Abridged version appeared in The Journal of Medical Educa-
         tion (Evanston, Ill.) 36:3 (March 1961), pp. 223-28.

2195   SCHULTZ, MYRON GILBERT.   "The challenge of Schweitzer."
         The New Physician (St. Louis, Mo.) 9:9 (Sept. 1960),
         pp. 43-47.

2196   SCHULZE, KÄTHE.   "Unter dem Sonnenschirmbaum von Lambarene."
         RUNDBRIEF 19 (Jan. 14, 1962), pp. 37-41.

2197   SCHWAB, TH.   "Die medizinische Bedeutung Lambarénés."
         BERICHTE 34 (Aug. 1972), pp. 8-9.

Medicine

2198 SILVER, ALI. "De verzorging van onze lepralijders."
Tijdschrift voor Ziekenverpfleging (Amsterdam) 3:8
(April 15, 1950), pp. 185-88.

2199 SKILLINGS, EVERETT. "Albert Schweitzer, humanitarian." In:
JUBILEE, pp. 87-118.

2200 "Some facts and figures." BRITISH BULLETIN 27 (Jan. 14, 1965),
pp. 4-6.

2201 STALDER, HANS. "Arzt und Patient in Afrika." In: HALFEN,
pp. 228-37.

2202 STAEWEN, CHRISTOPH. "Die Geistes- und Gemütskranken
Patienten des Spitals Lambarene." RUNDBRIEF 24
(June 15, 1964), pp. 26-29. Reprinted in: DOKUMENTE,
pp. 78-82; translated as "Die gestelijk gestoorde
patienten van Lambarene's ziekenhuis." NIEUWS 13:2
(Nov. 1964), pp. 3-4f.

2203 STEINER, ANDREAS. "Bericht van de geneisheer-directeur."
EERBIED 27:2 (Aug. 1978), pp. 8-10.

2204 _____. "Der Chefarzt, Dr. Andreas Steiner, Berichtet."
RUNDBRIEF 45 (May 1978), pp. 10-12.

2205 _____. "Rapport médical." A.I.S.L. Bulletin 4 (July 1977),
pp. 6-17.

2206 _____. "Rapport médical." A.I.S.L. Bulletin 5 (Nov. 1977),
pp. 31-32.

2207 _____. "Rapport médical." A.I.S.L. Bulletin 8 (Nov. 1978),
p. 43.

2208 STOEVESANDT, KARL. "Albert Schweitzer als Arzt und Helfer
der Menschheit." Evangelische Theologie (Munich) 15:3
(March 1955), pp. 97-114.

2209 "Surgery in the jungle" (editorial). Modern Medicine
(Minneapolis, Minn.) 24:17 (Aug. 21, 1961), pp. 28ff.

2210 TAKAHASHI, I. "Medical ethics of Albert Schweitzer, in honor
of his 90th birthday." Journal of the Japan Medical
Association 52 (Nov. 15, 1964), pp. 983-90.

2211 TENBRINCK, MARGARET S. "Blood pressure comparisons in
tropical Africans (Lambarene Hospital) and Peruvians."
New York State Journal of Medicine 64:20 (Oct. 15, 1964),
pp. 2584-87.

2212 _____. "Follow-up studies in tropical Africans." New York
       State Journal of Medicine 67:5 (March 1, 1967), pp. 724-25.

2213 _____. "Hospital practice in Equatorial Africa." Journal of
       the American Medical Women's Association (Nashville, Tenn.)
       17:2 (Feb. 1962), pp. 129-33. Also issued as a reprint.

2214 _____. "Hospital practice in Equatorial Africa. A revisit
       and an appraisal." Journal of the American Medical
       Women's Association (Nashville, Tenn.) 20:4 (April 1965),
       pp. 329-32.

2215 THEOPHRASTUS (pseud.). "Die kulturelle Mission des Arztes."
       Berliner Ärzteblatt 65:18 (Sept. 16, 1952), pp. 325-26.

2216 TOWN, ARNO E. "Opthamological Safari. A visit to Dr. Albert
       Schweitzer is included in the journey in which eye work
       was emphasized." Guildcraft (Philadelphia) 31:11
       (Nov. 1957), pp. 33-35.

2217 TRENSZ, FRÉDÉRIC and K. THOMAS. "Albert Schweitzer als Arzt."
       Wege zum Menschen (Göttingen) 7:1 (Jan. 1955), pp. 1-9.

2218 TRENSZ, FRÉDÉRIC. "Le médicin." In: ETUDES, pp. 203-24;
       second edition, pp. 173-90. Reprinted in: RAYONNEMENT,
       pp. 208-16.

2219 _____. "Rapport de mon voyage à Lambaréné." CAHIERS 19
       (June 1968), pp. 24-27.

2220 VAN WIJNEN, ARY. "Die Kinderabteilung." BERICHTE 30
       (Sept. 1967), pp. 21-23.

2221 WAWRO, N. WILLIAM. "A recent visit with Dr. Albert Schweitzer."
       Journal of the American Medical Association (Chicago),
       195:4 (Jan. 24, 1966), pp. 246-48.

2222 WEISS, ROBERT. "Schweitzer, pharmacien." In: HOMMAGE,
       pp. 112-18. Reprinted in: RAYONNEMENT, pp. 225-28.

2223 WICHT, ANDRE. "Rapport technique." A.I.S.L. Bulletin 8
       (Nov. 1978), pp. 55-57.

2224 WOODBURY, M. A. et al. "Psychiatric care at the Albert
       Schweitzer Hospital." Mental Hospitals (Washington,
       D.C.) 16:5 (May 1965), pp. 145-50. Illus.

2225 WOYTT-SECRETAN, MARIE. "Souvenirs d'une infirmière." In:
       RAYONNEMENT, pp. 228-40.

Medicine

2226   ZELLWEGER, HANS. "Grosskampftag im Spital." In: HALFEN,
          pp. 84-99.

2227   _____. "Looking back at Schweitzer." The Iowa Alumni Review
          (Iowa City, Iowa) 14:2 (Feb. 1961), pp. 4-11. Excerpted
          in An Understanding of Albert Schweitzer, no. 274 above,
          pp. 142-43.

2228   ZUROVSKY, BAYLE. "Albert Schweitzer . . . 'Reverence for
          Life.'" Postgraduate Medicine (Minneapolis, Minn.) 4:5
          (Nov. 1948), pp. 457-67.

VI. Philosophy

A. GENERAL

1. Books by Schweitzer

DIE RELIGIONSPHILOSOPHIE KANTS VON DER KRITIK DER REINEN VERNUNFT
BIS ZUR RELIGION INNERHALB DER GRENZEN DER BLOSSEN VERNUNFT
(The Religious Philosophy of Kant from the "Critique of Pure Reason"
to "Religion within the Bounds of Mere Reason")

In his autobiography, Albert Schweitzer has written: "By the advice
of Theobald Ziegler, I determined that I would take in hand next the
dissertation for the degree of Doctor in Philosophy. At the end of
the term (1898) he suggested to me . . . that my subject should be
the religious philosophy of Kant, a suggestion which greatly attracted me. Towards the end of October 1898 I went to Paris to study
philosophy at the Sorbonne. . . ." This was a disappointing experience for Schweitzer, and, instead, he sometimes attended lectures at
the Protestant Theological Faculty; but then he "resolved without
more ado to write the thesis without troubling with the literature,
and to see what results I could get by burying myself in the Kantian
writings themselves. . . . In the middle of March 1899 I returned to
Strasburg and read my finished work aloud to Theobald Ziegler. He
expressed himself as being strongly in agreement with it. It was
settled that I should take my degree at the end of July."[1] Schweitzer
spent the summer in reading philosophy in Berlin and, returning as
planned to Strassburg, took his degree at the end of July 1899. His
dissertation, "Die Religionsphilosophische Skizze der Kritik der
reinen Vernunft," was immediately elaborated and enlarged and appeared as a book before the end of the year.

2229   Die religionsphilosophische Skizze der Kritik der reinen
        Vernunft. Inauguraldissertation zur Erlangung der Doktor
        Würde bei der philosophischen Fakultät der Kaiser

---

[1]Out of My Life and Thought. New York: Holt, Rinehart and Winston,
1961, pp. 16, 19, 21.

General

Philosophy

Wilhelms-Universität zu Strassburg i.E., von Albert
Schweitzer, Kandidat der Theologie zu Strassburg i.E.
Freiburg im Breisgau: C. A. Wagner, 1899. 72 pp.

2230 Die Religionsphilosophie Kants von der Kritik der reinen
Vernunft bis zur Religion innerhalb der Grenzen der
blossen Vernunft. Freiburg i. B., Leipzig and Tübingen:
J. C. B. Mohr (Paul Siebeck), 1899. viii, 325 pp.

2231 Same. Nachdruck der ausg. 1899. Hildesheim, New York:
G. Olms, 1974. viii, 325 pp.

English

2232 The Essence of Faith; Philosophy of Religion. Translated and
edited, and with a foreword by Kurt F. Leidecker. New
York: Philosophical Library (distributed to the trade by
Book Sales, Inc.), 1966. 124 pp.

See also A Treasury of Albert Schweitzer, no. 66 above.

Japanese

Kanto no Shūkyo-tetsugaku. Tr. Giichi Saito and Shizutero
Yeda. Tokyo: Hakusuisha, 1959-60. See Collected Works,
no. 15 above.

KULTURPHILOSOPHIE
I. VERFALL UND WIEDERAUFBAU DER KULTUR
II. KULTUR UND ETHIK
(Philosophy of Civilization: I. The Decay and
Restoration of Civilization; II. Civilization and Ethics)

Kulturphilosophie was begun in Lambarene in 1914, while Schweitzer
was under house arrest as an enemy alien and was forbidden all activity in his hospital. He relates that the "first incitement to take
up this subject" came to him in Berlin while he was studying there
in the summer of 1899. "As early as my first years at the university
I had begun to feel misgivings about the opinion that mankind is con-
stantly developing in the direction of progress. My impression was
that the fire of its ideals was burning low without anyone noticing
it or troubling about it."[1] It was not until his sudden enforced
inactivity, however, that he found opportunity to initiate work on
the subject. When his internment was finally lifted, writing

---

[1]Out of My Life and Thought. New York: Holt, Rinehart and Winston,
1961, p. 146.

212

continued during night hours after hospital duties were finished.

In 1917 the French compelled Dr. Schweitzer and his wife, as German citizens, to leave Lambarene and undergo a second period of internment in Southern France. After their eventual return to Strasbourg, work on the Philosophy of Civilization continued, although Schweitzer could bring with him from Africa only a very rough draft of the original, and much of the manuscript had to be rewritten. In 1920 the first part of the book was finished and immediately provided material for a series of lectures to be delivered by Schweitzer at the University of Uppsala by invitation of the Olaus Petri Foundation. The lectures were also given in 1922 at Mansfield College, Oxford, and invitations followed from other European universities.

"In the spring of 1923," Schweitzer wrote, "the first two volumes of the Philosophy of Civilization were finished, and they were published the same year. The first bears the title of Verfall und Wiederaufbau der Kultur and the second that of Kultur und Ethik. In the first I describe the relations which subsist between Civilization and attitude toward life. . . . In Civilization and Ethics I unroll the history of the tragic struggle of European thought to attain an ethical acceptance of the world and life."[1] Projected third and fourth volumes in the series, to be devoted to reverence for life and the civilized state have never been published.

Part I

2233   Verfall und Wiederaufbau der Kultur. Kulturphilosophie.
        Erster Teil. Bern: Paul Haupt Akademische Buchhandlung
        vorm. Max Drechsel; Munich: C. H. Beck'sche
        Verlagsbuchhandlung (Oskar Beck), 1923. vii, 65 pp.
        (Olaus Petri-Vorlesungen an der Universität Upsala.)
        2. unveränd. Aufl., 1925; 3. Aufl., 1928; 4. Aufl., 1929;
        5. Aufl., 1931; 7. Aufl., 1941; 8. Aufl. Munich:
        Biederstein Verlag, 1946; 9. Aufl. Munich: Biederstein
        Verlag, 1948; 10. Aufl., 1951; 11. Aufl., 1953; 12. Aufl.,
        1955; 13. Aufl., 1958; "Sonderausgabe," 1960 (combined
        edition, see no. 2256 below.)

Arabic

2234   Falsafat al-hadārah (combined edition). Tr. Abd-al-Rahmān
        Badawī. Al-Qāhirah: Al-Mu'assasah al-'Amman Lil-ta'līf,
        1963. 419 pp.

---

[1]Ibid, pp. 197f.

213

General

Philosophy

Chinese

2235 Wen ming ti Shuai Pai Ho Fu Hsing. Tr. Liu Shu Hsien.
Taichung: Chung Yang Book Co., 1958. 78 pp.

2236 Same. Taiwan: Central Book Co., 1972. 78 pp.

2237 [The Philosophy of Civilization, combined edition.] Tr.
Anthony T. A. Cheng. Taiwan: Chih Wen Publishing Co.,
1974. 184 pp.

Czech

2238 Křesťanska Sociální Etika. Úpadek a nová vystavba Kultury.
Tr. Terezie Havlenová Kühnová. Prague: UCN, 1964. 79 pp.

Danish

2239 Kulturens Forfald og Genrejsning. Tr. Hans Wind. Copenhagen:
W. Pios Boghandel-Povl Branner, 1925. 90 pp.

2240 (Second edition). Tr. Johs. Novrup. Copenhagen: Det danske
Forlag, 1946. 82 pp. (Europaeisk Kulturbibliotek 2.)
2. Oplag., 1948; 3. Oplag., 1951; 4. Oplag., 1953; 5.
Oplag., 1956.

Dutch

2241 Verval en Weder-opbouw der Cultuur. Cultuur Philosophie, dl.
I. Tr. J. Eigenhuis. Haarlem: H. D. Tjeenk Willink &
Zoon, 1928. (Olaus Petri-lesingen aaan de Universiteit
van Upsala.)

English

2242 The Decay and the Restoration of Civilization. The Philosophy
of Civilization, Part I. Tr. C. T. Campion. London:
A. and C. Black, 1923. xvi, 105 pp. (The Dale Memorial
Lectures, delivered at Mansfield College, Oxford University, 1922.) 2nd impression, 1932; 3rd impr., 1947; 4th
impr., 1950; 5th impr., 1955. Also New York: Macmillan,
1933.

2243 (Paperback edition). Tr. C. T. Campion. London: Unwin
Books, published in association with Adam and Charles
Black, 1961. 91 pp. (Unwin Books, 19).

2244 The Philosophy of Civilization (combined edition). Tr. C. T.
Campion. Part I: The Decay and the Restoration of

Civilization. Part II: Civilization and Ethics. First
American Edition. New York: The Macmillan Co., 1949.
xvii, 347 pp. Reprinted, 1951.

2245 (Paperback edition). Two parts in one volume. New York:
Macmillan, 1960. xvii, 347 pp. (Macmillan Paperbacks,
12.)

2246 (Talking book for the blind). From the edition of the
Macmillan Company, 1949. 2 parts. Read by Kermit Murdock,
1951. American Foundation for the Blind. 24 records.

Italian

2247 Agonia della civiltà. Tr. M. Tássoni. Milan: Edizioni di
Comunità, 1963. 94 pp. (Humana civiltas, 16.)

Japanese

2248 Bunka no Botsuraku to Saiken (Bunka Tetsugaku, I.) Tr. Hyo
Pi yaku Ishihara. Tokyo: Shinkyo Shuppansha, 1951.
187 pp., port., illus.

Bunka no Taihai to Saiken. Tr. Koji Kunimatsu. Tokyo:
Hakusuisha, 1957. See Collected Works, no. 6 above.

Kannada (India)

2249 Badukuvadari. Tr. K. S. Haridasa Bhatta. Udupi: Mahatma
Gandhi Memorial College, 1956. 21 pp.

Korean

2250 Mun'hwa'eui Mol'lag'gwa Jae'geon. Tr. Ji Myeong-gwan. Seoul:
A'ca'de'mi, 1959. 108 pp.

Norwegian

2251 Du skal bygge opp (combined edition). Tr. Carl Engelstad.
Oslo: Johan Grundt Tanum, 1954. 312 pp. Contains
Kulturens Forfall og Gjenreisning, pp. 11-65, and Kultur
og Etikk, pp. 69-310.

Portuguese

2252 Decadência e regeneraçāo da culturá (Filosofia da culturá).
Conferências da Série "Olaus Petri" feitas na Universidade
de Upsala, Suécia. Traducāo, Prefacio e Notas de Pedro
de Almeida Moura. São Paulo: Edicões Melhoramentos,

Philosophy

> 1948. 110 pp., front. (port.), cover illus. Second edi-
> tion, 1959; third edition, 1964, 184 pp. 1964 edition
> contains as appendices the nuclear test ban broadcasts of
> April 28-30, 1958 and "The Problem of Ethics. . .,"
> see no. 2328 below.

Spanish

2253 Decaimiento y Restauración de la Civilizatión. Filosofía de
      la Civilización I. Buenos Aires: Sur, 1962. 105 pp.

Swedish

2254 Kulturens degeneration och regeneration. Kulturfilosofi,
      Förste delen. Tr. Oskar Krook. Stockholm: Svenska
      Kyrkans Diakonistyrelses Bokförlag, 1924. xxiii, 69 pp.
      (Olaus Petriföreläsningar vid Uppsala Universitet.)

Part II

2255 Kultur und Ethik. Kulturphilosophie. Zweiter Teil. Bern:
      Paul Haupt Akademische Buchhandlung vorm. Max Drechsel;
      Munich: C. H. Beck'sche Verlagsbuchhandlung (Oskar Beck),
      1923. xxiii, 280 pp. (Olaus Petri-Vorlesungen an der
      Universität Upsala.) 2. unveränderte Aufl., 1924; 3. Aufl.,
      1925; 4. Aufl., 1926; 5. Aufl., 1929; 6. Aufl., 1947; 7.
      Aufl., 1948; 8. Aufl., 1951; 9. unveränd. Aufl., 1953,
      xxvi, 269 pp.; 10. Aufl., 1955; 11. Aufl., 1958.

2256 Same. "Sonderausgabe" mit Einschluss von Verfall und
      Wiederaufbau der Kultur. Munich: C. H. Beck, 1960.
      372 pp. (Kulturphilosophie I and II.) Reprinted 1972.

Chinese

2257 [The Philosophy of Civilization (combined edition).] Tr.
      Anthony T. A. Cheng. Taiwan: Chih Wen Publ. Co., 1974.
      184 pp.

Danish

2258 AErefrygten for Livet. Tr. Herman Kleener. Copenhagen:
      Det danske Forlag, 1946. 111 pp. (Europaeisk Kultur-
      bibliotek, 3.) 2. opl., 1951, 108 pp.

2259 Kultur og Etik. Kulturphilosofi, 2. Del. Tr. Herman Kleener.
      Copenhagen: Det danske Forlag, 1953. 346 pp. 2. opl.,
      1954.

General

Dutch

2260   Cultuur en ethiek. Cultuur-philosophie, Dl. II. Tr. J.
          Eigenhuis. Haarlem: H. D. Tjeenk Willink & Zoon, 1931.
          xviii, 319 pp.

English

2261   Civilization and Ethics. The Philosophy of Civilization, II.
          Tr. John Naish. London: A. and C. Black, 1923. xxvi,
          298 pp. (The Dale Memorial Lectures delivered at
          Mansfield College, Oxford University, 1922.)[1]

2262   (Second edition, revised). Tr. C. T. Campion. London:
          A. and C. Black, 1929. xxiv, 289 pp.

2263   (Third edition, revised by Mrs. C. E. B. Russell). London:
          A. and C. Black, 1946. xxviii, 284 pp. Reprinted 1947,
          1949, 1951, 1955. Also issued with the imprint of the
          Macmillan Co., New York, 1947.

2264   (Paperback edition). London: Unwin Books, published in
          association with A. and C. Black, 1961. 248 pp. (Unwin
          Books, 20.)

2265   The Philosophy of Civilization (2 parts in one volume). Tr.
          C. T. Campion. Revised by Mrs. C. E. B. Russell. Part I:
          The Decay and the Restoration of Civilization. Part II:
          Civilization and Ethics. First American Edition. New
          York: The Macmillan Co., 1949. xvii, 347 pp. Reprinted,
          1951.

2266   (Paperback edition). Two parts in one volume. New York:
          Macmillan, 1960. xvii, 347 pp. (Macmillan Paperbacks,
          12.)

French

2267   La civilisation et l'éthique. Tr. M. Horst. Avant-propos
          Robert Minder. Préf. du Georges Marchal. Colmar: Ed.
          Alsatia, 1976. 216 pp.

---

[1]While the lectures were delivered in French, Schweitzer wrote out
his final copy for publication in German. Thus this manuscript is
a translation from the German rather than the French.

Philosophy

Japanese

2268   Bunka to Rinri. Tr. Yoshiyuki Yokoyama. Tokyo: Shinkyo
            Shuppansha, 1953. 430 pp.

        Same. Tr. Hidehiro Higami. Tokyo: Hakusuisha, 1957. See
            Collected Works, no. 7 above.

Norwegian

2269   Du skal bygge opp (combined edition). Tr. Carl Engelstad.
            Oslo: Johan Grundt Tanum, 1954. 312 pp.

Portuguese

2270   Cultura e ética. Tr. Herbert Caro. São Paulo: Ediçoes
            Melhoramentos, 1959. 295 pp., cover illus.

Russian

2271   Kul'tura i Êtika. Tr. N. A. Zaharcĕnko and G. V. Kolsanskij.
            Intro. Prof. Karpuschin. Moscow: Progress, 1973. 343 pp.

Spanish

2272   Civilización y Ética. Filosofía de la Civilización II.
            Tr. Héctor Vaccaro. Buenos Aires: Sur, 1962. 390 pp.

Swedish

2273   Kultur och Etik. Tr. Alvarik Roos. Stockholm: Bokförlaget
            Natur och Kultur, 1946. 315 pp., front. (port.).
            (Olaus Petriföreläsningar vid Uppsala Universitet).

DIE WELTANSCHAUUNG DER INDISCHEN DENKER
(Indian Thought and Its Development)

Mrs. Charles E. B. Russell, a close friend of Albert Schweitzer and
translator of several of his books, wrote that "he did not set out
to write a book on Indian thinkers. It came almost against his will.
In the preparation of the third volume of the Philosophy on which he
has been working for years, he found the Indian material he had collected was assuming an enormous bulk, and in order to keep within
bounds of the book he hopes at last to publish next year, he decided

to throw off much of this material in a separate preliminary
volume. . . ."[1]

   Schweitzer himself writes in his preface that the book was written "in the hope that it may help people in Europe to become better
acquainted than they are at present with the ideas [Indian thought]
stands for and the great personalities in whom these ideas are em-
bodied." He continues: "Indian thought has greatly attracted me
since in my youth I first became acquainted with it through reading
the works of Arthur Schopenauer. From the very beginning I was convinced that all thought is really concerned with the great problem
of how man can attain to spiritual union with infinite being. My
attention was drawn to Indian thought because it is busied with this
problem and because by its nature it is mysticism. What I liked
about it also was that Indian ethics are concerned with the behaviour
of man to all living beings and not merely with his attitude to his
fellow-man and to human society. . . . The deliberate brevity of my
treatise may give occasion to all kinds of misunderstanding. I had
no intention of describing Indian philosophy in detail, but only
wanted to show how it regards the great problems of life and how it
undertakes to solve them."[2]

2274   Die Weltanschauung der indischen Denker. (Mystik und Ethik.)
          Munich: C. H. Beck'sche Verlagsbuchhandlung; Bern:
          Paul Haupt, 1934. xi, 201 pp. Reissued, 1935.

2275   Same. 2., auf der Grund der Englischen Ausgabe von 1935
          Neugefasste Auflage. Munich: C. H. Beck, 1965. xii,
          218 pp. Includes a chapter on Gandhi, translated from
          the 1935 English edition.

2276   (Third edition). Munich: C. H. Beck, 1978. xii, 217 pp.
          (Beck'sche Sonderausgabe.)

Danish

2277   Indisk Taenkning og Mystik. Bearbejdet og oversat af Børge
          Friis. Copenhagen: Branner og Korch, 1956. 239 pp.

---

[1]Hibbert Journal (London) 33 (July 1935), pp. 630-34.

[2]Indian Thought and Its Development. Boston: Beacon Press, 1957.
pp. v-viii.

General

Philosophy

Dutch

2278 De wereldbeschouwing der indischen denkers. Mystiek en
        ethiek. Tr. Jan Eigenhuis. Haarlem: H. D. Tjeenk
        Willink & Zoon, 1935. 180 pp.

English

2279 Indian Thought and its Development. Tr. Mrs. Charles E. B.
        Russell. London: Hodder and Stoughton; New York:
        Henry Holt and Co., 1935. xii, 272 pp. Reprinted, 1956.

2280 Same. London: A. and C. Black, 1951. xii, 272 pp.
        Reissued, 1956.

2281 Same. Boston: The Beacon Press, 1952. xii, 272 pp. Paper-
        back edition, 1957, xii, 272 pp. Second printing,
        Sept. 1957; Third printing, June 1960.

2282 Same. Tr. Mrs. Charles E. B. Russell. Bombay: Wilco Pub-
        lishing House, 1960. 255 pp. (Wilco Books, W 42.)

French

2283 Les grands penseurs de l'Inde. Étude de philosophie comparée.
        Paris: Payot, 1936. 238 pp. (Bibliothèque Scientifique.)
        Reprinted 1945, 1952, 1956.

2284 Same. Tr. J.-L. Perrenoud. Paris: Petite Bibliothèque
        Payot, 1962. 209 pp. (Petite Bibliothèque Payot, 1.)

Italian

2285 Grandi Pensatori dell'India. Rome: Astrolabio. 208 pp.

Japanese

Indo Shisōka no Sekaikan. Shimpi-shugi to Rinri. Tr. Hiroshi
        Nakamura and Koshiro Temaki. Tokyo: Hakusuisha, 1957.
        See Collected Works, no. 9 above.

Norwegian

2286 Indinsk ög Kinesisk Tenkning. Tr. Bjørn Braaten. Innledning
        av Johan B. Hygen. Oslo: H. Aschehoug (W. Nygaard), 1972.
        132 pp.

Spanish

2287   El pensamiento de la India. Tr. Antonio Ramos-Oliveira.
       Mexico, Buenos Aires: Fondo de Cultura Económica, 1952.
       231 pp. (Breviaros del Fondo de Cultura Económica, 63.)
       Second edition, 1958.

Swedish

2288   Indisk livssyn. Mystik och Etik. Tr. Hugo Hultenberg.
       Stockholm: Svenska Krykans Diakonistyrelses Bokförlag,
       1935. 192 pp.

2. Shorter Writings by Schweitzer

2289   "Das Abenteuer Mensch zu sein. Die Organisierte
       Gedanklosigkeit im Jahrhundert der Angst." Europa
       (Bad Reichenall) 14:12 (1963), pp. 44-47.

2290   "Die Abhängigkeit der Individuen von der Gemeinschaften in
       der Gegenwart" (aus Kulturphilosophie, vol. 1, pp. 16ff.).
       Philosophie und Leben (Osterwieck/Harz) 1:4 (April 1925),
       pp. 147-49.

2291   "Albert Schweitzer." In: Alles Leben strömt aus Dir!
       Konfirmandenbuch. Hrsg. von Martin Werner und Julius
       Kaiser. Bern: Paul Haupt, 1926, pp. 82-84.

2292   "Albert Schweitzer." In: Deutsche Aphorismen. Ausgewählt
       von Hans Margolius. Bern: Alfred Scherz, 1953, pp. 46-
       48. (Parnass-Bücherei, Nr. 94.) 13 selections.

2293   "Albert Schweitzer in an interview over Radio Brazzaville,
       1953." In: ALBUM, pp. 153-54. Reprinted in: BRABAZON,
       pp. 245-46.

2294   "Albert Schweitzer on the truly human man." Rotarian
       (Evanston, Ill.) 96 (May 1960), p. 19.

2295   "Albert Schweitzer schreibt." In: FACKELTRÄGER, pp. 45-56.
       Selections.

2296   "Albert Schweitzer: zur Charakterologie der ethischen
       Persönlichkeit und der philosophischen Mystik." In:
       Jahrbuch für Charakterologie I and II, 1926. Excerpts
       from letters to Oskar Kraus, Jan. 2, 1924; Feb. 5, 1926;
       and Jan. 30, 1927. Reprinted in: Kraus, Oskar. Albert
       Schweitzer: Sein Werk und seine Weltanschauung. 2nd ed.

Philosophy

> Berlin, 1929, pp. 38f and 77f; translated in Kraus, Oskar.
> Albert Schweitzer: his work and his philosophy. London:
> Adam and Charles Black, 1944, pp. 42, 71-72; Excerpted in:
> BRABAZON, pp. 148-49, 303-04; excerpted in: Rosen, George
> and Beate Caspari-Rosen, eds. 400 Years of a Doctor's
> Life. New York: Henry Schuman, 1947, p. 414.

2297   "Bedreigde Cultuur." NIEUWS 6:2 (Dec. 1957), p. 10.

2298   "Bewahrt den Idealismus durchs ganze Leben." Der Speyerer
       Protestant (Speyer, Germany) 1 (March 1930), pp. 42-44.
       Excerpt from Aus meiner Kindheit und Jugendzeit.

2299   "Die Bitte für den Nächsten." Weg und Wahrheit (Frankfurt
       a.M.) 14:9 (Jan. 24, 1960), p. 2.

2300   "By Albert Schweitzer." COURIER, May 1974, pp. 6-7. Short
       selections.

2301   "Culture spirituelle et culture matérielle (Declarations qu'il
       a fait à son visiteur)." Bulletin du Bibliophile et du
       Bibliothecaire (Paris) 4 (1951), pp. 205-06. Reprinted
       from Figaro, July 5, 1951.

2302   "L'éthique dans le monde moderne. Un texte inédit du
       docteur Schweitzer." Les Lettres Francaises (Paris)
       1096 (Sept. 9/15, 1965), p. 6.

2303   "En Etisk mentalitet menneskenes redning." Aftenposten
       (Oslo) 95:511 (Nov. 5, 1954), p. 2.

2304   "Une étude philosophique en 1936." CAHIERS 30 (Spring 1974),
       pp. 9-12.

2305   Excerpts from Kulturphilosophie. In: Gollancz, Victor. A
       Year of Grace; Passages Chosen and arranged to express
       a mood about God and man. Middlesex, England: Penguin
       Books, 1955, pp. 217-22, 517-38. Shorter excerpts on
       pp. 9, 210, 309, 339, 424, 476.

2306   "Extrait de sa philosophie culturelles." CAHIERS 28
       (Spring 1973), pp. 3-8.

2307   "From the wisdom of Albert Schweitzer." Wisdom (Beverly Hills,
       Calif.) 1:2 (Feb. 1956), pp. 28-31.

2308   "Für Menschen einen Mensch sein." Die Kultur (Munich) 1:2
       (Oct. 15, 1952), p. 3.

2309   "De gevaarlijke ziekte." NIEUWS 2:5 (July 1954), p. 67.

2310   "Die Grundidee des Guten." RUNDBRIEF 41 (Feb. 1976), p. 48.

2311   "He that loses his life shall find it." In: Anshen, Ruth,
       ed. Moral Principles of Action: Man's ethical imperative.
       New York: Harper, 1952, pp. 673-91. (Science of Culture
       Series, vol. 6.)

2312   "Die Heilung von der Weltangst." Universitas (Stuttgart) 7:1
       (1952), pp. 93-94.

2313   "Der heutige Mensch." Allgemeine Zeitung (Mainz) Feuilleton,
       Nr. 11 (Jan. 14, 1960), p. 7.

2314   "'Humanism is the only true spirituality!' wrote Albert
       Schweitzer." The Humanist (Schenectady, N.Y.) 22:5
       (Sept./Oct. 1962), pp. 157-60. Includes a letter from
       Albert Schweitzer.

2315   "Humanität." Universitas (Stuttgart) 17:6 (June 1962),
       pp. 563-66. Dedicated by the author to his friend,
       Prof. Dr. Eduard Spränger, on his 80th birthday. Re-
       printed in: Die Lehre von der Ehrfurcht vor dem Leben,
       no. 2702 below, pp. 129-32; translated as "Humanity."
       Universitas (English language edition) 5:3 (1962),
       pp. 225-28.

2316   "Die Kraftquellen unseres geistigen Daseins." Universitas
       (Stuttgart) 18:5 (May 1963), pp. 449-56. "Der Verfasser
       schrieb diesen bisher ungedruckten Text 1962 in Lambarene."
       Reprinted in RUNDBRIEF 22 (April 18, 1963), pp. 12-18;
       translated as "The sources of our spiritual existence."
       Universitas (English language edition) 6:2 (1964), pp. 109-
       15; also as "Sources d'energie de notre être spiritual."
       CAHIERS 10 (Dec. 1963), pp. 3-7.

2317   "Die Lebenskraft der Ideale." Die Friedensrundschau 9:9
       (Sept. 1955), p. 1.

2318   "Limites de notre connaissance du monde et principe du
       vouloir-vivre." CAHIERS 33 (Winter 1975), pp. 3-7.
       Excerpted from Philosophy of Civilization.

2319   "The meaning of ideals in life." The Silcoatian (Silcoates
       School, Wakefield, Yorkshire, England) New Series, No. 25
       (Dec. 1935), pp. 781-86. Reprinted in part in BRITISH
       BULLETIN 13 (Autumn 1936), pp. 5-6.

Philosophy

2320   ["A la mémoire d'Albert Schweitzer--deux fragments de Kultur
        und Ethik choises et traduits par Eja Lazari-Pawlowska."]
        In: Fritzhand, Marek, ed. Ethyka II. Warsaw:
        Panstwowe Wydawniectwo Naukowe, 1967.

2321   "Moralische Erzählungen aus dem alten chinesischen Buch 'Von
        Lohn und von der Strafe.'" KIRCHENBOTE 49:7 (Feb. 14, 1920),
        p. 39.

2322   "O mundo de hoje vacile entre a inumanidade e o ideal de
        humanidade." Folha de São Paulo (São Paulo), March 25,
        1962.

2323   "Die organisierte Gedankenlosigkeit." Mannheimer Morgen,
        June 11, 1952. Reprinted in Die Kultur (Munich) 2:20-21
        (1953), p. 1. Reprinted in Plus 1:1 (Nov. 20, 1959),
        pp. 15-17. Illus.

2324   "Peace must be waged." Colliers 136:13 (Dec. 23, 1955),
        p. 29. Adapted from Philosophy of Civilization. One of
        a series of statements from 7 living Nobel Peace Prize
        winners.

2325   "Philosophie de la civilisation (extraits)." CAHIERS 29
        (Summer 1973), pp. 3-6.

2326   "Die Philosophie und die allgemeine Bildung im Neunzehnten
        Jahrhundert." In: Wolf, Georg, compiler. Das
        Neunzehnte Jahrhundert. 24 Aufsätze zur Jahrhundertende.
        Strassburg: Kommissionverlag der Strassburger Druckerei
        u. Verlagsanstalt, 1900, pp. 61-68.

2327   "Por uma visao unificade do munco." A Tribuna da Imprensa
        (Rio de Janeiro), Jan. 16, 1965.

2328   "Le Problème de l'éthique dans l'evolution de la pensée
        humaine." Revue des travaux de l'Académie des Sciences
        morales et politiques et Comptes rendus de sesseances
        1952 (2e semestre), pp. 36-46. Manuscript of a paper
        presented by Schweitzer at the October 20, 1952 meeting
        of the Academy of Moral and Political Sciences. Also
        issued as an offprint. Reprinted in: Feschotte, Jacques.
        Albert Schweitzer. Paris: Editions Universitaires, 1952,
        pp. 118-25; translated as "The problem of ethics in the
        evolution of human thought." In: Feschotte, Jacques.
        Albert Schweitzer: an Introduction. London: A. and C.
        Black, 1954; reprinted in: FESTSCHRIFT, pp. 125-40;
        Reprinted with the title "The problem of ethics for
        twentieth century man." The Saturday Review (New York)

36:24 (June 13, 1953), pp. 9-11, 46-48; reprinted in The
Saturday Review Treasury. New York: Simon and Schuster,
1957, pp. 450-61; reprinted in: Pollock, Thomas C. et al,
eds. Explorations: reading, thinking, discussion, writing. Englewood Cliffs, N.J.: Prentice-Hall, 1956, pp.
708-19; reprinted with the title "The problem of ethics in
the development of human thought." Universitas (English
language edition) 1:2 (1957), pp. 113-24; reprinted in
A.D. Report 4:2 (Feb. 1975), pp. 30-31; reprinted as "Evolution of ethics." The Atlantic Monthly (Boston) 202:5
(Nov. 1958), pp. 69-73. Translated as "Das Problem des
Ethischen in der Entwicklung des menschlichen Denkens."
In: Albert Schweitzer. Genie der Menschlichkeit.
Frankfurt am Main: Fischer, 1955, pp. 223-39; reprinted
in Die Lehre von der Ehrfurcht vor dem Leben, see no.
2702 below, pp. 99-112; reprinted as "Die Bedeutung des
Ethik für den Menschen des 20. Jahrhunderts." Kontinente
(Vienna) 7:4 (Dec. 1953), pp. 2-7, 33; translated as "O
probleme da ética na evolucão do pensamento." In
Decadência e Regeneracão da Cultura, 3rd edition (no.
2252 above). Translated as "Zsady etyki w rozwoju mysli
ludzkiej." Przeglad Lekarski-Oswiecim (Auschwitz) 22:1
(1966), pp. 58-64. Illus.

2329   "Questions of a journalist, Copenhagen, 1959." In: ALBUM,
        pp. 161.

2330   "Dei Religionsphilosophie Kants von der Kritik der reinen
        Vernunft." Kantstudien (Berlin) 5 (1901), pp. 218-21.

2331   "The renunciation of thought." The Saturday Review (New York)
        32:3 (Jan. 15, 1949), pp. 22-23. Excerpt from Out of My
        Life and Thought. Reprinted in: Hamalian, Leo and
        Edmond L. Volpe, eds. Great Essays by Nobel Prize Winners.
        New York: Noonday, 1960, pp. 212-16; reprinted in:
        Barnhart, Thearle A., William A. Donnelly and Lewis C.
        Smith, eds. Viewpoints: Readings for Analysis.
        Englewood Cliffs, N.J.: Prentice-Hall, 1954, pp. 139-43.

2332   "Romantische und rationale Weltanschauung." Philosophie und
        Leben (Osterwieck/Harz) 1:3 (March 1925), pp. 97-98.
        Excerpted from Kulturphilosophie.

2333   "Rosa Luxemburgs Gedanken in Gefängnis." KIRCHENBOTE 50:5
        (Jan. 29, 1921). Excerpted in: Pierhal, Jean. Albert
        Schweitzer; das Leben eines guten Menschen. Munich:
        Kinder Verlag, 1955; translated in: Pierhal, Jean.
        Albert Schweitzer: the life of a great man. London:
        Lutterworth, 1956, p. 123; also in Pierhal, Jean.

Philosophy

        <u>Albert Schweitzer, the story of his life</u>. New York:
        Philosophical Library, 1957, p. 123.

2334   "Schweitzer's answer to a journalist's question about suicide.
        Copenhagen, 1959." In: ALBUM, p. 65.

2335   "Schweitzer's words: light in the jungle." <u>New York Times</u>
        <u>Magazine</u>, Jan. 9, 1955, p. 73.

2336   "The state of civilization." <u>The Christian Register</u> (Boston)
        126:8 (Sept. 1947), pp. 320-23. Based on an interview
        with Schweitzer by Melvin Arnold and Charles R. Joy.
        Summarized in "Schweitzer sees the end of civilization."
        <u>The Christian Century</u> (Chicago) 64:40 (Oct. 1, 1947),
        p. 1165; translated as "Über die Lage unserer Kultur.
        Ein Interview zwischen Wasser und Urwald." <u>Südamerika</u>
        (Buenos Aires) 5:3 (Nov./Dec. 1954), pp. 257-59.

2337   "Über Glaube und Weltanschauung." <u>Welt-Stimmen</u> (Stuttgart)
        24:3 (1955), pp. 97-99. Excerpted from <u>Denken und Tat</u>,
        see no. 30 above.

2338   "Wer sein Leben verliert. . . ." <u>Die Friedensrundschau</u> 8
        (Feb. 1954), pp. 8-9.

2339   "Der Wille zur Wahrhaftigkeit." <u>Die Friedensrundschau</u> 10:9
        (Sept. 1956), pp. 19-21.

2340   "Words to live by." <u>Reader's Digest</u> (Pleasantville, N.Y.)
        65 (Nov. 1954), p. 125. Quotations from Schweitzer.

2341   "Words to live by--discover your true worth." <u>This Week</u>
        <u>Magazine</u> (New York <u>Herald Tribune</u>), Nov. 29, 1959,
        Section 10, p. 2.

2342   "Your second job" (as told in an interview with Fulton
        Oursler). <u>Reader's Digest</u> (Pleasantville, N.Y.) 55
        (Oct. 1949), pp. 1-5. Reprinted in: <u>Thirtieth Anniver-</u>
        <u>sary Reader's Digest Reader</u>. New York: Doubleday, 1951,
        pp. 104-08; reprinted as "Your second job: do unto
        others." <u>Reader's Digest</u> 79 (Oct. 1961), pp. 69-71;
        translated as "Uw tweede taak op aarde." NIEUWS 2:2
        (Sept. 1953), pp. 27-30; translated as "Die zweite
        Aufgabe im Leben." In: <u>Das Beste aus Reader's Digest</u>
        3:1 (1950), pp. 1-5.

3. Works by Others About Schweitzer

    a. Books

2343   BABEL, HENRY ADALBERT. La pensée d'Albert Schweitzer. Sa significance pour le théologie et la philosophie contemporaines. Neuchâtel: H. Messeiller, 1954. 239 pp. Summary in English. See also Dissertations, no. 4310 below.

2344   _____. Que pense Albert Schweitzer? Introduction à la pensée du docteur de Lambaréné. Publié à l'occasion du Congrès International pour la Tolérance, Geneve, 21, 22 et 23 août 1953. Geneva, Paris: Editions Jeheber, 1953. 46 pp.

2345   BAUR, HANS. Albert Schweitzer, der Führer zur Renaissance der Ethik. 192-? 4 pp.

2346   BIRNBAUM, WALTER. Organisches Denken; Vortrag zur Feier des 85. Geburtstages von Albert Schweitzer, am 14. Januar 1960 in München. Tübingen: J. C. B. Mohr, 1960. 43 pp. (Sammlung gemeinverständlicher Vorträge und Schriften aus dem Gebiet der Theologie und Religionsgeschichte, 231.)

2347   BLEEKER, C[LEAS] J[OUCO]. Inleiding tot het denken van Schweitzer. Assen: Born, 1953. 47 pp. (Hoofdfiguren van het menselijk denken, 10.)

2348   BURI, FRITZ. Albert Schweitzer und Karl Jaspers. Zürich: Artemis-Verlag, 1950. 29 pp. (Schriften zur Zeit, H.20.) Vortrag, gehalten am 29. Juni, 1950, vor der Basler Studentschaft.

2349   _____. Albert Schweitzer und unsere Zeit. Zürich: Artemis-Verlag, 1947. 53 pp. (Schriften zur Zeit, H. 15.) Eine Vorlesung gehalten am. 14. Januar 1947, Albert Schweitzers 72. Geburtstag, in der Universität Zürich. Also Kassel: Karl Winter Verlag, 1948. 47 pp.

2350   _____. Albert Schweitzers Wahrheit in Anfechtung und Bewährung. Zürich, Stuttgart: Artemis Verlag, 1960. 47 pp. (Schriften zur Zeit 23.) Festansprache, gehalten am 15. und 18. Januar 1960 . . . Berlin . . . Feier zum 85. Geburtstag Albert Schweitzers.

    _____. Christentum und Kultur bei Albert Schweitzer. See Theology and Religion, no. 2878 below.

Philosophy

2351   CLARK, HENRY. The Ethical Mysticism of Albert Schweitzer; a
           study of the sources and significance of Schweitzer's
           philosophy of civilization. With two essays by Albert
           Schweitzer. Boston: Beacon Press; Toronto: S. J.
           Reginald Saunders, 1962. 241 pp.
           (British edition). The Philosophy of Albert Schweitzer.
              London: Methuen, 1964. 241 pp.

2352   CORYLLIS, PETER. Im Lichtbereich der Ethik Albert Schweitzers.
           Kleine Texte unsere Freunde. Dülmen: Verlag der Steg im
           Kreis der Freund, 1977. 64 pp.

2353   DOMINGUEZ CABALLERO, DIEGO. Albert Schweitzer y la crisis
           moral de neustra civilización. Panama: Sociedad
           Panameña de Filosofía, 1953. 23 pp. (Cuadernos de la
           Sociedad Panameña de Filosofía no. 1. Serie: Critica.)

        FURR, LESTER SEYMOUR. The Philosophy of Albert Schweitzer and
           its exemplification in his life. See Dissertations,
           no. 4317 below.

2354   GRABS, RUDOLF. Albert Schweitzer; Gelebtes Denken. Berlin:
           Steuben Verlag, Paul G. Esser, 1948. 45 pp.

2355   _____. Lebensführung im Geiste Albert Schweitzers. Jena:
           Wartburg Verlag M. Kessler in Arbeitsgemeinschaft mit der
           Evangelischen Verlagsanstalt, Berlin, 1954. 80 pp.
           Second edition, 1960.
           (3., bearb. Aufl.) Berlin: Evangelische Verlagsanstalt
              (in Verbindung mit dem Wartburg-Verlag Kessler, Jena),
              1967. 130 pp.

2356   _____. Sinngebung des Lebens; aus Geist und Gedankenwelt
           Albert Schweitzers. Hamburg: R. Meiner, 1950. 157 pp.

        TRANSLATIONS

        Om at vaere menneske. Fra Albert Schweitzers ideverden.
           Tr. Børge Friis. Copenhagen: Branner og Korch, 1954.
           134 pp.

2357   GROOS, HELMUT. Albert Schweitzer, Grösse und Grenzen. Eine
           kritische Würdigung des Forschers und Denkers. Munich,
           Basel: Ernst Reinhardt Verlag, 1974. 841 pp.

2358   HIDDING, KLAUS ALDERT HENDRIK. Mystiek en ethiek in
           Schweitzer's geest; een anthropologische studie. Haarlem:
           Tjeenk Willink, 1938. 102 pp.

2359   HOMMEL, THEODOR. Ein Turnier Parzivals un den Gral mit
          Albert Schweitzer und Oswald Spengler. Bad Aibling/
          Oberbayern: Bundesverlag d. Gottesfreunde, 1954. 48 pp.

2360   HORSTMEIER, MARIE. Albert Schweitzer: ein Wegweiser der
          Kulturerneuerung. Berlin: Comenius Verlag, 1949. 38 pp.

2361   HYGEN, JOHAN BERNITZ. Albert Schweitzers tanker am kulturen.
          Oslo: Land og Kirke, 1954. 107 pp.

          TRANSLATIONS

       Albert Schweitzers Kulturkritik; eine Einführung. Göttingen:
          Vandenhoeck und Ruprecht, 1955. 70 pp.

       ICE, JACKSON LEE. A Critique of Albert Schweitzer's Philoso-
          phy of Civilization. See Dissertations, no. 4322 below.

       KAEMPF, BERNARD. Fondements de actualité de l'éthique
          d'Albert Schweitzer. See Dissertations, no. 4324 below.

2362   KRAUS, OSKAR. Albert Schweitzer, sein Werk und seine
          Weltanschauung. Charlottenburg: R. Heise, 1926. 63 pp.
          Originally appeared in Jahrbuch für Charakterologie, 1926,
          see no. 2540 below. Second enlarged edition, 1929.

          TRANSLATIONS

       Albert Schweitzer, his work and his philosophy. Tr. E. G.
          McCalman. With an introduction by A. D. Lindsay. London:
          A. and C. Black, 1944. x, 75 pp.

2363   LANGFELDT, GABRIEL. Albert Schweitzer. Oslo: H. Aschehoug
          (W. Nygaard), 1958.

          TRANSLATIONS

       Albert Schweitzer, a study of his philosophy of life. Tr.
          Maurice Michael. London: George Allen and Unwin; New
          York: George Braziller, 1960. 119 pp.

       LAZARI-PAWLOWSKA, IJA. Schweitzer. See Life and Work,
          no. 272 above.

       LIN, PO-CHEN. A Critical Analysis of Albert Schweitzer's
          Philosophy of Civilization. See Dissertations, no. 4328
          below.

Philosophy

2364   LIND, EMIL. Ein Meister der Menschheit: Albert Schweitzer;
       der Beitrag des Philosophen und Menschenfreundes Albert
       Schweitzer zur Lösung der Kulturkrise der Gegenwart.
       Bühl-Baden: Verlag Konkordia, 1954. 95 pp. (Grosse
       Erzieher der Menschheit, Bd. 4.)

2365   LÖNNEBO, MARTIN. Albert Schweitzers etisk-religiösa ideal.
       Zusammenfassung: Das ethisch-religiöse Ideal Albert
       Schweitzers. Stockholm: Diakonistyrelsens Bokförlag,
       1964. 352 pp. (Uppsala. Universitet. Acta Studia
       doctrinae Christianae Upsaliensia, 2.)

       MURRY, JOHN MIDDLETON. The Challenge of Schweitzer. See
       Theology and Religion, no. 2885 below.

       PACEWICKA-BECZEK, RENATA. [Albert Schweitzer's Philosophy of
       Civilization.] See Dissertations, no. 4335 below.

2366   PHILLIPS, HERBERT M. Albert Schweitzer: Prophet of Freedom.
       Evanston, Ill.: Cherokee Copy Co., 1957. 52 pp. Illus.

2367   PREMINGER, MARIAN MILL. Albert Schweitzer, his Philosophy and
       Influence on the Century. San Francisco, 1956. 14 pp.

2368   REES, THEOPHIL. Albert Schweitzer: Ehrfurcht vor dem Leben.
       Karlsruhe: C. F. Müller, 1947. 46 pp. "Den nachfolgenden
       Ausführungen liegt ein Vortrag zu Grunde. Er wurde
       gehalten in Karlsruhe in der Vortragsreihe vom 'Deutschen
       Genius' der Katholischen und Evangelischen
       Arbeitsgemeinschaft, ausserdem in Freudenstadt bei der
       Eröffnung des Volksbildungswerkes."

       REGESTER, JOHN DICKINSON. Immediate Intuition in the New
       Rationalism of Albert Schweitzer. See Dissertations,
       no. 4338 below.

2369   RUSSELL, LILIAN M. (Mrs. Charles E. B.). The Path to Recon-
       struction, a brief introduction to Albert Schweitzer's
       philosophy of civilization. London: A. and C. Black,
       1941.

       SEAVER, GEORGE. Albert Schweitzer; a vindication. See
       Theology and Religion, no. 2887 below.

2370   SPEAR, OTTO. Albert Schweitzers Ethik; Ihre Grundlinien in
       seinem Denken und Leben. Hamburg: Herbert Reich
       Evangelischer Verlag, 1978. 104 pp. (Evangelische
       Zeitstimmen 80.)

STREGE, MARTIN. Albert Schweitzers Religion and Philosophie.
   See Theology and Religion, no. 2889 below.

2371   _____. Der Neue Mensch in einer neuen Welt. Zum 90.
            Geburtstag von Albert Schweitzer am 14. Januar 1965.
            Wülfrath bei Düsseldorf, 1964. 46 pp.

         WILD, THOMAS. Fondements et actualité de la pensée d'Albert
            Schweitzer. See Dissertations, no. 4344 below.

2372   WOLFRAM, AUREL. Albert Schweitzer und die Krise des
            Abendlandes. Vienna: Gerold, 1947. 47 pp. (Führer
            zur Menschlichkeit, Heft 1.)

      b. Articles, Parts of Books

2373   ALBERS, A. "Albert Schweitzer." In: Almanach der
            Rupprechtspresse. Munich: C. H. Beck, 1923/1925,
            pp. 14-15. Port.

2374   _____. "Ein Heldenleben. Der Charakterologie Albert
            Schweitzers." Münchner Neueste Nachrichten (Munich)
            306 (Nov. 5, 1926), pp. 1-2.

2375   _____. "Schweitzer ist ein Lebensbejaher." NEUES 5
            (Aug. 1925), pp. 11-12.

2376   "Albert Schweitzer." Geist und Tat (Hamburg) 5:9
            (Sept. 1950), pp. 423-24.

2377   "Albert Schweitzer's policies." The Presbyterian Outlook
            (Richmond, Va.) 143:3 (Jan. 16, 1961), p. 12.

2378   AMADOU, ROBERT. "Homme du vingtième siècle, Albert
            Schweitzer." La Gazette des Lettres (Paris) 6:108
            (Feb. 18, 1950), pp. 1f.

2379   _____. "La pensée d'Albert Schweitzer." In: RAYONNEMENT,
            pp. 138-50.

2380   _____. "Le philosophe." In: ETUDES, pp. 83-110; second
            edition, pp. 73-96.

2381   AMES, EDWARD SCRIBNER. "The greatness of Albert Schweitzer"
            and "Studies in Schweitzer." The Scroll (Chicago) XLV:
            7-10 (Sept.-Dec. 1948); XLVI:1-3, 8-10 (Jan.-June, 1949),
            various pages in each issue.

Philosophy

2382 AMORIM, DEOLINDO. "Albert Schweitzer e o destinodo da
      cultura." Jornal do Comércio (Rio de Janeiro),
      Sept. 11, 1949.

2383 ANGYAL, ANDREAS. ["Begegnung und Erkenntnis."] In: DENKEN
      UND WEG, pp. 84-86.

2384 ARBRELL, RONALD L. "Albert Schweitzer: educator for a
      season." Contemporary Education (Terre Haute, Ind.) 46:1
      (Fall 1974), pp. 28-33.

2385 ASTER, ERNST VON. "Albert Schweitzers Kulturfilosofi." In:
      MANNEN, pp. 73-88.

2386 AUGUSTINY, WALDEMAR. "Albert Schweitzer und du." Die
      Schwarzburg (Hamburg) 63:6 (Dec. 1954), pp. 98-104.
      Excerpt from the author's book of the same title, no. 227
      above.

2387 _____. "Arzt der Menschheit." Rhein-Neckar Zeitung
      (Heidelberg), Jan. 12, 1955.

2388 BABEL, HENRY. "Albert Schweitzer annonciateur du XXIe
      siècle." CAHIERS 24 (Winter 1970/71), pp. 16-18.

2389 BÄHR, HANS WALTER. "L'Éthique cosmique d'Albert Schweitzer
      et les problèmes de l'éthique naturelle." REVUE 56:1-2
      (1976), pp. 97-117.

2390 BALCAR, JOSEF. "Albert Schweitzer's Denken und der Weg zum
      Frieden." In: DENKEN UND WEG, pp. 534-38.

2391 BARTHEL, ERNST. "Elsässische Geistesschicksale unter
      Europäischen Gesichtspunkt: 4. Albert Schweitzer."
      Elsass-Lothringen Heimatstimmen (Berlin) 5:11
      (Nov. 15, 1927), pp. 636-48. Later enlarged and pub-
      lished in Elsässische Geistsschicksale. Ein Beitrag zur
      Europäischen Verstandigung. Gebweiler: Alsatia Verlag;
      Heidelberg: Carl Winters Universitätsbuchhandlung, 1928,
      pp. 217-79. (Schriften der Elsass-Lothringischen
      Wissenschaftlichen Gesellschaft zu Strassburg. Reihe A.
      Alsatica und Lothringen, Bd. 5.)

2392 BAUR, HANS. "Albert Schweitzer ist auf dem Wege zur
      Menschheitshilfe." Schweizerisches Protestantenblatt
      (Basel) 47:7 (Feb. 16, 1924), p. 53.

2393 _____. "Albert Schweitzer und Immanuel Kant." Schweizerisches
      Protestantenblatt (Basel) 47:18 (May 3, 1924), pp. 133-34.

2394   _____. "Albert Schweitzer tourné vers l'avenir." In:
        RAYONNEMENT, pp. 259-61.

2395   BAUR, HERMANN. "Albert Schweitzer als Erzieher. Vortrag
        gehalten an der Pestalozzi-Feier 1968 in Bern."
        Schweizerische Lehrerzeitung 27/28 (1968). Reprinted in
        RUNDBRIEF 31 (1968).

2396   _____. "Albert Schweitzer et Pestalozzi, educateurs."
        CAHIERS 20 (Dec. 1968), pp. 11-13. Reprinted in
        NOUVELLES 30 (Jan. 1969), pp. 18-23.

2397   _____. "Albert Schweitzer und der Arztschriftsteller."
        In: DEBRECEN, pp. 13-17.

2398   _____. "Albert Schweitzer und unsere Zukunft. Vortrag aus
        Anlass der Eröffnung und Einweihung der Albert-Schweitzer-
        Gedankstätte und des Archivs am 14. Februar 1969 in
        Frankfurt/Main." RUNDBRIEF 34 (Dec. 1, 1971), pp. 9-21.
        Also issued as an offprint.

2399   _____. "Denken und Willen." Schweizerisches Reformiertes
        Volksblatt (Basel), Dec. 1967. Also issued as a 3-page
        offprint.

2400   _____. "Die Humanität in Albert Schweitzers Denken."
        RUNDBRIEF 23 (Jan. 14, 1964), pp. 41-44. Also RUNDBRIEF
        33 (Oct. 10, 1970), pp. 36-37.

2401   _____. "Vermächtnis der Hoffnung." RUNDBRIEF 40 (1975),
        pp. 23-25.

2402   BAVINK, BERNHARD. "Kultur und Ethik, Albert Schweitzers
        Kulturphilosophie." Unsere Welt (Bielefeld) 21 (1929),
        No. 1, pp. 1-7; No. 2, pp. 36-47.

2403   BERENDSON, WALTER A. "Albert Schweitzer und die Idee der
        Humanität." In: BEGEGNUNG, pp. 324-27.

2404   BERESZTOCZY, MIKLOS. "Wie die Töne einzigen Akkordes. . . ."
        In: BEITRÄGE, pp. 29-35.

2405   BERGHOLZ, HARRY. "Albert Schweitzers Kulturphilosophie."
        Modern Language Journal (Ann Arbor, Mich.) 38:3
        (March 1954), pp. 122-28.

2406   _____. "Albert Schweitzer's message." The Midwest Journal
        (Jefferson City, Mo.) 6:4 (Winter 1954/55), pp. 5-15.

Philosophy

2407   BERNARD, ALBERT. "Das grosse Ziel." Les Dernières Nouvelles
        du Haut-Rhin (Colmar), Jan. 14, 1960, pp. 9-10.

2408   BERTELSON, AAGE. "Albert Schweitzers Kulturtanker."
        Jyllands-Posten (Aarhus), May 24, 1950.

2409   BHARATI, A. "Albert Schweitzers Denken in indischer Sicht."
        In: DENKEN UND WEG, pp. 48-57.

2410   BIXLER, JULIUS SEEYLE. "Albert Schweitzer's unity of life
        and thought." In: The Student Seeks an Answer. Edited
        by John Alden Clark. Waterville, Maine: Colby College
        Press, 1960, pp. 123-38. (Ingraham Lectures in Philosophy
        and Religion at Colby College, 1951-1959.)

2411   _____. ["Begegnung und Erkenntnis."] In: DENKEN UND WEG,
        pp. 87-89.

2412   _____. "Dr. Schweitzer's one answer to the problems of the
        many." In: FESTSCHRIFT, pp. 3-10. Translated as
        "Albert Schweitzers Einheit in der Vielfelt." In:
        EHRFURCHT, pp. 233-38.

2413   _____. "The miracle of Lambaréné" (editorial). The Saturday
        Review (New York) 38:3 (Jan. 15, 1955), p. 24. Also
        issued as a reprint by the Albert Schweitzer Fellowship,
        New York.

2414   _____. "Productive tensions in the work of Albert
        Schweitzer." In: JUBILEE, pp. 69-86.

2415   _____. "Schweitzer reverenced 'truth' also!" Religious
        Humanism (Yellow Springs, Ohio) 9:4 (Autumn 1975),
        pp. 146-49.

2416   BOCK, EMIL. "Europa-Bilanz in Afrikanischen Urwald." Die
        Christengemeinschaft (Stuttgart) 22:1/2 (Jan./Feb. 1950),
        pp. 43-44.

2417   BOEKE, RICHARD F. "A twentieth-century Faust." In: PROPHET,
        pp. 22-24.

2418   BOLLNOW, OTTO FRIEDRICH. "Die Forderung des Menschlichkeit."
        In: DENKEN UND WEG, pp. 495-510.

2419   "De boodschap van Dr. Schweitzer aan de mensheid." Militia
        Christi (Lochem) 12:10 (May 18, 1957), pp. 3-7. Port.,
        illus.

234

2420   BOURKE, V. J. "Tensions in Schweitzer's ethics." In:
        CENTENNIAL. Reprinted in the Journal of Value Inquiry
        (The Hague) 11:1 (Spring 1977), pp. 41-43.

2421   BRANN, HENRY WALTER. "'Menschlichkeit der Kern aller Dinge'
        erklärt Schweitzer." New Yorker Staats-Zeitung und Herold
        (New York), June 29, 1949, pp. 1-2.

2422   BREMI, WILLI. "Albert Schweitzers elementare Ethik." In:
        Krisenzeit und Jesusforschung. Werdegang, Resultate und
        Ausblick. Basel, 1972, pp. 14-17.

2423   _____. "Das erste Albert-Schweitzer-Gespräch in Basel."
        Schweizerisches Reformiertes Volksblatt (Basel), Nov. 19,
        1967. Also issued as a 3-page offprint.

2424   BRET, PAUL. "Souvenirs sur Albert Schweitzer." Arts (Paris)
        283 (Oct. 27, 1950), p. 8. Port.

2425   BRINKMANN, DONALD. "Albert Schweitzer und die Welt technik."
        Technische Rundschau (Bern) 51:53 (1959), pp. 1f. Re-
        printed in Universitas (Stuttgart) 15:1 (Jan. 1960),
        pp. 101-06; reprinted in: DENKEN UND WEG, pp. 539-45.

2426   BRONSART, HUBERTA VON. "Ein Mythos stirbt. Missbrauchter
        Albert Schweitzer." Christ und Welt (Stuttgart) 14:39
        (Sept. 29, 1961), p. 2. For letters to the editor in
        reply, see Christ und Welt 14:43 (Oct. 27, 1961), p. 9.

2427   BRUNNER, HELLMUT. "Albert Schweitzers universelle Ethik und
        die alteste Hochkultur der Menschheit." In: DENKEN UND
        WEG, pp. 58-65.

2428   BURGER, C. B. "Schweitzer en Pearl Buck." NIEUWS 2:2
        (Sept. 1953), pp. 30-31.

2429   _____. "Albert Schweitzer als Denker." RUNDBRIEF 24
        (June 15, 1964), pp. 43-45.

2430   _____. "Het wetenschappelijk werk van Albert Schweitzer.
        Culturfilosofie." NIEUWS 19:2 (Dec. 1970), pp. 38-39.

        BURI, FRITZ. "Albert Schweitzer in der theologischen und
        philosophischer Lage der Gegenwart." See Theology and
        Religion, no. 2950 below.

2431   _____. "The belief of Schweitzer in the power of the spirit."
        In: FESTSCHRIFT, pp. 14-24.

Philosophy

2432   _____. "Schweitzer--prophet among nihilists." The Christian
        Register (Boston) 130:9 (Oct. 1951), p. 21.

2433   _____. "The significance of Albert Schweitzer for the problem
        'power of struggle against power of spirit.'" Faith and
        Freedom (Oxford) 5 (Oct. 1, 1952), pp. 107-13.

2434   CANIVEZ, ANDRÉ. "Albert Schweitzer et la réalité de la
        souffrance." REVUE 56:1-2 (1976), pp. 143-53.

2435   _____. "Personalité et philosophie d'Albert Schweitzer."
        CAHIERS 19 (June 1968), pp. 7-8.

2436   _____. "Raison, éthique et vie dans la philosophie d'Albert
        Schweitzer." In: RAYONNEMENT, pp. 125-38.

2437   CANNEGIETER, HENDRIK GERRIT. "Onrijpe vrijheid." NIEUWS 2:5
        (July 1954), p. 76.

2438   CARPEAUX, OTTO MARIA. "Motivos de Schweitzer." O Jornal
        (Rio de Janeiro), Dec. 25, 1949.

2439   CASSIRER, ERNST. "Albert Schweitzer as critic of nineteenth
        century ethics." In: JUBILEE, pp. 239-57.

2440   CHATTERJI, SUNITI KUMAR. "Eine Huldigung aus Indian." In:
        BEITRÄGE, pp. 36-40.

2441   CHRISTOU, CHR. "Albert Schweitzer." Nea Hestia 53-54:633
        and 634 (1953), pp. 1665-68, 1801-08.

2442   COOMARASWAMY, ANANDA K. "What is civilization?" In: JUBILEE,
        pp. 259-74.

2443   DACHERT, ALFRED. "De la philosophie de Schweitzer (à propos
        de son livre sur les grands penseurs de l'Inde)." La
        Revue du Christianisme Social (Paris) 50:3 (April/May
        1937), pp. 338-42.

2444   DAVENPORT, MANUEL M. "A statement" (philosophy and criticisms
        of Albert Schweitzer). In: THE CONVOCATION RECORD,
        pp. VI/5.

2445   DAVIS, SAMUEL. "Schweitzer's moral theories." Holborn Review
        (London) 18 (July 1927), pp. 344-53.

2446   DECKER, FRITZ. "Das geistige Profil Albert Schweitzers."
        Strassburger Monatshefte (Hünenburg/Unter-Elsass) 2:1
        (Jan. 1938), pp. 33-35.

2447   DEL VECCHIO, GIORGIO. "Sull'etica di Albert Schweitzer."
       Rivista Internazionale di Filosofia del Diritto (Milan)
       37 (May-June 1960), pp. 496-98.

2448   DELGADO, HONORIO. [Dank an Dr. Albert Schweitzer zum 85.
       Geburtstag.] Universitas (Stuttgart) 15:1 (Jan. 1960),
       pp. 31-32. Reprinted in: DENKEN UND WEG, pp. 94-95.

2449   "Dienaar des vredes." NIEUWS 2:3 (Dec. 1953), p. 36.

2450   DIESNER, HANS-JOACHIM. "Würzel für Schweitzers Handeln."
       Neue Zeit (East Berlin) 49 (Feb. 27, 1960), p. 5.

2451   "DIOGENES." "Albert Schweitzer." Time and Tide (London)
       36:49 (Dec. 3, 1955), pp. 1551-52. For letters to the
       editor in reply, see J. Anthony Byers, Time and Tide 36:51
       (Dec. 17, 1955), pp. 1670-71; Clement C. Chesterman and
       Santhi Rangarao, Time and Tide 36:52 (Dec. 24, 1955),
       pp. 1701-02; and "Sniping at greatness." Time and Tide
       36:53 (Dec. 31, 1955), p. 1721.

2452   DOMINGUEZ CABALLERO, DIEGO. "Albert Schweitzer y la tragedia
       moral de nuestra civilización." Universidad (Panama) 32,
       segundo sem estre (1952/1953), pp. 123-39.

2453   DOSENHEIMER, ELISE. "Albert Schweitzer, Gelehrter." Die Tat
       (Jena) 19:10 (Jan. 1928), pp. 744-56.

2454   DUCHESNE, JULES ["Begegnung und Erkenntnis."] In: DENKEN
       UND WEG, pp. 97-98.

2455   DUVE, HELMUTH. "Albert Schweitzer. Werk und Menschheit."
       Der Braunschweiger GNC-Monatsschrift (Braunschweig) 15
       (1928), pp. 395-99.

2456   _____. "Albert Schweitzers Werk und Menschentum." Deutsche
       Monatshefte (Leipzig) 5:2 (1929), pp. 249-52. Reprinted
       in Natur and Kultur (Vienna) 27/28 (1930), pp. 173-76;
       also in Übersee--und Kolonialzeitung 42:22 (Nov. 15, 1930),
       pp. 46-48.

2457   DYRSSEN, CARL. "Die Lebensethik Albert Schweitzer." Die
       Christliche Welt (Gotha) 39:24/25 (June 18, 1925),
       cols. 540-46.

2458   EIGELSREITER, F. "Albert Schweitzer, Arzt eines kranken
       Jahrhunderts." Der Grosse Entschluss (Vienna) 22
       (Dec. 1966), pp. 132-36. Reprinted in RUNDBRIEF 33
       (Oct. 10, 1970), pp. 51-64.

Philosophy

2459 EINARSSON, SIGURBJÖRN. "Lifsskooun Albert Schweitzers."
      Visir, Nov. 1955.

2460 EISSFELDT, FRITZ. "Von tragenden Grund. Albert Schweitzer
      als Theolog und Philosoph." Wege zum Menschen
      (Göttingen) 7:1 (Jan. 1955), pp. 9-14.

2461 ELIOT, FREDERICK M. "Albert Schweitzer's Out of my Life and
      Thought." In: Classics of Religious Devotion. Boston:
      The Beacon Press, 1950, pp. 103-14. Originally delivered
      as a Lenten lecture, Phillips Brooks House, Harvard Uni-
      versity, February/March 1948.

2462 ELST, RAYMOND VANDER. "L'oeuvre humanitaire et la pensée
      humaniste d'Albert Schweitzer." Cahiers Européens/
      Europäische Hefte/Notes from Europe (Munich) 2:1
      (Jan. 1975), pp. 20-23.

2463 ENDICOTT, JAMES G. "Stimme des Gewissens." In: BEITRÄGE,
      pp. 44-46.

2464 ENKO, RYSZARD. "Postep naukowotechniczny a kuyzys moralny
      naszego czasu w perspektywie poyladow Alberta Schweitzera."
      Studia Filozoficzne (Warsaw) 7 (92) (1973), pp. 105-18.

2465 ERNST, WILHELM. "Das Erziehungsmotiv in der Kulturphilosophie
      Albert Schweitzers." Die Evangelische Pädagogik
      (Leipzig) 8 (1933), pp. 86-89.

2466 EVERETT, JOHN R. "Albert Schweitzer and philosophy." In:
      THE CONVOCATION RECORD, pp. V/3-15. Reprinted in Social
      Research (New York) 33:4 (Winter 1966), pp. 513-30.

2467 F., E. "Kultur und Ethik. Hinweis auf Albert Schweitzer."
      Württemburgerische Lehrerzeitung (Stuttgart) 86:36
      (Sept. 9, 1926), pp. 336-37.

2468 FASCHER, ERICH. "Der Tierfreund." In: BEITRÄGE, pp. 47-51.

2469 FINA, CONSOL. "Albert Schweitzer: ecos de su obra." Pregon
      en Defensa de los Animales 106 (1977). Reprinted in the
      A.I.S.L. Bulletin 4 (July 1977), p. 25.

2470 _____. "Albert Schweitzer: ecos de su obra." Pregon en
      Defensa de los Animales 107 (1977). Reprinted in the
      A.I.S.L. Bulletin 5 (Nov. 1977), pp. 44.

2471 FLÜCKIGER, KURT. "Ruckbesinning auf einen Weisen: drei
      Ökumenische Abende in Lenzburg über Albert Schweitzer."

Aargauer Tagblatt, August 28, 1976. Reprinted in the
A.I.S.L. Bulletin 2 (Nov. 1976), p. 12.

2472 _____. "Umweltsethik an der Wurzel: Fazit der ökumenischen
Lenzburger Abende über Albert Schweitzer." Aargauer
Tagblatt, Sept. 4, 1976. Reprinted in the A.I.S.L.
Bulletin 2 (Nov. 1976), p. 13.

2473 FRICK, HEINRICH. "Albert Schweitzer als Kulturphilosoph."
Theologische Blätter (Leipzig) 3:3 (March 1924), cols.
56-59.

2474 FRIEDEMANN, KÄTE. "Albert Schweitzers Irrtum." Neues
Abendland (Munich) 8:7 (July 1953), pp. 437-40.

2475 FROMM, ERICH. "Albert Schweitzer und die Zwiespältigkeit
des Fortschritts" (Vortrag). Evangelische Kommentare
(Stuttgart) 8:12 (Dec. 1975), pp. 757-58.

2476 FUCHS, D. EMIL. "Symbol der helfenden Liebe--das Beispiel
Albert Schweitzers." Neue Zeit (East Berlin) 11
(June 14, 1960), p. 3.

2477 GELL, CHRISTOPHER W. M. "The life and thought of Albert
Schweitzer." The Dalhousie Review (Halifax, Nova Scotia)
33:3 (Autumn 1953), pp. 141-48; 33:4 (Winter 1953),
pp. 248-56; 34:1 (Spring 1954), pp. 389-96.

2478 _____. "The philosophy of Albert Schweitzer." The Cambridge
Journal (Cambridge, Eng.) 6:10 (July 1953), pp. 605-14.

2479 _____. "Schweitzer and Radhakrishnan; a comparison." The
Hibbert Journal (London) 51:3 (April 1953), pp. 234-41.
See also Goodwin, no. 2489 below.

2480 GEOHEGAN, WILLIAM DAVIDSON. "Albert Schweitzer's covenant
with life." Religion in Life (Nashville) 30:2
(Spring 1961), pp. 256-67.

2481 GILTAY, H. "De nieuwe cultuur." De Groene Amsterdammer
(Amsterdam), July 28, 1928.

2482 GITTLEMAN, DAVID. "Albert Schweitzer's timely gospel: an
appeal to man's nobler potentialities." The Churchman
(New York) 173:3 (March 1959), pp. 11-12.

2483 GLASEKNAPP, HELMUTH VON. "Lebensbejahung und Lebensverneinung
bei den Indischen Denker." Jahrbuch der Schopenhauer
Gesellschaft (Heidelberg) 22 (1935), pp. 177-94.

Philosophy

2484 GOEBEL, ROBERT. "Gegenwartsfragen im Lebensschicksal Albert
        Schweitzers." Die Christengemeinschaft (Stuttgart) 10:10
        (Jan. 1934), pp. 307-09.

2485 GÖTTING, GERALD. "A. Schweitzer dans les pays de l'est; un
        militant de l'humanisme." CAHIERS 29 (Summer 1973),
        pp. 8-9.

2486 _____. "Albert Schweitzer: Vorbild im Wirken für Frieden
        und Humanität." In: VERMÄCHTNIS UND WIRKLICHKEIT,
        pp. 5-18.

2487 _____. "Albert Schweitzer vu par les pays de l'Est." In:
        RAYONNEMENT, pp. 270-71.

2488 _____. "Was uns Albert Schweitzer bedeutet." RUNDBRIEF 40
        (1975), pp. 77-78. From his foreword to Ausgewählte Werke
        in fünf Banden, 1971, see no. 21 above.

2489 GOODWIN, WILLIAM F. "Mysticism and ethics: an examination
        of Radhakrishnan's reply to Schweitzer's critique of
        Indian thought." Ethics (Chicago) 67:1 (Oct. 1956),
        pp. 25-41.

2490 GRABS, RUDOLF. "Das geistige Erbe Albert Schweitzers."
        Glaube und Gewissen (Halle) 12:1 (Jan. 1966), pp. 4-7.

2491 GRESSEL, HANS. "Kultur und Ethik bei Albert Schweitzer."
        Die Friedensrundschau 11:1 (Jan. 1957), pp. 16-19.

2492 GROTJAHN, MARTIN. "A psychoanalyst looks at Albert
        Schweitzer." In: REALMS, pp. 295-301.

2493 GRÜBER, HEINRICH. "Albert Schweitzer." Spandauer Volksblatt
        (Berlin), Jan. 14, 1965. Reprinted in: CHARISMATISCHE
        DIAKONIE, pp. 23-25.

      GRÜBER, PROBST. "In Lambarene vollendet sich seine
        charismatische Diakonie." See Theology and Religion,
        no. 2988 below.

2494 GRÜTZMACHER, RICHARD H. "Ein universaler Denker und ganzer
        Mensch. Albert Schweitzer." La Revue Rhénane/Rheinische
        Blätter (Mayence) 10:3 (Dec. 1929), pp. 10-16.

2495 GUERRA, J. "A focca das idéias--filósofa e idolo." Diario
        de São Paulo, Supplement, Aug. 20, 1950.

2496   HÄRTLE, HEINRICH. "Politik und Ethik. Betrachtung zum
       Ableben von Albert Schweitzer." Deutsche Wochenzeitung
       (Hannover), Sept. 17, 1965.

2497   HAMMERSCHMIDT, WILHELM. "Albert Schweitzers Ethik--vergessene
       Weisheit?" Die Schwarzburg (Hamburg) 67:2 (1958),
       pp. 25-28. Reprinted in Der Convent (Mannheim-Sandhofen)
       9:9 (1958), pp. 193-95.

2498   HANG, T. ["Begegnung und Erkenntnis."] In: DENKEN UND WEG,
       pp. 99-101.

2499   HASSOLD, ERNEST CHRISTOPHER. "Schweitzer's philosophy of cul-
       ture." In: Hagemann, E. R., ed. Albert Schweitzer.
       Louisville, Ky.: University of Louisville, 1969.

2500   HAUCH, ERNST. "Albert Schweitzer, sein Grenzmarkschicksal
       und Geistesringen." Der Quell (Munich) 13:3 (Feb. 9, 1961),
       pp. 97-103.

2501   HAUTER, CHARLES. "Les grands penseurs de l'Inde à propos du
       livre de Schweitzer." REVUE 19 (1939), pp. 172-78.

2502   HEARD, GERALD. "The pattern of prestige." In: FESTSCHRIFT,
       pp. 48-51.

2503   HENNING, AUG. "Albert Schweitzer's Kultursyn." In:
       Kristendom og Samfundsliv. Bevaegelser og Personligheder.
       Copenhagen: Grønholt Pedersens Forlag, 1946, pp. 34-43.

2504   HERMAN, A. L. "Again, Albert Schweitzer and Indian thought."
       Philosophy East and West (Honolulu) 12:3 (Oct. 1962),
       pp. 217-32.

2505   HEYM, HANS. "Ein neuer Weg." Protestantenblatt (Bremen) 57
       (1924), pp. 13-17.

2506   HEYNS, JOHAN ADAM. "Albert Schweitzer." In: Denkers deur
       die eeue. Kaapstad: Tafel-berg-Uitg., 1967, pp. 120-32.

2507   HIDDING, K. A. H. "Ethiek en mystiek bij Albert Schweitzer."
       Theologie en Practijk (Lochem) 10:5/6 (May-June 1950),
       pp. 104-17.

2508   _____. "Het problem: Schweitzer." Kerk en Wereld (Assen)
       49:16 (Aug. 1957), p. 3; 49:18 (Sept. 13, 1957), pp. 4-5.

2509   HOCKE, GUSTAVE R. "Geist und Tat--eine neue Synthese. Die
       Verbindung von Mystik und Ethik. Zum Werk Schweitzer."
       Das Bunte Leben (Cologne) 25 (Abendblatt), Jan. 14, 1935.

Philosophy

2510   HOCKING, W. E. "Schweitzer's outlook on history." In:
       REALMS, pp. 204-18.

2511   HOGG, A. C. "To the rescue of civilization" and "The ethical
       teaching of Dr. Schweitzer." International Review of
       Missions (London) 14 (Jan. 1925), pp. 45-58; (April 1925),
       pp. 237-51.

2512   HOLZ, KARL. "Die Botschaft Albert Schweitzers." Neue
       Schweizer Rundschau (Zürich) 9:2 (June 1941), pp. 77-88.

2513   HÜBSCHER, ARTHUR. "Albert Schweitzer." In: Philosophen der
       Gegenwart. Fünfzig Bildnesse. Munich: Piper Verlag,
       1949, pp. 127-29, 170-71.

2514   HUNNEX, MILTON D. "Mysticism and ethics: Radhakrishnan and
       Schweitzer." Philosophy East and West (Honolulu) 8:3-4
       (Oct. 1958-Jan. 1959), pp. 121-36.

2515   HYGEN, JOHAN B. "Albert Schweitzers Kulturphilosophie und
       Kulturkritik." Universitas (Stuttgart) 15:1 (Jan. 1960),
       pp. 3-12. Excerpted from Albert Schweitzers Kulturkritik,
       see no. 2361 above. Reprinted as "Niedergang und
       Wiederaufbau der Kultur--die Kulturphilosophie Albert
       Schweitzers." In: DENKEN UND WEG, pp. 3-18; translated
       as "Decline and revival of culture--the cultural philoso-
       phy of Albert Schweitzer." Universitas (English language
       edition) 7:1 (1964), pp. 3-18.

2516   ICE, JACKSON LEE. "Ecological crisis: radical monotheism
       vs. ethical pantheism." Religion in Life (New York) 44:2
       (Summer 1975), pp. 203-11.

2517   "Interpreters of our faith: Albert Schweitzer." A.D. Report
       4:2 (Feb. 1975), p. 29. Illus.

2518   JACOBI, ERWIN R. "Gekurzte Wiedergabe des am 23.2.1968 im
       grossen Hörsaal des Kantonspitals Zürich gehaltenen
       Einführungsvortrags zu Dokumentarfilmen über das Albert-
       Schweitzer-Spital in Lambarene." KSZ Nachrichten,
       Hauszeitung für das Personal des Kantonspitals (Zürich)
       18 (March 1968), pp. 2-6, 21.

2519   JORDAN, VILHELM LASSEN. "To Livssyn--Albert Schweitzer og
       Simone Weil." Det Danske Magasin (Copenhagen) 3:1
       (1955), pp. 35-42. Ports.

2520   JUNGK, ROBERT. "Der Mensch gegen den Übermenschen." In:
       Pierhal, Jean. Albert Schweitzer, das Leben eines Guten

Menschen, see no. 291 above, pp. 5-16. Reprinted in
Münchner Merkur (Munich), Merkur am Sonntag 13
(Jan. 15/16, 1955), p. 1; reprinted in: BEGEGNUNG,
pp. 249-53; also issued as an offprint.

2521   JUNOD, MICHEL. "Schweitzer ou l'anti progrès." In:
          DEBRECEN, pp. 81-87.

2522   KAPF, RUDOLF. "Was ist uns Schweitzer?" Göppinger Volkskirche
          Zeitung (Göppingen) 4 (1931), p. 66.

2523   KARIMSKIJ, A. M. ["Albert Schweitzer et l'humanisme bourgeois
          du XXe siècle."] Vestnik Moskovskogo Universiteta
          Filosofija (Moscow) 1 (1975), pp. 22-31.

2524   KARPOUCINE, W. A. "L'éthique d'Albert Schweitzer." CAHIERS
          31 (Summer 1974), p. 14.

2525   KASTLER, A. "L'éthique d'Albert Schweitzer." In: ACADEMIE.

2526   KEATING, GEORGE T. "When I saw thee sick." In: REALMS,
          pp. 262-68.

2527   KEINTZEL, WALDEMAR. "Albert Schweitzer als Mensch und als
          Ethiker." Klingsor (Kronstadt, Romania) 8:1 (Jan. 1931),
          pp. 19-25.

2528   KEMLEIN, W. "Der Arzt--ein Mann zwischen den Ständen."
          RUNDBRIEF 20 (Sept. 1, 1962), pp. 25-29.

2529   KERNSTOCK, FRIEDRICH. "Philosoph und Urwalddoktor: Albert
          Schweitzers lebendiger Grundstein zum Aufbau einer neuen
          Menschheit." Leben und Gesundheit (Hamburg) 45:5 (1950),
          pp. 8-9. Ports.

2530   KESSLER, JOHANNES. "Ein Universalgenie." In: Ich glaube an
          den Sinn des Lebens. Berlin: Martin Warneck, 1938,
          pp. 127-56.

2531   KIK, RICHARD. "Albert Schweitzers Kulturproblem."
          Wurttemburgische Lehrerzeitung (Stuttgart) 90
          (June 19, 1930), pp. 290-300. Reprinted in RUNDBRIEF 8
          (Nov. 1, 1955), pp. 50-51.

2532   KLEINE, H. O. "Albert Schweitzer, der Baumeister einer neuen
          Ordnung." Hippokrates (Stuttgart) 26:1 (Jan. 15, 1955),
          pp. 2-9. Excerpts reprinted as "Religiöse Duldsamkeit."
          RUNDBRIEF 9 (Jan. 1, 1956), pp. 41-43; reprinted in:
          DOKUMENTE, pp. 306-07.

Philosophy

2533 _____. "Albert Schweitzer en het existentialism." NIEUWS
5:1 (April 1956), pp. 6-7.

2534 _____. "Albert Schweitzer en Immanuel Kant." NIEUWS 7:2
(Dec. 1958), pp. 11-12.

2535 KLENK, G. FRIEDRICH. "Albert Schweitzer." Stimmen der Zeit
(Freiburg i. B.) 146:7 (April 1950), pp. 29-37.

2536 _____. "Auszug aus dem Abendland?" Stimmen der Zeit
(Freiburg i. B.) 81:158 (1955/56), pp. 403-04.

2537 KOCH, THILO. "Albert Schweitzers Kulturphilosophie."
Berliner Hefte für geistiges Leben 2:6 (June 1947),
pp. 445-50.

2538 KOLLER, PETER. "Albert Schweitzer--zweiter Durchgang im
Hinblick auf 'Protestantismus in Lebenskonfigurationen.'"
In: Todestrieb im Protestantismus: Eigentümlichkeiten
protestantischen Lebens analysiert an Pfarrer-
Autobiographien . . . mit einer Reflexion über
psychoanalytische Denkstruktur. Zürich: TVZ-Verlag,
1976, pp. 57-145.

2539 KRAUS, OSKAR. "Albert Schweitzer, der Denker und Urwaldarzt."
Die Medizinische Welt (Stuttgart) 3:42 (Oct. 19, 1929),
pp. 1528-31.

2540 _____. "Albert Schweitzer. Zur Charakterologie der ethischen
Persönlichkeit und der philosophischen Mystik." Hrsg. von
Emil Ututz. Jahrbuch der Charakterologie, Bd. II/III.
Berlin: Pan Verlag Rolf Heise, 1926, pp. 287-332. Later
published as Albert Schweitzer, sein Werk und seine
Weltanschauung, see no. 2362 above. Excerpted as "Albert
Schweitzer, sein Leben und sein Werk." RUNDBRIEF 18
(July 15, 1961), pp. 21-36.

2541 _____. "Die Europäische Philosophie und die ethische
Weltanschauung. Erster Vortrag Albert Schweitzers."
Deutsche Zeitung Bohemia (Prague) 96:6 (Jan. 10, 1923),
pp. 5-6; "Zweite Vortrag Albert Schweitzers: die
Weltanschauung der Ehrfurcht vor dem Leben." Deutsche
Zeitung Bohemia (Prague) 8 (Jan. 12, 1923), p. 6.

2542 _____. "Epilog für einer Prager Albert-Schweitzer-Woche."
Deutsche Hochschulwarte (Bud-Weis-Prag) 2:10 (March 1923),
pp. 181-83.

2543   _____. [Selection without title.] In: BEGEGNUNG, pp. 130-38.
        Excerpted from his Albert Schweitzer, sein Werk und seine
        Weltanschauung, see no. 2362 above.

2544   KRIEGER, ERHARD. "Albert Schweitzer, ein Leben der 'Ehrfurcht
        vor dem Leben.'" In: Weltbürger des Menschseins und der
        Tat: Schweitzer, Nansen, Rolland, Bernadotte, Ghandi.
        Bad Homberg vor der Höhe: Verlag des Viergespann, 1960,
        pp. 11-37.

2545   KÜHN, GERHARD. "Geistiges Werk: die geistige Krise unserer
        Zeit und der Stellenwert des Denkens." RUNDBRIEF 46
        (Nov. 1978), pp. 37-39.

2546   KYLHAMMER, OLLE. "Schweitzers Kulturfilosofi." Svenska
        Morgonbladet (Stockholm), Jan. 19, 1950.

2547   LAZARI-PAWLOWSKA, IJA. "Humanizm Alberta Schweitzera."
        Studia filozoficzne (Warsaw) 11 (1974), pp. 169-83.
        Fragment from the author's book Schweitzer, see no. 272
        above.

2548   LEE, PETER H. "Albert Schweitzers Denken und die
        konfuzianische Geisteswelt." In: DENKEN UND WEG,
        pp. 75-82. Translated, without title, in Universitas
        (English language edition) 7:1 (1964), pp. 99-102.

2549   LEVADA, Y. A. ["Albert Schweitzer. Thinker and man."]
        Voprosy Filosofi (Moscow) 19:12 (1965), pp. 91-98.
        With English summary, p. 185.

2550   LEVI, ALBERT WILLIAM. "In search of culture." The Journal
        of Aesthetic Education (Urbana, Ill.) 11:4 (Oct. 1977),
        pp. 9-33. Schweitzer, pp. 31-32.

2551   LIN YUTANG. "Albert Schweitzer é o único homen no mundo
        diante do qual me ajoelho." Diário de São Paulo,
        Oct. 10, 1959.

2552   LIND, EMIL. "Albert Schweitzer als Erzieher. Persönlichkeit
        und Werk." Der Westmark (Neustadt a/Hardt) 2:7
        (April 1935), pp. 374-77.

2553   _____. "Auf den Wegen des Bergpredigers das Erdreich
        gewinnen. Albert Schweitzer, Künder von der Macht des
        Geistes." Das Parlament (Bonn) 5:3 (Jan. 19, 1955),
        p. 9. Port.

Philosophy

2554 _____. "Die Wahrhaftigkeit als Grundmotiv in Albert
        Schweitzers Leben und Denken." Freies Christentum
        (Frankfurt a.M.) 7:1 (Jan. 1, 1955), cols. 6-7.

2555 LINDESKOG, GÖSTA. ["Begegnung und Erkenntnis."] In: DENKEN
        UND WEG, pp. 111-13.

2556 LITT, THEODOR. "Albert Schweitzer." In: DENKEN UND WEG,
        pp. 207-09. Reprinted in: BEGEGNUNG, pp. 71-73.

2557 LOTAR, PETER. "Für den 'unbekannten Leser.'" In: EHRFURCHT,
        pp. 155-58.

2558 _____. "Vom Sinn des Lebens. Ein Gespräch aus Werk und
        Leben Albert Schweitzers gestaltet von Peter Lotar."
        Das Werk (Gelsenkirchen) 4, Ausgabe A: 1 (1955),
        pp. 3-10. From the author's book of the same title,
        see no. 70 above.

2559 LOUVARIS, NIKOLAUS. "Albert Schweitzer, symbol der Humanität."
        Universitas (Stuttgart) 15:1 (Jan. 1960), pp. 80-81.
        Reprinted with title [Begegnung und Erkenntnis.] In:
        DENKEN UND WEG, pp. 113-14.

2560 LUDWIG, WERNER. "Im Geiste wahren Menschentums." In:
        BEITRÄGE, pp. 97-102.

2561 LUTHER, ERNST. "Bewusstsein der Verantwortung." RUNDBRIEFE/
        DDR 29 (1976), pp. 1-7.

2562 MARCHAL, GEORGES. "Le paradoxe dans la pensée Albert
        Schweitzers." In: EHRFURCHT, pp. 82-89. Reprinted
        as "Paradoxe et respect de la vie dans la pensée d'Albert
        Schweitzer." In: HOMMAGE, pp. 65-73; excerpted in
        CAHIERS 1 (April 1959), pp. 17-18.

2563 MARGOLIUS, HANS. "Die Ethik Albert Schweitzers." RUNDBRIEF
        5 (June 1, 1954), pp. 40-46.

2564 _____. "Die Ethik Albert Schweitzers und das Judentum."
        RUNDBRIEF 37 (Sept. 4, 1973), pp. 35-40.

2565 MARKAKI, YOULIA. [Les deux grandes apôtres de la charité.
        Ghandi. Schweitzer.] Athens, 1968. 126 pp. Illus.

2566 MASTE, ERNST. "Vorrang der Ethik. Albert Schweitzers
        Kulturphilosophie." Europäische Rundschau (Vienna) 3:21
        (1948), pp. 988-90.

2567   MC ELROY, HOWARD C. "Albert Schweitzer." In: <u>Modern</u>
         <u>Philosophers: Western Thought since Kant</u>. New York:
         Moore, 1950, pp. 229-34.

2568   MECKEL, N. "Albert Schweitzers religiös-ethische
         Weltanschauung." <u>Die Kirche in der Welt</u> (Munster) 7:1
         (1954), pp. 47-52.

2569   MESSER, AUGUST. "Albert Schweitzers Kulturphilosophie."
         <u>Philosophie und Leben</u> (Osterwieck/Harz) 1:3 (March 1925),
         pp. 77-97.

2570   _____. "Albert Schweitzer." <u>Philosophie und Leben</u>
         (Osterwieck/Harz) 6:1 (Jan. 1930), pp. 2-7.

2571   _____. "Zur Ethik Albert Schweitzers." <u>Philosophie und Leben</u>
         (Osterwieck/Harz) 9:1 (Jan. 1953), pp. 1-11. For replies
         to this essay, see <u>Philosophie und Leben</u> 9:4 (April 1933),
         pp. 101-06.

2572   MEYER, EDOUARD. "Kulturphilosophische Wandlungen. Albert
         Schweitzer zum 75. Geburtstag." <u>Deutsche Universitäts-</u>
         <u>Zeitung</u> (Göttingen) 5:2 (Jan. 27, 1950), pp. 14-15.

2573   MEYER, ERICH. "Albert Schweitzer und die Ehrfurcht."
         <u>Freies Christentum</u> (Frankfurt a.M.) 6:6 (June 1, 1954),
         col. 78.

2574   MEYER, HERMANN J. "Albert Schweitzers Analyse dieses
         Zeitalters und seiner Kultur." In: DENKEN UND WEG,
         pp. 511-33.

2575   _____. "Albert Schweitzers Doktorarbeit über Kant." In:
         DENKEN UND WEG, pp. 66-74.

2576   MILOSCHEFF, BORIS. "Enzyklopädie der christlichen Moral."
         In: BEITRÄGE, pp. 103-07.

2577   GILMORE, MAX (ROBERT MINDER). "Albert Schweitzer."
         <u>Elsässische Literaturblatt</u> (Strasbourg) 1:9 (June 1, 1930),
         p. 4; 1:10 (July 1, 1930), p. 8.

2578   MITSCHISCHEK, ERHARD. "Objektive und subjektive Motivation--
         Bemerkungen zu Schweitzers Ethik." RUNDBRIEF 40
         (Jan. 14, 1975), pp. 93-101.

2579   MITZENHEIM, MORITZ. "Bahnbrecher der Mitmenschlichkeit."
         In: BEITRÄGE, pp. 108-110.

Philosophy

2580 MONTGOMERY, W. "Schweitzer's ethic." <u>The Hibbert Journal</u>
(London) 23:4 (July 1925), pp. 695-708.

2581 MOURA, TARCISIO. "Dr. Albert Schweitzer ou um diagnostico
da cultura." <u>Reflexão</u> (Campinas) 5 (1977), pp. 25-48.

2582 MUMFORD, LOUIS. <u>The Conduct of Life</u>. New York: Harcourt,
Brace and Co., 1951, pp. 207-15.

2583 MURRY, JOHN MIDDLETON. "The impasse of Albert Schweitzer"
and "The religion of Albert Schweitzer." In: <u>Love,
Freedom, and Society</u>. London: J. Cape, 1957, pp. 127-59
and 160-201.

2584 MUSSCHE, A. J. "Albert Schweitzer." <u>De Stem</u> (Arnhem) 5:1
(1925), pp. 150-53.

2585 NEKOLNY, K. F. R. "Essay over de absolute intelligente."
NIEUWS 5:2 (Oct. 1956), pp. 7-9.

2586 NEUENSCHWANDER, ULRICH. "Albert Schweitzer." In: <u>Denker
des Glaubens</u>. Gütersloh: Verlagshaus Mohn, 1974,
pp. 47-70. (Gütersloher Taschenbücher 81.)

_____. "Albert Schweitzer und das 20. Jahrhundert." See
Theology and Religion, no. 3069 below.

2587 _____. "La suite de la <u>Philosophie de la Civilisation</u> dans
les <u>Manuscrits Posthumes d'Albert Schweitzer</u>." REVUE
56:1-2 (1976), pp. 81-96.

2588 NIEBUHR, REINHOLD. "Can Schweitzer save us from Russell?"
<u>The Christian Century</u> (Chicago) 42:36 (Sept. 3, 1925),
pp. 1093-95.

2589 NITZBERG, A. SOREL "Réflexions sur l'éthique d'Albert
Schweitzer." In: HOMMAGE, pp. 93-97.

2590 NÖLLE, W. "Die Weltanschauung der Indischen Denker."
<u>Universitas</u> (Stuttgart) 15:1 (Jan. 1960), p. 115.

2591 NOVRUP, JOHS. "Albert Schweitzer." <u>Tidsskrift for Dansk
Røde Kors</u> (Copenhagen) 1 (1952), pp. 12-16. Port., illus.

2592 O'BRIEN, JOHN A. "Schweitzer: philosopher in the jungle."
<u>The Catholic World</u> (New York) 170:1018 (Jan. 1950),
pp. 290-91.

2593 O'HARA, MARY LOUISE. "Youth should be served." Friends
Journal (Philadelphia) 14:10 (May 15, 1968), pp. 247-48.

2594 OERTHEL, KURT VON. "Albert Schweitzer und die Jugend."
Aufbau (Berlin) 4:4 (1948), pp. 334-36.

2595 OTTO, BERND. "Strukturwandlungen der menschlichen Person--
ein Vergleich der Anfassungen J. H. Pestalozzis und
A. Schweitzers." RUNDBRIEF 32 (1969).

2596 OXNAM, G. BROMLEY. "The missionary as social reformer:
Albert Schweitzer." In: Personalities in Social Reform.
New York, Nashville: Abingdon-Cokesbury, 1950,
pp. 145-72. Based on a series of lectures given at
Drew Theological Seminary. Excerpted as "Albert Schweitzer:
Reform, revolution, regeneration!" In: FESTSCHRIFT,
pp. 72-75; translated as "Albert Schweitzer. Erneuerung,
Umgestaltung, Wiedergeburt." In: EHRFURCHT, pp. 228-30.

2597 PAFFRATH, LESLIE. "Remarks" (Albert Schweitzer's philosophy).
In: THE CONVOCATION RECORD, pp. I/5-9.

2598 PATNAIK, D. P. "Schweitzer and Indian philosophy." In:
Hagemann, E. R., ed. Albert Schweitzer. Louisville, Ky.:
University of Louisville, 1969.

2599 PETRITZKI, WILLI. "Schweitzer und Tolstoi." In: BEITRÄGE,
pp. 131-36.

2600 PFEIFFER, HERMANN. "Albert Schweitzer oder die Wiedergeburt
der Kultur aus dem Denken." Die Sammlung (Göttingen) 1
(Aug./Sept. 1946), pp. 642-48.

2601 PICHT, WERNER. "Albert Schweitzer in Lambarene." Wort und
Wahrheit (Freiburg i.B.) 15:4 (April 1960), pp. 292-305.

2602 PIETSCH, Dr. Med. "Rede vor die Albert-Schweitzer-Gruppe der
Strafanstalt Kassel-Welheiden zur Feier eines
Geburtstages von Albert Schweitzer." RUNDBRIEF 15
(Jan. 14, 1960), pp. 60-67.

2603 PILGRAM, PAUL. "Was hat uns Albert Schweitzer für das
Schwesternleben zu sagen." In: Lebenshilfe für das
Schwernleben. Berlin-Zehlendorf: Verlag des
Evangelischen Diakonievereins, 1928, pp. 9-40. Second
edition, 1929, p. 5-43.

2604 PIRE, DOMINIQUE. "Wherein do we differ?" In: REALMS,
pp. 201-03.

Philosophy

2605   PLANCK, REINHOLD. "Der sittliche Wille in seinem Verhältnis
        zur Natur" (Albert Schweitzer und Karl Planck). Die
        Christliche Welt (Gotha) 49:7 (April 1, 1935), pp. 303-10;
        49:8 (April 13, 1935), pp. 380-87.

2606   POHLMANN, JULIE. "Albert Schweitzers grosser Beitrag."
        Geist und Tat (Hamburg) 6:10 (Oct. 1951), pp. 309-12.

2607   RADHAKRISHNAN, SARVEPALLI. "Mysticism and ethics in Hindu
        thought." In: Eastern Religions and Western Thought.
        Oxford: Clarendon Press, 1939, pp. 64-114; New York:
        Oxford University Press, 1959. Radhakrishnan's reply to
        Schweitzer's critique of Indian thought. Translated as
        "Mystik und Ethik im Hindu-Denken." In: Die Gemeinschaft
        des Geistes. Östliche Religionen und westliches Denken.
        Tr. Franz Thierfelder. Darmstadt and Genf: Halle, 1952,
        pp. 78-129.

2608   RANLEY, ERNEST W. "Albert Schweitzer's philosophy of civili-
        zation." Thought (Bronx, N.Y.) 38:149 (Summer 1963),
        pp. 237-54.

2609   RANSON, GUY H. "The ethics of Albert Schweitzer." The
        Review and Expositor (Louisville) 47 (1950), pp. 21-32.
        Paper read before a meeting of the Missouri Philosophical
        Association, Washington University, St. Louis, Oct. 28-29,
        1949.

2610   RASMUSSEN, EGIL. "Albert Schweitzers etiske livsfordring."
        Aftenposten (Oslo) 95:501 (Oct. 30, 1954), pp. 2f.

2611   RAUSCHER, JOSEF. Krise der Menschlichkeit. Vienna: Verlag
        Forum Humanum, 1974.

2612   REGESTER, JOHN D. "Albert Schweitzer and existentialism."
        The College of Puget Sound Review (Tacoma, Wash.) 1:2
        (Spring 1957), pp. 17-20.

2613   _____. "Schweitzer's impact on philosophy; a positive
        existentialism." In: PROPHET, pp. 27-30.

2614   _____. "A statement" (Albert Schweitzer's philosophy). In:
        THE CONVOCATION RECORD, p. VI/15.

2615   _____. [Tribute without title.] In: DENKEN UND WEG,
        pp. 117-19.

2616   REICHARDT, HORST PETER. "Albert Schweitzers Ethos: ein
        Beweggrund für ärztliches Wirken verantwortungsbewusste

Christen in unser Gesellschaft." In: VERMÄCHTNIS UND
WIRKLICHKEIT, pp. 59-66.

2617 RICHTER, JULIUS. "Albert Schweitzer als Mystiker." Freies
Christentum (Frankfurt a.M.) 17:10 (Oct. 1965), cols.
149-55; 17:11 (Nov. 1965), cols. 163-69. Illus.

2618 RICHTER, WERNER. "Humanismus und Pädagogik." In: BEITRÄGE,
pp. 162-64.

2619 ROLFFS, ERNST. "Albert Schweitzer als ethisches phänomen
und theologisches Problem." Deutsches Pfarrblatt 35
(April 21, 1931), pp. 241-45; (April 28, 1939), pp. 257-59;
(May 5, 1931), pp. 271-78; (May 12, 1931), pp. 289-90.

2620 ROOS, ALARIK. "Liberalismus etiker" (based on John Middleton
Murry's The Challenge of Schweitzer, no. 2885 below).
Stockholms Tidening, Feb. 21, 1949.

2621 _____. "En rationalist och etiker" (Albert Schweitzer,
Bertrand Russell, Lecomte du Noüys). Stockholms Tidening,
Aug. 7, 1948.

2622 ROSTAND, JEAN. "L'apôtre de Lambaréné." Les Nouvelles
Littéraires (Paris) 43:1984 (Sept. 9, 1965), p. 1. Illus.

2623 RUSSELL, LILIAN M. "Dr. Schweitzer's ethics in relation to
animals." The Animal's Friend (London) 39:1 (Jan. 1933),
pp. 10-12.

2624 S., E. "Ein Vortrag Albert Schweitzers in Zürich." Elsass-
Lothringen Heimatstimmen (Berlin) 6:3 (March 10, 1928),
p. 187.

2625 SABISTON, CAMPBELL. "'Humanism is the only true spirituality'
wrote Albert Schweitzer." The Humanist (Schnectady, N.Y.)
22:5 (Sept./Oct. 1962), pp. 157-60.

2626 SACHSE, WOLFGANG. "Aesthetische Reflexionen." Allgemeine
Musikzeitung (Berlin, Cologne) 56:49 (Dec. 6, 1929),
pp. 1203-04.

2627 SACK, ARNOLD. "Albert Schweitzers Persönlichkeit als Arzt,
Denker und Mensch." Münchener Medizinische Wochenschrift
(Munich) 76:26 (June 28, 1929), pp. 1089-91. Also issued
as an offprint: Munich: E. Mühlthalers Buch- und
Kunstdruckerei. 11 pp.

Philosophy

2628   SALOMON, ALBERT. ["Albert Schweitzer."] In: Aertzliche
        Ethik und Umgangspsychologie für Studenten und Aerzte.
        Zürich: Rascher Verlag, 1947, pp. 25-39.

2629   SARTON, GEORGE. "The scholar's dilemma." In: JUBILEE,
            pp. 459-65. Translated as "Der Gelehrte im Dilemma der
            Gegenwart." In: DENKEN UND WEG, pp. 557-61.

2630   SCHAB, GÜNTER. "Ideal persönlichen Menschentums." Rhein-
            Neckar Zeitung (Heidelberg), May 1, 1950.

2631   SCHEFOLD, KARL. "Die Ehrfurcht vor dem Leben und das Ethos
            der Baukunst." In: DENKEN UND WEG, pp. 299-306.

2632   SCHLIPP, PAUL ARTHUR. "Schweitzer's practical moral judgments
            and his ethical theory." In: REALMS, pp. 228-42.

2633   SCHLOSSER, JULIE. "Albert Schweitzer, Mensch und Kreatur."
            Die Christliche Welt (Gotha) 43:2 (Jan. 19, 1929),
            pp. 66-68.

2634   SCHMIDT-WODDER, JOHANNES. "Die geistige Linie Albert
            Schweitzers." Zeitschrift für Geopolitik (Heidelberg)
            23 (1952), pp. 643-44.

2635   SCHOLL, ROBERT. "'Durch Denken religiös werden.' Über
            Frommigkeit und Denken bei Albert Schweitzer." Zeitwende
            (Hamburg) 38:5 (May 1967), pp. 294-309.

2636   SCHÜTZ, ROLAND. "Bilderreichtum--eine künstlerische Note
            in Albert Schweitzers Sprache." RUNDBRIEF 18
            (July 15, 1961), pp. 13-20.

2637   _____. [Essay without title.] In: BEGEGNUNG, pp. 83-84.

2638   _____. "Selig sind die Friedfertigkeit." Universitas
            (Stuttgart) 15:1 (Jan. 1960), pp. 131-32. Reprinted as
            "Friedfertigkeit und Brüderschaft." In: DENKEN UND WEG,
            pp. 392-98. Also reprinted in: SCHWEITZER, pp. 155-58.

2639   SCHWABE, GERHARD HELMUT. "Von der Selbstbedrohung des
            heutigen Menschen." Schweizerisches Reformiertes
            Volksblatt (Basel), Jan. 6, 1968. Also issued as a
            4-page offprint.

2640   SCHWARTZ, EUGENE. "Ethics and police: a Schweitzer per-
            spective?" In: CENTENNIAL.

2641 SCOTT, GABRIEL. "Albert Schweitzers livsgjerning; se på ham, ungdom, laer av ham, ungdom." Aftenposten (Oslo) 94:505 (Oct. 31, 1953), p. 11.

2642 SEAVER, GEORGE. "Albert Schweitzer." In: Harcourt, Melville, ed. Thirteen for Christ. New York: Sheed and Ward, 1963, pp. 93-118.

2643 _____. "The natural and the spiritual." In: REALMS, pp. 326-38.

2644 SIEBURG, FRIEDRICH. "Wozu grosse Männer?" Frankfurter Allgemeine Zeitung, Ausgabe D, Feb. 2, 1960, p. 1.

2645 SIMON, SACHA. "Le bon toubib." In: RAYONNEMENT, pp. 241-43. Extrait d'une vocation manquée, Le Figaro, 14. Oct. 1970.

2646 SKÅNLAND, HALFDAN. "I livets of Fredens tjeneste--Albert Schweitzer: Vi bygger opp." Pedagogen (Oslo) 8:1 (Jan. 1955), pp. 43-47.

2647 SØRENSØEN, B. ESBYE. "Albert Schweitzer. Kulturfilosoffen i urskoven." Tåge Hornet (Aarhus) 5:5 (April/May 1947), pp. 106-10.

2648 SONNTAG, WOLFGANG. "Ein heilender Denker." Niedersächsische Lehrerzeitung (Hannover) 2:13 (Sept. 15, 1951), p. 24.

2649 SOROKIN, PITRIM A. "Albert Schweitzer" and "Critical examination of the theories of Northrop, Kroeber, Schubart, Berdyaev, and Schweitzer." In: Social Philosophies of an Age of Crisis. Boston: Beacon Press, 1950, pp. 176-83 and 244-72. Unabridged and unaltered edition, with title Modern Historical and Social Philosophers. New York: Dover; Canada: McClelland and Stewart; London: Constable and Co., 1963. German edition, 1953, Kulturkrise und Gesellschafts-Philosophie; Spanish edition, 1954, Las Filosofías sociales de nuestra época de crisis; also published in Portuguese and Hindi, 1963 and 1964.

2650 SPEAR, OTTO. "The Albert Schweitzer discussion, Basle, 1967." Universitas (English Language edition) 10:4 (1968), pp. 351-62.

2651 _____. "Kein Vorrecht auf Glück und auf Rang--Albert-Schweitzer-Reflexionen." Universitas (Stuttgart) 27:3 (March 1972), pp. 297-306. Reprinted with title "Kein Vorrecht auf Leben, Glück und Rang--Reflexionen zu Albert Schweitzers Ethik." RUNDBRIEF 42 (Oct. 1976), pp. 32-41.

Philosophy

2652 _____. "Vernünftigkeit und Menschlichkeit--ein Gebot der
Stunde." RUNDBRIEF 36 (Jan. 14, 1973), pp. 63-65.

2653 _____. "Zweites Albert Schweitzer Gespräch." Universitas
(Stuttgart) 26:7 (July 1971), pp. 773-75. Translated as
"Problems of ethics in the second Albert Schweitzer
colloquium." Universitas (English language edition) 14:1
(1971), pp. 69-78.

2654 SPIEGELBERG, HERBERT. "Albert Schweitzer's other thought:
good fortune obligates." Africa: Journal of the Philosophical Assoc. of Kenya 1 (1973), pp. 11-17. Presented
at the Fifteenth World Congress of Philosophy in Varna,
Bulgaria. Enlarged and revised as "Good fortune obligates:
Albert Schweitzer's second ethical principal." Ethics
(Chicago) 85:3 (April 1975), pp. 227-34; reprinted in:
CENTENNIAL; condensed as "Schweitzer's second ethical
principle: good fortune obligates." In: PROPHET,
pp. 32-36; abridged in COURIER, Spring 1976, pp. 14-19;
translated as "Albert Schweitzers 'anderer Gedanke':
Glück verpflichtet. Philosophische Aspekte." Universitas
(Stuttgart) 29:10 (Oct. 1974), pp. 1077-87.

2655 SPRÄNGER, EDUARD. "Der Idealismus." Universitas (Stuttgart)
15:1 (Jan. 1960), pp. 13-16. Reprinted in: DENKEN UND
WEG, pp. 19-23; reprinted in: BEGEGNUNG, pp. 52-55;
translated as "Idealism." Universitas (English language
edition) 7:1 (1964), pp. 33-36.

2656 STAHLER, ROBERT. "L'universel, l'humain, le chrétien chez
Albert Schweitzer." In: EHRFURCHT, pp. 90-103. Reprinted in Le Protestant (Geneva) 89:1 (Jan. 15, 1955),
pp. 1ff.

2657 STEINBÜCHEL, THEODOR. "Zur Problematik der Ethik in der
Gegenwart." Zeitschrift für Theologie und Seelsorge
(Düsseldorf) 1:3 (March 1924), pp. 294-97.

2658 STERN, ALFRED. "Albert Schweitzer, une vie exemplaire, une
philosophie vie cue." Atenea (University of Puerto Rico)
9 (1972), pp. 75-88.

2659 STEUBING, H. "Kulturethik und Christentum. Eine kritische
Auseinandersetzung mit Albert Schweitzers
Kulturphilosophie." Neue Kirchliche Zeitschrift
(Leipzig and Erlangen) 41:10 (1930), pp. 649-86.

2660 STREGE, MARTIN. "Albert Schweitzer als Mystiker." Freies
Christentum (Frankfurt a.M.) 6:1 (Jan. 1, 1954), col. 3.

2661   _____. "Albert Schweitzer und der Zeitgeist." RUNDBRIEF 36
        (Jan. 14, 1973), pp. 45-62.

2662   _____. "Der Mensch in der Daseinsmitte. Jenseits von
        Philosophie und Theologie." RUNDBRIEF 13 (Dec. 15, 1958),
        pp. 44-50.

2663   STRÖLE, ALBRECHT. "Albert Schweitzers als Kulturphilosoph."
        RUNDBRIEF 9 (Jan. 1, 1956), pp. 32-41; Reprinted in:
        DOKUMENTE, pp. 298-305.

2664   SWIERZAWSKI, KS. WACLAW. "Odwie Dziny w Grunsbach."
        Tygodnik Powszechny (Krakow) 26:2 (9 stydznia 1972), p. 3.

2665   TAPPEN, M. "Albert Schweitzer und die Aufklärung." Geist
        und Tat (Hamburg) 8:12 (Dec. 1953), pp. 19-21.

2666   TATHAGATANANDA, SWAMI. "Albert Schweitzer--a profile."
        Modern Review (Calcutta) 121 (1) (Jan. 1967), pp. 11-13.

2667   TAU, MAX. "Albert Schweitzer." Fränkische Nachrichten
        (Tauberbischofsheim, Germany) 6:184 (Aug. 10, 1951).

2668   _____. Förord. In: Aerefrykt for Livet. Et ulvalg
        av Albert Schweitzers verker. Redigert av Rudolf Grabs.
        Oslo: Johan Grundt Tanum Verlag, 1951, pp. 7-20.

2669   THIOUT, MICHEL. "Albert Schweitzer, homme de coeur et de
        pensée." France-Asie (Saigon) 70 (March 1952),
        pp. 966-71.

2670   THYGESEN, ENGDAHL. "Der grosse Mensch Albert Schweitzer."
        Hamburger Anzeiger (Hamburg), Jan. 14, 1955.

2671   TRUEBLOOD, D. ELTON. "A philosophy in action." The Christian
        Century (Chicago) 48:17 (April 29, 1931), pp. 575-77.

2672   TURNER, VINCENT. "Albert Schweitzer, his work and his philos-
        ophy." The Dublin Review 215:430 (July 1944), pp. 575-77.

2673   VACHET, PIERRE. "Schweitzer, moraliste. . . ." In: DEBRECEN,
        pp. 65-67.

2674   VAN DALEN, W. S. HUGO. "Flamme des Friedens und der
        Menschenliebe." In: BEITRÄGE, pp. 41-43.

2675   VANDENRATH, JOHANNES. "Albert Schweitzer und Schopenhauer."
        Schopenhauer Jahrbuch für das Jahr 1968. Hrsg. von
        Arthur Hübscher. Frankfurt a.M.: W. Kramer, 1968,
        pp. 52-84.

Philosophy

2676 _____. "Wege zur Verwirklichung der Ethik Albert Schweitzers."
      In: GESTERN-HEUTE, pp. 65-68.

2677 VOGT, WILHELM. "Albert Schweitzer, der baumeister einer neuen
      Ordnung." RUNDBRIEF 12 (June 15, 1958), pp. 45-48.

2678 WACH, JOACHIM. "On understanding." In: JUBILEE, pp. 131-46.

2679 WANG TEH-CHIAO. "Albert Schweitzer und Wang Yang-ming."
      Minchu-p'ing-lun 5:19 (May 10, 1954).

2680 WARTENWEILER, FRITZ. "Ein Manuskript 'Albert Schweitzer' aus
      dem Jahr 1930." RUNDBRIEF 20 (Sept. 1, 1962), pp. 29-32.

2681 WARTENWEILER-HAFFTER, FRITZ. "Albert Schweitzer."
      Schweizerische Volkshochschule (Bern) 4:3 (April 1925),
      pp. 70-75.

2682 "Was uns nottut. Die Kultur setzt freie voraus. Albert
      Schweitzer." Der Landschäftler (Liestal) 24
      (Jan. 29, 1955).

2683 "Der Weg zur Regeneration der Kultur." Neue Zürcher Zeitung
      144:426 (March 29, 1923), Erstes Morgenblatt; 435
      (March 31, 1923), Erstes Morgenblatt; 442 (April 3, 1923),
      Zweites Morgenblatt.

2684 WEGMANN, HANS. "Albert Schweitzers Lebens- und
      Weltanschauung." Sonntagspost (Winterthur, Switz.) 65:2
      (Jan. 13, 1945), pp. 10-11.

2685 WEHRUNG, GEORG. "Albert Schweitzer und seine Zeitspiegel."
      Der Türmer (Stuttgart) 26:10 (July 1924), pp. 677-81.

2686 WENZEL, FRITZ. "Der einzelne und die Gemeinschaft bei Albert
      Schweitzer." Ethik (Halle/Saale) 13:3-5 (Jan.-June 1937),
      pp. 120-27, 157-64, 211-15. Reprinted in: Wenzel, Fritz.
      Wandlung des Herzens. Sieben Aufsätze über Albert
      Schweitzer, u.a. Braunschweig: Limbach, 1949, pp. 21-47.

2687 WERNER, HELMUT. "Hoffnung der studentischen Jugend."
      Universitas (Stuttgart) 15:1 (Jan. 1960), pp. 133-34.
      Reprinted in: BEGEGNUNG, pp. 247-48.

2688 W., M. (WERNER, MARTIN). "Albert Schweitzer in theologisch-
      philosophischen Geistesleben." Neue Zürcher Zeitung
      1792 (Nov. 30, 1924), p. 5; 1801 (Dec. 1, 1924), p. 10.

2689 _____. "Religion and human rights." Universitas (English
language edition) 7:1 (1964), pp. 45-50.

2690 WESTRA, P. "Albert Schweitzers philosophische en religieuze
ideen." De Gids (Utrecht) 116:6 (June 1953), pp. 392-401.

2691 WETZEL, ANDRÉ. "La pensée d'Albert Schweitzer." CAHIERS 13
(June 1965), pp. 9-13.

2692 WICKE, HELMUTH. "Albert Schweitzer-Mensch und Denker."
RUNDBRIEF 26 (June 15, 1965), pp. 34-38.

2693 WIRTH, GUNTER. "Kulturphilosophisches Denken und ethisches
Handeln." In: VERMÄCHTNIS UND WIRKLICHKEIT, pp. 19-28.

2694 WISSER, RICHARD. "Karl Jaspers und Albert Schweitzer, ihr
philosophisches Denken über Probleme der heutigen
Menschheit." Universitas (Stuttgart) 28:5 (May 1973),
pp. 497-506. Reprinted as "Albert Schweitzer und Karl
Jaspers." RUNDBRIEF 37 (Sept. 4, 1973), pp. 41-47.

2695 WOYTT, GUSTAV. "Die Philosophie und die allgemeine Bildung
im neunzehnten Jahrhundert." RUNDBRIEF 37 (Sept. 1973),
pp. 28-32.

2696 ZIMMERMAN, WALTER. "Albert Schweitzer und wir. Beiträge zu
seiner Pädagogik und Unterrichtsmethodik des gesunden
Menschenverstands." RUNDBRIEF 20 (Sept. 1, 1962),
pp. 42-44.

B.   Reverence for Life

The concept of Reverence for Life first came to Schweitzer in the
course of a journey on the Ogowe River in September 1915. "Lost in
thought, I sat on the deck of the barge, struggling to find the
elementary and universal conception of the ethical which I had not
discovered in any philosophy. Sheet after sheet I covered with dis-
connected sentences, merely to keep myself concentrated on the problem. Late in the third day, at the very moment when, at sunset, we
were making our way through a herd of hippopotamuses, there flashed
upon my mind, unforeseen and unsought, the phrase 'Reverence for
Life.' The iron door had yielded: the path in the thicket had become visible. Now I had found my way to the idea in which affirmation of the world and ethics are contained side by side!"[1] The

---

[1] Out of My Life and Thought. New York: Holt, Rinehart and Winston,
1961, pp. 156-57.

Philosophy

central concept of this philosophy is described as follows by
Schweitzer: ". . . the man who has become a thinking being feels
a compulsion to give to every will-to-live the same reverence for
life that he gives to his own. He experiences that other life in
his own. He accepts as being good: to preserve life, to promote
life, to raise to its highest value life which is capable of development; and as being evil: to destroy life, to injure life, to
repress life which is capable of development. This is the absolute,
fundamental principle of the moral, and it is a necessity of
thought."[1]

I have attempted in this section to isolate those books and
articles which deal specifically with this aspect of Schweitzer's
philosophical thought. Many of the more general treatises on philosophy undoubtedly contain additional material on the subject.

1. Books by Schweitzer

DIE LEHRE DER EHRFURCHT VOR DEM LEBEN
(The Teaching of Reverence for Life)

"This book grew out of a proposal which Gerald Götting made to me
during a visit to Lambarene in August, 1961. Albert Schweitzer."[2]

2697   Die Lehre der Ehrfurcht vor dem Leben. Berlin: Union Verlag,
        1963. 75 pp., front. (port.). 4th edition, 1967, 74 pp.;
        5th edition, 1968; 6th edition, 1969. CONTENTS: Das
        Problem der Ethik in der Höherentwicklung des menschlichen
        Denkens--Ethische Kultur--Mensch zu Mensch--Mensch zu
        Kreatur--Friede oder Atomkrieg--Los von der Gesinnung
        der Unmenschlichkeit! Los von den Atomwaffen!

2698   Same. Included in: Götting, Gerald. Albert Schweitzer,
        Pionier der Menschlichkeit. Berlin: Union Verlag, 1970,
        pp. 107-41.

English

2699   The Teaching of Reverence for Life. Tr. Richard and Clara
        Winston. New York: Holt, Rinehart and Winston, 1965.
        63 pp.

---

[1]Ibid, p. 158.

[2]From the back flyleaf of the American edition.

Estonian

2700   Arkartus elu ees. Tr. Peeter Tulviste. Tallin: Periodika,
            1972.   56 pp.

Polish

2701   Zycie. Tr. Jerzy Piechowski. Warsaw: Pax, 1964.   78 pp.
            Second edition, 1971.

DIE LEHRE VON DER EHRFURCHT VOR DEM LEBEN:
GRUNDTEXTE AUS FÜNF JAHRZEHNTEN

The idea for this collection, which was intended to consolidate
Schweitzer's basic texts on reverence for life into one volume, "und
durch diesen Band des Ganze seiner Erkenntnis, ihre Ausformungen,
ihren Werdegang und ihre Auseinandersetzung mit den Problemen der
Gegenwart darzustellen,"[1] was conceived in the summer of 1963.
Schweitzer himself was too occupied with the affairs of his hospital,
and so the project was placed in the hands of Hans Walter Bähr. The
selections included in the volume come from various sources, both
published and unpublished, and are arranged in chronological order.

2702   Die Lehre von der Ehrfurcht vor dem Leben: Grundtexte aus
            fünf Jahrzehnten. Im Auftrag des Verfassers hrsg. von
            Hans Walter Bähr. Munich: C. H. Beck, 1966. 160 pp.
            Second edition, 1976. CONTENTS: Die Entstehung der
            Lehre der Ehrfurcht vor dem Leben und ihre Bedeutung für
            unsere Kultur (manuscript from 1963)--Die Ehrfurcht vor
            dem Leben (from Strassburger Predigten)--Die Forderung
            der neuen Lehre (from Kultur und Ethik)--Die Krise der
            Kultur und ihre geistige Ursache (from Kultur und Ethik)--
            Jugenderinnerungen (from Aus Meiner Kindheit und
            Jugendzeit)--Ethik als Leben im Geiste Jesu Christi (from
            Die Mystik des Apostels Paulus)--Philosophie und
            Tierschutzbewegung--Das Problem des Ethischen in der
            Entwicklung des menschlichen Denkens ("Le Problème de
            l'éthique dans l'évolution de la pensée humaine")--Das
            Problem des Friedens in der heutigen Welt (Nobel Peace
            Prize address)--Humanität (manuscript from 1961)--Der
            Weg des Friedens heute (manuscript from 1963)--Rückblick
            und Ausblick (from Aus meinem Leben und Denken).

---

[1]Bahr, H. W. "Einleitung" to Die Lehre von der Ehrfurcht vor dem
    vor dem Leben.

Philosophy

2. Shorter Writings by Schweitzer

2703   "Albert Schweitzer." In: Davidson, Robert F., et al, eds.
        The Humanities in Contemporary Life. New York: Holt,
        1960, pp. 619-28. Epilogue to Out of my Life and Thought.

2704   "Albert Schweitzer speaks out." The World Book Year Book
        1964. Chicago: 1964, pp. 133-48. Reprinted in COURIER,
        May 1964, pp. 135-48; reprinted with the title "The
        philosophy of Dr. Schweitzer--'approach all life with
        reverence.'" Philadelphia Inquirer, Today's World,
        June 7, 1964, p. 1; Reprinted with some omissions as
        "Albert Schweitzer writes on 'Reverence for Life.'"
        National Wildlife 3:3 (April-May 1965), pp. 34-35.

2705   "Ehrfurcht vor dem Leben." Westdeutsche Rundschau
        (Wuppertal-Barmen) 11 (Jan. 14, 1960), p. 12.

2706   "Eine Ethik, die nur mit unseren Verhältnis zur anderen
        Menschen zu tun hat, ist unvollständig." Das Tier.
        Internationale Tierillustrierte (Bern) 7:4 (1967), p. 3.

2707   "Die Entstehung der Lehre der Ehrfurcht vor dem Leben und ihre
        Bedeutung für unsere Kultur." Universitas (Stuttgart)
        18:11 (Nov. 1963), pp. 1145-60. Reprinted in RUNDBRIEF
        23 (Jan. 14, 1964), pp. 2-16.

2708   "The Ethics of reverence for life." Christendom (Chicago)
        1:2 (Winter 1936), pp. 225-39. Reprinted in: Clark,
        Henry. The Ethical Mysticism of Albert Schweitzer,
        see no. 2351, pp. 180-94.

2709   "L'éthique du respect de la vie." CAHIERS/BELGE (Nov. 1960),
        pp. 32-33. Reprinted in CAHIERS/BELGE 5 (April 1965),
        pp. 6-7.

2710   "From elemental thinking: reverence for life." In: Burnett,
        Whit, ed. This is my Philosophy: twenty of the world's
        outstanding thinkers reveal the deepest meanings they
        have found in life. New York: Harper, 1957, pp. 53-70.
        Epilogue from Out of my Life and Thought.

2711   "L'homme et la souffrance des animaux." CAHIERS 30 (1974),
        pp. 3-8. Extr. du sermon du troisième dimanche de
        l'Avent 1908 (Strasbourg, Église St. Nicholas).

2712   Letter to Warren Steinkraus (dated Lambarene, 26.12.64). In:
        Steinkraus, Warren. "Borden P. Bowne and Albert
        Schweitzer." The Personalist (Los Angeles) 50:1
        (Winter 1969), pp. 82-83; German original, p. 84.

2713   "Man belongs to man." Reader's Digest (Pleasantville, N.Y.)
          87:519 (July 1965), pp. 77-78. Condensed from The
          Teaching of Reverence for Life.

2714   "Nochmals Falkenjägerai." Atlantis (Zürich), March 1932,
          pp. 175-76. Translated as "Valkenjacht." NIEUWS 2:1
          (May 1953), pp. 7-9; also as "The revival of falconry."
          The Animal's Friend (London) 38:11-12 (Nov.-Dec. 1932),
          pp. 319-20.

2715   "La notion du respect de la vie." CAHIERS 11 (July 1964),
          pp. 2-7.

2716   "Philosophy and the movement for the protection of animals."
          International Journal of Animal's Protection (Edinburgh),
          May 1936, pp. 5-7. Translated as "Philosophie und
          Tierschutzbewegung." International Tierschutzzeitung
          (Edinburgh), May 1936, pp. 5-7; translation reprinted in
          Die Lehre von der Ehrfurcht vor dem Leben, no. 2702
          above, pp. 92-98.

2717   "Le respect de la vie et ses problèmes." CAHIERS 27
          (Summer 1972), pp. 3-7.

2718   "Reverence for life." The Animal's Magazine, Oct. 1935,
          pp. 3-4.

2719   "Reverence for life." In: Burnett, Whit, ed. Spirit of Man:
          great stories and experiences of spiritual crisis, inspi-
          ration and the joy of life by forty famous contemporaries.
          Hawthorn Books, 1958. British Edition: The Human Spirit.
          London: George Allen and Unwin, 1960, pp. 307-10. Ex-
          cerpt from Out of my Life and Thought.

2720   "Reverence for Life." Friends Journal (Philadelphia) 21:3
          (Feb. 1, 1975), pp. 67-69. Excerpt from Out of my Life
          and Thought.

2721   "Reverence for Life." In: MacGregor, Geddes, and J. Wesley
          Robb, eds. Readings in Religious Philosophy. Boston:
          Houghton Mifflin, 1962, pp. 246-52. Excerpt from Philoso-
          phy of Civilization.

2722   "Tierschutz." (Letter from Albert Schweitzer to Christ und
          Welt in reply to its article "Tierschutz" of Nov. 13,
          1964). Christ und Welt (Stuttgart) 18:4 (Jan. 22, 1965),
          p. 12.

Philosophy

2723 "Von der Ehrfurcht vor dem Leben." Europäische Revue (Berlin)
 9:3 (March 1933), pp. 151-57.

2724 "Von der Ehrfurcht vor dem Leben." In: Deutscher Geist:
 Kulturdokumente der Gegenwart. Erster Jahresband 1933:
 Der Ruf. Hrsg. von Carl Lange und Ernst A. Dreyer.
 Leipzig: R. Voigtlander, 1933, pp. 15-21.

2725 "Von der Ehrfurcht vor dem Leben." Evangelisches
 Sonntagsblatt für Bonn und Umgegend 109:45 (Nov. 6, 1966),
 p. 11. From the book Durchs Jahr mit Albert Schweitzer,
 see no. 53 above.

2726 "Von der Ehrfurcht vor dem Leben." Werk (Gelsenkirchen) 2
 (1953), pp. 206-09.

2727 "With regard to experiments carried out on animals" (prepared
 by Schweitzer in response to a request from groups in the
 United States, 1962). In: ALBUM, p. 49.

3. Works by Others About Schweitzer

 a. Books

 ARBRELL, R. L. A Study of Albert Schweitzer's Precept of
 Reverence for Life. . . . See Dissertations, no. 4309
 below.

 BLACKWELL, DAVID M. Reverence for Life as an Educational
 Ideal. See Dissertations, no. 4311 below.

2728 FRIEDMAN, RICHARD. Reverence for Life: the Ethics of
 Dr. Albert Schweitzer (a lecture). Portland, Ore.:
 1963. 24 pp.

 JESCHKE, REUBEN P. Reverence for Life as an Ethical Ideal.
 See Dissertations, no. 4323 below.

2729 O'HARA, MARY LOUISE R. Everyone needs a philosophy of life:
 Albert Schweitzer's philosophy of reverence for life.
 Great Barrington, Mass.: Albert Schweitzer Friendship
 House, 1979. 73 pp. Includes extensive quotes from
 Albert Schweitzer and others.

2730 RHEE, TIMOTHY YILSUN. Reverence for Life and World Peace,
 speeches and reminiscences. Seoul: Guideposts, 1975.
 Speech titles: Ehrfurcht vor dem Leben und christliche
 Ethik; Ehrfurcht vor dem Leben und Menschenrecht;
 Ehrfurcht vor dem Leben und medizinische Ethik.

2731   RÍOS, JOSÉ. <u>Albert Schweitzer y su veneración por la vida;</u>
       <u>ensayo</u>. Montevideo, 1967. 67 pp.

2732   STREGE, MARTIN. <u>Ehrfurcht vor dem Leben</u>. Eine kurze,
       allgemeinverständliche Darstellung d. Grundlehre Albert
       Schweitzers. Speyer/Rh.: Wichernbuchhandlung, 1963.
       28 pp.

       WESTERLUND, C. K. The Reverence for Life Philosophy of Albert
       Schweitzer. See Dissertations, no. 4343 below.

   b. Articles, Parts of Books

2733   AEBI, H. "Ehrfurcht vor dem Leben und die Moderne Medizin."
       RUNDBRIEF 47 (May 1979), pp. 34-39.

2734   "Albert Schweitzer: humanism based on reverence for life."
       <u>Saint Louis Quarterly</u> (Baguio City, Philippines) 3:4
       (Dec. 1965), pp. 678-82.

2735   BABEL, HENRY. "Die Ethik der Ehrfurcht vor dem Leben--eine
       Darstellung." In: DENKEN UND WEG, pp. 24-30. Translated
       excerpts from the author's book <u>La Pensée d'Albert</u>
       <u>Schweitzer</u>, see no. 2343 above.

2736   _____. "L'éthique du respect de la vie." NOUVELLES 35
       (Sept. 1974), p. 4.

2737   BÄHR, HANS WALTER. "Die universelle Erweiterung der Ethik
       im Denken Albert Schweitzers." <u>Universitas</u> (Stuttgart)
       15:1 (Jan. 1960), pp. 89-100. Reprinted with title "Die
       Verantwortung für die Natur im Denken Albert Schweitzers."
       In: DENKEN UND WEG, pp. 36-47; reprinted with title
       "Über die Ethik der Ehrfurcht vor dem Leben." In:
       BEGEGNUNG, pp. 288-97; reprinted with title "Die Lehre
       der Ehrfurcht vor dem Leben." In: SCHWEITZER, pp. 130-
       47; translated as "The universal expansion of ethics as
       conceived by Albert Schweitzer." <u>Universitas</u> (English
       language edition) 5:4 (1963), pp. 327-38 and 7:1 (1964),
       pp. 57-68; translated as "La responsibilité de l'homme
       envers la nature dans la pensée d'Albert Schweitzer."
       CAHIERS 10 (Dec. 1963), pp. 15-20; reprinted in:
       RAYONNEMENT, pp. 261-66.

2738   _____. "Die universelle Ethik der Ehrfurcht vor dem Leben."
       RUNDBRIEF 40 (1975), pp. 42-47.

2739   BAUR, HERMANN. "Albert Schweitzers Ethik der Ehrfurcht vor
       dem Leben." <u>Hippokrates</u> (Stuttgart) 36:7 (April 15, 1965),
       pp. 275-79. Reprinted in: DEBRECEN, pp. 89-98.

Philosophy

2740 _____. "Kernkraft und Ehrfurcht vor dem Leben."
Schweizerisches Reformiertes Volksblatt (Basel),
Aug. 1977.

2741 _____. "Kreativität und Ehrfurcht vor dem Leben." A.I.S.L.
Bulletin 3 (Feb. 1977), p. 22.

2742 _____. "Ursprung und Wirking der Ehrfurcht vor dem Leben."
Schweizerisches Reformiertes Volksblatt (Basel),
April 1967. Also issued as a 3-page reprint. Reprinted
in BERICHTE 30 (Sept. 1967), pp. 32-34.

2743 BERGEL, KURT. "Albert Schweitzer's reverence for life."
The Humanist (Schnectady, N.Y.) 6:1 (May 1946), pp. 31-34.
Translated as: "Albert Schweitzers Beiträge zur
Erneuerung unserer Ethik." Neue Auslese (Munich) 1:10
(Nov. 1946), pp. 90-93.

2744 BOLLNOW, OTTO FRIEDRICH. "Die Ethik der Ehrfurcht vor dem
Leben. Überlegungen zu Albert Schweitzers Werk."
Evangelische Kommentare (Stuttgart) 9 (1976), pp. 527-30.
Translated as "Le Respect de la vie considéré comme
principe fondamental de l'éthique." REVUE 56:1-2 (1976),
pp. 118-42.

2745 BOTHMA, J. H. "Eerbied vir lewe." South African Verpleegsters
(Johannesburg) 21:9 (Sept. 1955), pp. 24f.

2746 BRINKEL. "Ehrfurcht vor dem Leben." Glabue und Heimat
(Jena) 2:15 (1947), p. 3.

2747 BRÜHL, RUDOLF. Chapter 6 in: Der Streit um die Menschlichkeit.
Stuttgart: Kreuz Verlag, 1974. (Vol. 5 of the series
Massstäbe des Menschlichen.)

2748 BUSKES, JOHANNES JACOBUS, JR. "Eerbied voor het leven."
Tijk en Taak (Amsterdam), 1950. Reprinted in NIEUWS 2:1
(May 1953), p. 11.

2749 DEML, FERDINAND. "Die Ethik der Ehrfurcht vor dem Leben."
Deutsche Hochschulwarte (Budweis/Prag) 2:10 (March 1923),
pp. 178-80.

2750 DIBELIUS, OTTO. "'Ehrfurcht vor dem Leben.' Albert
Schweitzers theologisches und philosophisches Werk."
Die Welt (Essen) Ausgabe D, Number 211 (Sept. 11, 1965),
p. 1.

2751   DOYLE, JAMES. "Schweitzer's extension of ethics to all life."
         In: CENTENNIAL. Reprinted in Journal of Value Inquiry
         (The Hague) 11:1 (Spring 1977), pp. 43-46.

2752   DRESSLER, MAX. "Ehrfurcht vor dem Leben." Die Pyramide
         (Karlsruhe) 13:52 (Dec. 28, 1924), p. 295.

2753   ERICSON, EDWARD L. "Albert Schweitzer and the ethical ecology
         of life." Religious Humanism (Yellow Springs, Ohio) 9:2
         (Spring 1975), pp. 50-54.

2754   FREE, ANN COTTRELL. "Some sort of help to animals. . . ."
         COURIER, Summer 1977, pp. 7-11.

2755   FUNKE, GERHARD. "Die Philosophie der Ehrfurcht vor dem Leben."
         Zeitschrift für Religions- und Geistesgeschichte
         (Cologne) 11:4 (Dec. 1959), pp. 356-73. Translated as
         "La filosofía del respeto por la vida. Albert Schweitzer
         y nosotros." Cultura Universitaria (Caracas) 68-69
         (July-Dec. 1959), pp. 7-21.

2756   GRABS, RUDOLF. "Zur Lehre der Erhfurcht vor dem Leben."
         In: BEITRÄGE, pp. 62-69.

2757   HÄRLE, WILIFRIED. "Unverfügarkeit des Lebens oder Freiheit
         zum Tode: Euthanasie als ethisches Problem." Zeitschrift
         für Evangelische Ethik (Gütersloh) 19 (May 1975),
         pp. 143-59. Schweitzer, pp. 152-54.

2758   HEDIGER, HEINI. "Albert Schweitzer und die Tiere." RUNDBRIEF
         47 (May 1979), pp. 25-33. Reprinted in: TIERE, pp. 22-30.

2759   HEITLER, W. "Ehrfurcht vor dem Leben--warum?" In: DEVENTER,
         pp. 9-21. Reprinted in RUNDBRIEF 47 (May 1979),
         pp. 40-42.

2760   HOFFMAN, LIESELOTTE. "Albert Schweitzer." In: Ihr Herz
         schlug für das Tier. Bedeutende Menschen als Fürsprecher
         der Tiere. Basel: Friedrich Reinhardt, 1958, pp. 177-89.

2761   HOLMBOE, THOROLF. "Vereratio vitae, Albert Schweitzers
         kulturfilosofi." Kirke og Kultur (Oslo) 46 (1939),
         pp. 154-72.

2762   KATAYAMA, T. "Aozora no shita de, sei eno ikei." New Age
         (Tokyo), July 1956, pp. 16-17.

2763   KRETSCHMER, WOLFGANG. "Albert Schweitzers Lehre von der
         Ehrfurcht vor dem Leben und die Behandlung seelischer

Philosophy

       Krankeiten." <u>Universitas</u> (Stuttgart) 16:7 (July 1961),
       pp. 755-64. Reprinted with title "Albert Schweitzers
       Ethik und die moderne Psychiatrie." In: DENKEN UND WEG,
       pp. 326-35.

2764   LANCZKOWSKI, GÜNTER. "Ehrfurcht vor dem Leben." <u>Denkendes</u>
       <u>Volk</u> (Braunschweig, Berlin, Hamburg) 2:11 (Nov. 1948),
       pp. 354-58. Illus., port.

2765   LANGE, G. "Die Grundsätze der 'Ehrfurcht vor dem Leben.'
       Bestimmen die Tradition der 'Albert Schweitzer Oberschule'
       für Körperbehinderte in Leipzig." In: VERMÄCHTNIS UND
       WIRKLICHKEIT, pp. 84-88.

2766   MAI, H. "Ehrfurcht vor dem Leben." RUNDBRIEF 46 (Nov. 1978),
       pp. 40-43. Sermon, preached at Münster-Gremmendorf, 1975.

2767   MARSHALL, GEORGE. "Schweitzer, prophet of ecology." In:
       PROPHET, pp. 7-9.

2768   MARTIN, HANS. "'I am the life that wills to live,' the inner
       meaning of Albert Schweitzer's reverence for life." <u>The</u>
       <u>Christian Register</u> (Boston) 128:7 (Aug. 1949), pp. 15-16.
       Port.

2769   MILLER, DAVID M. "The idea of reverence for life and the
       problems of health care, with special emphasis on those
       of the developing world." In: DEVENTER, pp. 89-102.
       Summaries in German, French and Dutch.

       NISSEN, RUDOLF. "Die Konsequenter der Ehrfurcht vor dem
       Leben für die Medizin." See Medicine, no. 2176 above.

2770   PAWLOWSKA, I. "Ehrfurcht vor dem Leben, das ethisches Ideal."
       In: DEVENTER, pp. 37-48. Summaries in French, English
       and Dutch.

2771   PETRICKIJ, V. [L'evolution du principe du respect de la vie
       dans la pensée philosophique et éthique d'Albert
       Schweitzer.] Ucenye Zapiski des Chaires de Sciences
       Sociales les Establissements d'enseignement Superieur
       (VUZY) de Leningrad 6 (Section de Philosophie), 1965,
       pp. 183-90.

2772   PINDRED, JAMES. "Dr. Albert Schweitzer." <u>St. Bartholomew's</u>
       <u>Hospital Journal</u> (London) 64:11 (Nov. 1965), p. 451.

2773   REINER, HANS. "Die Zukunft der Ethik Albert Schweitzers."
       <u>The Journal of Value Enquiry</u> (The Hague) 2:2-3 (Fall 1968),

pp. 157-65. Text eines Vortrags in der Allg. Philosrel.
Vereinigung in München, 14.1.1966. For a reply, see
Smith, T. G., no. 2778 below.

2774 ROSTAND, JEAN. "Philosophie du respect de la vie." In:
HOMMAGE, pp. 105-07. Reprinted in CAHIERS 31
(Summer 1974), pp. 12-13.

2775 SAKAHIAN, WILLIAM S. "Albert Schweitzer: reverence for life."
In: Ethics: an Introduction to Theories and Problems.
New York: Barnes and Noble, 1974, pp. 187-91.

2776 "Schweitzer the environmentalist." COURIER, Summer 1975,
p. 11.

2777 SEAVER, GEORGE. "Reverence for life: an interpretation."
In: FESTSCHRIFT, pp. 86-96. Translated as "Ehrfurcht
vor dem Leben." In: EHRFURCHT, pp. 147-54.

2778 SMITH, T. G. "Reiner on the future of Schweitzer's ethics."
The Journal of Value Inquiry (The Hague) 5 (Spring 1971),
pp. 131-35. Reply to Hans Reiner, no. 2773 above.

2779 SPEAR, OTTO. "Albert Schweitzer on the right to life and
happiness." Universitas (English language edition) 19:3
(1977), pp. 126-28.

2780 SPITALER, ARMIN. "Albert Schweitzer und die Tierschutz."
Universitas (Stuttgart) 15:1 (Jan. 1960), pp. 126-28.

2781 _____. "Die Ethik der Ehrfurcht vor dem Leben und der Schutz
für die Kreatur." In: DENKEN UND WEG, pp. 546-52.

2782 STEGANGA, P. "Albert Schweitzers Ehrfurcht vor dem Leben als
Prinzip der Ethik" (lecture given in Sondershausen).
Zeitschrift für Systematische Theologie (Berlin) 14:2
(1937), pp. 225-43.

2783 STEINKRAUS, WARREN. "Borden P. Bowne and Albert Schweitzer."
The Personalist (Los Angeles) 50:1 (Winter 1969),
pp. 75-84.

2784 STREGE, MARTIN. "Mystik der Ehrfurcht vor dem Leben."
RUNDBRIEF 40 (Jan. 14, 1975), pp. 108-110.

TERBORGH-DUPUIS, HELEEN. Medical ethics in perspective.
See Dissertations, no. 4342 below.

Philosophy

2785   TUCK, WILLIAM P. "Schweitzer's reverence for life." Theology Today (Princeton) 30:4 (Jan. 1974), pp. 39-45.

2786   ULBRICHT, WALTER. "Die Deutsche Demokratische Republik handelt in sinne Albert Schweitzers." In: BEITRÄGE, pp. 11-13.

2787   VEDETTE. "Round and about." Atlantic Advocate (University Press of New Brunswick) 55:9 (May 1965), p. 66. Port.

2788   WARTENWEILER, FRITZ. "Albert Schweitzers Weltanschauung der Ehrfurcht vor dem Leben." In: WÜRDIGUNG, pp. 11-13. Translated as "Albert Schweitzers beschouwing van de eerbied voor het Leven." NIEUWS 3:3 (Oct. 1954), pp. 86-87.

2789   WEISSBERG, B. "Le Respect de la vie est-il un 'donnée immédiate'?" CAHIERS 19 (June 1968), pp. 11-12. Reprinted in NOUVELLES 30 (Jan. 1969), pp. 23-25.

2790   WEITBRECHT, OSKAR. "Ehrfurcht vor dem Leben und Nächstenliebe bei Albert Schweitzer." RUNDBRIEF 11 (Aug. 1, 1957), pp. 52-54.

2791   WELLMAN, CARL. "An analysis of reverence for life." In: CENTENNIAL. Reprinted in The Journal of Value Inquiry (The Hague) 11:1 (Spring 1977), pp. 46-48.

2792   WERGELAND, HÅKON. "Hongvrydnaden for livet." Vårtland (Oslo) 8:245 (Oct. 29, 1952), p. 3.

2793   WERNER, MARTIN. "Albert Schweitzers 'Weltanschauung der Ehrfurcht vor dem Leben' in philosophischer Sicht." In: FESTGABE, pp. 43-76.

2794   ZETTERHOLM, TORE. "Vördnad for Livet." Samtid och Framtid (Stockholm) 4:4 (May 1947), pp. 245-58.

VII. Theology and Religion

A. General

1. Books by Schweitzer

DAS ABENDMAHL
(The Last Supper)

The first part of Albert Schweitzer's history of the Last Supper was presented to the Faculty of Theology of the University of Strasbourg as his dissertation for the degree of Licentiate in Theology, and was published in 1901. The second part, concerning the Secret of Jesus' Messiahship and Passion, served to procure for him at the same university, in 1902, the position of Privat-docent. In his autobiography Dr. Schweitzer writes: "When, after finishing my work on Kant, I returned to theology, the most obvious thing to do was to put together my studies on the problems of the life of Jesus which had occupied me since my first year at the University, and to work them up into a dissertation for my Licentiate examination. But my study of the Last Supper had widened my outlook and my interest. From the field of the problems of the life of Jesus I had stepped straightaway into the problems of primitive Christianity. The problem of the Last Supper belongs to both fields. It stands at the central point in the development of the faith of Jesus into the faith of primitive Christianity. . . .

"I formed the plan of writing a history of the Last Supper in connexion with the life of Jesus and the history of primitive Christianity. A preliminary investigation was to define my attitude in regard to previous research into the question of the Last Supper, and throw light upon the problem as a whole. A second section would give a picture of the thought and activities of Jesus as a condition of understanding the Supper which He celebrated with His disciples. A third was to treat of the Supper in the Primitive Church and in the two first centuries of Christianity. . . . The Study I had in view as a third volume on the development of the Last Supper in the primitive and later periods was indeed completed and delivered in lectures, as was also the companion study on the history of Baptism in the New

Theology and Religion

Testament and in primitive Christianity. Neither work was printed,
however . . . [and] the History of the Last Supper and Baptism in
the Early Christian Period has remained in the condition of manuscript for lectures . . . the thoughts which underlie it are put
forward in my book, The Mysticism of Paul the Apostle."[1]

2795   Kritische Darstellung unterschiedlicher neuerer historischer
            Abendmahlsauffassungen . . . Dissertation zur Erlangung
            des Grades seines Licentiaten der Theologie bei der
            theologische Fakultät zu Strassburg i.E. Freiburg i. B.:
            C. A. Wagners Universitäts-Buchdruckerei, 1901. 37 pp.
            (This "Critical Presentation" forms the first 8 chapters
            of Das Abendmahlsproblem. . . , no. 2796 below).

2796   Das Abendmahl im Zusammenhang mit dem Leben Jesu und der
            Geschichte des Urchristentums. Tübingen and Leipzig:
            J. C. B. Mohr (Paul Siebeck), 1901.
                Erstes Heft. Das Abendmahlsproblem auf Grund der
            Wissenschaftlichen Forschung des 19. Jahrhunderts und
            der historischen Berichte. xv, 62 pp.
                Zweites Heft. Das Messianitäts- und Leidensgeheimnis.
            Eine Skizze des Lebens Jesu. xii, 109 pp.

2797   Same. Zweite, photomechanisch gedruckte Auflage. Tübingen:
            J. C. B. Mohr (Paul Siebeck), 1929. This is an unaltered
            reprint, mechanically produced, of the original of 1901.
            The two parts are unchanged, and the pagination is the
            same.

2798   Das Messianitäts- und Leidensgeheimnis. Eine Skizze des
            Lebens Jesu. 3. unveränderte Auflage. Tübingen:
            J. C. B. Mohr (Paul Siebeck), 1956. xii, 109 pp. The
            "Erstes Heft" has not been reissued since 1929.

English

2799   The Mystery of the Kingdom of God; the Secret of Jesus'
            Messiahship and Passion. Translated, and with an intro-
            duction by Walter Lowrie. London: Adam and Charles
            Black; New York: Dodd Mead and Co., 1914. 275 pp.
            (Since 1929, this second part of Das Abendmahl has been
            published as a separate text, the first part having never
            been translated into another language.)

---

[1]Out of My Life and Thought. New York: Holt, Rinehart and Winston,
1961, pp. 32-34.

General

2800   Same.   Translated and with an introduction by Walter Lowrie.
New York: The Macmillan Co., 1950. xv, 174 pp. Reprinted, 1954.

2801   Same. New York: Schocken Books, 1964. 275 pp. (Schocken
Paperbacks, SB 78.) Reprinted in 1970.

French

2802   Le secret historique de la vie de Jésus. Tr. Annie Anex-
Heimbrod. Préface de Henry Babel. Paris: Albin Michel,
1961, 220 pp.

Japanese

2803   Jesu no Himitsu. Tr. Hachiro Tezuka. Tokyo: Kumonohashira-
sha, 1926. 130 pp.

2804   Jesus no Shōgai. Tr. Seiji Hagii. Tokyo: Iwanami Shoten,
1957. 240 pp.

Iesu Shōden. Tr. Bansetsu Kishida. Tokyo: Hakusuisha, 1957.
See Collected Works, no. 8 above.

2805   Meshiya to Jyunan no Himitsu. Tr. Seiji Hagii. Tokyo:
Shinkyo Shuppansha, 1956. 229 pp.

Spanish

2806   El Secreto Histórica de la Vida de Jesús. Tr. Julio Jacobson.
Buenos Aires: Ediciones Diglo Veinte, 1967. 198 pp.

VON REIMARUS ZU WREDE: EINE GESCHICHTE
DER LEBEN-JESU FORSCHUNG
(The Quest of the Historical Jesus,
a Critical Study of Its Progress from Reimarus to Wrede)

This work, completed in 1906, is a survey of the attempts of scholars,
from the late 18th century to the time of its writing, to investigate
the public ministry of Jesus and place him in the proper historical
background. In Schweitzer's words: "Incitement to occupy myself
with the history of research on the life of Jesus was given me by a
conversation with students who had attended a course of lectures by
Professor Spitta on the life of Jesus, but had learned practically
nothing about previous investigations into the subject. I therefore
resolved . . . to lecture . . . during the summer term of 1905 on the
history of research on the life of Jesus. The material took such
hold of me that when I had finished the course of lectures, I became

Theology and Religion

completely absorbed in it. . . . John Samuel Reimarus (1694-
1768) . . . was the first to attempt . . . an explanation of the
life of Jesus which started from the assumption that he shared the
eschatological expectations about a Messiah which were held by his
contemporaries. . . . William Wrede (1859-1907) . . . made the
first thoroughgoing attempt on a bold scale to deny that Jesus enter-
tained any eschatological ideas at all. . . . Since these two names
indicate the two poles between which the investigation moves, it was
from them that I made up the title of my book."[1]

The 1913 edition is enlarged and revised; Schweitzer included
in it new books which had appeared on the subject since 1906, and
reworked some sections with which he was dissatisfied. Unfortunately,
the English editions of this work have all been based on the earlier
1906 edition, and do not include these revisions.

2807   Von Reimarus zu Wrede: Eine Geschichte der Leben-Jesu
          Forschung. Tübingen: J. C. B. Mohr (Paul Siebeck),
          1906. 418 pp. Anhang: I. Die durch D. Fr. Straussens
          Leben-Jesu hervorgerufene Literatur; II. Die von Renan's
          Leben-Jesu hervorgerufene Literatur.

2808   Geschichte der Leben-Jesu Forschung. 2., neu bearbeitete und
          vermehrte Auflage des Werkes "Von Reimarus zu Wrede."
          Tübingen: J. C. B. Mohr (Paul Siebeck), 1913. 659 pp.
          Reprinted 1921, 1926, 1933.

2809   Same. 6., photomechanisch gedruckte Auflage. Tübingen: Mohr,
          1951. Includes a new preface by Schweitzer.

2810   Same. Einführung von James M. Robinson. Munich: Siebenstern
          Taschenbuch Verlag, 1966. 651 pp. 2 vol. Zweite Auflage
          1972.

2811   Same. Gütersloh: Gütersloher Verlagshaus/VVA (Lizenz d.
          Verlag Mohr, Tübingen), 1977. 3. Auflage. 340, 310 pp.
          (Gütersloher Taschenbücher Siebenstern 77, 78.)

Danish

2812   Jesu Liv. Af "Jesu-Liv-Forskningens Historie." (Udvalg og
          oversaettelse af Geschichte der Leben-Jesu-Forschung, 2.
          Udgave, 1913, ved. Johs Novrup.) Copenhagen: Det Danske
          Forlag, 1955. 260 pp.

---

[1]Out of My Life and Thought. New York: Holt, Rinehart and Winston,
1961, pp. 43-44.

General

English

2813   The Quest of the Historical Jesus. A Critical Study of its
Progress from Reimarus to Wrede. Tr. W. Montgomery.
Preface by F. C. Burkitt. London: A. and C. Black;
New York: The Macmillan Co., 1910. x, 410 pp. Second
edition, 1911. Reissued, 1922, 1926, 1931, 1936, 1945,
1948, 1952. The impressions of 1922 and 1948 appeared
also with the imprint of the Macmillan Co., New York.
Translation of the 1906 edition.

2814   Same. Third edition, with a new introduction by the author.
London: A. and C. Black, 1954. xxii, 410 pp. Reissued
1956, 1963.

2815   Same. (New, reset American edition, printed in the United
States.) New York: The Macmillan Company, 1948. ix,
413 pp. Reissued, 1950, 1955. Paperback edition, 1961,
ix, 413 pp. (Macmillan Paperbacks 55.)

2816   Same. With a new introduction by James M. Robinson. New
York: Macmillan, 1968. 413 pp.

Japanese

2817   Kiristo-den Ronsōshi. Tr. from the English by Toyohiko Kagawa.
Tokyo: Keischisha, 1913. 353 pp. (Contains selections
from Von Reimarus zu Wrede.)

      Iesuden-kendyûshi. Tr. Akira Endō and Yūzaburo Morita.
Tokyo: Hakusuisha, 1960-61. See Collected Works, nos.
17-19 above.

Norwegian

2818   Jesu Liv i Forskningens Lys. Tr. Rune Slagstad. Oslo:
Glydendal, 1969. 201 pp.

Swedish

2819   Jesu liv i forskningens ljus. Med inledning av Alf Ahlberg.
Tr. Alf Ahlberg. Stockholm: Kooperativa Förbundets
Bokförlag, 1955. 219 pp. 2nd ed., 1955. (Contains
selections from Geschichte der Leben Jesu Forschung.)

Theology and Religion

GESCHICHTE DER PAULINISCHEN FORSCHUNG
VON DER REFORMATION BIS AUF DIE GEGENWART
(Paul and His Interpreters: A Critical History)

Albert Schweitzer wrote concerning this study: "When near the conclusion of my medical studies, I could once more find time for theology, it seemed to me to be plainly indicated that I should produce a
history of scientific research into the thought-world of S. Paul, to
be a companion volume to the Quest of the Historical Jesus and an
introduction to an exposition of Pauline doctrine. . . . Immediately
after completing the Quest of the Historical Jesus I had gone on to
study the teaching of St. Paul. From the very beginning I had been
left unsatisfied by the explanations of it given by scientific theology, because they represented it as something complicated and loaded
with contradictions, an account of it which seemed irreconcilable
with the originality and greatness of the thought revealed in it . . .
I had thought at first that [a] literary-historical study could be
treated so briefly that it would form just an introductory chapter to
the exposition of the eschatological significance of the Pauline
teaching. But as I worked, it became clear that it would expand into
a complete book."[1] The volume, Geschichte der paulinischen Forschung,
was published in 1911, the same year in which Schweitzer completed
his medical studies at the University of Strasbourg.

2820   Geschichte der paulinischen Forschung von der Reformation bis
          auf die Gegenwart. Tübingen: J. C. B. Mohr (Paul
          Siebeck), 1911. xii, 197 pp.

2821   Same. 2. photomechanisch gedruckte Auflage. Tübingen:
          J. C. B. Mohr (Paul Siebeck), 1933. xii, 197 pp.

English

2822   Paul and his Interpreters: a Critical History. Tr. W.
          Montgomery. London: A. and C. Black; New York: The
          Macmillan Co., 1912. xiii, 253 pp. Reprinted 1948,
          1950, 1956.

2823   Same. New York: The Macmillan Co., 1951. xii, 252 pp.

2824   Same. New York: Schocken Books, 1964. xiii, 255 pp.
          (Schocken Paperbacks, SB 79.)

---

[1]Out of My Life and Thought. New York: Holt, Rinehart and Winston,
1961, pp. 34, 118, 120.

General

DIE MYSTIK DES APOSTELS PAULUS
(The Mysticism of Paul the Apostle)

Albert Schweitzer began writing his book on the mysticism of Saint Paul in 1906; the incentive to develop this subject had come to him as far back as 1902, when he delivered his inaugural lecture on the Logos doctrine in the Fourth Gospel before the Theological Faculty of the University of Strasbourg. The manuscript was temporarily laid aside while he wrote another book, Paul and His Interpreters, which had grown out of an introductory chapter, and while he prepared the second enlarged edition of Geschichte der Leben-Jesu-Forschung. Then, due to the establishment of Schweitzer's hospital in Lambarene, the First World War, his work on Kulturphilosophie, and many duties in Europe and Africa, work on the manuscript was continued only at long intervals. The book was not completed until 1929, the last chapter being written on shipboard during the author's return to Africa in December of that year. Pastor Georges Marchal, in his preface to the French translation of that book, writes: "This work, the last which Schweitzer devoted to theological problems, forms, with Le Secret historique de la vie de Jésus, a kind of trilogy to which all the other theological works of the author may easily be related."

As Schweitzer says in his introduction to the work: "With this exposition . . . I bring the theological work I have hitherto undertaken to a kind of conclusion. When still a student I conceived the plan of explaining the evolution of thought in the first generation of Christianity on the basis of the axiom . . . that the Preaching of the Kingdom of God by Jesus was in itself eschatological, and that it was so understood by those who heard it. . . . My studies . . . turn about the two questions--whether besides the eschatological interpretation of the Preaching of Jesus there was any room for another, and how the original completely eschatological faith of Christians fared in the course of the substitution of the Hellenistic for the eschatological way of thinking."[1]

2825   Die Mystik des Apostels Paulus. Tübingen: J. C. B. Mohr
        (Paul Siebeck), 1930. xv, 407 pp.

2826   Same. 2., photomechanisch gedruckte Auflage. Tübingen:
        J. C. B. Mohr (Paul Siebeck), 1954. xv, 407 pp.

English

2827   The Mysticism of Paul the Apostle. Tr. William Montgomery.
        Preface by F. C. Burkitt. London: A. and C. Black;

---

[1]Schweitzer's preface to the 1968 Seabury Press edition, p. viii.

Theology and Religion

New York: Henry Holt and Co., 1931. xvi, 411 pp. 2nd edition, 1953, xv, 411 pp.

2828   ("Cheaper edition.") London: A. and C. Black, 1937.

2829   Same. New York: The Macmillan Co., 1955. xv, 411 pp. Reprinted, by photo offset, 1956.

2830   (Paperback edition.) New York: Seabury Press, 1968. xv, 411 pp.

French

2831   La mystique de l'apôtre Paul. Tr. Marcelle Guéritot. Préface de Georges Marchal. Paris: Albin Michel, 1962. xviii, 338 pp.

Japanese

Shito Paulo no Shinpishugi. Tr. Kazuo Mutō and Bensetsu Kishida. Tokyo: Hakusuisha, 1957-58. See Collected Works, no. 11 above.

DAS CHRISTENTUM UND DIE WELTRELIGIONEN
(Christianity and the Religions of the World)

Albert Schweitzer writes that having again settled in Strasbourg after the First World War, waiting for his original manuscript on the Philosophy of Civilization to arrive from Africa, "I occupied myself with studying the great world-religions and the world-views which they implied. Just as I had already examined philosophy up to today to see how far it represents ethical acceptance of the world as providing the impulse to civilization, so I now sought to make clear to what extent acceptance and rejection of the world and ethics are contained in Judaism and Christianity, in Islam, in the religion of Zarathustra, in Brahminism, Buddhism, and Hinduism, and in the religious side of Chinese thought."[1]

It was this study which later was developed by Schweitzer into lectures, Christianity and the Religions of the World, which he delivered at the Selly Oak Colleges, in Birmingham, England, in February 1922. The lectures "define the nature of these religions from the philosophic standpoint according to the greater or smaller degree of importance allowed in the convictions underlying them to

---

[1]Out of My Life and Thought. New York: Holt, Rinehart and Winston, 1961, pp. 181-82.

world- and life-affirmation, to world- and life-negation, and to
ethics. Unfortunately, I was obliged to confine within too small a
compass this epitome of my examination of these religions, since I
had to publish it in the form of those lectures."[1] The book was
published in the English translation before it appeared in its
original German.

2832   Das Christentum und die Weltreligionen. Munich: C. H.
            Becksche Verlagsbuchhandlung Oskar Beck; Bern: Paul
            Haupt, Akademische Buchhandlung, vorm. Max Drechsel,
            1924. 60 pp. 2. Aufl., 1925 (59 pp.). Reprinted 1928
            (also Heitz & Cie, Strasbourg), 1932 (Biederstein Verlag),
            1939 (Biederstein Verlag), 1947 (Biederstein Verlag),
            1949 (Biederstein Verlag), 1952, 1953, 1955, 1957, 1962
            (50 pp.).

2833   Same. Zwei Aufsätze zur Religionsphilosophie. Mit einer
            Einführung in das Denken Albert Schweitzers von Ulrich
            Neuenschwander. Munich: Beck, 1978. 110 pp. (Beck'sche
            Schwarze Reihe, 181.)

Danish

2834   Kristendommen og Verdensreligionerne. Tr. Julius Ellehauge.
            Copenhagen: V. Pio, Povl Branner, 1925. 62 pp.
            (Published previously in Kirke og Kultur (Kristiania),
            1924, no. 2862 below).

2835   Same. 2. oplag (new edition). Copenhagen: Branner og Korch,
            1954. 63 pp.

Dutch

2836   Het Christendom en de wereldgodsdiensten. Tr. Henriette
            Crommelin. Met een inleiding door J. de Zwann. Haarlem:
            H. D. Tjeenk Willink & Zoon, 1927. xvi, 96 pp. 2^c druk,
            1930.

English

2837   Christianity and the Religions of the World. Lectures de-
            livered at the Selly Oak Colleges, Birmingham, February
            1922 . . . Tr. Johanna Powers . . . with a foreword by
            Nathaniel Micklem. . . . London: George Allen and Unwin,
            1923. 86 pp. (Selly Oak Colleges, Central Council

---

[1]Ibid.

Theology and Religion

    Publications, III.) Second impression, 1924; Third imp.,
    1936; Fourth imp., 1951; Fifth imp., 1953; Sixth imp.,
    1960.

2838 Same. New York: George H. Doran Co., 1923. xv, 19-93 pp.
    (Selly Oak Colleges, Central Council of Publications, III.)
    Reissued by Doubleday, Doran and Co., (Garden City, N.Y.),
    1923. xv, 19-93 pp. The same plates were reissued by
    Henry Holt and Co., New York, 1939. xix, 86 pp. They
    were later reissued (fourth impression) by the Macmillan
    Co., New York, 1951. xix, 86 pp.

2839 Same. Reissue. Grand Rapids, Mich.: Zondervan Publishing
    House, 1934. 85 pp.

French

2840 Les Religions Mondiales et le Christianisme. Tr. Charles
    Schweitzer. Rev. et Annotée par Anne Baudraz et Bernard
    Reymond. Présent de Bernard Reymond. Lausanne: Editions
    l'Age d'Homme, 1975. 76 pp. (Coll. Alethina 13.)

Italian

2841 Il Christianésimo e la grandi religioni, bramanismo, buddismo,
    confucismo, induismo. Discorsi tradutti da G. G. Milan:
    Doxa Editrice, 1933. 99 pp.

Japanese

2842 Kirisutokyō to Sekaishūkyō. Tr. Toshiro Suzuku. Tokyo:
    Iwanami Shoten, 1956. 99 pp.

    Kirisutokyō to Sekai no Shūkyō. Tr. Yasusama Oshima. Tokyo:
    Hakusuisha, 1957. See Collected Works, no. 8 above.

2843 Shukyokagaku yori mitaru Kiristokyo. Tr. Genjiro Roshida.
    Tokyo: Keiseisha, 1925. 137 pp.

Korean

2844 Kidokkyo wa Segye Chonggyo. 1959. 113 pp. (Bound with
    Das Problem des Friedens in der Heutigen Welt.)

Spanish

2845 El cristianismo y las religiones universales. Tr. Adam Wolff.
    Buenos Aires: "La Aurora," 1950. 97 pp.

General

2846   El Christianismo y las Religiones Mundiales. Tr. I. G. Klever.
            Buenos Aires: Ediciones Siglo Veinte, 1964. 94 pp.

Swedish

2847   Kristendomen och Världsreligionerna. Tr. Bengt Oxenstierna.
            Jämto ett företal av oversattaren. Uppsala: J. A.
            Lindblad, 1924. 83 pp.

REICH GOTTES UND CHRISTENTUM
(The Kingdom of God and Primitive Christianity)

This work was conceived in 1950-51 and discovered in manuscript form
by Schweitzer's daughter after his death. According to Richard Hiers,
it "fills the need for a full statement of Schweitzer's mature position with respect to New Testament eschatology."[1] It is comprised
of four parts: 1. Das Reich Gottes bei den Propheten und im
Spätjudentum; 2. Das Reich Gottes bei Jesus; 3. Der Urchristlichen
Glaube an das Reich Gottes; and 4. Das Reich Gottes bei Paulus. In
his introduction to the English edition Ulrich Neuenschwander describes this work as "an historical investigation of the biblical
belief in the Kingdom from the Old Testament prophets to the Apostle
Paul" (p. v.). Indications are that Schweitzer intended to expand
the manuscript further, at least through the later New Testament
writings, and perhaps up through the later Christian era as well.

2848   Reich Gottes und Christentum. Hrsg. und mit einem Vorwort
            versehen von Ulrich Neuenschwander. Tübingen: J. C. B.
            Mohr, 1967. xii, 212 pp.

English

2849   The Kingdom of God and Primitive Christianity. Edited and
            with an introduction by Ulrich Neuenschwander. Tr. L. A.
            Garrard. New York: Seabury; London: A. and C. Black,
            1968. xiv, 193 pp.

Japanese

2850   Schweitzer Chosaku Shû. Tokyo: Hakusuisha, 1972. 470 pp.
            (Bound with Strassburger Predigten.)

---

[1]Hiers, R. H. "Kingdom of God and Primitive Christianity." Journal
of the American Academy of Religion 38 (March 1970), pp. 94-98.

Theology and Religion

2. Shorter Writings by Schweitzer

2851   "Albert Schweitzer antwortet Gustav Wyneken; kein Abschied
        vom Christentum." Christ und Welt (Stuttgart) 17:4
        (April 4, 1964), p. 12. "Albert Schweitzer . . . hat das
        Buch von Gustav Wyneken (Abschied vom Christentum) . . .
        gelesen und uns diese Stellungnahme zugeschickt."
        Reprinted in: Franz, Günther, ed. Jahrbuch des Archivs
        der Deutschen Jugendbewegung, Bd. 3 (1971).

2852   "As one unknown he comes." The American Home (New York) 55
        (Dec. 1955), p. 41. Excerpt from The Quest of the His-
        torical Jesus, as quoted from Albert Schweitzer: An
        Anthology.

2853   [Concluding statement from Die Geschichte der Leben-Jesu
        Forschung.] In: Clark, Henry. The Ethical Mysticism of
        Albert Schweitzer, see no. 2351 above, pp. 195-205.

2854   "A declaration of faith" (letter, translated from the original
        German text, sent to the delegates of the conference of
        the International Association for Liberal Christianity and
        Religious Freedom-I.A.R.F.- Berne, Switzerland, dated
        'Lambarene, August 10, 1947.'). Faith and Freedom
        (Oxford) 1:1 (Oct. 1947-June 1948), p. 48.

2855   "Der Geist Jesu and der Geist der Welt." KIRCHENBOTE[1] 49:52
        (Dec. 25, 1920), pp. 264-65.

2856   "Geschichte der paulinischen Forschung. Zusammenfassung und
        Problemstettung." In: Ringstorf, Karl Heinrich, ed.
        Das Paulusbild in der neueren deutschen Forschung.
        Darmstadt: 1964.

2857   "Gespräche über das Neue Testament." Series of 24 articles
        which appeared in KIRCHENBOTE between 1902 and 1904.
        They are as follows:
        "Pharisäer und Sadducäer." Jan. 18, 1902, pp. 18-20.
        "Die Messianischen Hoffnung des Volkes Israel."
            Feb. 22, 1902, pp. 59-61.
        "Johannes der Täufer." April 3, 1902, pp. 150-52.
        "Jesu Taufe und Versuchung." May 24, 1902, pp. 176-78.
        "Der See Genezareth." June 14, 1902, pp. 200-02.
        "Der erste Sabbat in Kapernaum." July 12, 1902, pp. 229-34.

---

[1]Schweitzer served as editor of this weekly publication from
December 1, 1918, to April 2, 1921. Volumes 47-50 contain many
contributions by him, both signed and unsigned.

"Die Wunder Jesu." Aug. 2, 1902, pp. 256-59.
"Wie lang hat Jesu öffentlich gewirkt?" Aug. 30, 1902,
    pp. 288-90.
"Die Rückkehr nach Kapernaum." Sept. 17, 1902,
    pp. 320-22.
"Die ersten Gleichnisse Jesu" (Mark 4, Matthew 13).
    Dec. 16, 1902, pp. 403-07.
"Die Seligpreisungen" (Matthew 5:3-12; Luke 6:20-26).
    Jan. 3, 1903, pp. 4-6.
"Jesus und das Gesetz." Feb. 28, 1903, pp. 66-68.
"Jesus und die Heiden." June 13, 1903, pp. 189-91.
"Jesus und die Reichen." June 27, 1903, pp. 206-07.
"Jesus und der Staat." July 11, 1903, pp. 221-22.
"Lebensernst und Lebensfreudigkeit." July 25, 1903,
    pp. 238-39.
"Jesus und die Weisen." Nov. 21, 1903, pp. 380-82.
"Die Missionsreise der Jünger." Dec. 12, 1903, pp. 405-07.
"Nach der Aussendung." Jan. 9, 1904, pp. 11-13.
"Wer sagen die Leute, dass ich sei?" April 16, 1904,
    pp. 132-33.
"Warum musste Jesus leiden." May 14, 1904, pp. 165-66.
"Jerusalem." July 30, 1904, pp. 254-55.
"Worte des Anstosses." Sept. 10, 1904, pp. 300-02.
"Jesu letzte Weissagungen." Oct. 22, 1904, pp. 356-57.

2858 "How can we attain the kingdom of God: a meditation." The
         Christian Century (Chicago) 72 (Sept. 7, 1955), pp. 1021-
         22. Dated Lambarene, July 2, 1955. Originally written by
         Schweitzer for Dr. James E. Doty, minister of the First
         Methodist Church in Lynn, Mass., while Dr. Doty was visit-
         ing Lambarene. Originally in German; English translation
         also by Schweitzer.

2859 "How we read the Bible in the Jungle." Bible Society Record
         (New York) 106:1 (Jan. 1961), pp. 4-5. Illus.

2860 "Die Idee des Reiches Gottes im Verlauf der Umbildung des
         eschatologischen Glaubens in den uneschatologischen."
         Schweizerische Theologische Umschau (Bern) 23:1-2
         (Feb. 1953), pp. 2-20. Reprinted as "Die Idee des
         Reiches Gottes und unsere Zeit." Universitas (Stuttgart)
         8:7 (1953), pp. 673-77; translated as "The conception of
         the kingdom of God in the transformation of eschatology."
         In: Mozley, E. N. The Theology of Albert Schweitzer,
         see no. 65 above, pp. 87-117 (American edition), 79-108
         (British edition); reprinted in: Kaufmann, W. A., ed.
         Religion from Tolstoy to Camus. New York: Harper, 1961,
         pp. 407-24.

Theology and Religion

2861   "Jesus--an imperious ruler." In: Kepler, Thomas S., compiler,
        Contemporary Thinking about Jesus: an Anthology. New
        York: Abingdon-Cokesbury, 1944, pp. 387-91. From The
        Quest of the Historical Jesus.

2862   "Kristendommen og Verdens-Religionerne." Kirche og Kultur
        (Kristiania) 31 (1924), pp. 181-99, 262-77.

2863   "Die Lage des Protestantismus in Frankreich." KIRCHENBOTE
        49:17 (April 24, 1920), pp. 86-87. Excerpted in:
        Pierhal, Jean. Albert Schweitzer: das Leben eines guten
        Menschen, see no. 291 above, p. 122 (English edition).

2864   Letters to Martin Buber, 1932, 1936, 1951. In: Buber, Martin.
        Briefwechsel aus sieben Jahrzehnten. Hrsg. v. Grete
        Schaeder. Bd. II: 1918-1938. Heidelberg: Lambert
        Schneider, 1973, pp. 453, 625-26; Bd. III: 1938-1965.
        Heidelberg: Lambert Schneider, 1975, pp. 274-76.

2865   "Liberal Christianity." Le Monde Religieux. Editions
        d'Histoires Modernes des Religions. 7th year, no. 1,
        vol. XXI. Mulhouse: Imprimerie Bader et Cie, 1948,
        pp. 41-44.

2866   "Die literarischen und theologischen Probleme der Briefe an
        Timotheus und Titus. Verzeichnis der Vorlesungen der
        Universität Strasbourg. Strasbourg: 1910.

2867   "The Pauline epistles." In: Kepler, Thomas S. Contemporary
        Thinking about Paul. New York: Abingdon-Cokesbury, 1950,
        pp. 239-46. Excerpted from The Mysticism of Paul the
        Apostle.

2868   "Pfingsten 1919. Thessalonischer 5, 19: 'Den Geist dampfet
        nicht.'" KIRCHENBOTE 48:23 (June 7, 1919), p. 93.

2869   "Der Prophet Amos. Eine Adventsgestalt." KIRCHENBOTE
        47:49/50 (Dec. 1918).

2870   "Der Protestantismus und die Theologische Wissenchaft.
        Vortrag." Wesen und Werden des Protestantismus.
        Strassburg: E. van Hauten, 1903.

2871   "Das Recht der Wahrhaftigkeit in der Religion." Die
        Christliche Welt (Gotha) 46:20 (Oct. 1932), pp. 941-42.

2872   "Religion in modern civilization." The Christian Century
        (Chicago) 51:47 (Nov. 21, 1934), pp. 1483-84; 51:48
        (Nov. 28, 1934), pp. 1519-21. A summary of Schweitzer's

lectures at Manchester College, Oxford, Oct. 16-25, 1934.
Reprinted as "Dr. Schweitzer on war and peace." The
Expository Times (Edinburgh) 46:3 (Dec. 1934), pp. 141-43.
Excerpts from the lectures; reprinted in Seaver, George.
Albert Schweitzer, the Man and his Mind, see no. 300 above,
pp. 335-42 (1947 edition) and 359-66 (1955 edition).

2873   "14. Sonntag nach Trinitatis." KIRCHENBOTE 49 (Sept 4, 1920),
        p. 185.

2874   "Valeur impérissable de la mystique Paulienne." CAHIERS 8
        (Dec. 1962), p. 18.

2875   "Zum Totensonntag." KIRCHENBOTE 49:47 (Nov. 20, 1920), p. 233.

2876   "Der zweite Iesaja, eine Adventsgestalt." KIRCHENBOTE 47:51
        (Dec. 22, 1918), pp. 209-11.

3. Writings by Others About Schweitzer

    a. Books

        BABEL, HENRY ADALBERT. La Pensée d'Albert Schweitzer. See
            Philosophy, no. 2343 above. See also Dissertations,
            no. 4310 below.

        BROWARZIK, ULRICH. Glaube, Historie und Sittlichkeit. . . .
            See Dissertations, no. 4313 below.

2877   BURI, FRITZ. Albert Schweitzer als theologe heute.
            Schaffhausen: Verlagsverein "Christ und Welt," 1955.
            32 pp. (Schriften für lebensbejahendes Christentum.)
            "Herausgegeben unter dem patronat des Schweizerischen
            Vereins für freies Christentum und des Schweizerischen
            Zwinglibundes."

2878   _____. Christentum und Kultur bei Albert Schweitzer; eine
            Einführung in sein Denken als Weg zu einer christlichen
            Weltanschauung. Bern, Leipzig: P. Haupt, 1941.

        CHAN, MARGERY. A Study of Albert Schweitzer's Theory of
            Religious Experience. See Dissertations, no. 4314 below.

        CLARK, HENRY. The Ethical Mysticism of Albert Schweitzer.
            See Philosophy, no. 2351 above.

2879   FLÜCKIGER, FELIX. Der Ursprung des christlichen Dogmas; eine
            Auseinandersetzung mit Albert Schweitzer und Martin Werner.

        Zollikon-Zürich: Evangelischer Verlag, 1955. 216 pp.
        Based on a lecture given at the University of Basel.

2880   GARRARD, LANCELOT AUSTIN. The Historical Jesus: Schweitzer's
        Quest and Ours after Fifty Years. London: Lindsey Press,
        1956. 29 pp. (Essex Hall Lecture, 1956.)

2881   GITTLEMAN, DAVID. Albert Schweitzer: the Man and his Timely
        Gospel. 1959. 22 pp.

        GRABS, RUDOLF. Albert Schweitzer als Religiöser Charakter.
        See Dissertations, no. 4318 below.

2882   _____. Albert Schweitzer, Denker aus Christentum. Halle/
        Saale: M. Niemeyer, 1958. 208 pp.

2883   _____. Die Weltreligionen im Blickpunkt Albert Schweitzers.
        Berlin: Evangelische Verlagsanstalt, 1953. 76 pp.

        GROOS, HELMUT. Albert Schweitzer, Grösse und Grenzen. See
        Philosophy, no. 2357 above.

2884   ICE, JACKSON LEE. Schweitzer: Prophet of Radical Theology.
        Philadelphia: Westminster Press, 1971. 208 pp.

        KASAI, KEIJI. Die Bedeutung des Christentums in der heutigen
        Welt bei Albert Schweitzer und Paul Tillich. See Dis-
        sertations, no. 4325 below.

        KRAUS, OSKAR. Albert Schweitzer, sein Werk und seine
        Weltanschauung. See Philosophy, no. 2362 above.

        LÖNNEBO, MARTIN. Albert Schweitzer's etisk-religiöse Ideal.
        See Philosophy, no. 2365 above. See also Dissertations,
        no. 4330 below.

        MC CALL, WILLIAM E. An Analysis of Albert Schweitzer's Inter-
        pretation of the New Testament. See Dissertations, no.
        4331 below.

        MERZ, NIKLAUS. Reich Gottes im theologischen und
        philosophischen Denken von Albert Schweitzer. See Dis-
        sertations, no. 4332 below.

        MOZLEY, EDWARD NEWMAN. The Theology of Albert Schweitzer for
        Christian Inquirers. See Anthologies, no. 65 above.

2885   MURRY, JOHN MIDDLETON. The Challenge of Schweitzer. London:
        Jason Press, 1948. 133 pp. Reprinted in limited edition

of 150 copies: Folcroft, Pa.: Folcroft Press, 1970.
133 pp. See Seaver, no. 2887 below, for a reply.

OGNIBENI, BRUNO. Das Abendmahlsproblem in exegetischen Werk
von Albert Schweitzer. See Dissertations, no. 4333 below.

2886 PRIBNOW, HANS. Jesus im Denken Albert Schweitzers. Hanau:
1964. 36 pp. Schriftenreihe Freies Christentum, Beiheft
50 and 51.

2887 SEAVER, GEORGE. Albert Schweitzer, a Vindication; being a
reply to The Challenge of Schweitzer by John Middleton
Murry. London: James Clarke, 1950; Boston: Beacon Press,
1951. 120 pp.

2888 _____ . Albert Schweitzer: Christian Revolutionary. New York
and London: Harper Brothers, 1944. 130 pp.

(Second edition, revised and enlarged). London: Adam
and Charles Black; New York: Harper, 1955. 128 pp.

TRANSLATIONS

Albert Schweitzer und das Christentum. 1956. (German)

2889 STREGE, MARTIN. Albert Schweitzers Religion und Philosophie:
eine systematische Quellenstudie. Tübingen: Katzmann,
1965. 148 pp.

2890 _____ . Das Eschaton als gestaltende Kraft in der Theologie:
Albert Schweitzer und Martin Albertz. Stuttgart:
Evangelische Verlagswerk, 1955. 106 pp.

2891 _____ . Zum sein Gott durch Denken. Eine Darstellung der
ethischen Mystik Albert Schweitzers. Bern, Leipzig:
P. Haupt, 1937. 106 pp.

2892 STUCKI, ALFRED. Albert Schweitzer, ein Christ der Tat.
Basel: H. Majer, 1952. 131 pp. Second edition, 1954,
130 pp.

2893 WERNER, MARTIN. Albert Schweitzer und das Freie Christentum.
Zürich: Beer et Cie, 1924. 31 pp.

2894 _____ . Das Weltanschauungsproblem bei Karl Barth und Albert
Schweitzer. Munich: Beck, 1924. 136 pp.

WOUDENBERG, PAUL RICHARD. Pauline Eschatology in the Writings
of R. H. Charles and Albert Schweitzer. See Dissertations,
no. 4348 below.

Theology and Religion

    b. Articles, Parts of Books

2895   AHLBERG, ALF. "Den eskatologiska Jesusbilden." In: <u>Har</u>
         <u>Jesus levat och ved kunna vi veta om honom?</u> Stockholm:
         Natur och Kultur, 1929.

2896   "Albert Schweitzer." <u>Alt-Katholisches Volksblatt</u> (Bonn) 7
         (Feb. 1955), p. 14.

2897   ["Albert Schweitzer in Unitarian ranks?"] <u>Time</u> (New York)
         78:23 (Dec. 8, 1961), p. 39.[1]

2898   "Albert Schweitzer kein Unitarier." <u>Evangelisches Gemeindeblatt</u>
         <u>für München</u> 65:23 (June 1962), p. 4.

2899 **"Albert Schweitzer og kristendommen." <u>Fast Grun</u> (Bergen,
         Norway) 10:2 (1957), pp. 93-94.[2]

2900   ALLEN, E. L. "A new liberal theology: Fritz Buri of Basel."
         <u>Religion in Life</u> (Nashville, Tenn.) 30:2 (Spring 1961),
         pp. 209, 210f, 216.

2901   ALTHAUS, PAUL. "Das Christentum und die Weltreligionen."
         <u>Universitas</u> (Stuttgart) 15:1 (Jan. 1960), pp. 112-14.
         Reprinted with title "Schweitzers Schrift 'Das
         Christentum und die Weltreligionen.'" In: DENKEN UND
         WEG, pp. 200-03.

---

[1]This short item includes Schweitzer's comments on his supposed conversion to Unitarianism. In April of 1961 George Marshall, Minister of the Church of the Larger Fellowship, Unitarian Universalist, in Boston, wrote asking Schweitzer to become an honorary member of the Unitarian Church. Schweitzer accepted and Marshall published his letter, producing great controversy. Schweitzer eventually replied that he had no intention of breaking with the Lutheran Church, but wished to be on good terms with all Protestant denominations. For further comments, see numbers 2898, 2951, 3007, 3083, 3125, and 3139 below.

[2]This and certain other entries in this section are concerned with the theological controversy in Norway during the years 1956 through 1958 (principally among Langfeldt, Riisøen, and Schelderup) as to whether Schweitzer was a Christian. All entries related to this controversy will be marked with two asterisks (**). See also Dr. Langfeldt's book <u>Albert Schweitzer, a Study of his Philosophy</u>, no. 2363 above.

2902 AMBROSIANO, ANTONIO. L'Eucaristia nell-esegesi di Oscar
Cullman. Naples: M. d'Aufia, Editore Pontificio, 1956,
pp. xviii, 2f, 6, 57f, 142.

2903 ANDREWS, CHARLES FREER. "Albert Schweitzer." In: What I
Owe to Christ. London: Hodder and Stoughton, 1932,
pp. 200-212; 1933, 1934, "Cheap edition," pp. 98-105.
New York: Abingdon Press, 1932, pp. 181-92. Translated
in: Rnānjali. Calcutta: Writers' Syndaicat, 1960;
translated as "A-êrh-pa-t'ê Hsi-wa-sa-êrh." In: Wo So
ti'i yen ti Chi-tu. Shanghai: Association Press, 1934,
pp. 108-16; translated in: Wat ik aan Christus te danken
heb. Utrecht: Erven J. Bijkeveld, 1933, pp. 152-62;
translated in: Was ich Christus Verdanke. Bad Pyrmont:
Leonhard Friedrich, 1947, pp. 147-59.

2904 **B., A. "En Schweitzer-studie." Dagen (Bergen) 113
(May 20, 1958), p. 4.

2905 BABEL, HENRY ADALBERT. "Albert Schweitzer, théologian."
La Gazette de Lausanne, Jan. 14, 1960. Reprinted in
CAHIERS 3 (June 1960), pp. 23-24; reprinted with the
title "Albert Schweitzer, théologien protestant."
Journal de Geneve 11 (Jan. 14, 1960), p. 1.

2906 _____. "Équisse d'un philosophie de l'histoire du
Christianisme." In: MISÉRICORDE, pp. 95-97f.

2907 _____. Préface. In: Schweitzer, Albert. Le sécret
historique de la vie de Jésus. Paris: Albin Michel,
1961, pp. 11-17. Excerpted in NOUVELLES 27 (July 1961),
pp. 7-8.

2908 BALLARD, C. M. "Albert Schweitzer." Contemporary Review
(London) 207:1198 (Nov. 1965), pp. 225-28.

2909 **BALSVIK, PER-DAGFINN. "Langfeldt-Schweitzer." Verdens Gang
(Oslo) 66 (March 19, 1957), p. 2.

2910 BARRETT, C. K. "Albert Schweitzer and the New Testament."
The Expository Times (Edinburgh) 87:1 (Oct. 1975),
pp. 4-10. Lecture given on April 10, 1975 as part of
the Albert Schweitzer Centenary Celebration.

2911 BARTHA, TIBOR. "Taten, die das Wort authentisch machen."
In: BEITRÄGE, pp. 23-28.

2912 BARTHEL, ERNST. "Albert Schweitzer als Theologe."
Theologische Studien und Kritiken (Gotha) 98/99:3/4

Theology and Religion

(1926), pp. 445-62. Translated, with title "Dr. Albert
Schweitzer as Theologian." The Hibbert Journal (London)
26:4 (July 1928), pp. 720-35.

2913   BAUR, HANS. "Albert Schweitzer und das freie Christentum."
Schweizerisches Protestantenblatt (Basel) 56:50
(Dec. 16, 1933), pp. 398-99; 51 (Dec. 23, 1933),
pp. 404-05; 52 (Dec. 30, 1933), pp. 415-16.

2914   _____. "Der Anwalt der religiösen Denkens Albert Schweitzers."
Protestantenblatt (Bremen) 66 (1933), pp. 115-20.

2915   _____. "Karl Barth und Albert Schweitzer." Schweizerisches
Protestantenblatt (Basel) 47:35 (Aug. 30, 1924),
pp. 277-79; 47:36 (Sept. 6, 1924), pp. 284-86.

2916   BEINTKER, HORST. "Albert Schweitzer als Theologe." Neue
Zeit (East Berlin) 9 (Jan. 12, 1955), p. 3.

2917   _____. "Albert Schweitzers theologische Bedeutung."
Wissenschaftliche Zeitschrift der Ernst-Moritz-Arndt
Universität (Greifswald) 4 (1954/55), pp. 233-44.

2918   _____. "Eschatologie und Ethik." Zeitschrift für
systematische Theologie (Berlin) 23:4 (1954), pp. 418,
424-25ff.

2919   BENTUÉ, A. "Albert Schweitzer: eschatologia y hermenéutica
(a la memoria de Albert Schweitzer, en el centario de
su nacimienio)." Teologia y Vida (Santiago de Chile)
16:2-3 (1975), pp. 152-64.

2920 **BERG, ARTHUR. "Ope brev til Biskop Kristian Schjelderup."
Dagen (Bergen, Norway) 48 (Feb. 26, 1957), p. 2.

2921 **_____. "Schweitzer, sin etikk." Dagen (Bergen, Norway) 148
(July 1, 1958), p. 3.

2922 **_____. "Schweitzer som Teolog. Svar til forretningsfører
Ivar Samset." Dagen (Bergen, Norway) 151, 152
(July 4 and 5, 1958), p. 3.

2923   BESGEN, ACHIM. "Albert Schweitzer und die 'Wahrheit Jesu.'"
Hochland (Munich) 44:4 (April 1952), pp. 338-45.

2924   BETZ, OTTO. "Albert Schweitzer Jesusdeutung im Lichte der
Qumran-Texte." In: DENKEN UND WEG, pp. 159-71.

2925   BJERKELUND, CARL J. "Albert Schweitzer som Paulusforsker."
       Kirke og Kultur (Oslo) 58:1 (Jan. 1953), pp. 37-41.

2926   _____. "Albert Schweitzers Paulus-Forskning-en-karakteristik."
       Norsk Teologisk Tidsskrift (Oslo) 58:2 (1957), pp. 65-89.

2927   BLACK, M. "From Schweitzer to Bultmann: the modern quest of
       the Historical Jesus." McCormick Quarterly 20 (May 1967),
       pp. 271-83.

2928   BLEECKER, C. J. "Albert Schweitzer als godsdiensthistoricus."
       Theologie en Practijk (Lochem) 10:5/6 (May-June 1950),
       pp. 117-21. Reprinted in NIEUWS 6:2 (Dec. 1957),
       pp. 11-13.

2929   _____. "Schweitzers Blick auf die asiatischen Weltreligionen."
       In: DENKEN UND WEG, pp. 193-99. Also issued as a reprint:
       Tübingen: Mohr, 1962, 6 pp.

2930   BOISEN, ANTON T. "What did Jesus think of himself?" The
       Journal of Bible and Religion (Baltimore) 20:1 (Jan. 1952),
       pp. 7-12.

2931 **BONNEVIE, CARL. "Hvem kan met rette kalles kristan?"
       Verdens Gang (Oslo) 123 (June 2, 1958), p. 2.

2932   BOUTTIER, MICHEL. "La mystique de l'apôtre Paul, rétrospective
       et prospective." REVUE 56:1-2 (1976), pp. 54-67.

2933   BOWMAN, JOHN WICK. "From Schweitzer to Bultmann." Theology
       Today (Princeton) 11:2 (July 1954), pp. 160-78. Trans-
       lated as "De Schweitzer à Bultmann." Etudes Théologiques
       et Religieuses (Montpelier) 30:2 (1955), pp. 3-23.

2934   _____. "The quest of the historical Jesus." Interpretation
       (Richmond, Va.) 3:2 (April 1949), pp. 184-93. Based on
       Schweitzer's book of the same name.

2935   BREMI, WILLY. "Albert Schweitzer." In: Tendenzen der
       Theologie des 20. Jahrhunderts. Eine Geschichte in
       Porträts. Hrsg. von H. J. Schultz. Stuttgart: Kreuz
       Verlag; Olten: Walter-Verlag, 1966, pp. 145-49.

2936   _____. "Albert Schweitzers theologische Arbeit im Rahmen
       seiner Biographie." In: FESTGABE, pp. 9-42.

2937   _____. "Albert Schweitzers theologische Vorstoss 1901/1913."
       In: Krisenheit und Jesusforschung. Werdegang, Resultate
       und Ausblick. Basel, 1972, pp. 10-13.

Theology and Religion

2938   . Der Weg des protestantischen Menschen von Luther bis
      Albert Schweitzer. Zürich: Artemis Verlag, 1953, pp. 111,
      126f. 255, 271, 368ff, 384, 437-51, 494, 532ff, 562.

2939   BRINKERINK, J. "Het Christendom en de wereldgodsdiensten."
      NIEUWS 2:5 (July 1954), pp. 72-73.

2940   BROCK, ERICH. "Albert Schweitzer und sein Leben Jesu."
      Neue Zürcher Zeitung, Oct. 20, 1963, p. 5.

2941   BUBER, MARTIN. "Ein Realist des Geistes." In: EHRFURCHT,
      pp. 203-04. Reprinted in: Die Brücke zur Welt
      (Sonntagsbeilage zu Stuttgarter Zeitung) 5 (Jan. 8 1955),
      p. 17; reprinted in Neue Schweizer Rundschau (Zürich) 5:12
      (April 1955), pp. 728-29; reprinted in: Buber, Martin.
      Nachlese. Heidelberg: Lambert Schneider, 1965, pp. 30-32;
      reprinted in: GESTERN-HEUTE, pp. 26-27; reprinted in:
      BEGEGNUNG, pp. 286-87; translated as "A realist of the
      spirit." In: FESTSCHRIFT, pp. 11-13.

2942   BÜLCK, WALTER. "Albert Schweitzers Bedeutung für die
      religiöse Lage der Gegenwart." Christliche Gegenwart
      (Hamburg) 1/2 (1948), pp. 5-17.

2943   BULTMANN, RUDOLF. "Urchristentum und Religionsgeschichte."
      Theologische Rundschau (Tübingen) 4:11 (1932), pp. 1-21.

2944   BUONAIUTI, ERNESTO. "Die Mystik des Apostels Paulus, 1930."
      Richerche Religiose (Rome) 6 (1930), pp. 361-63.

2945   BURGER, C. B. "Lezing van Prof. Dr. J. N. Sevenster ('Albert
      Schweitzer als Nieuw Testamenticus')." NIEUWS 1:3
      (July 1952), p. 51.

2946   . "Het wetenschappelijk Werk van Albert Schweitzer.
      De betekenis van Paulus' visie op het evangelie."
      NIEUWS 19:1 (June 1970), pp. 17-19.

2947   . "Het wetenschappelijk werk van Albert Schweitzer.
      Het christendom temidden der wereldgodsdiensten." NIEUWS
      21:1 (May 1972), pp. 13-15.

2948   BURI, FRITZ. "Albert Schweitzer." In: Peerman, Dean G. and
      Martin E. Marty, eds. Handbook of Christian Theologians.
      Cleveland: World Publishing, 1965, pp. 112-24.

2949   . "Albert Schweitzer als Forcher, Denker und Christ."
      Schweizerische Theologische Umschau (Bern) 25:1/2
      (Feb. 1955), pp. 2-11. Also issued as a 12-page offprint

by Buchdruckerei Bückler and Co., Bern. Reprinted in
National-Zeitung, Sonntagsbeilage (Basel) 54
(Feb. 2, 1955).

2950   _____. "Albert Schweitzer in der theologischen und
philosophischer Lage der Gegenwart. Eine Würdigung zu
sein Geburtstag." Schweizerische Theologische Umschau
(Bern) 34:3/4 (Dec. 1964), pp. 98-106.

2951   _____. "Die amerikanischen Unitarier und Albert Schweitzer."
Schweizerisches Reformiertes Volksblatt (Basel) 81:48
(Dec. 6, 1947), pp. 382-84.

2952   _____. "Der extentielle Charakter des konsequenteschato-
logischen Jesus-Verständnisses Albert Schweitzers.
Dargestelle im Zusammenhang mit der heutigen Debatte
zwischen Bultmann, Barth und Jaspers." In: EHRFURCHT,
pp. 44-58. Reprinted in Neue Zürcher Zeitung.
Sonntagsausgabe: Literatur und Kunst (Zürich) 7
(Jan. 8, 1955), pp. 3, 6; 10 (Jan. 11, 1955).

2953   _____. "Das hermeneutische in der Protestantischen
Theologie der Gegenwart." Schweizerische Theologische
Umschau (Bern) 27 (June 1957), pp. 29-51.

2954   _____. "Kontroverse. Zur Diskussion des Problems der
Ausgebliebenen Parusie." Theologische Zeitschrift
(Basel) 3:6 (Nov./Dec. 1947), pp. 422-28.

2955   _____. "Zur gegenwärtigen Diskussion über das Problem
Hoffnung." Theologische Zeitschrift (Basel) 22:3
(May-June 1966), pp. 196-211.

2956   CAMPION, CHARLES THOMAS. From Christianity to Spiritualism.
London: George Allen and Unwin, 1935, pp. 9-11, 64-65,
69-73, 93, 97-98, 100-101. Translated by Elio Falchi as
Dal Cristianesimo allo spiritualismo scientifico.
Verona: Case editrice Europa, 1947. (Collana di
"Problema dell'anima" v. 3.)

2957   CANNON, WILLIAM R. "Eschatology in the light of current
theological discussions." Religion in Life (New York)
24:4 (Autumn 1955), pp. 524-36.

2958   CHAMBERLAIN, ARTHUR D. "Till the son of man be come."
Interpretation (Richmond, Va.) 7:1 (Jan. 1953), pp. 3-13.

2959   CLARK, HENRY. "Albert Schweitzer's contribution to theology."
In: THE CONVOCATION RECORD, pp. V/17-30.

Theology and Religion

2960   CONRAD, OTTO. "Albert Schweitzer im Religionsunterricht der
        höheren Schulen." <u>Monatsblätter für den Evangelischen
        Religionsunterricht</u> (Göttingen) 22 (1929), pp. 144-50.

2961   CULLMANN, OSCAR. "Albert Schweitzers Auffassung der
        urchristlichen Reichsgottesoffnung im Lichte der heutigen
        neutestamentlichen Forschung." <u>Evangelische Theologie</u>
        (Munich) 25:11 (1965), pp. 643-56. Reprinted in:
        CHARISMATISCHE DIAKONIE, pp. 37-50.

2962   _____. "La signification de la Sainte-Cène dans le
        christianisme primitif." REVUE 16:1 (1936), pp. 1-22.

        DAVENPORT, MANUEL M. "The aesthetic foundation of
        Schweitzer's ethics." See Music, no. 3241 below.

2963   DAVIES, W. D. <u>Paul and rabbinic Judaism</u>. London: SPCK,
        1948. 2nd ed., 1958. 3rd ed., 1970, pp. 287ff.

2964   DAWE, DONALD G. "Schweitzer on the paranoia of Jesus."
        <u>Minnesota Medicine</u> (St. Paul) 49:1 (Jan. 1966), pp. 181-82.

2965   DEMPE, HELLMUTH. "Albert Schweitzer und die Religion."
        <u>Zeitschrift für Religions- und Geitesgeschichte</u> 30:4
        (1978), pp. 337-45.

2966   DIBELIUS, MARTIN. "Glaube und Mystik bei Paulus." <u>Neue
        Jahrbücher für Wissenschaft und Jugendbildung</u> (Leipzig/
        Berlin) 7:8 (1931), pp. 683-99. Reprinted in: <u>Botschaft
        und Geschichte: Gesammelte Aufsätze von Martin Dibelius</u>.
        Tübingen: J. C. B. Mohr, 1956, Vol. II, pp. 94-116.

2967   DINGLE, REGINALD J. "The historical Jesus, an approach of
        faith?" <u>The Clergy Review</u> (London) 38:5 (May 1953),
        pp. 280-89.

2968   DOBSCHÜTZ, ERNST VON. "The Eschatology of the gospels, I,
        II, III, and IV" (four lectures). <u>The Expositor</u> (London)
        36th year, seventh series, vol. IX, no. 50 (Feb. 1910),
        pp. 97-113. Schweitzer discussed, pp. 105-06. Other
        versions appear in: Dobschütz, Ernst von. <u>Eschatology
        of the Gospels</u>. London: Hodder and Stoughton, 1910,
        pp. 56-58; "The significance of early Church eschatology."
        In: <u>Transactions of the Third International Congress for
        the History of Religions</u>. Oxford: Clarendon Press, 1908,
        vol. II, pp. 312-20.

2969   DUNGAN, DAVID L. "Disillusionment with the historical recon-
        struction of the life of Jesus." <u>Perkins School of
        Theology Journal</u> (Dallas) 29 (Spring 1976), pp. 27-48.

2970   EDDY, HOWARD C. "This I believe." Faith and Freedom (Oxford)
          13:38 (Spring 1960), pp. 56-60.

       EISSFELDT, FRITZ. "Vom tragenden Grund. Albert Schweitzer
          als Theologe und Philosoph." See Philosophy, no. 2460
          above.

2971   EMMET, CYRIL W. "The eschatological question in the Gospels
          as interpreted by Schweitzer." In: The Eschatological
          Question in the Gospels; and other studies in recent New
          Testament criticism. Edinburgh: T. and T. Clark, 1911,
          pp. 3-77.

2972   FRIDRICHSEN, ANTON. "Albert Schweitzer som teolog." Kirke
          og Kultur (Kristiania) 42:46 (1935), pp. 360-69. Reprinted
          in: MANNEN, pp. 60-72.

2973   _____. "Jesus och Paulus." Svenska Dagbladet (Stockholm),
          April 27, 1930.

2974   _____. "Paulus-Kronik" (Die Mystik des Apostels Paulus).
          Svensk Teologisk Kvartalskrift (Lund) 6:3 (1930),
          pp. 280-90.

2975   FULTON, AUSTIN A. "Schweitzer on the mysticism of Paul:
          a criticism." The Evangelical Quarterly (London) 20:3
          (July 15, 1948), pp. 172-83.

2976   GAEBLER, MAX D. "The roots of an ethic-centered religion."
          In: PROPHET, pp. 17-20.

2977   GEORGI, DIETER. "Schweitzers theologisches Erbe."
          Süddeutsche Zeitung (Munich) 3:3 (Dec. 31, 1965/
          Jan. 1-2, 1966), feuilleton, pp. 70-71.

2978   GIBSON, COLIN J. "The Kingdom of God: in refutation of the
          eschatological theory." Faith and Freedom (Oxford) 12:35
          (Spring 1959), pp. 71-80.

2979   GIESECKE, HANS. "Wort, Welt, und Gemeinde." Die Zeichen
          der Zeit (Berlin) 10:7 (1956), pp. 252-58.

2980   GILMOUR, SAMUEL MAC LEAN. "Schweitzer's Jesus of history."
          Religion in Life (New York) 18:3 (Summer 1949), pp. 427-33.

2981   GLASSON, T. FRANCIS. "Jesus and his gospel, since Schweitzer."
          The London Quarterly and Holborn Review Vol. 176
          (Sixth series, vol. 20), (April 1951), pp. 104-13.

Theology and Religion

2982 _____. "Schweitzer's influence: blessing or bane?" The
 Journal of Theological Studies 28 (Oct. 1977), pp. 289-302.

2983 GOGUEL, MAURICE. "L'Éxégetè." In: ETUDES, pp. 157-202;
 second edition, pp. 135-72.

2984 _____. "Albert Schweitzer: Von Reimarus zu Wrede." REVUE 44
 (1906), pp. 276-83.

2985 _____. "La mystique paulienne d'après Albert Schweitzer."
 REVUE 3 (March/April 1931), pp. 185-210. Reprinted in:
 Goguel, Maurice. Trois études sur la pensée religieuse
 du christianisme primitif. Paris: Librarie Félix Alcan,
 1931. (Cahiers de la Revue d'histoire et de philosophie
 religieuses publiés par la faculté de théologie protestante
 de l'Université de Strasbourg, no. 23.)

2986 GRABS, RUDOLF. "Albert Schweitzer." In: Die Religion in
 Geschichte und Gegenwart. Handwörterbuch für Theologie
 und Religionswissenschaft. Hrsg. von Kurt Galling. 3.
 neubearbeitete Auflage. 5 volumes. Tübingen: J. C. B.
 Mohr (Paul Siebeck), 1961, cols. 1607-08.

2987 _____. "Albert Schweitzer als religiöse wegweisende
 Persönlichkeit." Glaube und Tat (Giessen) 2:8 (1951),
 pp. 1-3.

2988 GRÜBER, PROBST. "In Lambarene vollendet sich seine
 charismatische Diakonie." Die Zeit (Hamburg) 20:37
 (Sept. 14, 1965), p. 5. Reprinted in: CHARISMATISCHE
 DIAKONIE, pp. 7-10.

2989 HALL, G. STANLEY. Jesus, the Christ, in the light of psychology. Garden City, N.Y.: Doubleday, Page and Co., 1917,
 Vol. II, pp. 397-400, 413.

2990 HANSELMANN, GERHARD. "Ehrfurcht vor dem Leben. Albert
 Schweitzers Denken als Frage und Aufgabe an die Theologie."
 Für Arbeit und Besinnung (Stuttgart) 9:6 (March 15, 1955),
 pp. 82-92.

2991 HEIDRICH, PETER. "Differenzierte Urteile und anregende
 Darstellung. Zu Albert Schweitzers wissenschaftlichen
 Werk." Standpunkt: Evangelische Monatsschrift (Berlin)
 3:1 (Jan. 1975), pp. 18-20.

2992 HEILER, FRIEDRICH. [Tribute without title.] In: DENKEN UND
 WEG, pp. 104-06.

2993   HERING, JEAN. "De H. J. Holtzmann à Albert Schweitzer." In:
        EHRFURCHT, pp. 21-29. Also issued as an offprint: Bern:
        P. Haupt, 1955. 11 pp.

2994   HESS, M. WHITCOMB. "The apotheosis of Albert Schweitzer."
        The Catholic World (New York) 174:1044 (March 1952),
        pp. 425-29.

2995   "Heute Vortrag Prof. Schweitzer über des geschichtliche und
        geistige Jesus." Deutsche Zeitung Bohemia (Prague) 9
        (Jan. 13, 1923), p. 6.

2996   HEWETT, A. PHILIP. "The religion of Albert Schweitzer."
        Ghandi Marg (New Delhi) 9(2) (April 1965), pp. 154-59.

2997   HIERS, RICHARD H. "The historical Jesus vs. modern theology;
        ethics and eschatology." In: Jesus and Ethics. Four
        Interpretations. Philadelphia: The Westminster Press,
        1968, pp. 39-78. Based on the author's dissertation,
        see no. 4320 below.

2998   _____. "Interim ethics; an essay in tribute to Albert
        Schweitzer." Theology and Life 9:3 (Fall 1966),
        pp. 220-33.

2999   HODGES, GEORGE. "Christ among the doctors." The Atlantic
        Monthly (Boston) 107:4 (April 1911), pp. 483-90.

3000   HOLM, SÖREN. "Zu Ehren von Albert Schweitzer." Schweizerische
        Theologische Umschau (Bern) 30:4 (Dec. 1960), pp. 255-60.

        HOLMSTRÖM, FOLKE. Det Eskatologiska Motivet i Nutida
        Theologi. See Dissertations, no. 4321 below.

3001   HOLTZMANN, HEINRICH JULIUS. "Der gegenwärtige Stand der
        Leben-Jesu-Forschung." Deutsche Literaturzeitung
        (Leipzig) 27:38 (Sept. 28, 1906), cols. 2357-64; 27:39
        (Sept. 29, 1906), cols. 2413-22; 27:40 (Oct. 6, 1906),
        cols. 2477-83; 27:41 (Oct. 13, 1906), cols. 2541-46.

3002   HOOYKAAS, C. E. "Jesus, heer der Toekomst. De
        eschatologische Christusbeschouwing. Over het werk van
        Prof. Albert Schweitzer." De Stroom, Feb. 9 and March 9,
        1929.

3003 **HOVSTAD, JOHAN. "Albert Schweitzer og kristendommen. Svar
        til Sverre Riisøen fra Johan Hovstad." Verdens Gang
        (Oslo) 125 (June 4, 1958), p. 2.

Theology and Religion

3004 **_____. "Albert Schweitzer og nordsk kulturdebatt."
<u>Dagbladed</u> (Oslo) 201 (Aug. 30, 1956), pp. 3-4.

3005 **_____. "Svar til pastor Sverre Riisøen fra Johan Hovstad."
<u>Verdens Gang</u> (Oslo) 131 (June 11, 1958), p. 2.

3006 [HUNTEMANN, GEORG.] "Schweitzers revolutionäres Christentum.
Pastor Georg Huntemann deutete die religiösen Anschauungen
des grossen Arztes." <u>Weser-Kurier</u> (Bremen) 18
(Jan. 22, 1959), p. 9.

3007 I.A.R.F. "Die amerikanischen Unitarier und Albert
Schweitzer." <u>Christliche Gegenwart</u> (Hamburg) 1/2 (1948),
pp. 64-66.

3008 ICE, JACKSON LEE. "Did Schweitzer believe in God?" <u>The
Christian Century</u> (Chicago) 93 (April 7, 1976), pp. 332-34.
Reprinted in COURIER, Summer 1977, pp. 17-22.

3009 _____. "Schweitzer's radical Christianity and its impact
today." In: CENTENNIAL. Reprinted as "The impact of
Schweitzer's radical Christianity on today." In: PROPHET,
pp. 11-15.

3010 _____. "Was Schweitzer a mystic after all?" <u>Christian
Century</u> (Chicago) 95:8 (March 8, 1978), pp. 237-40.

3011 JENSSEN, HANS HEINRICH. "Die Bedeutung Albert Schweitzers
für eine geistige neuorientierung der Christen in der
DDR." In: VERMÄCHTNIS UND WIRKLICHKEIT, pp. 41-50.

3012 JULICHER, ADOLF. "Die Epoche 1901 (Albert Schweitzer)."
In: <u>Neue Linien in der Kritik der evangelischen
Überlieferung</u>. Giessen: Alfred Töpelmann, 1906, pp. 1-13.

3013 JUNG, ADAM. "War Jesus eschatologisch orientiert?"
<u>Pfälzisches Pfarrerblatt</u> (Essingen) 44 (1953), no. 4,
pp. 19-21; no. 7, pp. 46-50; no. 8, pp. 53-57; no. 9/10,
pp. 64-68; no. 11, pp. 78-81.

3014 JUNGHEINRICH, HANSJÖRG. "Albert Schweitzer und die
evangelische Kirche. <u>Freies Christentum</u> (Frankfurt a.M.)
13:4 (April 1, 1961), col. 46.

3015 KEGLER, HARTMUT. "Der Kern aller Religiosität." <u>Neue Zeit</u>
(East Berlin) 67 (March 19, 1960), p. 5.

3016 KESSLER, LINA. "Albert Schweitzers 'Mystik des Apostels
Paulus' und die religiös-bildliche Erkenntniss."

Die Christliche Welt (Gotha) 47:8 (April 22, 1933),
pp. 339-44.

3017 KIBBLEWHITE, KEITH N. "Albert Schweitzer the theologian and
      philosopher." Peace News (London) 968 (Jan. 14, 1955),
      p. 4.

3018 KOBAYASHI, M. "Shinpi-shugi to shūmatsu shisō." Shūkyo
      Kenkyū (Tokyo) 125 (April 1951).

3019 KOCH, TRAUGOTT. "Albert Schweitzers Kritik des christologischen
      Denkens--und die sachgemässe Form einer gegenwärtigen
      Beziehung auf den geschichtlichen Jesus." Zeitschrift
      für Theologie und Kirche (Tübingen) 73:2 (June 1976),
      pp. 208-40.

3020 KOEHLER, LUDWIG. "Eine Handvoll Neues Testament." In:
      EHRFURCHT, pp. 71-80.

3021 KÖTSCHER-BARK, URSULA. "Vortrag über Albert Schweitzer in
      Düsseldorf. 'Albert Schweitzer, die geistige Position
      eines undogmatischen Christen unserer Tage.'" Freies
      Christentum (Frankfurt a.M.) 9:3 (March 1, 1957),
      cols. 35-36.

      KOLLER, PETER. "Albert Schweitzer--zweiter Durchgang im
      Hinblick auf Protestantismus in Lebenskonfigurationen."
      See Philosophy, no. 2538 above.

3022 KRAUS, FRITZ. "Ehrfurcht vor dem Leben. Die Religiösen
      Wurzeln Albert Schweitzer." RUNDBRIEF 17 (Jan. 14, 1961),
      pp. 29-40.

3023 KRAUS, OSKAR. "Halle-Vortrag Schweitzers 'Der historische
      Jesu.'" Deutsche Zeitung Bohemia (Prague) 10
      (Jan. 14, 1923), p. 4.

3024 KÜMMEL, WERNER GEORG. "Albert Schweitzer als Jesus- und
      Paulusforscher." In: Albert Schweitzer als Theologe.
      Zwei akademische Reden . . . von Werner Georg Kümmel und
      Carl Heinz Ratschow. Marburg: Elwert, 1966, pp. 9-27.

3025 _____. "Albert Schweitzer et l'apôtre Paul." REVUE 56:1-2
      (1976), pp. 37-53.

3026 _____. "L'eschatologie conséquente d'Albert Schweitzer
      jugée par des contemporaines." REVUE 37:1 (1957),
      pp. 58-70. Translated as "Die konsequente Eschatologie
      Albert Schweitzers im Urteil der Zeitgenossen." In:

Theology and Religion

Kümmel, Werner Georg. Heilsgeschehen und Geschichte. Marburg, pp. 328ff; translation reprinted in Kümmel, W. G. Gesammelte Aufsätze 1933-1964. Hrsg. von Erich Grässer und anderen. Marburg: N. G. Elwert Verlag, 1965.

3027   _____. Das neue testament. Geschichte der Erforschung seiner Probleme. Munich: Karl Alber, 1970. 2., überbearbeitete und ergänzte Auflage, pp. 298-309. (Orbis Academus Band, III/3). Translated as The New Testament: the History of the Investigation of its Problems. Tr. S. M. Gilmour and H. C. Kee. Nashville, New York: Abingdon, 1972, pp. 235-44.

3028   LAKE, KIRSOPP. "Albert Schweitzer's influence in Holland and England." In: JUBILEE, pp. 425-40.

3029   **LANGFELDT, GABRIEL. "Albert Schweitzers Innsats." Jyllands-Posten (Aarhus) 35 (Nov. 5, 1958), p. 9.

3030   **_____. "Albert Schweitzers livssyn." Verdens Gang (Oslo) March 19, 1957, p. 3.

3031   **_____. "Albert Schweitzers syn pa religion og moral." Verdens Gang (Oslo) 43/44 (Feb. 20, 21, 1957), pp. 3f.

3032   **_____. "Albert Schweitzers syn pa religion og moral." Samtiden (Oslo) 66:9 (1957), pp. 548-56. This version differs from the previous entry.

3033   **_____. "Human-etikken og Albert Schweitzer." Verdens Gang (Oslo) 1 (Jan. 2, 1957), p. 3.

3034   **_____. "Schweitzers etikk og hans teologi." Verdens Gang (Oslo) 147 (June 30, 1958), p. 3. Reprinted in Dagen (Bergen) 147 (June 30, 1958), p. 3.

3035   **_____. "Sverre Riisøens manglende kjennskap til Schweitzers livssyn." Verdens Gang (Oslo) 133 (June 13, 1958), p. 3.

3036   **_____. "Sverre Riisøens retrett." Verdens Gang (Oslo) 139 (June 9, 1958), p. 3.

LANGLEY, JAMES A. A Critique of Contemporary Interpretations of the Sermon on the Mount. See Dissertations, no. 4326 below.

3037   LEA, F. A. The Seed of the Church. London: Sheppard Press, 1948, pp. 9, 121-28, 130-31, 136, 139-42.

3038   LEENHARDT, FRANZ J. "Le docteur Schweitzer et l'apôtre Paul."
        Foi et Vie (Paris) 33 (April 1932), pp. 371-81.

3039   LINDESKOG, GÖSTA. "Mästaren och hans Lärjunge." Arsbok för
        Kristen Humanism (Lund) 18 (1956), pp. 11-20.

3040   LINTON, OLOF. "Albert Schweitzers interpretation of St. Paul's
        theology." In: JUBILEE, pp. 441-56.

3041   LLOYD, ROGER B. "The effects of Albert Schweitzer." In:
        The Church of England in the Twentieth Century. New York
        and London: Longmans, Green and Co., 1946, Vol. 1,
        pp. 70-76, 79, 92, 93.

3042   LOHMEYER, ERNST. "Vom urchristlichen Abendmahl." Theologische
        Rundschau (Tübingen) 9:3 (1937), pp. 168-227.

3043   LONICER, HEINZ. "Hans Pribnow. Der Sechste Vortrag
        (Arbeitstagung in Stuttgart-Hohenheim, 1963). Jesus im
        Denken Albert Schweitzers." Freies Christentum
        (Frankfurt a.M.) 15:10 (Oct. 1, 1963), cols. 118-19.

3044   MAGILL, FRANK N., ed. "The quest of the historical Jesus."
        In: Masterpieces of Christian Literature in Summary Form.
        New York: Harper and Row, 1963, pp. 847-51.

3045   MARCHAL, GEORGES. Introduction to Le Mystique de l'apôtre
        Paul par Albert Schweitzer. Paris: Albin Michel, 1962,
        pp. ix-xvii. Reprinted, with some omissions, in CAHIERS
        8 (Dec. 1962), pp. 14-17; translated as "Albert Schweitzers
        Paulusdeutung." In: DENKEN UND WEG, pp. 172-77.

3046   _____. "La pensée religieuse d'Albert Schweitzer." Le Monde
        non Chrétien 79-80 (July-Dec. 1966), pp. 63-69. Also in
        L'Orgue (Paris) 119 (July-Sept. 1966), pp. 89-94.

3047   _____. "La théologie et la musique d'Albert Schweitzer."
        In: ACADEMIE.

3048   _____. "Le théologien." In: ETUDES, pp. 111-56; 2nd
        edition, pp. 97-134.

3049   _____. "Vue d'ensemble." In: RAYONNEMENT, pp. 153-73.

3050   MARGOLIUS, HANS. "Albert Schweitzer. His links with the
        teachings of Judaism." Jewish Affairs (Johannesburg,
        South Africa), Jan. 1975, pp. 37-41.

Theology and Religion

3051   MARSHALL, GEORGE N. "The religious liberalism of Albert
            Schweitzer." The Crane Review (Medford, Mass.) 5:2/3
            (Winter/Spring 1963), pp. 68-81. Adapted as "Is Schweitzer
            a Christian?" The Inquirer (London) 118:6329
            (Oct. 26, 1963), pp. 4-5; translated as "Der religiöse
            Freisinn Albert Schweitzers." Eleusis (Kulmbach, Germany)
            19:3 (May/June 1964), pp. 132-48.

3052   MARTIN, ALFRED VON. "Albert Schweitzer--ein Mahner unserer
            Zeit." Una Sancta (Stuttgart) 3:1 (1927), pp. 65-84.

3053   MC COWN, CHESTER C. "Albert Schweitzer." In: The Search
            for the Real Jesus. New York: Scribners, 1940,
            pp. 239-53.

3054   _____. "The eschatology of Jesus reconsidered." Journal of
            Religion (Chicago) 16:1 (Jan. 1936), pp. 30-46.

3055   MEHL, ROGER. "La spiritualité d'Albert Schweitzer." Le
            Monde (Paris) 6422 (Sept. 7, 1965), pp. 1f.

3056   MEILI, KONRAD. "Die Lehre von Gott und die Lehre von Christus
            bei Albert Schweitzer." Theologische Blätter (Leipzig)
            13:7 (July 1934), cols. 204-12.

3057   MENSING, KARL. "Christusmystik." Die Christliche Welt
            (Gotha) 52:5 (March 5, 1938), cols. 169-71.

3058   MERK, OTTO. "Albert Schweitzer, sein Denken und sein Weg."
            Nachrichten der Evang.-Luth. Kirche in Bayern 30 (1975),
            pp. 26-29.

3059   MICHEL, OTTO. "Albert Schweitzer und die Leben-Jesu-Forschung
            heute." Universitas (Stuttgart) 15:1 (Jan. 1960),
            pp. 33-42. Reprinted in: DENKEN UND WEG, pp. 125-34;
            reprinted in expanded form with title "Albert Schweitzer--
            konsequenzen aus der Leben-Jesu-Forschung." In:
            BEGEGNUNG, pp. 312-21.

3060   MONTGOMERY, W. "Dr. Schweitzer on the interpretation of
            St. Paul." The Expository Times (Edinburgh) 23 (1912),
            pp. 209-11.

3061   MORGENSTERN, OTTO. "Die Leben-Jesu-Forschung." Freies
            Christentum (Frankfurt a.M.) 5:6 (June 1, 1953),
            cols. 62-64.

3062   MÜLLER, ERNST. "Die Messianitäts und Leidensgeheimnis.
            Geschichte der Leben-Jesu Forschung." Universitas
            (Stuttgart) 15:1 (Jan. 1960), pp. 107-110.

3063   _____. "Die säkulare Bedeutung Schweitzers für die Leben-
        Jesu-Forschung." In: DENKEN UND WEG, pp. 146-58.
        Translated and condensed as "The secular significance
        of Schweitzer's research into the life of Jesus."
        Universitas (English language edition) 7:1 (1964),
        pp. 75-80.

3064   MUIRHEAD, L. A. "The 'mythical Christ' and the 'historical'
        Jesus: a critical study." Review of Theology and Philoso-
        phy (Edinburgh) 6:10 and 6:11 (1911), pp. 577-86 and
        633-46.

3065   MUNDLE, WILHELM. "Die Christus Mystik des Apostels Paulus:
        Schweitzer-Lohmeyer-Liechtenhan." Die Christliche Welt
        (Gotha) 44:16 (Aug. 16, 1933), pp. 765-72.

3066   MURET, MAURICE. "Le christianisme appliqué d'Albert
        Schweitzer." Journal des Débats (Paris) 2 (Oct. 21, 1932),
        pp. 675-78.

        MURRY, JOHN MIDDLETON. "The religion of Albert Schweitzer."
        See Philosophy, no. 2583 above.

3067   NEILL, STEPHEN. The Interpretation of the New Testament
        1861-1961. London: Oxford University Press, 1964,
        pp. 191-200. (The Firth Lectures, 1962).

3068   "Die neue Diskussion über die Frage nach dem historischen
        Jesus." Schweizerische Theologische Umschau (Bern)
        31:13 (Oct. 1961), pp. 140ff.

        NEUENSCHWANDER, ULRICH. "Albert Schweitzer." In: Denker
        des Glaubens. See Philosophy, no. 2586 above.

3069   _____. "Albert Schweitzer und das 20. Jahrhundert." Von des
        Christen Freude und Freiheit (Zürich) 7:201 (July/
        Aug. 1960), pp. 22-31. Reprinted in RUNDBRIEF 17
        (Jan. 14, 1961), pp. 40-50; reprinted in BERICHTE 27
        (July 1, 1961), pp. 8-17; reprinted in: DENKEN UND WEG,
        pp. 568-78; excerpted as "Een vreemdeling in enze rijd."
        NIEUWS 11:2 (Nov. 1962), pp. 8-9. Reprinted in:
        Neuenschwander, Ulrich. Gott und dem nichts. Bern:
        P. Haupt, 1980.

3070   _____. "Albert Schweitzers theologische Bedeutung." Neue
        Zürcher Zeitung 8 (Jan. 11/12, 1975), p. 52. Reprinted in:
        Neuenschwander, Ulrich. Gott und dem nichts. Bern:
        P. Haupt, 1980.

3071   _____. "Auswirkungen der Gedanken Albert Schweitzers in der
        gegenwärtigen Theologie." Schweizerische Theologische
        Umschau (Bern) 25:1 (Feb. 1955), pp. 16-23.

Theology and Religion

3072 _____. "Begegnung mit Albert Schweitzer als Theologen--
heute." In: GESTERN-HEUTE, pp. 53-57.

3073 NEUENSTEIN, M. VON. "'Es gibt hier kein Mitteldinge!' Albert
Schweitzer--Pfarrer von Ars." Der Christliche Sonntag
(Freiburg im Breisgau) 9:8 (Feb. 24, 1957), pp. 61-62.
For a reply from Pfarrer H. and Neuenstein's reply, see
Der Christliche Sonntag 9:12 (March 24, 1957), p. 96.

3074 NICOL, IAIN G. "Schweitzer's Jesus: a psychology of the
heroic will." The Expository Times (Edinburgh) 86:2
(Nov. 1974), pp. 52-55.

3075 NITSCHKE, AUGUST. "Albert Schweitzer. Ein historiker in
Auseinandersetzung mit der modernen Theologie." RUNDBRIEF
30 (1967).

3076 NIVEN, W. D. "Eschatology and the primitive church." The
Expository Times (Edinburgh) 50:7 (April 1939), pp. 325-30.

3077 OKADA, MINORU. "Schweitzer wa Idaina Christian de aru ka?"
Kirisuto-Sha (Tokyo) 6 (Summer 1954).

3078 OXENSTIERNA, BENGT. "Albert Schweitzer" (behandlande
Schweitzers teologi). Dagens Tidning (Stockholm),
Dec. 28 and 29, 1921.

3079 PELIKAN, JAROSLAV. "Albert Schweitzer, theologian and
thinker." Saturday Review (New York) 48:39
(Sept. 25, 1965), pp. 21-22. For a letter to the editor
in reply by Eugene Exman, see 48:24 (Oct. 16, 1965), p. 41.

3080 PERRIN, NORMAN. The Kingdom of God in the Teaching of Jesus.
London: SCM Press, 1963, pp. 28-35.

3081 PFISTER, OSKAR. "Albert Schweitzer und die ökumenische
Bewegung." In: EHRFURCHT, pp. 205-19.

3082 PIPER, OTTO. "Das Problem des Lebens Jesu seit Schweitzer."
In: Verbum dei manet in aeternum. Eine Festschrift für
Otto Schmitz zu seinem siebzigsten Geburtstag. Hrsg.
von Werner Foerster. Witten/Ruhr: Luther-Verlag, 1953,
pp. 73-93.

3083 PRIBNOW, HANS. "Albert Schweitzer und die Unitarier."
Freies Christentum (Frankfurt a.M.) 14:5 (May 1, 1962),
cols. 56-58. Reprinted in RUNDBRIEF 20 (Sept. 1, 1962),
pp. 34-36.

3084 _____. "Jesus im Denken Albert Schweitzers." RUNDBRIEF 25
(Jan. 14, 1965), pp. 41-74. Reprinted from the brochure
of the same name, see no. 2886 above.

3085 "R." (M. RADE). "Ist das liberales Jesusbild modern?"
Die Christliche Welt (Gotha) 21:14 (April 4, 1907),
cols. 336-41.

3086 RADHAKRISHNAN, SARVEPALLI. "For whom religion is a reality."
In: FESTSCHRIFT, pp. 76-77. Reprinted with the title
"His religion: a reality, not a profession." The
Christian Register (Boston) 134:1 (Jan. 1955), p. 18.

3087 RASKER, ALBERT. "Eschatologie und Ethik." In: BEITRÄGE,
pp. 147-50.

3088 RATSCHOW, CARL-HEINZ. "Die geistesgeschichtliche Bedeutung
Albert Schweitzers." In: Albert Schweitzer als Theolog.
Zwei akademische Reden von W. G. Kümmel und C.-H.
Ratschow. Marburg: Elwert, 1966, pp. 29-40.

3089 RATTER, MAGNUS. "The Lord's Prayer--before and after
Schweitzer." Faith and Freedom (Oxford) Vol. 16,
part 3, no. 48 (Summer 1963), pp. 121-24.

3090 REGESTER, JOHN DICKINSON. "Albert Schweitzer: another apostle
out of season." The Christian Advocate (New York) 107:25
(June 23, 1932), pp. 651-62.

3091 REGNER, FRIEDEMANN. "Johannes Weiss: Die Predigt Jesu vom
Reiche Gottes. Gegen eine theologiegeschichtliche Fable
convenu." Zeitschrift für Kirchengeschichte (Stuttgart)
84:1 (1973), pp. 82-92.

3092 REITZENSTEIN, R. "Religionsgeschichte und Eschatologie."
Zeitschrift für die Neutestamentliche Wissenschaft
(Giessen) 13:1 (1912), pp. 1-28.

3093 RICHTER, JULIUS. "Die 'konsequente Eschatologie' im Feuer
der Kritik." Zeitschrift für Religions- und Geistes-
geschichte (Cologne) 12:2 (1960), pp. 146-66.

3094 RIGAUX, BÉDA. "La Redécouverte de la dimension eschatologique
de l'évangile." REVUE 56:1-2 (1976), pp. 3-27.

3095 **RISSØEN, SVERRE. "Duplikk til Dr. Philos. Johan Hovstad."
Verdens Gang (Oslo) 127 (June 6, 1958), p. 3.

Theology and Religion

3096 **_____. "Kameleon-theologi." Verdens Gang (Oslo) 112
          (May 19, 1958), p. 3.

3097 **_____. "Mer kelapp-kultusen nok en gang. Svar til
          professor dr. med. G. Langfeldt." Verdens Gang (Oslo)
          114 (June 26, 1958), p. 3.

3098 **_____. "Realiteter og etiketter. Svar til Dr. philos.
          Johan Hovstad." Verdens Gang (Oslo) 123 (June 2, 1958),
          p. 3.

3099 **_____. "Svar til Ragnar Kvam." Verdens Gang (Oslo) 123
          (June 2, 1958), p. 3.

3100 **_____. "Takk til Professor dr. med. G. Langfeldt." Verdens
          Gang (Oslo) 136 (June 17, 1958), p. 3.

3101 RODGERS, HENRY A. "Albert Schweitzer." In: Hunt, George L.
          Ten Makers of Modern Protestant Thought. New York:
          Association Press, 1958. (A Reflection Book). Revised
          and expanded version: Twelve Makers of Modern Protestant
          Thought. New York: Association Press, 1971, pp. 25-31.

3102 RÖHR, HEINZ. "Buddhismus und Christentum. Untersuchung zur
          Typologie zweier Weltreligionen." Zeitschrift für
          Religions- und Geistesgeschichte (Cologne) 25:4 (1973),
          pp. 289-303. Contains a section entitled "A. Schweitzer:
          Buddhas 'Ethik des Mitleids'--Jesu 'Ethik der tätigen
          Lebe,'" pp. 301-03.

3103 ROLOFF, JÜRGEN. "Schweitzer--der nahe unbekannte." In:
          Motiv des Glaubens. Eine Ideengeschichte des Christentums
          in 18 Gestalten. Hrsg. von Johannes Lehmann. Hamburg:
          1968, pp. 161-68.

3104 SACHS, W. "Geschichte der Paulinischen Forschung und Mystik
          des Apostels Paulus." Universitas (Stuttgart) 15:1
          (Jan. 1960), pp. 110-12. Reprinted in: DENKEN UND WEG,
          pp. 178-83.

3105 SALVATORELLI, LUIGI. "Da Locke a Reitzenstein." Rivista
          Storica Italiana (Torino) 46, new series 7 (Jan./April
          1929), pp. 5-66. Schweitzer: pp. 25-29, 43-45, 50, 58.

3106 **SAMSET, IVAR. "Schweitzer som teolog." Dagen (Bergen,
          Norway) 154 (July 8, 1958), p. 3.

3107 **_____. "Spørsmal til redaktør A. Berg." Dagen (Bergen,
          Norway) 150 (July 3, 1958), p. 3.

3108   SANDAY, WILLIAM. "The apocalyptic element in the gospels."
          The Hibbert Journal (London) 10:1 (Oct. 1911), pp. 83–109.
          Schweitzer: pp. 83–85, 103.

3109   SANDERS, E. P. Paul and Palestinian Judaism. London: SCM,
          1977, pp. 434–41, 446–48, 453–56, 476–81.

3110   SCHACHT, ROBERT H., JR. "'The greatest soul in Christendom'
          and his stand on free religion." The Christian Register
          (Boston) 128:7 (Aug. 1949), pp. 17–20; 8 (Sept. 1949),
          pp. 17–19f.

3111   SCHÄR, HANS. "Albert Schweitzers konsequent-eschatologische
          Deutung des Neuen Testaments als Element einer
          Seelengeschichte." In: EHRFURCHT, pp. 59–70.

3112 **SCHJELDERUP, KRISTIAN. "Albert Schweitzer og Kristendommen."
          Dagen (Bergen, Norway) 51 (March 1, 1957), p. 2.

3113 **_____. "Veien tel deg selv. Albert Schweitzer i
          fredsbiblioteket." Samtiden (Oslo) 66:1 (1957), pp. 11–17.

3114   SCHMIDT, MARTIN. "Albert Schweitzer als Theologe." In:
          Hallier, Christian, ed. Studien der Erwin von Steinbach
          Stiftung. Vol. 2, 1968.

3115   SCHNEIDER, ADOLF. "Leben-Jesu-Forschung und Christus-
          botschaft." Zeitwende (Hamburg) 3 (1927), pp. 63–74.

3116   SCHOLDER, KLAUS. "Albert Schweitzer und Ferdinand Christian
          Baur." In: DENKEN UND WEG, pp. 184–92.

       SCHOLL, ROBERT. "Durch Denken religiös werden." See
          Philosophy, no. 2635 above.

3117   SCHÜTZ, ROLAND. "Albert Schweitzers Christentum und
          theologische Forschung." RUNDBRIEF 9 (Jan. 1, 1956),
          pp. 12–29. Reprinted in: DOKUMENTE, pp. 282–97.

3118   SCHUSTER, HERMANN. "Die konsequente Eschatologie in der
          Interpretation des Neuen Testaments, kritisch betrachtet."
          Zeitschrift für die Neutestamentliche Wissenchaft (Giessen)
          47 (1956), pp. 1–25.

3119   _____. "Zeitgemässe Theologie." Die Christliche Welt (Gotha)
          50:10 (May 23, 1945), pp. 454ff.

3120   SCHWEITZER, WOLFGANG. "Und Jesus kam nicht wieder. . . ."
          Die Zeichen der Zeit (Berlin) 10:7 (1956), pp. 241–46.

Theology and Religion

3121　"Schweitzer and religious freedom." The Modern Churchman
　　　　(Oxford) 38:2 (June 1948), pp. 84-85.

3122　**"Schweitzer-Schjelderup og kristendommen." Vårt Land (Oslo),
　　　　March 5, 1957.

3123　"Schweitzer's confessio fidei." The Modern Churchman
　　　　(Oxford) 40:4 (Dec. 1950), pp. 342-44.

3124　SEVENSTER, J. N. "Schweitzer als Nieuwtestamenticus."
　　　　Theologie en Practijk (Lochem) 10:5/6 (May-June 1950),
　　　　pp. 96-104.

3125　SIEGFRIED, KARLA. "Um Albert Schweitzer" (about his Unitar-
　　　　ian membership). Freies Christentum (Frankfurt a.M.)
　　　　14:2 (Feb. 1, 1962), cols. 22-23.

3126　SILBERMAN, L. H. "Apocalyptic revisited: reflections on
　　　　the thought of Albert Schweitzer." American Academy of
　　　　Religion Journal (Missoula, Mont.) 44:3 (Sept. 1976),
　　　　pp. 489-501. Paper read in a slightly different form at
　　　　Chandler School of Theology, Emory University, during the
　　　　celebration of the centenary of Albert Schweitzer's birth,
　　　　April 1975.

3127　SLENCZKA, REINHARD. "Albert Schweitzer's 'Geschichte der
　　　　Leben-Jesu Forschung.'" In: Geschichtlichkeit und
　　　　Personsein Jesu Christi. Göttingen: Vandenhoek and
　　　　Ruprecht, 1967, pp. 26-33. (Forschungen zur system-
　　　　atischen und ökumenischen Theologie, Bd. 18.)

3128　SPEAR, OTTO. "Reich Gottes und Christentum--und Judentum.
　　　　Schweitzer und Buber." RUNDBRIEF 45 (May 1978), pp. 41-46.

3129　SPIEGELBERG, HERBERT. "Albert Schweitzer and Quakerism."
　　　　Friends Journal (Philadelphia) 21:3 (Feb. 1, 1975),
　　　　pp. 70-71.

3130　STREGE, MARTIN. "Albert Schweitzers Bedeutung für
　　　　Weltanschauung, Theologie und Kirche." RUNDBRIEF 26
　　　　(June 15, 1965), pp. 41-44. Reprinted in RUNDBRIEF 33
　　　　(Oct. 10, 1970), pp. 41-43.

3131　_____. "Albert Schweitzers Ruf zum 'Reich Gottes.'"
　　　　Freies Christentum (Frankfurt a.M.) 3:9 (Sept. 1, 1951),
　　　　cols. 1-2.

3132　_____. "Die Bedeutung der 'konsequenten Eschatologie' Albert
　　　　Schweitzers für die Theologie." Pfälzisches Pfarrerblatt
　　　　(Essingen) 44:3 (1953), pp. 11-14.

3133 SZYLKARSKI, WLADIMIR. "Albert Schweitzer und die Leben-Jesu
         Forschung." In: KDA: Blätter der deutschen Katholischen
         Akademikerschaft (Cologne) 2:2 (1950-51), pp. 18-19.

3134 THIELICKE, HELMUT. "Verehrt, verleumdet, verherrlicht.
         Albert Schweitzer wird heute 90 Jahre alt." Die Welt
         (Hamburg) 11 (Jan. 14, 1965), p. 3. Port. Reprinted in:
         BEGEGNUNG, pp. 275-81; reprinted in: RUNDBRIEF 40 (1975),
         p. 18f.

3135 THISELTON, ANTHONY C. "Biblical Classics, Part 6:
         Schweitzer's interpretation of Paul." Expository Times
         (Edinburgh) 90 (Feb. 1979), pp. 132-37.

3136 TISSERANT, EUGÈNE. "Miséricorde chrétienne." In: MISÉRICORDE,
         pp. 399-400. Translated as "Christliche Barmherzigkeit."
         In: SCHWEITZER, pp. 79-80.

3137 TROCMÉ, ETIENNE. "Albert Schweitzer et la vie Jésus."
         REVUE 56:1-2 (1976), pp. 28-36.

3138 TRUMPP, JULIUS. "Zum Boycott Albert Schweitzers."
         Süddeutsche Zeitung (Munich) 171 (July 18/19, 1951),
         unnumbered pp.

3139 TWINN, KENNETH. "Die Unitarier und Dr. Albert Schweitzer."
         Freies Christentum (Frankfurt a.M.) 14:7 (July 1, 1962),
         cols. 80-81.

3140 VAN DER LOOS, H. "Schweitzers eschatologische visie op het
         Nieuwe Testament." Theologie en Practijk (Lochem) 10:5/6
         (May-June 1950), pp. 81-96.

3141 VAN DER MEIDEN, ANNE. "Gathering People." In: DEVENTER,
         pp. 51-57. Summaries in French, German and Dutch.

3142 VAN LEEUWEN, A. TH. "Onopgeloste problemen der eschatologie.
         I: Van Albert Schweitzer tot Oscar Cullman." Nederlands
         Theologisch Tijdschrift (Wageninen, Netherlands) 5
         (1950/51), pp. 65-77.

3143 VERHEUS, S. L. "Albert Schweitzer de man van Lambarene.
         Lijden stond ook in zijn theologisch denken centraal."
         Algemeen Handelsblad (Amsterdam), Sept. 6, 1965, p. 12.

3144 VOGELSANGER, PETER. "Albert Schweitzer als Theologe."
         Reformatio (Zürich) 4:1 (Jan. 1955), pp. 8-20.

Theology and Religion

3145   WARNER, T. E. "Professor Dodd and Albert Schweitzer." The
        Modern Churchman (Oxford) 29:8 (Nov. 1939), p. 462.

3146   WEBER, A. E. "Die Mystik des Apostels Paulus, 1930."
        Theologisches Literaturblatt (Leipzig) 51:26
        (Dec. 19, 1930), cols. 403-07.

3147   WEINEL, HEINRICH. "Ist unsere Verkündigung von Jesus
        unhaltbar geworden?" Zeitschrift für Theologie und Kirche
        (Tübingen) 20:1 (1910), pp. 1-38; 20:2 (1910), pp. 89-129.

3148   WEINEL, HEINRICH. "Kommt das Heil von der Mystik?" Die
        Christliche Welt (Gotha) 49:10 (May 18, 1935), cols. 457ff.

3149   WELLE, IVAR. "Schweitzers theologi og filosofi." Fast Grun
        (Bergen, Norway) 7:1 (1954), pp. 23-31.

        W., M. (MARTIN WERNER). "Albert Schweitzer in theologisch-
        philosophischen Geistesleben." See Philosophy, no. 2688
        above.

3150   WERNER, MARTIN. "Albert Schweitzers Antwort auf die Frage
        nach dem historischen Jesus." In: EHRFURCHT, pp. 13-20.
        Reprinted in Neue Zürcher Zeitung 58 (Jan. 9, 1955), p. 4;
        translated as "The answer of Albert Schweitzer to the
        search for the historical Jesus." In: FESTSCHRIFT,
        pp. 104-13.

3151   _____. "Albert Schweitzer Beitrag zur Frage nach dem
        historischen Jesus." In: DENKEN UND WEG, pp. 135-44.

3152   _____. "Die Bedeutung der Theologie Albert Schweitzers für
        den christlichen Glauben." In: Werner, Martin. Glaube
        und Aberglaube. Aufsätze und Vorträge. Gesammelt aus
        Anlass seines 70. Geburtstages. Bern, Stuttgart: Paul
        Haupt, 1957, pp. 7-9, 96-114.

3153   _____. "Die heutige Entwicklung der liberalen Theologie."
        Schweizerische Theologische Umschau (Bern) 25:3/4
        (July 1955), pp. 49-60.

3154   _____. "Die religiöse Botschaft Albert Schweitzers."
        Schweizerische Theologische Umschau (Bern) 25:1
        (Feb. 1955), pp. 12-16.

3155   WERNLE, PAUL. "Schweitzer. Von Reimarus zu Wrede."
        Theologische Literaturzeitung (Leipzig) 31:18
        (Sept. 1, 1906), cols. 501-06.

3156   WIEFEL, WOLFGANG. "Albert Schweitzers Eintritt in die
       neutestamentliche Wissenschaft." Wissenschaftliche
       Zeitschrift der Martin Luther-Universität Halle-Wittenberg.
       Gesellschafts- und Sprachwissenschaftliche Reihe (Halle/
       Saale) 21:3 (1972), pp. 91-100.

3157   WILDER, AMOS. "Albert Schweitzer and the New Testament in the
       perspective of today." In: REALMS, pp. 348-62.

3158   _____. Eschatology and Ethics in the Teachings of Jesus.
       New York: Harper and Brothers, 1939, pp. 28-33 ff., 41,
       222, 225, 241.

3159   WINKLER, ROBERT. "Eschatologie und Mystik; zur Auseinder-
       setzung mit Albert Schweitzer und Hans Emil Weber."
       Zeitschrift für Theologie und Kirche (Tübingen) 12:2
       (1931), pp. 147-63.

3160   WOLFF, J. "Kann das Christentum 'entmythologisiert'
       werden?" Schweizerische Theologische Umschau (Bern)
       25:5 (Sept. 1955), pp. 97-115. For a letter to the
       editor in reply, see Marti, P. "Zur Frage der
       entmythologisierung." Schweizerische Theologische Umschau
       (Bern) 25:6 (Dec. 1955), pp. 132-39.

3161   WOOD, HERBERT G. "Albert Schweitzer and eschatology." The
       Expository Times (Edinburgh) 65:7 (April 1954), pp. 206-09.

B.   Sermons by Schweitzer

1. Collections

STRASSBURGER PREDIGTEN
(Reverence for Life)

Schweitzer was active as a preacher for many years. He began preaching in 1898 as a substitute for his father at Günsbach. From 1899-
1913, and again from 1918-1921, he was active at St. Nicolai in
Strasbourg. He said of his preaching: ". . . to me preaching was
a necessity of my being. I felt it as something wonderful that I
was allowed to address a congregation every Sunday about the deepest
questions of life."[1]

----

[1]Out of My Life and Thought. New York: Holt, Rinehart and Winston,
1961, p. 25.

Theology and Religion

This volume consists of seventeen of Schweitzers finished sermons
from the period 1900-1919. They were selected to give an all-around
impression of Schweitzer as a preacher, and to show his development
over this period. The sermons included are as follows:

Dritte Predigt über die Seligspreisungen. May 24, 1900.
Passions predigt über den Sinn des Todes Jesu. February 23, 1902.
Die Rückkehr der Siebzig. May 11, 1902.
Predigt auf Sonntag nach Ostern. April 24, 1904.
Predigt zum Erntedankfest über die Dankarbeit gegen Gott.
   November 20, 1904.
Adventspredigt. December 18, 1904.
Predigt zum Missionsfest. January 6, 1905.
Jesus auf dem Meere Wandelnd. November 19, 1905.
Zum Totengedächtnis. November 17, 1907.
Ein Wort an die Neukonfirmierten. April 4, 1909.
Letzte Nachmittagspredigt über die Treue. February 25, 1912.
Letzte Predigt vor der Abreise nach Lambarene. March 9, 1913.
Erste Predigt nach der Rückkehr von Lambarene und aus dem Lager
   von St. Remy de Provence. October 13, 1918.
Zum Gedächtnis der Totens des Weltkrieges. December 1, 1918.
Erste Predigt über die Ehrfurcht vor dem Leben. February 16,
   1919.
Zweite Predigt über die ethischen Probleme und die Ehrfurcht
   vor dem Leben. February 23, 1919.
Doppelpredigt über die Dankarbeit. July 27, 1919.

3162   Strassburger Predigten. Hrsg. von Ulrich Neuenschwander.
      Munich: C. H. Beck; Bern: P. Haupt, 1966. 168 pp.
      Nachwort der Herausgebers, "Albert Schweitzer als
      Prediger," pp. 159-69.

Dutch

3163   Strasburger Preken. Kampen, Holland: Kok. IN PREPARATION.

English

3164   Reverence for Life. Tr. Reginald H. Fuller. New York:
      Harper and Row, 1969. 153 pp. Includes Ulrich
      Neuenschwander's postscript "Albert Schweitzer as
      preacher," pp. 143-53. Reprinted New York: Pilgrim
      Press, 1980.

3165   Same. London: Society for Propagation of Christian Knowledge,
      1970. 153 pp.

Sermons by Schweitzer

French

3166 Vivre, dix Huit Sermons. Tr. Madeleine Horst. Préface de
         Georges Marchal (pasteur). Postface d'Ulrich
         Neuenschwander. Paris: Albin Michel, 1970. 229 pp.

Japanese

3167 Kokoru wa Yûhi yorimo Akaruku; Strassburg Sekkyôshû. Tr. Shin
         Aizu. Tokyo: Shinkyô Shuppansha, 1967. 218 pp.

3168 Schweitzer chosaku shû. Tokyo: Hakusuisha, 1972. 470 pp.
         (Bound with Reich Gottes und Christentum).

Norwegian

3169 Ord i Takknemlight. Utg. av Ulrich Neuenschwander. Tr.
         Johann B. Hygen. Oslo: H. Aschehoug (W. Nygaard), 1967.
         148 pp.

WAS SOLLEN WIR TUN?

This collection, published after Schweitzer's death, contains twelve
sermons on ethical problems preached at St. Nicolai, Strasbourg, from
February to August 1919. Before the First World War, in Africa,
Schweitzer had been working on his massive Philosophy of Civilization.
During his subsequent internment as a prisoner of war, and upon his
return to Günsbach, he did not have this manuscript available to work
on. He was still engaged, however, in trying to work out the ethical
aspects of life. He was studying to what extent ethics was accepted
or rejected by the major religions of the world, leading to a "full
confirmation of [his] view that civilization is based upon ethical
acceptance of the world."[1] In 1920, shortly after these sermons were
delivered, he delivered his series of lectures in Uppsala, in which
he coalesced the thoughts "which [he] had been carrying about with
[him] for five years. In the last lecture . . . [he] developed the
fundamental ideas of the ethic of Reverence for Life."[2]

These sermons on ethical problems, then serve as a valuable
reflection of the direction of Schweitzer's thinking during this

---

[1] Out of My Life and Thought. New York: Holt, Rinehart and Winston,
1972, p. 182. (Holt paperback.)

[2] Ibid., p. 185.

Theology and Religion

crucial time of his life. Three of the texts had appeared earlier
in Strassburger Predigten (see no. 3162 above.) The others were put
together from manuscripts in the possession of friends and coworkers.
The sermons included are as follows:

Erste Predigt über die moralischen Probleme. February 16, 1919.
2. Predigt über ethische Probleme. February 23, 1919.
III Predigt über ethische Probleme. March 2, 1919.
IV Predigt über ethische Probleme. March 16, 1919.
5te Predigt über ethische Probleme. March 30, 1919.
6te Predigt über ethische Probleme. May 3, 1919.
VII^{te} Predigt über ethische Probleme (Über den Besitz).
   May 11, 1919.
VIII^{te} Predigt über ethische Probleme. 2te Predigt über Besitz.
   May 25, 1919.
IX^{te} Predigt über ethische Probleme. 3te Predigt über Besitz.
   June 1, 1919.
X^{te} Predigt über ethische Probleme. June 15, 1919.
Predigt über ethische Probleme. July 1919.
Ethische Predigten. Dankarbeit I and II. July 27 and
   August 17, 1919.

3170   Was Sollen wir tun?   12 Predigten über ethische Probleme.
          Aus dem Nachlass hrsg. von Martin Strege und Lothar
          Stiehm. Nachwort Martin Strege. Heidelberg:
          L. Schneider, 1974. 192 pp.

Chinese

3171   [Was sollen wir tun?] Tr. Cheng Hsuan. Taiwan: Evergreen
          Cultural Enterprise, 1974. 120 pp.

Japanese

3172   Warera nani o Nasubekika? Tokyo: Shinkyo Shuppansha. 184 pp.

Norwegian

3173   Hva kan vi gjøre? Tr. Johan B. Hygen. Oslo: H. Aschehoug,
          1975. 123 pp.

2. Inclusion in Periodicals and Books by Others

Due to the fact that many of the sermons listed are not dated, no
attempt has been made to put all versions or excerpts of the same
sermon together. Entries are merely listed alphabetically by title.

Theology and Religion

3174   "The call to mission." Sermon preached at St. Nicolai,
          Jan. 6, 1905. Excerpted in: MARSHALL AND POLING, p. 58.
          Also excerpted in: BRABAZON, pp. 160-61.

3175   "Derriere la Charrue" (extract of a sermon, Dec. 18, 1904).
          In: RAYONNEMENT, pp. 25-26. Reprinted from Vivre dix
          huit Sermons, no. 3166 above. Excerpts of same appeared
          in CAHIERS 22 (Dec. 1969), pp. 3-4.

3176   "Eerbied voor het leven. Uit een preek van Schweitzer op 23
          Februari 1919." NIEUWS 19:2 (Dec. 1970), pp. 34-35.
          Excerpts from the same sermon, with the same title,
          appeared in NIEUWS 21:1 (May 1972), p. 12.

3177   "L'engant sur le pont" (extract from a sermon, Nov. 17, 1907).
          In: RAYONNEMENT, pp. 27-28. Reproduced from Vivre dix
          huit Sermons, no. 3166 above.

3178   Excerpts from a sermon preached at St. Nicolai, Nov. 19, 1905.
          In: BRABAZON, pp. 176-77.

3179   "En expiation des violences" (extracts of a sermon, Jan. 6,
          1905). NOUVELLES 35 (Sept. 1974), pp. 17-19.

3180   "Forgiveness," a sermon. The Christian World Pulpit
          (London) Nov. 1, 1934, p. 11.

3181   "Gottesdienst im Spital zu Lambarene." FAMILIEN-KALENDAR 38
          (1931), pp. 79-81. Also issued as a 7-page offprint.
          Reprinted in RUNDBRIEF 9 (Jan. 1, 1956); reprinted in:
          DOKUMENTE, pp. 308-12; translated as "Un culte du dimanche
          en forêt vierge." Les Cahiers Protestants (Strasbourg-
          Neudorf) 15:2 (March 1931), pp. 122-28; Also issued as a
          7-page offprint by Imprimerie Wilch, Strasbourg-Neudorf;
          translated as "Sunday at Lambarene." The Christian Century
          (Chicago) 48:11 (March 18, 1931), pp. 373-76; reprinted
          in: Fey, Harold E. and Margaret Firkes, eds. The Chris-
          tian Century Reader. New York: Associated Press, 1962,
          pp. 359-65; same, translated by Mrs. C. E. B. Russell in
          The Spectator (London) 146:5362 (April 4, 1931), pp. 540-
          41; translation from the French entitled "A sermon by
          Schweitzer." The Friends Intelligencer (Philadelphia)
          112:3 (Jan. 15, 1955), p. 33.

3182   "Jesus der Herr" (sermon preached at St. Nicolai, Strassburg,
          May 27, 1906). In: Picht, Werner. Albert Schweitzer:
          Wesen und Bedeutung, see no. 290 above, pp. 288f (German
          edition); translated as "Jesus the Lord," pp. 257-60
          (English edition).

Theology and Religion

3183   "Meditation sur la mort" (sermon, Nov. 17, 1907). CAHIERS
           23 (June 1970), pp. 3-6.

3184   "On immortality" (Sunday sermon, Nov. 17, 1907, morning
           service at St. Nicolai, Strasbourg, France). Boston:
           Church of the Larger Fellowship, 196-. 4 pp. Part of
           the Church of the Larger Fellowship sermon series.

3185   "The one-talent people" (sermon of the month). The Christian
           Herald (New York) 72:9 (Sept. 1949), p. 24.

3186   "'Pardonner sept fois,' sermon preche à nois noirs par le
           Docteur Albert Schweitzer." Cahiers Alsaciens et Lorraine
           (Strasbourg) 6:5 (May 1931), pp. 74-76. Text of a sermon
           preached at Lambarene.

3187   "Paulus der Befreier" (sermon preached at St. Nicolai,
           Strasbourg, 1906). In: Picht, Werner. Albert Schweitzer:
           Wesen und Bedeutung, see no. 290 above. Translated as
           "Paul the Liberator" in the American edition of same,
           pp. 260-64.

3188   "Predigt auf den Sonntag-Morgen vor Wiehnachten 1909.
           St. Nicolai/Sermon prononcé à l'église Saint Nicolas
           en 1909, le dimanche matin avant noël." REVUE 56:1/2
           (1976), pp. 194-201. German, with French translation
           by Madeleine Horst.

3189   "Ein Predigt über das Verziehen." Seelsorger (Vienna) 29
           (58-59), pp. 181-82.

3190   "La Retour des Soixante dix. Sermon prononcé 11. mai, 1902,
           à l'église Sainte-Nicolas de Strasbourg." CAHIERS 19
           (June 1968), pp. 5-6.

3191   "Un Sermon du Dr. Schweitzer." Notre Chemin (Lyon) 48:2
           (Feb. 1958), p. 1.

3192   "Un Sermon du Docteur Schweitzer à Lambaréné." NOUVELLES 4
           (June 1958), pp. 3-4. Illus.

3193   "Sermon prononcé après pâques le dimanche 24 avril 1904 à
           l'église Saint-Nicolas de Strasbourg." NOUVELLES 30
           (Jan. 1969), pp. 3-8.

3194   "Sermon sur les colonies, prononcé le dimanche 6 janvier 1905,
           à l'église St. Nicolas de Strasbourg." CAHIERS 20
           (Dec. 1968), pp. 3-6.

3195   "Sur la fidélité" (extrait du sermon du 25-11-1912). CAHIERS
        24 (Winter 1970-71), pp. 6-8.

3196   "Ter nagedachtenis aan de doden uit de wereldoorlog. Preek
        van Albert Schweitzer." NIEUWS 19:1 (June 1970), pp. 14-15.

3197   "The tornado and the spirit." A sermon by Albert Schweitzer,
        recorded at Lambarene, translated by Charles R. Joy. The
        Christian Register (Boston) 126:8 (Sept. 1947), p. 328.
        Reprinted in: Skillings, Everett. "Experiencing Albert
        Schweitzer." Religion in Life (New York) 17:3
        (Summer 1948), pp. 432-33; translated as "Eine Predigt
        Albert Schweitzers. Der Sturm und der Geist."
        Schweizerisches Reformiertes Volksblatt (Basel) 82:1
        (Jan. 3, 1948), pp. 3-4.

3198   Zwei Predigten. Erlautert von Takashi Oshio. Tokyo:
        Ikubundo, 1957. 34 pp.

3. Articles About Schweitzer as a Preacher

3199   BURI, FRITZ. "Albert Schweitzers Theologie in seinen
        Predigten" (Vorträge Tübingen, Jan. 1975, Strasbourg,
        May 1975). Theologia Practica (Bielefeld) 10:4 (1975),
        pp. 224-36. Strasbourg speech appears as "La Théologie
        d'Albert Schweitzer dans ses Predications." REVUE 56:1/2
        (1976), pp. 68-82.

3200   HORST, MADELEINE. "La presbytère du quai Saint-Nicholas."
        In: RAYONNEMENT, pp. 176-78.

3201   HORST, PAUL-LOUIS. "Le prédicateur." In: RAYONNEMENT,
        pp. 173-76.

3202   JENSSEN, HANS HEINRICH. "Albert Schweitzer--ein engagierter
        Prediger." Standpunkt: Evangelische Monatsschrift
        (Berlin) 3:1 (Jan. 1975), pp. 16-18.

3203   MARCHAL, GEORGES. "Preface d'un nouveau livre d'Albert
        Schweitzer 'Vivre.'" CAHIERS 24 (Winter 1970/71),
        pp. 3-5. From his preface to Vivre dix huit Sermons,
        see no. 3166 above.

3204   NEUENSCHWANDER, ULRICH. "Albert Schweitzer als Prediger."
        BERICHTE 33 (Sept. 1971), pp. 19-21.

3205   _____. "Bei Albert Schweitzer in der Predigt." BERICHTE 34
        (Aug. 1972), pp. 21-23.

Theology and Religion

3206　_____. "Nachwort des Herausgebers--Albert Schweitzer als
　　　Prediger." In: Strassburger Predigten, see no. 3162
　　　above, pp. 159-69.

3207　PETER, RODOLPHE. "Un Sermon inedit d'Albert Schweitzer."
　　　REVUE 56:1/2 (1976), pp. 186-92.

3208　WARTENWEILER, FRITZ. "Ein wenig bekannte Seite in Schweitzers
　　　Wirken:　als Seelsorger an St. Nicolai in Strassburg 1901-
　　　1913." In:　EHRFURCHT, pp. 104-14.

3209　WOYTT, GUSTAV. "Ein Zeugnis christlicher Humanität.　Albert
　　　Schweitzers Predigt zum Gedächtnis der Toten des ersten
　　　Weltkrieges in der Kirche St. Nicolai in Strasbourg."
　　　RUNDBRIEF 44 (Nov. 1977), pp. 50-53.

VIII. Music

A. General

1. Writings by Schweitzer

    a. Anthology

3210   <u>Music in the Life of Albert Schweitzer</u>, with selections from
his writings. By Charles R. Joy. New York: Harper and
Brothers; Boston: The Beacon Press, 1951. xvii, 300 pp.
Illus. Contains excerpts from <u>J. S. Bach le musicien-
poète</u>; Die Reform unseres Orgelbaues; Warum es so schwer
ist in Paris einen guten Chor zusammensobringen; Souvenirs
et Appreciations (M. J. Erb); Souvenirs d'Ernest Munch;
Zur Geschichte des Kirchenchors zu St. Wilhelm; <u>Eugene
Munch</u>; Mes Souvenirs sur Cosima Wagner; Der Runde
Violinbogen; Zur Reform des Orgelbaues; Questionnaire
on Organ Construction; <u>Deutsche und Französische
Orgelbaukunst und Orgelkunst</u>; Siegfried Ochs; The 1927
Epilogue (to <u>Deutsche und Französische Orgelbaukunst und
Orgelkunst</u>).

        Same. Freeport, N.Y.: Books for Libraries Press, 1971.
300 pp. Illus. (Essay Index Reprint Series.)

        (First British edition). London: Adam and Charles Black,
1953. xvi, 279 pp. Port., illus.

    b. Eugène Munch

Albert Schweitzer's first published work was a memorial tribute to
his first music master, Eugène Munch, organist of St. Stephen's
Reformed Church in Mülhausen, Alsace, who died in the prime of his
life. To the influence of this young musician and Bach scholar may
be traced Albert Schweitzer's lifelong devotion to the music of Bach.
In his tribute he acknowledges his debt to his teacher for the organ
instruction he had enjoyed with him from his fifteenth year and for
his acquaintance with the works of Bach at an early age. He writes:
"When in the autumn of 1898 he died of typhoid fever in the flower
of his age, I perpetuated his memory in a small booklet written in

317

Music

French. It was published in Mülhausen, and was the first product of my pen to appear in print."[1]

3211 <u>Eugène Munch, 1857-1895</u>. Mülhausen: Imprimerie J. Brinkmann, 1898, pp. (3)-28. In French. Signed "A. S." Albert Schweitzer's tribute is the first of three memorials to Eugène Munch in this brochure, the two following being "Discours de Mr. le Pasteur Stricker" (pp. 28-31), and "Discours de Monsieur J. B. Kirchner" (pp. 32-33). For English and German translations, and a reprint, see nos. 3210, 3214, 3221.

   c. Shorter Writings

3212 Albert Schweitzer évoque un musicien. "Tel était Marie-Joseph Erb." CAHIERS 22 (Dec. 1969), pp. 11-14.

3213 "Erinnerungen an Cosima und Siegfried Wagner. . . ." <u>Bayreuther Festspiele 1955</u>, "Der Fliegende Hollander." Program, German/English/French. Hrsg. von der Festspielleitung. Bayreuth: Verlag der Festspielleitung, 1955, pp. 4-16.

3214 "Eugene Munch." RUNDBRIEF 37 (1973).

3215 Anonymous translation of JAËLL, MARIE. <u>Le Toucher. Ensiegnement du piano basé sur la physiologie</u>. Vol. 1. Paris, 1895. German edition entitled <u>Neues Klavierstudium auf physiologischer Grundlage</u>. Leipzig, 1902.

3216 "Mes souvenirs sur Cosima Wagner." <u>L'Alsace Française</u> (Strasbourg) 13:7 (Feb. 12, 1933), pp. 124-25.

3217 "Professor Ernst Münch und die Elsassische Kirche." KIRCHENBOTE 49:33 (Aug. 14, 1920), p. 172.

3218 "Die Sängerin Aglaja Orgeni." <u>Münchner Neueste Nachrichten</u>, Sept. 11, 1931.

3219 Selections. In: Barth, Herbert. <u>Allgewalt Musik, Bekenntnisse von Musikern und Dichtern</u>. Ebenhausen bei München: Langewiesche-Brandt, 1953, pp. 12, 49-50, 191-93.

---

[1]<u>Out of My Life and Thought</u>. New York: Holt, Rinehart and Winston, 1961, p. 3.

3220 "Souvenirs d'Ernest Munch." In: Jung, Erik, ed. Le Choeur
de St. Guillaume de Strasbourg. Un chapitre de l'histoire
de la musique en Alsace. Documents récueilles et publies
par Erik Jung. Préface de Arthur Honneger. Strasbourg:
P. H. Heitz, 1947, pp. 51-62.

3221 "Souvenirs d'Eugène Munch." CAHIERS 4 (Dec. 1960), pp. 20-21.

3222 "Souvenirs et Appreciations." In: Un Grand Musicien Francais,
Marie-Joseph Erb, sa Vie et son Oeuvre. Strasbourg,
Paris: La Roux, 1948, pp. 83-88.

3223 "Theodor Gerholds 'Sängerfibel' und die Hebung des volkstüm-
lichen Chorgesangs." Elsass-Lothringische Gesang- und
Musikzeitung 10 (1909).

3224 "Warum es so schwer ist in Paris einen guten Chor zusammensobringen. Eine sozial-musikalische Studie." Die Musik
(Berlin and Leipzig) 36:4 (July 1910), pp. 23-30.

3225 "Zur Geschichte des Kirchenchors zu St. Wilhelm." In: Jung,
Erik, ed. Le Choeur de St.- Guillaume de Strasbourg. Un
Chapitre de l'histoire de la musique en Alsace. Documents
récueilles et publies par Erik Jung. Préface de Arthur
Honneger. Strasbourg: P. H. Heitz, 1947, pp. 13-17.

2. Works About Schweitzer by Other Authors

  a. Books

3226 JACOBI, ERWIN R. Albert Schweitzer und die Musik.
Jahresgabe der Internationalen Bachgesellschaft, 1975.
Wiesbaden: Breitkopf und Härtel, 1975.

3227 _____. "Die Konzerttätigkeit von Albert Schweitzer,
einschliesslich seiner Plattenaufnahemn und seiner
Vorträge." (Maschr. Ma.) 1976.

  b. Articles, Parts of Books

3228 "Albert Schweitzer als Musiker." Neue Zürcher Zeitung,
Sept. 10, 1965.

3229 "Albert Schweitzer de man van Lambarene. In zijn Orgelspel
was hij en 'bevrijder' van Bach." Algemeen Handelsblad
(Amsterdam), Sept. 6, 1965, p. 12. Port.

Music

3230   "Albert Schweitzer, organist, physician and thinker." The
       Times (London), Feb. 12, 1954, p. 6.

3231   "Albert Schweitzer und Max Drischner." Schlesische Rundschau
       (Wangen/Allgau) 7:7 (March 5, 1955), p. 5.

3232   BANGERT, EMILIUS. "Albert Schweitzer, der Musiker." In:
       WÜRDIGUNG, pp. 28-30. Translated as "Albert Schweitzer,
       de musicus." In: Albert Schweitzer, naar zijn waarde
       geschat. Vertaald door Mevr. A.D. W-Br. Deventer:
       A. E. Kluwer, 1934, pp. 35-37.

3233   _____. "Noble erindringer om Albert Schweitzer (I anledning
       af hans 60 aars. Fødelsdag den 14. Januar 1935)."
       Medlemsblad for Dansk Organist- of Kantorsamfund af 1905
       1:3 (Feb. 1935), pp. 25-38; 1:4 (April 1935), pp. 46-47,
       50-54; 1:5 (June 1935), pp. 66-70. Also issued as a
       15-page reprint: Slagelse, Sorø Amtstidende, 1935.

3234   BENDER, WILLIAM. "His lasting contribution to the world of
       music." New York Herald-Tribune, Sept. 6, 1965, p. 4.

3235   BLANKENBURG, WALTER. "Albert Schweitzer zum Gedächtnis."
       Die Musikforschung (Kassel and Basel) 19:1 (Jan./March
       1966), pp. 1-3. Port.

3236   BORLISH, HANS. "Der Musiker Albert Schweitzer." Standpunkt:
       Evangelische Monatsschrift (Berlin) 3:1 (Jan. 1975),
       pp. 20-22.

3237   BRINER, A. "Albert Schweitzer und die Musik." Musik und
       Gottesdienst (Zürich) 19:5 (1965), pp. 111-14.

3238   BROMAN, STEN. "Albert Schweitzer, 60ar" (Albert Schweitzer
       as musician). Sydsvenska Dagbladet Snällposten (Mälmo),
       Jan. 13, 1935.

3239   BÜLOW, PAUL. "Der Bayreuther Kulturkreis im Erlebnis Albert
       Schweitzers." Zeitschrift für Musik (Regensburg) 100:2
       (Feb. 1933), pp. 122-24.

3240   CHERNIAVSKY, DAVID. "Albert Schweitzer, the man and the
       musician." Etude (Philadelphia) 72:1 (Jan. 1954), p. 11.
       Port.

3241   DAVENPORT, MANUEL M. "The aesthetic foundation of
       Schweitzer's ethics." Southwestern Journal of Philosophy
       (Norman, Okla.) 5:1 (Spring 1974), pp. 39-46.

3242   DAVISON, ARCHIBALD T.   "The transcendentalism of Albert
         Schweitzer." In: JUBILEE, pp. 197-212.

3243   "Dr. Albert Schweitzer." Musical Opinion and Music Trade
         Review (London) 51:609 (June 1928), p. 912.

3244   EHLERS, ALICE. "Musical days with Albert Schweitzer." In:
         JUBILEE, pp. 227-38.

3245   ESCHRICHT, AUGUSTA. "Albert Schweitzer." Musik (Copenhagen)
         4:8 (Aug. 1, 1920), pp. 107-09.

3246   FESCHOTTE, JACQUES. "Albert Schweitzer et la musique."
         Journal Musical Francais, Journal des Jeunesses Musicales
         de France (Paris) 2:14 (Dec. 18, 1952), pp. 1, 8. Port.,
         illus.

3247   _____. "Albert Schweitzer et la musique." Musica (Paris) 55
         (Oct. 1958), pp. 2-5. Illus.

3248   _____. "Albert Schweitzer, servitor of music." In: REALMS,
         pp. 161-69.

3249   _____. Les Hauts-Lieux de la musique. Strasbourg: Istra;
         Paris: Société d'editions Francaises et Internationales,
         1950, pp. 114-17, 131, 132, 135.

3250   _____. "Le Musicien." In: ETUDES, pp. 225-28; second
         edition, pp. 190-218.

3251   _____ and ROBERT MINDER. "Albert Schweitzer et la musique en
         France." CAHIERS 4 (Dec. 1960), pp. 9-12.

3252   GODDARD, SCOTT. "Albert Schweitzer the musician." Peace News
         (London) 968 (Jan. 14, 1955), p. 5.

3253   HALÉVY, DANIEL. "L'ami des nègres et des orgues." In:
         Courrier d'Europe. Paris: Grasset, 1933, pp. 172-80.

3254   HERZ, GERHARD. "A statement" (Albert Schweitzer the musician).
         In: THE CONVOCATION RECORD, pp. III/11-14.

3255   _____. "Schweitzer the musician" and "Personal recollections."
         In: Hagemann, E. R., ed. Albert Schweitzer. Louisville,
         Ky.: University of Louisville, 1969.

3256   HINRICHSEN, MAX. "Schweitzer . . . music in Amberia" (the
         meeting of Albert Schweitzer and Pablo Casals in Zürich,
         Oct. 14, 1951). Music Book, Vol. VII of J. Hinrichsen's

Music

Musical Year Book (London, New York). Hinrichsen Edition
Limited, 1952, pp. 35-36.

3257 HULL, A. EAGLEFIELD. "A remarkable man: Dr. Albert
Schweitzer." Musical Opinion and Music Trade Review
(London) 45:535 (April 1922), pp. 616-17. Port.

3258 HUME, PAUL. "In celebration of Schweitzer the musician."
The Washington Post (Washington, D.C.), Jan. 12, 1975,
pp. G1, G4.

3259 JACOBI, ERWIN R. "Albert Schweitzer--der musiker."
Reformierte Schweiz 15:2 (Feb. 1958), pp. 87-89; 15:3
(March 1958), pp. 131-34. Later version in Schweizer
Musikpädogogische Blätter (Basel/Fribourg) 46:3
(July 1958), pp. 107-20; shortened version entitled "Der
Musiker Albert Schweitzer." Deutsche Zeitung und
Wirtsschafts Zeitung (Stuttgart) 55 (July 12, 1958),
p. 25; translated with title "Albert Schweitzer--
humusikai." Journal des Jeunesses Musicales d'Israel
(Tel Aviv) 3:3 (Jan. 1960), pp. 1-4.

3260 JACOBI, ERWIN R. "Albert Schweitzer 85 Jahre." Musica
(Kassel, Basel) 14:1 (Jan. 1960), pp. 44-45.

3261 _____. "Albert Schweitzer und Richard Wagner. Eine
Dokumentation." (Vortrag . . . gehalten auf Einladung
der Schweizerischen Richard Wagner-Gesellschaft in
Zürich am 20.2.1976). Tribschener Blätter, Zeitschrift
der Schweiz. Richard-Wagner Gesellschaft 41 (Dec. 1977),
pp. 1-17.

3262 _____. "Die Musik im Leben und Schaffen von Albert
Schweitzer" (Ansprache in Fraumünster Zürich am 28.1.1975).
Musik und Gottesdienst (Zürich) 29:1 (1975), pp. 2-15.
Reprinted RUNDBRIEFE/DDR 29 (1976), pp. 14-19; 30 (1977),
pp. 11-18; translated as "La musique dans la vie et
l'oeuvre d'Albert Schweitzer." REVUE 56:1-2 (1976),
pp. 154-73; reprinted in NOUVELLES 38 (Sept. 1976),
pp. 17-23; 39 (Jan. 1977), pp. 16-23; 40 (Sept. 1977),
pp. 17-22.

3263 _____. "Der musikalische Nachlass von Albert Schweitzer."
BERICHTE 38 (Sept. 1974), pp. 15-19. Reprinted in
RUNDBRIEF 40 (1975), pp. 87-92; reprinted in Der Bund
(Bern) Feuilleton, Aug. 3, 1975, p. 31.

3264 _____. "Schweitzer the musician" (lecture given at the
International Colloquium of UNESCO, June 12, 1975).

COURIER, Spring 1976, pp. 6-12. Translated as "Albert
Schweitzer musicien--son rayonnement sur notre temps."
Schweizerische Musikzeitung/Revue Musicale Suisse (Zürich)
116:3 (May-June 1976), pp. 179-82.

3265   JOSIMOVIC, R. "Svedocanstva o Schweitzeru." Zvuk;
jugoslovenska musicka revija (Beograd) 66 (1966),
pp. 15-25. Port.

3266   KLOTZ, HANS. "Albert Schweitzer und die Musik." Neue Zürcher
Zeitung 8 (Jan. 11/12, 1975), p. 52.

3267   LAUTERBERG, O. "Albert Schweitzer in Berner Oberland."
Musik und Gottesdienst (Zürich) 29:2 (1975), pp. 45-50.

3268   LAWSON, LUCIE CHENEVERT. "Albert Schweitzer was my teacher."
Edited by L. V. Brant. Etude (Philadelphia) 68:12
(Dec. 1950), pp. 13-15.

"The legacy of Albert Schweitzer." See Life and Work, no. 689
above.

MARCHAL, G. "La théologie et la musique d'Albert Schweitzer."
See Theology and Religion, no. 3047 above.

3269   MARTIN, HANS. "Der Musiker Albert Schweitzer." Die Gegenwart
(Freiburg i.B.) 1:14/15 (July 24, 1946), pp. 34-36.
Reprinted in part in: BEGEGNUNG, pp. 242-46.

3270   METZGER, HANS ARNOLD. "Erinnerung an Albert Schweitzer."
Musik und Kirche (Kassel) 35:5 (1965), pp. 225-27.

3271   MINDER, ROBERT. "Schweitzer, professeur de piano." In:
HOMMAGE, pp. 75-80. Reprinted in: BEGEGNUNG, pp. 143-50.

3272   _____. "Vue d'ensemble." In: RAYONNEMENT, pp. 95-113.
Excerpted as "A. Schweitzer et ses maîtres parisiens--
Widor, Jaëll, Philipp." CAHIERS 33 (Winter 1975),
pp. 17-21.

3273   MOREL, FRITZ. "Albert Schweitzer als Musiker." In: FESTGABE,
pp. 77-90. Reprinted as "Der Musiker Albert Schweitzer."
Musik und Gottesdienst (Zürich) 13:3 (May/June 1959),
pp. 65-76; reprinted in: SCHWEITZER, pp. 117-29.

3274   MOSIMANN, P. "Albert Schweitzer und die Musik." BERICHTE
36 (Sept. 1973), pp. 23-24.

Music

3275 "Der Musiker" (Albert Schweitzer). Sonntagsblatt, <u>Basler</u>
        <u>Nachrichten</u> (Basel) 49:2 (Jan. 16, 1955).

3276 RAICS, I. "Ismeretlen Schweitzer-level Muenchholz." <u>Musika</u>
        (Budapest) 12 (Aug. 1969), pp. 24-25.

3277 RANGEL, FELIX. "Souvenirs d'un musicien." CAHIERS 24
        (Winter 1970/71), pp. 14-15.

3278 ROLLAND, ROMAIN. "Une fête musicale en Alsace-Lorraine."
        <u>Revue de Paris</u> (Paris) 12:13 (July 1, 1905), pp. 134-52.
        Reprinted in his <u>Musiciens d'aujourd'hui</u>. Paris:
        Hachette et Cie, 1908, p. 178; translated as <u>Musicians</u>
        <u>of Today</u>. New York: Henry Holt, 1915, p. 210.

3279 SAINZ, HELGA. "Ma recontre musicale avec le Docteur
        Schweitzer." In: DEBRECEN, pp. 175-77.

3280 SCHRADE, LEO. "L'esthétique schweitzérienne dans ses rapports
        avec les théories de Wagner." In: RAYONNEMENT, pp. 119-20.

3281 "Schweitzer à Gunsbach." <u>L'Orgue</u> (Paris) 66 (Jan.-March 1953),
        pp. 17-19. Illus.

3282 "La scomparsa di Schweitzer e di varese." <u>Musica d'Oggi</u>
        (Milan) 8:8/10 (1965), pp. 248-49.

3283 SPIELER, H. "Musik und Menschlichkeit--zum 100. Geburtstag
        Albert Schweitzers." <u>Musik und Gesellschaft</u> (East Berlin)
        25 (Jan. 1975), pp. 40-41.

3284 STEINBERGER, HERMANN. "Albert Schweitzer und Richard Wagner."
        <u>Münchner Merkur</u> (Munich) 218 (Sept. 11, 1965), p. 4.

3285 STRICKER, NOÉMIE. "Albert Schweitzer et Pablo Casals."
        CAHIERS 30 (Spring 1974), pp. 13-17.

3286 TAGLIAVINI, LUIGI F. "In memoria di Albert Schweitzer."
        <u>Revista Italiana di Musicologia</u> (Firenze) 1:1 (1966),
        pp. 157-58.

3287 TURECK, ROSALYN. "Albert Schweitzer: in music, a new
        approach." <u>Saturday Review</u> (New York) 48:39
        (Sept. 25, 1965), pp. 23-24.

3288 URBAN, HERBERT. "Mitten in Erinnerungen an Albert Schweitzer.
        Zum 65. Geburtstag des Komponisten Max Drischner am 31.
        Januar 1956." <u>Schlesische Rundschau</u> (Wangen/Allgäu) 8:4
        (Feb. 5, 1956), p. 5.

3289   VALENTIN, ERICH.   "Der Musiker Albert Schweitzer. Ein Wort
           zu seinem 75. Geburtstag am 14. Januar." Zeitschrift für
           Musik (Regensburg) 111:2 (Jan. 1950), pp. 87-88.

3290   _____. "Praeceptor Hominum: Albert Schweitzers als Lehrer
           und Vorbild." Zeitschrift für Musik (Regensburg) 116:1
           (Jan. 1955), pp. 1-3. Port.

3291   VAN DER HORST, ANTHON.   "Albert Schweitzer. Gewone dingen
           uit het leven van een ongewone Mens." Het Parool
           (Amsterdam), Jan. 8, 1955. Port.

3292   VAN DER LEEUW, G.   "Albert Schweitzer, de muziek en not iets."
           Theologie en Practijk (Lochem) 10:5/6 (May/June 1950),
           pp. 121-22.

3293   V., C. (C. VEITS).   "Prof. Albert Schweitzer als Musiker."
           Deutsche Zeitung Bohemia (Prague) 96:4 (Jan. 6, 1923),
           p. 7.

3294   "Visita del Dr. Albert Schweitzer." Revista Musical Catalaña
           (Barcelona) 16:188-192 (Aug.-Dec. 1919), p. 231.

3295   WALSER, PAUL.   "Albert Schweitzer als Musiker." Sonntagspost
           (Winterthur, Switzerland) 65:2 (Jan. 13, 1945), p. 14.

3296   YSAYE, M. A.   "Albert Schweitzer musicien; une visite à
           Gunsbach." CAHIERS/BELGE 2 (Nov. 1961), pp. 9-13.

3297   ZERASCHI, H.   "Albert Schweitzer und sein Leipziger
           Musikverlag." Musik und Gesellschaft (East Berlin) 16
           (May 1966), pp. 315-20.

3298   "Zum 80. Geburtstag Albert Schweitzers." National-Zeitung
           (Basel) 20 (Jan. 13, 1955).

B.   Albert Schweitzer and Johann Sebastian Bach

1.   Writings by Schweitzer

a.   Books

J. S. BACH LE MUSICIEN-POÈTE

"While busy with the Quest of the Historical Jesus I finished a book
written in French on J. S. Bach. Widor, with whom I used to spend
several weeks in Paris every spring . . . had complained to me that

Music

there existed in French only biographical books about him, but none
that provided any introduction to his art. I had to promise that I
would spend the autumn vacation of 1902 in writing an essay on the
nature of Bach's art for the students of the Paris Conservatoire. . . .
At the end of the vacation I had, in spite of the most strenuous work,
not gotten further than the preliminary studies for the treatise. It
had also become clear that this would expand into a book on Bach.
With good courage I resigned myself to my fate.

"In 1903 and 1904 I devoted all my spare time to Bach. . . . In
the autumn of 1904 I was able to announce to Widor, who had spurred
me on and on again . . . that the undertaking was now so far advanced
that he must start upon the preface which he had promised me. This
he did at once. The book appeared in 1905. . . ."[1]

3299   <u>J. S. Bach le musicien-poète</u>. Avec la collaboration de
        M. Hubert Gillot. Préface de Ch. M. Widor. Leipzig:
        Breitkopf and Härtel; Paris: Costallat & Cie., 1905.
        xx, 455 pp., front. (port.), illus. (music). 2e tirage,
        1905; 3e tirage, 1913; 4e tirage, s.d. (1924?).

3300   Same. 5e tirage. Wiesbaden: Breitkopf & Härtel, 1950.
        xvi, 322 pp., front. (port.), illus. (music). 6e-7e tirage,
        1950. 8e tirage, 1967. 300 pp.

3301   Same. Lausanne: Maurice et Pierre Foetisch, 1951. xvi,
        322 pp., front. (port.), illus. (music). ("Publié avec
        l'authorisation de Breitkopf & Härtel à Wiesbaden.")
        The complete edition has also been produced on microfilm.
        Reprinted, 1953.

English

For sections of <u>J. S. Bach le musicien-poète</u> in English
translation, see <u>Music in the Life of Albert Schweitzer</u>,
no. 3210 above.

Italian

3302   <u>G. S. Bach. Il musicista poeta</u>. Pref. di C. M. Widor. Tr.
        P. A. Roversi. Milan: Suvini e Zerboni, 1952. 439 pp.,
        illus. (music), cover port. 2e edizioni, 1962, xv, 452 pp.

---

[1]<u>Out of My Life and Thought</u>. New York: Holt, Rinehart and Winston,
1972, pp. 60, 61, 63.

Spanish

3303   J. S. Bach, el músico poeta. Con la colaboración de M. Hubert
          Gillot . . . Prefacio de C. M. Widor. Traducción de Jorge
          D'Urbano. Buenos Aires: Ricordi Americana, 1955.
          379 pp., front. (port.), illus. (music). Illus. cover.
          Second edition, 1965.

J. S. BACH (1908)

"I was surprised and delighted that my work (J. S. Bach le musicien-
poète) met with recognition even in Germany as an enrichment of the
study of Bach, whereas I had written it merely to fill a gap in
French musical literature. In the Kunstwart von Lüpke raised the
question of a translation. Consequently in the autumn of that year,
1905, a German edition was agreed upon, to be published by Breitkopf
and Härtel.

"When in the summer of 1906 . . . I turned to work on the German
edition of Bach, I soon became conscious that it was impossible for
me to translate myself into another language, and that if I was to
produce anything satisfactory, I must plunge anew into the original
materials of my book. So I shut the French Bach with a bang, and
resolved to make a new and better German one. Out of the book of
455 pages there sprang, to the dismay of the astonished publisher,
one of 844. . . .

"The German edition appeared early in 1908, and is the text from
which the English translation was made by the clever pen of Ernest
Newman."[1]

3304   J. S. Bach. Vorrede von Charles Marie Widor. Leipzig:
          Breitkopf & Härtel, 1908. xvi, 844 pp., 3 pls. including
          front. (port.), illus. (music), 2 facsimilies (music).
          Reprinted 1915, 1920, 1921, 1922, 1928, 1929, 1930, 1934
          (xvi, 843 pp., 5 pls.), 1937, 1942, 1947, 1948 (6 pls.).

3305   Same. Leipzig: Breitkopf and Härtel, 1951. xvi, 791 pp.,
          6 pls. (including front.), illus. (music), 2 facsimilies
          (music). Reprinted 1952, 1954, 1955, 1957, 1958, 1959,
          1961, 1963, 1967, 1969 (some with Wiesbaden rather than
          Leipzig imprint). 8. Auflage, 1972. Dertiende Druk,
          1978. 924 pp.

---

[1]Out of My Life and Thought. New York: Holt, Rinehart and Winston,
1961, pp. 63-64.

Music

Danish

3306 J. S. Bach. Introduktion af Charles Marie Widor. Oversat og
          bearbejdet af Børge Friis. Copenhagen: Branner og Korch,
          1953. 276 pp., illus. (The text includes only the first
          part, the biography, of the original edition.)

English

3307 J. S. Bach. With a preface by C. M. Widor. English transla-
          tion by Ernest Newman. 2 vols. Leipzig and London:
          Breitkopf and Härtel, 1911. xiv, 428, 498 pp. (English
          translation from the German edition, with alterations and
          additions by the author.) Reissued, 1912.

3308 Same. 2 vols. London: A. and C. Black, 1923. xvi, 428,
          vii, 498 pp. Reissued 1935, 1938, 1945, 1947, 1949, 1950,
          1952, 1955, 1962. Issued also with the imprint of the
          Macmillan Company, New York, 1935.

3309 (Paperback edition). Replica of the British edition of 1923.
          2 vols. Boston: Bruce Humphries, 1964. xvi, 428, viii,
          498 pp.

3310 Same. 2 vols. New York: The Macmillan Company, 1950. xvi,
          428, vii, 498 pp. (Printed in Great Britain). Reprinted,
          1952.

3311 (Paperback). 2 vols. Boston: Branden, 1962.

3312 (Paperback edition). Unabridged republication of the 1911
          Breitkopf and Härtel edition. New York: Dover, 1966.
          2 vols., 428, 498 pp.

3313 Same. Magnolia, Mass.: Peter Smith, 1970.

Hebrew

3314 Johann Sebastian Bach (I, II). Tr. Yizhak Hirshberg. Tel
          Aviv: Idid, 1958. 836 pp.

Japanese

3315 Bach (I, II). Tr. Soichi Tsuji and Ginji Yamane. Tokyo:
          Iwanami Shoten, 1955, 1958. 431, 493 pp. (Part I con-
          tains chapters I-VI; Part II contains Chapters VII-XVIII
          of the original work.)

328

Music

Same. Tr. Masao Asai, Keiichi Uchigaki, and Yoshimu Sugiyama.
3 vols. Tokyo: Hakusuisha, 1957–58. See Collected Works,
nos. 12–14 above.

3316   Bach Kenkyu. Tr. Yosiyuki Yokoyama. Tokyo: Bach-Kyokai
Shuppanbu, 1933. 142 pp. (Contains Chapters I, VII and
XIV of J. S. Bach and the preface, "Einführung in des
Schaffen Bachs" from Klassiker der Tonkunst, no. 3328
below.)

3317   Bach no geijutsu. Tr. Shuichi Tsugawa. Tokyo: Shinko
Ongaku Shuppansha, 1942. 306 pp. (Includes Chapters
XIII through XVIII of J. S. Bach.)

3318   Bach no Shogai. Tr. Suichi Tsugawa. Tokyo: Hakusuisha,
1940. 314 pp. (Includes Chapters VII through XII of
J. S. Bach.) Reissued by Shinko Ongaku Shuppansha, 1942.
314 pp.

Polish

3319   Jan Sebastian Bach. Tr. M. Kurecka and W. Wirpsza. Pref.
C. M. Widor. Postowie Bohdan Pociej. Krakow: Polski
Wydawn. Muzyizne, 1963. 854 pp. Reprinted 1972, 856 pp.
Translation of the 1963 Breitkopf and Härtel edition.

Russian

3320   J. S. Bakh. Perevod Z. F. Savelovoi pod redaktziyei M. V.
Ivanova-Boretskovo. Moskva: Muzgiz, 1934. 16, 272 pp.
(Problemy Musykosnaniya, Istorichiskaya Bibliotcka.)
Predisloviye, Ivanova-Boretukovo, pp. 3–4.

3321   J. S. Bakh. Moscow: Ed. "La Musique," 1965. 725 pp.

PUBLISHED MUSIC BY JOHANN SEBASTIAN BACH
COMPLETE ORGAN WORKS

"That before starting for Africa I was busy again with Bach was due
to a request from Widor. The New York publisher, Mr. G. Schirmer,
had asked him to prepare an edition of Bach's organ music with direc-
tions about the best rendering of it, and he agreed to do so on condition that I shared the work. Our collaboration took the form of my
preparing rough drafts which we afterwards worked out together. . . .

. . . We considered our task to be that of showing to organists
acquainted with modern organs only and therefore strangers to the
organ style of Bach, what registration and what changes of keyboard

329

Music

had to be considered for any particular piece on the organs with which Bach had to reckon. . . . In matters of phrasing what Widor and I had to say is given to the player in the introduction.

"It was only the first five volumes of the new edition containing the Sonatas, the Concertos, the Preludes and the Fugues that we could complete before my departure for Africa. The three volumes containing the Choral Preludes we intended to complete during my first period of leave in Europe, on the foundation of rough drafts to be made by me in Africa.

"By the publisher's desire, the work was published in three languages. . . . Widor and I had agreed that in the French edition his ideas, which fitted better the peculiarities of the French organs, should be dominant, while in the German and the English mine should, taking, as they did, more into account the character of the modern organ. . . .

I have again and again been obliged to postpone the publication of the three volumes of Choral Preludes."[1]

In 1912, a small selection of "Eight Little Preludes and Fugues of the First Master Period" (no. 3325 below) and a series of single works selected from the Complete Organ Works of Bach (no. 3325 below) were edited and published by Widor and Albert Schweitzer. In 1954, the sixth volume of the original English edition of the Complete Organ Works ("Miscellaneous Compositions on the Chorale") was edited and published by Edouard Nies-Berger and Albert Schweitzer. Volumes 7 and 8, also done in collaboration with Nies-Berger, appeared in 1967, in English only.[2]

3322   Johann Sebastian Bach. Complete Organ Works. A critico-
        practical edition in eight volumes. Provided with a
        preface containing general observations on the manner of
        performing the preludes and fugues and suggestions for
        the interpretation of the compositions contained in each
        volume. By Charles Marie Widor, Professor in the Con-
        servatoire at Paris and Organist at the Church of St.
        Sulpice, and Dr. Albert Schweitzer, Privatdozent at
        Strassburg University and Organist for the Bachgesellschaft
        of Paris. Vols. I-V. Albert Schweitzer and Edouard

---

[1]Out of My Life and Thought. New York: Holt, Rinehart and Winston, 1961, pp. 130, 133.

[2]For an interesting account of the publication of these volumes, see Hans Heinsheimer's article, no. 3376 below.

Music

Nies-Berger, Vols. VI-VIII. New York: G. Schirmer, 1912-
1967. 8 vols.

Contents

I. Preludes and Fugues of the Youthful Period. 1912.
xxxix, 119 pp.
II. Preludes and Fugues of the First Master-Period. 1912.
xxv, 109 pp.
III. Preludes and Fugues of the Mature Master-Period,
Part 1. 1913. xxix, 114 pp.
IV. Preludes and Fugues of the Mature Master-Period,
Part 2. 1913. xxvi, 107 pp.
V. Organ Concertos and Organ Sonatas. 1913. iv, 147 pp.
VI. Miscellaneous Compositions on the Chorale. Edited by
Edouard Nies-Berger and Albert Schweitzer. 1954.
lxiii, 122 pp.
VII. The Orgelbüchlein--the Catechism Hymns. Edited by
Edouard Nies-Berger and Albert Schweitzer. 1967.
112 pp.
VIII. Schübler Chorales--Eighteen Chorales--Chorale
Variations. Edited by Edouard Nies-Berger and Albert
Schweitzer. 1967. 133 pp.

French

3323 Jean-Sébastien Bach. Oeuvres Complètes pour orgue. Édition
critique et practique en huit volumes. Précédée d'une
Préface contenant les observations générales sur l'inter-
prétation et l'analyse des compositions contenues dans
chaque volume par Charles Marie Widor . . . et Dr. Albert
Schweitzer. New York and London: G. Schirmer, 1914-1924.
3 vols.

German

3324 Johann Sebastian Bach. Sämmtliche Orgelwerke. Eine
kritischpraktische Ausgabe in acht Bänden mit einer
allgemeinen Vorrede zur Orientierung über die Prinzipien
der Ausführung der Praeludien und Fugen und mit Rat- und
Vorschlägen für die Wiedergabe jedes der in dem betraffende
Bände enthaltenen Stücke versehen von Charles-Marie
Widor . . . und Dr. Albert Schweitzer, 1914. 5 vols.

Selections

3325 Selected compositions from the Complete Organ Works edited by
Charles-Marie Widor and Albert Schweitzer, published by
G. Schirmer, New York, 1912, in separate format:

Music

    Eight Little Preludes and Fugues of the First Master
       Period. xii, 31 pp. (Schirmer's Library of Musical
       Classics, vol. 1456.)
    Prelude and Fugue in D Major. 18 pp.
    Prelude and Fugue in E Major (St. Anne's). v, 21 pp.
    Prelude and Fugue in E Minor (The Cathedral). iii, 5 pp.
    Prelude and Fugue in G Minor (The Great). vii, 15 pp.
    Prelude and Fugue in A Minor. 15 pp.
    Prelude in G Minor (The Little). 7 pp.
    Passacaglia and Thema Fugatum in C Minor. 19 pp.
    Toccata and Fugue in D Minor. 13 pp.
    Fugue in D Minor (The Giant). Later again edited by
       Edward Shippen Barnes, 1923. 9 pp.

  b. Writings by Schweitzer in Periodicals and Books by Others

    (1) Bach--General

3326   "A propos de Bach, le Musicien-Poète," une lettre d'Albert
       Schweitzer à Jacques Feschotte. La Revue Internationale
       de Musique (Paris) 10 (Spring/Summer 1951), pp. 418-20.
       Dated Lambarene, Jan. 4, 1951.

3327   "Albert Schweitzer kompozytor przy pracy" (excerpt from his
       book J. S. Bach le musicien-poète). Ruch Muzyczny
       (Warsaw) 9:20 (1965), pp. 3-4.

3328   "Einführung in das Schaffen Bachs." Introduction to a selec-
       tion of the best piano works of Bach. In: Klassiker der
       Tonkunst. Ausgabe ausgewählter Klavierwerke von J. S.
       Bach, edited by H. Neumayr. Vienna and Leipzig: Universal
       Edition A.G., 1929, pp. III-XIII.

3329   Excerpts from J. S. Bach le Musicien-Poète. In: Corredor,
       J. Ma. Conversations avec Pablo Casals. Paris: Albin
       Michel, 1955. Translated as Conversations with Pablo
       Casals. London: Hutchinson, 1956; New York: Dutton,
       1957; translated as Gespräche mit Casals. Bern: Scherz,
       1954; also as Conversaciones con Pablo Casals. Buenos
       Aires: Sudamericana, 1955; also as Casals. Hovory s
       Pablem Casalem. Prague: Státní Nakladatelství Krasné
       Literatury, Hubdy a Umění, 1958.

3330   "J. S. Bach als Tondichter." Kunstwart (Munich) 19:14
       (April 1906), pp. 60-64. (Excerpt from J. S. Bach le
       musicien-poète).

3331   "Johann Sebastian Bachs Künstlerpersönlichkeit." Die
       Musikwelt, Bach-Heft 9 (1921).

3332   "Juan Sebastian Bach" (Excerpt from <u>El Camino hacia ti Mismo</u>).
        <u>Psallite</u> (La Plata, Argentina) 24:93 (1975), pp. 18-19.

3333   Letter to Gustav Bret, c. 1908, in: Bret, Gustav. "Bach,
        Schweitzer et la Société J-S Bach de Paris." <u>Saisons</u>
        <u>d'Alsace</u> (Strasbourg) 2:2 (Spring 1930), p. 161.

3334   "O Wykonywaniu dziel Jana Sebastiano Bacha" (excerpt from
        J. S. Bach le musicien-poète). <u>Ruch Muzyczny</u> (Warsaw)
        7:1 (1963), pp. 1-2.

3335   "La passió segons Sant Mateu de Joan Sebastià Bach." <u>Revista</u>
        <u>Musical Catalaña</u> (Barcelona) 18:205-07 (Jan.-March 1921),
        pp. 1-14. Reprinted from concert program.

3336   "Schweitzer's views on correct tempos for works of Bach."
        <u>The Diapason</u> (Chicago) 41:12 (Nov. 1, 1950), p. 22.

3337   "Siegfried Ochs als Bachinterpret." Fest-Programm des
        Berliner Philharmonischen Chors, Dec. 5, 1932, pp. 11-13.

3338   "Sobre la personalitat y l'art de Bach." Conferencie donada
        al Palau de la Música Catalana pel Doctor Albert Schweitzer
        la nit del 21 d'octubre de 1908. <u>Revista Musical Catalaña</u>.
        Butlletí Mensual de l'Orfeó Català (Barcelona) 5:59
        (Nov. 1908), pp. 207-12; 5:60 (Dec. 1908), pp. 230-33.
        Reprinted as "Sobre la personalidad y el arte de J. S.
        Bach." <u>Universitas</u> (Spanish edition) 13:2 (Dec. 1975),
        pp. 145-62; translated as "Concerning the art and person-
        ality of J. S. Bach." <u>Universitas</u> (English Language edi-
        tion) 17:3 (1975), pp. 203-18. Also issued as a reprint.
        Most of a lecture given by Schweitzer in Barcelona, 1908;
        translated as "Von Bachs Persönlichkeit und Kunst."
        Mitgeteilt von Erwin R. Jacobi. RUNDBRIEF/DDR 31 (1977),
        pp. 10-18; 32 (1978), pp. 3-15.

3339   "Le Symbolisme de Bach" (excerpt from <u>J. S. Bach le musicien-</u>
        poète). <u>Musica</u> (Chaix) 140 (Nov. 1965), pp. 18-19.
        Reprinted in <u>Revue Germanique</u> (Paris) 1 (1905), pp. 69-81;
        translated as "Bachs Symbolismus." <u>Der Kunstwart</u> (Munich)
        20:22 (Aug. 1907), pp. 556-62.

3340   "Über die Wiedergabe der Präludien und Fugen für Orgel von
        J. S. Bach." Aus D. Arbeiten für Amerikan Ausgabe d.
        Orgelwerke Bachs von C. M. Widor and A. Schweitzer.
        <u>Die Orgel</u> 7 (1910). Reprinted Leipzig: Klinner, 1910
        (Kirchenmusikalisches Archive, Heft 7.) Reprinted Bremen:
        Lilienthal, 1976. 27 pp. (Eres Edition).

Music

3341   "Views and comments: Albert Schweitzer." In: Herz, Gerhard,
       ed. Bach, Johann Sebastian. Cantata No. 140: Wachtet
       auf, Ruft uns die Stimme. New York: W. W. Norton, 1972,
       pp. 159-61. Excerpts from J. S. Bach.

3342   "Von Bachs Tod bis zur ersten Wiederaufführung der
       Matthäuspassion. Eine Geschichte der Anfanges Bachkults."
       Die Musik (Berlin) 7:2 (1907/08), pp. 76-78.

3343   "Vorschläge zur Wiedergabe der Orgelpräludien und Orgelfugen
       J. S. Bach." Bremen, 1911. Kirchenmusikalisches Archiv,
       Vol. X.

3344   "Was ist mir Johann Sebastian Bach und was bedeutet er für
       unsere Zeit?" Die Musik (Berlin) 5:1 (1905/06), pp. 75-
       76. Translated as "Ce que signifie Bach pour moi et notre
       temps." In: RAYONNEMENT, pp. 29-30.

3345   with C. M. Widor. "Wie sind J. S. Bachs Präludien und Fugen
       auf unseren modernen Orgeln zu registrieren." Die Musik
       (Berlin) 10:2 (Zweites Oktoberheft 1910-11), pp. 67-80;
       10:3, pp. 143-57.

3346   "Zum 28. Juli, dem Todestage Bachs." Gegenwart (Berlin) 37:74,
       no. 31 (Aug. 1, 1908), pp. 74-76.

       (2) The Round Violin Bow

3347   "De l'archet à utiliser dans l'exécution des oeuvres pour
       violin seul de Bach." Part of a souvenir program entitled
       XIIe festival de Strasbourg, deuxiéme centenaire de la
       mort de Jean-Sébastien Bach, sous la présidence d'honneur
       du docteur Albert Schweitzer, 8-22 juin, 1950. Strasbourg,
       1950, pp. 110-14.

3348   "Die für Bachs Werke für Violine solo erforderte Geigenbogen."
       In: Matthae, Karl, ed. Bach-Gedenkschrift 1950, im
       auftrag der Internationalen Bach Gesellschaft. Zürich:
       Atlantis Verlag, 1950, pp. 75-83. Issued also as a
       9-page offprint. Translated by Edouard Nies-Berger as
       "Reconstructing the Bach violin bow." Musical America
       (New York) 70:8 (July 1950), pp. 5, 34.

3349   "Der Geigenbogen für polyphones Spiel. Zur Frage der
       wiedergabe der Werke Bachs für violine Solo." Der Musik-
       Student 4 (1952), pp. 85-90.

3350   "A new violin bow for unaccompanied violin music." Tr.
       Margaret Deneke. The Musical Times and Singing-Class
       Circular (London) 74:1087 (Sept. 1933), pp. 792-95.

3351   "Les oeuvres pour violin seul de Bach. De l'archet à utiliser
         pour leur exécution." Saisons d'Alsace (Strasbourg) 2:2
         (Spring 1950), pp. 139-45. Revised version of original
         round bow study.

3352   "Om Bach-Buen." Dansk Musiktidsskrift (Copenhagen) 25:6-7
         (1950), pp. 118-21.

3353   "Der Runde Violinbogen. Zum Bach-Konzert von Konsertmeister
         Rolph Schroeder im Tonkunstlerverein zu Strassburg, am
         24. Januar 1933." Schweizerische Musikzeitung (Zürich)
         73:6 (March 15, 1933), pp. 197-203. Also issued as a
         7-page offprint.

2.   Works by Others About Schweitzer

     a.   Books

3354   LIND, EMIL. Albert Schweitzer, ein Leben für Johann
         Sebastian Bach. Speyer: Leibeling, 1950. 84 pp. Illus.
         (Schriftenreihe: Albert Schweitzer. Bd. 2. Meisenheimer
         Vorträge, Heft 1.)

     b.   Articles, Parts of Books

3355   ALTMANN, WILHELM. "Der 60jährige Albert Schweitzer."
         Allgemeine Musikzeitung (Berlin, Köln) 62:2 (Jan. 11, 1935),
         pp. 23-24.

3356   ASHBY, A. B. "Schweitzer on Bach." Music and Letters
         (Taunton, Eng.) 26:2 (April 1945), pp. 102-112. A reply
         to Gordon Sutherland's "Schweitzerian Heresy," see no.
         3413 below.

3357   BALDENSPERGER, FERNAND. [Reaction to J. S. Bach le musicien-
         poète.] Le Courier Musical (Paris), March 15, 1905.
         Reprinted in: RAYONNEMENT, pp. 117-19.

3358   BASER, FRIEDRICH. "Köpfe in Profile. Albert Schweitzer-
         Otakar Sevcik-Hans Weisbach." Die Musik (Berlin) 23:5
         (Feb. 1931), pp. 334-37.

3359   BESCH, HANS. Johann Sebastian Bach. Frömmigkeit und Glaube.
         Volume I: Deutung und Wirklichkeit. Gütersloh:
         C. Bertelsmann, 1938. See index for numerous references
         to Schweitzer.

3360   BIXLER, JULIUS SEELYE. "The greatest of preachers." The
         American-German Review (Philadelphia) 16:6 (Aug. 1950),
         pp. 5-6f.

Music

3361 BLUME, FRIEDRICH. <u>Johann Sebastian Bach im Wandel der</u>
<u>Geschichte</u>. Kassel: Bärenreiter Verlag, 1947,
pp. 33-35, 37, 39. (Musikwiss. Arbeiten, hrsg. von der
Gesellschaft für Musikforschung, 1.) Translated by
Stanley Godman as <u>Two Centuries of Bach</u>. London: Oxford
University Press, 1950, pp. 73-77.

3362 BORDES, CHARLES. "Albert Schweitzer. J. S. Bach le musicien-
poète." <u>La Tribune de Saint-Gervais</u> (Paris) 11:3
(March 1905), pp. 91-94. Illus.

3363 BORREL, E. Review of Norbert Duforcq--<u>J. S. Bach, la mâitre</u>
<u>de l'orgue</u> (see no. 3370 below). <u>Revue de Musicologie</u>
(Paris) 32:93/94 (July 1950), p. 62. Makes assertions
about <u>J. S. Bach le Musicien-poète</u>.

3364 BRET, GUSTAV. "Albert Schweitzer et la Société de J.-S. Bach
de Paris." In: WÜRDIGUNG, pp. 31-33. Reprinted in
<u>Saisons d'Alsace</u> (Strasbourg) 2 (Spring 1950), pp. 155-63;
reprinted in CAHIERS 4 (Dec. 1960), pp. 13-17; reprinted
in: RAYONNEMENT, pp. 113-16; translated as "Bach,
Schweitzer und die Pariser Bach-Gesellschaft." In:
DENKEN UND WEG, pp. 287-93; reprinted in: BEGEGNUNG,
pp. 124-29.

3365 BRINER, ANDRES. "Albert Schweitzer als Musiker." <u>Neue</u>
<u>Zürcher Zeitung</u> 123 (Jan. 14, 1955). Reprinted in
<u>Schweizerische Musikzeitung</u> (Zürich) 95:2 (Feb. 1, 1955),
pp. 45-46.

3366 CASTEDO, LEOPOLDO. "La Interpretación de Bach según las
Ideas de Albert Schweitzer." <u>Revista Musical Chilena</u>
(Santiago) 6:38 (1950), pp. 82-94.

3367 CHERNIAVSKY, D. "Albert Schweitzer." <u>The Canon</u> (Sydney,
Australia) 7:7 (Feb. 1954), pp. 260-65.

3368 DOWNES, OLIN. "Albert Schweitzer: 70th birthday of musician,
theologian, and healer--his kinship to Rolland." The
New York <u>Times</u>, Jan. 14, 1945, sect. 2, p. X5.

3369 DRUSKIN, M. "Al'bert Shveytser i voprosy bakhovedeniya."
<u>Sovetskaya Muzyka</u> (Moscow) 24:3 (March 1960), pp. 61-70.

3370 DUFOURCQ, NORBERT. <u>Jean-Sébastien Bach. Le mâitre de l'Orgue</u>.
Paris: Floury, 1948, pp. 340, 353-55, 361, 374, 378.

3371 "Er lehrte Bachs Sprache." <u>Musikhandel</u> (Bonn) 16:1
(Jan. 1965), p. 3.

3372   FESCHOTTE, JACQUES. "Un éxegetè de Bach en Afrique noire:
        Albert Schweitzer." Jeunesses Musicales de France
        (Paris), March 1, 1950, pp. 1, 12.

3373   GALL, HUGHES-R. "L'heritier de Jean-Sébastien. Une interview
        de Marcel Dupré." Les Nouvelles Littéraires (Paris)
        43:1984 (Sept. 9, 1965), p. 9. Illus.

3374   GRABS, RUDOLF. "Johann Sebastian Bach--Gestalt und Deutung
        durch Albert Schweitzer." RUNDBRIEFE/DDR 20 (1972),
        pp. 3-10.

3375   GREW, SYDNEY. "Schweitzer and Bach." The Choir (London)
        27:324 (Dec. 1936), pp. 267-70; 28:325 (Jan. 1937),
        pp. 6-9; 28:326 (Feb. 1937), pp. 33-35; 28:327
        (March 1937), pp. 57-58.

3376   HEINSHEIMER, HANS W. "The saga of Schweitzer's Bach edition."
        (New York City Ballet Program). The New York State Theatre
        Program, Oct. 1965, pp. 30, 33, 36-39. Updated version in
        Music, the AGO and RCCO Magazine 9 (Jan. 1975), pp. 30-33.

3377   HULL, A. EAGLEFIELD. "Two great Bach commentators (Albert
        Schweitzer and Andre Pirro)." Monthly Musical Record
        (London) 52:616 (April 1, 1922), pp. 78-79.

3378   JACOBI, ERWIN R. "Schweitzer über Bachs Ornamentik."
        (Zusammenfassung des Referats über "Albert Schweitzers
        hinterlassene Manuskripte über die Ornamente in Johann
        Sebastian Bachs Komponistionen," gehalten am 2-5. 1971
        in Bloomington/Indiana, USA, auf der Frühjahrstagung der
        American Musicological Society.) RUNDBRIEFE/DDR 20
        (1972), p. 32.

3379   _____. "Zur Entstehung des Bach-Buches von Albert Schweitzer,
        auf Grund unveröffentlichter Briefe." Bach Jahrbuch 1975.
        Berlin, 1976, pp. 141-61.

3380   JOLLES, HENRY. "Os 70 anos de Bach-Schweitzer." O Estado
        de São Paulo, Jan. 21, 1945, p. 4.

3381   KELLER, H. "Johann Sebastian Bach." Universitas
        (Stuttgart) 15:1 (Jan. 1960), pp. 116-18. Reprinted in:
        DENKEN UND WEG, pp. 294-98; translated as "Albert
        Schweitzer's book on Bach." Universitas (English
        language edition) 7:1 (1964), pp. 69-74.

3382   KELLER, WILHELM. "Das Thema der 'Kunst der Fuge.'"
        Zeitschrift für Musik (Regensburg) 111:2 (Jan. 1950),
        pp. 71-73. Port.

Music

3383 KÖHLER, JOHANNES ERNST. "Albert Schweitzers Verdienst um
Johann Sebastian Bach und die Orgel." In: VERMÄCHTNIS
UND WIRKLICHKEIT, pp. 51-58.

3384 KRAUS, FRITZ. "Bach-Dichter und Maler in Musik. Albert
Schweitzers Standard-Werk." Die Neue Zeitung (Munich)
186 (Aug. 9/10, 1952), p. 19.

3385 LÜDICKE, HEINO. "Lebendige Zweisprache mit der Musik: Der
Bach Forscher und Organist Albert Schweitzer." Neue Zeit
(East Berlin) 11 (Jan. 14, 1960), p. 3.

3386 M., A. "Albert Schweitzer on Bach's motets" (editorial).
American Choral Review (New York) 8:2 (Dec. 1965),
pp. 1-2. Port.

3387 MICHAELIS, OTTO. "Strassburg und die Bach-Schütz-Pflege.
Eine Erinnerungen zum Bach-Handel-Schütz-Jahr" (Albert
Schweitzer und Ernst Munch). Elsass-Lothringen
Heimatstimmen (Berlin) 13:6 (July 28, 1935), p. 283.

3388 MILLET, LUIS. "El Dr. Albert Schweitzer." Revista Musical
Catalaña. Butlletí di l'Orfeó Catalá (Barcelona) 5:59
(Nov. 1908), pp. 206-07.

3389 MONTADON, C. M. [Reaction to J. S. Bach le musicien- poète.]
La Femme Contemporaine (Paris) 4:30 (March 1906), p. 271.
Reprinted in: RAYONNEMENT, pp. 116-17.

3390 MOSER, HANS JOACHIM. "Das Bachbild Albert Schweitzers."
Zeitschrift für Musik (Regensburg) 116:1 (Jan. 1955),
pp. 3-4.

3391 MÜLLER, FRITZ. "Albert Schweitzer als Musiker und Bach-
kenner." Neue Musik-Zeitschrift (Munich) 4:5 (May 1950),
pp. 130-32.

3392 MÜLLER-BLATTAU, JOSEPH. "Albert Schweitzer und das Bach-
Bild des 20. Jahrhundert." In: BEGEGNUNG, pp. 301-09.

3393 _____. "Albert Schweitzers Weg zur Bach-Orgel und zu
seiner neuen Bach-Auffassung." In: DENKEN UND WEG,
pp. 243-61.

3394 MÜNCH, FRITZ. "Bach à Strasbourg." Saisons d'Alsace
(Strasbourg) 2 (Spring 1950), p. 154.

3395 OSTERGAARD, JENS. "Schweitzers bog om Bach." Aalborg
Stiftstidende (Aalborg, Denmark), April 8, 1954.

3396   "Palau de la Música Catalaña. Concerts de Quaresma."
          Revista Musical Cataraña (Barcelona) 9:99 (March 1912),
          pp. 80-82.

3397   "Palau de la Música Cataraña. Festivals Bach." Revista
          Musical Cataraña (Barcelona) 8:96 (Dec. 1911), pp. 375-85.

3398   "Palau de la Música Cataraña. Festivals Bach." Revista
          Musical Cataraña (Barcelona) 8:95 (Nov. 1911), pp. 337-39.

3399   R., J. "Albert Schweitzer och J. S. Bach." Göteborgs-
          Handelsoch Sjofarts-Tidning (Göteborg, Sweden),
          Jan. 21, 1922.

3400   RAMIN, GUNTHER. "Johan Sebastian Bach als Ende und Anfang
          und seine Bedeutung für die geistige Entwicklung der
          Jugend." In: EHRFURCHT, pp. 184-92.

3401   _____. "Dem Vater der Bachpflege. Grusswort zum 80.
          Geburtstag von Albert Schweitzer." Musica (Kassel) 9:1
          (Jan. 1955), p. 10.

3402   RIEDEL, JOHANNES. "Albert Schweitzer's Bach." The Christian
          Century (Chicago) 77:12 (March 23, 1960), pp. 348-50.

3403   RIEMENSCHNEIDER, ALBERT. "Bach Biographies and their authors."
          In: Hinrichsen's Musical Year Book, Music Book, Vol. VII.
          Edited by Max Hinrichsen. London, New York: Hinrichsen
          Edition Ltd., 1952, pp. 536-38. Port.

3404   ROBERT, GUSTAVE. Le descriptif chez Bach. Paris: Fischbacher,
          1909. Numerous references to Schweitzer, especially
          pp. 24-25, 33-34 and 71-72.

3405   ROHM, KARL. "Albert Schweitzers Bach-Bild." Österreichische
          Furche (Vienna) 6:20 (1950), p. 3.

3406   ROSENWALD, HANS. "Schweitzer, Goethe und Bach." In: THE
          CONVOCATION RECORD, pp. III/5-9.

3407   SCHAEFFER, LOUIS EDOUARD. "Das Verschwiegene Bachkonzert."
          In: Weltenbürger, Porträts von Meistern und Freunden.
          Strasbourg: Schaeffer, 1950, pp. 63-72. Impressions of
          a recorded Bach concert by Schweitzer, October 1936.

3408   SCHALLENBERG, E. W. "Albert Schweitzer en J. S. Bach."
          De Gids (Utrecht) 96:4 (Nov. 1932), pp. 188-206.

Music

3409   SCHMITZ, EUGEN. "Das poetisierende Element in Bachs Musik"
         (review of J. S. Bach le musicien-poète). Hochland
         (Munich) 4:3 (Dec. 1906), pp. 354-60.

3410   SCHONBURG, HAROLD C. "Schweitzer's Bach: a study in symbols."
         The New York Times, Jan. 17, 1965, section 2, p. X-11.

3411   SCHRADE, LEO. "Schweitzer's aesthetics: an interpretation
         of Bach." In: JUBILEE, pp. 173-96. Translated as "Die
         Äesthetik Albert Schweitzers. Eine Interpretation Bachs."
         Universitas (Stuttgart) 15:1 (Jan. 1960), pp. 61-78;
         Reprinted in: DENKEN UND WEG, pp. 262-80.

3412   STUCKENSCHMIDT, H. H. "Das persönliche Opfer Albert
         Schweitzers." Frankfurter Allgemeine Zeitung, Jan. 13,
         1965. Reprinted in Berichte und Informationen des
         Österreichischen Forschungsinstituts für Wirtschaft und
         Politik (Salzburg) 20:964 (1965), pp. 14-15; reprinted in:
         BEGEGNUNG, pp. 108-11.

3413   SUTHERLAND, GORDON. "The Schweitzerian heresy." Music and
         Letters (Taunton, Eng.) 23:4 (Oct. 1942), pp. 265-89.
         For a reply, see Ashby, no. 3356 above.

3414   TAUTER, PETRE. "J. S. Bach as commented and interpreted by
         Albert Schweitzer, or figural music." In: DEBRECEN,
         pp. 151-65.

3415   VALENTINE, CYRIL HENRY. "Schweitzer on Bach." The Hibbert
         Journal (London) 48:4 (July 1950), pp. 383-87.

3416   VOIGT, WALDEMAR. "Zu Bachs Weihnachts Oratorium. Teil 1
         bis 3." Bach Jahrbuch 5 (1908), pp. 1-48. Schweitzer
         mentioned in pp. 6, 12, 14, 18, 19, 20, 27.

         C. Organs, Organ Construction, and Organ Concerts

1. Works by Schweitzer

   a. Books

         DEUTSCHE UND FRANZÖSISCHE ORGELBAUKUNST UND ORGELKUNST
   (The Art of Organ-Building and Organ-Playing in Germany and France)

"As a corollary to the book on Bach there appeared in the autumn of
1905, before I began my medical studies, an essay on organ building. . . . I was curiously affected by the organs which were built

toward the end of the nineteenth century. Although they were lauded
as miracles of advanced technical skill, I could find no pleasure in
them. . . . My foreboding that the modern organ meant . . . a step
not forward but backward, suddenly became a certainty. In order to
convince myself finally of this fact and to find the reasons for it,
I used my free time in the next few years [after 1896] in getting to
know as many organs, old and new, as possible. I also discussed the
matter with all the organists and organ builders with whom I came in
contact. The pamphlet . . . was understood at first by only a few
people. . . . I acknowledge in it a preference for the French style
of organ building as compared with the German, because in several
respects it has remained faithful to the traditions of the art."[1]

3417   Deutsche und französische Orgelbaukunst und Orgelkunst.
       Leipzig: Breitkopf und Härtel, 1906. 51 pp. (Appeared
       originally under the same title in Die Musik, see no.
       3427 below.)

3418   Same. Faksimilierter Nachdruck der 1. Auflage von 1906.
       Wiesbaden: Breitkopf und Härtel, 1962. 51 pp. 3.
       Auflage, 1968.

3419   Same. Mit Nachwort über den gegenwärtigen Stand der Frage
       des Orgelbaues 1927. Leipzig: Breitkopf und Härtel,
       1927. iii, 73 pp. (Nachwort von 1927, pp. 49-70.)

English

"The Art of Organ Building and Organ Playing in Germany and
France." See Music in the Life of Albert Schweitzer,
no. 3210 above.

"The 1927 Epilogue." See Music in the Life of Albert
Schweitzer, no. 3210 above.

III. KONGRESS DER INTERNATIONAL MUSIKGESELLSCHAFT,
WIEN 25. BIS 29. MAI 1909 (SEKTION Vc)
HAYDN-ZENTENARFEIER
(Third Congress of the International Music Society, Vienna)

Albert Schweitzer, along with Abbe Dr. Franz Xaver Mathias,[2] held an
important position in Section Vc of the Third Congress of the

---

[1]Out of My Life and Thought. New York: Holt, Rinehart and Winston,
1961, pp. 70-71.

[2]Dr. Xaver Mathias was Lecturer in Church Music on the Catholic
Theological Faculty, University of Strasbourg.

Music

International Music Society, held in Vienna in May 1909. This section, "Orgelbaufragen," was concerned with questions of organ construction. Previous to the meeting, Dr. Schweitzer sent to organ-players and organ-builders in the Germanic and Romance countries a questionnaire relating to the building of organs (Die allgemeine Umfrage bei Orgelspielern und Orgelbauern in deutschen und romanischen Ländern). His address to section Vc of the Congress (Die Reform unseres Orgelbaues . . .) and the deliberations which followed it were based on the replies he had received to his questionnaire. The Internationales Regulativ für Orgelbau, which resulted from the discussions, were drawn up and signed jointly by Albert Schweitzer and the Abbe Mathias on behalf of the committee and were incorporated into the report of the congress. They were also published in German and French in the same year as independent books and, later, in Italian. Although the report of Section Vc of the congress was not exclusively the work of Dr. Schweitzer, the various texts relating to it are included here because of the important work which he contributed to the organization and writing of the report.[1]

1. The Questionnaire

3420   Die allgemeine Umfrage bei Orgelspielern und Orgelbauern in deutschen und romanischen Ländern. In: III. Kongress der Internationalen Musikgesellschaft, Wien, 25. bis 29. Mai 1909. Vienna: Artaria & Co.; Leipzig: Breitkopf & Härtel, 1909, pp. 581-83.

See also no. 3457 below.

English

"The Questionnaire on Organ Construction." See Music in the Life of Albert Schweitzer, no. 3210 above.

2. Schweitzer's Address

3421   Die Reform unseres Orgelbaues auf Grund einer allgemeinen Umfrage bei Orgelspielern und Orgelbauern in deutschen und romanischen Ländern. In: III. Kongress der Internationalen Musikgesellschaft, Wien, 25. bis 29. Mai 1909. Vienna: Artaria & Co.; Leipzig: Breitkopf & Härtel, 1909, pp. 581-607.

---

[1]For further information on Schweitzer's involvement in these issues, see Out of My Life and Thought (Holt, Rinehart and Winston, 1961), p. 76; and Music in the Life of Albert Schweitzer, pp. 177, 202-05.

English

"The Organ that Europe Wants." See <u>Music in the Life of Albert Schweitzer</u>, no. 3210 above.

3. The Regulations

3422   Internationales Regulativ für Orgelbau. Von Albert Schweitzer und F. Xaver Mathias. In: <u>III. Kongress der Internationalen Musikgesellschaft, Wien, 25. bis 29. Mai 1909</u>. Vienna: Artaria & Co.; Leipzig: Breitkopf und Härtel, 1909, pp. 636-79. Published also as independent books in German, French and Italian, as follows:

3423   <u>Internationales Regulativ für Orgelbau</u>. Entworfen und bearbeitet von der Sektion für Orgelbau auf dem Dritten Kongress der Internationalen Musikgesellschaft (Wien, 25. bis 29. Mai 1909). Deutsche Ausgabe. Vienna: Artaria & Co.: Leipzig: Breitkopf & Härtel, 1909. 46 pp.

French

3424   <u>Règlement général international pour la facture d'orgues</u>. Elaboré et dressé par la Section de Facture d'Orgues au IIIe Congrès de la Société Internationale de Musique (Vienne, 25-29 mai 1909). Édition française. ("Au nom du Comité du IIIe Congrès de la Société internationale de Musique: Dr. Albert Schweitzer et l'abbé Dr. Franz Xaver Mathias.") Vienna: Artaria & Co.; Leipzig: Breitkopf & Härtel, 1909. 46 pp.

Italian

3425   <u>Regolamente generale internazionale per la costruzione degli organi</u>. 3. Congresso della Societa Internazionale di Musica a Vienna, 25-29 Maggio 1909. (Albert Schweitzer e Xaver Mathias. In Nome del Comitato del 3. Congresso della Soc. Int. di Musica.) Bronte, 1914, pp. 7-122. (Appendix by the translator, D. Carmelo Sangiorgio, pp. 123-70.)

ZUR DISKUSSION ÜBER ORGELBAU (1914)

The manuscript of this work was found by Erwin R. Jacobi among Schweitzer's papers after his death. It was originally written for the periodical <u>Die Orgel</u> in 1914, but the periodical ceased publication in that year, before the piece could be printed.

Music

3426   Zur Diskussion über Orgelbau (1914). Hrsg. von Erwin R.
            Jacobi. Berlin: Verlag Merseburger, 1977. 48 pp.
            Documenta Organologica, Band 1. Vierundfünfzigste
            Veröffentlichen der Gesellschaft der Orgelfreunde.

    b. Shorter Writings by Schweitzer

3427   "Deutsche und französische Orgelbaukunst und Orgelkunst."
            Die Musik (Berlin) 5:14 (1905/06) pp. 75-90; 5:15
            (1905/06), pp. 139-54. Translated as "Art compare de la
            facture et du jeu de l'orgue en France et en Allemagne."
            L'Orgue (Paris) 122-23 (1967), pp. 40-62. Introd. de
            Pierre Vallotton.

3428   "Ch. M. Widor's Sinfonia Sacra für Orgel und Orchester."
            In: Die Strassburger Sängerhaus-Orgel. Strassburg i.
            Els.: J. Manias, 1909.

3429   "El arte de construir y el arte del organo en Alemania y
            Francia" (excerpt from El Camino hacia ti Mismo).
            Psallite (La Plata, Argentina) 24:93 (1975), pp. 9-10.

3430   "Französische und deutsche Orgelbaukunst und Orgelkunst."
            Zeitschrift für Orgel-, Harmonium- und Instrumentenbau
            (Graz) 4:8 (Aug. 15, 1906), pp. 61-64; 4:9 (Sept. 15, 1906),
            pp. 73-74; 4:10 (Oct. 15, 1906), pp. 81-82; 4:11 (Nov. 15,
            1906), pp. 89-91; 4:12 (Dec. 15, 1906), pp. 98-99; 5:3
            (March 15, 1907), pp. 17-18; 5:4 (April 15, 1907), pp. 25-
            27; 5:5 (May 15, 1907), pp. 33-34; 5:6 (June 15, 1907),
            pp. 41-43.

3431   "Gutachten über die Orgel zu St. Jacobi in Hamburg." In:
            Mehrkens, Karl. Die Schnitgerorgel in der Hauptkirche
            St. Jacobi in Hamburg. Kassell: Bärenreiter Verlag,
            1930, pp. 15ff.

3432   Letter to Reverend Weinland from Albert Schweitzer and Fritz
            Dickert (on rebuilding the Günsbach organ), 1959. In:
            ALBUM, p. 33.

3433   "M. J. Erb's Symphonie für Orchester und Orgel." In: Die
            Strassburger Sängerhaus-Orgel. Strassburg i. Els.:
            J. Manias, 1909.

3434   "Reform in organ building." Musical America (New York) 459
            (1950), pp. 217-24.

3435   "Über den Orgelbau" (excerpt from Aus meinem Leben und Denken).
            Welt-Stimmen (Stuttgart) 24:3 (1955), pp. 97-99.

2. Works by Others About Schweitzer and the Organ

    a. Books

3436   FERINGA, K. Terugblik op Albert Schweitzers Orgelconcerten in
        Nederland. Deventer: Albert Schweitzer Centrum, 1977.

3437   PHELPS, L. I. A Short History of the Organ Revival. St.
        Louis: Concordia, 1967. 20 pp.

3438   QUOIKA, RUDOLF. Albert Schweitzers Begegnung mit der Orgel.
        Berlin: C. Merseburger, 1954. 96 pp. Illus., ports.
        (Gesellschaft der Orgelfreunde. Veröffentlichungen, 7.)
        Second edition, 1958.

3439   _____. Ein Orgelkolleg mit Albert Schweitzer. Giesenfeld/
        Obb: Staudt-Druck, 1970. 47 pp.

3440   SONNER, RUDOLF. Dr. Albert Schweitzer und die Orgelbewegung
        (Vortrag gehalten am 4. Juni 1955 in Colmar). Colmar:
        Hohner, 1955. 8 pp. Port.

    b. Articles, Parts of Books

3441   "Albert Schweitzer som orgelspelare." Lunds Dagblad
        (Lund, Sweden), Dec. 5, 1921.

3442   "Albert Schweitzer speelt Bach." NIEUWS 1:1 (Dec. 1951),
        pp. 12-13.

3443   "Albert Schweitzer spielt Bach (am 28. und 29. Juli in der
        St.-Thomas-Kirche in Strasbourg)." Badische Zeitung,
        Aug. 3, 1954. Reprinted in RUNDBRIEF 6 (Dec. 1, 1954),
        p. 27; reprinted in: DOKUMENTE, pp. 229-30.

3444   ANDREAS, BENGT. "Besök hos en fransk orgelmästare."
        Musikrevy (Sweden) 10 (1955), pp. 29-30, 36.

3445   ARGENTORATENSIS. "À propos d'un recital d'orgue du Docteur
        Schweitzer" (extraits d'un article parue dans le journal
        Les Dernières Nouvelles du Haut Rhin, le 1er Octobre
        1952). L'Orgue (Paris) 73 (Oct.-Dec. 1954), pp. 116-17.

3446   BALSIGER, M. U. "Die Orgelhartstoeht van Albert Schweitzer."
        EERBIED 27:2 (Aug. 1978), pp. 21-23.

3447   BANGERT, EMILIUS. "Albert Schweitzer som orgeldonstnär."
        In: MANNEN, pp. 89-90.

Music

3448 _____. "Albert Schweitzer und die Orgel." In: EHRFURCHT,
pp. 174-83.

3449 BARNES, WILLIAM H. "Some corrections." The American Organist
(Staten Island, N.Y.) 18:7 (July 1935), pp. 280-81.

3450 BAUR, HANS. "Schonet die alten orgeln!" Schweizerisches
Protestantenblatt (Basel) 49:22 (May 20, 1926),
pp. 180-81.

3451 BECKETT, HENRY. "Schweitzer gives organ recital in a barn."
New York Post, July 21, 1949.

3452 BIGGS, E. POWER. "A statement" (Albert Schweitzer and old
organs in Europe). THE CONVOCATION RECORD, pp. III/15-24.

3453 BILLETER, BERNHARD. "Albert Schweitzer en zijn Orgelbouwer."
Acta Organologica (Berlin), 1977.

3454 BIRTNER, HERBERT. "Die Probleme der Orgelbewegung."
Theologische Rundschau (Tübingen) 4:1 (1932), pp. 39-66,
122-30. Albert Schweitzer, pp. 40, 42-46, 125.

3455 BROM, A. "Albert Schweitzer en de orgelbouw." NIEUWS 1:3
(July 1952), p. 42.

3456 BUNK, GERARD. "Albert Schweitzer an der Orgel." Christ und
Welt (Stuttgart) 7:15 (April 15, 1954), p. 10. Port.

_____. "Onmoeting met Albert Schweitzer." See Visits, no.
1137 above.

3457 BUSCH, H. J. "Zur Situation des europaeischen Orgelbaus am
Beginn des 20. Jahrhunderts--zum Gedenken an den 100.
Geburtstag Albert Schweitzers am 14. Januar 1975."
Ars Organi (Esslingen/Neckar) 23:46 (1975), pp. 2080-86.
Includes Schweitzer's questionnaire on organs, see nos.
3420 above.

3458 C., H. "With Schweitzer at the organ." The Musical Times
and Singing-Class Circular (London) 76 (Dec. 1935),
p. 1116.

3459 "Dr. Schweitzer examines an organ mechanism in Boston."
Musical America (New York) 69:11 (Sept. 1949), p. 34.

3460 DU FOURCQ, NORBERT. "Albert Schweitzer et l'Esthétique de
l'orgue au tournant du XXe siècle." REVUE 56:1-2 (1976),
pp. 174-81.

3461 EHLERS, ALICE. "Albert Schweitzers Orgelspiel." In:
       WÜRDIGUNG, pp. 34-35.

3462 EPSTEIN, PETER. "Die Orgel als Kunstdenkmal." Monatsschrift
       für Gottesdienst und Kirchliche Kunst (Göttingen) 31:12
       (Dec. 1926), pp. 300-04.

3463 ERDMAN, JERZY. "Poglady Alberta Schweitzera na organy i
       muzyke organowa." Ruch Muzyczny (Warsaw) 17 (1976),
       pp. 3-5.

3464 "Erstes Orgelkonzert Albert Schweitzers." Deutsche Zeitung
       Bohemia (Prague) 96:10 (Jan. 14, 1923), p. 8.

3465 FESCHOTTE, J. "Albert Schweitzer et l'orgue: evocation et
       souvenirs." L'Orgue (Paris) 118 (April-June 1966),
       pp. 49-55. Port.

3466 FETT, HARRY. "Albert Schweitzer og de gamle norske orgler."
       Aftenposten (Oslo) 95:512 (Nov. 5, 1954), pp. 3, 6.
       Illus.

3467 GURLITT, WILIBALD. "Zur gegenwärtigen Orgelerneuerungsbewegung
       in Deutschland." Musik und Kirche (Kassel) 1:1
       (Jan./Feb. 1929), pp. 15-27.

3468 HANSEN, L. W. "Orgelsaken i Stavanger og Albert Schweitzer."
       In: Foreningen til Norske Fortidsminnesmerkers Bewaring
       (Oslo), Annual Report, 1935, pp. 21-30. Port., illus.
       Also issued as a 9-page reprint: Oslo: Grondahl and
       Sons, 1935.

3469 HASSE, KARL. "Karl Straub als Orgelkünstler." In: Karl
       Straub zu seinem 70. Geburtstag. Gaben der Freunde.
       Leipzig: Koehler and Amelang, 1943. Albert Schweitzer:
       pp. 167-83, 191. Port.

3470 HEROLD, WILH. "Deutsche und französische Orgelbaukunst
       und Orgelkunst. . . ." Siena (Gütersloh) 35:1 (1910),
       pp. 1-2.

3471 HÖGNER, FRIEDRICH. "Die deutsche Orgelbewegung." Zeitwende
       (Munich) 7 (1931), pp. 56-71. Albert Schweitzer,
       p. 60-61.

3472 KÖHLER, JOHANNES-ERNST. "Schweitzers Verdienst um die wahre
       Orgel." In: BEITRÄGE, pp. 88-90.

Music

3473   [LENEL, LUDWIG]. "Reminiscences of Albert Schweitzer as
         organist and teacher" (an interview with Ludwig Lenel).
         Church Music (St. Louis) 67:1 (1967), pp. 31-34.

3474   LLIURA, T. F. "Konzert" (Orfeó Catalá, Barcelona). Die
         Musik (Berlin) 8:6 (1908/09), pp. 372-73.

3475   LOR, RAINE. "Albert Schweitzer in Frankfurt: das
         Orgelkonzert." Elsass-Lothringen Heimatstimmen
         (Berlin) 6:12 (Dec. 6, 1928), pp. 753-54.

3476   MAHRENHOLZ, CHRISTHARD. "Fünfzehn Jahre Orgelbewegung.
         Rückblick und Ausblick. Vortrag auf dem Fest der
         deutschen Kirchen-Musik. . . ." Musik und Kirche
         (Kassel) 10:1 (Jan./Feb. 1938), pp. 8-28.

3477   MC KINNEY, HOWARD D. "Organs and organ building." The New
         Music Review and Church Music Review (New York) 32
         (Oct. 1933), pp. 381-84.

3478   METZGER, H. A. "Das Leben Albert Schweitzer auf einer
         Konzertreise in Holland." In: WÜRDIGUNG, pp. 36-40.
         Translated into Dutch as "Het leven van Albert Schweitzer
         op een concertries." In: Albert Schweitzer naar zijn
         waarde geschat. Vertaald door Mevr. A.D. W.-Br. Deventer:
         A. E. Kluwer, 1934, pp. 44-49.

3479   METZGER, HANS A. "Mit Albert Schweitzer auf holländischen
         Orgeln." Musik in Württemburg (Ludwigsburg) 5 (1932),
         pp. 111-16.

3480   MITSCHISCHEK, ERHARD. "Eugen Münch, Klavier- und Orgellehrer
         Albert Schweitzers." RUNDBRIEF 37 (Sept 4, 1973),
         pp. 16-27.

3481   NIES-BERGER, EDOUARD. "Albert Schweitzer et l'orgue de
         Gunsbach." CAHIERS 33 (Winter 1975), pp. 14-16. Trans-
         lated as "Die Guensbacher Orgel und Albert Schweitzer."
         Ars Organi (Esslingen/Neckar) 24:51 (1976), pp. 14-17;
         translated as "The Gunsbach Organ and Albert Schweitzer."
         Music (New York) 10:5 (May 1976), pp. 50-51. Reprinted in
         The Organ (Bournemouth) 57:225 (July 1978), pp. 1-4.

3482   NOEHREN, ROBERT. "Commends opinions of Dr. Schweitzer to
         organ designers." The Diapason (Chicago) 45:3
         (Feb. 1, 1954), p. 22.

3433   NOLL, RAINER. "Albert Schweitzer und mein Weg zur Orgel-
         Summe und Bekenntnis." BERICHTE 39 (March 1975),
         pp. 18-21.

3484   QUOIKA, RUDOLF. "Albert Schweitzer ein Neunziger." Musica
       (Kassel and Basel) 18:6 (Dec. 1964), p. 323.

3485   _____. "Albert Schweitzer und Würtemmberger Orgeln."
       Kultus und Unterricht (Stuttgart) 4:1 (1955),
       Nichtamtlicher Teil, pp. 1-3.

3486   _____. "Albert Schweitzer und die Orgel." Zeitschrift für
       Musik (Regensburg) 116:1 (Jan. 1955), pp. 5-7.

3487   _____. "Orgelspiel und Urwald." Musica (Kassel) 9:1
       (Jan. 1955), pp. 13-14.

3488   _____. "Die Reform des Orgelbaus." Universitas (Stuttgart)
       15:1 (Jan. 1960), pp. 128-30.

3489   RUPP, EMIL. Die Entwicklungsgeschichte der Orgelbaukunst.
       Einsiedeln: Benziger and Co., 1929, pp. 332-34, 339,
       350-51, 361, 371.

3490   _____. "Die Orgel der Zukunft." Zeitschrift für
       Instrumentenbau (Leipzig) 27:4 (Nov. 1, 1906), pp. 91-92;
       27:6 (Nov. 21, 1906), pp. 155-56; 27:7 (Dec. 1, 1906),
       p. 190; 27:9 (Dec. 21, 1906), p. 253; 27:13 (Feb. 1, 1907),
       pp. 372-73; 27:14 (Feb. 11, 1907), p. 404; 27:27 (June 21,
       1907), pp. 836-38; 27:36 (Sept. 21, 1907), p. 1135.

3491   SATTLER, ERWIN. "Einweihung der neuen Orgel in der
       protestantischen Kirche in Strassburg-Neudorf (Elsass)."
       Musikund Kirche (Kassel und Basel) 36:3 (May-June 1966),
       pp. 141-42. Illus.

3492   SAWADE, HEINZ. "Schweitzer und die Mühlhäuser Bachorgel."
       In: BEITRÄGE, pp. 167-70.

3493   SCHLEICHER, BERTHA. "Albert Schweitzer, ein Meister der
       Orgel." Michael (Munich) 6:5 (June 1, 1948), p. 8.

3494   "Schweitzer speelde Bach in Strassburg" (editorial). Vrij
       Nederland (Amsterdam) 11:50 (Aug. 11, 1951), p. 5.

3495   "Schweitzers Bachkonzert" (in Prag). Deutsche Zeitung Bohemia
       (Prag) 11 (Jan. 16, 1923), p. 6.

3496   SEAVER, GEORGE. "Die Rettung der alten Orgel." Musica
       (Kassel) 9:1 (1955), pp. 11-12. Excerpt from Albert
       Schweitzer als Mensch und Denker.

Music

3497   STOOB, HEINZ. "Albert Schweitzer und die Arp-Schnitger-
          Orgel." In: 700 Jahre St. Jacobi zu Hamburg 1255-1955.
          Festschrift.

3498   SUMNER, W. L. "Paris organs and organists in the 'twenties'--
          some reminiscences." Organ Yearbook 2 (1971), pp. 51-57.
          Illus. Albert Schweitzer, p. 54.

3499   THOMPSON-ALLEN, AUBREY. "Information given" (autobiographical
          notes). Music (New York) 6:6 (June 1972), pp. 24-27.
          Illus., port.

3500   VALLOTON, PIERRE. "Albert Schweitzer et la facture d'orgues."
          L'Orgue (Paris) 122-23 (1967), pp. 33-39.

3501   WEINRICH, CARL. "Albert Schweitzer's contribution to organ-
          building." In: JUBILEE, pp. 213-26.

                        D. Discography

1. Recordings by Schweitzer

Schweitzer's first recordings of organ music were done in 1928 at
Queen's Hall, London, for His Master's Voice. He next (1935) recorded six works of Bach's for the Bach Organ Music Society on the
organ of All Hallows in the Tower. In 1936 he recorded additional
works for the society, this time on the organ of St. Aurelia in
Strasbourg. Both of these sets were recorded by Columbia. A fourth
set of recordings was completed in November 1952 at the organ of the
Günsbach Parish Church.

3502   Bach: Prelude and Fugue in E Minor. Chorale preludes: Wenn
          wir in höchsten Nöten sind; Herzlich tut mich verlangen.
          Felix Mendelssohn-Bartholdy: Fugue and Finale from Sonata
          no. 6 for the Organ. Recorded in 1928 on the organ of
          Queen's Hall, London, for His Master's Voice. Released
          1929. V-9741.

3503   Genius at the Keyboard: Compositions for Piano and Organ by
          Bach, Beethoven, Chopin, Debussy, Paderewski, Prokofiev,
          Rachmaninoff and Schubert, performed by Paderewski,
          Prokofiev, Rachmaninoff, Rosenthal, and Schweitzer.
          Part of "A Treasury of Golden Performances" series.
          Victor LCT-1000. Released 1951.

3504   Bach Organ Society, Album I. Fantasia and fugue, G minor;
          "Little" fugue, G minor; Preludes and fugues in C major,

F minor, G major; Toccata and fugue, D minor. Albert
Schweitzer, organ of All Hallows, Barking by the Tower,
England. Columbia Masterworks 270. Accompanying text
by Harvey Grace. Recorded 1935, released 1936. Re-
released in 1964, with text by Walter Munz.

 Historical re-issue of the above: "Schweitzer plays
  Bach organ works." Angel Records GR 2085, part of their
  "Great Recordings of the Century" series. Manufactured
  under license by Toshiba-Emi Ltd., Japan. 4-page pro-
  gram notes in Japanese inserted in the container.
  (Additional number on labels COLC 89).

3505 Bach Organ Society, Album II. Chorale Preludes: An
  Wasserflüssen Babylon; Christ lag in Todesbanden;
  Christum wir sollen loben schon; Christus der uns selig
  macht; Da Jesu an dem Kreuze stand; Erschienen ist der
  Herrliche Tag; Jesu Christus unser Heiland; Liebster Jesu
  wir sind hier; Mit Fried und Freud ich fahr' dahin; O
  Lamm Gottes unschuldig; O Mensch bewein' dein' Sünde
  gross; Schmücke dich, o liebe Seele; Sei gegrüsset,
  Jesu Gütig. Albert Schweitzer, organ of St. Aurélie,
  Strasbourg. Columbia Masterworks 310. Recorded 1936,
  released 1937. Appeared together with Bach Organ Society
  Album III (see next entry). Accompanying text for both
  by Alec Robertson.

3506 Bach Organ Society, Album III. Preludes and fugues in C minor,
  C major, E minor; Fugue, A minor. Albert Schweitzer,
  organ of St. Aurélie, Strasbourg. Columbia Masterworks
  320. Recorded 1936, released 1937, together with Bach
  Organ Society Album II, see previous entry.

  Historical re-issue of the above was made on Odeon COLH
   316.

3507 Bach. Toccata and fugue in D minor; Preludes and Fugues in
  E minor, A minor, C major, C minor. (ML 5040)
  Toccata and fugue in D minor (Dorian); Preludes and
  fugues in A major, F minor, H minor. (ML 5041)
  Passacaglia and fugue in C minor; Prelude and fugue in G
  major; Chorale preludes: Ein feste Burg ist unser Gott;
  Gottes Sohn ist reich; Alle Menschen müssen sterben;
  Variation XI on Sei gegrüsset, Jesu gütig. (ML 5042)
  Albert Schweitzer, organ of Parish Church, Günsbach,
  Alsace. 3-record set, recorded in 1951-52, released in
  1953. Number for set is SL 223. Record liners include
  extensive analyses by Albert Schweitzer, translated by
  Nathan Broder.

Discography

Music

3508   Albert Schweitzer plays Bach. 3 records. Columbia SL 175.
            Volume 1--Fugue, from fantasia and fugue, G minor; Prelude
                and fugue, A minor; Toccata, adagio and fugue, C major.
                (ML 4600)
            Volume 2--Chorale preludes: Gelobet seist du, Jesu Christ;
                Herzlich tut mich verlangen; Ich ruf' zu dir, Herr Jesu
                Christ; Nun komm, der Heiden Heiland; O Mensch, bewein'
                dein' Sünde gross; Wenn wir in höchsten Nöten sind.
                (ML 4601)
            Volume 3--Canzona, D minor; Preludes, C major and D major;
                Mendelssohn-Bartholdy, Felix. Sonata number 6 in D
                minor. (ML 4602)
            Albert Schweitzer, organ of Parish Church, Günsbach.
                Recorded in 1952-1953.

3509   Albert Schweitzer plays Bach. Prelude in C major; Toccata,
            adagio and fugue in C major; Fugue in A minor; Fantasia
            and fugue in G minor "the Great"; Prelude in D major;
            Canzona in D minor; Chorale preludes: Ich ruf' zu dir,
            Herr Jesu Christ; Wenn wir in höchsten Nöten sind; O
            Mensch, bewein' dein' Sünde gross; Gelobet seist du,
            Jesu Christ; Herzlich tut mich verlangen; Nun komm, der
            Heiden Heiland. Part of the Legendary Performances Series,
            famous recordings originally released by Columbia Master-
            works. Recorded at the Parish Church, Günsbach. Program
            notes by Albert Schweitzer. Two records. Odyssey
            32-26-0003. Released 1967. If purchased separately,
            record numbers are 32-16-0063 and 32-16-0065.

3510   Bach. Organ works. Chorale preludes: Jesus Christus, unser
            Heiland; O Mensch, bewein' dein' Sünde gross; Christ lag
            in Todesbanden; Liebster Jesu, wir sind hier; Fantasy and
            fugue in G minor; Prelude and fugue in C major; Prelude
            and fugue in E minor; Toccata and fugue in D minor. Albert
            Schweitzer, organ. HMV HLM 7003. Released c. 1972.

3511   Franck, Cesar. Choral No. 1 in E major; Choral no. 2 in B
            minor; Choral no. 3 in A minor. A new (1958) release of
            recordings originally put on tape in 1952, at the Parish
            Church, Günsbach. Program notes by Albert Schweitzer on
            the slipcase. Columbia ML 5128.

3512   Mendelssohn-Bartholdy, Felix. Organ sonata No. 4, Opus 65,
            B^b major. Widor, C. M. Symphony no. 6, Opus 42, no. 2,
            G minor--selections (the intermezzo is omitted). Together
            on Columbia ML5290. Jacket notes by Albert Schweitzer,
            translated by Nathan Broder. Released 1958.

3512a   Franck, Cesar. Choral No. 1 in E major for Organ. Columbia
            X-100.

Discography

2. Reviews and Discussions of Recordings

3513   A., P. "Cesar Franck--3 Chorals" (ML 5128). <u>Records in Review</u>. Great Barrington, Mass.: Wyeth Press, 1958, pp. 66-67.

3514   B., J. "Johann Sebastian Bach. Chorals pour Orgue. . . ." <u>Disques</u> (Paris) 67 (Sept.-Oct. 1954), p. 528.

3515   B., N. [Review of Angel COLC 89.] <u>Records in Review</u>. Great Barrington, Mass.: Wyeth Press, 1964, pp. 14-15.

3516   "Bach organ music--Albert Schweitzer, organ: Passacaglia and fugue in C minor, Prelude and fugue in G major, six chorale-preludes." <u>Columbia Record Club Magazine</u> (New York) 3:3, p. 3.

3517   BRICO, ANTONIA. "A statement" (preparation for recording Bach). In: THE CONVOCATION RECORD, pp. VI/1-2.

3518   ELBIN, PAUL N. "Portrait--the phonograph discovers the organ." <u>Etude</u> (Philadelphia) 71:4 (April 1953), pp. 17ff. Port. Review of SL-223.

3519   E., R. (ERICSON, RAY). "Records in Review: Bach: Organ works. . . ." <u>High Fidelity</u> (Great Barrington, Mass.) 3:1 (March-April 1953), pp. 49-50. Review of SL 175.

3520   G., H. "Gramophone notes: Columbia." <u>The Musical Times and Singing-Class Circular</u> (London) 78 (Aug. 1937), p. 708. (Review of Bach Organ Society recording.)

3521   "Gramophone notes: Albert Schweitzer." <u>The Musical Times and Singing-Class Circular</u> (London) 77 (Aug. 1936), pp. 713-14. (Review of Bach Organ Society recording.)

3522   HAGGIN, B. H. "Records." <u>The Nation</u> (New York) 176:8 (Feb. 21, 1953), p. 175. (Review of SL 175.)

3523   HEBB, DAVID. "Schweitzer returns." <u>The Saturday Review</u> (New York) 35:52 (Dec. 27, 1952), p. 52. (Review of SL 175).

3524   KUPFERBERG, HERBERT. "Schweitzer's Bach." The New York <u>Herald Tribune</u> Book Review (Section 6), Oct. 16, 1955, p. 17.

3525   L., C. J. "Schweitzer plays Bach." <u>American Record Guide</u> (New York) 19:7 (March 1953), pp. 215-16. (Review of SL 175).

Music

3526   P., A. "Le 1ᵉʳ disque de Albert Schweitzer. . . ." Disques
        (Paris) 6:59 (Sept.-Oct. 1953), p. 534. (Review of
        SL 175.)

3527   P., R. "J. S. Bach on Organ: the Schweitzer legend now is
        actuality." The New York Times, Jan. 18, 1953, Sect. 2,
        p. 8. (Review of SL 175).

3528   R., A. "Bach . . . Albert Schweitzer (organ). . . ."
        Gramophone (Harrow) 31:366 (Nov. 1953), pp. 193-94.
        (Review of part of SL 175).

3529   _____. "Bach. Chorale preludes. . . ." Gramophone (Harrow)
        31:367 (Dec. 1953), pp. 241-42. (Review of chorale
        preludes sections of SL 175).

3530   REED, PETER HUGH. "Records and radio." Etude (Philadelphia)
        55:1 (Jan. 1937), p. 18. Port. (Review of Columbia 270).

3531   [Review of HMV-HLM 7003.] Hi Fi Notes and Record Review
        (London), July 1972, p. 1284.

3532   [Review of SL 175.] Musical America (New York) 73:7
        (May 1953), p. 17.

3533   SCHONBERG, HAROLD C. [Review of SL 175.] In: The Guide
        to Long-Playing Records: Chamber and Solo Instrument
        Music. New York: Knopf, 1955, pp. 276-77.

IX. Albert Schweitzer and Wolfgang von Goethe

Schweitzer's first attempt to deal with Goethe came while he was studying philosophy at Strasbourg. He could not reconcile Goethe's loyalty to the natural philosophy of the Stoics and Spinoza with his own enthusiasms for the great speculative philosophers Kant, Fichte, and Hegel. Eventually, however, Schweitzer himself turned to a nature philosophy similar to Goethe's and "realized that Goethe was the man who had held out at the abandoned post where we were once more mounting guard. . . ."[1] He discovered a further kinship with Goethe when he began to study the natural sciences in pursuit of his medical degree.

These and many other debts which Schweitzer felt he owed to Goethe were described in his 1928 Goethe Prize address (numbers 3534-3541 below). Over the years, Schweitzer wrote several speeches and articles on the subject. As he states in a letter to Charles R. Joy: "Goethe is the personality with which I have been most deeply concerned. . . . What attracts me to him is that he is a man of action at the same time that he is a poet, a thinker, and in certain domains a savant and a man of research. And what binds us together in the deepest depths of our beings is his philosophy of nature. . . . I cannot tell exactly the extent and the intensity of Goethe's influence upon me. It is impossible to determine in what he has influenced me and in what he has only confirmed me in the way I was already taking. I believe that the latter rather than the former is the more important."[2]

A. Works by Schweitzer

Listed below are the titles of four addresses and an essay written by Schweitzer concerning Goethe. Included in this section are all published versions of these works, both those published as monographs and those published in periodicals or books by others.

---

[1] Goethe. Five Studies. Boston: Beacon Press, 1961, p. 23.

[2] Ibid., pp. 3, 17-18.

Schweitzer and Goethe

      1) Goethe Prize Address (<u>Ansprache bei der Verleihung des Goethepreises</u>), delivered on the occasion of receiving the Goethe Prize from the city of Frankfurt-am-Main, August 28, 1928.

      2) Address delivered at the Centennial Celebration of Goethe's Death (<u>Gedenkrede gehalten bei der Feier der 100. Wiederkehr seines Todestages</u>), Frankfurt-am-Main, March 22, 1932.

      3) "Goethe--Thinker" ("Goethe--Penseur"), an essay contributed to a special Goethe issue of the French review <u>Europe</u>, April 15, 1932.

      4) Goethe as Thinker and Man (<u>Goethe als Denker und Mensch</u>), an address delivered in Ulm, Germany, July 9, 1932. This address has never been independently published, but has appeared only in various editions of the collected addresses.

      5) Goethe: his personality and his work (<u>Goethe, l'homme et l'oeuvre</u>). Address delivered, first in French and later in German, at the International Convocation to Commemorate the Bicentenary of Goethe's Birth, Aspen, Colorado, July 6, 8, 1949. The address was delivered twice, in French and German. The French version was translated and published in Bergstraesser (no. 3560 below); the German version is much longer and differs from the French in other ways. Joy's <u>Goethe. Five Studies</u> contains a new English translation utilizing both versions.

1. Ansprache bei der Verleihung des Goethespreises

  a. Monographs

3534 "Ansprache bei der Verleihung des Goethespreises am 28. August 1928 (Nach dem Stenogram)." Frankfurt a.M.: (Selbstverlag), 1929. 8 pp. Offprint of same from <u>Jahrbuch des Freien Deutschen Hochstifts</u>, 1928, see no. 3536 below.

3535 <u>Goethe</u>. New York: Henry Holt, 1929. 8 pp. Brochure, reprinted from <u>The Hibbert Journal</u>, see no. 3539 below.

  b. Inclusion in Periodicals and Books by Others

3536 "Ansprache bei der Verleihung des Goethespreises am 28. August 1928 (nach dem Stenogram)." <u>Jahrbuch des Freien</u>

Schweitzer and Goethe

Deutschen Hochstifts, 1928. "Im Auftrag der Verwaltung
hrsg. von Ernst Beutler." Frankfurt a.M.: Selbstverlag,
1928, pp. 254-61.

3537   "Ansprache bei der Verleihung des Goethespreises am 28.
August 1928." Elsass-Lothringische Mittellungen
(Strasbourg), 1928, pp. 434ff.

3538   "Discours sur Goethe, 1928" (Extrait). In: HOMMAGE,
pp. 127-35.

3539   "Dr. Albert Schweitzer and Goethe." Tr. C. T. Campion. The
Hibbert Journal (London) 27:4 (July 1929), pp. 684-90.

3540   "Goethe Prize Address." In: Seaver, George. Albert
Schweitzer: the Man and his Mind (see no. 300 above),
1947 edition, pp. 329-34; 1955 edition, pp. 353-58.
Translated in Albert Schweitzer als Mensch and als Denker,
pp. 376-81.

3541   "In welcke apzichten voelt Albert Schweitzer zich verbonden
aan Goethe? De hier folgende Toespraak werd door Prof.
A. Schweitzer op 28. Aug. 1928 in't Goethehuis te
Frankfort bij 't in ontrangst nemen van den 'Goetheprijs'
gehouden." Het Parool (Amsterdam), Aug. 13, 1949.

2. Gedenkrede bei der Feier der 100. Wiederkehr seines
Todestages in seiner Vaterstadt

    a. Monographs

3542   Goethe. Gedenkrede gehalten bei der Feier der 100. Wiederkehr
seines Todestages in seiner Vaterstadt, Frankfurt a.M.,
am 22. März 1932. Munich: C. H. Beck, 1932. 50 pp.
Reprinted 1933.

3543   Goethe. Tr. Takanori Oguri. Tokyo: Nagasake Shoten, 1942.
280 pp.

3544   Goethe. Tokyo: Shinkyo Shuppansha, 1949. 155 pp.

3545   Goethe. Discurso commemorative proferido nas solenidades do
1.⁰ centenáirio de sua morte, a 22 de Marco de 1932 em
Francfurt sóbre-o-Meno, cidado natal de poeta. Tr. Pedro
de Almeida Houra. São Paulo: Edicões Melhoramentos,
1949. 33 pp. (Colecao Goetheana, vol. 1.)

Schweitzer and Goethe

    b. Inclusion in Periodicals, Books by Others

3546   "Goethe's Botschaft an uns." <u>Die Pädagogische Provinz</u>
        (Frankfurt a.M.) 3:8 (Aug. 1949), pp. 475-78. Reprint of
        the final portion of the address.

3547   "Goethe's message for our time." In: Unger, William, ed.
        <u>The Goethe Year/Das Goethe Jahr, 1747-1947</u>. . . . London:
        Maxon and Company, 1952, pp. 27-30. German and English.
        Excerpts only.

3. Goethe, Penseur

3548   "Goethe, Penseur." <u>Europe</u> (Paris) 28:112 (April 15, 1932),
        pp. 175-99.

4. Goethe, l'homme et l'oeuvre

    a. Monographs

3549   "Goethe, der Mensch und das Werk. Ein Vortrag." Amsterdam:
        Bermann-Fischer, 1949, 26 pp. Offprint from <u>Die Neue</u>
        <u>Rundschau</u>, see no. 3559 below.

3550   "Goethe: der Mensch und das Werk/Goethe: his personality
        and his work." Phonodisc. Lecture in German, Aspen,
        Colorado, July 1949. Translation by Thornton Wilder.
        Introduction by G. A. Borghese. German text with English
        translation following intermittently. Winchester Records
        D9-CC-1638-1641.

3551   <u>Goethe: His personality and his work. Address to the Goethe</u>
        <u>Bicentennial Convocation, Aspen, Colorado, July 6 and 8,</u>
        <u>1949</u>. Chicago: Albert Schweitzer Foundation, 1959. 7 pp.
        Reprinted from Bergstraesser, Arnold, ed. <u>Goethe and the</u>
        <u>Modern Age</u>, see no. 3560 below.

3552   "Goethe, l'homme et l'oeuvre. Texte de la conférence faite
        à Aspen (Colorado, U.S.A.) lors de la fête du bicentenaire
        de la naissance de Goethe, organisde par la Société Goethe
        américaine." 15 pp. Offprint from <u>Saisons d'Alsace</u>, see
        no. 3561 below.

3553   <u>Goethe 200-nen Kinen-Koen</u>. Tr. Minoru Nomura. Tokyo:
        Shinkyo Shuppansha, 1950. 64 pp. Reprinted from
        <u>Kirisutokyo-Bunka</u>, see no. 3562 below.

b.   Inclusion in Periodicals, Books by Others

3554   "Albert Schweitzers Bekenntnis zu Goethe. Der Wortlaud des
        Festrede des Arztes und Menschenfreundes bei der
        Zweijahrhundertfeier in Aspen, Colorado." New Yorker
        Staats-Zeitung und Herold (New York), July 7, 8, 9, 1949.

3555   "Albert Schweitzers Goethe-Rede." NIEUWS 1:1 (Dec. 1951),
        pp. 10-11; 1:2 (March 1952), pp. 28-30; 1:3 (July 1952),
        pp. 39-40; 1:4 (Dec. 1952), pp. 60-62.

3556   "Albert Schweitzers Goethe-Rede." IFL Nieuws (The Hague),
        June 1952, pp. 4-6.

3557   BORGESE, ELISABETH MANN. "Goethe and the unity of mankind."
        Common Cause (Chicago) 3:3 (Oct. 1949), pp. 122-24.
        Includes excerpts from Schweitzer's address.

3558   "Goethe, der Mensch und das Werk." Einleitung, Erwin R.
        Jacobi. Radio DRS August 2, 18 and 25, and September 1,
        1978. Reprinted in: BERICHTE 46 (Oct. 1978), pp. 26-27.

3559   "Goethe, der Mensch und das Werk. Ein Vortrag." Die Neue
        Rundschau (Amsterdam) 15 (Summer 1949), pp. 340-65.

3560   "Goethe: his personality and his work." In: Bergstraesser,
        Arnold, ed. Goethe and the Modern Age. The International
        Convocation at Aspen, Colorado, 1949. Chicago: Henry
        Regnery Co., 1950, pp. 95-110.

3561   "Goethe, l'homme et l'oeuvre. . . ." Saisons d'Alsace
        (Strasbourg) 1 (Winter 1950), pp. 13-31. Includes
        facsimile reproduction of a page of the author's manu-
        script, four full-page portraits, and a reproduction of
        a bronze head by Robert Forrer. Accompanied by a digest
        of the address in English.

3562   "Goethe 200-nen Kinen-Koen." Tr. Minoru Nomura. Kirisutokyo-
        Bunka (Tokyo) 46 (May 1950), pp. 8-25.

5.   Collected Addresses

3563   Goethe. Drei Reden. Herausgegeben aus den Verlag C. H. Beck.
        München: Biederstein Verlag, 1949. 67 pp. Contents:
        Ansprache bei der Verleihung des Goethepreises der
        Stadt Frankfurt--Gedenkrede gehalten bei der Feier der
        100. Wiederkehr von Goethes Todestag. . . .--Goethe als
        Denker und Mensch.

Schweitzer and Goethe

3564   Goethe. <u>Vier Reden</u>. (2. und 3. erweiterte Aufl.) München:
        C. H. Beck'sche Verlagsbuchhandlung, 1950. 101 pp.
        Reprinted, 1953, 1955, 1956, 1970. Contents: Ansprache
        bei der Verleihung des Goethepreises der Stadt Frankfurt--
        Gedenkrede gehalten bei der Feier der 100. Wiederkehr
        von Goethes Todestag. . . .--Goethe als Denker und Mensch--
        Goethe, der Mensch und das Werk.

3565   Goethe. [Drei Studien.] Olten [Schweiz]. Vereinigung Oltner
        Bücherfreunde. 1953. 87 pp. Neunundfünfzigste
        Veröffentlichung auf Veranlassung von William Matheson
        für die Vereinigung Oltner Bücherfreunde, 28. August, 1953,
        nr. 59. Limited edition of 686 numbered copies,
        "Bibliophile Ausgabe." Contents: Ansprache bei der
        Verleihung des Goethepreises der Stadt Frankfurt. . . .--
        Goethe als Denker und Mensch--Goethe, der Mensch und das
        Werk.

Danish

3566   <u>Goetheana</u>. I udvalg og oversaettelse ved Ingeborg Buhl.
        Copenhagen: Steen Hasselbalchs Forlag, 1963. 58 pp.,
        port. (Hasselbalchs Kultur-Bibliotek, Bd. 219.) Contents:
        Extracts from Ansprache bei der Verleihung des Goethe-
        preises der Stadt Frankfurt in the preface--Gedenkrede
        gehalten bei der Feier der 100 Wiederkehr von Goethes
        Todestag--Goethe als Denker und Mensch--Goethe, der Mensch
        und das Werk--Goethe Penseur. Aufsatz aus <u>Europe</u>, XXVIII,
        1932.

English

3567   <u>Goethe</u>. London: Adam and Charles Black, 1949. ix. 84 pp.
        Contents: My debt to Goethe (address delivered at
        Frankfurt am Main on receiving the city's Goethe Prize
        "for services to humanity," 28 August, 1928)--Goethe's
        message for our time (address delivered at the celebration
        of the 100th anniversary of his death in the city of his
        birth . . . 22 March, 1932)--Goethe--Thinker (an essay
        contributed to the special number of the French review
        <u>Europe</u>. . . .).

3568   Goethe. <u>Two Addresses</u>. Edited and translated by Charles R.
        Joy and C. T. Campion, with an introduction by Charles R.
        Joy. Boston: The Beacon Press, 1948. 74 pp. Contents:
        A Memorial Address delivered at the celebration of the
        100th anniversary of Goethe's death . . . March 22, 1932--
        An Address delivered at the Goethe House . . . on receiv-
        ing the Goethe Prize . . . August 28, 1928.

3569   <u>Goethe. Four Studies</u>. Translated, with an introduction, by
        Charles R. Joy. Enlarged bicentennial edition. Boston:
        The Beacon Press; Toronto: S. J. Reginald Saunders, 1949.
        116 pp. Contents: The 100th anniversary address delivered
        at the centennial celebration of Goethe's death . . .
        March 22, 1932--Goethe, the Philosopher, an article from
        <u>Europe</u>, April 15, 1932--Goethe as Thinker and man, an
        address given at Ulm, Germany, July 9, 1932--The Goethe
        Prize address, delivered at the Goethe House, Franfurt on
        the Main . . . August 28, 1928.

3570   <u>Goethe. Five Studies</u>. Translated, with an introduction, by
        Charles R. Joy. Boston: Beacon Press, 1961. 143 pp.
        Paperback edition. (BP 116.) Contents: The Goethe
        Prize Address, delivered at the Goethe House, Frankfurt
        on the Main . . . August 28, 1928--Goethe: his Personal-
        ity and His Work, an address given at the Goethe Bicen-
        tennial Convocation . . . at Aspen, Colorado, July 6 and
        8, 1949--The One Hundredth Anniversary Memorial Address,
        delivered at the Centennial Celebration of Goethe's death,
        in his native city, Frankfurt on the Main, March 22, 1932--
        Goethe the Philosopher, an article from <u>Europe</u>, April 15,
        1932--Goethe as Thinker and Man, an address given at Ulm,
        Germany, July 9, 1932.

Japanese

3571   <u>Goethe. Eien no Goethe</u>. Tr. Takanori Oguri. Tokyo: Misuzu
        Shobo, 1953. 142 pp. Contents: Goethe der Mensch und
        das Werk. Vortrag gehalten in Aspen am 8. Juli 1949--
        Goethe als Denker und Mensch. Vortrag gehalten in Ulm,
        1932--Goethe der Philosoph. Ein Aufsatz aus <u>Europe</u>,
        15. April 1932--Ansprache bei der Verliehung des
        Goethepreises der Stadt Frankfurt am 28. August 1928.

       <u>Goethe</u>. Tr. Tomio Tezuka. Tokyo: Hakusuisha, 1957. See
        Collected Works, Vol. 6, no. 6 above.

Portuguese

3572   <u>Goethe. Estudos sōbre o poeta através de quatro discursos</u>.
        Tr. e pref. e notas de Pedro de Almeida Moura. São
        Paulo: Melhoramentos, 1961. 159 pp., front.

Schweitzer and Goethe

    B. Writings by Others About Schweitzer and Goethe

  a. Books

3573 <u>Goethe. Bicentennial Convocation and Music Festival, 1949</u>.
        Aspen, Colorado, U.S.A., June 27-July 16. Chicago:
        Goethe Bicentennial Foundation, n.d. 12 pp. Port.

      HAYNES, ROBERT. Albert Schweitzer's View of Goethe. See
        Dissertations, no. 4319 below.

3574 LIND, EMIL. <u>Die universalmenschen Goethe und Schweitzer</u>.
        <u>Parallelen zwischen Weimar und Lambarene</u>. (Zum 90.
        Geburtstag.) Neustadt a/d. Weinstrasse: Pfalzische
        Verlagsanstalt, 1964, 310 pp.

      WOODHULL, ALICE SUMNER. Albert Schweitzer und Johann
        Wolfgang von Goethe. See Dissertations, no. 4347 below.

  b. Articles, Parts of Books

3575 "Albert Schweitzer Goethepreisträger." <u>Elsass-Lothringische</u>
        <u>Mitteilungen</u> (Berlin) 10:1 (Jan. 1, 1928), pp. 434-35.

3576 "Albert Schweitzer, Träger des Goethepreises." <u>Mitteilungen</u>
        <u>des Verlages Breitkopf & Härtel</u> (Leipzig) 146 (Dec. 1928),
        pp. 1-2.

3577 BAUR, HANS. "Albert Schweitzer, Träger des Goethepreises."
        <u>Schweizerisches Protestantenblatt</u> (Basel) 51:35
        (Sept. 1, 1928), p. 285.

3578 BELZNER, EMIL. "Albert Schweitzers drei Goethe-Reden."
        <u>Rhein-Neckar Zeitung</u> (Heidelberg), Aug. 30, 1949.

3579 BORGESE, ELISABETH MANN. "Goethe and the unity of mankind."
        A report on the Goethe Bicentennial Convocation in
        Aspen . . . <u>Common Cause</u> (Chicago) 3:3 (Oct. 1949),
        pp. 122-24.

3580 COARACY, VIVALDO. "Goetheana." <u>O Estado de São Paulo</u> (São
        Paulo), Oct. 18, 1949, p. 20.

3581 COBBAERT, A.-M. "Commend ecrivait Schweitzer?" <u>Germinal</u>
        (Brussels) 827 (Sept. 10, 1965), p. 5.

3582 "Die deutsche millionen endeckt. Die deutsche Propagandastelle
        bekennt--Der Bandenführer v. Goethe als Mittelsmann--Die
        Politzei deckt durch Zufall die Zusammenhänge auf. . . ."

Schweitzer and Goethe

Das Narrenschiff (Strasbourg) 10 (Sept. 8, 1928), p. 2.
Satire on the award of the Goethe Prize to Albert
Schweitzer. Reprinted as "Um Albert Schweitzers Goethe-
Preis." Elsass-Lothringen Heimatstimmen (Berlin) 6:11
(Nov. 3, 1928), pp. 700-01.

3583   DOWNES, OLIN. "Albert Schweitzer calls Bach and Goethe
         painters." The New York Times, July 10, 1949, p. X5.

3584   E., DR. "Goethe als Denker und Mensch. Vortrag von Prof.
         Dr. Albert Schweitzer, Ulm, 9. Juli 1932." Ulmer Tagblatt
         (Ulm), July 10, 1932. Reprinted in RUNDBRIEF 19
         (Jan. 14, 1962), pp. 54-55.

3585   FIELDS, SIDNEY. "The thirteenth apostle." Sunday Mirror of
         Sunday Daily Mirror (New York), July 10, 1949, p. 27.

3586   GILTAY, H. "Schweitzer en Goethe." NIEUWS 2:4 (March 1954),
         pp. 59-60.

3587   "Goethe and Schweitzer" (editorial). The Christian Century
         (Chicago) 66:29 (July 20, 1949), pp. 862-63.

3588   "Der Goethepreis für Lambarene." Eckart (Berlin-Steglitz)
         4:10 (Oct. 1928), p. 447.

3589   GRABS, RUDOLF. "Ehrfurcht bei Goethe und Schweitzer."
         Freies Christentum (Frankfurt a.M.) 20:6 (June 1968),
         cols. 86-88.

3590   "Grosse Rede Prof. Albert Schweitzers bildete den Höhepunkt
         der Goethe-Feierlichkeiten in Aspen, Col." New Yorker
         Staats-Zeitung und Herold (New York), July 10, 1949.

3591   KIRCHNER, FRANZ. "Albert Schweitzer und Goethe." In:
         VERMÄCHTNIS UND WIRKLICHKEIT, pp. 67-74.

3592   LANDMANN, LUDWIG. [Official address delivered on the occasion
         of his presentation of the Goethe Prize to Albert
         Schweitzer on behalf of the City of Frankfurt am Main,
         28 August 1928.] In: Jahrbuch des Freien Deutschen
         Hochstifts 1928. Hrsg. von Ernst Beutler. Frankfurt
         am Main, 1928, pp. 249-53.

3593   LENEL, LUISE. "Goethe and Schweitzer." In: Hammer, Carl,
         ed. Goethe after Two Centuries. Baton Rouge, La.:
         Louisiana State University Press, 1952, pp. 105-09.
         (Humanity Series, no. 1.)

Schweitzer and Goethe

3594   LIND, EMIL. "Albert Schweitzer and Goethe." RUNDBRIEF 13
           (Dec. 15, 1958), pp. 8-28.

3595   _____. "Die Goethe-Reden Albert Schweitzers." In: DENKEN
           UND WEG, pp. 307-10.

3596   _____. [Selection without title.] In: BEGEGNUNG, pp. 192-95.
           From his book Albert Schweitzer. Aus seinem Leben und
           Werk, see no. 273 above.

3597   MATHOW, ERICH. "Albert Schweitzer in der Nachfolge Goethes."
           RUNDBRIEF 17 (Jan. 14, 1961), pp. 50-59.

3598   MINDER, ROBERT. "Le Prix Goethe de 1928--Albert Schweitzer."
           Revue d'Allemagne et des Pays de Langue Allemande (Paris)
           13/14 (Nov. 1928), pp. 538-42.

3599   _____. "Zu Albert Schweitzers Begegnung mit Goethe."
           Universitas (Stuttgart) 15:1 (Jan. 1960), pp. 43-48.
           Reprinted in: DENKEN UND WEG, pp. 281-86; reprinted in
           RUNDBRIEF 40 (Jan. 14, 1975), pp. 50-54; translated as
           "Albert Schweitzer's relationship to Goethe." Universitas
           (English language edition) 7:1 (1964), pp. 51-56.

3600   MÖCKEL, KARL. "Albert Schweitzer und Goethe." RUNDBRIEFE/DDR
           7 (Jan. 1966), pp. 10-14.

3601   "Neue Ehrung Albert Schweitzers. Verleihung des Goethepreises
           der Stadt Frankfurt a. M." Elsass-Lothringen Heimatstimmen
           (Berlin) 6:8/9 (Sept. 1, 1928), p. 572.

3602   OE., W. "Verleihung des Goethepreises an Albert Schweitzer."
           Evangelisches Missionsmagazin (Basel) 72 (Oct. 1928),
           pp. 315-17.

3603   PAQUET, ALFONS. "Der Goethe-Preis. Ein Rundfunkvortrag."
           Die Literatur (Stuttgart, Berlin) 31 (Oct. 1928/
           Oct. 1929), pp. 21-26.

3604   RATTER, MAGNUS. "Schweitzer's debt to Goethe." Faith and
           Freedom (Leeds) 2 (Oct. 1948/June 1949), pp. 17-20.

3605   REUBER, KURT. "Albert Schweitzer und Goethe." Die
           Christliche Welt (Gotha) 46:15 (Aug. 1, 1952), pp. 682-87.

           ROSENWALD, HANS. "Schweitzer, Goethe, and Bach." See Music--
           Bach, no. 3406 above.

3606 SCHÜTZ, ROLAND. "Ehrfurcht--von Goethe zu Albert Schweitzer."
RUNDBRIEF 13 (Dec. 15, 1958), pp. 39-43.

3607 "Schweitzer here for Goethe event." The New York Times,
June 29, 1949, p. 15.

3608 "Schweitzer meets students of Goethe." The New York Times,
July 8, 1949, p. 17.

3609 STEFFAHN, HARALD. "Goethe und Albert Schweitzer. Ein Versuch."
RUNDBRIEF 22 (April 18, 1963), pp. 19-37.

3610 STEVENS, AUSTIN. "Schweitzer calls U.S. aid 'spiritual.'
Philosopher at Goethe session points to Americans behind
material lift to Europe (Marshall Plan)." The New York
Times, July 6, 1949, p. 22.

3611 _____. "Schweitzer says Goethe philosophy would help mankind
seek liberty." The New York Times, July 7, 1949, p. 23.

3612 STRESEMANN, WOLFGANG. "Die Bedeutung Albert Schweitzers als
Interpret Goetheschen Geistes." New Yorker Staats-
Zeitung und Herold (New York), July 14, 1949, p. 8.

3613 WALTER, HEINRICH. "Albert Schweitzers Weg zu Goethe."
New Yorker Staats-Zeitung und Herold (New York),
July 6, 1949, p. 4.

3614 WINSOR, ELLEN and REBECCA WINSOR EVANS. "Reservations on
Goethe and Schweitzer." The Christian Century (Chicago)
66:33 (Aug. 17, 1949), p. 965. For a letter to the
editor in response, see Johnson, F. E. "Schweitzer out
of context." The Christian Century (Chicago) 66:37
(Sept. 14, 1949), p. 1074.

3615 ZEYDEL, E. H. "Goethe's message and Schweitzer's, America to
hear 'the new Faust incarnate' during the 200th anniver-
sary." The Christian Register (Boston) 138:6 (June 1949),
pp. 14-16.

X. Albert Schweitzer and World Peace

Albert Schweitzer's concern with peace was deeply rooted in his basic philosophy of reverence for life and his concern with the crisis of modern civilization. As James Brabazon says in his biography of Schweitzer, "Before 1914 he was already warning the world against rampant nationalism, the dehumanizing effects of technology, and the growth of vast, soul-demanding organizations, whether commercial or political. In the Second World War irreverence for life had reached new levels. . . . Things that human beings would never . . . dream of doing on their own behalf, they did cold-bloodedly in the name of some national or political mystique."[1] In 1951 Schweitzer was awarded the Friedenspreis des Deutschen Buchhandels for his efforts to create an ethical world society (see nos. 3639-52); in his acceptance speech, he declared that the way to peace was for men to become able to trust one another. His thoughts on the ethical foundation of world peace were summarized in his Nobel Peace Prize address in Oslo in 1954 (see nos. 3653-83 below).

Schweitzer had also been concerning himself with the issue of atomic development. He had been in touch with Einstein and Oppenheimer and had done research into the effects of the atomic explosions at Nagasaki and Hiroshima. But he did not speak out publicly on this issue until 1954, when he published a letter in the London Daily Herald (no. 3779 below) urging individual scientists to speak out against the dangers of atomic weaponry. In 1957 he decided that he should express his concern publicly and arranged for his "Declaration of Conscience" (nos. 3712-22 below) to be broadcast over Radio Oslo. He followed this with three more broadcasts on April 28, 29, and 30, 1958 (nos. 3723-44 below). He continued his work against the bomb in letters and articles until his death in 1965.

---

[1]Brabazon, James. Albert Schweitzer: a Biography. New York: G. P. Putnam, 1975, p. 418.

General

World Peace

A. General

1. Shorter Writings by Schweitzer

3616   "Geleitwort von Albert Schweitzer." Kriegesblinden Jahrbuch
          8:1 (1958), pp. 1-2.

3617   Letter to Dwight Eisenhower, Jan. 10, 1957. In: Cousins,
          Norman. Dr. Schweitzer of Lambarene. New York: Harper,
          1960, pp. 189-90. Reprinted in: BRABAZON, p. 432.

3618   "Schuldig der Unmenschlichkeit (1952)." In: Italiaander,
          Rolf, compiler. Frieden in der Welt, aber wie? Gedanken
          der Friedens-Nobelpreisträger. Mit einem Vorwort von
          Carl Friedrich von Weizsäcker. Stuttgart: J. Fink,
          1967, pp. 67-69. (Politikum-Reihe, Band 15.)

3619   "Der Weg zum Frieden." Schweizer Frauenblatt (Zürich) 33:53
          (1954).

2. Writings About Schweitzer by Others

    a. Books

        AVILES FABILA, RENE. Albert Schweitzer. See Life and Work,
            no. 228 above.

3620   OTTO, BERND. Albert Schweitzers Beitrag zur Friedenspolitik.
          Geleitwort von Ulrich Neuenschwander. Hamburg: Herbert
          Reich Evangelischer Verlag, 1974. 125 pp. (Evangelische
          Zeitstimmen 67/68). See also Dissertations, no. 4334
          below.

3621   TAU, MAX. Albert Schweitzer und der Friede. Hamburg:
          Meiner, 1955. 32 pp. Illus. Also Leipzig: Dt. Buch-
          Export-u.-Import in Komm., 1957. 34 pp.

3622   WINNUBST, BENEDICTUS. Das Friedensdenken Albert Schweitzers.
          Amsterdam: Rodopi, 1974. 219 pp. See also Dissertations,
          no. 4345 below.

    b. Articles, Parts of Books

3623   BAUR, HERMANN. "Albert Schweitzer--Friede und Zukunft."
          In: GESTERN-HEUTE, pp. 24-25. Shortened version of a
          speech given by Baur in Saarburcken, Oct. 29, 1971.

General

3624 CHEN WU FU, ALBERT. "The way to world peace." Medicine and
         Ministry 10:2 (May 15, 1976), pp. 1-3. Reprinted in
         A.I.S.L. Bulletin 2 (Nov. 1976), pp. 25-27.

3625 FISCHER, GERHARD. "Die Dimensionen von Albert Schweitzers
         Friedensdienst." Standpunkt: Evangelische Monatsschrift
         (Berlin) 3:1 (Jan. 1975), pp. 9-10.

3626 GÖTTING, GERALD. "Dem Pionier der Friedensgesinnung."
         RUNDBRIEFE/DDR 6 (1965), pp. 6-16.

3627 _____. "Streiter für Humanität und Frieden." In: Albert
         Schweitzer Komitee beim Präsidium des Deutschen Roten
         Kreuzes in der DDR. 100. Geburtstag von Albert Schweitzer.
         Festveranstaltung, pp. 6-18.

3628 _____. "Wegbereiter der Friedensgesinnung." RUNDBRIEFE/DDR
         27 (1975), pp. 1-10.

3629 HAMMARSKJÖLD, D. "Dernière lettre." In: RAYONNEMENT, p. 269.

3630 LUDWIG, WERNER. "Seine Mahnung zum Frieden wirkt fert."
         RUNDBRIEFE/DDR 19 (1972), pp. 2-8.

3631 PIRE, DOMINIQUE. "Gespräch mit Dr. Albert Schweitzer über
         den Frieden, 1959." Universitas (Stuttgart) 15:1
         (Jan. 1960), pp. 121-22. Reprinted as "Gespräch über
         den Frieden." In: DENKEN UND WEG, pp. 566-67; reprinted
         in: BEGEGNUNG, pp. 266-67; reprinted as "Aus dem Gespräch
         mit Dr. Albert Schweitzer über den Frieden, 1959." In:
         GESTERN-HEUTE, p. 58; translated as "Believing in God."
         Universitas (English language edition) 7:1 (1964),
         pp. 91-92.

3632 POLAK, MARTIN WILLEM. "Albert Schweitzer en de vrede."
         Vrij Nederland (Amsterdam) 13 (Nov. 27, 1954), p. 15.

3633 ROSENBLATT, THEO. "Mit den Waffen von Ghandi und Schweitzer."
         Die Friedensrundschau 9:9 (Sept. 1955), p. 24.

3634 SHIGI, T. "Was sollen wir heute tun?" In: DENKEN UND WEG,
         pp. 562-65.

3635 SPEAR, OTTO. "Schweitzers und unsere Sorge um den Frieden."
         RUNDBRIEF 44 (Nov. 1977), pp. 39-49.

3636 STREGE, MARTIN. "Der Weg zum Frieden ist Albert Schweitzers
         'elementare Religion.'" RUNDBRIEF 35 (June 15, 1972),
         pp. 22-33.

World Peace

3637   UITZ, FRANZ ADALBERT. "Albert Schweitzer und das Problem des
          Friedens." RUNDBRIEF 12 (June 15, 1958), pp. 30-43.

3638   WINNUBST, BENEDICT. "Albert Schweitzer und der Friede in
          unserer Zeit." RUNDBRIEF 40 (1975), pp. 11-17.

   B.   Peace Prize Address (Friedenspreis des Deutschen
             Buchhandels, 16. September 1951)

On September 16, 1951, in Frankfurt am Main, Schweitzer was awarded
a 10,000-mark prize by the West German Association of Book Publishers
and Sellers for his efforts in promoting world peace. The following
lists include reprints of Schweitzer's address, as well as articles
commenting on or relating to it.

1.   Schweitzer's Address

3639   "Auszug aus der Frankfurter Rede vom 16. September 1951."
          In: Oswald, Suzanne. Geist der Humanität, see no. 286
          above.

3640   [Peace Prize Address.] In: Börsenblatt für den Deutschen
          Buchhandel (Stuttgart) 7:82 (Oct. 1951), pp. 367-69.

3641   "Festansprache (beim Empfang des Friedenspreises)." In:
          Friedenspreis des Deutschen Buchhandels. Reden und
          Würdigungen 1951-1960. Frankfurt am Main: Börsenverein
          des Deutschen Buchhandels, 1961, pp. 24-31.

3642   "Albert Schweitzer." In: Freiheit und Verantwortung, vier
          Ausprachen anlässlich der Verleihung des Friedenspreises
          des deutschen Buchhandels an. Frankfurt: Deutscher
          Verleger-und-Buchhändler Verbände, 1951, pp. 31-38.

3643   "Die Kraft der Humanitätsgesinnung." In: Mensch und
          Menschlichkeit, eine Vortragsreihe. With contributions
          by Paul Althaus, Karl Barth, and others. Stuttgart:
          Kröner, 1956, pp. 123-32.

2.   Works About Schweitzer in Periodicals and
     Books by Others

3644   "Albert Schweitzer erhält Friedenspreis des Buchhandels."
          Offenbach Post 175 (July 31, 1951), p. 2.

3645   "German publishing industry honors Albert Schweitzer."
       Publishers Weekly (New York) 160 (Nov. 3, 1951), p. 1808.

3646   HEUSS, THEODOR. "Ansprache der Bundespräsidenten Professor
           Theodor Heuss anlässlich der Verleihung des Friedens-
           preises des deutschen Buchhandels an Professor Albert
           Schweitzer auf dem Ersten Deutschen Buchhändlertag am
           16. September 1951 in der Paulskirche zu Frankfurt am
           Main." Börsenblatt für den deutschen Buchhandel
           (Stuttgart) 7:82 (Oct. 12, 1951), pp. 365-67. Reprinted
           in: Friedenspreis des Deutschen Buchhandels. Reden und
           Würdigungen 1951-1960. Frankfurt am Main: Börsenverein
           des Deutschen Buchhandels, 1961, pp. 17-23; reprinted in
           Freiheit und Verantwortung, vier Ausprachen Anlässlich
           der Verleihung des Friedenspreises des deutschen
           Buchhandels an. Frankfurt: Deutscher Verleger-und-
           Buchhändler Verbände, 1951, pp. 21-27; reprinted as
           "Albert Schweitzer." In: Heuss, Theodor. Würdigungen:
           Reden, Aufsätze und Briefe aus den Jahren 1949-1955.
           Hrsg. von Hans Bott. Tübingen: Rainer Wunderlich, Verlag
           Hermann Leins, 1955, pp. 271-79; reprinted in: BEGEGNUNG,
           pp. 233-38; reprinted in: EHRFURCHT, pp. 194-99; reprinted
           with title "Ein grosse Wagnis." In: GESTERN-HEUTE,
           pp. 40-41; translated as "Speech on Albert Schweitzer.
           The man and his way for mankind." Universitas (English
           language edition) 7:1 (1964), pp. 19-24.

3647   KNECHT, JOSEF. [Speech made at the presentation.] In:
           Freiheit und Verantwortung, vier Ausprachen anlässlich
           der Verleihung des Friedenspreises des deutschen Buch-
           handels an. Frankfurt: Deutscher Verleger-und-Buchhändler
           Verbände, 1951, pp. 11-18.

3648   KOLB, WALTER. [Speech made at the presentation.] In:
           Freiheit und Verantwortung, vier Ausprachen anlässlich
           der Verleihung des Friedenspreises des deutschen Buch-
           handels an. Frankfurt: Deutscher Verleger-und-Buchhändler
           Verbände, 1951, pp. 7-8.

3649   "M. Albert Schweitzer recoit le Prix de la Paix fondé par
           l'Association des éditeurs allemande." Le Figaro (Paris)
           125:2184 (Sept. 17, 1951), p. 2.

3650   "Schweitzer given peace award" (editorial). The Christian
           Century (Chicago) 68:41 (Oct. 10, 1951), p. 1148.

3651   "'Solange in Deutschland solche Not herrscht . . . Albert
           Schweitzer will Preis nicht annehmen." Abendpost
           (Frankfurt a.M.) 201 (Aug. 30, 1951), p. 2.

World Peace

3652   TAU, MAX. "Albert Schweitzer." <u>Börsenblatt für den deutschen</u>
           <u>Buchhandel</u> (Stuttgart) 7:63 (Aug. 7, 1951), p. 261.

                    C. Nobel Peace Prize

1. Schweitzer's Nobel Peace Prize Address

                   LE PROBLÈME DE LA PAIX
              (Das Problem des Friedens in der Heutigen Welt/
              The Problem of Peace in the World of Today)

Albert Schweitzer was awarded the 1952 Nobel Peace Prize in absentia
on October 30, 1953; he returned to Europe to deliver his Peace Prize
address in Oslo on November 4, 1954. In his speech, "The Problem of
Peace in the World of Today," delivered in French, he discusses the
world situation of that time, sketches various historical approaches
to the problems of peace, and concludes: "I am profoundly convinced
that the solution is this; we should reject war for ethical reasons--
because, that is to say, it makes us guilty of the crime of
inhumanity."[1]

     The following lists publications of Schweitzer's address, both in
monographs and in periodicals and books by others, and discussions of
the address by other authors.

     a. Monographs

3653   <u>Le Problème de la Paix</u>. Stockholm: P. A. Norstedt and Söner,
           1955.

3654   <u>Le Problème de la Paix</u>. Discours d' Oslo, 4 Novembre 1954.
              Seraing: Assoc. Belge des Amis d'Albert Schweitzer. 15 pp.

3655   <u>Message de la Paix</u>. Paris: P. de Tartas, 1958. 61 pp.
           Illus.

                            <u>Danish</u>

3656   <u>Fredens Problem</u>. Tale Holdt ved Modtagelsen af Nobelfred-
              prisen i Oslo den 4. November 1954. Tr. Børge Friis.
              Copenhagen: Branner og Korch, 1954. 16 pp.

_____

[1]<u>The Problem of Peace in the World of Today</u>. London: A. and C.
Black, 1955, p. 19.

                               372

World Peace

Dutch

3657   Nobelprijs-Rede van Dr. Albert Schweitzer. Vertaald door
       Harold E. Robles. Deventer: Nederlands Albert Schweitzer
       Centrum. 12 pp.

English

3658   The Problem of Peace in the World of Today. Nobel Peace
       Prize Address. New York: Harper, 1954. 19 pp.

3659   The Problem of Peace in the World of Today. London: A. and
       C. Black, 1954. 20 pp. Reprinted 1954, 1955.

German

3660   Das Problem des Friedens in der Heutigen Welt. Rede bei der
       Entgegennahme des Nobel-Friedenspreises in Oslo am 4
       November 1954. Munich: C. H. Beck, 1955. 20 pp.

International Language

3661   La Problemo dil Paco. Diskurso okasion la distributo dil
       Nobel Premio dil Paco en Oslo. Tradukita ek la Franca
       al Linguo Internaciona Ido da Ed. Wakerkotte. Colmar,
       Zürich: Suis Uniono por la Linguo Internaciona, n.d.,
       11 pp.

Korean

3662   Hyŏndae ŭi segye p'yŏngwa munje. 1959. 113 pp. (With Das
       Christentum und die Weltreligionen).

b. Inclusion in Periodicals, Books by Others

3663   "Le Problem de la Paix." Foi et Vie (Paris) 53:3
       (May-June 1955), pp. 226-39. Published also as an
       offprint.

3664   "Discours d'Oslo, 1954." (Extracts of Nobel Peace Prize
       Speech, Nov. 4, 1954). In: HOMMAGE, pp. 137-41.

3665   "Discours d'Oslo, 1954, lors de la remise du Prix Nobel"
       (extrait). In: RAYONNEMENT, pp. 272-74.

Dutch

3666   "Albert Schweitzer's Rede te Oslo. 'Houdt vrede met alle
       mensen!'" Vrij Nederland (Amsterdam) 15:11
       (Nov. 13, 1954), pp. 1-2. Port.

World Peace

3667   "Het probleem van de vrede. Rede op 4 November 1954 te Oslo
         gehouden." NIEUWS 4:2 (May 1955), pp. 3-12.

3668   "De weg naar de vrede." (Rede ter gelegenheid van de
         aanvaarding van de Nobelprijs voor de Vrede 1954.)
         De Kern (Amsterdam) 24:12 (Dec. 1954), pp. 570-75. Port.,
         cover port.

English

3669   "Excerpts from the Nobel Peace Prize Address by Dr. Schweitzer
         in Oslo." The New York Times, Nov. 5, 1954, p. 4.

3670   "Peace." In: FESTSCHRIFT, pp. 143-58.

3671   "The problem of peace. Dr. Albert Schweitzer's Nobel Peace
         Prize lecture." Peace News (London) 959 (Nov. 12, 1954),
         pp. 2-3.

3672   "The problem of peace." The Norseman (London) 12:6
         (Nov./Dec. 1954), pp. 361-69.

3673   "The problem of peace." In: Haberman, Frederick W., ed.
         Peace 1951-1970: Nobel Lectures, including presentation
         speeches and laureates' biographies. Amsterdam, London,
         New York: Elsevier, 1972, Vol. III, pp. 46-57.

3674   "The problem of peace in the world of today." The Christian
         Register (Boston) 134:1 (Jan. 1955), pp. 11-15.

3675   "The problem of peace in the world of today." COURIER,
         special edition (April 1968), 16 pp.

German

3676   "Albert Schweitzer: nie wieder Krieg! Die Friedensrede des
         Nobelpreisträgers in Oslo. Ruf nach dem Geist der Ethik."
         Münchner Merkur (Munich) 265 (Nov. 5, 1954), p. 11.

3677   "Friedensrede Albert Schweitzers in Oslo. Nationalismus
         übelster Art grösstes Hindernis--Appell an die Völker."
         Stuttgarter Zeitung 259 (Nov. 5, 1954), p. 1.

3678   "Das Problem des Friedens. Albert Schweitzers Nobelpreisrede
         in Oslo." Mannheimer Morgen (Nov. 5, 1954), p. 14.

3679   "Das Problem des Friedens. Rede bei der Entgegennahme des
         Nobelfriedenspreises in Oslo am 4. November 1954." Die
         Schwarzburg (Hamburg) 64:2 (May 1955), pp. 25-33.

3680   "Das Problem des Friedens in der heutigen Welt." In: Röhrs,
          Hermann, ed. Friedenspädagogik. Erziehungswissen-
          schaftliche Reihe, Bd. 1. Frankfurt am Main, 1970,
          pp. 3-14.

3681   "Das Problem des Friedens in der heutigen Welt." In: Die
          Lehre von der Ehrfurcht vor dem Leben, see no. 2702
          above, pp. 113-28.

3682   [Phonodisc.] Das Problem des Friedens in der heutigen Welt
          (und) Aus meiner Kindheit und Jugendzeit. Stimme der
          Wissenschaft 21/1. 1966. Recorded in Oslo, Nov. 4-5,
          1954.

3683   "Über das Problem des Friedens. Aus der Rede bei der
          Überreichung des Friedens-Nobelpreises in November 1954."
          Das Werk (Gelsenkirchen) 4:1 (1955), pp. 11-12.

2.   Writings About Schweitzer by Others

3684   [Award of the Nobel Peace Prize for 1952.] Life (New York)
          35:19 (Nov. 9, 1953), p. 54. Port.

3685   C., L. "Albert Schweitzer, Premio Nobel." Revista Musical
          Chilena (Santiago) 9:44 (Jan. 1954), pp. 99-101.

3686   "Doctor Schweitzer honored." The Nation (New York) 177:21
          (Nov. 21, 1953), p. 421.

3687   "Enthusiasm in Oslo for Dr. Schweitzer--most popular winner
          of peace prize." The Times (London), Nov. 3, 1954, p. 4f.

3688   GUNTHER, JOACHIM. "'Es ist stärkend an Sie zu denken!' Zur
          Verleihung des Friedensnobelpreises an Albert Schweitzer."
          Die Neue Zeitung (Munich) 256 (Nov. 1, 1953), p. 5.

3689   H., F. "Friedenspreis für Albert Schweitzer." Neues
          Abendland (Munich) 6:9 (1951), p. 505.

3690   HEUSS, THEODOR. "Den menschen tröstendes Symbol. Bundes-
          präsident Prof. Dr. Theodor Heuss zur Verleihung des
          Friedens-Nobelpreises an Albert Schweitzer." (Würdigungs-
          Ansprache über den Nordwestdeutschen Rundfunk am 31.
          Oktober 1953). Das Parlament (Bonn) 3:45 (Nov. 11, 1953),
          p. 3.

3691   "Honored: Albert Schweitzer." Newsweek (New York) 44:20
          (Nov. 15, 1954), p. 87.

World Peace

3692   HYGEN, JOHAN B. "Albert Schweitzer og vi tale i Oslo rådhus
          5 November." Morgenbladet (Oslo) 258 (Nov. 6, 1954),
          p. 3.

3693   ITALIAANDER, ROLF. "Hat die Katze junge bekommen?
          Schweitzer glaubte nicht an den Nobelpreis." Hamburger
          Abendblatt (Hamburg) 290 (Dec. 12/13, 1953), p. 9.

3694   _____. "Schweitzer geloofde neit aan de Nobel prijs."
          Vrij Nederland (Amsterdam) 15 (Dec. 5, 1953), pp. 1f.
          Reprinted in NIEUWS 2:3 (Dec. 1953), pp. 43-44.

3695   JAHN, GUNNAR. [Selection without title.] In: BEGEGNUNG,
          pp. 239-41. Text prepared for the Siebenstern-Taschenbuch
          edition of Aus meinem Leben und Denken.

3696   LINDEMANN, HELMUT. "Ein Mensch gegen den geist der Zeit.
          Zur Verleihung des Friedens-Nobel-preises an Albert
          Schweitzer." Stuttgarter Zeitung 256 (Nov. 2, 1953),
          p. 2.

3697   MARCHAL, GEORGES. "Albert Schweitzer, Prix Nobel de la Paix."
          In: Boegner, Marc, et al. Dynamisme du Protestantisme
          français. Paris: Fischbacher, 1954/55, pp. 26-27. A
          short radio talk.

3698   MICHALTSCHAFF, THEODOR. "Albert Schweitzer erhielt den
          Friedensnobelpreis." Die Friedensrundschau 8 (Feb. 1954),
          pp. 7-8.

3699   "En misjonaer far Nobelprisen." Norsk Misjonstidende
          (Stavanger) 108:36 (Nov. 14, 1953), p. 8. Port.

3700   "Nobel Prize to Dr. Schweitzer." The Diapason (Chicago)
          45:1 (Dec. 1, 1953), p. 20.

3701   "Nobelman Schweitzer." Time (New York) 64 (Nov. 15, 1954),
          p. 48.

3702   "De Nobelprijs toegekend" (and) "De uitreiking." NIEUWS 2:3
          (Dec. 1953), p. 42.

3703   NOVRUP, JOHS. "Nobelpristagerin Albert Schweitzer."
          Verdens Gang (Oslo) 7:10 (Dec. 1953), pp. 374-77.

3704   "Le Prix Nobel de la Paix pour 1952 au Dr. Albert Schweitzer."
          Magazin Ringier (St. Louis, France) 47 (Nov. 21, 1953),
          pp. 3-4.

World Peace

3705   [ROSS, EMORY.] "An unusual choice" (editorial). <u>National
        Council Outlook</u> (New York) 3:10 (Dec. 1953), p. 16.

3706   "Schweitzer and Marshall Nobel Prizemen." <u>The Christian
        Century</u> (Chicago) 70:45 (Nov. 11, 1953), p. 1283.

3707   TAU, MAX. "Albert Schweitzer i forbindelse med hand besök
        i Norge." <u>Aftenposten</u> (Oslo), Jan. 15, 17, 1953.

3708   THIOUT, MICHEL. "Dans le triste monde qui est le nôtre voici
        un grand homme. Albert Schweitzer. Prix de Paix."
        <u>L'Alsace Illustrée</u> (Mulhouse) 8:22 (Nov. 15, 1953),
        pp. 8, 17. Illus., ports.

3709   "'Vi venter paaen forsoningens aans.' Fredsprisvinderen hyldes
        i Oslo en intraengende Appel til sllr lsnde om at fjerne
        frygten for krig." <u>Politiken</u> (Copenhagen), Nov. 5, 1954,
        pp. 1-2.

3710   WIBERG, INGRID SEGERSTEDT. "Den Goda Viljans Seger (Albert
        Schweitzer)." <u>Världshorisont</u> (Stockholm) 8:12 (Dec. 1954),
        pp. 27-29.

3711   "Zur Verleihung des Friedens-Nobelpreises" (in deutsche
        Sprache). <u>Les Dernieres Nouvelles d'Alsace</u> (Strasbourg),
        Nov. 1, 1953. Reprinted in RUNDBRIEF 4 (Jan. 14, 1954),
        p. 16; reprinted in: DOKUMENTE, pp. 196-97.

D.   Schweitzer's Opposition to Nuclear Testing

Schweitzer first voiced his opposition to nuclear testing in a letter
to the <u>London Daily Herald</u> in 1954. On April 23, 1957, an address by
him on the danger of atomic-bomb experiments was broadcast by
Norwegian Radio from Broadcast House, Oslo, Norway. The broadcast
was in Norwegian (for home service) and in the English, French,
German, and Russian languages by short wave.

A second address, "Friede oder Atomkrieg?" (Peace or Atomic War?),
originally written in German by Dr. Schweitzer and delivered on
three successive days, was broadcast to the world a year later, on
April 28, 29, and 30, 1958. It, too, was sent from Olso, in
Norwegian (for home service), and in English, French, German, and
Russian by short wave. The text was also broadcast in either English, French, German, or Norwegian to practically all radio stations
in Europe, Africa, Asia, Australia, South America, and the United
States, a total of ninety-six stations.

World Peace

    The entries below are in two sections. The first, "Monographs,"
includes the titles of the addresses published in book or brochure
form and citations for the mimeographed transcripts used in the
various broadcasts. Included also are entries for Dr. Schweitzer's
own typescripts for the 1957 and 1958 broadcasts, now in the archives
of Norwegian Radio.

    The addresses were widely published in periodicals or newspapers
of many countries, and entries for them, so far as they could be discovered by the compiler, appear in the second section, "Inclusion in
Periodicals and Books by Others." This section also includes other
works by Schweitzer on this subject.

1. Monographs

1957

3712   Die Gefahr welche die bei Versuchen mit Atombomben entstehenden
        radioaktiven Elemente für die Menschheit bedeuten.
        20 pp. Dr. Schweitzer's original typescript, with his
        corrections added in ink.

        Mimeographed Transcripts for the 1957 Broadcasts

Norwegian

3713   Faren ved forsøk med atombomber. Om den fare som fölger med
        de radioaktive stoffer som oppstår ved atombombepröver.
        10 pp. Radioappell: Norsk Rikskringkasting, Oslo,
        23 april 1957. This is the official radio transcript
        authorized by Albert Schweitzer.

English

3714   The radio activity created by the testing of atom bombs is a
        peril to the human race. 17 pp.

French

3715   Sur les dangers que représentent pour l'humanité les éléments
        radioactifs liberés à la suite des essais avec la bombe
        atomique. 16 pp.

German

3716   Die Gefahr welche die bei Versuchen mit Atombomben entstehenden
        radioaktiven Elemente für die Menschheit bedeuten. 13 pp.

378

2. Books and Brochures

Danish

3717 Albert Schweitzers Radiotale om Radioaktivitetens Farer.
      Tr. Georg Rona. Copenhagen: Det Danske Forlag, 1957.
      14 pp.

Norwegian

3718 Faren ved forsøk med atombomber. Lest av direktor Gunnar Jahn
      i Norsk Rikskringkasting 23. april 1957. Oslo: Aas &
      Wahle, 1957. 15 pp., illus., cover port.

3719 Same. Bergen: Utg. av Bergens Tidende og J. W. Eikes
      Boktrykkeri, 1957. 28 pp.

Swedish

3720 Faran med atombombsexperimenten. Föredrag av Albert Schweitzer
      utsänt i norsk radio på norska, engelska, franska, tyska
      och ryska måndagen den 23 april 1957. Göteberg:
      Götebergskretsen av Internationella Kvinnoförbundet för
      Fred och Frihet, Västsvenska FN-föreningen, 1957. 11 pp.

3721 Rädda Mänskligheten! Ett radioföredrag om faren av
      Atombombsprov. Uppsala: J. A. Lindblad, 1957. 15 pp.,
      cover port.

1958

3722 Friede oder Atomkrieg? Erster Appell: Versicht auf Versuchs-
      explosionen. 18 pp. Zweiter Appell: Versicht auf Atom-
      waffen. 35 pp. Dr. Schweitzer's original typescript,
      with his corrections added in ink, for the broadcasts on
      April 28, 29, and 30, 1958.[1]

Mimeographed Transcripts for the 1958 Broadcasts

Norwegian

3723 Fred eller atomkrig? Foredrag i Norsk Rikskringkasting, Oslo,
      1958. 24 pp. (Parts 1 and 2/I-II). Förste foredrag:

---

[1]It should be noted that in the original German version of the 1958
addresses, there were only two parts. In the official mimeographed
transcripts, the second part was divided and broadcast in two parts.
Later, for publication, the addresses appeared in three parts.

World Peace

> Stans prövene med kjernefysiske våpen! 8 pp. 28. April
> 1958. Andre foredrag, 2/I: Gi avkall på atomvåpene!
> 8 pp. 29. Apr. 1958. Annet foredrag, 2/II: Forhandlinger
> på höyeste plan. 8 pp. 30. Apr. 1958. This is the offi-
> cial radio transcript authorized by Albert Schweitzer.

English

3724 Peace or Atomic War? First Appeal: The renunciation of
   nuclear tests. 8 pp. Second Appeal, Part I: The risk
   of a nuclear war. 8 pp. Second Appeal, Part II: Negotiations at the highest level. 9 pp.

French

3725 Paix ou guerre atomique? Premier discours: La renonciation
   aux expériences nucléaires. 9 pp. Deuxième discours:
   Le danger de la guerre atomique. 9 pp. Troisième
   discours: Les négociations au sommet. 9 pp.

German

3726 Friede oder Atomkrieg? Erster Vortrag: Verzicht auf
   Versuchexplosionen. 10 pp. Zweiter Vortrag, Teil I:
   Verzicht auf Atomwaffen. 10 pp. Zweiter Vortrag,
   Teil II: Rapackiplan und Verhandlungen. 10 pp.

Russian

3727 [Transcript in Russian.] Tr. Rostislav Jankow.

Books and Brochures

Dutch

3728 Vrede of Atoomoorlog. Drie radio-redevoeringen uitgezonden
   door Radio-Oslo op 28, 29, en 30 april 1958. Tr. A. Wempe.
   Haarlem: H. D. Tjeenk Willink & Zoon, 1958. iv, 63 pp.
   Eerste Appel: Staben van de kernproeven. Tweede Appel:
   De gevaren van een atoomoorlog. Derde Appel: Onder
   handelingen op hoogste niveau.

English

3729 Peace or Atomic War? Three appeals broadcast from Oslo on
   April 28, 29, 30, 1958. London: Adam and Charles Black,
   1958. 28 pp. I. The Danger of Nuclear Tests. II. The
   Danger of an Atomic War. III. Negotiations at the
   Highest Level.

3730   Same. New York: Henry Holt and Co., 1958. 47 pp. Reissued
          Port Washington: Kennikat Press, 1972. 47 pp.

3731   Same. Bombay: Asia Publishing House, 1958. 45 pp.

3732   "An Obligation to Tomorrow." New York, 1958, 8 pp. Reprinted
          from Saturday Review, May 24, 1958.

3733   The Rights of the Unborn and the Peril Today. Statement by
          Albert Schweitzer with reference to the Present Nuclear
          Crisis in the World. Chicago: Albert Schweitzer Educa-
          tion Foundation, 1958. 11 pp. Cover port. Part I.
          Annihilation without Representation. Part II. Disaster
          by Devices. Part III. Sermon on the Summit.

French

3734   Paix ou guerre atomique? Paris: Albin Michel, 1958. 60 pp.
          Premier Appel: La renonciation aux expériences nucléaires.
          Deuxième Appel: Le danger de la guerre atomique.
          Troisième Appel: Les négociations au sommet.

German

3735   Albert Schweitzer an die Völker der Erde. Der neue Appel des
          Grossen Menschenfreundes in vollen Wortlaut. Zürich:
          Schweizerische Zentralstelle für Friedensarbeit, 1958.
          4 pp. Illus.

3736   Albert Schweitzer warnt vor dem Atommord. Drei Reden im
          April 1958. . . . Darmstadt: Stimme-Verlag, 1958. 8 pp.

3737   Friede oder Atomkrieg? Drei Appelle. Munich: C. H. Beck;
          Bern: Paul Haupt, 1958. 47 pp. Die hier vereinigten
          drei Appelle Albert Schweitzers hat Radio Oslo am 28.,
          29., und 30.4.1958 gesendet. Erster Appell: Verzicht
          auf Versuchsexplosionen; Zweiter Appell: Die Gefahr
          eines Atomkrieges; Dritter Appell: Verhandlungen auf
          höchsten Ebene.

3738   Same. Tokyo: Ikubundo Verlag, 1958. 33 pp.

Italian

3739   I popoli devono sapere. Tr. di Piero Bernardini Marzolla.
          Torino: Giulio Einaudi, 1958. 43 pp. Primo Appello:
          Rinunziare agli esperimente nucleari. Secondo Appello:
          Il pericolo di una guerra atomica. Terzo Appello:
          Trattative al massino livello.

World Peace

Japanese

3740   Friede oder Atomkrieg? (text in Japanese characters). Tokyo:
          Hakusuisha, 1958. 32 pp.

Korean

3741   [Peace or Atomic War?] Three appeals broadcast from Oslo on
          April 28, 29 and 30, 1958. Seoul: Sungnohaksa, 1958.
          7 pp. Text in Korean characters.

Norwegian

3742   Fred eller atomkrig? Tr. Knut Johansen. Disse foredrag av
          Albert Schweitzer ble av Norsk Rikskringkasting sendt ut
          28., 29. og 30.4.1958. Oslo: H. Aschehoug and Co.
          (W. Nygaard), 1958. 43 pp. I. Stans Prövene med
          kjernefysiske våpen. II. Gi avkall på atomvåpene.
          III. Forhandlinger på høyeste plan.

Portuguese

See Decadência et Regeneracão da Cultura, 3rd edition, no.
2252 above.

Spanish

3743   ¿ Paz o Guerra Atómica? Los tres llamados aquí reunidos se
          difundieron por la Radio de Oslo los días 28, 29, y 30
          de abril de 1958. México, Buenos Aires: Fondo de
          Cultura Económica, 1958. 69 pp. Port. Premier Llamado:
          Renuncia a las explosiónes de prueba. Segunda Llamado:
          El peligre de una guerra atómica. Tercer Llamado:
          Negociaciones en el plano supremo.

Swedish

3744   Fred eller atomkrig? Tre ratioforedrag våren 1958. Tr. Kurt
          Andersson. Uppsala: J. A. Lindblad, 1958. 36 pp. Cover
          port. I. Sluta upp med kärnvapenproven! II. Faran av
          ett atombombkrig. III. Förhandlingar på högsta nivä.

3. Inclusion in Periodicals, Books by Others

3745   "Albert Schweitzer." In: Urquhart, Clara, ed. A Matter of
          Life. London: Jonathan Cape; Boston: Little Brown, 1973,
          pp. 199-205.

3746   "Albert Schweitzer an die Völker der Erde. Der neue Appell
des grossen Menschenfreundes in vollen Wortlaut."
(Unabridged text, in German of 1958 broadcasts.) <u>Neue
Wege</u> (Zürich) 52:6 (June 1958). Also issued as an offprint, see no. 3735 above.

3747   "Albert Schweitzer. Die Gefahr wächst von Tag zu Tag.
Auszüge aus den drei Vorträgen, die der Arzt und
Philosoph in Norwesischen Rundbunk hielt." <u>Die Welt</u>
(Hamburg) 101 (May 1, 1958), p. 7. Port.

3748   "Albert Schweitzer mahnt die Welt. Auszüge aus seiner Osloer
Rede in Wortlaut." <u>Mannheimer Morgen</u> 95 (April 24, 1957),
pp. 2f.

3749   "Albert Schweitzer warnt die Menschheit von der Atomgefahr."
In: FACKELTRÄGER, pp. 57-62.

3750   "Albert Schweitzer. 2. Oslo-Appell (1958)." In: HEIPP,
p. 109.

3751   "Albert Schweitzers Appell an die Menschheit." RUNDBRIEF 11
(Aug. 1, 1957), pp. 31-40. Reprinted in: HEIPP,
pp. 49-56.

3752   "Albert Schweitzer's erste Mahnung." <u>Münchner Merker</u> (Munich)
12:99 (April 24, 1957).

3753   "Appeal to humanity" (first broadcast from Oslo, 1957.)
<u>Faith and Freedom</u> (Oxford) 11:part 1, no. 31 (Autumn 1957),
pp. 33-40.

3754   "Apelos prō cessacāo das experiências atômicas (3 apelos)."
<u>Mundo Melhor</u> (Sao Paulo) 1:8 (Aug. 1958), pp. 108-20.
Port.

3755   "L'appel du docteur Schweitzer contre les expériences des
bombes atomiques" (reprint of the Oslo broadcast of 1958,
laid in, 4 unnumbered pages). NOUVELLES 4 (June 1958).

3756   "En Appell." <u>Verdens Gang</u> (Oslo) 94 (April 24, 1957), p. 2.

3757   "Appell von Albert Schweitzer." <u>Geist und Zeit</u> (Düsseldorf)
3 (1957), pp. 9-18.

3758   "Appell zur Einstellung der Atombombenversuche." <u>Jahrbuch
der Deutschen Akademie für Sprache und Dichtung in
Darmstadt Heidelberg</u> (1957), pp. 99-111.

World Peace

3759   "Atomaufrüstung bricht Völkerrecht. Der volle Wortlaut der
        Osloer Reden von Albert Schweitzer" (aus den Englischen
        übertragen von Georg Gogert). <u>Die Kultur</u> (Munich) 6:107
        (May 1, 1958), pp. 1, 4-6.

3760   "Die Atomgefahr, in der wir leben." <u>Brille</u>, die ungefarbte
        Kulturkritische Zeitschrift (Göttingen) 2:3-4 (1956-57),
        pp. 218-28.

3761   "Die Atomgefahr in der wir heute leben. Albert Schweitzer an
        die Welt." In: Elsner, Richard, et al. <u>Gesamtdeutsche
        Ostpolitik: Deutschland, Russland, Poland</u>. Göttingen:
        R. Elsner, 1957, pp. 90-100.

3762   "Die Atomgefahr in der wir heute leben." <u>Frankfurter
        Allgemeine Zeitung</u> 95 (April 24, 1957), p. 7.

3763   "De Boodschap van Dr. Schweitzer aan die mensheid." <u>Militia
        Christi</u> (Lochem) 12:10 (May 18, 1957), pp. 3-7. Port.,
        illus.

3764   "Brief an John F. Kennedy," August 25, 1963. In: HEIPP,
        pp. 15-16.

3765   "Contre les armes nucleaires. Le nouvel appel du docteur
        Schweitzer." <u>Paix et Liberté</u> (Gilly, Belgium) 58:27
        (July 6, 1958), p. 3.

3766   "A declaration of conscience." <u>The Saturday Review</u> (New York)
        40:20 (May 18, 1957), pp. 17-20. Illus. Excerpts also
        in <u>The Reporter</u> (New York) 16:10 (May 16, 1957), p. 26;
        reprinted in <u>Bulletin of Atomic Scientists</u> (Chicago) 13
        (June 1957), pp. 204-05; reprinted in: SELECTION,
        pp. 45-52; reprinted in: Pauling, Linus. <u>No More War!</u>
        New York: Dodd, Mead, 1958, pp. 225-37; reprinted in:
        Ludwig, Richard M., ed. <u>Essays Today 3</u>. New York:
        Harcourt, Brace and Co., 1957, pp. 165-72.

3767   "Dr. Albert Schweitzer: 'Gevaar van radioactiviteit neem nog
        steeds toe.' Brief aan Japanse College (Dr. Nomura)."
        <u>Het Parool</u> (Amsterdam) 4075 (April 25, 1958), p. 4.

3768   "Dr. Albert Schweitber talar till världen." <u>Fredsmissionären</u>.
        Organ för världsfredmissionaren i Sverige (Gökalund)
        38:5-6 (May-June 1957), pp. 3, 4, 7.

3769   "Dr. Schweitzer's appeal to humanity." In: MacLeod, Sir
        George Fielding, Bart. <u>Bombs and Bishops</u>. Glasgow:
        Iona Community Publishing Dept., 1957, pp. 13-23. "An
        Iona Community Pamphlet."

3770   "Dr. Schweitzer's appeal to the nations." British Weekly
          (London) 141:3730 (May 8, 1959), p. 5.

3771   "Dr. Schweitzers dramatischer Appell an die Menschheit."
          Die Freiheit (Mainz) 11:50 (April 26, 1957), p. 4.

3772   "Ehrfurcht vor dem Leben! (Abschaffung der Atomwaffen
          notwendig)." Kirchenblatt für die reformierte Schweiz
          (Basel) 120 (1964), pp. 74-75.

3773   "Faren ved forsøg med atombomber." Dansk Udsyn (Askov)
          37:3 (June 1957), pp. 137-46.

3774   "Faren ved forsøkmed atombomber." (Text of radio broadcast
          from Oslo, April 1957). Morgenbladets Kronikk (Oslo)
          I:95 (April 24, 1957), pp. 3ff; 96 (April 25, 1957),
          pp. 3ff.

3775   "Fred eller atomkrig." Tr. H. Moe. Dansk Udsyn (Askov) 38:3
          (1958), pp. 131-38.

3776   "Friede oder Atomkrieg. Drei Appelle von Albert Schweitzer
          von Radio Oslo in die Welt gesendet am 28. 29. u.
          30.4.1958." RUNDBRIEF 12 (June 15, 1958), pp. 3-23.

3777   "From a letter to a Polish doctor." In: ALBUM, p. 121.

3778   "Die Gefahr, in der wir leben." Das Werk (Gelsenkirchen)
          29 (1957), pp. 69-71.

3779   "The H-bomb." Daily Herald (London), April 11, 1954, p. 4.
          Reprinted in: FESTSCHRIFT, p. 141; reprinted with title
          "Scientists must speak up. . . ." Saturday Review
          (New York) 37 (July 17, 1954), p. 23; reprinted in
          Science (Washington, D.C.) 120 (Sept. 10, 1954), p. 11a;
          reprinted in Science Monthly 79 (Oct. 1954), p. 208;
          reprinted in Bulletin of Atomic Scientists (Chicago) 10
          (Nov. 1954), p. 339; reprinted in: HEIPP, pp. 25-26.

3780   "Haltet endlich ein! Albert Schweitzer fordert Einstellung
          der Atomversuche." Die Kultur (Munich) 5:83 (May 1, 1957),
          p. 12.

3781   Letter to Albert Einstein. In: MARSHALL AND POLING, p. 240.

3782   Letter to Martin Buber. In: Buber, Martin. Briefwechsel
          aus sieben Jahrzehnten. Hrsg. v. Grete Schaeder. Vol.
          III: 1938-1965. Heidelberg: Lambert Schneider, 1975,
          pp. 451-52.

World Peace

3783 "Lettre d'Albert Schweitzer sur la bombe atomique." CAHIERS
      2 (Dec. 1959), p. 22.

3784 "Modelle für Atombrief" (two letters from Albert Schweitzer,
      Lambarene). In: Winnubst, Benedictus. Das
      Friedensdenken Albert Schweitzer, see no. 3622 above,
      pp. 213-15.

3785 "My last message to mankind." Paix et Liberté 32
      (Jan.-March 1967), p. 7. Translated as "Mein Wort an die
      Menschen (1964)." BERICHTE 30 (Sept. 1967); reprinted in
      RUNDBRIEFE/DDR 6 (1965), pp. 3-5; phonodisc "Mein Wort an
      die Menschen." Stimmen der Zeit. Available G. Heipp.
      6661 Reischweiler, Pfarrhaus.

3786 "Neuer appell Albert Schweitzers an die Menschheit."
      Münchner Merkur (Munich) 13:102 (April 29, 1958), p. 2.

3787 "Notes on the nuclear crisis." Fellowship (Nyack, N.Y.)
      24:13 (July 1958), p. 27.

3788 "An Obligation to tomorrow" (translation of Schweitzer's radio
      broadcasts on the problem of atomic testing). Saturday
      Review (New York) 41 (May 24, 1958), pp. 21-28. Also
      issued as a 8-page offprint, see no. 3732 above. Re-
      printed in: Rudman, Harry W. and Irving Rosenthal, eds.
      A Contemporary Reader, Essays for Today and Tomorrow.
      New York: Ronald Press, 1961, pp. 342-57.

3789 "Peace or atomic war? A new appeal by Dr. Schweitzer." The
      full texts of his Oslo broadcasts of April 28-30, 1958.
      Peace News (London) 1,140 (May 2, 1958), special supple-
      ment, 4 pp., laid in.

3790 "Peace or atomic war?" The Norseman (London) 16:3
      (May-June 1958), pp. 145-60.

3791 "Peace or Atomic War?" Texts of addresses from 4/24/57 and
      4/58. In: Cousins, Norman. Dr. Schweitzer of Lambarene.
      New York: Harper, 1960, pp. 227-54.

3792 "Renuncia a las explosiones de proeba." Cultura Universitaria
      (Caracas) 65 (1958), pp. 7-13. Reproduction of first
      chapter of Paz o Guerra Atómica, see no. 3743 above.

3793 "Schluss mit den Atombomben-Versuchen!" Die Friedensrundschau
      11:5 (May 1957), pp. 2-8.

World Peace

3794   "Schweitzer speaks to peace workers" (an interview with
            Albert Schweitzer at Lambarene in Africa by Signe Hojer,
            President of the Swedish section of the Women's Inter-
            national League for Peace and Freedom). The American
            Friend (Berne, Ind.) 46:14, p. 210. Excerpted as
            "Schweitzer (I've been dubbed a Communist): keep public
            opinion alive." Peace News (London) 1,146 (June 13, 1958),
            p. 1.

3795   "Schweitzer urges world opinion to demand end of nuclear
            tests; excerpts from message by Dr. Schweitzer." The
            New York Times 106 (April 24, 1957), pp. 1, 4, 5. Port.

3796   "Schweitzer's appeal" (editorial). The Christian World
            (London) 101:5,273, p. 1.

3797   "Stans prøvene!" (text of Schweitzer's broadcast from Oslo
            April 1957). Verdens Gang Kronikk (Oslo) 941
            (April 24, 1957), pp. 3, 8.

3798   "Telegramm an die 3. Christliche Friedenskonferenz in Prag,
            September 1960." In: HEIPP, p. 45.

3799   "A time for trust and responsibility" (extracts from the 1958
            appeals from Oslo). Toward a World Disarmed (New York)
            4:9 (May 1958), pp. 3-4. Reprinted in Concern 13:19
            (June 13, 1958), p. 6; reprinted in The Christian-
            Evangelist (St. Louis, Mo.) 96:25 (June 23, 1958),
            pp. 16-17. Article distributed by the Albert Schweitzer
            Fellowship in New York, taken from Schweitzer's radio
            broadcasts of April 28-30.

3800   To Live or to Die. The H-Bomb vs. Mankind. Public statements
            by Albert Schweitzer and others. With a foreword by
            W. E. B. DuBois. New York: New Century Publishers, 1957.

3801   "To the men of Geneva" (letter signed by Albert Schweitzer
            and 18 others). The Saturday Review (New York) 41:47
            (Nov. 22, 1958), p. 22.

3802   "Voor de gedenkdag van Hiroshima 1960." EERBIED 23:2
            (Dec. 1974), p. 31.

3803   "Vrede of atoomoorlog. Microfoon uitsprak op 16, 23 en 30
            mei 1958. Vertaald dor J. B. Th. Hugenholtz." NIEUWS
            7:1 (July 1958), pp. 9-27.

3804   "Wir machen uns mitschuldig" und "Die Wissenschaftler müssen
            zur Welt sprechen." Die Friedensrundschau 9:9
            (Sept. 1955), p. 6.

World Peace

3805   "Der Wortlaut von Albert Schweitzers Appell." <u>Frankfurter</u>
          <u>Neue Presse</u> 12:95 (April 24, 1957), p. 9.

4. Writings About Schweitzer in Periodicals
     and Books by Others

3806   AALBERS, BERT. "Toen Schweitzer over kernproeven sprak kreeg
          hij veel vijanden." EERBIED 27:2 (Aug. 1978), pp. 17-20.

3807   "Albert Schweitzer mahnt: beendet die Atomversuche. Appell
          an die Staatsmänner." <u>Die Welt</u> (Hamburg) 95
          (April 24, 1957), pp. 1f. Port.

3808   "Albert Schweitzer protesta contra las provos atómicas."
          <u>O Estado</u>, April 29, 1958.

3809   "Albert Schweitzer sprach zur Welt." <u>Kirchliches Monatsblatt</u>
          <u>für Evangelisch-Lutherische Gemeinden in Amerika</u>
          (Philadelphia) 14:8 (Aug. 1957), p. 237.

3810   "Albert Schweitzer waarschuwt de wereld. Oproep tot
          bezinning." NIEUWS 6:1 (May 1957), p. 7.

3811   "Albert Schweitzers Mahnruf an die Welt." <u>Österreichische</u>
          <u>Furche</u> (Vienna) 13:18 (May 4, 1957), p. 5.

3812   ALFRINK, BERNARD. "Reverence for life--foundation of society
          and basis of civilization." In: DEVENTER, pp. 23-34.
          Summaries in French, German and Dutch.

3813   ALLARD, ANTOINE. "Denken und Handeln im Einklang." In:
          BEITRÄGE, p. 16.

3814   ANDREAS, BENGT. "Albert Schweitzers kamp mit Atombomben."
          In: <u>Vördnad för livet</u>, see no. 30 above, pp. 225-36.

3815   "En Appell" (editorial). <u>Verdens Gang</u> (Oslo) 94
          (April 24, 1957), p. 2.

3816   "Un avertissement du Dr. Schweitzer: la radioactivité met
          l'humanite en danger." <u>Le Figaro</u> (Paris) 131:3929
          (Aug. 24, 1957), pp. 1, 3.

3817   "Botschaft des Urwalddoktors. Friedens-Nobelpreisträger
          Albert Schweitzer zum Abstimmung über das Atomwaffenverbot."
          <u>National-Zeitung</u> (Basel), March 24, 1962.

3818 BROWN, HARRISON. "What is a 'small risk'?" <u>Saturday Review</u>
(New York) 40 (May 25, 1957), pp. 9-10.

3819 "Die 'christliche' Presse unterdrückt Schweitzers Stimme"
(editorial). <u>Voix d'Alsace</u> (Geudertheim) 6:21 (1958),
pp. 1-2.

3820 COUSINS, NORMAN. "Entretien avec Albert Schweitzer à Lambaréné
sur les problèmes atomiques (1952)." In: RAYONNEMENT,
pp. 266-69.

3821 _____. "Mr. Cousins' comments on Dr. Schweitzer's stand."
<u>U.S. News and World Report</u> (Washington, D.C.) 43:5
(Aug. 2, 1957), p. 90.

3822 _____. "An open letter to David Lawrence." <u>The Saturday
Review</u> (New York) 40:27 (July 6, 1957), pp. 20-21.

3823 _____. "Remarks" (nuclear test ban). In: THE CONVOCATION
RECORD, pp. II/3-9.

3824 _____. "The Schweitzer declaration. Introduction." <u>The
Saturday Review</u> (New York) 40:20 (May 18, 1957), pp. 13-16.

3825 "Devant des déclarations du docteur Schweitzer, l'opinion de
ceux de nos savants qui travaillent de problème (sa
déclaration sur les ravages de la radioactivité)." <u>Le
Figaro Littéraire</u> (Paris) 12:576 (May 4, 1957), p. 11.

3826 DOBIAS, F. M. [Essay without title.] <u>Universitas</u>
(Stuttgart) 15:1 (Jan. 1960), pp. 28-30. Reprinted in:
DENKEN UND WEG, pp. 95-97.

3827 "Dr. Schweitzer stirs world conscience" (editorial). <u>The
Christian Century</u> (Chicago) 74:19 (May 8, 1957), pp. 579-80.

3828 "Dr. Schweitzer vs. Archbishop Godfrey" (editorial). <u>America</u>
(New York) 99:6 (May 10, 1958), p. 188. Replies by
Edward Morin and A. C. Malmsten. <u>America</u> 99:11
(June 14, 1958), p. 321.

3829 FRANKENBERG, EGBERT VON. "In gemeinsamen Kampf."
<u>Standpunkt: Evangelische Monatsschrift</u> (Berlin) 3:1
(Jan. 1975), pp. 10-11.

3830 "'Friede oder Atomkrieg.' Zum 10. Todestag Albert
Schweitzers." <u>Deutsche Volkszeitung</u> (Düsseldorf) 39
(Sept. 25, 1975), p. 6.

World Peace

3831   "I have one wish." Newsweek (New York) 55:20 (May 16, 1960),
       p. 78. Port.

3832   JUNGK, ROBERT. "Der Menschenfreund gegen die Atomversuche."
       In: Pierhal, Jean. Albert Schweitzer (see no. 291
       above), pp. 378-91. Excerpted with title "Für eine
       humane neue Welt!" In: GESTERN-HEUTE, pp. 43-46.

3833   KAWAGUCHI, J. "Hiroshima 1945 und Albert Schweitzers
       Mahnung an die Welt." In: DENKEN UND WEG, pp. 482-85.

3834   KRAJA, NORBERT. "Albert Schweitzers Kampf gegen die
       Atomkriegsgefahr--bleibender Auftrag an die
       Friedliebenden Christen." In: VERMÄCHTNIS UND
       WIRKLICHKEIT, pp. 29-40.

3835   L., J. "Your radiation diary." The Saturday Review (New York)
       40 (May 25, 1957), p. 13.

3836   LAVERGNE, VARNARD. "Kämpfer gegen die Atomkriegsgefähr."
       In: BEITRÄGE, pp. 94-96.

3837   LEAR, JOHN. "The shrinking margin." The Saturday Review
       (New York) 40 (May 25, 1957), pp. 11-13f.

3838   LIBBY, WILLARD F. "An open letter to Dr. Schweitzer." The
       Saturday Review (New York) 40 (May 25, 1957), pp. 8-9.

3839   NIETHAMMER, PROF. "Urwald Arzt studiert Atome. Zwei Forscher
       besuchte Albert Schweitzer." Offenbach Post 185
       (Aug. 13, 1959), p. 8.

3840   OSCHILEWSKI, WALTHER G. "Stimme des Weltgewissens.
       A. S.: Samariter der Barmherzigkeit." Telegraf
       (West Berlin) 97 (April 26, 1957), p. 3.

3841   "The Peril of strontium 90." Time (New York) 69:18
       (May 6, 1957), p. 24. Port.

3842   "Schweitzer pede a suspensão das experiências nucleares."
       O Estado, April 24, 1957.

3843   "Schweitzer's new 'halt tests' call." Peace News (London)
       1,140 (May 2, 1958), p. 1.

3844   SIEBERT, HANS EBERHARD. "Albert Schweitzer mahnt die Welt."
       Die Schwarzburg (Hamburg) 66:2 (1957), pp. 25-32.

3845   "Die Völker müssen ihre Stimme erheben. Der Appell Albert
       Schweitzers gegen die Atomgefahr--Kernwaffenversuche

World Peace

untergraben Existenz der Menschheit." <u>Der Demokrat</u> 106
(May 10, 1957), p. 3. Port.

3846   WAGNER, FRIEDRICH. "Albert Schweitzer und die Atomproblem."
         <u>Universitas</u> (Stuttgart) 15:1 (Jan. 1960), pp. 49-60.
         Revised version in: DENKEN UND WEG, pp. 437-55.

3847   WENZL, ALOYS. "Albert Schweitzers Reden zum Friedensproblem."
         In: DENKEN UND WEG, pp. 553-56.

3848   "What's back of the 'fall-out scare'?" <u>U.S. News and World
         Report</u> (Washington, D.C.) 42:23 (June 7, 1957), pp. 27-28.

3849   WÜNSCH, GEORG and HANS PRIBNOW. "Dankadresse an Albert
         Schweitzer." RUNDBRIEF 11 (Aug. 1, 1957), pp. 41-42.

XI. Miscellaneous Writings
by Albert Schweitzer

A. Letters (Published in Books or Periodicals)

The following is a chronological list of Schweitzer's letters which have appeared in books or periodicals. Letters which deal with one of the specific subject areas of this bibliography have been included in the appropriate subject section.

3850   Letter to Suzanne Oswald, Freitag vor Weihnachten, 1898. In: BERY, pp. 77-80 (French); pp. 202-04 (German).[1] Translated in: BRABAZON, pp. 92-93.

3851   A. Schweitzer à Marie Jaëll, Berlin, 1899. In: Lange, Madeleine and Theodore, eds. Albert Schweitzer 1875-1975. Strasbourg: Bibliothèque Nationale et Universitaire, 1975. pp. 122-23.

3852   Letter to Suzanne Oswald, Berlin, June 1899. In: BERY, pp. 80-83 (French); pp. 204-06 (German). Excerpts translated in: BRABAZON, pp. 101-02.

3853   Letter to Gustav von Lüpke (October 1905?). In: Pierhal, Jean. Albert Schweitzer (see no. 291 above), p. 59. Reprinted in: BRABAZON, p. 177.

3854   Zwei Briefe Albert Schweitzers aus frühen Jahren, 1905 und 1908. RUNDBRIEF 41 (Feb. 1976), pp. 51-55.

3855   Letter to Suzanne Oswald, Jan. 21, 1913. In: BERY, p. 84 (French).

3856   Letter to Suzanne Oswald, Dated Lambarene, 18. May 1913. In: BERY, pp. 84-85 (French); pp. 206-07 (German).

---

[1]Letters appear in this source in German, French, or both. Each entry will indicate which language(s) a particular letter appears in.

Misc. Writings by Schweitzer

3857   Letter to M. Boegner, Société des Missions Evangeliques
        (1913?). In: ALBUM, p. 28.

3858   Letter (portion) written to the Société des Missions
        Evangeliques de Paris. <u>Journal de Société des Missions</u>
        <u>Evangeliques de Paris</u> 89 (Feb. 1914), pp. 152-53.

3859   Letters to Romain Rolland, Aug. 25, 1915 and Nov. 10, 1915.
        In: Rolland, Romain. <u>Journal des Années de Guerre,</u>
        <u>1914-1919</u>. Texte établie par Marie Romain Rolland.
        Préface de Louis Martin-Cauffier. Paris: Albin Michel,
        1952, pp. 505, 603. Translated as <u>Zwischen den Völkern,</u>
        <u>Aufzeichnungen und Dokumente aus den Jahren 1914-1919</u>.
        Stuttgart: Deutsche Verlage Anstalt, 1954; excerpted in:
        Pierhal, Jean. <u>Albert Schweitzer</u>, see no. 291 above,
        pp. 100-01.

3860   Letter to Suzanne Oswald. Dated Lambarene, May 1916. In:
        BERY, p. 87 (German).

3861   A. Schweitzer au Directeur du Camp d'internes civils de
        Garaison, Nov. 25, 1917; Dec. 24, 1917; Jan. 24, 1917.
        In: Lange, Madeleine and Theodore, eds. <u>Albert Schweitzer</u>
        <u>1875-1975</u>. Strasbourg: Bibliothèque Nationale et
        Universitaire, 1975, pp. 124-28.

3862   Letter to Theodore Baker, Dec. 1919. In: Heinsheimer, Hans W.
        "The Saga of Schweitzer's Bach edition." <u>Music</u> (New York)
        9 (Jan. 1975), pp. 30-33.

3863   Letter to Suzanne Oswald, June 1920. In: BERY, pp. 100-01
        (German).

3864   Letter to Jean Bianquis, April 30, 1922. In: BRABAZON,
        pp. 295-97.

3865   Ein Brief von Albert Schweitzer an Wilibald Gurlitt.
        <u>Musik und Kirche</u> (Kassel) 45:2 (March-April 1975),
        pp. 53-54. Dated Lambarene, 23.2.26.

3866   Ein Brief Albert Schweitzers ("16. September 1928").
        <u>Schweizerisches Protestantenblatt</u> (Basel) 51:38
        (Sept. 22, 1928), p. 316.

3867   Letters from Albert Schweitzer to Margit Jacobi, covering
        period from Dec. 11, 1929 to Jan. 20, 1937. In: Jacobi,
        Erwin. "Albert Schweitzer: unveröffentlichen Briefe an
        Margit Jacobi." <u>Librarium</u> 19:1 (May 1976), pp. 2-21.

3868   "Schweitzer letter presented by librarian"; excerpts from
        letter to Rudolf Bultmann, Oct. 11, 1931. Wilson Library
        Bulletin 40 (Nov. 1965), pp. 217f.

3869   Letters from Schweitzer to Mr. and Mrs. Donald Francis Tovey,
        1932/33, 1934, 1935. In: Grierson, Mary. Donald Francis
        Tovey: a Biography based on Letters. London: Oxford
        University Press, 1952, pp. 268, 284-85, 289-90.

3870   Letter to Martin Buber, Jan. 15, 1935. In: Buber, Martin.
        Briefwechel aus sieben Jahrzehnten. Hrsg. von Grete
        Schaeder. Band II: 1918-1938. Heidelberg: Lambert
        Schneider, 1973. p. 562.

3871   Letters to Gerald Herz, Nov. 20, 1935; Nov. 26, 1934; Nov.
        1936; Nov. 28, 1942; March 20, 1942; June 4, 1947. In:
        Herz, Gerald. "Schweitzer the musician" and "Personal
        recollections," see no. 3255 above.

3872   Letter to Suzanne Oswald, Palm Sunday, 1940. In: BERY,
        p. 111 (French); pp. 207-08 (German).

3873   Letter to Suzanne Oswald, Lambarene, May 9, 1940. In: BERY,
        pp. 111-12 (French); pp. 207-08 (German).

3874   Letters to J. Seelye Bixler, June 12, 1940 through Dec. 5,
        1946. In: Bixler, J. S. "Letters from Dr. Albert
        Schweitzer in the Colby Library." Colby Library Quarterly
        (Waterville, Me.) 6:9 (March 1964), pp. 373-82.

3875   Letter to Suzanne Oswald, Lambarene, Aug. 4, 1940. In: BERY,
        p. 113 (French); p. 208 (German).

3876   Letter to Charles R. Joy, Jan. 23, 1945. In: MARSHALL AND
        POLING, pp. 220-21.

3877   Dr. Schweitzer writes. The Christian Century (Chicago)
        62:12 (March 21, 1945), pp. 380-81. "Recent" letter from
        A. S. to the Albert Schweitzer Fellowship.

3878   Letter to Reuben Jacobi, June 12, 1945. In: Jacobi, Erwin.
        "Albert Schweitzer: unveröffentlichen Briefe an Margit
        Jacobi." Librarium 19:1 (May 1976), pp. 2-21.

3879   Letter to Charles R. Joy, October 19, 1946. In: MARSHALL
        POLING, pp. 220-21.

3880   Letter to Albert Einstein, April 30, 1948. In: BRABAZON,
        pp. 375-77. Also in: MARSHALL AND POLING, pp. 231-33.

Misc. Writings by Schweitzer

3881   Lettre au Tailleur. New York, July 1, 1949. To Jean
        Baptiste Kempf. In: RAYONNEMENT, pp. 28-29.

3882   Letter to Suzanne Oswald, Lambarene, May 17, 1950. In: BERY,
        pp. 116-17 (German).

3883   Letter to Suzanne Oswald. Am Weihnachstag 1950. In: BERY,
        pp. 117-18 (German).

3884   Albert Schweitzer and Emmy Martin. Letters from Lambarene
        to Mr. Hanstein, Carl Schurz Memorial Foundation, 1951.
        The American-German Review (Philadelphia) 17:5
        (June 1951), pp. 38-39. In German with English
        translation.

3885   Albert Schweitzer and Israel. Letter dated "Lambarene
        8.3.51," translated from German into English. Jerusalem
        Post, Nov. 13, 1953. Port.

3886   Albert Schweitzer grüsst Memmingen. Der Urwaldarzt dankt
        dem "Hochwürdigen Magistrat der Stadt Memmigen" (In
        eine mundatierten Brief aus Lambarene für die Benennung
        einer Albert-Schweitzer-Strasse). Memminger Zeitung 83
        (April 29, 1952), p. 8.

3887   Letter to Suzanne Oswald, May 13, 1952. In: BERY,
        pp. 118-19 (German).

3888   Letter to a Lieutenant (JG) in the United States Navy who was
        on his way to Korea. Lambarene, Dec. 27, 1952. In:
        ALBUM, p. 68.

3889   To the publisher Felix Meiner in Hamburg on the occasion of
        his 70th birthday (dated Lambarene, Feb. 13, 1953). In:
        Felix Meiner zum 70. Geburtstag, 25. März 1953. Hamburg:
        1953, pp. 15-18. Reprinted in: ALBUM, p. 138.

3890   To the students of a school for nurses who asked me for a
        motto. Lambarene, Feb. 20, 1953. In: ALBUM, p. 74.

3891   Miscellaneous letters, Jan.-May 1953. RUNDBRIEF 4
        (Jan. 14, 1954). Reprinted in: DOKUMENTE, pp. 189-93.

3892   Une lettre du Docteur Schweitzer (dated Lambarene, March 14,
        1953). Les Cignognes de Pfastatt-le-Château (organ
        périodique des établissements Schaeffer et Cie,
        Pfastatt-le-Château, Haut-Rhin) 21 (Oct. 1953), pp. 12-13.

3893   Letter, in French, with English translation, from Albert
        Schweitzer in acknowledgement of the Wellcome Bronze
        Medal and a cheque for £50 from the Royal African Society.
        African Affairs 53:210 (Jan. 1954), pp. 1-3.

3894   Letter to Dag Hammarskjold (Jan. 1954?). In: BRABAZON,
        p. 416.

3895   Letter to Suzanne Oswald, March 22, 1954. In: BERY, p. 126
        (German).

3896   Brief vom 11.4.1954 aus Lambarene an sein Patenkind Jurgen
        Gerhold zu dessen Konfirmation. RUNDBRIEF 5 (June 1, 1954),
        p. 14. Reprinted in: DOKUMENTE, pp. 206-07; reprinted in
        Freies Christentum (Frankfurt a.M.) 10:3 (March 1, 1958),
        col. 34; translated in: ALBUM, p. 62.

3897   Two letters from Albert Schweitzer to Rudolf Quoika,
        Aug. 2 and Aug. 8, 1954. In: Quoika, Rudolf. Ein
        Orgelkolleg mit Albert Schweitzer. Greisenfeld: Staudt,
        1970.

3898   Letter to Max Tau, Oct. 29, 1954? In: Tau, Max. Auf dem
        Weg zur Versöhnung. Hamburg: Hommand and Campe, 1968,
        pp. 223-24.

3899   Letter to Henry Babel, dated Günsbach, Dec. 15, 1954. Le
        Protestant (Geneva), Jan. 15, 1955, p. 5.

3900   Anonymous. "Albert Schweitzer, 80 Jahre, Gedanken des grossen
        Wissenschaftlers und uneigennützigen Menschenfreundes."
        Includes a letter from A. S. Berliner Lehrerzeitung
        (Berlin), Jan. 15, 1955, p. 9.

3901   Letter to Einstein's niece, June 18, 1955. In: MARSHALL AND
        POLING, pp. 240-41.

3902   Une Lettre d'Albert Schweitzer à propos du Journal des Années
        de Guerre, 1914-1918 (dated Lambaréné, 30 Juillet 1955,
        addressed to Madame Rolland). Europe (Paris) 43:439/440
        (Nov./Dec. 1965), pp. 155-56.

3903   Albert Schweitzer zum Heimgang von Pfarrer Erich Meyer.
        Freies Christentum (Frankfurt a.M.) 7:8 (Aug. 1, 1955),
        col. 102.

3904   Une lettre de Lambaréné (Feb. 2, 1956). Le Figaro Littéraire
        (Paris), Feb. 11, 1956, p. 9.

Misc. Writings by Schweitzer

3905   Letter from A. S. dated 15.8.1956. In: Müller, Herbert.
       "Ein Verzeichnis der Albert-Schweitzer-Literatur."
       Bücher und Bildung (Reutlingen) 8:12 (Dec. 1956),
       pp. 481-82.

3906   Extracts of letters written to Richard Kik from Lambarene,
       Feb. to Oct. 1956. RUNDBRIEF 10 (Dec. 1, 1956), p. 66.

3907   Letter to Adlai Stevenson, Aug. 14, 1956. Excerpted in:
       BRABAZON, p. 434.

3908   A Letter from Albert Schweitzer. In response to President
       Chatelain's invitation to speak at the Convention (centen-
       nial convention). Journal of the American Institute of
       Architects (Washington, D.C.) 28:2 (June 1957), p. 80.

3909   Letter to Marc Chalufour, 1957. In: Cousins, Norman.
       Dr. Schweitzer of Lambarene. New York: Harper, 1960,
       pp. 188-89.

3910   Ein Brief Albert Schweitzers (aus Lambarene. Absage auf
       die Einladung der Stadt München zu ihrer 800-Jahrfeier).
       Münchner Stadtanzeige (Beilage der Süddeutsche Zeitung,
       Munich) 27 (July 5, 1957), p. 3.

3911   Letter (facsimile) from Albert Schweitzer to Willy Brandt,
       Bürgermeister of Berlin, reply to an invitation to visit
       Berlin. Telegraf (West Berlin) 137/13 (June 15, 1958),
       p. 1.

3912   Letter to Erhard Krieger, May 27, 1958. In: Krieger, Erhard.
       Weltbürger des Menschseins und der Tat. Bad Homberg vor
       der Höhe: Verlag des Viergespann, 1960, p. 31.

3913   An Suzanne Oswald, Jan. 21, 1959. In: BERY, pp. 177-78.

3914   Litterae ab Musicis. Letter of Feb. 24, 1959 to Elinore
       Barber. Bach III/4 (Oct. 1972), pp. 25-27.

3915   Albert Schweitzer an das Jugendsozialwerk. Letter from A. S.
       to the "Leiter des Lehrlings von heimes des Jugend-
       sozialwerks, Stuttgart, Hansenbergsteige." Tübinger
       Brief, Mitteilungen, Berichte, Notizen aus den Jugend-
       sozialwerk 5:5 (1959). Reprinted in Freies Christentum
       (Frankfurt a.M.) 12:1 (Jan. 1, 1960), p. 11.

3916   Albert Schweitzer dankt brieflich für 10,000 dm. Geburts-
       tagsgeschenk der Stadt München." Münchner Merker
       (Munich) 59 (March 9, 1960), p. 11.

Letters

3917   Extrait d'une lettre d'Albert Schweitzer du 23 fevrier 1960
        et du 14 octobre 1960. NOUVELLES 27 (July 1961), pp. 3-6.

3918   Letter from Albert Schweitzer to a high-school student in
        Wimmelburg bei Eisleben. Neue Zeit (East Berlin) 220
        (Sept. 20, 1961), p. 8.

3919   JACOBI, ERWIN R. "Fromm sein--gedanken zu einem Brief von
        Albert Schweitzer." Divine Light (Winterthur, Switz.),
        2:1 (June 1967), pp. 1-6. Text of a letter from A. S.,
        May 10, 1962.

3920   Litterae ab musicis. Letter from Schweitzer to Elinore Barber,
        May 19, 1963. Bach II/2 (April 1971), pp. 20-21.

3921   Letter to J. Seelye Bixler, July 28, 1963. In: Bixler, J.
        Seelye. "Letters from Dr. Albert Schweitzer in the
        Colby Library." Colby Library Quarterly (Waterville, Me.)
        6:9 (March 1964), pp. 373-82.

3922   Portion of a letter from A. S. dated Nov. 1963. In: Pribnow,
        Hans. "Albert Schweitzer wird am 14. Januar 89. Jahre
        alt." Freies Christentum (Frankfurt a.M.) 16:1
        (Jan. 1964), col. 10.

3923   An Suzanne Oswald. Lambarene, Jan. 26, 1964. In: BERY,
        pp. 178-80.

3924   Albert Schweitzers Brief an dem Kongress. . . . Freies
        Christentum (Frankfurt a.M.) 16:11 (Nov. 1, 1964),
        cols. 136-37.

3925   Letter to Miriam Rogers, Aug. 20, 1964. In: TRIBUTE,
        pp. 30-31. German facsimile, with English translation
        by Ali Silver.

3926   Letter to George N. Marshall, Feb. 15, 1965. In: MARSHALL
        AND POLING, pp. 295-96.

3927   An Prof. Dr. H. W. Bähr, April 2, 1965. Quoted in the intro-
        duction to Die Lehre von der Ehrfurcht vor dem Leben,
        see no. 2702 above.

3928   Zwei Briefe Albert Schweitzers an Gerald Götting, May 5, 1965
        and May 27, 1965. In: BEITRÄGE, pp. 7-11.

3929   Brief van Dr. Schweitzer. (facsimile of a letter from A. S.
        addressed to "Dominee D. Lamberts . . . Deventer," dated
        9.5.1965.) Deventer Dagblad (Deventer, Holland),
        Sept. 25, 1965, p. 3.

Misc. Writings by Schweitzer

B.   Speeches, Addresses, Lectures

This section includes speeches, addresses, lectures, etc., on topics
not included in the various subject areas above.

3930   "Albert Schweitzer in Münster." RUNDBRIEF 40 (1975), pp. 104-
         07. Text of a speech given Oct. 6, 1959 at the Anatomical
         Institute of the University of Münster-Westfalen.

3931   "Bibellese von Albert Schweitzer gehalten in Lambarene von
         2.5.1963 to 10.4.1964." Nach der Stenogram von Siegfried
         Neukirch. Freiburg: Siegfried Neukirch, n.d.

3932   "Discours du docteur Albert Schweitzer" (le prix de la
         Fondation Joseph Lemaire). CAHIERS/BELGE 1 (Nov. 1960),
         pp. 7-12. Illus. Translated as "Ansprache bei
         Entgegennahme des Belgischen Joseph-Lemaire Preises,
         18. November 1955." RUNDBRIEF 19 (Jan. 14, 1962).

3933   "A humanity of culture" (from a speech to school children,
         Hamburg, 1959). In: ALBUM, p. 146.

3934   "I am one of you." Address, in part, at Rotary Club of
         Colmar, France, 1952. Rotarian (Evanston, Ill.) 80:3
         (March 1952), p. 8.

3935   "Lieber Schuler!" Address to the pupils of the Albert-
         Schweitzer-Gymnasium, Marl i Westfalen, 7. Oktober 1959.
         RUNDBRIEF 16 (Oct. 1, 1960), pp. 20-22.

3936   Rede in der Albert-Schweitzer-Schule in Hamburg, Oct. 3, 1959.
         RUNDBRIEF 23 (1964).

3937   Rede in der Albert-Schweitzer-Schule in Hannover, Oct. 5,
         1959. RUNDBRIEF 36 (1973).

3938   "Rede vom Albert Schweitzer." In: Zusammenkunft von
         Mitarbeitern und Freunden des Spitals in Lambarene mit
         Albert Schweitzer am 22. September 1957 in Kammermusiksaal
         des Kongresshauses in Zürich. Zürich, 1957, pp. 7-15.

C.   Prefaces in Books by Others

3939   DOTY, JAMES EDWARD. Postmark Lambarene: a Visit with Albert
         Schweitzer. Indianapolis: John Woolman Press, 1965.
         Foreword (facsimile and text) in English by Albert
         Schweitzer.

3940   ECCARD, FRÉDÉRIC. Le Livre de la vie. Préf. de Albert
        Schweitzer. Neuchâtel: V. Attinger; Strasbourg:
        Editions Oberlin, 1951. 352 pp.

3941   GÖTTINGER ARBEITSKREIS. Dokumente der Menschlichkeit aus der
        Zeit des Massenaustreibung, gesammelt und hrsg. von
        Göttinger Arbeitskreis. 2. Auflage. Zum Geleite von
        Albert Schweitzer. Würzburg: Holzner-Verlag, 1960.
        342 pp.

        TRANSLATIONS

        Documents of Humanity during the Mass Expulsions. Compiled
        by K. O. Kurth. Tr. Helen Taubert and Margaret Brooke.
        Foreword by Albert Schweitzer. New York: Harper, 1954.
        Foreword, dated Lambarene, January 12, 1954, pp. 9-10.

3942   HOCHHUTH, ROLF. The Deputy. Tr. Richard and Clara Winston.
        New York: Grove Press, 1964. Letter to Rowohlt Verlag,
        dated Lambarene, June 30, 1963, serves as the preface.
        (The original German version, Der Stellvertreter, lacks
        this preface.)

3943   JOY, CHARLES R. Anthologia tōn ergōn tou Albertou Svaitzer.
        Tr. Agnes N. Diamantopoulou. Athens, 1963. 174 pp.
        Letter from Schweitzer to translator, in French and Greek,
        serves as preface.

3944   LIPPENS, LOUIS. Face aux dangers nucléaires. Préf. d'Albert
        Schweitzer. Linselles (Nord): Elan, 1964.

3945   Der Mann in der Brandung. Ein Bildbuch um Martin Niemöller.
        Frankfurt a.M.: Stimme Verlag, 1962.

3946   MARCHAL, GEORGES. Essais sur le fait religieux. Lettre-
        préface d'Albert Schweitzer. Paris: Berger-Levrault,
        1954.

3947   MERCIER, ANNE MARIE. Lambarene. Paris: Editions des
        Horizons de France, 1958. Preface signed Albert
        Schweitzer.

3948   "A Note from Albert Schweitzer." In: A Picture-History of
        the Bible and Christianity in 1000 Pictures, with the
        inspiring stories of all the world's great religions.
        Los Angeles: Year, the Annual Picture-History, 1952, p. 5.

3949   ORR, MYRIAM. Ils vivent pour la Paix. Préf. du Albert
        Schweitzer. Tr. Jacqueline Baron. Geneva: Perret-Gentil,
        1962. 136 pp.

Misc. Writings by Schweitzer

3950   Reverence for Life. Concept: Gerhard Kühn and Carl Zeiss.
        Picture editor: Bernd von Gleich. Aalen, Stuttgart:
        Leben im Bild, 1965.

3951   ROLLAND, ROMAIN. Zwischen den Völkern, Aufzeichnungen und
        Dokumente aus den Jahren 1914-1919 (German edition of his
        Journal des Années de Guerre, 1914-1919). Stuttgart:
        Deutsche Verlags Anstalt, 1954, Vol. 1, p. 5. Letter
        from Schweitzer, July 30, 1953, serves as preface. Re-
        printed as "Preface à l'édition allemande de'Journal de
        la guerre de 1914-1919' de Romain Rolland." In:
        RAYONNEMENT, pp. 271-72.

3952   ULRICH, HENRI. Chasser sans Tuer. Carnets d'un Naturaliste.
        Woerth (Bas-Rhin): Editions Sutter, 1954. Letter from
        Schweitzer to Dr. Ulrich, March 4, 1953, serves as the
        preface.

3953   WERNER, MARTIN. Glaube und Aberglaube: Aufsätze und
        Vorträge gesammelt aus Anlass seines 70. Geburtstages.
        Bern: P. Haupt, 1957, pp. 7 ff. Letter from Schweitzer
        to Werner on March 29, 1957, on the occasion of Werner's
        70th birthday, serves as the preface.

D. Miscellaneous

3954   "Albert Schweitzer: Auszüge aus seinen Schriften."
        RUNDBRIEF 40 (1975), pp. 57-76.

3955   "Albert Schweitzer grüsst den Dritten Deutschen Kongress für
        Freies Christentum, Mülheim a.d. Ruhr." Freies
        Christentum (Frankfurt a.M.) 4:10 (Oct. 1, 1952),
        col. 122.

3956   "An unsere Leser zum Neujahr 1921." KIRCHENBOTE 50:1
        (Jan. 1, 1921), pp. 1-2.

3957   "Chinesische Tierschutzgeschichten." KIRCHENBOTE 48:38
        (Sept. 20, 1919), p. 155.

3958   "Ein Tag in Oberammergau." KIRCHENBOTE (Oct. 27, 1900),
        pp. 340-42.

3959   "Frühe Unruhe in Kolmar." New Yorker Staats-Zeitung und
        Herold, July 30, 1949, p. 4.

3960   "My debt to the universities." University of Chicago Faculty
        News Bulletin 1:8 (Aug. 1949).

Miscellaneous

3961 "À l'occasion de son 75e anniversaire. Quel ques pensées
         d'Albert Schweitzer. Le Figaro Littéraire (Paris) 5:195
         (Jan. 14, 1950), p. 7.

3962 "Sätze von Albert Schweitzer" (five selections from his
         writings). Volksrecht (Zürich) 11 (Jan. 14, 1955).

3963 "Some random observations. Selections from Albert Schweitzer:
         an Anthology." The Christian Register (Boston) 126:8
         (Sept. 1947), pp. 328-31.

3964 "Vom alten zum neuen Jahr." KIRCHENBOTE 49:1 (Jan. 3, 1920),
         pp. 1-2. Excerpted in: Pierhal, Jean. Albert Schweitzer,
         see no. 291 above, p. 121 (English translation).

3965 "Was ich Teenagern rate." Evangelisches Sonntagsblatt für
         Bonn und Umgegend 109:3 (Jan. 16, 1966), p. 4.

3966 "Worte von Albert Schweitzer." In: Woytt-Secretan, Marie.
         Albert Schweitzer: der Urwalddoktor von Lambarene.
         Bern: P. Haupt, pp. 181-88.

3967 "Zum hundertsten Todestage des Philosophen Kant." KIRCHENBOTE
         33:7 (Feb. 13, 1904), p. 54.

3968 "Zur Reorganisation unserer Kirchenbehörde." KIRCHENBOTE 48
         (Jan. 5, 1919), p. 4.

3969 "Zwei Anekdoten aus Schweden." FAMILIEN-KALENDAR (1923), p. 5.

XII. Miscellaneous Writings About Albert Schweitzer

A. Honors and Awards

This section includes, in chronological order, articles about the various honors and awards given Albert Schweitzer. For convenience, various honorary degrees, postage stamps, and miscellaneous awards have been grouped in separate sections following the chronological listings. The German Peace Prize, the Nobel Peace Prize, and the Goethe Prize are omitted, as they are covered in previous sections.

French Academy--elected 1951; acceptance speech 1952

Note: Publications of Schweitzer's speech are included in Philosophy, no. 2328 above.

3970 CHAPELAN, MAURICE. "Albert Schweitzer à l'Institut." Le Figaro Littéraire (Paris) 7:340 (Oct. 25, 1952), pp. 1-2.

3971 "Schweitzer must make another speech." The Christian Century (Chicago) 68:51 (Dec. 19, 1951), p. 1415.

See also no. 3972 below.

Prince Carl Medal, Sweden--1952

3972 [Albert Schweitzer . . . has returned to Lambarene . . . inducted into French Academy and given the Prince Carl Medal by Sweden.] The Christian Century (Chicago) 69:51 (Dec. 17, 1952), p. 1462.

3973 "King of Sweden bestows medal on Dr. Schweitzer." The Diapason (Chicago) 43:24 (April 1, 1952).

3974 "König Gustav von Schweden hat Albert Schweitzer für sein verdienstvolles humanitäres Wirken mit der Prinz-Carl-Medaille ausgezeichnet." Börsenblatt für den Deutschen Buchhandel (Stuttgart) 8:21 (March 11, 1952), p. 94.

Misc. Writings About Schweitzer

3975   "Le professeur Schweitzer recoit le médaille du Prince
            Charles pour l'année 1952." Le Figaro (Paris) 126:2324
            (Feb. 28, 1952), p. 7.

Paracelsus Medal--September 1952

3976   "Albert Schweitzer--Medal winner." Time (New York) 60:16
            (Oct. 20, 1952), p. 46. Port.

3977   FRITON, B. "Begebenheit um einen grossen Arzt. Wie Professor
            Dr. Albert Schweitzer Ehrenmitglied der Internationalen
            Paracelsus-Gesellschaft wurde." Medizinische Technik
            (Berlin) 73:1 (Jan. 1953), pp. 130-31.

        NEUFFER, PROF. DR. "Albert Schweitzer 80 Jahre alt." See
            Life and Work--Visits, no. 1179 above.

German Order Pour le Mérite--January 13, 1955

3978   "German honor for scholars." The Times (London), Jan. 14,
            1955, p. 6c.

3979   "Professor Albert Schweitzer wurde Ritter des 'Pour le
            mérite.'" Offenbach Post 11 (Jan. 14, 1955), p. 1.

Order of Merit, Britain--1955

3980   "Albert Schweitzer--Queen's favorite." Time (New York) 66
            (Oct. 31, 1955), p. 28. Port.

3981   CHESTERMAN, CLEMENT C. "Schweitzer at the palace" (letter to
            the editor). The Times (London), Dec. 24, 1971, p. 11.

3982   "Dr. Schweitzer at the palace." The Times (London) 53,356
            (Oct. 20, 1965), p. 10.

3983   "Dr. Schweitzer in London, Oct. 17-24, 1955." BRITISH
            BULLETIN 23 (July 1957), pp. 9-10. Illus. (Also about
            LLD, Cambridge).

3984   "Now it's Albert Schweitzer O.M., one of world's 24." The
            Christian Register (Boston) 134:6 (July 1955), p. 38.

3985   "Portrait. The Queen honors a famous missionary and musician
            with the Order of Merit: Dr. Albert Schweitzer." The
            Illustrated London News 226 (March 5, 1955), p. 394.

3986   "Queen gives Schweitzer Merit Medal." The New York Times,
            Oct. 20, 1955.

3987   "Royal Tribute." Newsweek (New York) 46:18 (Oct. 31, 1955),
        p. 52.

3988   "A Sage's reception (in London to receive the Order of Merit
        and honorary degree from Cambridge). Life (New York)
        39:18 (Oct. 31, 1955), pp. 32-33. Illustrations only.

3989   "Schweitzer given Britain's highest distinction" (editorial).
        The Christian Century (Chicago) 72:44 (Nov. 2, 1955),
        p. 1262.

3990   "Scientists in the news--Albert Schweitzer (Order of Merit,
        England)." Science (Washington, D.C.) 122:3175
        (Nov. 4, 1955), p. 868.

Sonning Prize--1959

3991   [Award of the Sonning Prize, Copenhagen.] Time (New York)
        74:15 (Oct. 12, 1959), p. 43.

3992   "The University of Copenhagen has awarded the Sonning Peace
        Prize. . . ." The Christian Century (Chicago) 76:14
        (Oct. 14, 1959), p. 1174.

Honorary Degrees (all degrees are listed in Chronology)

3993   "Albert Schweitzer Ehrendoktor der Universität Münster
        (Westfalen)." Offenbach Post 232 (Oct. 7, 1959), p. 1.

3994   "Albert Schweitzer zu Besuch in Tübingen. Feier in der
        Universität." Stuttgarter Zeitung 236 (Oct. 13, 1959),
        p. 14.

3995   "Dr. Schweitzer in London, October 17-24, 1955." BRITISH
        BULLETIN 23 (July 1957), pp. 9-10. Illus. (Honorary LLD,
        Cambridge).

3996   EASTVOLD, S. C. "Albert Schweitzer, P.L.C.'s newest alumnus."
        In: Around the World in 180 Days. Minneapolis: Augsburg
        Publishing House, n.d., pp. 55-65. (Pacific Lutheran
        College, Washington).

3997   "Ehrendoktorwürde für Dr. Albert Schweitzer." Universitas
        (Stuttgart) 13:1 (Jan. 1958), pp. 94-96. (Tübingen.
        Mostly a reprint of Otto Michel's tribute to Schweitzer
        at this time.)

3998   "Elogien von Universitäten." In: DENKEN UND WEG, pp. 428-33.

Misc. Writings About Schweitzer

3999   "Eulogies from Universities." <u>Universitas</u> (English language
         edition) 7:1 (1964), pp. 107-12. Zürich, honorary doc-
         torate, 1920; Edinburgh, Dr. theol. h.c., 1929;
         Edinburgh, Dr. phil. h.c., 1929; Münster, Dr. med. h.c.,
         1958; Oxford, Dr. theol. h.c., 1932; Marburg, Dr. theol.
         h.c., 1952; Cambridge, Dr. jur. h.c.; Tübingen, Dr. theol.
         h.c.

4000   "Honorary Doctorate for Dr. Albert Schweitzer." <u>Universitas</u>
         (English language edition) 2:2 (1958), pp. 207-09.
         (Tübingen).

4001   "Die philos. Fakultät der Dt. Univ. Prag hat Prof. Dr. Albert
         Schweitzer den Titel eines Dr. h.c. verleihen." <u>Deutsche
         Literaturzeitung</u> (Berlin) 4:12 (March 19, 1927), col. 578.

4002   SPENCER, MARCUS A. "Dr. Albert Schweitzer honored at
         Edinburgh University." <u>The Christian Century</u> (Chicago)
         49:32 (Aug. 10, 1932), p. 987.

4003   "Universität Tübingen zur Verleihung des Dr. theol. h.c."
         <u>Universitas</u> (Stuttgart) 15:1 (Jan. 1960), p. 136.

4004   WEITBRECHT, OSKAR. "Albert Schweitzer Ehrendoktor von
         Tübingen." <u>Freies Christentum</u> (Frankfurt a.M.) 10:1
         (Jan. 1, 1958), p. 7.

Postage Stamps

4005   BRENET, A. "Histoire philatélique d'Albert Schweitzer."
         <u>Communautés et Continents</u> (Paris) 67:37 (Jan.-March 1975),
         pp. 35-36.

4006   [Four postage stamps in honor of Albert Schweitzer.] <u>The
         Christian Century</u> (Chicago) 71:41 (Oct. 13, 1954), p. 1229.

4007   KÜHN, G. "Albert Schweitzer. Briefmarken von 36 Staaten
         ehren sein Andenken." <u>Schwäbische Post</u>, May 23, 1979.
         Reprinted in the <u>A.I.S.L. Bulletin</u> 10 (Oct. 1979), p. 13.

4008   LIDMAN, DAVID. "Stamps--sale on the high seas--fight on
         leprosy." The New York <u>Times</u>, Sunday, Feb. 20, 1966,
         section 2, p. 28. Illus. (About 2 Schweitzer stamps
         issued by Ruwanda.)

4009   _____. "Stamps--U.N. World Federation--Schweitzer." The New
         York <u>Times</u>, Sunday, March 30, 1975, section 2, p. 35.
         Illus. (3 from Gambia, 7 from Hungary, 1 each from
         Pakistan, France, West Germany, East Germany, South Korea,
         Turkey, Rumania, Mali.)

Miscellaneous

4010 AMMAN, ARNOLD. "Hebel Preis für Professor Albert Schweitzer."
      Deutsche Tagespost (Würzburg) 57 (May 19, 1951), p. 8.

4011 "Ein Denkmal für Albert Schweitzer in Weimar. Gerhard Geyer
      beantwortete einige Frage der Redaktion." Bildende Kunst
      (Dresden) 17:4 (1969), pp. 200-02. Illus.

4012 "Dr. Albert Schweitzer is named man of the century." The
      Diapason (Chicago) 42:33 (Feb. 1, 1951), p. 22. (Named
      by National Arts Foundation.)

4013 DURANT, THOMAS M. "Dr. Albert Schweitzer: our new honorary
      fellow." Transactions and Studies of the College of
      Physicians of Philadelphia 30:2 (Oct. 1962), pp. 51-54.
      Port. Contains facsimile letter from A. S., dated
      Lambarene, June 25, 1962.

4014 "Ehrfurcht vor dem Leben." (Medal of Honor awarded to Albert
      Schweitzer by the American Institute for the Protection
      of Animals . . . designed by Gustav Bohland and struck in
      gold, 1955). Süddeutsche Zeitung (Munich), Feb. 1, 1955.

4015 "Four of ten 'most admired men' are religious leaders."
      The Sunday Bulletin (Philadelphia), Jan. 1, 1956, sect. 1.

4016 HANNON, LESLIE F. "The greatest ten of our time." Maclean's
      Magazine (Toronto) 63 (Jan. 1, 1950), pp. 10-11.

4017 HARTKE, WERNER. "Dem Ehrenmitglied der Deutschen Akademie
      der Wissenschaften zu Berlin." In: BEITRÄGE, pp. 70-73.

4018 HOLL, ALBERT. "Staatliche Münze prägt Schweitzer-
      gedenkmedaille. Zum 85. Geburtstag Albert Schweitzers
      am 14. Januar wurde von Professor Albert Holl eine
      Gedenkmedaille geschaffen." Stuttgarter Zeitung 9
      (Jan. 13, 1960), p. 14. Illus.

4019 _____. "Zum 50. Jahrestag der Gründung der Urwaldspitals in
      Lambarene durch Albert Schweitzer hat der deutsche
      Münzplastiker Prof. Albert Holl eine Gedenkmedaille
      geschaffen, die bei allen Banken und Sparkassen . . .
      erhältlich ist." National-Zeitung (Basel) 174
      (April 17, 1963), p. 1. Illus.

4020 "Inauguration du Monument Albert Schweitzer à Gunsbach."
      CAHIERS 22 (Dec. 1969), pp. 5-10. Includes texts of
      speeches given at the time.

Misc. Writings About Schweitzer

4021 JUNGHEINRICH, HANSJÖRG. "Albert Schweitzer würde Ehrenbürger
der Stadt Frankfurt." Freies Christentum (Frankfurt a.M.)
12:2 (Feb. 1, 1960), p. 26.

4022 PATTERSON, WILLIAM D. "The hour and the men--SRL reader poll
on the greatest living persons (Albert Schweitzer)." The
Saturday Review (New York) 34:1 (Jan. 6, 1951), pp. 10-11.

4023 "Schweitzer-Gedenkmedaille: zum 85. Geburtstag Albert
Schweitzers, von Professor Albert Holl geschaffen."
Schwarzwälder-Bote (Oberndorf am Neckar) 10 (Jan. 14, 1960),
p. 3. Illus.

B. The Schweitzer Influence

1. Education

One area into which Schweitzer's influence has extended is that of
education. As of 1966 there were forty-five elementary schools in
Germany which bore Schweitzer's name, as well as many in other coun-
tries. The New York State Legislature at one time funded five Albert
Schweitzer Chairs in the Humanities at New York State colleges. In
addition, there has been an Albert Schweitzer College in Corcelles,
Switzerland, and the Albert Schweitzer Education Foundation in
Chicago, now defunct, founded in 1958 by Herbert Phillips to further
Schweitzer's philosophy of life through lectures, a library, and
sponsored research.

Several centers for the study of Schweitzer's work have also
been set up. The Albert Schweitzerhuis in Holland, opened in 1951,
was intended as an international study center and residence for
students. The Albert Schweitzer Center in Great Barrington, Mass.,
was set up to educate people, especially young people concerning
Schweitzer's work through lectures, films, and exhibits. Its
extensive library of Schweitzer materials is also available to
researchers. Maison Albert Schweitzer in Günsbach, Alsace, houses
the central Albert Schweitzer Archives, including letters, films,
records, tapes, photographs, and paintings.

The Albert Schweitzer Centrum in Deventer, Holland, was begun
by Harold Robles in 1970. The center has a large library, as well
as archives containing Schweitzer photos, letters, and documents.
The Albert Schweitzer archives in Frankfurt contain letters and
books by and about Schweitzer, as well as pictures, newspaper

---

[1]Formerly Albert Schweitzer Friendship House.

Misc. Writings About Schweitzer

clippings, and early Rundbriefe. There are also collections of
Schweitzer materials at Princeton University and Chapman College.

4024   [. . . Albert Schweitzerschool in Hannover.] NIEUWS 2:5
         (July 1954), pp. 74-75.

4025   ANDERSON, ERICA. "Ein inneres Licht wurde angezündet."
         In: GESTERN-HEUTE, pp. 13-16. (History of Albert
         Schweitzer Friendship House.)

4026   _____. "Das 'Albert Schweitzer Friendship House.'" BERICHTE
         34 (Aug. 1972), pp. 24-25.

4027   "Archives centrales Albert Schweitzer à Gunsbach." NOUVELLES
         31 (May 1970), pp. 4-10.

4028   BEEKHUIS, ALEID. "Albert Schweitzer College." NIEUWS 5:2
         (Oct. 1956), p. 14.

4029   BURGER, C. B. "Het Albertschweitzerhuis te Amsterdam."
         NIEUWS 1:2 (March 1952), pp. 23-26. Illus.

4030   _____. "Een Bezoek aan Gunsbach." NIEUWS 19:1 (June 1970),
         pp. 6-7.

4031   CAHILL, EDWARD A. "The founding of Schweitzer College." The
         Christian Register (Boston) 132:1 (Jan. 1953), pp. 21-22.

4032   CUMMINGS, JUDITH. "Albany ends funds for $50,000 chairs at
         colleges in state." The New York Times, April 23, 1976,
         pp. 1, 33. Albert Schweitzer Chairs.

4033   FARBER, M. A. "States' $50,000 stipend cut upsets 'super-
         teachers.'" The New York Times, Dec. 23, 1972, p. 27.
         Includes a list of holders of Schweitzer chairs. For a
         letter to the editor in reply, see Tholfsen, Trygve.
         "Education: state vs. 'superteachers.'" The New York
         Times, Dec. 30, 1972, p. 20.

4034   [FEISSER, J. J. LOUËT.] "Toespraak der Gelegenheid van de
         Opening van het Albert Schweitzer Huis op 23 November
         1951. . . ." NIEUWS 1:3 (July 1952), pp. 44-46.

4035   "Günsbach." COURIER, May 1974, n.p. (13-14).

4036   [L'Institut Albert Schweitzer--Albert Schweitzer College at
         Churwalden.] NOUVELLES 27 (July 1961), p. 17.

4037   LEMBURGER, H. "Albert Schweitzer Education Foundation."
         Universitas (Stuttgart) 15:1 (Jan. 1960), p. 133.

411

.

Misc. Writings About Schweitzer

4038   MILLER, RHENA SCHWEITZER. "Albert Schweitzer Friendship
       House." A.I.S.L. Bulletin 2 (Nov. 1976), p. 14.

4039   MINDER, R. "Das Albert-Schweitzer-Zentral-Archiv in Günsbach."
       BERICHTE 31 (June 1969), pp. 33-35.

       PHILLIPS, MC CANDLISH. "Casals dedicates Schweitzer Library."
       See Life and Work, no. 800 above.

4040   PIEPENHORN, CHARLOTTE. "Das Holländischen Albert Schweitzer
       Centrum in Deventer." A.I.S.L. Bulletin 5 (Nov. 1977),
       pp. 2-3.

4041   PRIAL, FRANK J. "Trouble bedeviling Schweitzer chairs."
       The New York Times, Sunday, Dec. 13, 1970, p. 79.

4042   PWALOWSKA, IJA. "Günsbach." A.I.S.L. Bulletin 3 (Feb. 1977),
       p. 12.

4043   REITER, ELISABETH. "Das Albert Schweitzer Archiv in
       Frankfurt ist umgezogen." RUNDBRIEF 45 (May 1978), p. 35.

4044   ROSENWALD, HANS. "The Albert Schweitzer College," In: THE
       CONVOCATION RECORD, pp. IV/9-15.

4045   SCHWEITZER, RHENA. "Inauguration d'une Albert Schweitzer
       library à Great Barrington (USA)." CAHIERS 26
       (Winter 1971/72), pp. 22-24.

4046   SCHWEITZER-MILLER, RHENA. "Einweihung einer Albert Schweitzer
       Bibliothek in Great Barrington." RUNDBRIEF 35
       (June 15, 1972), pp. 37-39.

4047   "Schweitzer Centers." COURIER, Spring 1976, p. 20. About
       Albert Schweitzer Friendship House and Gunsbach.

4048   SILVER, ALI and TONY VAN LEER. "Das Albert-Schweitzer-Haus
       in Günsbach." RUNDBRIEF 45 (May 1978), pp. 33-34. Illus.

4049   STELLWAG, H. W. F. "Rede van Prof. H. W. F. Stellwag van de
       raad van bestuur van het international studiecentrum . . .
       van de opening van het Albert Schweitzer Huis." NIEUWS
       1:3 (July 1952), pp. 47-48.

4050   STOLZ, H. "Nederlands Albert Schweitzer archief." BERICHTE
       36 (Sept. 1973), pp. 24-25.

4051   W., S. R. "The Albert Schweitzer Collection (at Chapman
       College)." A.I.S.L. Bulletin 10 (Oct. 1979), p. 33.

4052   WERNER, D. A. "Internationaal studiecentrum in Oostenrijk
          gevestigd." NIEUWS 2:5 (July 1954), pp. 71-72.

4053   "Zentralarchiv in Gunsbach." RUNDBRIEF 33 (Oct. 10, 1970),
          pp. 26-30.

2. Hospitals

The example of Albert Schweitzer and Lambarene inspired several other
doctors to set up hospitals on his model. Besides those discussed
below, there are others: "Hospital Albert Schweitzer," opened by
Dr. Humberto M. Sa in Guarapuano, Brazil, in March 1963; The Ullong-do
Hospital, founded by Rev. Timothy Yilsun Rhee, M.D., in Ullong-do,
Korea; the Albert Schweitzer Clinic, founded by Dr. Carl van Aswegan,
Lesotho, South Africa; the Albert Schweitzer Clinic, Maseru,
Basutoland, Africa.

Hôpital Albert Schweitzer, Haiti

This hospital was founded by Larimer and Gwen Mellon in the
Artibonite Valley of Haiti in June 1956. The Mellons had been
millionaire ranchers in Arizona when they read an article about
Schweitzer's work in 1947. In 1948 they moved to New Orleans, where
Larimer Mellon studied medicine at Tulane, and his wife trained in
medical technology and hospital administration. As of the summer of
1977, their hospital had 200 beds and was staffed by twelve physicians, thirty registered nurses, and thirty nurses' aides.

        "Albert Schweitzer Hospital." See Youth, no. 4261 below.

4054   "Albert Schweitzerhospital in Haiti." NIEUWS 6:2 (Dec. 1957),
          pp. 5-6.

4055   ALPERIN, SHIRLEY HOPE. "In the footsteps of Albert Schweitzer."
          Nursing World (New York) 133:12 (Dec. 1959), pp. 25-27.
          Illus.

4056   "Un Américain construit un noveau Lambaréné." NOUVELLES 4
          (June 1958), p. 7.

4057   "The assurance that somebody cares." COURIER, Summer 1977,
          pp. 14-16.

4058   BARNES, BARBARA. "Pennsylvania-born doctor in Haiti follows
          the path of Albert Schweitzer." The Sunday Bulletin
          (Philadelphia), July 23, 1961, section 2, pp. 1-2.

Misc. Writings About Schweitzer

4059   BARTHÉLEMY, GUY et GREET. "L'Hôpital Schweitzer en Haiti."
        In: Au coeur du Gabon. Recontre avec Albert Schweitzer.
        Paris: A.I.D. and P.F.A.H., 1962, pp. 103-09.

4060   BRACKMAN, HENRIETTA. "Millionaire into medical missionary."
        Sunday Mirror (New York), Sept. 30, 1956, pp. 4-5. Illus.

4061   "Bronze head of Schweitzer will be accepted by Dr. Mellon for
        hospital in Haiti." Carillon (Newsletter of the Riverside
        Church, New York) 1:22 (Nov. 5, 1959), p. 1.

4062   C., N. (COUSINS, NORMAN). "The business of Larimer and Gwen
        Mellon." The Saturday Review (New York) 40:50
        (Dec. 10, 1960), pp. 26-27f.

4063   FEY, H. E. "In Haiti reverence for life." The Christian
        Century (Chicago) 74:12 (March 20, 1957), pp. 351-52.

4064   "Haiti Schweitzer hospital inspired by Beacon book." The
        Christian Register (Boston) 139:3 (March 1955).

4065   "L'hôpital 'Albert Schweitzer' en Haiti." CAHIERS 2
        (Dec. 1959), pp. 23-24.

4066   "Hospital in Haiti named for Schweitzer" (editorial). The
        Christian Century (Chicago) 71:52 (Dec. 29, 1954),
        p. 1573.

4067   "In Schweitzer's footsteps." Time (New York) 68:2
        (July 9, 1956), p. 33.

4068   JACKSON, JOY. "Haiti to have its own Dr. Schweitzer."
        Times-Picayune (New Orleans), Feb. 20, 1955, section 2,
        p. 1.

4069   KENNEDY, PAUL P. "Dream inspires Haiti hospital." The New
        York Times, Jan. 22, 1956.

4070   LA COSSITT, HENRY. "'Miracle of the spirit.'" Reader's
        Digest (Pleasantville, N.Y.) 68:408 (April 1956),
        pp. 182-88. Issued also as a 5-page reprint. Reprinted
        in The Orange Disc (Magazine of the Gulf Companies,
        Pittsburgh, Pa.) 12:6 (May/June 1956), pp. 14-16.

4071   "A life of purpose." Newsweek (New York) 45:25 (June 20, 1955),
        p. 92. Illus.

        MC GAVRAN, GRACE W. "Because somebody cared." See Youth,
        no. 4288 below.

Misc. Writings About Schweitzer

4072 MC GRADY, MIKE. "Paths of greatness." In: Jungle Doctors.
          Philadelphia: J. B. Lippincott, 1962, pp. 67-73.

4073 MELLON, (WILLIAM) LARIMER, JR. "Response to presentation of
          a bronze head of Albert Schweitzer, Riverside Church,
          New York City, November 11, 1959." In: REALMS, pp. 372-77.

4074 _____. "Road to happiness." This Week Magazine, New York
          Herald Tribune, Dec. 15, 1957.

4075 MORGAN, THOMAS B. and ERICA ANDERSON. "Mellon's miracle in
          Haiti; a millionaire American doctor follows the example
          of Albert Schweitzer." Look Magazine (New York) 20:22
          (Oct. 30, 1956), pp. 54-58.

4076 MORRIS, JOE ALEX. "Doctors vs. witchcraft." The Saturday
          Evening Post (Philadelphia) 234:37 (Sept. 16, 1961),
          pp. 48ff. Also issued as a 5-page reprint.

4077 OLDS, JAMES M. "Country doctor--jungle style." Today's
          Health (Chicago) 34:7 (July 1958), pp. 43-46. Translated
          by Glenn D. Kittler in Amepnka (Washington, D.C.) 45
          (196_), pp. 20-23. Illus.

4078 PHILLIPS, HERBERT M. "A spark leaps the seas." The Christian
          Century (Chicago) 73:26 (June 27, 1956), pp. 771-72.

4079 REED, HOWARD. "A month at l'hôpital Albert Schweitzer in
          Haiti." The Canadian Medical Association Journal
          (Toronto) 90 (Oct. 2, 1965), pp. 752-55.

4080 [ROSS, EMORY.] "We participate in a modern miracle."
          Forward (Park Avenue Christian Church, New York) 57:13
          (Dec. 9, 1954), unpaged.

4081 ROWLAND, STANLEY, JR. "Schweitzer inspires U.S. couple to
          operate own hospital." The New York Times, Jan. 28, 1957.

4082 SAVACOOL, HARRY. "The millionaire doctor carries on."
          Church Management (Cleveland) 35:3 (Dec. 1958), pp. 16f.

4083 SCHOFIELD, JOHN. "Haiti, West Africa of the Indies." The
          National Geographic Magazine (Washington, D.C.) 114:2
          (Feb. 1961), pp. 241, 243, 246-47.

4084 SHIRER, W. LLOYD. "Haiti's valley of opportunity." World
          Call (Indianapolis) 10:3 (March 1958), pp. 15-17. Illus.

Misc. Writings About Schweitzer

4085   _____. "Hôpital Albert Schweitzer." The Tulanian (New
         Orleans) 32:1 (Sept. 1958), pp. 5-7. Illus.

4085a   TORROP, HILDA M. "With reverence for all life." Practical
         Nursing (New York) 9:4 (April 1959), pp. 10-11. Illus.

4086   VESTAL, ADDISON A. "The stature of a man." The Christian-
         Evangelist (St. Louis, Mo.) 94:11 (March 1956), pp. 5-7.
         Issued also as an 11-page reprint by the Albert Schweitzer
         Fellowship, New York, 1955.

4087   WICK, ANDRE. "Une visite à l'Hôpital Albert Schweitzer à
         Deschapelles (Haiti)." CAHIERS 6 (Dec. 1961), pp. 14-15.

Hospital Amazónico Albert Schweitzer, Pucallpa, Peru

In 1956 Dr. Theodor Binder and his wife left a thriving private practice in Lima to open a temporary clinic in Pucallpa. This action was
based on a decision made by Binder at the age of 11, after meeting
Albert Schweitzer, to become a missionary. The hospital officially
opened in January of 1960. It has since been closed, and Dr. Binder
has started a second hospital in Mexico (see no. 4091 below).

4088   "Das Amazonas-Hospital Albert Schweitzer in Peru." RUNDBRIEF
         17 (Jan. 14, 1961), p. 77. Illus.

4089   BURKS, EDWARD C. "Schweitzer admirer (Dr. Theodor Binder)
         seeks aid for hospital in Peruvian jungle." The New York
         Times, Nov. 23, 1959, p. 33.

4090   CARLEY, AUSTIN J. "Theodor Binder: Peru's Albert Schweitzer."
         Américas (Pan American Union, Washington, D.C.) 19:3
         (March 1967), pp. 1-6. Illus.

4091   "Centro hospitalaria y de asistencia agropecuaria y artesanal
         "Albert Schweitzer" in Santa Ana Nichi/Mexico 1977."
         A.I.S.L. Bulletin 4 (July 1977), p. 28.

4092   "Deutscher baut Hospital im Urwald von Peru (Dr. Theodor
         Binder). Albert Schweitzers Lambarene als Vorbild des
         'Hospitals der Menschlichkeit.'" Schweinfurter
         Volkszeitung 1:47 (Nov. 24, 1959), p. 8.

4093   "Hilfe im Geist Albert Schweitzers. Ein Hilfsverein für das
         peruanische Urwaldhospital des Lörrachers Dr. Binder."
         Stuttgarter Zeitung 17 (Jan. 22, 1959), p. 15.

4094   "Hospital Amazonico Albert Schweitzer." Journal of the Amer-
         ican Medical Women's Association (Nashville) 17:2
         (Feb. 1962), p. 136.

Misc. Writings About Schweitzer

4095   LANDMANN, HERBERT. "Hospital im Amazonas. Dr. Binder schuf
       in Peru ein Krankenhaus im Sinne Albert Schweitzer."
       Neue Zeit (East Berlin) 12 (Jan. 14, 1961), p. 3. Illus.

4096   MEILACH, DONA Z. "Jungle doctor in Peru." Américas (Pan
       American Union, Washington, D.C.) 12:9 (Sept. 1960),
       pp. 6-10. Illus. Published in English, Spanish and
       Portuguese.

4097   MENDELSOHN, JACK. The Forest calls Back. Boston, Toronto:
       Little, Brown, 1965, 267 pp. Illus.

4098   MEYER, WALTER C. "In the spirit of Dr. Schweitzer." New
       York Sunday News, Feb. 19, 1967, pp. 21-23.

4099   PACHAS, AIDA. "Aus dem Amazonas-spital 'Albert Schweitzer'
       in Peru." RUNDBRIEF 19 (Jan. 14, 1962), pp. 57-59. Illus.

4100   "Skandal am Amazonas. Urwaldarzt Binder im Kreuzfeuer der
       Meinungen." Christ und Welt (Stuttgart) 18:3
       (Jan. 15, 1965), p. 6. Illus.

4101   TENBRINCK, MARGARET S. "Hospital Amazonico Albert Schweitzer,
       Pucallpa, Peru." In: THE CONVOCATION RECORD,
       pp. IV/22-26.

4102   _____. "Hospital practice on the edge of the Amazon Jungle."
       Journal of the American Medical Women's Association
       (Nashville) 18:12 (Dec. 1963), pp. 569-75.

4103   TORRES, AUGUSTÍN. "Obra de Schweitzer inspira construcão de
       hospital em Plena Selva Peruana." Diario de São Paulo,
       Jan. 17, 1960.

4104   TRENDE, WULF. "Der Humanität ein Bresche." RUNDBRIEFE/DDR
       19 (1972), pp. 34-36.

Albert Schweitzer Memorial Hospital, Balsam Grove, N.C.

The idea for this hospital was conceived by Dr. Gaine Cannon, who
went to the North Carolina mountains from Pickens, S.C., to recover
from overwork in 1953. He worked until 1963 in a clinic and as a
traveling doctor in the hills, meanwhile building a hospital with
the help of clinic patients. Unfortunately, the hospital was never
finished and today the building stands empty and unused.

4105   BLYTHE, LEGETTE. Mountain Doctor. Photographs by Bruce
       Roberts. New York: William Morrow, 1964. 221 pp.

Misc. Writings About Schweitzer

4106   CASTAN, SAM. "Blue Ridge Samaritan." Look Magazine (New
        York) 27:17 (Aug. 27, 1963), pp. 82-86. Illus.

4107   MELLON, WILLIAM L. III. "Mountain Samaritan--Dr. Gaine
        Cannon. . . ." The American Weekly/Journal American
        (New York), Dec. 24, 1961, pp. 12-13. Illus.

4108   "Mountain medicine" (picture study). MD (New York) 6:7
        (July 1962), pp. 91-95. Illus.

4109   TENBRINCK, MARGARET S. "Hospital practice in Appalachia.
        Report on the Albert Schweitzer Memorial Hospital,
        Balsam Grove, North Carolina." Journal of the American
        Medical Women's Association (Nashville) 21:7 (July 1966),
        pp. 578ff.

3. Supporting Committees

Soon after Albert Schweitzer started his work in Lambarene, he began
the practice of writing report letters describing the conditions
which he encountered, the state in which the natives lived, the
total lack of medical care, the magnitude of the work to be done,
and the surprising response of the natives to the medical services
which he offered. The letters were privately printed and circulated
to friends and colleagues who had contributed to his venture. Cir-
cles of friends, first in Switzerland and later in many other countries, organized themselves into committees with the purpose of
sending supplies and raising funds for the needs of the hospital.
Many of these committees later began to publish periodicals to be
circulated to supporters. The work of the committees has inspired
many hundreds of people within their orbits to follow the concepts
of Schweitzer and to share in the work of the Lambarene hospital.

    The following is a list of these supporting committees, with
their addresses. While the addresses were the most recent available,
they may not be accurate in all cases. A list of articles which discuss the committees follows, as does a section listing the periodicals published by the various groups.

            Association Internationale de l'Hôpital Albert Schweitzer
                à Lambaréné et son Oeuvre
                P.O. Box 15
                7400 AA Deventer/Holland

            Albert Schweitzer Association Colombo
                23/51 Magazine Road
                Colombo 8, Ceylon

Misc. Writings About Schweitzer

The Albert Schweitzer Fellowship
    866 United Nations Plaza
    New York, NY 10017

The Albert Schweitzer Fellowship of Japan
    2-3-18-23 Nishwaseda
    Shinjuku Ku--Tokyo
    Japan

The Albert Schweitzer Fellowship of Taiwan, Republic of
    China
    89-5 Chung-Chun Road
    Taipei, Taiwan, R.O.C.

Albert-Schweitzer-Komitee in der DDR
    Kaitzer Strasse 2
    DDR 801, Dresden

Albert Schweitzer Komitee Polen
    Trynitarska 11, 31-061 Krakow
    Poland

Amigos del Dr. Alberto Schweitzer
    Calle Loria 117
    Buenos Aires, Argentina

Association Belge des Amis d'Albert Schweitzer
    41 Rue du Ruisseau
    B-4100 Seraing, Belgium

Association Francaise des Amis d'Albert Schweitzer
    5 Rue Bellini
    F-92806 Puteaux, France

Association Italiana Amici de Albert Schweitzer
    Palazzo del Governo
    Via Anfiteatro 4, 1-74100
    Taranto, Italy

Dänischer Hilfsverein: Dr. Albert Schweitzer Hospital
    Strandveig 18
    Copenhagen, Denmark

Deutscher Hilfsverein für das Albert-Schweitzer-Spital in
    Lambarene
    Sertürner Strasse 23
    D-44, Münster, Germany

Misc. Writings About Schweitzer

>   Dr. Schweitzer's Hospital Fund
>   7 Parsifal Road
>   London NW 6 IUG
>   England
>
>   Schweizer Hilfsverein für das Albert Schweitzer-Spital
>   in Lambarene
>   Bürglenstrasse 15A
>   CH-3600, Thun, Switzerland
>
>   Stichtung Nederlands Albert Schweitzer Fonds
>   Brink 89
>   Deventer/Holland
>
>   Svenska Albert Schweitzer Förenigen
>   Nackgrand 1
>   S-58243 Linkoeping, Sweden
>
>   Vereinigung der Österreichischen Freunde des Albert
>   Schweitzer-Spitals in Lambarene
>   Kalvarienberggase 5/1/14
>   A-1170 Wien, Austria

4110   "Activité du comité de Paris." CAHIERS 6 (Dec. 1961), p. 22.

4111   "The Albert Schweitzer Fellowship." COURIER, Autumn 1968,
         inside front cover.

4112   "Associations Albert Schweitzer dans le monde." CAHIERS 4
         (March 1965), pp. 7-11.

4113   "Compte-rendu de l'Assemblée Générale qui s'est tenue le
         12 janvier 1962." CAHIERS 7 (Sept. 1962), pp. 13-15.

4114   CORTOT, ALFRED. "Albert Schweitzer à Paris. Sa reception
         par l'Association Francaise." CAHIERS 2 (Dec. 1959),
         pp. 3-6.

4115   "Friends of Doctor Schweitzer grow out of Boston efforts."
         The Christian Register (Boston) 135:5 (May 1956), p. 27.

4116   GAERTNER, HENRYK A. "Kropla i potok" (Polish Albert
         Schweitzer committee). Zwiastun 18/33/:21 (1978),
         pp. 331-32.

4117   _____. "Pezy lozku chorego" (Albert Schweitzer Committee in
         Poland). Kierunki 23:3 (1978), p. 7.

Misc. Writings About Schweitzer

4118   "Interview: wie wir Schweitzers Werk lebendig erhalten."
         Standpunkt: Evangelische Monatsschrift (Berlin) 3:1
         (Jan. 1975), pp. 14f.

4119   LAFONTAINE, LEON. [L'Association Belge des Amis d'Albert
         Schweitzer.] CAHIERS/BELGE 1 (Nov. 1960), p. 4.

4120   "Meet the officers of the Albert Schweitzer Fellowship."
         COURIER, April-May 1966, pp. 23-26.

4121   MINDER, ROBERT. "But de l'Association et rôle des Cahiers."
         CAHIERS 1 (April 1959), pp. 3-5.

4122   PAFFRATH, LESLIE. "The Albert Schweitzer Fellowship." In:
         THE CONVOCATION RECORD, pp. VII/3-6.

4123   "Reorganize for support of Schweitzer" (editorial). The
         Christian Century (Chicago) 63:8 (Feb. 20, 1946), p. 229.

4124   ROGERS, MIRIAM. "History of the Friends of Albert Schweitzer."
         In: SELECTION, pp. 67-69.

4125   _____. "How the Friends of Albert Schweitzer came into being."
         In: REALMS, pp. 406-11.

4126   _____. "A report about the Friends." In: TRIBUTE,
         pp. 24-27.

4127   ROSS, EMORY. "The Albert Schweitzer Fellowship." In: REALMS,
         pp. 365-70.

4128   SCHÜTZ, ROLAND. "Rundbriefe für den Freundeskreis von Albert
         Schweitzer." Freies Christentum (Frankfurt a.M.) 8:1
         (Jan. 1, 1956), col. 11.

4129   "Svenska Förbundet för stod till Albert Schweitzers verksamhet."
         In: MANNEN, pp. 251-52.

4130   W., D. A. (WERNER, D. A.) "Mogelijkheden tot oprichting van
         een Albert Schweitzercomite in Belgie." NIEUWS 6:2
         (Dec. 1957), p. 6.

4. Periodicals Published by Supporting Committees

4131   A.I.S.L. Bulletin. Published in Deventer, Holland since 1976
         by the Association Internationale d l'Hôpital Albert
         Schweitzer à Lambaréné et de son Oeuvre. H. E. Robles,
         editor. Multi-lingual, mimeographed.

Misc. Writings About Schweitzer

4132   A.S.F.H. Newsletter. Published since 1977 by the Albert
            Schweitzer Friendship House, Great Barrington, Mass.
            Recently re-named Reverence.

4133   Berichte aus Lambarene. Hrsg. vom Schweizer Hilfsverein für
            das Albert Schweitzer Spital in Lambarene. Published
            since 1924. Since 1955 there has been a French version,
            Nouvelles de Lambarene, see below. From 1924-1930 it
            was entitled Neues von Albert Schweitzer.

4134   Briefe aus dem Lambarene Spital. Published as a sequel to the
            book Briefe aus Lambarene. Written by Schweitzer from
            1930-1954 to inform his German friends about his activi-
            ties. Superceded by Rundbrief, see no. 4145 below.

4135   Les Cahiers de l'Association Belge des Amis d'Albert
            Schweitzer. Published since November 1960 in Seraing,
            Belgium.

4136   Cahiers Albert Schweitzer. Published from 1959-1976 under the
            title Cahiers de l'Association Française des Amis d'Albert
            Schweitzer. Published twice annually in Paris.

4137   The Courier. Published irregularly by the Albert Schweitzer
            Fellowship, New York.

4138   Dr. Schweitzer's Hospital Fund. British Bulletin. Published
            in London since 1925.

4139   Eerbied voor het Leven en Nieuws uit Lambarene. Published
            from 1930-1974, in Assen, as Nieuws uit Lambarene.
            Currently published in Deventer, Holland, by the
            Nederlands Albert Schweitzer Fonds. Editor: Harold E.
            Robles.

4140   Lettres de l'hôpital du docteur Schweitzer à Lambaréné.
            14 letters, covering the period 1930-1954. Published
            by Imprimerie Alsacienne, Strasbourg.

4141   Meddelanden från professor Albert Schweitzers Verksamhet.
            Published in Stockholm by the Svenska Förbundet til stöd
            för Albert Schweitzer's Verksamhet. Begun in 1925.

4142   Nouvelles de Lambaréné et de l'oeuvre d'Albert Schweitzer
            dans le Monde. Published by the Association Suisse de
            l'aide à l'hôpital, Section de la Suisse romande,
            Montreux.

Misc. Writings About Schweitzer

4143 Rapports sur Lambaréné. Published since May 1959 by the
Société d'entre'aide pour l'hôpital Albert Schweitzer de
Lambaréné, Bâle. Issued in French and German language
editions.

Reverence. See no. 4132 above.

4144 Revue Hôpital Albert Schweitzer Lambaréné. Hrsg. von der
Fondation Internationale de l'Hôpital du Dr. Albert
Schweitzer à Lambaréné. Begun in 1978.

4145 Rundbrief für den Freundeskreis von Albert Schweitzer und den
Deutschen Hilfsverein e.V. Founded in 1947 by Richard Kik
under the title Rundbrief für den Freundeskreis von
Albert Schweitzer. The title changed in 1966 with the
28th Rundbrief. During 1967/68, a few issues were issued
by the German Hilfsverein für das Albert Schweitzer Spital
in Lambarene. Current editor, Manfred Hänisch.

4146 Rundbriefe der Albert Schweitzer Komitee in der Deutschen
Demokratischen Republik. Issued twice yearly since 1963.

5. Villages

One Albert Schweitzer village was founded by Guy Barthélemy, a journalist who visited Lambarene in 1959 and 1960, and his wife, Greet,
who was formerly a surgeon there. The first village, intended as a
rural center for orphaned and deserted children, refugees, and the
handicapped, was founded in Paunat, Dordogne, in 1960. It was later
moved to Senez (Alpes des Hautes Provence) and has since been dis-
banded. Another Albert Schweitzer Kinderdorf for refugees and abandoned children was founded by M. Gutoehrlein in Waldenburg,
Württemburg, Germany. A third village has been registered in Liege,
Belgium.

a. Books

4147 BARTHÉLEMY, GUY. Lettre à Albert Schweitzer. Village Albert
Schweitzer, Paunat (Dordogne). Bergerac: Imprimerie
Robert Taillandier, 1966. 145 pp.

b. Articles, Parts of Books

4148 "Albert-Schweitzer Village." CAHIERS 2 (Dec. 1959), p. 5.

4149 BARTHÉLEMY, GUY. "Die gute Saat." In: GESTERN-HEUTE, p. 19.

4150 _____. "Lettre du village Albert Schweitzer à Paunat."
CAHIERS 7 (Sept. 1962), pp. 21-22.

Misc. Writings About Schweitzer

4151   _____. "Lettre du village Albert Schweitzer à Paunat."
        CAHIERS 6 (Dec. 1961), pp. 19-20.

4152   _____. "Le village Albert Schweitzer à Vaudune (Dordogne)."
        CAHIERS/BELGE 5 (April 1965), pp. 34-35.

4153   _____ et GREET. "Nouvelles du Village Albert Schweitzer,
        Paunat (Dordogne)." CAHIERS 5 (Sept. 1961), pp. 15-17.

4154   _____. "Le Village Albert Schweitzer, Paunat (Dordogne)."
        In: Au coeur du Gabon. Recontre avec Albert Schweitzer.
        Paris: A.I.D. and P.F.A.H. 1962, pp. 113-17.

4155   "Inauguration d'un village européen 'Albert Schweitzer.'"
        La Vie Protestant 21:33 (Sept. 12, 1958), p. 5.

4156   "Jeunesse Albert Schweitzer et village Albert Schweitzer à
        Vaudune." CAHIERS/BELGE 2 (Nov. 1961), pp. 17-19.

4157   "Nouvelles de Paunat." CAHIERS 11 (July 1964), p. 23; 12
        (Dec. 1964), p. 20.

4158   "Nouvelles du Village Albert Schweitzer à Paunat." CAHIERS
        9 (May 1963), p. 23.

4159   SCHÜTZ, ROLAND. "Albert-Schweitzer-Kinderdorf." Freies
        Christentum (Frankfurt a.M.) 11:5 (May 1, 1959),
        cols. 71-72. Also 10:9 (Sept. 1, 1958), cols. 118-19.

4160   "Village Albert Schweitzer fonde par le R. P. Pire." CAHIERS
        1 (April 1959), p. 25.

4161   "Village d'enfants et de refugies-centre rural Albert
        Schweitzer." CAHIERS 4 (Dec. 1960), pp. 8, 27.

4162   WOYTT-SECRETAN, MARIE. "Ein Besuch im Albert-Schweitzer-
        Kinderdorf bei Paunat." RUNDBRIEF 23 (Jan. 14, 1964),
        pp. 64-68. Illus.

6. Bobby Hill

Bobby Hill was the son of a U.S. Army sergeant stationed in Italy.
In 1959 he read about Schweitzer's hospital and decided to contribute
a bottle of aspirin. When he asked the United States Air Force to
deliver the aspirin to the hospital in Lambarene, an Italian radio
station broadcast the story, and donations poured in. The result
was $400,000 worth of medical supplies, which were flown into
Lambarene on planes donated by the French and Italian governments.

4163   "A boy's dream comes true." The Christian Century (Chicago)
         76:30 (July 29, 1959), p. 870.

4164   JUNGHEINRICH, HANSJÖRG. "Bobby Hill brachte Albert Schweitzer
         Medikamente." Freies Christentum (Frankfurt a.M.) 12:2
         (Feb. 1, 1960), col. 26.

4165   MC GURN, BARRETT. "Georgia boy, 13, sparks big gift for
         Dr. Schweitzer." New York Herald Tribune, July 14, 1959,
         p. 3, Illus.

4166   PUNER, MORTON. "To Dr. Schweitzer--with love." Coronet
         (Chicago) 47:6 (April 1960), pp. 37-41.

4167   "Schweitzer mission aided by U.S. Boy." The New York Times,
         July 9, 1959.

7. Miscellaneous

4168   "Albert Schweitzer en Belgique." CAHIERS/BELGE 1 (Nov. 1960),
         p. 6.

4169   "Der Albert Schweitzer Preis." A.I.S.L. Bulletin 5 (Nov. 1977),
         pp. 21-24 (German); pp. 25-28 (French).

4170   BABEL, HENRY. "A. Schweitzer et la Chine." CAHIERS 29
         (Summer 1973), p. 7.

4171   BALCAR, JOSEF. "Albert Schweitzer et la Tchecoslovaquie."
         Les Amis d'Albert Schweitzer (Paris), Dec. 1954, pp. 3-5.

4172   BAUR, HERMANN. "Albert Schweitzer und die Schweiz, 1975."
         BERICHTE 39 (March 1975), pp. 10-12. Reprinted in
         Communautés et Continents (Paris) 67:37 (Jan.-March 1975),
         pp. 19-22.

4173   _____ and ROBERT MINDER. "Bericht über das geistige Werk
         1969/70." BERICHTE 32 (Sept. 1970), pp. 35-37.

        DE FREITAS, DWALDO GASPAR. "O Doutor Schweitzer e o Brasil."
        See Bibliography, no. 4807 below.

4174   GAERTNER, HENRYK. "Bericht 1976-Juni 1977" (activities in
         Poland). A.I.S.L. Bulletin 4 (July 1977), pp. 22-23.

4175   GORFINKLE, PRISCILLA. "Boston University's Station WBUR-FM
         and the program 'Presenting Albert Schweitzer.'" In:
         SELECTION, pp. 65-66.

Misc. Writings About Schweitzer

4176   HAUSWALD, LEONORE. "Sein Name ist verpflichtung und
       Anregung." In: BEITRÄGE, pp. 74-77.

4177   LABUSCHAGNE, P. W. [Tribute without title.] (Albert
       Schweitzer's influence in South Africa). In: DENKEN
       UND WEG, pp. 408-10.

4178   LAFONTAINE, LÉON. "Albert Schweitzer et la Belgique."
       Communautés et Continents (Paris) 67:37 (Jan.-March 1975),
       p. 34.

4179   LAGERFELT, GRETA. "Albert Schweitzer et la suède." In:
       WÜRDIGUNG, pp. 25-27.

4180   MC MANUS, FRANK. "Labour's new M.P. followed Schweitzer's
       advice." Peace News (London) 1,171 (Dec. 5, 1958), p. 3.

4181   MILLER, RHENA SCHWEITZER. "Le rayonnement de mon père aux
       Etats Unis." Communautés et Continents (Paris) 67:37
       (Jan.-March 1975), pp. 13-15.

4182   MINDER, R. "Bericht über das geistige Werk." BERICHTE 33
       (Sept. 1971), pp. 13-15.

4183   _____. "Rapport sur l'activité de l'oeuvre spirituelle
       1970/1971." NOUVELLES 32 (Sept. 1971), pp. 18-26.
       Reprinted in CAHIERS 26 (Winter 1971/72), pp. 19-21.

4184   _____. "Wurzel und Triebe." BERICHTE 34 (Aug. 1972),
       pp. 15-18.

4185   _____. "Wurzel und Triebe." RUNDBRIEFE/DDR 21 (1973),
       pp. 20-23.

4186   _____ and HERMANN BAUR. "Wurzel und Triebe. Bericht der
       Komission für das geistige Werk, 1972-73." RUNDBRIEF
       37 (Sept. 4, 1973), pp. 48-54. Reprinted in BERICHTE
       36 (Sept. 1973), pp. 12-17.

4187   "Le Musée Albert Schweitzer." Le Monde (Paris), June 27, 1967,
       p. 13.

4188   NOMURA, MINORU. "Lambarene and Japan." In: BEITRÄGE,
       pp. 111-15.

4189   PETRIZKIJ, WILLI. "Albert Schweitzer in der UdSSR."
       RUNDBRIEFE/DDR 30 (1977), pp. 21-24.

4190   "Le Prix Albert Schweitzer." Cahiers Européens/Europäische
       Hefte/Notes from Europe (Munich) 2:1 (Jan. 1975), p. 25.
       Prize offered by the Johann Wolfgang von Goethe
       Foundation.

4191   REICHELT, GEORG. "Seinem Vorbild verpflichtet." RUNDBRIEFE/
       DDR 29 (1976), pp. 23-25.

4192   RHEE, TIMOTHY. "A Statement" (influence of Schweitzer).
       In: THE CONVOCATION RECORD, pp. VI/19-23.

4193   ROBLES, HAROLD E. "Albert Schweitzer in Polen." EERBIED
       27:2 (Aug. 1978), pp. 25-26.

4194   "Schweitzer peace award winners." The Times (London)
       May 26, 1969, p. 3.

4195   SILVER, ALI. "Rayonnement d'Albert Schweitzer in Japan."
       CAHIERS 20 (Dec. 1968), pp. 19-22.

4196   STINZI, MARIE-PAUL. "Le Prix Albert Schweitzer." Cahiers
       Européens/Europäische Hefte/Notes from Europe (Munich)
       2:1 (Jan. 1975), pp. 26-31.

4197   _____. "Remise des 'Prix Albert Schweitzer 1970' à
       Bruxelles." CAHIERS 24 (Winter 1970/71), pp. 19-22.

4198   TIGERSTRÖM, HARALD. "Albert Schweitzer et la suède."
       Communautés et Continents (Paris) 67:37 (Jan.-March 1975),
       p. 33.

4199   _____. [Tribute without title.] (Albert Schweitzer's
       activities and affiliations in Sweden since 1920.)
       In: DENKEN UND WEG, pp. 424-27.

4200   UCHIMURA, YUSHI. "Der ärztliche Weg der Humanität." In:
       DENKEN UND WEG, pp. 336-39. About Schweitzer's influence
       in Japan.

4201   VANDENRATH, JOHANNES. "Albert Schweitzer et l'Italie."
       Communautés et Continents (Paris) 67:37 (Jan.-March 1975),
       pp. 22-24.

4202   WANSELL, GEOFFREY. "Schweitzer medal for Samaritans founder."
       The Times (London), Oct. 13, 1972, p. 3.

4203   WERNER, D. A. "Albert Schweitzer et la Hollande: rayonnement
       et influence." Communautés et Continents (Paris) 67:37
       (Jan.-March 1975), pp. 28-31.

Misc. Writings About Schweitzer

4204   WOLFF, ANTHONY. "Schweitzer awards." Saturday Review
            (New York) 3 (Nov. 15, 1975), p. 6. Awards given by
            Southeastern North Carolina Educational, Historical and
            Scientific Foundation.

                        C. Works for Youth

1. Books

4205   AMUNDSON, SVERRE SALVESEN. Oganga. Den Store Medisin-mannen.
            En Biografi for ungdom. Oslo: Ansgar, 1966. 87 pp.
            Illus.

4206   ANDERSON, ERICA. Erica Anderson Presents Albert Schweitzer.
            Philadelphia: Chilton Company, 1961. 122 pp. (Meet
            your Great Contemporaries Series.)

4207   ASAI, MASAO. Genshirin no Dokutoru. Tokyo: Chikumashobo,
            1953. 182 pp. (Junior high school edition.)

4208   BARTHÉLEMY, GUY. Chez le Docteur Schweitzer. Témoignages.
            Avec quatre Illustrations. Paris, Fountainbleau:
            Editions Gilles, 1952. 132 pp.
            (Same). Paris: Diffusion le Guide, avec 11 illustrations.
                121 pp.
            (Same). Lausanne: Plaisir de Lire, 1953. 131 pp.
                4 illus. (Plaisir de Lire 88).

        TRANSLATIONS

        Wie ich Lambarene erlebte. Ein junger Mensch besucht Albert
            Schweitzer. Tr. Marie Woytt-Secretan. Munich: C. H.
            Beck, 1953, 1954. 99 pp. Ports.

4209   BERRILL, JACQUELYN. Albert Schweitzer, Man of Mercy.
            Illustrated with drawings by the author and with photo-
            graphs. New York: Dodd, Mead & Co., 1956. 200 pp.
            Illus. (For junior and senior high school.)

            (Same). 90th birthday edition, revised, 1965. 202 pp.
                Port., illus.

4210   CHO, P'UNG-YŎN. Sibaitchō Paksa. 1975. 216 pp. Illus.
            (Ŭryu sonyŏn mun'go.)

4211   DAHL, TITT FASMER. Eventyret om Albert Schweitzer. Med
            illustrasjoner av Oscar Reynert Olsen. Oslo: Gyldendal
            Norsk Forlag, 1954. Tiende Opplag, 1975. 114 pp.

Misc. Writings About Schweitzer

TRANSLATIONS

(Danish). Copenhagen: Det Dansk Forlag, 1956. 104 pp.

L'histoire marveilleuse d'Albert Schweitzer. Tr. Marguerite
Gay and Gerd de Mautort. Paris: Éditions G. P., 1955.
179 pp. Illus. (Bibliothèque rouge et or.)

(Same). Paris: Presses de la Cité, 1967. 252 pp. Illus.

Lakaren i Urskogen. En Bok om Albert Schweitzer. Tr.
Elisabeth Akesson. Lund: C. W. K. Gleerup, 1955.
112 pp. Ports., illus. (C. W. K. Gleerup's
Ungdomsböcker 124.)

La Maravillosa Historia de Alberto Schweitzer. Santiago de
Chile: Zig-zag, 1957. 107 pp. Illus. (Biblioteca
Juvenil. Serie Amarilla.)

Mit Albert Schweitzer zum Ogowestrom. Tr. Elisabeth Ihle.
Hamburg: Agentur des Rauhen Hauses, 1956. 112 pp.
Illus. 2nd edition, 1957.

Örnek insan Doktor Schweitzer. Tr. Pervin Esenkova.
Istanbul, 1960. 133 pp. 2nd edition, 1963.

4212   DANIEL, ANITA. The Story of Albert Schweitzer. Illustrated
with photographs by Erica Anderson and drawings by W. T.
Mars. New York: Random House, 1957. 179 pp. Ports.,
illus. (World Landmark Books, W 33). Grades 7-9.

(Brit. ed.) All about Albert Schweitzer. London:
W. H. Allen. 1961. 127 pp. Illus., plates.

(Phonodisc). Bell, Elise. The Story of Albert Schweitzer.
Enrichment Records EWR 302, 1964. American (i.e. World)
Landmarks. A dramatization with music and sound effects,
adapted from the World Landmark Book of the same title by
Anita Daniel. Second side is author's Julius Caesar.

TRANSLATIONS

Albert Schweitzer. Tr. Annette van Henscle. Amsterdam:
C. P. J. van der Peet, 1961. 123 pp. Illus.

Albert Schweitzer. Tr. Habibeh Fouoozat. Tehran: Niland
Amirkabira, 1960. 131 pp.

Albert Schweitzer. Tr. Luis Mejia. Medellin, Colombia:
Ediciones Albon, 1963. 181 pp.

Misc. Writings About Schweitzer

<u>La Storia di Albert Schweitzer</u>. Tr. E. Cappelli. Milan:
Fratelli Fabbri (D. Negri), 1964. 194 pp. Illus.
(Linri del Sapere, 25.)

4213 DIAZ-PLAJA, AURORA. <u>El doctor Schweitzer</u>. Ilustraciones de
Azpelicueta. Barcelona: Editorial Juventud, 1962.
75 pp. Illus.

4214 EDSCHMID, KASIMIR (Eduard Schmid). <u>Albert Schweitzer</u>.
Düsseldorf: August Bagel Verlag, 1949. 70 pp.
(Schulausgabe.)

4215 ENGELHARDT, EMIL. <u>Albert Schweitzer</u>. Mit Zeichnungen von
Helma Stumper. Herausgegeber: Arbeitsgemeinschaft
Bremer Schüle. Bremen: Eilers und Schünemann, 1952.
43 pp. (Bremen Bogen--Unsere Schüle.)

4216 ESSEL, FRANK TH. (Samuel Gullberg). <u>Läkaren i Urskogen. Ur
Albert Schweitzers liv och gärning i Ekvatorialafrikas</u>.
Stockholm: Harriers Bokförlag, 1942. 93 pp. Illus.
(Bragd och Hjältedad, 6.)

4217 FRANCK, FREDERICK. <u>My Friend in Africa</u>. Illustrated with
drawings by the author. Indianapolis, Ind.: Bobbs-
Merrill, 1960. 94 pp. Illus.

TRANSLATIONS

(Dutch). <u>Mijn Vriend in Afrika</u>.

4218 FRIIS, BØRGE. <u>Jeg Hedder osse Albert--men kald mig bare
Peter</u>. Copenhagen: Branner og Korch, 1961.

4219 FRITZ, JEAN. <u>The Animals of Doctor Schweitzer</u>. Illustrated
by Douglas Howland. New York: Coward-McCann, 1958.
64 pages, unnumbered. Illus. Grades 3-5.

4220 GOEDSCHE, CURT RUDOLF and W. E. GLAETTLI. <u>Schweitzer</u>.
New York: American Book Company, 1957. 71 pp. Illus.
Revised edition, 1966. (Cultural graded readers, alter-
nate German Series: I. Elementary.)

4221 GOETZ, BERNHARD. <u>Albert Schweitzer. Ein Mann der guten Tat</u>.
Göttingen: W. Fischer Verlag, 1955. 79 pp. Illus.
(Göttinger Jugend-Bände.) For 12-15 year olds.

4222 GÓMEZ, ORTIZ MANUEL. <u>El Brujo Blanco de Lambarené, el Doctor
Schweitzer</u>. Madrid: Ediciones PPC, 1966. 88 pp.
Illus. (Colleción "Lo Impossible" 45.)

Misc. Writings About Schweitzer

4223   GRAAFLAND, B. Schweitzer, Eerbied voor het Leven. Illus.
         F. Wijnand. Hoorn: "West-Friesland," 1955. 153 pp.
         Illus. (Klimopreeks no. 13.)

4224   HAGII, SEIJI. Schweitzer. Tokyo: Kaneko Shoten, 1955.
         242 pp.

4225   HEIPP, GÜNTHER. Der Arzt von Lambarene. Aus dem Leben
         Albert Schweitzers. Murnau, Munich, Innsbruck, Olten:
         Verlag Lux, 1956. 32 pp. (Lex-Lesebogen Natur- und
         Kulturkundliche Hefte. Kleine Bibliothek des Wissens.)
         5th edition, 1965. 6th edition, 1967.

         TRANSLATIONS

         Le docteur de Lambaréné. Souvenirs de la vie d'Albert
             Schweitzer. 14 Janvier 1875-4 septembre 1965. Vevey,
             1972.

4226   HENRICH, RUTH. They thought he was Mad (Albert Schweitzer).
         New York: Friendship Press; London: Edinburgh House
         Press, 1940. 32 pp. See also numbers 4276-77 below.

4227   ITALIAANDER, ROLF. Der weisse Oganga, Albert Schweitzer; eine
         Erzählung aus Äquatorialafrika. Hannover: Oppermann,
         1954. 155 pp. Illus. (Oppermanns Jugendbücher, Bd. 12.)

         TRANSLATIONS

         De Blanke Oganga. Albert Schweitzer. Een verhaal uit
             Equatorial Afrika met een nawoord van E. D. Spelberg.
             Rotterdam: Ad. Donker, 1957. 148 pp. Port., illus.

4228   KIK, RICHARD. Beim Oganga von Lambarene; Geschichten aus
         dem Leben Albert Schweitzers. Reutlingen: Ensslin und
         Laiblin, 1954. 79 pp. Illus. Reprinted 1958. Ages
         10-15.

         TRANSLATIONS

         Beim Oganga von Lambarene. Tr. J. van Ewijk. Zutphen:
             W. J. Thieme and Co., 1960. 70 pp. Illus.

         Hos Oganga i Lambarene. Tr. F. Asmussen. Copenhagen:
             Hernovs Forlag, 1957. 92 pp.

         With Schweitzer in Lambarene. Tr. Carrie Bettelini.
             Philadelphia: Christian Education Press, 1959. 87 pp.
             Illus.

Misc. Writings About Schweitzer

4229   KRIEGER, ERHARD. Der Doktor im Urwald, Albert Schweitzer.
        Christ der Tat. Wuppertal-Wichlinghausen: Montanus and
        Ehrenstein, n.d. 32 pp.

4230   LANGLEY, NINA. Dr. Schweitzer, O.M. The story of his life
        and work for the new generation. London: Harrap, 1956.
        108 pp. Illus.

        TRANSLATIONS

        Doctor Schweitzer. Tr. R. Orta Manzano. Barcelona:
            Juventud, 1966. 189 pp.

4231   MANTON, JO. The Story of Albert Schweitzer. Illus. Astrid
        Walford. London: Methuen, 1955. 176 pp. Illus.
        Grades 5-10.

            (Same). New York: Abelard-Schuman, 1955. 223 pp.
                Illus.

            (Same). Eau Claire, Wis.: E. M. Hale, 1957. 179 pp.

        TRANSLATIONS

        A. Schweitzer. Il Medico dei Lebbrosi. Tr. M. Pavan. Milan:
            U. Mursia, 1970. 163 pp.

        Alberto Schweitzer. Tr. Isaura Correia dos Santos. Porto:
            Civilizacäon, 1960. 238 pp. Illus.

        Un destin: Albert Schweitzer. Tr. Renée Dardel et Juliette
            Maquemer. Paris: Michel, 1956. 220 pp. Illus.
            Reprinted 1963.

        Den Store Doktoren. Historien om Albert Schweitzer.
            Tr. F. Fasmer. Stavanger: Misjonsselskapets Forlag,
            1957. 161 pp.

4232   MARTIN, NANCY. The Great Doctor: the Story of Albert
        Schweitzer. Exeter, Eng.: Religious Education Press,
        1978.

4233   MARUYAMA, YOSHIJI. Ai to Hikari no Shito. Tokyo: Keisli-sha,
        1952. 318 pp. (Stories of Great Men series.)

4234   MELZER, FRISO. Albert Schweitzer und sein Werk. Stuttgart:
        Evangelische Missionsverlag, 1953. 16 pp. 2nd edition,
        1954. (Auf den Strassen der Welt; Missionshefte der
        Jungen Gemeinde, nr. 21.)

Works for Youth

4235   MERRETT, JOHN. The True Book about Albert Schweitzer. Illus.
         N. G. Wilson. London: F. Muller, 1960. 141 pp. Illus.
         (Grades 7-9).

         (American edition). The True Story of Albert Schweitzer,
            Humanitarian. Chicago: Children's Press, 1964.
            143 pp. Illus.

4236   MONTGOMERY, ELIZABETH RIDER. Albert Schweitzer, Great
         Humanitarian. Champaign, Ill.: Garrard, 1971. 144 pp.
         Illus. (Grades 4-7.)

4237   NORTHCOTT, WILLIAM CECIL. Forest Doctor: The Story of Albert
         Schweitzer. London: Lutterworth, 1955. 93 pp. Illus.
         (Stories of Faith and Fame.) Grades 3-7.

         (Same). New York: Roy Publishers, 1957. 92 pp. Illus.

4238   OSWALD, SUZANNE. Im Urwaldspital von Lambarene. Photographs
         by Erica Anderson, from Die Welt von Albert Schweitzer.
         Zürich: Schweizerisches Jugendschriftenwerk, 1955. 48 pp.
         Illus. (Schweizerisches Jugendschriftenwerk nr. 546.)

4239   OTERDAHL, JEANNA and KAJ BECKMAN. Albert Schweitzer, pojken
         som inte kunde döda. Stockholm: Svenska Kyrkans
         Diakonistyreles, 1965. 21 pp. Grades 1-4.

         TRANSLATIONS

      Albert Schweitzer: the Boy who could not Kill. Tr. Gene and
         Louise Lund. Minneapolis: Augsburg Pub. House, 1967.
         23 pp. Illus.

4240   PAYNE, PIERRE STEPHEN ROBERT. The Three Worlds of Albert
         Schweitzer. New York: Thomas Nelson, 1957. 252 pp.
         See also no. 4294 below.

         (Paperback edition). Bloomington, Ind.: Indiana
            University Press, 1961. 252 pp. (Midland Books, 29.)

         (British edition). Schweitzer: Hero of Africa. London:
            Robert Hale Ltd., 1957. 194 pp.

         TRANSLATIONS

      Albert Schweitzer und seine drei Welten. Tr. Margaret
         Carroux. Konstanz, Zürich: Diana Verlag, 1964. 269 pp.

      (Dutch). De Driewoudige Wereld van Albert Schweitzer.
         187 pp.

Misc. Writings About Schweitzer

4241 PETRIZKI, WILLI. [Light in the Jungle.] Leningrad: Detskaja
        Literatura, 1972.

        TRANSLATIONS

        Licht im Dschungel. Tr. Ilse Berger. Illus. Erich Gürtzig.
            Berlin: Kinderbuchverlag, 1975. 280 pp.

4242 REINHART, JOSEF. Der Menschenfreund im Urwald. Aarau:
        Sauerländer, 1934. 40 pp. Illus. (Reprinted from Helden
        und Helfer. Aarau: Sauerländer, 1931, pp. 295-331.)

4243 RICHARDS, KENNETH G. Albert Schweitzer. Chicago: Children's
        Press, 1968. 94 pp. Illus. (People of Destiny: a
        Humanities Series.)

4244 ROBLES, HAROLD E. Albert Schweitzer. Kampen: J. H. Kok,
        1978. 27 pp. Illus. (Lantaarn Reeks 31.) Ages 8-10.

4245 RUSSELL, LILIAN M. My Monkey Friends. London: A. and C.
        Black, 1938. 126 pp. 2nd edition, 1948. 127 pp.
        Illus.

        TRANSLATIONS

        Meine Freunde, die Affen; Mensch und Tier in Albert Schweitzers
            Lambarene und anderswo. Tr. Marie Woytt-Secretan.
            Stuttgart: Günther, 1950. 178 pp. Illus.

        SCHIFFMAN, EVELYN. Albert Schweitzer, jungle doctor: a story
            reference for children. See Dissertations, no. 4340
            below.

4246 SCHOMBURG, EBERHARD. Albert Schweitzer. Ein Leben
        unmittelbaren Dienens. Braunschweig, Berlin, Hamburg:
        G. Westermann, 1948. 56 pp. Reprinted 1950, 1952, 1954.
        (Helden des Friedens.)

4247 SILVER, ALI. Albert Schweitzer voor de kinderen verteld.
        Amsterdam: Internationale uit geversmaatschappij het
        wereldvenster, 1951. 47 pp. Illus.

4248 SIMON, CHARLIE MAY (HOGUE), pseud. All Men are Brothers; a
        Portrait of Albert Schweitzer. Photos by Erica Anderson.
        New York: Dutton, 1956. 192 pp. Illus. 5th printing,
        1959. Grades 7-10.

        (British Edition). London: Blackie, 1959. 190 pp.

        (New edition). Glasgow: Blackie, 1970.

Misc. Writings About Schweitzer

TRANSLATIONS

Ningen wa mina Kyodai. Tr. Minoru Nomura. Tokyo:
    Hakusuisha, 1959. 246 pp.

4249   SINGER, KURT DEUTSCH and JANE SHERROD. Dr. Albert Schweitzer,
    medical missionary; a biographical sketch of a man who
    had dedicated his life to others. Minneapolis: T. S.
    Denison, 1962. 163 pp. Reprinted 1963. (Denison's Men
    of Achievement series).

4250   SŎNU, NAM. Nam ŭl Wihae Sanun Saram. 1961. 58 pp. Illus.

4251   STEINITZ, BENNO. Albert Schweitzer, Leben-Werk-Botschaft.
    Vienna, 1955. 144 pp. 2. Vermehrte und verbesserte
    Auflage, 1959. 178 pp. (Schriftenreihe der
    Österreichischen UNESCO-Kommission, Bd. 16).

4252   SUGIYAMA, KATSUEI. Shubaitsā. 1969. 182 pp. (Kodomo no
    Denki Zenshŭ, 19.)

4253   TEUFEL, WILHELM. Der Urwalddoktor. Stuttgart: Quell-Verlag,
    16 pp. Series: Immergrün. (Erzählungen für die Jugend
    #340.)

4254   THOMAS, M. Z. Unser grosser Freund, Albert Schweitzer.
    Munich: Schneider, 1960. 128 pp.

TRANSLATIONS

Albert Schweitzer. London: Oliver and Boyd, 1962, 1965.
    Richmond, Va.: John Knox Press, 1965.

Albert Schweitzer van kind tot man. Tr. J. J. Human.
    Kaapstad: H.A.U.M., 1960. 112 pp. Illus.

Vägen till Lambarene. Tr. Ulf Schenkmanis. Illus. Werner
    Kulle. Stockholm: Svenska Diakonistyrelses Bogforlag,
    1961. 138 pp. Illus.

Vår venn Albert Schweitzer. Tr. Ottar Odland. Oslo:
    Det Norsk Samlaget, 1962. 114 pp.

4255   VETHAKE, KURT. Das Weisse Haus im Dschungel. Kiel: Neumann
    und Wolff, 1954. 77 pp. 2nd edition, 1955, 81 pp.
    (Taschengeld-Taschenbücher, 1.)

4256   WARTENWEILER, FRITZ. Der Urwalddoktor Albert Schweitzer.
    Zürich: Schweizerisches Jugendschriftenwerk, 1930.

Misc. Writings About Schweitzer

> 32 pp. 4th edition, 1951. Reprinted 1955 for Schweitzer's
> 80th birthday in cooperation with "Freunde Schweizerischer
> Volksbilddungsheime, Basel." 9th edition, 1961.
> (Schweizerisches Jugendschriftenwerk, nr. 49.)

> TRANSLATIONS

> Albert Schweitzer, le médecin des noirs. Le docteur de la
>   forêt vierge Albert Schweitzer à Lambaréné. Adaptation:
>   Louis Germond. Illus. René Merminod. Zürich: Oeuvre
>   suisse des lectures pour la jeunesse, 1953. 32 pp. Illus.
>   (Oeuvre suisse des lectures pour la jeunesse 481.)

> Urskogslaekjaren Albert Schweitzer. Tr. Sigurd Sandvik.
>   Oslo: Leif H. Anderson and Co., 1957. 63 pp.

4257 WENZEL, LENE and FERDINAND BECHTLE. Albert Schweitzer--
      Lambarene einst und jetzt. Stuttgart: Quell-Verlag und
      Buchhandlung d. Ev. Gesellschaft in Stuttgart, 1975.
      48 pp. Illus.

4258 WINKLER, JOHAN. Ik Kom u Helpen Doktor. Amsterdam:
      Ploegsma, 1955. 120 pp.

> TRANSLATIONS

> Ek kom u help, Doktor. Illus. Alie Evers. Johannesburg:
>   Afrikaanse Pers-Boekhandel, 1960. 109 pp. Illus.

> Ich komme Ihnen helfen, Herr Doktor! Tr. Hans Cornioley.
>   Zeichnungen von Edgar Ruf. Aarau und Frankfurt a.M.:
>   Sauerländer, 1957. 156 pp. Illus.

4259 WYMER, NORMAN. Albert Schweitzer. London: Oxford University
      Press, 1959. 31 pp. Illus. (Lives of Great Men and
      Women, Series 4, No. 8.) See also no. 4308 below.

4260 ZINTL, MARTIN. Menschenfreund in Lambarene, ein Lebensbild
      des Urwaldarztes Dr. Albert Schweitzer. Munich:
      Bayerischer Schulbuch, 1950. 48 pp. Illus. (Die Welt
      im Speigel der Geschichte.)

2. Articles, Parts of Books

4261 "Albert Schweitzer Hospital." Junior World (St. Louis, Mo.)
      82:34 (Aug. 23, 1959), pp. 268-69. About Haiti Hospital.

4262   ARMSTRONG, MARJORIE MOORE. "In the footsteps of Albert
       Schweitzer." Crusader (Memphis) 1:7 (April 1971), pp. 4-6.

4263   BACH, MARCUS. "Albert Schweitzer." In: The Circle of Faith.
       New York: Hawthorn Books, 1956, pp. 147-81.

4264   BARTLETT, ROBERT. "Reverence for life . . . Albert Schweitzer."
       In: They Stand Invincible. Men who are Reshaping our
       World. New York: Thomas Y. Crowell, 1959. pp. 51-73.

4265   BRIDGES, THOMAS CHARLES (Christopher Beck) and HUBERT HESSELL
       TILTMAN. "Fighting disease in the jungle: Albert
       Schweitzer's work of healing in darkest Africa." In:
       More Heroes of Modern Adventure. Boston: Little, Brown
       and Co., 1930, pp. 160-72; London: George S. Harrap,
       1931. Translated as "I kamp mot sjukdomar i djungeln.
       Albert Schweitzers verksamhet som läkare i mörkaste
       Afrika." In: Med livet på spel. Verklighetsskildringer
       från upptäcktsfard och äventyrsstrat. Tr. Gosta Dahk.
       Stockholm: Fahlcrantz and Co., 1932, pp. 177-91. Illus.
       (Moderna Hjältar, III).

4266   BULL, NORMAN J. One Hundred Great Lives. Amersham,
       Buckinghamshire, England: Hulton Educational Publica-
       tions, 1972, pp. 334-36. Illus.

4267   CARLEBERG, GÖSTA. "Albert Schweitzer, filosof, teolog,
       musiker, och missionär." In: Kristendom in Funktion.
       Kristna Gestalter under 1900-talet. Biografier för
       Ungdom. Uppsala: J. A. Lindblads Förlag, 1952,
       pp. 47-73.

4268   CLARKE, MAURICE. "The ambassador to Lambaréné." In: Adven-
       tures in Church Worship. Milwaukee: Morehouse Publish-
       ing Co., 1933, pp. 80-84. (Christian Nurture Series).

4269   DESCOEUDRES, ALICE. "Albert Schweitzer." In: Encore des
       héros. La Chaux-de-Fonds: Imprimerie des Coopératives
       Réunirs, 1934, pp. 215-60. Port.

4270   DOUMA, SIOERD and M. C. CAPELLE. "Dr. Albert Schweitzer.
       Dienaar der lijdende mensheid." In: Groot Vertelboek
       van de Zending. Baarn: Bosch & Keuning, 1954,
       pp. 166-74.

4271   FRANCK, FREDERICK. "Lambaréné revisited." In: African
       Sketchbook. New York: Holt, Rinehart and Winston, 1961,
       pp. 151-68. Illus.

Misc. Writings About Schweitzer

4272   GARLICK, PHYLLIS. "Albert Schweitzer." In: <u>Six Great</u>
       <u>Missionaries</u>. London: Hamish Hamilton, 1955, pp. 177-214.

4273   _____. "Albert Schweitzer, the jungle doctor." In: <u>Pioneers</u>
       <u>of the Kingdom</u>. London: The Highway Press, n.d., Part II,
       pp. 133-44.

4274   GUNTHER, JOHN. "Jungle Philosopher." In: <u>Great Lives,</u>
       <u>Great Deeds</u>. Pleasantville, N.Y.: The Reader's Digest
       Association, 1964, pp. 113-18.

4275   HAMPE, JOHANN CHRISTOPH, comp. <u>Das soll dir bleiben. Ein</u>
       <u>Brevier für jungen Menschen</u>. Stuttgart: Kreuz Verlag,
       1956, pp. 58-59.

4276   HENRICH, RUTH. "They thought he was mad." In: <u>Eagle Omnibus</u>
       <u>Number Five</u> (True stories of real people. . .). London:
       The Livingston Press, 1948, pp. 65-94. (Eagle Books,
       nos. 26-31.)

4277   _____. "Albert Schweitzer. Man dacht dat hij niet goed
       wijs was." In: <u>Pioniers van Christus</u>, uit het engels
       bewerkt door A. H. Oussoren. Kampen: J. H. Kok N. V.,
       1950, pp. 123-50.

4278   HOWARTH, DAVID. "Albert Schweitzer." In: <u>Heroes of Nowadays</u>.
       With drawings by Leonard Rosoman. London: Collins,
       1957, pp. 169-86. Translated as <u>Vår tids Helter</u>. Tr. Per
       Wollebaek. Oslo: J. W. Cappelans Forlag, 1958, pp. 110-23.

4279   HUGHES, LANGSTON. "Albert Schweitzer: Missionary." In:
       <u>The First Book of Africa</u>. New York: Franklin Watts,
       1960, pp. 23-24. Illus.

4280   JERAN, URSULA. "Albert Schweitzer--Arzt in Urwald." In:
       Meinhof, I. and R. Riemeck, eds. <u>Freunde und Helfer der</u>
       <u>Menschheit</u>. Oldenburg/Hamburg: Stalling, 1948,
       pp. 21-26.

4281   KELEN, IMRE. <u>Fifty Voices of the Twentieth Century</u>.
       New York: Lothrop, Lee and Shepard, 1970.

4282   KENWORTHY, LEONARD S. "Albert Schweitzer. Doctor in the
       jungle." In: <u>Twelve Citizens of the World</u>. Illus.
       William Sharp. Garden City, N.Y.: Doubleday, 1944,
       pp. 199-220. Reprinted 1945, 1946, 1953.

4283   KEPLER, THOMAS S. "Albert Schweitzer." In: <u>A Journey with</u>
       <u>the Saints</u>. Cleveland, New York: The World Publishing
       Co., 1951, pp. 138-41.

4284   KOHN, HAROLD E. "The measure of a man." In: A Touch of
          Greatness. Grand Rapids, Mich.: William B. Eerdmans
          Publishing Co., 1965, pp. 148-51. Illus.

4285   LAMB, GEOFFREY FREDERICK. "Albert Schweitzer." In: Six
          Good Samaritans. . . . London: Oxford University Press,
          Geoffrey Cumberlege, 1947, pp. 74-88. (Living Names
          Series).

4286   LOEPER, JOHN J. "Albert Schweitzer." In: Men of Ideas.
          Illus. James and Ruth McCree. New York: Atheneum Press;
          Canada: McClelland and Stewart, 1970, pp. 101-05.

4287   MARSDEN, C. "Boy named Laugher." The Instructor (Dansville,
          N.Y.) 76:8 (April 1967), pp. 39f.

4288   MC GAVRAN, GRACE W. "Because somebody cared." Junior World
          (St. Louis, Mo.) 82:14 (April 5, 1959), pp. 108f. (About
          Mellons' Haiti hospital.)

4289   MC NEER, GRACE and LYND WARD. "Jungle doctor, Albert
          Schweitzer." In: Armed with Courage. New York,
          Nashville: Abingdon Press, 1957, pp. 90-112.

4290   MEYER, EDITH PATTERSON. "The good doctor of the jungle.
          Albert Schweitzer, 1952." In: Champions of Peace,
          winners of the Nobel Peace Prize. Boston: Little, Brown
          and Co., 1959, pp. 156-74. Illus.

4291   NAGANO, Y. "Shin no yusha." Shinjoen (Tokyo), July 1943.

4292   NIEBUHR, HULDA. "A zinc-lined piano." In: Greatness Passing
          By: Stories to tell to Boys and Girls. New York:
          Charles Scribner's Sons, 1931, 1947, pp. 26-32.

4293   NORTHCOTT, CECIL (WILLIAM). "Jungle doctor (Albert
          Schweitzer)." In: Venturers of Faith. London:
          Edward Arnold, 1950, pp. 158-74. Illus. (Merlin Books.)

4294   PAYNE, (PIERRE STEPHEN) ROBERT. "The three worlds of Albert
          Schweitzer." In: Greene, Jay E., ed. Four Complete
          Biographies. New York: Globe Book Co., 1962, pp. 261-458.

4295   PEET, HUBERT. "Oganga, the forest doctor." In: Mathews,
          Basil, ed. The Race of Heroes. Illus. Ernest Piater.
          London: S. W. Partridge, 1924, pp. 63-82. Reprinted,
          with slight omissions and additions, as "Oganga of the
          African Forest." The World Outlook (Nashville, Tenn.)
          33:7 (July 1933), pp. 252-53ff; 33:8 (Aug. 1933),

Misc. Writings About Schweitzer

> pp. 290-92ff; translated as "Oganga der Negerdoktor." <u>Schweizerische Jugendblätter</u> (Basel) 3:7 (July 25, 1925), pp. 202-07; 3:8 (Aug. 1925), pp. 231-35.

4296 SEILER, GRACE. "Shaggy face frightens Schweitzer." <u>Music Journal</u> (New York) 30:2 (Feb. 1972), p. 30.

4297 SPANN, MENO and CURT RUDOLF. "Schweitzer. Ein moderner Christ." In: <u>Deutsche Denker und Forscher</u>. New York: Appleton-Century-Crofts, 1954, pp. 54-63.

4298 STEINECKE, C. TH. "Beim Urwalddoktor von Lambarene." <u>Dein Freund</u> (Hamburg) 2:8 (April 1951), pp. 243-46.

4299 STEVENS, WILLIAM OLIVER. "Albert Schweitzer." In: <u>Famous Humanitarians</u>. New York: Dodd, Mead, and Co., 1953, pp. 123-30.

4300 TERPSTRA, K. "Albert Schweitzer." In: <u>Leidende Figuren</u>. Korte levens beschrijving van een tiental geestelijke leiders. Utrecht: Vrijzinnig Christelijke Jeugd Centrale, 1938, pp. 11-17.

4301 THOMAS, HENRY (Henry Thomas Schnittkind) and DANA LEE THOMAS (Dana Arnold Schnittkind). "Albert Schweitzer." In: <u>50 Great Modern Lives</u>: inspiring biographies of men and women who have guided mankind to a better world. Garden City, N.Y.: Hanover House, 1956, pp. 377-86.

4302 VANDERVELDE, MARJORIE. "A dream becomes a reality." <u>Twelve Fifteen</u> (Nashville, Tenn.) 11:5 (May 1962), pp. 5f. Illus.

4303 VASNER, COLETTE ELSE FERNAND. "I live at the Schweitzer hospital." In: Joy, Charles R. <u>Young People of Africa, Their Stories in their own Words</u>. New York: Duell, Sloan and Pearce, 1961, pp. 168-74.

4304 WALKER, V. E. and E. H. SPRIGGS. "The conquest of pain (Dr. Schweitzer of Lambarene.)" In: <u>Hero Stories: A Book of Christ's Followers</u>. London: Edinburgh House Press, 1929, pp. 64-70. Illus.

4305 WALLACE, ARCHER. "Albert Schweitzer, a hero in the African jungle." In: <u>Heroes of Peace</u>. London: Student Christian Movement Press, n.d., pp. 20-28. Also Garden City, N.Y.: Doubleday, 1929, Chapter III.

4306   WARTENWEILER, FRITZ. "Der Urwalddoktor Albert Schweitzer."
        In: Meister und Diener: Lebensbilder für junge Leute.
        Erlenbach-Zürich: Rotapfel Verlag, 1934, pp. 56-64.
        Port.

4307   WOYTT-SECRETAN, MARIE. "Albert Schweitzer der Urwaldarzt."
        In: Bauer, Ida Marie and Otto Heinrich Müller, eds.
        Der Mensch im Wandel der Zeiten, Bd. II. Braunschweig,
        Berlin, Hamburg, Kiel: Westermann, 1950, pp. 180-88.

4308   WYMER, NORMAN. "Albert Schweitzer." In: Medical Scientists
        and Doctors. London: Oxford University Press, 1958.
        (Lives of Great Men and Women, series 4.) Also issued as
        a 31-page offprint, see no. 4259 above.

                    D. Dissertations

4309   ARBRELL, RONALD LANE. A Study of Albert Schweitzer's Precept
        of Reverence for Life with some Implications for Educa-
        tion. Doctoral dissertation, Montana State University,
        1972. 268 pp.

4310   BABEL, HENRY ADALBERT. La Pensée d'Albert Schweitzer; sa
        Signification pour la Théologie et la Philosophie
        Contemporaines. Theol. Diss., Leiden, 1954. Later
        published, see no. 2343 above.

4311   BLACKWELL, DAVID M. Reverence for Life as an Educational
        Ideal, with special reference to the ethical thought of
        Albert Schweitzer. Master's thesis, McDonald, 1969/70.

4312   BOURDIER, ROLAND. La Vie et la Pensée d'Albert Schweitzer.
        Plaidoyer pour un nouvel humanisme médical. Université
        de Clermont-Ferrand, Faculté de Médecin, 1976.

4313   BROWARZIK, ULRICH. Glaube, Historie und Sittlichkeit; eine
        systematische Unterzuchung über die theologischen
        Prinzipien im Denken Albert Schweitzers. Inauguraldiss.,
        Erlangen, 1959. 114 pp.

4314   CHAN, MARGERY MAY. A Study of Albert Schweitzer's theory of
        Religious Experience: an analysis of the basic categories
        of a theory of religious experience of Albert Schweitzer.
        Ph.D. dissertation, New York University, 1954. 158 pp.

4315   DOTY, JAMES EDWARD. Reverence for Life in the Career of
        Albert Schweitzer. Ph.D. Dissertation, Boston University,
        1959. 310 pp.

Misc. Writings About Schweitzer

4316   FANONI, ROY H. Peter Parker and Albert Schweitzer: elements
         contributing to their missionary accomplishments.
         Master's thesis, Biblical Seminary, 1950.

4317   FURR, LESTER SEYMOUR. The Philosophy of Albert Schweitzer
         and its Exemplification in his Life. B.D. thesis, Duke
         University Divinity School, 1936. 144 pp.

4318   GRABS, RUDOLF. Albert Schweitzer als religiöser Charakter
         und als religionswissenschaftlicher Denker. Leipzig,
         1954. 280 pp.

4319   HAYNES, ROBERT. Albert Schweitzer's view of Goethe and the
         Ethical Precept of Vita Activa. Master's thesis, Univer-
         sity of Vermont, 1973.

4320   HIERS, RICHARD HYDE. The Teaching of Jesus in Christian
         Ethical Theory as Interpreted by New Testament Scholar-
         ship. Ph.D. Dissertation, Yale University, 1961. 414 pp.

4321   HOLMSTRÖM, FOLKE. Det eskatologiska motivet i nutida teologi.
         Tre etapper i 1900-talets teologiska tankeutveckling.
         Horvördiga Teologiska Faculteten vid Lunds Universitet,
         1933. Lund: Berlingska Boktryckeriet, 1933, pp. 57-62,
         73-103, 425-37, 451-55, 458-73, 487-88, plus other
         single-page references. Translated as: Das eschatologische
         Denken der Gegenwart. Tr. Harald Kruska. Gutersloh:
         C. Bertelsmann, 1936, pp. 54-55, 58-60, 72-102, 246-51.

4322   ICE, JACKSON L. A Critique of Albert Schweitzer's Philosophy
         of Civilization: a systematic presentation and critical
         evaluation of the social and ethical philosophy of Albert
         Schweitzer. Ph.D., Harvard University, 1955.

4323   JESCHKE, REUBEN P. Reverence for life as an ethical ideal,
         with special reference to Albert Schweitzer. Ph.D.,
         Columbia University, 1951.

4324   KAEMPF, BERNARD. Fondements de actualité de l'éthique
         d'Albert Schweitzer. Faculté de Théologie Protestante,
         Université des Sciences Humaines de Strasbourg, 1975.
         224 pp.

4325   KASAI, KEIJI. Die Bedeutung des Christentums in der heutigen
         Welt bei Albert Schweitzer und Paul Tillich. Dissertation
         zur Erlangung der Doktorwürde der Theol. Fakultät der
         Universität Basel, 1977.

Dissertations

4326 LANGLEY, JAMES A. A critique of contemporary interpretations
of the Sermon on the Mount with special reference to
Albert Schweitzer, Reinhold Niebuhr and C. H. Dodd.
Ph.D., Southwestern Baptist Theological Seminary, 1957.

4327 LEWIS, MELVA JEAN. Significance and Contributions of Albert
Schweitzer's medical work in Africa. Master's thesis,
Berkeley Baptist, 1957.

4328 LIN, PO-CHEN. A Critical Analysis of Albert Schweitzer's
Philosophy of Civilization with Special Reference to his
Ethical Conception of Reverence for Life. Ph.D., Univer-
sity of Southern California, 1953.

4329 LINSI, URS. Das Entwicklungsprojekt Lambarene im Wandel der
Zielvorstellungen über die Entwicklungspolitik.
Diplomarbeit, Hochschule St. Gallen, 1974.

4330 LÖNNEBO, MARTIN. Albert Schweitzer's etisk-religiöse Ideal.
Dr. theol., University of Uppsala, Sweden, 1964. Later
published, see no. 2365 above.

4331 MC CALL, WILLIAM EARNEST. An Analysis of Albert Schweitzer's
Interpretation of the New Testament. Th.D., Baptist
Theological Seminary, New Orleans, 1975. 155 pp.

4332 MERZ, NIKLAUS. Reich Gottes im theologischen und
philosophischen Denken von A. Schweitzer. Akzessarbeit,
Universität Basel, 1975.

4333 OGNIBENI, BRUNO. Das Abendmahlsproblem in exegetischen Werk
von Albert Schweitzer. Eine methodolische Forschung.
University of Freiburg, 1971.

4334 OTTO, BERND. Albert Schweitzers Beitrag zur Friedenspolitik.
Dr. Phil., Paedagogische Hochschüle Braunschweig, 1974.
Later published, see no. 3620 above.

4335 PACEWICKA-BECZEK, RENATA. [Albert Schweitzer's Philosophy of
Civilization.] Catholic University, Lublin, Poland,
1978. 80 pp.

4336 POZZONI, NANDO. Albert Schweitzer. Apologie eines Apostels
der Humanität. University of Milan, 1973.

4337 RAAB, KARL. Albert Schweitzer. Persönlichkeit und Denken.
Düsseldorf: G. H. Nolte Dissertations-Verlag, 1937.
Inaugural-Dissertation zur Erlangung der Doktorwürde
der hohen philosophischen Facultät der Friedrich-
Alexanders-Universität Erlangen, 1936. 95 pp.

Misc. Writings About Schweitzer

4338   REGESTER, JOHN DICKINSON. Immediate Intuition in the New
            Rationalism of Albert Schweitzer. Ph.D., Boston
            University, 1928. 335 pp.

4339   SCHALTENBRAND, EDITH. Pädagogisches Denken und Handeln
            Albert Schweitzers. Lehrerseminar Liestal, Schweiz, 1976.

4340   SCHIFFMAN, EVELYN. Albert Schweitzer, Jungle Doctor: A Story
            Reference for Children. Master's thesis, Newark State,
            1958/59.

4341   SHARP, WILLIAM JAMES. A sociological interpretation of the
            life and work of Albert Schweitzer. Master's thesis,
            University of Southern California, 1952.

4342   TERBORGH-DUPUIS, HELEEN. "Albert Schweitzer, the ethics of
            reverence for life." In: Medical Ethics in Perspective.
            Leiden, Holland, 1976.

4343   WESTERLUND, CHARLES KENNETH. The Reverence for Life Philosophy
            of Albert Schweitzer: an Existential Model in an
            Ethically-oriented education. Master's, Alberta, 1970.

4344   WILD, THOMAS. Fondements et actualité de la pensée d'Albert
            Schweitzer. University of Strasbourg, 1975.

4345   WINNUBST, BENEDICT. Das Friedensdenken Albert Schweitzers.
            1974. Later published, see no. 3622 above.

4346   WORBOYS, LAWRENCE W. The Missionary Principles and Methods
            of Albert Schweitzer. Doctor's dissertation, Biblical
            Seminary, 1950.

4347   WOODHULL, ALICE SUMNER HAWLEY. Albert Schweitzer and Johann
            von Goethe: a Comparative Study of their Contributions
            to the Field of Education. Doctoral dissertation,
            University of Buffalo, 1954.

4348   WOUDENBERG, PAUL RICHARD. Pauline Eschatology in the Writings
            of R. H. Charles and Albert Schweitzer. Ph.D., Boston
            University, 1959. 215 pp.

E. Drama and Films

1. Actual Works

The following is a list of those plays, films, filmstrips, and slide
shows on which information was available. Some may be of purely historical interest, and may no longer be available for rental.

4349   Africa and Schweitzer (motion picture). Cathedral Films, 1961.
          Black and white. 28 minutes. Narrator: Lowell Thomas.
          Photographer: Sven Nykvist.

4350   Albert Schweitzer (slide show). FWV Productions, Munich.
          13 black and white slides with text.

4351   Albert Schweitzer (filmstrip). Common Ground, London.
          Released in the United States by United World Films, 1951.
          40 frames, black and white, 35 mm. "Lives of great
          Christians" series.

4352   Albert Schweitzer (motion picture). Louis de Rochemont
          Associates, 1957. Color, 80 mins., 16 mm. Producer and
          director: Jerome Hill. Narration: Albert Schweitzer.
          Narrators: Frederic March and Burgess Meredith. Music:
          Alec Wilder. Photographer: Erica Anderson. Commentary:
          Thomas Bruce Morgan. Available in English, French and
          German versions, Albert Schweitzer himself speaking the
          narration in the French and German versions.

4353   Albert Schweitzer (filmstrip). Released by the Albert
          Schweitzer Fellowship, 1960. Photographed by Erica
          Anderson. 100 color frames.

4354   Albert Schweitzer baut Lambarene (motion picture). 1930.
          Black and white, 16 mm. Available from the
          Schmalfilmzentrale Bern, Erlacherstrasse 21, Bern,
          Switzerland. Order number 35-2382.

4355   Albert Schweitzer: der Lebensweg eines Menschenfreundes
          (slide show). Collected and composed by Heidi Stolz.
          42 slides with commentary. Deals with Schweitzer's life
          and the development of his hospital, 1913-1965.

4356   Albert Schweitzer in seinem Urwaldhospital (motion picture).
          16 mm. color film. 24 minutes in duration. Available
          through Kreis- und Landebildstellin.

Misc. Writings About Schweitzer

4357   Albert Schweitzer: the Power of his Life (color-sound
            filmstrip). Lyceum Productions, Inc., P.O. Box 1226,
            Laguna Beach, Calif., 92652, 1974. Written by Elizabeth
            Hazelton. Photographs by Erica Anderson and Ann Atwood.
            Part I covers through World War I--65 frames, 17 minutes
            running time. Part II--68 frames, 18 minutes. Suitable
            for grades 6-14.

4358   Albert Schweitzer: the Three Avenues of a Mind (motion
            picture). Released by the University of Southern
            California, Division of Cinema, 1962.

4359   Albert Schweitzer und Bach. Color. 14 minutes. Available
            from the Schmalfilmzentrale Bern, Erlacherstrasse 21,
            Bern, Switzerland. Order number 35-2026.

4360   Albert Schweitzer--Urwalddoktor und Christ der Tat (slide
            show). 45 black and white slides. Available through
            the Evangelischen Medienzentralen der Landeskirchen für
            Baden-Württemburg, Z-B7, Stuttgart 1, Theodor Heuss-
            Strasse 23.

4361   Albert Schweitzers Spital im Urwald. Color. 40 minutes.
            Available from the Schmalfilmzentrale Bern, Erlacher-
            strasse 21, Bern, Switzerland. Order number 35-7345.

4362   CESBRON, GILBERT. "Il est minuit, Docteur Schweitzer! Pièce
            en deux actes." France Illustration. Supplement Theatral
            et Littéraire (Paris) 90 (Sept. 8, 1951), pp. 1-24. Illus.
            Reprinted in Les Ouevres Libres (Paris, Librairie Arthème
            Fayard) 290:64 (Sept. 1951), pp. 243-314; reprinted in
            volume with Briser la Statue. Paris: Robert Laffont,
            1952, 156 pp.; film adaptation made in 1952, directed by
            André Haguet; Photographs from film adaptation in:
            Pierre Fresnay incarne le Docteur Schweitzer. Par André
            Legrand et André Haguet. Paris: La Colombe, 1952; Play
            translated as Es ist Mitternacht, Dr. Schweitzer.

4363   For all that Lives. The Words of Albert Schweitzer (color-
            sound filmstrip). Edited by Ann Atwood and Erica
            Anderson. Lyceum Productions, Inc., P.O. Box 1226,
            Laguna Beach, Calif., 92652. 1974. 58 frames, 13 1/2
            minutes running time. See also Anthologies, no. 54
            above.

4364   The Living Work of Albert Schweitzer (motion picture).
            Produced by Erica Anderson and Rhena Eckert-Schweitzer,
            1966. Photographed by Erica Anderson. From this film,

the Institut für Wissenschaft und Bild, Munich, made a 28-minute film for schools in Germany.

4365   L'oeuvre vivante du Dr. Albert Schweitzer. Jerome Hill and Erica Anderson, 1951-55.

4366   ROBACK, A. A. "Scenes in a great life" (a playlet). In: REALMS, pp. 63-77.

SCHMIDTBONN, WILHELM. "Ein Mann erklärt einer Fliege den Krieg." See Poetry, no. 4855 below.

4367   Schweitzer and Bach (motion picture). Jerome Hill and Erica Anderson, 1951-52. 16 mm., color, 11 minutes. Available in French, German or English texts, all with Schweitzer's voice in German.

4368   60 Jahre Urwaldspital Lambarene. Color film report prepared by Swiss television, April 18, 1973. 20 minutes. Available from the Schmalfilmzentrale Bern, Erlacherstrasse 21, Bern, Switzerland. Order number 35-2340.

Other films about Lambarene:

4369   English film made by Fritz Rosenberg, 1960. 16 mm., black and white, 20 minutes.

4370   Swedish film made by Lars Sundh, 1960. 16 mm., color, 20 minutes.

4371   Film made by Japanese television, 1964. 25 minutes, 16 mm., black and white, silent.

4372   Film made by British Broadcasting Corp., 1955. Black and white, 16 mm., 30 minutes. English text spoken by Michael Redgrave.

2. Reviews of Works

4373   "Albert Schweitzer: the Power of his Life." The Booklist (Chicago) 71:4 (March 15, 1975), p. 735.

4374   "De Albert Schweitzerfilm" (editorial). NIEUWS 7:1 (July 1958), p. 3.

4375   ALPERT, HOLLIS. "The Schweitzer story." The Saturday Review (New York) 40 (Jan. 5, 1957), pp. 25-26. (Review of no. 4353 above.)

Misc. Writings About Schweitzer

4376   "La biographie filmée d'Albert Schweitzer." CAHIERS 1
        (April 1959), p. 26.

4377   CAUVIN, O. "Pour-ou-contre: Il est minuit Dr. Schweitzer."
        L'Illustré Protestant (Lyon) 7 (March 1953), p. 27. Illus.

4378   CROWTHER, BOSLEY. "Like the good old days." The New York
        Times, Jan. 19, 1957, Section 2, p. 1. (Review of no.
        4353 above.)

4379   DRIVER, TOM F. "'Wide soul, small screen'--a review of film,
        Albert Schweitzer." The Christian Century (Chicago) 74:14
        (April 3, 1957), p. 425.

4380   "Es ist Mitternacht, Dr. Schweitzer." Christ und Welt
        (Stuttgart) 6:5 (Jan. 29, 1953), p. 8. Illus.

4381   H., P. "Albert Schweitzer: the Power of his Life . . . For
        all that Lives." The Horn Book Magazine (Boston) 52:3
        (June 1976), p. 312.

4382   JORDAAN, L. J. "Het is middernacht, Dr. Schweitzer."
        NIEUWS 2:1 (May 1953), pp. 12-15.

4383   KIK, RICHARD. "Der Albert-Schweitzer-Farbfilm von Erica
        Anderson." RUNDBRIEF 11 (Aug. 1, 1957), pp. 57-60.

4384   "Life of Dr. Schweitzer as motion picture subject." The
        Diapason (Chicago) 43:33 (May 1952), p. 33. (About film
        version of Il est Minuit, Dr. Schweitzer.)

4385   MC CARTEN, JOHN. "Proteus in Africa." The New Yorker
        (New York) 32:50 (Feb. 2, 1957), pp. 99-100. Review
        of no. 4353 above.

4386   "Presentation du film documentaire sur A. Schweitzer à
        Strasbourg." CAHIERS 2 (Dec. 1959), p. 26.

4387   RATTNER, D. S. [Review of no. 4353 above.] Film and TV
        Music (New York) 16 (Spring 1957), p. 17.

4388   "Schweitzer film in New York run." Musical America (New
        York) 77 (March 1957), p. 47. (Review of no. 4353 above.)

4389   "Two views of Schweitzer." Fellowship (Nyack, N.Y.) 25:9
        (May 1, 1959), pp. 32, 24. (Reviews of nos. 4352 and
        4353 above.)

Misc. Writings About Schweitzer

4390   WEILER, A. H. "By way of report: Dr. Schweitzer's movie
              portrait--addenda." The New York Times, Sept. 5, 1954,
              p. x5. (Preview of no. 4353 above.)

4391   WERNER, RUDOLF. "Dichtung und Wahrheit um Albert Schweitzer.
              (Gedanken zu einem Film um das Leben des grossen Arztes.)"
              Medizinische Klinik (Berlin) 48:19 (May 8, 1953), p. 681.
              (About Il est minuit, Dr. Schweitzer!)

4392   WINKLER, JOHAN. "'Il est minuit, Docteur Schweitzer!'"
              NIEUWS 1:3 (July 1952), p. 4.

4393   ZUNSER, JESSE. "Schweitzer, exponent of 'reverence for life.'"
              Cue (New York) 26:4 (Jan. 26, 1957), p. 8. Illus.

F.   Reviews

Entries are divided by the English title of the work discussed.
Arrangement of sections is alphabetical by title; arrangement within
sections is alphabetical by author or title of article.

General

4394   "Neues über und von Albert Schweitzer." Elsass-Lothringen
              Heimatstimmen (Berlin) 7:10 (Oct. 18, 1929), pp. 621-22.

4395   ROUVILLE, MARGUERITE DE. "Albert Schweitzer" (series of
              essays on Albert Schweitzer's books published prior to
              1925). Nieuwe Rotterdamsche Courant 82:174
              (April 25, 1925), pp. 3-5; 82:175 (May 2, 1925), pp. 2-5;
              82:176 (May 9, 1925), pp. 5-7.

Anthologies and Selected Works

4396   A., G. "Charles R. Joy: Music in the Life of Albert
              Schweitzer." Monthly Musical Record (London) 84:954
              (Feb. 1954), p. 49.

4397   "Albert Schweitzer an Anthology." The New Yorker 23
              (Dec. 20, 1947), p. 93.

4398   "Albert Schweitzer on Music." The Times Literary Supplement
              (London), Feb. 26, 1954, p. 132. (Music in the Life of
              Albert Schweitzer.)

4399   BOSTROM, OTTO H. "Vördnad for Livet. Anthology of Albert
              Schweitzer's Works. Edited by Rudolf Grabs." The
              Lutheran Quarterly (Gettysburg, Pa.) 4:1 (Feb. 1952),
              p. 117.

Reviews

Misc. Writings About Schweitzer

4400   BREMI, WILLI. "Besprechung" (Albert Schweitzer's Ausgewählte
           Werke in fünf Bänden). BERICHTE 34 (Aug. 1972), pp. 28-30.

4401   CHERNIAVSKY, DAVID. "Music in the Life of Albert
           Schweitzer. . . ." The Musical Times and Singing-Class
           Circular (London) 95:1336 (June 1954), p. 313.

4402   COOPER, MARTIN. "Schweitzer the musician--Music in the Life
           of Albert Schweitzer." The Spectator (London) 192:6552
           (Jan. 22, 1954), p. 106.

4403   D., H. F. "Albert Schweitzer. An Anthology." Blackfriars
           (London) 34:296 (March 1953), p. 155.

4404   D., J. S. "Music in Schweitzer's life" (Music in the Life of
           Albert Schweitzer). The Diapason (Chicago) 42:8
           (July 1, 1951), p. 12.

4405   DEVOE, ALAN. "The Animal World of Albert Schweitzer." New
           York Herald Tribune Book Review, April 22, 1951, p. 17.

4406   DILLISTONE, FREDERICK W. "The Theology of Albert Schweitzer
           for Christian Inquirers. . . ." The Anglican Theological
           Review (Evanston, Ill.) 35:1 (Jan. 1953), p. 59.

4407   "Dr. Schweitzer's writings: Albert Schweitzer. An
           Anthology. . . ." The Times Literary Supplement
           (London) 2666 (March 6, 1953), p. 157.

4408   FENDT, EDWARD C. "The Theology of Albert Schweitzer by
           E. N. Mozley." The Lutheran Quarterly (Gettysburg, Pa.)
           4:1 (Feb. 1952), pp. 115-16.

4409   FUCHS, EMIL. "Albert Schweitzer. Selbstzeugnisse. . . ."
           Deutsche Literaturzeitung (Berlin) 81:2 (Feb. 1960),
           col. 105.

4410   G., W. E. "The Animal World of Albert Schweitzer." The
           Christian Century (Chicago) 67:51 (Dec. 20, 1950), p. 1524.

4411   _____. "The Wit and Wisdom of Schweitzer." The Christian
           Century (Chicago) 67:1 (Jan. 4, 1950), p. 18.

4412   GARDNER-SMITH, P. "The Theology of Albert Schweitzer for
           Christian Inquirers. . . ." The Cambridge Review
           (Cambridge, Eng.) 72:1761 (April 21, 1951), pp. 434, 436.

4413   H., H. "A great organist (Music in the Life of Albert
           Schweitzer. . . .)." Musical Opinion and Music Trade
           Review (London) 77:919 (April 1954), pp. 413-14.

Misc. Writings About Schweitzer

4414   HARRIS, EMERSON W.   "Music in the Life of Albert Schweitzer."
        The Churchman (New York) 165:12 (July 1951), p. 15.

4415   HARRISON, WILLIAM.   "Albert Schweitzer. An Anthology."   The
        Churchman (New York) 162:8 (April 15, 1948), p. 17.

4416   HEISLER, AUGUST.   "Albert Schweitzer: Denken und Tat. . . ."
        Universitas (Stuttgart) 5:5 (May 1950), pp. 597-98.

4417   JENSSEN, H. H.   "Schweitzer, Albert. Ausgewählte Werke in
        fünf Bänden. . . ."   Theologische Literaturzeitung
        (Leipzig) 98:10 (Oct. 1973), pp. 732-34.

4418   LAWSON, O. GERALD.   "Albert Schweitzer. An Anthology."   The
        Library Journal (New York) 72:21 (Dec. 1, 1947), p. 1687.

4419   LEWY, IMMANUEL.   "Albert Schweitzer an Anthology."   Journal
        of Philosophy (New York) 45:4 (Feb. 12, 1948), pp. 107-08.

4420   MENDEL, ARTHUR.   "Some self-revelations."   The Saturday Review
        (New York) 34:21 (May 26, 1951), pp. 21f.   (Music in the
        Life of Albert Schweitzer).

4421   "Music in the Life of Albert Schweitzer." NIEUWS 2:4
        (March 1954), p. 63.

4422   PARSONS, ARRAND.   "Schweitzer the Musician--Music in the Life
        of Albert Schweitzer."   The Christian Century (Chicago)
        68:23 (June 6, 1951), pp. 686-87.

4423   SCHACHT, ROBERT H., JR.   "One of the greatest souls since
        Jesus. Albert Schweitzer: an Anthology."   The Christian
        Register (Boston) 126:11 (Dec. 1947), p. 490.

4424   SCHLÖTERMANN, HEINZ.   "Albert Schweitzer: Denken und Tat."
        Philosophischer Literaturanzeiger (Munich) 2:6 (1950),
        pp. 264-69.

4425   SCHROEDER, JOHN C.   "The spirit and thought of Schweitzer:
        Albert Schweitzer. An Anthology."   Yale Review (New
        Haven) 37:3 (March 1948), pp. 535-37.

4426   STOLZ-HEID, HEDI.   [Review of Grabs' selected works.]
        Schweizerisches Reformiertes Volksblatt (Basel),
        Nov. 1970.

4427   WILLARD, C. LAWSON.   "The Animal World of Albert Schweitzer."
        The Churchman (New York) 165:7 (April 1, 1951), p. 18.

Reviews

Misc. Writings About Schweitzer

4428   WIRTH, GÜNTER. "Fünfbändige Ausgabe der Werke Albert
          Schweitzers." In: GESTERN-HEUTE, pp. 69-71.

4429   YOUNG, FRANKLIN W. "Albert Schweitzer an Anthology."
          Crozer Quarterly (Chester, Pa.) 25:3 (July 1948), p. 266.

          African Notebook (Afrikanische Geschichten)

4430   D., H. "African Notebook. . . ." The Saturday Review
          (New York), April 15, 1939, p. 18.

4431   F., W. "Afrikanische Geschichten." Algemeen Nederlands
          Tijdschrift voor wijsbegeerte en Psychologie (Assen) 34:2
          (Dec. 1940), pp. 95-96.

4432   "From my African Notebook." The New Statesman and Nation
          (London) 17:417 (Feb. 18, 1939), p. 260.

          The Art of Organ-Building and Organ Playing . . .
       (Deutsche und Französische Orgelbaukunst und Orgelkunst)

4433   BROCK, E. "Albert Schweitzer--Deutsche und französische
          Orgelbaukunst und Orgelkunst." Elsass-Lothringen
          Heimatstimmen (Berlin) 6:1 (Jan. 20, 1928), pp. 56-58.

4434   "Deutsche und französische Orgelbaukunst und Orgelkunst."
          Gregorius-Blatt für Deutschen Kirchenmusik (Aachen) 4
          (1917), p. 71.

       HEROLD, WILHELM. "Deutsche und französische. . . ." See
          Music--Organs, no. 3470 above.

          Christianity and the Religions of the World
           (Das Christentum und die Weltreligionen)

4435   ABERLY, JOHN. "Christianity and the Religions of the World."
          Lutheran Quarterly (Gettysburg, Pa.) 4:1 (Feb. 1952),
          p. 116.

4436   BRAREN, JÜRGEN. "Im Spiegel der Zeit--Das Christentum und die
          Weltreligionen." Die Christliche Welt (Gotha) 38:48/49
          (Dec. 4, 1924), cols. 1023-25.

4437   DRAOI, CIAN. "Comparative Religion: Christianity and the
          Religions of the World." Dublin Magazine 1:5 (Dec. 1923),
          pp. 449-50.

4438   EGGENBERGER, CHR. "Das Christentum und die Weltreligionen."
          Kirchenblatt für die Reformierte Schweiz (Basel) 105:4
          (Feb. 17, 1949), p. 63.

452

Misc. Writings About Schweitzer

4439   GOUNELLE, ANDRÉ. "Les Religions Mondiales et le
         Christianisme. . . ." Études Théologiques et
         Religieuses (Montpellier) 51:2 (1976), pp. 250-51.

4440   "Het Christendom en de wereldgodsdiensten . . . 1927." Nieuw
         Theologisk Tijdschrift (Haarlem) 17 (1928), pp. 389-90.

4441   HIRSCH, E. "Albert Schweitzer: Aus meiner Kindheit und
         Jugendzeit; Zwischen Wasser und Urwald; Das Christentum
         und die Weltreligionen." Theologische Literaturzeitung
         (Leipzig) 49:17 (Aug. 23, 1924), cols. 377-79.

4442   MEHL, R. "Les Religions Mondiales et le Christianisme. . . ."
         REVUE 56:1-2 (1976), pp. 217-18.

4443   PRAXMARER, K. "Das Christentum und die Weltreligionen und
         Aus meiner Kindheit und Jugendzeit." Werkland (Leipzig)
         4 (1924/25), pp. 311-12.

4444   SCHLÖTERMAN, HEINZ. "Albert Schweitzer . . . Christentum und
         die Weltreligionen." Philsophischer Literaturanzeiger
         (Munich) 1:1 (1949), pp. 19-22.

4445   WUNDERLE, G. "Das Christentum und die Weltreligionen."
         Literarische Handweiser (Freibach i.B.) 60 (1924),
         pp. 459-61.

Complete Organ Works (Sämmtliche Orgelwerke)

4446   [Complete Organ Works.] Notes (Music Lib. Assoc.) 12:4
         (Sept. 1955), pp. 646-47. Review of vol. 6.

4447   DENDY, JAMES S. "New issues for organ." The Diapason
         (Chicago) 46:3 (Feb. 1, 1955), p. 17. Review of vol. 6.

4448   MASON, MARILYN. "Johann Sebastian Bach's Complete Organ
         Works. . . ." Journal of Church Music (Philadelphia)
         10:8 (Sept. 1968), pp. 14-15. Review of vols. 7 and 8.

Goethe--Collected Addresses

4449   ALDRICH, V. C. ". . .Goethe: Two Addresses." Journal of
         Philosophy (New York) 46:2 (Jan. 20, 1949), pp. 53-54.

4450   BOGAN, LOUISE. "Goethe--four studies." The New Yorker 25:30
         (Sept. 17, 1949), p. 102.

4451   "From Alsace to Africa" (includes a review of Goethe: Two
         Addresses). The Times Literary Supplement (London),
         Sept. 25, 1948, p. 545.

Misc. Writings About Schweitzer

4452   G., W. E. "Goethe: Two Addresses. . . ." The Christian
       Century (Chicago) 65:29 (July 21, 1948), p. 734.

4453   KRACAUER, SIEGFRIED. "Schweitzer's Goethe--Two Addresses. . . ."
       The Saturday Review (New York) 31:27 (July 3, 1948), p. 9.

4454   MOELMAN, CONRAD H. "Goethe--Two Addresses." Crozer Quarterly
       (Chester, Pa.) 25:4 (Oct. 1948), p. 374.

Indian Thought and Its Development
(Die Weltanschauung der Indischen Denker)

4455   ALLO, E. BERN. "Die Weltanschauung der indischen Denker."
       Revue des Sciences Philosophiques et théologiques (Paris)
       24 (1935), pp. 530-31.

4456   B., E. "Albert Schweitzers neues Buch" (Die Weltanschauung
       der Indischen Denker). Elsass-Lothringen Heimatstimmen
       (Berlin) 13:3 (March 17, 1935), p. 142.

4457   DAS, TARANKNATH. "Indian Thought and its Development."
       Catholic Historical Review (Washington, D.C.) 24:3
       (Oct. 1938), pp. 392-93.

4458   GLASENAPP, H. VON. "Die Weltanschauung der indischen Denker."
       Kantstudien (Berlin) 40 (1935), pp. 287-88.

4459   HOFER, HANS. "Mystik und Ethik--die Weltanschauung der
       indischen Denker." Zeitwende (Berlin) 11:12 (Sept. 1935),
       pp. 368-71.

4460   MERKEL, R. F. "Die Weltanschauung der indischen Denker."
       Die Christliche Welt (Gotha) 49:15 (Aug. 3, 1935),
       pp. 695-96.

4461   NEIIENDAM, HENRIK. "Albert Schweitzer. Indisk taenkning og
       mystik." Ekstrabladet (Copenhagen), July 7, 1956.

4462   "Ein neuer Albert Schweitzer!" Der Speyerer Protestant
       (1934), p. 216.

       NÖLLE, W. "Die Weltanschauung der Indischen Denker." See
       Philosophy, no. 2590 above.

4463   OPPENHEIM, RALPH. "Albert Schweitzer: Indisk Taenkning og
       Mystik." Politiken (Copenhagen), Dec. 1, 1956.

4464   PALUDAN, JACOB. "Albert Schweitzer: Indisk Taenkning og
       Mystik." Dagens Nyheder (Copenhagen), Aug. 9, 1956.

Misc. Writings About Schweitzer

4465   RUSSELL, LILIAN M. "Albert Schweitzer on Indian thought."
        The Aryan Path (Bombay) 6:6 (June 1935), pp. 375-79.

4466   _____. "Die Weltanschauung der indischen Denker. . . ."
        The Hibbert Journal (London) 33:4 (July 1935), pp. 630-34.

4467   RHODE, PETER P. "Albert Schweitzer. Indisk taenkning og
        mystik." Information (Copenhagen), July 3, 1956.

4468   RUBEN, WALTER. "Schweitzer, Albert: Die Weltanschauung der
        indischen Denker. . . ." Orientalische Literaturzeitung
        (Leipzig) 38:10 (Oct. 1935), pp. 638-40.

4469   SANDEGREN, HERMAN. "Bland ruinerna av en urgammal
        världsåskådning." Svenska Morgonbladet (Stockholm),
        Jan. 29, 1936.

4470   SCHERMERHORN, W. D. "Schweitzer turns to India. . . ." The
        Christian Century (Chicago) 53:45 (Nov. 4, 1936),
        pp. 1460-61.

4471   SCHNEIDER, HERBERT W. "Indian thought and its
        development. . . ." Journal of Philosophy (New York)
        33:26 (Dec. 17, 1936), pp. 714-15.

J. S. Bach

4472   AIZU, SHIN. "Schweitzer no Bach." Ongaku Geijutsu (Tokyo)
        Sept. 1952.

4473   BAUMANN, F. "J. S. Bach (1908)." Literarisches Zentralblatt
        für Deutschland (Leipzig) 59:20 (May 16, 1908), col. 659.

4474   GRUNSKY, KARL. "Albert Schweitzer. J. S. Bach, 1908."
        Bayreuther Blätter (Bayreuth and Leipzig) 35:IV-VI
        (1912), pp. 159-60.

4475   HEUSS, ALFRED. "Über A. Schweitzers J. S. Bach." Zeitschrift
        der Internationalen Musikgesellschaft (Leipzig) 10:1
        (Oct. 1908), pp. 7-14.

4476   IWASZKIEWICZ, JAROSLAW. "Jan Sebastian Bach." Ruch Muzyczny
        (Warsaw) 8 (1973), pp. 3-4. Illus. Same in Zycie
        Warszawy 90 (1975), p. 7.

4477   "J. S. Bach. . . ." Athenaeum (London) 4390 (Dec. 16, 1911),
        pp. 778-79.

Misc. Writings About Schweitzer

4478   KACZYNSKI, TADEUSZ. "Jan Sebastian Bach." Nowe Ksiaj 7
       (1974), pp. 67-69. Illus.

       KELLER, H. "Johann Sebastian Bach." See Music--Bach,
       no. 3381 above.

4479   LÜPKE, GUSTAV VON. "Albert Schweitzer. Joh. Seb. Bach, 1908."
       Neue Musik-Zeitung (Stuttgart-Leipzig) 29:11
       (March 5, 1908), pp. 244-45.

4480   "A new light on Bach." The Academy and Literature (London)
       82:2080 (March 16, 1912), pp. 332-34.

4481   OPALSKI, JOSEF. "Jan Sebastian Bach." Odra 2 (1974),
       pp. 103-05.

4482   POCIEJ, BOHDAN. "Jan Sebastian Bach." Jazz (Warsaw) 2
       (1973), pp. 4-5. Illus.

4483   SABIN, ROBERT. "J. S. Bach up to date." American Record
       Guide (New York) 34:2 (Oct. 1967), p. 157.

4484   SCHERING, ARNOLD. "Albert Schweitzer. J. S. Bach, 1908."
       Die Musik (Berlin) 7:22 (Zweites August Heft, 1907/1908),
       pp. 234-35. See also no. 4492 below.

J. S. Bach le Musicien-Poète

       BORDES, CHARLES. "Albert Schweitzer. J. S. Bach le musicien-
       poète." See Music--Bach, no. 3362 above.

4485   COMBARIEU, JULES. "A. S.: J.-S. Bach, le musicien-
       poète. . . ." Revue Critique d'Histoire et Littérature
       (Paris) 60:40 (Oct. 7, 1905), pp. 277-79.

4486   "J. S. Bach le musicien-poète." Literarisches Zentralblatt
       für Deutschland (Leipzig) 56:31 (July 29, 1905),
       col. 1037.

4487   LOUIS, RUDOLF. "Albert Schweitzer: J. S. Bach, le musicien-
       poète. . . ." Die Musik (Berlin) 5:2 (1905/1906),
       pp. 112-14.

4488   _____. "J. S. Bach le musicien-poète." Süddeutsche
       Monatshefte (Munich and Leipzig) 2:6 (June 1905),
       pp. 511-13.

4489   LUDWIG, FRIEDRICH. "Albert Schweitzer. J. S. Bach le
       musicien-poète." Bach-Jahrbuch (1905), pp. 111-13.

4490   OCHS, SIEGFRIED. "J. S. Bach le musicien-poète." Deutsche
            Literaturzeitung (Leipzig) 26:48 (Dec. 2, 1905),
            pp. 3023-24.

4491   SCHERING, ARNOLD. "J. S. Bach le musicien-poète. . . ."
            Zeitschrift der Internationalen Musikgesellschaft
            (Leipzig) 7:1 (1905), p. 35.

4492   _____. "J. S. Bach le musicien-poète and J. S. Bach (1908)."
            Bach Jahrbuch 4 (1907), pp. 182-89.

        SCHMITZ, EUGEN. "Das poetisierende Element in Bachs Musik."
            See Music--Bach, no. 3409 above.

4493   SMEND, J. "J. S. Bach le musicien-poète. 1905."
            Monatsschrift für Gottesdienst und Kirchliche Kunst
            (Göttingen) 13:10 (1908), pp. 300-04.

                The Kingdom of God and Primitive Christianity
                    (Reich Gottes und Christentum)

4494   BRUCE, F. F. "Albert Schweitzer. Reich Gottes und
            Christentum." Erasmus (London) 19:19/20 (1967),
            col. 587-89.

4495   CAHILL, P. JOSEPH. "Albert Schweitzer. The Kingdom of God
            and Primitive Christianity. . . ." Catholic Biblical
            Quarterly (Washington, D.C.) 31:3 (July 1969), pp. 459-60.

4496   HIERS, R. H. "Kingdom of God and Primitive Christianity."
            Journal of the American Academy of Religion 38
            (March 1970), pp. 94-98.

4497   HUNT, B. "Kingdom of God and Primitive Christianity."
            Southwestern Journal of Theology 12 (Fall 1969),
            pp. 102-03.

4498   MOORE, C. "Albert Schweitzer. The Kingdom of God and
            Primitive Christianity." Cross and Crown (St. Louis, Mo.)
            21 (June 1969), p. 234.

4499   OSTEN-SACKEN, R. V. D. "Reich Gottes und Christentum."
            Lutheran World 14:4 (1967), p. 403.

4500   POLING, DAVID. "Theme of Reverence for Life. The Kingdom
            of God and Primitive Christianity. . . ." The New York
            Times Book Review, Nov. 24, 1968, pp. 24-26. Illus.

Misc. Writings About Schweitzer

4501   SEVENSTER, J. N. "Reich Gottes und Christentum." Nederlands
        Theologisch Tijdschrift (Wageninen) 22 (Fall 1968),
        pp. 219-20.

4502   "Talking points from books." The Expository Times
        (Edinburgh) 80:3 (Dec. 1968), pp. 65-66.

                The Last Supper (Das Abendmahl)

4503   BARTH. "Das Abendmahl im Zusammenhang mit dem Leben
        Jesu. . . ." Theologischer Literatur-Bericht (Gütersloh)
        25:10 (Oct. 1902), pp. 368-69.

4504   ENSLEN, MORTON S. "The Mystery of the Kingdom of God."
        Crozer Quarterly (Chester, Pa.) 27:3 (July 1950),
        pp. 280-81.

4505   FEINE, PAUL. "Das Abendmahl im Zusammenhang mit dem Leben
        Jesu. . . ." Theologisches Literaturblatt (Leipzig)
        24:37 (Sept. 11, 1903), cols. 439-41.

4506   H., G. "Das Abendmahl in Zusammenhang mit dem Leben
        Jesu. . . ." Literarisches Zentralblatt für Deutschland
        (Leipzig) 53:29 (July 19, 1902), col. 969-70.

4507   HOLIMAN, GEORG. "Das Abendmahl im Zusammenhang mit dem
        Leben Jesu." Theologische Literaturzeitung (Leipzig)
        27:17 (Aug. 16, 1902), col. 465-69.

        MÜLLER, ERNST. "Die Messianitäts und Leidensgeheimnis."
        See Theology and Religion, no. 3062 above.

4508   OEPKE, A. "Das Abendmahlsproblem . . . u. Das Messianitäts-
        und Leidensgeheimnis." Theologisches Literaturblatt
        (Leipzig) 51:12 (June 6, 1930), cols. 182-83.

4509   PRIBNOW, HANS. "Albert Schweitzer. Das Messianitäts u.
        Leidensgeheimnis. . . ." Freies Christentum
        (Frankfurt a.M.) 14:6 (June 1, 1962), cols. 70-71.

4510   SNYDER, RUSSELL D. "The Mystery of the Kingdom of God."
        The Lutheran Quarterly (Gettysburg, Pa.) 3:1 (Feb. 1951),
        pp. 95-96.

4511   TITUS, JOSEPH H. "The Mystery of the Kingdom of God." The
        Churchman (New York) 164:16 (Sept. 15, 1950), p. 15.

4512   TROCME, ETIENNE. "La secret historique de la vie de Jesus."
        REVUE 42 (1962), pp. 247-48.

Reviews

4513   WEINEL, HEINRICH. "Albert Schweitzer: Das Abendmahl in
       Zusammenhang. . . ." Theologische Rundschau (Tübingen)
       5:6 (1902), pp. 242-45.

4514   WENDT, H. H. "Das Abendmahl in Zusammenhang. . . ." Deutsche
       Literaturzeitung (Leipzig) 23:12 (March 22, 1902),
       pp. 710-14.

4515   WINTER, PAUL. "Das Messianitäts- und Leidensgeheimnis. . . ."
       The Hibbert Journal (London) 55 (Jan. 1957), pp. 197-98.

Die Lehre von der Ehrfurcht vor dem Leben

4516   MAURER, KARL W. "Albert Schweitzer. The man and his way for
       mankind." Universitas (English language edition) 10:3
       (1968), pp. 282-84.

4517   SCHREY, HEINZ-HORST. "Albert Schweitzer: Die Lehre von der
       Ehrfurcht. . . ." Theologische Rundschau (Tübingen)
       32:2 (July 1967), pp. 174-75.

Memoirs of Childhood and Youth
(Aus Meiner Kindheit und Jugendzeit)

4518   "Aan den zoom van het Oerwoud." Nieuwe Rotterdamsche Courant
       82:174 (April 25, 1925), supplement, p. 6.

4519   ACKERKNECHT, E. "Aus meiner Kindheit und Jugendzeit. . . ."
       Bücherei und Bildungspflege (Leipzig) 5 (1925), p. 126.

4520   B., D. "Albert Schweitzers Jugend-Biographie. . . ." New
       Yorker Staats-Zeitung und Herold, Sept. 17, 1949, p. 4.

4521   BOSTROM, OTTO H. "Memoirs of Childhood and Youth." The
       Lutheran Quarterly (Gettysburg, Pa.) 2:1 (Feb. 1950),
       p. 118.

4522   ENGELSTADT, CARL FREDRIK. "Den Uverdige. . . ." Morgenbladet
       (Oslo), Dec. 19, 1952. (Review of Fra min barndom og
       ungdom and Mellon elver og urskog.)

4523   GARRISON, W. E. "Schweitzer in person . . . Memoirs of
       Childhood and Youth. . . ." The Christian Century
       (Chicago) 66:33 (Aug. 17, 1949), pp. 964-65.

4524   GRÜTZMACHER, RICHARD H. "Aus meiner Kindheit und Jugendzeit."
       Theologie der Gegenwart (Leipzig) 19:2 (Feb. 1925),
       pp. 37-38.

Misc. Writings About Schweitzer

4525   HIRSCH, E. "Albert Schweitzer: Aus meiner Kindheit und
          Jugendzeit. . . ." Theologische Literaturzeitung
          (Leipzig) 49:17 (Aug. 23, 1924), cols. 377-79.

4526   "Memoirs of Childhood and Youth." The New Yorker 25:28
          (Sept. 3, 1949), pp. 66-67.

4527   "Memoirs of Childhood and Youth." The Times Literary
          Supplement (London), Dec. 24, 1954, p. 809.

4528   MORGENSTERN. "Aus meiner Kindheit und Jugendzeit." Hefte
          für Büchereiwesen (Vienna, Leipzig) 10:1/2 (1925), p. 19.

4529   PRAXMARER, K. "Das Christentum und die Weltreligionen und
          Aus meiner Kindheit und Jugendzeit." Werkland (Leipzig)
          4 (1924/25), pp. 311-12.

4530   R., J. "Uit mijn jeud." Mededeelingen Tijdschrift voor
          Zendings-Wetenschap (Oegstgeest, Netherlands) 69 (1925),
          pp. 191-92.

4531   R.-H., L. ". . .Albert Schweitzer: Souvenirs de mon enfance."
          Le Monde non-Chretien (Paris) 13 (Jan.-March 1950),
          pp. 115-16.

4532   RIISØEN, SVERRE. "Den ideele bok for ungdom. Albert
          Schweitzer: fra min barndom og ungdom." Morgenavisen
          (Copenhagen), Nov. 14, 1952.

4533   RYCHNER, MAX. "Aus meiner Kindheit und Jugendzeit." Wissen
          und Leben (Zürich) 17:25 (Dec. 20, 1924), pp. 1580-82.

4534   SAMPSON, GEORGE. "Memoirs of Childhood and Youth." The
          Bookman (London) 68 (June 1925), p. 164.

4535   "Souvenirs de mon enfance." Le Figaro Littéraire (Paris)
          5:217 (June 17, 1950), p. 7.

4536   WEREIDE, SOPHIE. "Retten til lykke. Albert Schweitzer. Fra
          min barndom og ungdom. . . ." Aftenposten (Oslo),
          Dec. 17, 1952.

4537   WUNDERLE, GEORG. "Aus meiner Kindheit und Jugendzeit."
          Literarischer Handweiser (Freiburg i. Br.) 60:10
          (Oct. 1924), col. 540.

Misc. Writings About Schweitzer

The Mysticism of Paul the Apostle
(Die Mystik des Apostels Paulus)

4538   ADAM. "Die Mystik des Apostels Paulus, 1930." Theologische
        Quartalschrift (Tübingen) 111 (1930), pp. 438-41.

4539   BAKEL, H. A. VAN. "Die Mystik des Apostels Paulus." Nieuw
        Theologisk Tijdschrift (Haarlem) 20 (1931), pp. 155-59.

4540   BOTTE, D. B. "Die Mystik des Apostels Paulus. . . ."
        Recherches de Théologie Ancienne et Médiévale (Louvain) 2
        (1930), pp. 437-38.

        BUONAIUTI, ERNESTO. "Die Mystik des Apostels Paulus." See
        Theology and Religion, no. 2944 above.

4541   BULTMANN, R. "Die Mystik des Apostels Paulus. 1930."
        Deutsche Literaturzeitung (Leipzig) 2:25 (June 12, 1931),
        cols. 1153-58.

4542   CARLYON, J. T. "Pauline Mysticism." Journal of Religion
        (Chicago) 12:3 (July 1932), p. 377.

4543   CAVE, SYDNEY. "The Mysticism of Paul the Apostle." The
        Congregational Quarterly (London) 10 (1932), pp. 107-11.

4544   CHARUE, A. "Die Mystik des Apostels Paulus." Revue d'Histoire
        Ecclésiastique (Louvain) 27 (1931), pp. 353-56.

4545   EASTON, BURTON SCOTT. "Die Mystik des Apostels Paulus. . . ."
        The Anglican Theological Review (Evanston, Ill.) 13:1
        (Jan. 1931), pp. 92-94.

        FRIDRICHSEN, ANTON. "Paulus-Kronik." See Theology and
        Religion, no. 2972 above.

4546   JACOB, ERNST. "Die Mystik des Apostels Paulus."
        Monatsschrift für Geschichte und Wissenschaft des
        Judentums (Breslau) 75 (1931), pp. 329-33.

4547   K., A. D. "The Mysticism of Paul the Apostle." The Living
        Church (Milwaukee, Wis.), May 7, 1932, p. 18.

        KESSLER, LINA. "Albert Schweitzers 'Mystik des Apostels
        Paulus' und die religiös-bildliche Erkenntnis." See
        Theology and Religion, no. 3016 above.

4548   KEYSERLING, H. "Mystik des Apostels Paulus." Der Weg zur
        Vollendung (Darmstadt) 25 (1939), p. 47.

Misc. Writings About Schweitzer

4549   LAGRANGE, M.-J. "Die Mystik des Apostels Paulus." La Revue
          Biblique (Paris) 42 (1933), pp. 114-23.

4550   LEMON, W. P. "Schweitzer on St. Paul." The Christian Century
          (Chicago) 49:18 (May 4, 1932), pp. 577-78.

4551   LEMONNYER, A. "Die Mystik des Apostels Paulus." Revue des
          Sciences Philosophiques et Théologiques (Paris) 20
          (1931), pp. 348-49.

4552   LINDBLOM, JOH. "Die Mystik des Apostels Paulus." Svensk
          Teologisk Kvartalskrift (Lund) 9 (1933), pp. 17-25.

4553   MOFFATT, JAMES. "Schweitzer on Paul's mysticism. . . ." The
          Expository Times (Edinburgh) 42:12 (Sept. 1931),
          pp. 566-67.

4554   MUNDLE, WILHELM. "Die Christus Mystik des Apostels Paulus:
          Schweitzer-Lohmeyer-Liechtenhan." Die Christliche Welt
          (Gotha) 44:16 (Aug. 16, 1930), pp. 765-72.

4555   "The Mysticism of Paul the Apostle." The New Statesman and
          Nation (London) 3:47 (Jan. 16, 1932), pp. 72-73.

4556   "Die Mystik des Apostels Paulus, 1930." Geistkampf der
          Gegenwart (Gütersloh) 66:12 (1930), pp. 478-79.

4557   "Die Mystik des Apostels Paulus." Journal of Religion
          (Chicago) 11:1 (Jan. 1931), p. 148.

4558   "Die Mystik des Apostels Paulus." Neue Allgemeine
          Missionszeitschrift (Gütersloh) 7 (1930), pp. 223-24.

4559   NAISH, J. P. "Die Mystik des Apostels Paulus." The
          Congregational Quarterly (London) 8:4 (Oct. 1930),
          pp. 490, 493-96.

4560   PAUST, ALBERT. "Die Mystik des Apostels Paulus."
          Literarisches Zentralblatt für Deutschland (Leipzig)
          81:20 (Oct. 31, 1930), col. 1393.

        SACHS, W. "Geschichte der Paulinischen Forschung und Mystik
        des Apostels Paulus." See Theology and Religion, no. 3104
        above.

4561   TELFORD, JOHN. "The Mysticism of Paul the Apostle." The
          London Quarterly Review 157 (July 1932), pp. 397-400.

Misc. Writings About Schweitzer

THISELTON, ANTHONY. "Biblical classics, pt. 6: Schweitzer's interpretation of Paul." See Theology and Religion, no. 3135 above.

4562 VELDHUIZEN, A. VAN. "Die Mystik des Apostels Paulus." Nieuwe Theologische Studien (Wageningen) 13 (1930), pp. 304-06.

WEBER, A. E. "Die Mystik des Apostels Paulus, 1930." See Theology and Religion, no. 3146 above.

4563 ZWANN, J. DE. "Die Mystik der Apostels Paulus." Nieuwe Theologische Studien (Wageningen) 14 (1931), pp. 146-47.

On the Edge of the Primeval Forest and More from the Primeval Forest (Zwischen Wasser und Urwald and Mitteilungen aus Lambarene)

1. Combined Editions

4564 BIERSTEDT, ROBERT. "Hospital in the jungle. . . ." Saturday Review (New York) 32:2 (Jan. 8, 1949), p. 18.

4565 G., W. E. "On the Edge of the Primeval Forest and More from the Primeval Forest. . . ." The Christian Century (Chicago) 66:4 (Jan. 26, 1949), p. 113.

4566 WARD, BARBARA E. "On the Edge of the Primeval Forest and More from the Primeval Forest." Man (London) 50:205 (Sept. 1950), p. 128.

2. On the Edge of the Primeval Forest

4567 "Aan den zoom van het oerwoud." Nieuwe Rotterdamsche Courant 82:174 (April 25, 1925), Supplement, p. 6.

4568 "Albert Schweitzer: Zwischen Wasser und Urwald." Therapie der Gegenwart (Berlin) 65:7 (July 1924), p. 323.

4569 B., D. "Prof. Albert Schweitzer schildert Erlebnisse. . . ." New Yorker Staats-Zeitung und Herold, Oct. 8, 1949, p. 4.

4570 B., P. "A l'orée de la forêt vierge by Albert Schweitzer." Journal des Société des Missions Evangéliques de Paris 99 (Jan. 1924), pp. 65-66.

4571 BECKER, MARY LAMBERTON. "On the Edge of the Primeval Forest." The Saturday Review of Literature (New York) 8:41 (April 30, 1932), p. 705.

Misc. Writings About Schweitzer

4572   BLOCK, JEAN RICHARD. "Albert Schweitzer--A l'orée de la forêt
          vierge. . . ." Europe (Paris) 4:14 (Feb. 15, 1924),
          pp. 247-48.

4573   CARVER, W. O. "On the Edge of the Primeval Forest." The
          Review and Expositor (Louisville) 29:2 (April 1932),
          pp. 250-51.

4574   ELLINGER, GEORG. "Zwischen Wasser und Urwald. . . ."
          Münchner Neueste Nachrichten (Munich) 79:54 (Feb. 23, 1956),
          pp. 1-2.

4575   ENGELSTADT, CARL FREDRIK. "Den Uverdige. . . ." Morgenbladet
          (Oslo), Dec. 19, 1952.

4576   FRICK, HEINRICH. "Zwischen Wasser und Urwald." Theologische
          Blätter (Leipzig) 2:12 (Dec. 1922), col. 278.

4577   HIRSCH, E. "Albert Schweitzer: . . . Zwischen Wasser und
          Urwald. . . ." Theologische Literaturzeitung (Leipzig)
          49:17 (Aug. 23, 1924), cols. 377-79.

4578   HOFFMAN, R. E. "On the Edge of the Primeval Forest."
          Missionary Review of the World (New York) 55:5
          (May 1932), p. 318.

4579   KAMMERER, J. "Zwischen Wasser und Urwald." Die Evangelischen
          Missionen (Berlin-Steglitz) 28 (April 1922), pp. 49-58.

4580   MEHL, R. "Albert Schweitzer: A l'orée de la forêt
          vierge. . . ." REVUE 34 (1954), pp. 185-86.

4581   MEINERTZ, M. "Zwischen Wasser und Urwald." Zeitschrift für
          Missionswissenschaft (Münster/Westfalen) 12 (1922),
          pp. 123-25.

4582   MORGENSTERN. "Zwischen Wasser und Urwald. . . ." Hefte für
          Büchereiwesen (Vienna, Leipzig) 9:2 (1924), p. 104.

4583   PASSAGE, HENRY DU. "Albert Schweitzer--a l'orée de la forêt
          vierge." Études (Paris) 275 (Nov. 1952), p. 271.

4584   PICHT, WERNER. "Zwischen Wasser und Urwald, 1922." Hochland
          (Munich) 19:6 (March 1922), pp. 757-59.

4585   SAUER, B. "Zwischen Wasser und Urwald. . . ." Bücherei und
          Bildungspflege (Leipzig) 6:2/3 (1926), p. 174.

4586   THORBECKE, F.   "Schweitzer, Albert.   Zwischen Wasser und
         Urwald. . . ."   Geographische Zeitschrift (Leipzig) 29:2
         (1923), p. 153.

4587   "Zwischen Wasser und Urwald."   Der Turmer (Stuttgart),
         June 1922, pp. 173-77.

4588   "Zwischen Wasser und Urwald, 1923."   Katholische Missions-
         arztliche Fürsorge (Aachen), 1924, pp. 67-70.

4589   "Zwischen Wasser und Urwald."   Deutsche Medizinische
         Wochenschrift (Stuttgart) 48:49 (Dec. 8, 1922), p. 1659.

   3.   More from the Primeval Forest

4590   G., W. E.   "Schweitzer Africanus."   The Christian Century
         (Chicago) 48:39 (Sept. 30, 1931), p. 1211.

4591   KLENK, G. FRIEDRICH.   "Albert Schweitzer: 1. Briefe aus
         Lambarene. . . ."   Stimmen der Zeit (Freiburg i.B.)
         80:8 (May 1955), p. 160.

4592   KOINKHAMMER, CARL.   "Mitteilungen aus Lambarene."
         Literarischer Handweiser (Freiburg i.B.) 66:2
         (Nov. 1929), col. 131.

4593   PEET, H. W.   "More from Dr. Schweitzer--More from the
         Primeval Forest."   International Review of Missions
         (London) 21 (1932), pp. 149-50.

4594   SCHLUNK, M.   "Mitteilungen aus Lambarene, II, 1926."
         Theologisches Literaturblatt (Leipzig) 48:19
         (Sept. 16, 1927), col. 317.

4595   Z., S. M.   "The Forest Hospital at Lambarene."   Missionary
         Review of the World (New York) 55:2 (Feb. 1932), p. 127.

Out of My Life and Thought
(Aus Meinem Leben und Denken)

4596   ALMSTEDT, HERMANN.   "Aus meinem Leben und Denken."   The
         Journal of English and Germanic Philology (Urbana, Ill.)
         32, pp. 434-35.

4597   ANDREWS, C. F.   "Dr. Schweitzer's autobiography. . . ."
         International Review of Missions (London) 23 (April 1934),
         pp. 282-84.

Misc. Writings About Schweitzer

4598   B., A. J. "Out of my Life and Thought." Missionary Review
        of the World (New York) 56:7 (July 1933), pp. 406-07.

4599   BAKEL, H. A. VAN. "Uit mijn leven en denken (1932)."
        Nieuw Theologisk Tijdschrift (Haarlem) 22 (1933), p. 273.

4600   BREIT, HARVEY. "Repeat performance appraised. . . ." The
        New York Times Book Review, July 10, 1949, p. 7.

4601   CASE, S. J. "Out of my Life and Thought." Journal of
        Religion (Chicago) 13:4 (Oct. 1933), p. 494.

4602   CERFAUX, L. "Aus meinem Leben und Denken." Revue d'Histoire
        Ecclésiastique (Louvain) 28 (1932), pp. 677-78.

4603   DEVARANNE. "Aus meinem Leben und Denken." Zeitschrift
        für Missionskunde und Religionswissenschaft (Berlin)
        47 (1932), pp. 281-82.

4604   "AUG. E." (ERNST, D. AUG.) "Ein neues Buch von Albert
        Schweitzer. . . ." Elsass-Lothringen Heimatstimmen
        (Berlin) 9:12 (Dec. 11, 1931), p. 553.

4605   FORST DE BATTAGLIA, OTTO. "Aus meinem Leben und Denken."
        Die Bücherwelt (Bonn am Rhein) 29:5 (Sept.-Oct. 1932),
        pp. 389-90.

4606   GARRISON, W. E. "Schweitzer in person. . . ." The Christian
        Century (Chicago) 66:33 (Aug. 17, 1949), pp. 964-65.

4607   HOBART, R. E. "'Reverence for Life'--My Life and Thought.
        An autobiography." The English Review (London) 56
        (April 1933), p. 459.

4608   HUTCHINSON, PAUL. "'Prodigious Schweitzer'--Out of my Life
        and Thought." The Christian Century (Chicago) 50:9
        (March 1, 1933), pp. 293-94.

4609   IRVINE, LYN Ll. "Albert Schweitzer. My Life and
        Thought. . . ." The New Statesman and Nation (London)
        5:113 (April 22, 1933), pp. 509-10.

4610   L. "Albert Schweitzer. Aus meinem Leben und Denken."
        Fortschritte der Medizin (Würzburg) 50:8 (April 15, 1932),
        p. 335.

4611   KATTENBUSCH, FERDINAND. "Aus meinem Leben und Denken, 1931."
        Zeitschrift für Kirchengeschichte (Gotha), 1932,
        pp. 359-60.

Reviews

4612   LEDERMANN, L. "Dr. Schweitzer's Autobiography: Ma Vie et
        ma Pensée. . . ." The Ecumenical Review (Geneva) 13:2
        (Jan. 1961), pp. 267-68.

4613   LINTON, OLOF. "Vördnaden för Livet" (review of Ur mitt liv
        och tänkande). Svenska Dagbladet (Stockholm),
        Nov. 8, 1936.

4614   MC KINNEY, HOWARD D. "Albert Schweitzer--antidote." The
        New Music Review and Church Music Review (New York)
        32:380 (Sept. 1933), pp. 349-52.

4615   MEHL, R. "Albert Schweitzer: Ma Vie et ma Pensée. 1960."
        REVUE 41:1 (1961), pp. 98-99.

4616   "Out of my Life and Thought." New York Herald Tribune Book
        Review, Sept. 25, 1949.

4617   "Out of my Life and Thought." Heterofonia: Revista Musical
        Bimestral (Mexico) 4:23 (1972), pp. 30-32.

4618   "Out of my Life and Thought." The New Yorker 25:23
        (July 30, 1949), pp. 67-68.

4619   REDMAN, BEN RAY. "Out of my Life and Thought. . . ." The
        Saturday Review (New York) 32:39 (Sept. 24, 1949),
        p. 33.

4620   REGESTER, JOHN D. "Out of my Life and Thought. . . ."
        Religion in Life (New York) 2:2 (Spring 1933),
        pp. 307-08.

4621   SCHURCK, PAUL. "Aus meinem Leben und Denken." Neue
        Literatur (Leipzig) 33:6 (June 1932), p. 281.

4622   TAU, MAX. "Selbstdarstellungen--Albert Schweitzer, Aus
        meinem Leben und Denken." Velhagen & Klasings
        Monatshefte (Beielfeld, Berlin, Darmstadt) 46:10
        (1931/32), pp. 357-59.

4623   USENER, WILHELM. "Aus meinem Leben und Denken."
        Theologische Literatur-Zeitung (Halle-Berlin) 57:24
        (Nov. 19, 1932), cols. 560-63.

4624   WAHL, JEAN. "Aus meinem Leben und Denken, 1931." Revue
        Philosophique de la France et de l'Étranger (Paris) 115
        (1933), pp. 140-41.

Reviews

Misc. Writings About Schweitzer

Paul and His Interpreters
(Geschichte der Paulinischen Forschung)

4625 BURKITT, F. C. "Geschichte der Paulinischen Forschung." The
       Journal of Theological Studies (Oxford, England) 13
       (July 1912), pp. 604-11.

4626 _____. "Three books on St. Paul." The Ecumenical Review
       (Geneva) 13:2 (July 1912), pp. 608ff.

4627 DAVIDSON, JOHN G. "Paul and his Interpreters." The Churchman
       (New York) 165:19 (Dec. 1, 1957).

4628 G., W. E. "Paul and his Interpreters. . . ." The Christian
       Century (Chicago) 69:3 (Jan. 16, 1952), p. 73.

4629 "Geschichte der Paulinischen Forschung, 1911." Literarisches
       Zentralblatt für Deutschland (Leipzig) 63:31
       (July 27, 1912), cols. 986-97.

4630 GUIGNEBERT, CH. "L'âge apostolique." Revue Historique
       (Paris) 110 (May-Aug. 1912), pp. 351-52.

4631 HEADLAM, ARTHUR C. "Some books on St. Paul." The Church
       Quarterly Review (London) 76 (April 1913), pp. 165-75.

4632 HOLTZMANN, OSCAR. "Geschichte der Paulinischen
       Forschung. . . ." Deutsche Literaturzeitung (Leipzig)
       33:16 (April 20, 1912), pp. 974-78.

4633 KOCH, W. "Geschichte der paulinischen Forschung."
       Theologische Quartalschrift (Tübingen) 95:1 (1913),
       pp. 144-45.

4634 KÖGEL, JULIUS. "Zur Geschichte der Paulinischen Forschung."
       Theologischer Literatur-Bericht (Gütersloh) 35:7
       (July 1912), pp. 225-30.

4635 KROPATSCHECK, F. "Geschichte der paulinischen Forschung."
       Zeitschrift für Kirchengeschichte (Gotha) 33 (1912),
       pp. 587-88.

4636 LAKE, KIRSOPP. "Geschichte der paulinischen Forschung."
       Theologisch Tijdschrift (Leiden) 46 (1912), pp. 262-68.

4637 MENZIES, ALLAN. "Paul and his Interpreters." Review of
       Theology and Philosophy (Edinburgh) 8:6 (1912), p. 315.

Misc. Writings About Schweitzer

MONTGOMERY, W. "Dr. Schweitzer on the Interpretation of St. Paul." See Theology and Religion, no. 3060 above.

4638 NATALI, GIACOMO. "Albert Schweitzer. Paulus and his Interpreters. . . ." Bilychnis (Rome) 2:3 (May/June 1913), pp. 214-17.

4639 OEPKE. "Geschichte der paulinischen Forschung." Theologisches Literaturblatt (Leipzig) 54:26 (Dec. 22, 1933), cols. 403-04.

4640 "Paul and his Interpreters. . . ." The Saturday Review of Politics, Literature, Science and Art (London) 115:2986 (Jan. 18, 1913), p. 83.

4641 "Paul and his Interpreters. . . ." The Academy and Literature (London) 84:2137 (April 19, 1913), pp. 489-90.

4642 R., S. "Albert Schweitzer. Geschichte der Paulinischen Forschung. . . ." Revue Archéologique (Paris) 23 (June 1914), pp. 449-50.

SACHS, W. "Geschichte der Paulinischen Forschung und Mystik des Apostels Paulus." See Theology and Religion, no. 3104 above.

4643 SNYDER, RUSSELL D. "Paul and his Interpreters." The Lutheran Quarterly (Gettysburg, Pa.) 4:1 (Feb. 1952), pp. 116-17.

4644 "St. Paul and his Interpreters. . . ." The Review and Expositor (Louisville) 10:2 (April 1913), p. 309.

4645 VAN DEN BERGH VAN EYSINGE, G. A. "Geschichte der Paulinischen Forschung." Nieuw Theologisk Tijdschrift (Haarlem) 2 (1913), pp. 110-13.

4646 VISCHER, E. PAULUS. "Geschichte der Paulinischen Forschung, 1911." Theologische Rundschau (Tübingen) 16:8 (1913), pp. 247-50.

4647 VOS, GEERHARDUS. "Paul and his Interpreters. . . ." The Princeton Theological Review 12 (1914), pp. 142-49.

4648 W. "Geschichte der Paulinischen Forschung." Zeitschrift für Wissenschaftlichen Theologie 55 (1914), pp. 173-74.

4649 WERNLE, PAUL. "Geschichte der paulinischen Forschung." Theologische Literaturzeitung (Leipzig) 39:17 (Aug. 22, 1914), cols. 516-19.

Misc. Writings About Schweitzer

<u>Peace</u>

4650   FOCKLER, HERBERT. "Albert Schweitzer. Peace or Atomic War?"
          <u>The Library Journal</u> (New York) 83:15 (Sept. 1, 1958),
          p. 2313.

4651   HÜBENER, ERHARD. "Albert Schweitzer. Das Problem des Friedens
          in der heutigen Welt." <u>Deutsche Literaturzeitung</u>
          (Berlin) 76:7/8 (July/Aug. 1955), cols. 481-83.

4652   JACK, HOMER A. "Science and conscience (Peace or Atomic
          War?). . . ." <u>The Christian Century</u> (Chicago) 75:51
          (Dec. 17, 1958), p. 1461.

4653   KLENK, G. FRIEDRICH. "Albert Schweitzer . . . Das Problem
          des Friedens in der heutigen Welt." <u>Stimmen der Zeit</u>
          (Freiburg i.B.) 80:8 (May 1955), p. 160.

<u>A Pelican Tells About His Life</u>
<u>(Ein Pelikan Erzählt Aus Seinem Leben)</u>

4654   E., E. "Glimt av Schweitzer. . . ." <u>Bergens Tidende</u>
          (Bergen), Dec. 18, 1954.

4655   JOUVÉ, R. "Docteur Schweitzer--Le Pelican du Docteur
          Schweitzer. . . ." <u>Études</u> (Paris) 273 (June 1952),
          p. 430.

<u>Philosophy of Civilization (Kulturphilosophie)</u>

4656   ADAM, MICHEL. "La civ. et l'éthique." <u>Revue Philosophique
          de la France et de l'Étranger</u> (Paris) 102 (Jan.-March
          1977), pp. 118-19.

4657   ALBRIGHT, W. F. "Albert Schweitzer. The Philosophy of
          Civilization." <u>The Hopkins Review</u> (Baltimore) 3:2
          (Winter 1950), pp. 45-47.

4658   BERGENDOFF, CONRAD. "The Philosophy of Civilization."
          <u>The Lutheran Quarterly</u> (Gettysburg, Pa.) 2:2 (May 1950),
          pp. 230-31.

4659   BOHLIN, TORSTEN. "Kulturens degeneration och regeneration,
          1925." <u>Svensk teologisk kvartalskrift</u> (Lund) 1:3
          (1925), pp. 300-09.

4660   BROCK, ERICH. "Albert Schweitzer. Verfall und Wiederaufbau
          der Kultur." <u>Logos</u> (Tübingen) 12:2 (1923/24), pp. 415-18.

Reviews

Misc. Writings About Schweitzer

4661   _____. "Kultur und Ethik." Logos (Tübingen) 13 (1924/25),
        pp. 264-69.

4662   BRUGH, E. J. VAN DER. "Cultuur en Ethiek. . . ." Nieuw
        Theologisk Tijdschrift (Haarlem) 23 (1934), pp. 392-94.

4663   EHRHARDT, EUG. "Kultur und Ethik. Kulturphilosophie."
        REVUE 5 (1925), pp. 274-79.

4664   ELERT. "Verfall und Wiederaufbau der Kultur." Theologisches
        Literaturblatt (Leipzig) 45:10 (May 9, 1924), col. 141-42.

4665   EMMEL, FELIX. "Albert Schweitzer. Kultur Philosophie. . . ."
        Preussischer Jahrbücher (Berlin) 195:3 (March 1924),
        pp. 293-96.

4666   FEHR, H. "Kulturphilosophie I and II." Neue Zürcher Zeitung,
        March 21, 1926.

4667   FISCHER, MAX. "Schweitzer, the philosopher." The Commonweal
        (New York) 51:9 (Dec. 9, 1949), pp. 271-72.

4668   FUCHS, EMIL. "Albert Schweitzer: Kultur und Ethik. . . ."
        Deutsche Literaturzeitung (Berlin) 85:5 (May 1964),
        cols. 386-90.

4669   G., H. Y. "Verval en wederopbouw der cultuur." Nieuw
        Theologisk Tijdschrift (Lund) 18 (1929), pp. 191-92.

4670   G., W. E. "The Philosophy of Civilization. . . ." The
        Christian Century (Chicago) 66:47 (Nov. 23, 1949), p. 1394.

4671   JOAD, C. E. M. "Dr. Schweitzer and Civilization." The
        Nation and the Athenaeum (London) 34:9 (Dec. 1, 1923),
        pp. 352-53.

4672   K., W. "Albert Schweitzers Kulturphilosophie." Basler
        Nachrichten (Basel) 19:383 (Aug. 19, 1923), pp. 1-2.

4673   KEYSERLING, HERMANN. "Bücherschau." Weg zur Vollendung
        (Darmstadt) 10 (1925), pp. 55-58.

4674   "Kulturphilosophie." Deutsche Arbeit 23:195 (1924),
        pp. 293-96.

4675   MEDICUS, FRITZ. "Albert Schweitzer: Kultur und Ethik."
        Wissen und Leben (Zürich) 18 (Aug. 1, 1925), pp. 829-34.

Misc. Writings About Schweitzer

4676   MEMEGOZ, FERNAND. "La Philosophie de la civilisation de
       M. Albert Schweitzer." REVUE 4 (1924), pp. 84-90.

4677   PFENNINGDORF, E. "Kultur, Ethik, Christendom--Verfall und
       Wiederaufbau der Kultur." Geisteskampf der Gegenwart
       (Gütersloh) 60:2 (1924), pp. 37-41.

4678   "Philosophy of Civilization." The New Yorker 25
       (Nov. 19, 1949), p. 168.

4679   "The Philosophy of Civilization." The Churchman (New York)
       164:2 (Jan. 15, 1950), p. 17.

4680   RUSSELL, BERTRAND. "Does ethics influence life?" The Nation
       and the Athenaeum (London) 34:8 (Feb. 2, 1924),
       pp. 635-36.

4681   SAWICKI, F. "Kultur und Ethik." Literarischer Handweiser
       (Freibach i.B.) 60:1/2 (1924), cols. 21-22.

4682   SCHLÖTERMANN, HEINZ. "Albert Schweitzer: Verfall und
       Wiederaufbau der Kultur; Kultur und Ethik. . . ."
       Philosophischer Literaturanzeiger (Munich) 1:1 (1949),
       pp. 19-22.

4683   SILBERSCHMIDT, BENNO DANIEL. "Decadência e Regeneracão da
       Culture." Revista do Arquivo Municipal (São Paulo)
       14:116 (1947), pp. 41-48.

4684   SNETHLAGE, J. E. "Kultur und Ethik. 1923." Nieuw Theologisk
       Tijdschrift (Haarlem) 15 (1926), pp. 243-47.

4685   STEIGER, HENRY W. "Albert Schweitzer. The Philosophy of
       Civilization." Christian Science Monitor (Boston)
       Dec. 29, 1949, p. 11.

4686   STOKES, S. E. "Civilization and Ethics." The Visva-Bharati
       Quarterly (Calcutta) 2 (Jan. 1925), pp. 380-84.

4687   "Verfall und Wiederaufbau der Kultur." Nieuwe Theologische
       Studien (Wageningen) 8 (1925), p. 305.

4688   WAKEFIELD, GEORGE W. "Philosophy of Civilization." The
       Library Journal (New York) 74:15 (Sept. 1, 1949), p. 1198.

4689   WIDGERY, A. G. "The Decay and Restoration of
       Civilization . . . Civilization and Ethics. . . ." Mind
       (London) 33:132 (Oct. 1924), pp. 467-69.

Misc. Writings About Schweitzer

The Psychiatric Study of Jesus
(Die Psychiatrische Beurteilung Jesu)

4690 ALDRICH, V. C. "The Psychiatric Study of Jesus (and) Goethe: Two Addresses." Journal of Philosophy (New York) 46:2 (Jan. 20, 1949), pp. 53-54.

4691 BELSER. "Die psychiatrische Beurteilung Jesu." Theologische Quartalschrift (Tübingen) 95:4 (1913), pp. 618-19.

4692 BUNDY, WALTER E. "The Psychiatric Study of Jesus." Crozer Quarterly (Chester, Pa.) 25:4 (Oct. 1948), pp. 351-52.

4693 CASWELL, WILBUR L. "The Psychiatric Study of Jesus." The Churchman (New York) 162:12 (June 15, 1948), p. 18.

4694 LEIPOLDT. "Die psychiatrische Beurteilung Jesu." Theologisches Literaturblatt (Leipzig) 34:21 (Oct. 10, 1913), cols. 489-90.

4695 LIGHTBOURNE, FRANCIS C. "The Psychiatric Study of Jesus." The Living Church (Milwaukee, Wis.) 136:18 (May 4, 1958), p. 6.

4696 LOISY, ALFRED. "Dis psychiatrische Beurteilung Jesu. . . ." Revue Critique d'Histoire et Littérature (Paris) 78 (Aug.-Dec. 1914), p. 152.

4697 MARCH, H. "Die psychiatrische Beurteilung Jesu. . . ." Theologisches Literaturblatt (Leipzig) 54:18 (Sept. 1, 1933), col. 277.

4698 PRUYSER, PAUL W. "The Psychiatric Study of Jesus. . . ." Pastoral Psychology (Great Neck, N.Y.) 9:86 (Sept. 1958), pp. 56-58.

4699 "The Psychiatric Study of Jesus. . . ." Chicago Review (University of Chicago) 12:2 (Summer 1958), p. 106.

4700 STAMM, RAYMOND T. "The Psychiatric Study of Jesus. . . ." The Lutheran Quarterly (Gettysburg, Pa.) 1:2 (May 1949), pp. 237-38.

4701 VAN DEN BERGH VAN EYSINGA, G. A. "Die psychiatrische Beurteilung Jesu, 1913." Nieuw Theologisk Tijdschrift (Haarlem) 3 (1914), p. 290.

Misc. Writings About Schweitzer

4702   WEBER. "Die psychiatrische Beurteilung Jesu, 1913."
         Theologische Literaturzeitung (Leipzig) 39:10
         (May 9, 1914), col. 296.

4703   WINDISCH, HANS. "Leben und Lehre Jesu. . . ." Theologische
         Rundschau (Tübingen) 16:12 (1913), pp. 439-41.

4704   ZIEHEN, TH. "Die psychiatrische Beurteilung Jesu, 1913."
         Deutsche Literaturzeitung (Leipzig) 34:42 (Oct. 18, 1913),
         pp. 2642-44.

The Quest of the Historical Jesus
(Von Reimarus zu Wrede)

4705   "Albert Schweitzers 'Leben Jesu.'" Schweizerisches
         Protestantenblatt (Basel) 48:11 (March 14, 1925),
         pp. 87-89; 48:12 (March 21, 1925), pp. 94-97; 48:13
         (March 28, 1925), pp. 101-04.

4706   BABEL, HENRY. "Le sécret historique de la vie de Jésus."
         NOUVELLES 27 (July 1961), pp. 7-8.

4707   BAKEL, H. A. VAN. "Geschichte der Leben-Jesu-Forschung.
         1933." Nieuw Theologisk Tijdschrift (Haarlem) 22
         (1933), pp. 273-75.

4708   BETHUNE-BAKER, J. F. "Quest of the Historical Jesus." The
         Journal of Theological Studies (Oxford, Eng.) 12 (1911),
         p. 148.

4709   "Biblische Wissenschaft." Vergangenheit und Gegenwart
         (Leipzig, Berlin) 5 (1915), p. 178.

4710   BRAIG, K. "Geschichte der Leben-Jesu-Forschung." Der
         Katholik (Mainz) 1916, pp. 456-58.

4711   BULLARD, ROGER A. "The Quest of the Historical Jesus . . .
         1968. . . ." Encounter 30:4 (Fall 1961), pp. 393-94.

4712   BULTMANN, RUDOLF. "Geschichte der Leben-Jesu-Forschung."
         Die Christliche Welt (Gotha) 28:27 (July 2, 1914), p. 643.

4713   CASE, SHIRLEY JACKSON. "Recent books on Jesus: Geschichte
         der Leben-Jesu-Forschung." American Journal of Theology
         (Chicago) 18 (1914), pp. 609-10.

4714   DIBELIUS, MARTIN. "Geschichte der Leben-Jesu-Forschung."
         Deutsche Literaturzeitung (Leipzig) 5:7 (Feb. 18, 1934),
         col. 292.

Misc. Writings About Schweitzer

4715   ERBES, K. "Von Reimarus zu Wrede. . . ." Zeitschrift für
           Kirchengeschichte (Gotha) 28 (1907), pp. 84-86.

4716   FRENCH, G. E. "The Quest of the Historical Jesus. . . ."
           The Hibbert Journal (London) 9:1 (Oct. 1910), pp. 203-06.

4717   G., W. E. "The Quest of the Historical Jesus. . . ." The
           Christian Century (Chicago) 65:52 (Dec. 29, 1948),
           p. 1431.

4718   "Geschichte der Leben-Jesu-Forschung." The Anglican Theo-
           logical Review (Evanston, Ill.) 15:2 (April 1933),
           p. 184.

4719   "Geschichte der Leben-Jesu-Forschung. Die Tat. Wege zum
           freien Menschentum (Leipzig) 15 (1923), pp. 284-95.

4720   "Geschichte der Leben-Jesu-Forschung." Nieuwe Theologische
           Studien (Wageningen) 10 (1927), p. 53.

4721   "Geschichte der Leben-Jesu-Forschung." Christentum und
           Wissenschaft (Leipzig) 2 (1926), pp. 346-48.

4722   GOGUEL, MAURICE. "Geschichte der Leben-Jesu-Forschung."
           Revue Critique d'Histoire et Littérature (Paris) 100:5
           (May 1933), pp. 200-01.

        _____. "Albert Schweitzer: Von Reimarus zu Wrede." See
           Theology and Religion, no. 2984 above.

4723   GUIGNEBERT, CH. "Antiquités Chrétiennes." Revue Historique
           (Paris) 120 (1915), pp. 360-61.

4724   HANSON, RICHARD. "The history and the 'historic' Jesus."
           The Church Quarterly Review (London) 96 (1923),
           pp. 84-102.

        HODGES, GEORGE. "Christ among the doctors." See Theology
           and Religion, no. 2999 above.

4725   HOLM, SØREN. "Albert Schweitzer. Jesu Liv." Berlingske
           Tidende (Copenhagen), Jan. 7, 1956.

4726   KENNEDY, H. A. A. "The life of Jesus in the light of recent
           discussions. . . ." American Journal of Theology
           (Chicago) 11 (1907), pp. 150-57.

4727   KIRCHOFF-LARSEN, CHR. "Albert Schweitzer. Jesu Liv."
           Børsen (Copenhagen), March 12, 1956.

Misc. Writings About Schweitzer

4728   KRAGH, TH. V. "Albert Schweitzer. Jesu Liv." Vejle Amts
          Folkeblad (Vejle, Jutland), Jan. 27, 1956.

4729   LAYMAN, C. M. "Quest of the Historical Jesus." Methodist
          History (Lake Junaluska, N.C.) 8 (Jan. 1970), pp. 57-58.

4730   LEIPOLDT. "Geschichte der Leben-Jesu-Forschung."
          Theologisches Literaturblatt (Leipzig) 34:15
          (July 18, 1913), cols. 345-46.

4731   LOISY, ALFRED. "Von Reimarus zu Wrede. . . ." Revue Critique
          d'Histoire et Littérature (Paris) 62:38 (Sept. 24, 1906),
          pp. 221-24.

4732   MEISNER, POVL. "Albert Schweitzer. Jesu Liv." Social-
          Demokraten, Jan. 13, 1956.

       MORGENSTERN, OTTO. "Die Leben-Jesu-Forschung." See Theology
          and Religion, no. 3061 above.

4733   MÜLLER, ERNST. "Geschichte der Leben-Jesu-Forschung."
          Universitas (Stuttgart) 15:1 (Jan. 1960), pp. 107-10.

4734   NÖSGEN, K.-F. "Von Reimarus zu Wrede." Theologisches
          Literaturblatt (Leipzig) 27:43 (Oct. 26, 1906),
          cols. 505-11.

4735   PFANMÜLLER, GUSTAV. "Schriften zur Jesusliteratur."
          Literarisches Zentralblatt für Deutschland (Leipzig)
          64:39 (Sept. 27, 1913), cols. 1259-60.

4736   "The Quest of the Historical Jesus. . . ." The Spectator
          (London) 104:4276 (June 11, 1910), pp. 978-79.

4737   R., S. "Albert Schweitzer: Geschichte der Leben-Jesu-
          Forschung." Revue Archéologique (Paris) 22
          (July-Dec. 1913), p. 315.

4738   REDMAN, BEN RAY. "The Quest of the Historical Jesus." The
          Saturday Review (New York) 32:7 (Feb. 12, 1949), p.27.

4739   ROHR. "Geschichte der Leben-Jesu-Forschung." Theologische
          Quartalschrift (Tübingen) 108 (1927), p. 360.

4740   SOLTAU. "Von Reimarus zu Wrede . . . 1906." Wochenschrift
          für Klassische Philologie (Berlin) 23:49 (Dec. 5, 1960),
          cols. 1338-45.

Misc. Writings About Schweitzer

4741   SPICQ. "Geschichte der Leben-Jesu-Forschung, 1951."
       Revue des Sciences Philosophiques et Théologiques (Paris)
       36 (1952), pp. 151-52.

4742   STEPHEN, H. "Von Reimarus zu Wrede." Literarisches
       Zentralblatt für Deutschland (Leipzig) 57:46
       (Nov. 10, 1906), col. 1545-47.

4743   VAN DEN BERGH VAN EYSINGA, G. A. "Geschichte der Leben-Jesu-
       Forschung, 1913." Nieuw Theologisk Tijdschrift (Haarlem)
       3 (1914), pp. 194-200.

4744   VOELTZEL, R. "Albert Schweitzer: Geschichte der Leben-Jesu-
       Forschung." REVUE 31 (1951), pp. 375-77.

4745   VOS, GEERHARDUS. "The Quest of the Historical Jesus."
       The Princeton Theological Review 9:1 (Jan. 1911),
       pp. 132-41.

       WERNLE, PAUL. "Schweitzer. Von Reimarus zu Wrede. . . ."
       See Theology and Religion, no. 3155 above.

4746   WINDISCH, HANS. "Leben und Lehre Jesu (Von Reimarus zu
       Wrede)." Theologische Rundschau (Tübingen) 12 (1909),
       pp. 146-48ff.

4747   _____. "Zum Streit um Geschichtlichkeit Jesu. . . ."
       Theologische Rundschau (Tübingen) 16:9 (1913), pp. 338-41.

       WOOD, HERBERT G. "Albert Schweitzer and Eschatology." See
       Theology and Religion, no. 3161 above.

The Religious Philosophy of Kant
(Die Religionsphilosophie Kants)

4748   GIGLIOTTI, G. "Die Religionsphilosophie Kants." Bollettino
       Bibliografico per le scienze morali et sociali (Rome)
       33/36 (1976), pp. 345-48.

4749   HÖHNE. "Die Religionsphilosophie Kants. . . ." Theologischer
       Literatur-Bericht (Gütersloh) 23:6 (June 1900),
       pp. 203-05.

4750   KATZER, DR. "Die Religionsphilosophie Kants. . . ."
       Kantstudien (Berlin) 7 (1902), pp. 132-41.

4751   MALTER, R. "Die Religionsphilosophie Kants." Kantstudien
       (Bonn) 66:2, p. 267.

Misc. Writings About Schweitzer

4752   MAYER, E. W. "Schweitzer, Dr. Albert. Die Religionsphilosophie Kants. . . ." <u>Theologische Literaturzeitung</u>
(Leipzig) 25:20 (1900), cols. 568-70.

4753   RABUS, L. "Die Religionsphilosophie Kants von der Kritik
der reinen Vernunft. . . ." <u>Theologisches Literaturblatt</u>
(Leipzig) 21:37 (Sept. 14, 1900), cols. 433-34.

4754   "Die Religionsphilosophie Kants. . . ." <u>Literarisches
Zentralblatt für Deutschland</u> (Leipzig) 52:10
(March 9, 1901), col. 403.

4755   "Die Religionsphilosophie Kants." <u>Athenaeum</u> (London) 3843
(June 22, 1901), pp. 781-82.

4756   "Die Religionsphilosophie Kants. . . ." <u>Die Christliche Welt</u>
(Gotha) 14:17 (April 26, 1900), col. 402.

4757   STANGE, CARL. "Die Religionsphilosophie Kants. . . ."
<u>Zeitschrift für Philosophie und Philosophische Kritik</u>
(Leipzig) 120:2 (1902), pp. 101-06.

Reverence for Life (Strassburger Predigten)

4758   C., J. B. "Vivre. 18 Sermons." <u>Foi et Vie</u> (Paris) 70:1
(1971), p. 97.

4759   EBOR, DONALD. "Reverence for Life. . . ." <u>Church Quarterly</u>
3:2 (Oct. 1970), p. 163.

4760   GRABS, RUDOLF. "Schweitzer, Albert: Strassburger Predigten."
<u>Theologische Literaturzeitung</u> (Leipzig) 93:6
(June 1968), p. 463.

4761   MAC QUEEN, ANGUS J. "Reverence for Life. . . ." <u>Canadian
Journal of Theology</u> 16:1-2 (Jan./April 1970), pp. 111-12.

4762   VASSAUX, P. "Vivre. 18 Sermons." <u>Études Théologiques et
Religieuses</u> 47:2 (1972), p. 251.

Selbstdarstellung

4763   ENGELHARDT, WALTHER. "Selbstdarstellung (1929)." <u>Die
Christliche Welt</u> (Gotha) 43:19 (Oct. 5, 1929), p. 957.

4764   GERBER. "Selbstdarstellung." <u>Theologisches Literaturblatt</u>
(Leipzig) 53:4 (Feb. 12, 1932), col. 5.

Misc. Writings About Schweitzer

4765   KATTENBUSCH, FERDINAND. "Selbstdarstellung, 1929."
Zeitschrift für Kirchengeschichte (Gotha) 49 (1930),
p. 390.

4766   SCHOMERUS, H. W. "Selbstdarstellung." Theologie der Gegenwart
(Leipzig) 25:4 (April 1931), pp. 91-92.

Was Sollen Wir Tun?

4767   MAHR, GERHARD. "Was Sollen wir Tun?. . . ." Rheinischer
Merkur (Cologne) 20 (May 17, 1974), p. 29.

4768   SPEAR, OTTO. "Was Sollen wir Tun? 12 Predigten über
ethische Probleme." RUNDBRIEF 41 (Feb. 1976), p. 47.

G. Meetings and Symposia

This section lists significant meetings and symposia held in honor
of Albert Schweitzer and their publications, if available. Any
articles which discuss the various meetings will be included immediately following the particular meeting concerned. Individual
papers presented at the various symposia are listed in the appropriate subject sections under the author's name.

4769   Académie des sciences morales et politiques, Paris. Céle-
bration du centenaire de la naissance d'Albert Schweitzer;
séance du lundi 27 Janvier 1975/Institut de France,
Académie des sciences morales et politiques. Paris:
Institut de France, 1975. 39 pp.

4770   The Albert Schweitzer Centennial Week in St. Louis, Missouri,
1975. Records. Mimeographed, unpaged.

4771   Albert Schweitzer Centennial Symposium. UNESCO, Paris, 1975.
No published proceedings.

4772   Albert Schweitzer: Conférences du Congrès international des
ecrivains-médecins, Debrecen, 1966. Debrecen
Orvostudomanyi Egyetem, 1966. 209 pp. Illus. Conference
of the International Federation of Medical Writers, held
August 26-30, 1966.

4773   Albert Schweitzer International Convocation, Aspen, Colorado,
1966. The Convocation Record. Aspen, Colorado, 1966.
Sponsored by the Aspen Institute for Humanistic Studies,
the Albert Schweitzer Fellowship, and the Johnson
Foundation.

Misc. Writings About Schweitzer

4774   "Dr. Albert Schweitzer and his work: International Con-
        vocation, Aspen, 1966." Pan Pipes of Sigma Alpha
        Iota (Menasha, Wis.) 58:3 (1966), p. 6.

4775   "International Convocation to evaluate Schweitzer's work."
        COURIER, April-May 1966, pp. 26-27.

4776   JACK, H. A. "Schweitzer Convocation at Aspen." The
        Christian Century (Chicago 83:26 (June 29, 1966),
        pp. 840-41.

4777   SCIPIO, CORNELIUS. "Is Schweitzer dead? Albert Schweitzer
        International Convocation, Aspen, Col. . . ." Atlantic
        Monthly (Boston) 218:2 (Aug. 1966), pp. 41-44. For
        comments, see the Atlantic Monthly 218: 4 (October 1966),
        p. 48; 218:6 (December 1966), p. 44.

4778   Albert-Schweitzer-Komitee beim Präsidium des Deutschen Roten
        Kreuzes in der DDR. 100 Geburtstag von Albert Schweitzer.
        Festveranstaltung. Records of a symposium held Dec. 6,
        1974 at the Deutschen Hygiene Museum, Dresden.

4779   The Atlanta Symposium of the Albert Schweitzer Centenary,
        April 4-12, 1975. No published proceedings. Main theme:
        Health in the developing world.

4780   SULLIVAN, WALTER. "Experts voice some hope despite the
        vast global scope of disease and malnutrition."
        The New York Times, April 14, 1975, p. 25.

4781   BAUR, DR. H. and PROF. DR. R. MINDER. Albert-Schweitzer-
        Gespräch Basel 1967. Hamburg: Herbert Reich Evangelischer
        Verlag, 1969. 104 pp. (Evangelische Zeitstimmen 42/43).
        Symposium auf Einladung des Schweizer Hilfsvereins für
        das Lambarene Spital und seiner Arbeitsgruppe für das
        geistige Werks Albert Schweitzers, Oct. 14 and 15, 1967.

        BREMI, WILLI. "Das erste Albert-Schweitzer-Gespräch in
        Basel." See Philosophy, no. 2423 above.

4782   MEYER, HERMANN J. "Internationales Albert-Schweitzer-
        Symporion in Basel." Universitas (Stuttgart) 23:4
        (April 1968), pp. 431-33.

        SPEAR, OTTO. "The Albert Schweitzer discussion, Basel,
        1967." See Philosophy, no. 2650 above.

4783   HAGEMANN, E. R., editor. Albert Schweitzer. Louisville, Ky.:
        University of Louisville, 1969. 33 pp. "The occasion
        for this symposium, December 6, 1965, was to commemorate

Misc. Writings About Schweitzer

Albert Schweitzer (1875-1965) as part of the faculty
lectures in the humanities at the University of Louisville."

4784   International Albert Schweitzer Symposium. 28 September-
            1 Oktober 1978 Deventer-Holland. 120 pp. Proceedings
            are available from the Albert Schweitzer Centrum, Postfach
            15, 7400AA, Deventer, Niederlande.

4785   "Albert-Schweitzer Symposium in Holland." A.I.S.L.
            Bulletin 8 (November 1978), pp. 3-12.

4786   "Deventer." COURIER, Winter 1978, pp. 26-27.

4787   "Deventer." RUNDBRIEF 46 (November 1978), p. 56.

4788   Revue d'Histoire et de Philosophie Religieuses (Strasbourg)
            56:1-2 (1976), pp. 1-201. Contains papers read at a
            colloquium held in Strasbourg on May 5-7, 1975, in honor
            of the centenary of Schweitzer's birth.

4789   Second International Conference on Albert Schweitzer
            (Spiritual Work). Milan, April 3 and 4, 1971. London:
            Photographic Service Ltd., 13 pp. Translated as: Zweites
            Internationales Albert-Schweitzer-Gespräch (Geistiges
            Werk). 14 pp.

            SPEAR, OTTO. "Zweites Albert Schweitzer Gespräch." See
                Philosophy, no. 2653 above.

4790   Tübinger Albert-Schweitzer-Woche Januar 1975. Programmheft.
            48 pp. Programmentwurf und Leitung: E. Mitschischek.
            Veranstalter: Deutscher Hilfsverein für das Albert-
            Schweitzer-Spital in Lambarene.

4791   Vermächtnis und Wirklichkeit; zum 100. Geburtstag Albert
            Schweitzers. Berlin: Union Verlag, 1974. Papers pre-
            sented at a colloquium held at the Zentrale Schulungs-
            stätte der CDU "Otto Nuschke" in Burgscheidungen.

4792   Wingspread Symposium. Racine, Wisconsin, October 1977. No
            published proceedings. Presentations are abstracted in
            COURIER, Winter 1978, pp. 4-25.

Misc. Writings About Schweitzer

H. Bibliographies

a. Books

4793   Albert Schweitzer: 1875-1975. Exposition. Bibliothèque
            Nationale et Universitaire de Strasbourg, Mai-Juin 1975;
            Bibliothèque Municipale de Colmar, Août-Septembre 1975.
            Catalogue établi par Madeleine et Théodore Lange (texte
            francais) et Gustave Woytt (texte allemande) avec le
            collaboration d'André Canivez et de J.-F. Collange.
            Strasbourg: Bibliothèque Nationale et Universitaire,
            1975. Annotated catalog of exhibit materials by and
            about Schweitzer. Text in German and French.

4794   AMADOU, ROBERT. Albert Schweitzer. Eléments de Biographie
            et de Bibliographie. Paris: L'Arche, 1952. 142 pp.
            Lists books and articles by and about Albert Schweitzer.

4795   BREVER, BEATE. Albert Schweitzer. Verzeichnis in der D.D.R.
            erschienenen Literatur. Leipzig: Fachschule für
            Bibliothekare an Wissenschaftlichen Bibliotheken, 1968.
            ix, 14 pp.

4796   HEINRICH, GISELA, comp. Albert Schweitzer. Wegweiser zu
            Büchern von ihm und über ihm. Ein Verzeichnis der in den
            Dortmunder Volksbüchereien vorhandenen Werke. Zusammen-
            gestellt anlässlich der Verleihung des Friedens-
            Nobelpreises. Dortmund: Städt. Volksbüchereien, 1954.
            23 pp. (Dichter und Denker unserer Zeit; eine
            Bücherverzeichnis-Reihe, 4.) For revised version,
            see Müller, no. 4798 below.

4797   Lankamp and Brinkman, bookshop, Amsterdam. Prof. Dr. Albert
            Schweitzer. Tentoonstelling van en over zijn werk,
            9-23 November 1935. Amsterdam: Lankamp and Brinkman,
            1935. 15 pp. Preface by J. Eigenhuis.

4798   MÜLLER, HERBERT and GISELA HEINRICH. Albert Schweitzer; ein
            Bücherverzeichnis. Duisburg: Stadtbücherei, 1956.
            41 pp.

4799   RICE, HOWARD C., JR., compiler. Albert Schweitzer, the
            Bibliographical Approach; catalogue of the exhibition in
            the Princeton University Library, January-March 1956.
            Princeton, N.J.: 1956. (Princeton University Library.
            Dept. of Rare Books and Special Collections. Exhibition
            Catalogues, no. 18.)

Misc. Writings About Schweitzer

4800   STAFFORDSHIRE COUNTY LIBRARY. Albert Schweitzer, 1875-1965. Stafford, 1965. 7 pp. Lists books by and about Schweitzer in the Staffordshire County Library.

4801   STUTTGART. KULTURAMT. Albert Schweitzer, ein Bücherverzeichnis. Stuttgart: Stadtbücherei, 1965. 41 pp.

    b. Articles, Part of Books

Note: Bibliographies listed from books are five or more pages in length.

4802   "Albert Schweitzer--the bibliographical approach." Universitas (English language edition) 1:1 (1956), pp. 90-92.

4803   "Albert-Schweitzer-Literatur seit 1965." In: CHARISMATISCHE DIAKONIE, pp. 90-93.

4804   BIXLER, J. SEELYE. "Letters from Dr. Albert Schweitzer in the Colby Library." Colby Library Quarterly (Waterville, Me.) 6:9 (1964), pp. 373-82.

4805   CLARK, HENRY. The Philosophy of Albert Schweitzer. London: Methuen, 1964, pp. 223-33. American edition: The Ethical Mysticism of Albert Schweitzer. Boston: Beacon Press, 1962, pp. 223-33. Includes books and articles by and about Schweitzer.

4806   D., E. "University hails Schweitzer at 81. Princeton opens big display of memorabilia." The New York Times, Jan. 15, 1956.

4807   DE FREITAS, DWALDO GASPAR. "O Doutor Schweitzer e o Brasil." In: DEBRECEN, pp. 131-50.

4808   GRABS, RUDOLF. Albert-Schweitzer, Denker aus Christentum. Halle/Saale: M. Niemeyer, 1958, pp. 184-92. Lists works by and about Schweitzer.

4809   _____. "Albert-Schweitzer-Literatur in der DDR." In: VERMÄCHTNIS UND WIRKLICHKEIT, pp. 75-83.

4810   GROOS, HELMUT. Albert Schweitzer: Grösse und Grenzen. Munich, Basel: Ernst Reinhardt, 1974, pp. 814-35. Includes books and articles by and about Schweitzer.

4811   HAGEDORN, HERMANN. Prophet in the Wilderness: The Story of Albert Schweitzer. New York: Macmillan, 1947,

Misc. Writings About Schweitzer

pp. 216-21; 1955, pp. 233-40. Includes materials by and about Schweitzer.

4812   JACK, HOMER A., ed. To Dr. Albert Schweitzer: a Festschrift commemorating his 80th birthday from a few of his friends. Evanston, Ill.: 1955, pp. 161-74.

4813   JOY, CHARLES R., ed. Albert Schweitzer, an Anthology. Boston: Beacon Press, 1955 (paperback edition), pp. x-xv; 1960, pp. 333-42; Harper, 1965, pp. 346-53. Lists only works by Schweitzer.

4814   KRAUS, OSKAR. "Das Gesamtwerk Albert Schweitzers." Das Deutsche Buch (Leipzig) 8:11/12 (1928), pp. 329-31. A discussion of works by Schweitzer. "Bibliographie der Werke A. Schweitzers," pp. 332-33.

4815   LAZARI-PALOWSKA, IJA. "Uczczenie Alberta Schweitzera w Niemieckiej Republice Demokratnycznej." Studie Filozoficzne (Warsaw) 6 (115) (1975), pp. 153-54.

4816   LIND, EMIL. Albert Schweitzer: aus seinem Leben und Werk. Bern: P. Haupt, 1948, pp. 196-203; Wiesbaden: Necessitas-Verlag, 1955, pp. 347-71. Includes works by Schweitzer and works about Schweitzer in German.

4817   LÖNNEBO, MARTIN. Albert Schweitzers etisk-religiosa Ideal. Stockholm: Diakonistyrelsens Bokförlag, 1964, pp. 339-48. Works by and about Schweitzer.

4818   MARSHALL, GEORGE N. and DAVID S. POLING. Schweitzer, a Biography. Garden City, N.Y.: Doubleday, 1971, pp. 319-25. Includes books by and about Schweitzer, recordings and motion pictures, and miscellaneous articles.

4819   MINDER, ROBERT, ed. Rayonnement d'Albert Schweitzer; 34 Etudes et 100 Temoignages. Publ. sous la Direction de Robert Minder. Colmar: Editions Alsatia, 1975, pp. 291-97. Includes works by and about Schweitzer, films, recordings, and periodicals.

4820   MÜLLER, HERBERT. "Ein Verzeichnis der Albert-Schweitzer-Literatur." Bücherei und Bildung (Reutlingen) 8:12 (Dec. 1956), pp. 481-82. About no. 4798 above.

4821   NEUENSCHWANDER, ULRICH. "A Statement" (unpublished books of Albert Schweitzer). In: THE CONVOCATION RECORD, pp. VI/33-34.

4822   "Out of Schweitzer's life and thought (notes on recent
         acquisitions)." Princeton University Library Chronicle
         (Princeton, N.J.) 21:4 (Summer 1960), pp. 246-51.

4823   "Reading List." COURIER (May 1974), pp. 15-16.

4824   REES, THEOPHIL. Albert Schweitzer: Ehrfurcht vor dem
         Leben. Karlsruhe: C. F. Muller, 1947, pp. 40-46.

       RICE, HOWARD C. "Albert Schweitzer: some bibliographical
         digressions." See Life and Work, no. 833 above.

4825   _____. "Albert Schweitzer. The bibliographical approach."
         The Princeton University Library Chronicle (Princeton,
         N.J.) 19:3-4 (Spring-Summer 1958), pp. 214-18.

4826   ROBACK, A. A. "A tentative bibliography of Albert
         Schweitzer." In: JUBILEE, pp. 469-84. Includes books
         and articles by and about Schweitzer.

4827   RUSSELL, LILIAN M. The Path to Reconstruction. London:
         A. and C. Black, 1941, pp. 64-68. Lists books and
         articles by and about Schweitzer.

4828   SCHÜTZ, ROLAND. "Über Bücher von Albert Schweitzer."
         RUNDBRIEF 12 (June 1958), pp. 53-59.

4829   SPEAR, OTTO. Albert Schweitzers Ethik. Hamburg: Herbert
         Reich Evangelischer Verlag, 1978, pp. 91-104. Includes
         works by and about Schweitzer.

4830   STEFFAHN, HARALD, ed. Albert Schweitzer in Selbstzeugnissen
         und Bilddokumenten. Reinbek bei Hamburg: Rowohlt, 1979,
         pp. 143-53. Includes works by and about Schweitzer.

4831   TAKAHASHI, I. "Saiken no Schweitzer Bunken." Gakutō
         (Tokyo) (Jan. 1955), pp. 40-44.

4832   WERNER, KARIN, compiler. "Förteckning över Professor Albert
         Schweitzers skrifter, samt ett urval böcker och uppsatser
         av andra författare, behandlande hans liv och verksamhet."
         In: MANNEN, pp. 240-50.

4833   WINNUBST, BENEDICTUS. Das Friedensdenken Albert Schweitzers.
         Amsterdam: Rodopi, 1974, pp. 202-11. Includes books,
         manuscripts, letters and speeches by Schweitzer and
         articles and books about him.

Misc. Writings About Schweitzer

4834 ZÜRCHER, JOHANN. "Auf der Suche nach dem richtigen Text.
      Arbeit am philosophischen und theologischen Nachlass
      Albert Schweitzers." Der Bund (Bern), Dec. 31, 1974.

4835 _____. "Stand und Fortführung der Arbeit an Albert
      Schweitzers philosophischem und theologischem Nachlass."
      A.I.S.L. Bulletin 5 (Nov. 1977), pp. 5-6.

                          I. Poetry

     a. Books

4836 BLUM, ROBERT. Offrande au Docteur Schweitzer. Poèmes.
      Paris: Editions de la Revue Moderne, 1955. 16 pp.
      (Collection "Rhythmes.")

4837 SCHNEIDER, CAMILLE. Albert Schweitzer. Strasbourg, 1962.
      14 pp. Illus. E. H. Cordier. (Mes poèmes bilingues, 3.)
      French and German on opposite pages. Limited edition.

4838 _____. Albert Schweitzer. Strasbourg, 1957, n.p. Illus.

     b. In Periodicals or Books

4839 "Albert Schweitzer." The Chinese Recorder (Shanghai) 64:2
      (Feb. 1933), p. 90.

4840 ALBRECHT, MAX. "Albert Schweitzer." NEUES 4 (March 1925),
      p. 3.

4841 _____. "Albert Schweitzers Urwald." Schweizerisches
      Protestantenblatt (Basel) 49:40 (Oct. 2, 1926), p. 334.

4842 BAUR, HANS. "Der Oganga kommt zurück." BERICHTE 20 (1937).
      Reprinted in: HALFEN, pp. 184-86.

4843 CHAKRAVARTY, AMIYA. "Poem." In: SELECTION, p. 15.

4844 _____. "African Signature." In: TRIBUTE, pp. 44-45.

4845 DORYAN, MIREIO. "Quel est ce passant?" In: DEBRECEN,
      pp. 128-29. Reprinted from En Alsace chez le Dr. Albert
      Schweitzer.

4846 GRABOWSKI, TADEUSZ. "Rzecz o Albercie Schweitzerze." In:
      Swiatlo Dzungli (Poezje). Warsaw: Pax, 1972, pp. I-XXIV.
      Zeszyty Poet, 1.

4847   HAUSHOFER, ALBRECHT. "Albert Schweitzer." In: Moabiter
        Sonette. Berlin: Lothar Blanvalet, 1946, p. 77.
        Reprinted in: GESTERN-HEUTE, p. 39.

4848   _____. "Albert Schweitzer." Wege zum Menschen (Göttingen)
        7:1 (Jan. 1955), p. 1.

4849   HAVEMANN, ROBERT. "Albert Schweitzer." In: BEGEGNUNG,
        pp. 77-78.

4850   HUNTER, ELIZABETH. "Hands to match the mind." The Christian
        Century (Chicago) 72:2 (Jan. 12, 1955), p. 43.

4851   KAUS, GUDRUN. "Albert Schweitzer zum Gedenken." RUNDBRIEFE/
        DDR 29 (1976), p. 35.

4852   KRETZ, T. "From a photograph: Albert Schweitzer (1875-1965);
        poem." Ave Maria (Notre Dame, Ind.) 102:21 (Nov. 20, 1965),
        p. 25.

4853   LYSOHORSKY, ONDRA. "Albert Schweitzers Tod." In: Der Tag
        des Lebens. Gedichte. Hrsg. von Paul J. Mark.
        Holzschnitte von Helene Salich. Geneva: Poesie Vivante,
        1971, pp. 68-69. (Collection "Le Grand Pavois" no. 4.)

4854   SCHAEFFER, LOUIS-EDOUARD. "Sonnet." CAHIERS 7 (Sept. 1962),
        p. 17.

4855   SCHMIDTBONN, WILHELM. "Ein Mann erklärt einer Fliege den
        Krieg. Szenen aus einem Hörbild." Eckart (Witten/Ruhr,
        Berlin) 7:1 (Jan. 1931), pp. 16-26.

4856   SCHMITT, CHRISTIAN. "An Albert Schweitzer." Schweizerisches
        Protestantenblatt (Basel) 47:41 (Oct. 11, 1924), p. 327.

4857   _____. "An Albert Schweitzer. Bei seinem zweiten Aufenhalt
        als Missionsarzt in Lambarene." NEUES III
        (Ende Oktober 1924), p. 1.

4858   _____. "Geburtstagsgruss an Albert Schweitzer. Zur
        Vollendung seines 50. Lebensjahres." NEUES 4
        (March 1925), p. 1.

4859   SCHNEIDER, CAMILLE. [Poem without title.] CAHIERS 7
        (Sept. 1962), pp. 10-12. Excerpt from her book Albert
        Schweitzer.

4860   SILKIN, JON. "The Forests" (on the occasion of Albert
        Schweitzer's visit to England, 1955). African Affairs
        55:218 (Jan. 1956), p. 46.

Fiction

Misc. Writings About Schweitzer

4861   STARKWEATHER, PAULINE. "Portraits of two Alberts." The
        Saturday Review of Literature (New York) 33:24
        (June 17, 1950), p. 40.

4862   STURZENEGGER, RASCHE. "An Albert Schweitzer." NEUES 7, p. 1.

4863   TRÜBE, MARTIN. "Albert Schweitzer zum Gedächtnis." Glaube
        und Gewissen (Halle) 12:1 (Jan. 1966), p. 8.

                        J.   Fiction

        a.   Books

            FRITZ, JEAN. The Animals of Dr. Schweitzer. See Youth,
                no. 4219 above.

4864   SCHMIED, LUISE MARIA. An den Ufern des Ogowe. Berlin:
        A. Holz, 1956. 186 pp. Illus.

            TRANSLATIONS

            Wij wachten op Dr. Schweitzer. Tr. H. Manger. Amsterdam:
                Ten Brink, 1960. (Kernpockets voor de Jeugd, no. 25.)

        b.   Articles, Parts of Books

4865   LIEBMANN-SMITH, RICHARD. "The Albert/Albert Exchange"
        (fantasy correspondence between Albert Einstein and
        Albert Schweitzer). Playboy (Chicago) 25:2 (Feb. 1978),
        pp. 123, 188-89.

4866   MALCOLM, DONALD. "'Dr. Schweitzer, I presume'. . . ." The
        New Republic (Washington, D.C.) 136:2 (March 25, 1957),
        p. 7. Satire on a suppositional visit by Vice President
        Richard Nixon to Albert Schweitzer at Lambarene.

4867   MAURICE, MICHAEL (Conrad Arthur Skinner). Blind Vision.
        London: Hutchinson and Co., n.d., pp. 137-62.

            K.   Complete Issues of Periodicals

Listed below are issued of periodicals devoted completely or in large
part to Albert Schweitzer. Articles included in these issues are
listed under authors' names in the appropriate subject sections.

4868   Aesculape 43 (Feb. 1960), pp. 3-61.

Complete Issues of Periodicals

4869   Cahiers Européens/Europäische Hefte/Notes from Europe
            (Munich) 2:1 (Jan. 1975), pp. 9-38.

4870   The Christian Register (Boston) 126:8 (Sept. 1947),
            pp. 314-31.

4871   The Christian Register (Boston) 134:1 (Jan. 1955), pp. 11-20.

4872   Communautés et Continents (Paris) 67:37 (Jan.-March 1975),
            pp. 1-36. "Centenaire de la Naissance d'Albert Schweitzer."

4873   Deventer Kerkbode (Deventer, Holland), April 20, 1928.

4874   France-Asie (Saigon) 70 (March 1952), pp. 957-71.

4875   Ghandi Marg (New Delhi) 9:2 (April 1965), pp. 133-59.

4876   Monatsschrift für Anthroposophie (Stuttgart), 1923.

4877   Monatsschrift für Sekundar- und Obere Primarschulen
            (Stuttgart), Nov./Dec. 1927.

4878   Ons Godsdienstig Leven. April 28, 1928.

4879   Revue d'Histoire et Philosophie Religieuses (Strasbourg)
            56:1-2 (1976), pp. 3-201. Contains papers read at a
            colloquium in Strasbourg on May 5-7, 1975.

4880   Saisons d'Alsace 10:14 (1965), pp. 120-58. Special section
            entitled "Albert Schweitzer dans sa Vérité. Hommage
            pour ses quatre-vingt-dix ans." Also issued as a reprint,
            see no. 1549 above.

4881   The Saturday Review (New York) 49:39 (Sept. 25, 1965),
            pp. 18-32. Special in memoriam issue; section entitled
            "Schweitzer--his life, his work, his thought."

4882   Schweizerische Theologische Umschau 25:1 (Feb. 1955),
            pp. 1-24. In honor of Schweitzer's 85th birthday.

4883   Standpunkt: Evangelische Monatsschrift (Berlin) 3:1
            (Jan. 1975), pp. 8-22.

4884   Theologie en Practijk (Lochem) 10:5/6 (May-June 1950),
            pp. 81-122.

4885   Universitas (Stuttgart) 15:1 (Jan. 1960), pp. 1-136. In
            honor of Schweitzer's 85th birthday.

Misc. Writings About Schweitzer

4886   Universitas (English Language Edition) 7:1 (1964), pp. 1-112.
        In honor of Schweitzer's 90th birthday. A good many of
        these articles are translations of those in the January
        1960 German edition.

4887   Wege zum Menschen (Gottingen) 7:1 (Jan. 1955). In honor of
        Schweitzer's 80th birthday.

4888   Das Werk (Gelsenkirchen) 2, Ausgabe B, Heft 9 (Nov. 1953),
        pp. 199-209.

                        L. Miscellaneous

4889   A., M. (ARNOLD, MELVIN). "International publishing projects
        launched for Schweitzer writings." The Christian Register
        (Boston) 126:8 (Sept. 1947), p. 314.

4890   "Albert Schweitzer besucht unsere Dedaktion" (editorial).
        New Yorker Staats-Zeitung und Herold, July 1, 1949, p. 4.

4891   "Albert Schweitzer in de familiekring." NIEUWS 1:4
        (Dec. 1952), pp. 66-67. Port.

4892   "Albert Schweitzer zum 73. Geburtstag. Ein Radiogruss nach
        Lambarene. Sendung des Schweiz. Rundspruche vom 13.
        Januar 1948 in 'Echo der Zeit.'" Zürich: Buchdruckerei
        A/d Sihl, 1948. 4 pp. Illus.

4893   BERGEVIN, D. DE. "Lettre de Dakar (Albert Schweitzer's
        arrival on board the SS Foucauld)." France Outre-Mer
        (Paris) 30:267 (Jan. 1952), p. 4. Port.

4894   BONDER, W. "Verslag van de Schweitzeravond in de Martinikerk
        te Groningen." NIEUWS 1:3 (July 1952), pp. 48-51. Illus.

4895   "Een borstbeeld van Albert Schweitzer . . . van de beeldhouwer
        F. Werner." NIEUWS 2:2 (Sept. 1953), p. 26. Illus.

4896   BUSSE, HERMANN. [Portrait of Albert Schweitzer and text by
        Hans A. Bühler.] Hans Adolf Bühler. Karlsruhe i.B.:
        C. F. Muller, 1931, pp. 132-35.

4897   "Cambridge welcomes Dr. Schweitzer." The Times (London),
        Oct. 24, 1955, p. 10.

4898   CANIVEZ, ANDRÉ. "Schweitzer et la jeunesse." In: HOMMAGE,
        pp. 25-30.

Miscellaneous

4899 "Le Cardinal Tisserant rend hommage au Docteur Albert
       Schweitzer." Les Dernières Nouvelles d'Alsace
       (Strasbourg) 100 (April 28, 1955), p. 22.

4900 CHESTERMAN, CLEMENT. "Un voyage du Docteur Albert Schweitzer
       en Grande-Bretagne." Communautés et Continents (Paris)
       67:37 (Jan.-March 1975), pp. 25-28.

4901 "Le docteur Schweitzer a confié aux editions Albin Michel
       la publication de deux de ses livres. . . ." Le Figaro
       Littéraire (Paris) 11:527 (May 26, 1956), p. 9.

4902 DORYAN, MIRÈIO. La Presence Passionnée. Vers et proses
       ornés de quarante pensées d'Albert Schweitzer. Editions
       Pierie Clairai.

4903 "Dr. Albert Schweitzer criticizes the U.N." (editorial).
       The Christian Century (Chicago) 80:4 (Jan. 23, 1963),
       p. 101.

4904 EGGINGTON, JOYCE. "Waiting for Dr. Schweitzer." The New
       Statesman and Nation (London) 50:1286 (Oct. 29, 1955),
       pp. 536ff.

4905 FISCHER, ANTOINE. "Merci, Albert Schweitzer." Saisons
       d'Alsace (Strasbourg) 3:1 (Winter 1951), p. 12.

4906 G., N. "Jan Eigenhuis en Albert Schweitzer." De Nieuwe Gids
       (Gravenhage) 51 (May 1936), pp. 462-64.

4907 GILLESPIE, NOEL M. "From an old letter by a former helper
       at Lambarene." In: REALMS, pp. 303-04.

4908 GIRSON, ROCHELLE. "Schweitzer in Alvastone." The Saturday
       Review (New York) 38:51 (Dec. 17, 1955), p. 13. Illus.
       Background history of the sculptured head of A. S. by
       Leo Cherne.

4909 GMÜNDER, PAUL. "Albert Schweitzer und der Maler." BERICHTE
       42 (Oct. 1976), pp. 26-28.

4910 GOLLANCZ, VICTOR. My dear Timothy. London, 1952, pp. 337-40.

4911 HAAS, ROBERT. "Notre plus illustré voyageur de 3e classe,
       le docteur Albert Schweitzer." La Vie du Rail (Paris)
       476 (Christmas 1954), p. 31. Port., illus.

4912 "The head of Schweitzer appears in one of the stained-glass
       windows in the Pittsburgh Educational Wing." The Chris-
       tian Register (Boston) 133:5 (May 1954), p. 22.

Misc. Writings About Schweitzer

4913   HEINTZELMAN, ARTHUR W. "Statement" (about Schweitzer's
         appearance, by a sculptor). In: SELECTION, pp. 16-17.

4914   HEMAR, MARIAN. Kantata na smierc doktora Alberta Schweitzera.
         Tydzien Polski 40:1 (1965).

4915   HOELL, ANDREAS. "Endelig." Dagbladed (Oslo) 225
         (Nov. 3, 1954), pp. 3-4.

4916   "Hommes et faits d'outremer (Albert Schweitzer) au Cercle de
         la France Outre Mer; le Sénateur Durand-Réville, Président,
         a recu le docteur Schweitzer. . . ." France d'Outre Mer
         (Paris) 30:278 (Dec. 1952), p. 4. Illus.

4917   HUNTEMANN, GEORG H. "Aus dem Geiste Albert Schweitzers.
         Zum 70. Geburtstag von Martin Werner. . . ." Freies
         Christentum (Frankfurt a.M.) 9:11 (Nov. 1, 1957),
         cols. 134-36.

4918   KARSH, YOUSUF. "Albert Schweitzer." In: Portraits of
         Greatness. New York: Thomas Nelson and Sons, pp. 178-79.
         Full-page portrait.

4919   _____. "Great faces in color, Dr. Albert Schweitzer."
         Maclean's Magazine (Toronto) 67:23 (Dec. 1, 1954),
         pp. 14-15. Port.

4920   _____. "A new gallery of Karsh" (two portraits of A. S.).
         Coronet (Chicago) 39:2 (Dec. 1955), pp. 166-67.

4921   KAZANTZAKIS, NIKO. "Die beiden Brüder" (Franz von Assisi
         und Albert Schweitzer). Epilog. In: Pierhal, Jean.
         Albert Schweitzer, see no. 291 above, pp. 392-96.
         Reprinted in: GESTERN-HEUTE, p. 47.

4922   KIK, RICHARD. "Kleine Mitteilungen." RUNDBRIEF 10
         (Dec. 1, 1956), pp. 67-68.

4923   KRAUS, OSKAR. "Eine Albert-Schweitzer-Woche in Prag."
         Deutsche Zeitung Bohemia (Prag) 96:3 (Jan. 5, 1923),
         p. 5.

4924   LAGERFELT, GRETA. "Hemma in Elsass. Minnen fran Strassburg
         och Gunsbach. . . ." In: MANNEN, pp. 204-39.

4925   LE COMPTE, ROWAN. "Windows in the Boardman Bay, Washington
         Cathedral" (stained glass window honoring Albert
         Schweitzer). The Cathedral Age (Washington, D.C.) 32:3
         (Autumn 1957), pp. 7f.

4926   MAI, HERMANN. "Geleitwort." In: GESTERN-HEUTE, pp. 11-12.

4927   MAYER, LOUIS. Bas Relief of Albert Schweitzer (1949).
       The Christian Register (Boston) 128:6 (June 1949), cover.

4928   "Music for medicine. Hartford organists join in national
       program to support hospital work of Albert
       Schweitzer. . . ." The Hartford Courant Magazine
       (Hartford, Conn.), March 6, 1955, p. 6.

4929   NEHMER, RUDOLF. "Überlegungen zu meiner Albert-Schweitzer-
       Grafik." In: VERMÄCHTNIS UND WIRKLICHEKIT, pp. 89-90.

4930   PETRIZKIJ, WILLI. "Schöpferische Tat des Künstlers."
       RUNDBRIEFE/DDR 29 (1976), pp. 8-11.

4931   PIETSCH, DR. MED. [Albert Schweitzer und Strafgefangene.]
       RUNDBRIEF 8 (Nov. 1, 1955), pp. 52-54. Reprinted in:
       DOKUMENTE, pp. 273-74.

4932   "Portrait. Dr. Schweitzer . . . with Sir Anthony Eden."
       The Illustrated London News 227 (Oct. 29, 1955), p. 749.

4933   "Portrait . . . Dr. Schweitzer by Mr. Augustus John. . . ."
       The Illustrated London News 227 (Nov. 12, 1955), p. 823.

4934   REIF, PAUL. "Reverence for life. A musical tribute to Albert
       Schweitzer in celebration of his 85th birthday. "Monsieur
       le Pelican." Epic BC 1065. 1960. 1 record, 40-page score.
       Walter Cassel, Baritone. Epic String Quartet. Leonid
       Hambro, Piano (first work), New York Wind Ensemble (second
       work).

4935   ROBACK, A. A. "The Iconography of Albert Schweitzer." In:
       REALMS, pp. 111-37. Ports.

4936   ROSS, EMORY and MYRTA. "Meditation for the meeting of the
       Albert Schweitzer Fellowship, Sept. 23, 1968." COURIER,
       Autumn 1968, pp. 10-13.

4937   SCHAFFNER, MANFRED. "Kraftquell unserer Arbeit." In:
       BEITRÄGE, pp. 171-72.

4938   SCHNABEL, ILSE. "Ansprache." In: Zusammenkunft von
       Mitarbeitern und Freunden des Spitals am 22. September
       1957 in Kammermusiksaal des Kongresshauses in Zürich,
       pp. 4-7.

Misc. Writings About Schweitzer

4939   SCHWEITZER, HELENE. "Briefe von Frau Schweitzer." RUNDBRIEF
       11 (Aug. 1, 1957), pp. 19-22. Reprinted in: DOKUMENTE,
       pp. 358-61.

4940   "Ein 'Schweitzer' Haus." NEUES II (Pfingsten 1924), pp. 5-6.

4941   "Schweitzer tentoonstelling." NIEUWS 4:1 (Jan. 1955),
       p. 111.

4942   TAU, MAX. "Albert Schweitzer und die Jugend. Ein
       Huldigungsgruss zu seinem 78. Geburtstag." Rhein-Neckar
       Zeitung (Heidelberg), Jan. 9, 1953. Reprinted in
       Schwarzwälder-Bote (Oberndorf am Neckar), Jan. 15, 1953.

4943   _____. "Albert Schweitzer och ungdommen." Världshorisont
       (Stockholm) 6:12 (Dec. 1952), pp. 16-20.

4944   _____. "Albert Schweitzer og ungdommen." Aftenposten
       (Oslo), Nov. 22 and 24, 1952.

4945   W., R. "Albert Schweitzer in Stuttgart." Elsass-Lothringen
       Heimatstimmen (Berlin) 7:3 (March 23, 1929), p. 196.

4946   WEITBRECHT, OSKAR. "Albert Schweitzer in Tübingen am 12.
       Oktober 1951." Freies Christentum (Frankfurt am Main)
       12:1 (Jan. 1, 1960), cols. 10-11.

4947   "With Dr. Schweitzer to America." BRITISH BULLETIN 19
       (June 1951), pp. 5-6.

Addendum

1. Anthologies, Collections

4948   KÜHN, GERHARD. Schriftenreihe 'Ehrfurcht vor dem Leben.'
       Frankfurt a.M.: Albert Schweitzer Archiv und Zentrum.
       11 in the series have appeared to date: "14 Thesen aus
       diesen Einsichten" (Dec. 1977); "Christentum und Welt-
       religionen" (Feb. 1978); "Die geistige Krise unserer Zeit
       und der Stellenwert des Denkens" (Sept. 1978); "Ehrfurcht
       vor dem Leben--die Grundhaltung" (Dec. 1978); "Die
       Einstellung zum Naturgesetz" (March 1979); "Die Ehrfurcht
       vor dem menschlichen Leben und was dies bedeutet"
       (Aug. 1979); "Ideal und Wirklichkeit" (Dec. 1979); "Das
       Zwischenmenschliche Verhältnis--Dienen und Helfen als
       ethische Aufgabe" (May 1980); "Das Zwischenmenschliche
       Verhalten--Höflichkeit und Anstand als ethische Aufgabe"
       (Sept. 1980); "Das Zwischenmenschliche Verhalten--
       Dankarbeit als ethisches Problem" (Dec. 1980); "Das
       Recht auf Besitz und das ethische Problem" (in preparation).

2. Life and Work

    a. General

4949   SCHWEITZER, ALBERT. Naeui Sanegaewa Sasang cheon Byeonghi.
       Seoul: Munye Chulpansa. 282 pp. (Korean translation
       of Aus meinem Leben und Denken.)

4950   ROSE, STEPHEN C. "Schweitzer: a hidden greatness." The
       Berkshire Courier, Thursday, Oct. 16, 1980.

4951   SALMON, A. E. The Great Doctor: the Story of Albert
       Schweitzer. Birmingham, Ala.: Religious Education Press,
       1978.

Addendum

   b. Friends

4952   BAUR, DR. "Robert Minder." <u>A.I.S.L. Bulletin</u> 12 (Dec. 1980),
         p. 17.

4953   DURAND-REVILLE, LUC. "Allocution du Président Durand-Reville,
         aux obsèques de . . . Professeur Minder. . . ." <u>A.I.S.L.</u>
         <u>Bulletin</u> 12 (Dec. 1980), pp. 4-5.

3. Lambarene

4954   BERTHOUD, ROGER. "Following in Albert Schweitzer's foot-
         steps." <u>The Times</u> (London) Sept. 1, 1978, p. 5.
         Interview with Max Caulet.

4955   BURGER, HANNES. "Lambarenes Weg vom Mythos zur Praxis. . . ."
         <u>Süddeutsche Zeitung</u> (Munich) 119 (May 27, 1978), p. 12.

4956   "Des hommes d'affaires à l'Hôpital Schweitzer." <u>L'Union</u>,
         Oct. 15, 1980. Reprinted in the <u>A.I.S.L. Bulletin</u> 12
         (Dec. 1980), p. 10.

4957   KEERDOJA, EILEEN. "Schweitzer's African legacy." <u>Newsweek</u>
         (New York) 93 (April 16, 1979), p. 20.

4958   LAMARK, BERND. "Lambarene gerettet. Ein Albert Schweitzer-
         Nachfolger kehrte heim." <u>Rheinischer Merkur</u> (Cologne) 1
         (Jan. 7, 1977), p. 13.

4959   MICHEL, H. "Reise an den Ogowe." <u>A.I.S.L. Bulletin</u> 12
         (Dec. 1980), pp. 18-19.

4960   N., L. B. "Il y 15 ans, mourait Albert Schweitzer."
         <u>L'Union</u>, Sept. 9, 1980. Reprinted in the <u>A.I.S.L.</u>
         <u>Bulletin</u> 12 (Dec. 1980), p. 8.

4961   SCHNEIDER, THOMAS. "Scheck für Lambarene verdoppelt sich in
         Brüssel." <u>A.I.S.L. Bulletin</u> 11 (June 1980), p. 18.

4962   SCHUFFENECKER, GERARD. "'In allem wird der Geist Albert
         Schweitzers respektiert.'" <u>Dernieres Nouvelles d'Alsace</u>,
         May 4, 1980. Reprinted in the <u>A.I.S.L. Bulletin</u> 11
         (June 1980), p. 16 (German), 33 (French). Interview
         with Max Caulet.

4963   TÉTAZ-NIEDERHAUSER, ERNA. "Zügiger Ausbau des Albert
         Schweitzer-Spitals. Finanzielle Mittel fürs erste
         gesichert." <u>Neue Zürcher Zeitung</u> 251 (Oct. 27, 1977),
         p. 4.

Addendum

4964   ZIMMERMAN, HORST. "Rettung für Urwald-Hospital Albert
        Schweitzers. . . ." *Der Tagespiegel* (Berlin) 9291
        (April 7, 1976), p. 3.

4. Philosophy

    a. General

4965   SCHWEITZER, ALBERT. *Reverence for Life*. Bombay: Bharatiya
        Vidya Bhavan, 1963. 43 pp. (Bhavan's book University)
        Reprint of Chapter XXI of the third edition of *Civiliza-
        tion and Ethics*.[1]

4966   SCHWEITZER, ALBERT. "Toward a new Culture." *Reverence*
        (Great Barrington, Mass.) 1 (1980), pp. 5-8. Transcrip-
        tion of a speech given on Nov. 6, 1959.

4967   ABRELL, RON. "The educational legacy of Albert Schweitzer."
        Vital Speeches 46:13 (April 15, 1980), pp. 391-95.
        Speech given at the University of Houston at Clear Lake
        City, Jan. 30, 1980.

4968   BOSIO, FRANCO. "Il significato della cultura e il fina della
        filosofia nel pensiero di Max Scheler." *Raccolta di
        Studi e Richerche* (Bari) 1 (1977), pp. 9-21.

4969   CHATTOPADHYAYA, BASANTA KUMAR. "Schweitzer on Indian philoso-
        phy." *Indian Philosophy and Culture* 2 (Sept. 1957),
        pp. 133-34.

4970   MUGAY, PETER. "Durch die Tat ehren." *Neue Zeit* (East Berlin)
        Nov. 5, 1980. Reprinted in the *A.I.S.L. Bulletin* 12
        (Dec. 1980), p. 31.

4971   _____. "Gemeinsamer Nenner im Miteinander der Völker."
        Neue Zeit (East Berlin), Nov. 6, 1980. Reprinted in the
        A.I.S.L. Bulletin 12 (Dec. 1980), p. 32.

4972   P., G. "Über das alte und neue Lambarene." *Osnabrück Ev.
        Zeitung*, Jan. 13, 1980. Reprinted in the *A.I.S.L.*

---

[1]In many sources, including the Library of Congress printed catalogue
and many library catalogues, this work is listed as a translation of
Strassburger Predigten. This is erroneous—it was published before
Strassburger Predigten, and includes a notation that it is a translation of chapter 21 of *Civilization and Ethics*.

Addendum

        Bulletin 11 (June 1980), p. 17. Interview with Harold
        Robles.

  b. Reverence for Life

4973   SCHWEITZER, ALBERT. *Nauka úcty k zivotu.* Tr. Vera
       Kovaricková. Prague: Supraphon. 85 pp. Ill.
       Czech translation of *Die Lehre der Ehrfurcht vor dem*
       Leben.

4974   "Ehrfurcht vor dem Leben--Vermächtnis und Pflicht." *Neue*
       Zeit (East Berlin), Oct. 25, 1980, pp. 1-2. Reprinted
       in the *A.I.S.L. Bulletin* 12 (1980), pp. 27-28.

5. Theology and Religion

4975   GRÄSSER, ERICH. *Albert Schweitzer als Theologe.* Tübingen:
       Mohr, 1979. x, 279 pp. (Beiträge zur historischen
       Theologie). Based on a lecture course given in 1976 at
       the Ruhr-Universität Bochum.

4976   KAUFMANN, WALTER ARNOLD. "Jesus vis-a-vis Paul, Luther and
       Schweitzer." In: *The Faith of a Heretic.* Garden City:
       Doubleday, 1961, pp. 219-60; 1963 paperback edition,
       pp. 207-48. Also New York, London: New American Library,
       1978, pp. 207-48.

4977   KLIEBISCH, UDO. "Hermeneutik der Unmittelbarkeit in
       Schweitzers 'Geschichte der Leben-Jesu-Forschung.'"
       Bochum, Germany, 1980.

4978   LATTKE, MICHAEL. "Neue Aspekte der Frage nach dem
       historischen Jesus." *Kairos: Zeitschrift für*
       Religionswissenschaft und Theologie (Salzburg) 21:4
       (1979), pp. 288-99.

4979   ROBERTS, T. A. "The Relevance of Liberal Christianity."
       Hibbert Journal (London) 59 (July 1961), pp. 320-30.

6. Music

  a. Bach

4980   DRUSKIN, MIKHAIL. "Iz istorii zarubezhnogo bakhovedeniya."
       Sovetskaya Muzyka (Moscow) 42 (March 1978), pp. 94-96.

Addendum

4981   PERSHING, D.   "The Bach-bow controversy." Journal of the
             Violin Society of America 3:2 (1977), pp. 72-81.

    b. Organs

4982   GRONDSMA, FOLKERT.   "Nationaal Albert Schweitzer
             Orgelfestival." Mens en Melodie 33 (Nov. 1978), pp. 382-84.

7. The Schweitzer Influence

    a. Education

4983   M., P. "Ferrenbach: 'Renovér le musée et soutenir
             l'hôpital.'" A.I.S.L. Bulletin 11 (June 1980), p. 30.

4984   MINDER, ROBERT. "Bericht des Präsidenten der Kommission
             'Geistiges Werk von Albert Schweitzer und Haus von
             Günsbach.'" A.I.S.L. Bulletin 11 (June 1980), pp. 4-9
             (German), 21-26 (French).

4985   OLSON, JUDITH. "Albert Schweitzer Collection." Daily Pilot,
             Nov. 6, 1980. Reprinted in the A.I.S.L. Bulletin 12
             (Dec. 1980), p. 13. About the collection at Chapman
             College.

    b. Hospitals

4986   CHWATSKY, ANN. "In Albert Schweitzers Fussstapfen."
             Für Uns, Nov. 1980. Reprinted in the A.I.S.L. Bulletin
             12 (Dec. 1980), pp. 33-34. (About Haiti Hospital.)

4987   MC CALL, C. "Mellon from Pittsburgh gives his life and
             fortune to help the poor of Haiti." People 12
             (April 28, 1980), pp. 24-31.

    c. Organizations

        Circulo de Amigos de Albert Schweitzer
             Vico 21
             Barcelona 21, Spain
             President: Dolores Marsans Comas

    d. Miscellaneous

4988   "Das Albert-Schweitzer-Komitee beim Präsidium des Deutschen
             Roten Kreuzes der Deutschen Demokratischen Republik."
             A.I.S.L. Bulletin 11 (June 1980), pp. 10-11.

Addendum

8. Works for Youth

4989   JOHNSON, SPENCER. The Value of Dedication: The Story of
       Albert Schweitzer. San Diego, Calif.: Value Communica-
       tions, Inc. (Distributed by Oak Tree Pubns.), 1979.
       Illus. Grades k-6.

9. Drama and Films

4990   36 slides with accompanying text by Gustav Woytt in French/
       German/English about Schweitzer's life and work and the
       continuation of his work in Lambarene after his death.
       Compiled and published by the Albert Schweitzer Center
       in Deventer, Holland, and available from them.

10. Reviews

     a. Zur Diskussion über Orgelbau

4991   Ars Organi (Singen) 26:55 (1978), p. 304.

4992   Der Kirchenmusiker (Kassel) 29:5 (1978), pp. 185-86.

4993   Musik und Gottesdienst (Zurich) 32:3 (1978), p. 98.

4994   Musik und Kirche (Kassel-Wilhelmshoehe) 48:2 (1978), p. 81.

4995   Musikhandel (Bonn) 30:1 (1979), p. 44.

11. Meetings and Symposia

4996   "Albert Schweitzer Aktuell." May 5-9, 1980, Strasbourg.

4997   de B, F. "Actualité de la pensée d'Albert Schweitzer."
       Dernieres Nouvelles d'Alsace 108 (May 8, 1980), p. V.
       Reprinted in the A.I.S.L. Bulletin 11 (June 1980), p. 29.

4998   "Eine Albert-Schweitzer-Woche." Dernieres Nouvelles d'Alsace,
       May 6, 1980. Reprinted in the A.I.S.L. Bulletin 11
       (June 1980), p. 15 (German); p. 28 (French).

4999   HORST, MADELEINE. "Beginn der Informationswoche in
       Strasbourg." Dernieres Nouvelles d'Alsace, May 6, 1980.
       Reprinted in the A.I.S.L. Bulletin 11 (June 1980), p. 14
       (German); p. 27 (French).

Addendum

5000   "Ehrfurcht für dem Leben--heute." International Albert
          Schweitzer Symposium, CDU "Otto Nuschke" in
          Burgscheidungen, October 23-October 26, 1980.

5001   "Ehrfurcht vor dem Leben verlangt, der Erhaltung des
          "Friedens zu dienen.'" Neue Zeit (East Berlin),
          Oct. 27, 1980. Reprinted in the A.I.S.L. Bulletin 12
          (Dec. 1980), pp. 29-30.

5002   "Ethos Albert Schweitzers aktuell für die Aufgaben von heute."
          Neue Zeit (East Berlin), Oct. 25, 1980, pp. 1f. Reprinted
          in the A.I.S.L. Bulletin 12 (December 1980), pp. 25-26.

5003   Homenaje al doctor Albert Schweitzer. Barcelona, Sept. 20,
          1980. Exposition, addresses, concert. Program repro-
          duced in the A.I.S.L. Bulletin 12 (Dec. 1980), p. 37.

Indexes

This index is an alphabetical list of names of authors; editors; compilers; writers of prefaces, etc.; subjects; and correspondents included in the bibliography. The names of subjects which have their own particular section in the bibliography (e.g., Goethe, Bach, Jesus) are not included. Correspondents are indicated by a (c) after their names; subjects by an (s); writers of letters to the editor by (le). Reference is to entry number rather than to page number.

Bell, Elise, 4212
Belser, 4691
Belzner, Emil, 400, 3578
Bender, William, 3234
Bentué, A., 2919
Berendson, Walter A., 2403
Beresztoczy, Miklos, 2404
Berg, Arthur, 2920, 2921, 2922
Berg, C. van den, 2098
Bergel, Kurt, 46, 2743
Bergendorf, Conrad, 4658
Bergevin, D. de, 4893
Berggrav, Eivind, 1537
Bergholz, Harry, 2405, 2406
Bergius, Yngve, 401
Bergmann, Hilda, 402
Bergstraesser, Arnold, 3551,
    3560
Bernadotte, 2544(s)
Bernard, Albert, 403, 404, 1076,
    1538, 2407
Bernsdorf, Otto, 405
Berrill, Jacquelyn, 4205
Bertelson, Aage, 2408
Besch, Hans, 3359
Besgen, Achim, 2923
Bessesen, Camilla Wing, 406
Bessuges, Jacques, 1454
Bethune-Baker, J. F., 4708
Betz, Otto, 2924
Beutler, Ernst, 3536, 3592
Bharati, A., 2409
Bianquis, J., 1974, 3864(s)
Bickers, William M., 407
Bierstedt, Robert, 4564
Biezais, H., 234
Biggs, E. Power, 3452
Bikoro, Simon Obame, 2185
Billeter, Bernhard, 3453
Billy, André, 408
Binder, Theodor, 409, 4088-
    4104(s)
Birnbaum, Walter, 2346
Birneburg, Kurt, 410
Birtner, Herbert, 3454
Biskarop, Dr., 411
Bixler, Julius Seelye, 94, 412,
    413, 414, 415, 416, 417,
    2410, 2411, 2412, 2413,
    2414, 2415, 3360, 3874(c),
    3921(c), 4804

Bjerhagen, Jakob, 1539
Bjerkelund, Carl J., 2925, 2926
Björkquist, Manfred, 418
Black, M., 2927
Blackwell, David M., 4311
Blandford, Linda, 1540
Blankenburg, Walter, 3235
Bleecker, C. J., 2928, 2929
Bleeker, Cleas Jouco, 2347
Block, Jean Richard, 4572
Blomberg, Harry, 1541
Blum, Robert, 4836
Blume, Friedrich, 3361
Blyth, Jeffrey, 419
Blythe, Legette, 4105
Bock, Emil, 2416
Boegner, Marc, 420, 421, 3697,
    3857(c)
Böhmer, Günter, 1543
Böhringer, H., 422
Böhringer, Marianne, 1544
Boeke, Richard F., 2417
Bogan, Louise, 4450
Bogardus, Emory S., 423
Bohland, Gustav, 4014
Bohlin, Torsten, 4659
Boisdeffre, Pierre de, 424
Boisen, Anton T., 2930
Bois-Reymond, Lili du, 1545
Bollnow, Otto Friedrich, 2418,
    2744
Bonder, W., 4894
Bonnevie, Carl, 2931
Booth, Edwin Prince, 82, 425
Borchard, Adolphe, 426
Bordes, Charles, 3362
Borgese, Elisabeth Mann, 3557,
    3579
Borghese, G. A., 3550
Borlish, Hans, 3236
Borrel, E., 3363
Bostrom, Otto H., 4399, 4521
Bothma, J. H., 2745
Bott, Hans, 1065, 3646
Botte, D. B., 4540
Bourdier, Roland, 4312
Bourk, V. J., 2420
Bouttier, Michel, 2932
Bowman, John Wick, 2933, 2934
Bowne, Borden P., 2712(s),
    2783(s)

Cameron, James, 449, 450, 451, 1555
Campbell, L. A., 478(1e)
Campion, Charles Thomas, 203, 755, 2956
Canivez, André, 2434, 2435, 2436, 4898
Cannegieter, Hendrik Gerrit, 452, 2437
Canning, John, 663, 2079
Cannon, Gaine, 4105-4109(s)
Cannon, William R., 2957
Canto, Gilberto de Ulhôa, 453
Capelle, M. C., 4270
Carleberg, Gösta, 4267
Carley, Austin J., 4090
Carlyon, J. T., 4542
Carpeaux, Otto Maria, 454, 455, 456, 2438
Carver, W. O., 4573
Cary, Mary, 457
Casals, Pablo, 800(s), 1064(s), 1138, 3256(s), 3285(s), 3329
Case, S. J., 4601
Case, Shirley Jackson, 4713
Caspari-Rosen, Beate, 210, 2296
Cassirer, Ernst, 2439
Castan, Sam, 4106
Castedo, Leopoldo, 3366
Caswell, Wilbur L., 4693
Catchpool, Frank, 2102, 2180
Caulet, Max, 1557, 1558, 1559, 1560, 1669(s), 1751, 1816, 1948
Caulet, Mirielle, 1105(s)
Cauvin, O., 4377
Cave, Sydney, 4543
Cerfaux, L., 4602
Cesbron, Gilbert, 237, 278, 458, 459, 460, 461, 462, 4362
Chaix-Ruy, J., 463
Chakravarty, Amiya, 464, 1080, 4843, 4844
Chalufour, Marc, 3909(c)
Chamberlain, Arthur D., 2958
Chambless, Bill, 1724
Chan, Margery May, 4314
Chapelan, Maurice, 3970
Charles, R. H., 4348
Charue, A., 4544
Chassé, Charles, 238

Chatterji, Suniti Kumar, 2440
Chauchard, P., 465
Chelminski, Rudolph, 1562
Chen Wu Fu, Albert, 3624
Cherniavsky, David, 3240, 3367, 4401
Chesterman, Clement C. C., 1563(1e), 1564, 2103, 2451(1e), 3981(1e), 4900
Chevallaz, Madeline, 1081
Cho, P'ung-yŏn, 4210
Choi, Ki-sik, 466
Christaller, Helene, 239
Christen, Ernest, 240, 467
Christou, Chr., 2441
Clark, Henry, 2351, 2708, 2853, 2959, 4805
Clark, John Alden, 2410
Clarke, Maurice, 4268
Clausen, Bernard C., 468
Clifford, Peter, 2106
Coarcy, Vivaldo, 3580
Cobbaert, A.-M., 3581
Cohn, Jonas, 469
Colao, Alberto, 36
Collier, Paulette, 470
Collin, Robert, 1082
Combarieu, Jules, 4485
Comenious, Jan Amos, 390(s)
Connaught, Vere, 1083
Conrad, Otto, 2960
Coolidge, Gloria, 1565, 1566
Coomaraswamy, Ananda K., 2442
Cooper, Martin, 4402
Corredor, J.-Ma., 1064, 3329
Corson, J.-P., 1567
Cortot, Alfred, 4114
Coruh, Hakki Sinasi, 241
Coryllis, Peter, 2352
Cousins, Norman, 37, 191, 242, 472, 473, 474, 475, 476, 477, 478, 1568, 1569, 1570, 1571, 3617, 3791, 3820, 3821, 3822, 3823, 3824, 3909, 4062
Cramer, R. S., 1001
Crowther, Bosley, 4378
Crucy, Francois, 479
Cullman, Oscar, 2902(s), 2961, 2962, 3142(s)
Cummings, Judith, 4032

Fett, Harry, 3466
Fey, Harold E., 3181, 4063
Fields, Albert, 2114
Fields, Sidney, 3585
Fierzova, Olga, 249
Fina, Consol, 2469, 2470
Fink, Robert, 1632, 1633, 1634,
 2115, 2116
Firkes, Margaret, 3181
Fischer, Antoine, 4905
Fischer, Edith, 542, 1090, 1635,
 1636, 1637, 1638, 2117
Fischer, Gerhard, 25, 250, 1639,
 1640, 3625
Fischer, Max, 4667
Fischer, Paul, 1128(s)
Fischer, R., 1641
Fischer, W. F. J., 543
Flachs, Charlotte, 1147
Fleischhack, Marianne, 1016,
 1957
Fletcher, A. H. S., 544
Fletcher, John P., 545
Fletcher, Marie, 546
Fliflet, Albert Lange, 1642,
 1643
Fluck, David A., 1644
Flückiger, Felix, 2879
Flückiger, Kurt, 2471, 2472
Fockler, Herbert, 4650
Foerster, Werner, 3082
Follereau, Raoul, 547
Foote, Arthur, 548
Forbech, Ragnar, 549
Forrest, A. C., 1645
Forst de Battaglia, Otto, 4605
Franck, Cesar, 3511
Franck, Frederick, 551, 1148,
 1459, 1647, 1648, 4217,
 4271
Frankenberg, Egbert von, 3829
Franz, Günther, 2851
Free, Ann Cottrell, 2754
French, G. E., 4716
Frey, Maurice, 2118
Freyer, Paul Herbert, 251, 1019,
 1649, 1650
Frick, Heinrich, 2473, 4576
Fridrichsen, Anton, 187, 2972,
 2973, 2974
Friedemann, Käte, 2474

Friedman, Richard, 2728
Friedrich, Lotte, 1651, 1652
Friis, Børge, 252, 552, 553,
 1149, 1150, 1151, 1292, 3306,
 4218
Friton, B., 3977
Fritz, Jean, 4219
Fritzhand, Marek, 2320
Fromm, Erich, 2475
Fuchs, Emil, 554, 1059(s), 2476,
 4409, 4668
Füllemann, Emmy, 1654
Fuerstner, C., 555
Füssli, O., 1655
Fulton, Austin A., 2975
Fulton, William, 556
Funck, Bernhard, 51
Funke, Gerhard, 2755
Furr, Lester Seymour, 4317

Gaebler, Max D., 2976
Gaertner, Henryk, 253, 559, 560,
 561, 1656, 1657, 2119, 4116,
 4117, 4174
Gagnebin, Edmonde, 1658, 2120
Gall, Hughes-R., 3373
Galling, Kurt, 2986
Galván, Enrique Tierno, 562
Gardner, Hy, 563
Gardner, Nellie, 564
Gardner, Percy, 565
Gardner-Smith, P., 4412
Garlick, Phyllis, 4272, 4273
Garrard, Lancelot Austin, 2880
Garrison, W. E., 4523, 4606
Gassen, Kurt, 1057
Geffert, Heinrich, 34
Geiser, Samuel, 1070
Gell, Christopher W. M., 566,
 567, 568, 2477, 2478, 2479
Geohegan, William Davidson, 2480
George, Manfred, 571, 1152
Georgi, Dieter, 2977
Gerber, 4764
Gerhold, Jurgen, 3896(c)
Gerhold, Lotte, 41, 1660
Gerhold, Theodor, 3223(s)
Geyer, Carl, 572
Geyer, Gerhard, 4011(s)
Ghandi, 2544(s), 2565(s), 3633(s)
Gibson, Colin J., 2978

Giesecke, Hans, 2979
Gigliotti, G., 4748
Gillespie, Noel-A., 1364, 1661, 1662, 1663, 2121, 4907
Gillot, Hubert, 3299, 3303
Gilmore, Max, 734, 2577
Gilmour, Samuel MacLean, 2980
Giltay, H., 2481, 3586
Giniger, Kenneth S., 472
Girson, Rochelle, 4908
Gittleman, David, 2482, 2881
Given-Wilson, F. G., 573
Glaettli, W. E., 4220
Glaseknapp, Helmuth von, 2483, 4458
Glasson, T. Francis, 2981, 2982
Gleich, Bernd von, 3950
Gmünder, Paul, 4909
Goddard, Mickey, 85
Goddard, Scott, 3252
Godfrey, Archbishop, 3828(s)
Godman, Stanley, 574
Goebel, Robert, 2484
Goedsche, Curt Rudolf, 4220
Götting, Gerald, 21, 86, 1460, 1664, 1665, 2485, 2486, 2487, 2488, 2698, 3626, 3627, 3628, 3928(c)
Goettmann, Alphonse, 87, 575
Goetz, Bernhard, 4221
Goguel, Maurice, 2983, 2984, 2985, 4722
Goldschmid, Ladislas, 576, 2122
Goldschmidt, Helmut, 577, 1020, 1092, 1093, 1666, 1667
Goldwyn, Robert M., 2123, 2124
Goletty-Brazzaville, Max, 1668
Gollancz, Victor, 2305, 4910
Gollomb, Joseph, 255
Gomez, Ortiz Manuel, 4222
Gonggrijp, Fritz, 1669
Gonser, Sofie, 1670
Goodall, Norman, 579, 580
Goodwin, William F., 2489
Gorfinkle, Priscilla, 4175
Gossett, Pierre, 1671
Gossett, Renée, 1671
Gottstein, Werner, 581, 2125
Gounelle, André, 4439
Gouzy, René, 1672
Graafland, B., 4223

Grabowski, Tadeusz, 4846
Grabs, Rudolf, 21, 26, 30, 43, 55, 101, 152, 256, 257, 258, 259, 260, 261, 539, 582, 583, 1153, 2354, 2355, 2356, 2490, 2668, 2756, 2882, 2883, 2986, 2987, 3374, 3859, 4318, 4760, 4808, 4809
Grace, Harvey, 3504
Grässer, Erich, 3026
Graf, C., 1674
Grashey-Straub, Irmingard, 1154
Gray, Tony, 584
Greene, Jay E., 4294
Gressel, Hans, 2491
Grew, Sydney, 3375
Grierson, Mary, 3869
Groeneweg, H., 1233
Groos, Helmut, 2357, 4810
Gross, Emanuel, 2126
Grotjahn, Martin, 2492
Grüber, Heinrich, 2493
Grüber, Probst, 2988
Grützmacher, Richard H., 2494, 4524
Grunsky, Karl, 4474
Guerra, J., 2495
Guggisburg, Kurt, 1677
Guignard, J. F., 2127, 2128
Guignebert, Ch., 4630, 4723
Guimarães, Ney, 589
Gullberg, Samuel, 4216
Gunther, Joachim, 3688
Gunther, John, 1678, 4274
Gurlitt, Wilibald, 3467, 3865(c)
Gussman, Lawrence, 1679, 1680, 1681
Guthrie, Vee, 40

Haantjes, Johannes, 590
Haas, Robert, 4911
Haberman, Frederick W., 591, 3673
Habicht, H., 2129
Habran, J., 592
Hacker, W., 1682
Häckermann, Ernst, 551(1e)
Hänisch, Manfred, 4145
Härle, Wilifried, 2757
Härtle, Heinrich, 2496
Haessig, George, 1308
Hagedorn, Hermann, 262, 593, 4811

Seymour, David M., 895
Seymour, Peter, 37
Seynes, J. de, 1974
Sharp, William James, 4341
Shepherd, R. H. W., 896
Sherrod, Jane, 4249
Shigi, T., 3634
Shimazaki, T., 897
Shirer, W. Lloyd, 4084, 4085
Shyr, Yee Tseur, 1478
Siebeck, Richard, 898
Sieber, Elfriede, 1043
Siebert, Hans Eberhard, 1200, 3844
Siebert, Theodor, 1201
Sieburg, Friedrich, 2644
Siefert, Jeanette, 1976
Siegfried, André, 77, 899
Siegfried, Karla, 3125
Siegfried, Ruth, 1977
Silberman, L. H., 3126
Silberschmidt, Benno Daniel, 4683
Silcox, Claris Edwin, 900
Silkin, Jon, 4860
Silver, Ali, 1978, 1979, 1980, 2198, 4048, 4195, 4247
Simmel, Georg, 1057(s)
Simon, Charlie May (Hogue), 4248
Simon, Sacha, 901, 2645
Simonsen, Sevald, 301
Simsa, Jaroslav, 902
Singer, Kurt Deutsch, 4249
Singh, Rahul, 903
Singh, Sundar, 1891(s)
Sithole, Ndabaningi, 1981
Sitte, Fritz, 1982
Sittler, Lucien, 904, 1115
Siwa, Remy-Andre, 905
Skånland, Halfdan, 2646
Skelton, Humphrey, 906
Skillings, Everett, 164, 907, 1387, 2199, 3197
Skillings, Mildred Davis, 1202
Skinner, Conrad Arthur, 4867
Slenczka, Reinhard, 3127
Sloan, Raymond P., 1984
Smend, J., 4493
Smith, Asbury, 908, 1985
Smith, Lewis C., 2331
Smith, T. G., 2778

Smith, W. Eugene, 1986
Snethlage, Hendrik Ann Constantijn, 302, 1987
Snethlage, J. L., 4684
Snyder, Russell D., 4510, 4643
Söderblom, Anna, 1066(s)
Söderblom, Nathan, 1067(s)
Soltau, 4740
Sonner, Rudolf, 3440
Sonntag, Wolfgang, 1988, 2648
Sonu, Nam, 4250
Sørensøen, B. Esbye, 2647
Sorokin, Pitrim A., 2649
Sosland, Henry A., 476(1e)
Soubeyran, Léon, 1989
Soupault, Philippe, 909
Spann, Meno, 4297
Spear, Otto, 1044, 2370, 2650, 2651, 2652, 2653, 2779, 3128, 3635, 4768, 4829
Speiser, Peter P., 1990
Spelberg, E. D., 206, 910, 4227
Spencer, Marcus A., 4002
Spencer, Steven S., 2167
Spengler, Wilhelm, 442
Sperisen-Schwenk, V., 1991
Spicq, 4741
Spiegelberg, Herbert, 2654, 3129
Spieler, H., 3283
Spitaler, Armin, 2780, 2781
Spränger, Eduard, 2655
Spriggs, E. H., 4304
Spyropoulos, N., 303
Staats, Walter, 1993
Stade, Frans, 911, 912
Staewen, Christoph, 2202
Stahler, Robert, 913, 2656
Stalder, Elise, 1994
Stalder, Hans, 914, 1479, 1995, 2201
Stamm, Frederick K., 915
Stamm, Raymond T., 4700
Stange, Carl, 4757
Starkweather, Pauline, 4861
Stassen, Harold E., 916
Steele, Robert, 917
Steere, Douglas V., 918, 1996, 1997
Steffahn, Harald, 304, 305, 919, 1117, 1480, 1998, 1999, 2000, 3609, 4830

B.   Title Index

In this index are listed titles of all works by and about Schweitzer,
with the exception of nondescriptive titles such as "Albert
Schweitzer," "Letter from . . . ," "Dr. Schweitzer's Report,"
"Erinnerungen an Albert Schweitzer," etc. The index is divided
into two parts:

   1.   Works by Albert Schweitzer. All works by Schweitzer are
listed by the title under which they were originally published.
The titles of translations are not included. When a work by
Schweitzer serves as the subject of an article or review, the
entry number is followed by an (s). This is only true, however,
when the title indicates that the article deals with a particular
work; other articles undoubtedly include discussion of specific
works. Reference throughout the index is by entry number rather
than page number. Articles that are merely short excerpts of
Schweitzer's works have been omitted. Contents of anthologies
have been included if they include all or most of a work.

   2.   Works by others about Schweitzer. These titles are listed
alphabetically, and reference is again to entry number. Here
again only the title of the article as it originally appeared is
given; titles of translations are not indexed. In the case where
an article about Schweitzer appears in an anthology or as a chapter of a larger work, the title of the article is listed, but not
that of the book in which it appears.

   In the interest of brevity, Albert Schweitzer has been abbreviated
throughout as AS. Articles are enclosed in quotation marks; all
entries without quotation marks are monographs.

1.   Works by Schweitzer

"A propos de Bach, le Musicien-Poète," 3326
Das Abendmahl im Zusammenhang mit dem Leben Jesu. . . , 2796,
   4503-15(s)
"Das Abenteuer Mensch zu sein. Die organisierte Gedanklosigkeit im
   Jahrhundert der Angst," 2289
"Die Abhängigkeit der Individuen von der Gemeinschaften in der
   Gegenwart," 2290
Afrikanische Geschichten, 5, 1310-1330, 4430-32(s)
Afrikanische Jagdgeschichten, 25, 1306-1309, 1347
Afrikanisches Tagebuch, 1939-1945," 25, 30, 1401
"Afrikanisches Tagebuch 1944-45," 1402
AS: a Self-Portrait, 191
AS: an Anthology, 28
"AS an das Jugendsozialwerk," 3915
"AS and Israel," 3885
"AS antwortet Gustav Wyneken; kein Abschied vom Christentum," 2851

"Jesu Taufe und Versuchung," 2857
"Jesus--an imperious ruler," 2861
"Jesus der Herr," 3182
"Jesus und das Gesetz," 2857
"Jesus und der Staat," 2857
"Jesus und die Heiden," 2857
"Jesus und die Reichen," 2857
"Jesus und die Weisen," 2857
Johann Sebastian Bach. Complete Organ Works, 3322-25, 4446-48(s)
"Johann Sebastian Bachs Künstlerpersönlichkeit," 3331
"Johannes der Täufer," 2857
"Josephine der zahme Wildschwein," 48, 1365
"Journal du Dr. Schweitzer. I. L'arrivée . . . II. Premièrs
    impressions. . . . III. Réglement . . . IV. Premieres
    observations," 1406
"Juan Sebastian Bach," 3332

Kein Sonnenstrahl geht verloren. Worte ASs, 58
"Die Kraftquellen unseres geistigen Daseins," 2316
"Das Krankenhaus in Afrika. Wie mein Lebenswerk entstand," 1366
"Krieg und Völkerrecht," 20
"Kriegsausbruch 1914," 207
"Kristendommen og Verdens-Religionerne," 2862
Kritische Darstellung underschiedlicher neuerer historischer
    Abendmahlsauffassungen, 2795
Kultur and Ethik, 6, 22, 2234, 2237, 2244, 2245, 2246, 2251,
    2255-73, 2402(s), 2467(s)
Kulturphilosophie, 2233-73, 2385(s), 2402(s), 2405(s), 2408(s),
    2430(s), 2465(s), 2491(s), 2515(s), 2537(s), 2546(s), 2569(s),
    2587(s), 2608(s), 2659(s), 4656-89(s)

"Die Lage des Protestantismus in Frankreich," 2863
Lambarene, mijn Werk aan de Zoour van het Oerwoud, 59
"Lambarene, 1946-1954," 1405
"Das Lambarenespital vom Herbst 1945 bis Frühjahr 1954," 25, 1404
"Lebensernst und Lebensfreudigkeit," 2857
"Die Lebenskraft der Ideale," 2317
Die Lehre der Ehrfurcht vor dem Leben, 2697-2701
Die Lehre von der Ehrfurcht vor dem Leben: Grundtexte aus fünf
    Jahrzehnten, 2702, 4516-17(s)
"Les Gendarmes," 208
"Letter fom Lambarene," 1367
"Liberal Christianity," 2865
"Ein Lichtbild aus Lambarenes Urwaldspital," 1368
"Lieber Schuler!", 3935
"Die literarischen und theologischen Probleme der Briefe an
    Timotheus und Titus," 2866

"M. J. Erb's Symphonie für Orchester und Orgel," 3433
"Man belongs to man," 2713
"Ein Marge de l'oeuvre médicale," 1369

"Pensées sur la Croix-Rouge," 1062
"Pfingsten 1919. Thessalonischer 5.19: 'Den Geist dampfet nicht,'"
    2868
"Pharisäer und Sadducäer," 2857
"Die Philosophie und die allgemeine Bildung im neunzehnten
    Jahrhundert," 30, 2326
"Philosophie und Tierschutzbewegung," 25, 48, 2716
"Playboy interview: AS, a candid interview with Africa's enigmatic
    doctor of the body and soul," 212
"Politik ohne öffentliche Meinung im Atomzeitalter," 20
"Por uma visao unificade do munco," 2327
"Ein Predigt über das Verziehen," 3189
"Premiers mois à Lambaréné," 1385
"Das Problem des Friedens in der heitigen Welt," See "Le Problème
    de la Paix"
"Le Problème de la Paix, 6, 64, 3653-83, 4650-53(s)
"Le Problème de l'éthique dans l'évolution de la pensée humaine," 6,
    25, 2328
"Professor Ernst Münch und die Elsassische Kirche," 3217
"Der Prophet Amos. Eine Adventgestalt," 2869
"Der Protestantismus und die Theologische Wissenschaft. Vortrag,"
    2870
Die psychiatrische Beurteilung Jesu, 5, 2085-89, 2091, 2964(s),
    4690-4704(s)

"Questions of a journalist, Copenhagen, 1959," 2329

"Das Recht der Wahrhaftigkeit in der Religion," 2871
"Reform in organ building," 3434
"Die Reform unseres Orgelbaues," 3210
Reich Gottes und Christentum, 24, 2848-50, 3128(s), 4494-4502(s)
"The relations of the white and colored races," 36, 60, 1386
"Religion in modern civilization," 8, 36, 60, 2872
Die Religionsphilosophie Kants von der Kritik der reinen Vernunft
    bis zur Religion innerhalb der Grenzen der blossen Vernunft, 15,
    16, 66, 2229-32, 2575(s), 4748-57(s)
"The renunciation of thought," 2331
"Le respect de la vie et ses problèmes," 2717
"Le retour des soixante dix," 3190
"Reverence for life," 2718, 2719, 2720, 2721
Reverence for Life. An anthology of selected writings, 60
"Rosa Luxemburgs Gedanken in Gefängnis," 2333
"Die Rückkehr nach Kapernaum," 2857
"Der runde Violinbogen," 3210, 3353

"Die Sängerin Aglaja Orgeni," 3218
Schriften aus dem Nachlass, 61
"Schuldig der Unmenschlichkeit," 3618
S no kotoba to shisô: heiwa e no susume, 62
"S plays Bach organ works," 3504
"S speaks to peace workers," 3794

"Utöver mattet av sina krafter," 1066

"Valeur impérissable de la mystique Paulienne," 2874
"En Valgörare for de primitiva invanarna Ogowe's urskogar," 1067
Verfall und Wiederaufbau der Kultur, 6, 22, 56, 2223-54, 2256, 2257,
    2265, 2266, 2269
"14. Sonntag nach Trinitatis," 2873
"Viktor Hugo," 1068
"Vom alten zum neuen Jahr," 3964
"Vom Regen und schön Wetter auf dem Äquator," 25, 48, 1393
Vom Sinn des Lebens. Ein Gespräch zu fünft, 70
"Von Bachs Tod bis zur ersten Wiederaufführung der
    Matthäuspassion. . . .," 3342
"Von der Ehrfurcht vor dem Leben," 2723, 2724, 2725, 2726
"Von der Mission. Gedanken und Erfahrungen," 1394
Von Reimarus zu Wrede: eine Geschichte der Leben-Jesu Forschung,
    2807, 2984(s), 3155(s). See also Geschichte der Leben-Jesu-
    Forschung
"Von unseren Tieren in Lambarene," 1395
"Voor de gedenkdag van Hiroshima 1960," 3802
"Vorschläge zur Wiedergabe der Orgelpräludien und Orgelfugen J. S.
    Bach," 3343

Waffen des Lichts. Worte aus den Werken von AS, 71
"The war on Katanga," 1396
"Warum es so schwer ist in Paris einen guten Chor zusammensobringen,"
    3210, 3224
"Warum musste Jesus leiden," 2857
"Was ich Teenagern rate," 3965
"Was ist mir Johann Sebastian Bach und was bedeutet er für unsere
    Zeit?," 3344
Was sollen wir tun?, 3170-73, 4767-68(s)
"Der Weg des Friedens heute," 25
"Der Weg zum Frieden," 3619
"Weinachten unter Palmen," 1397
Die Weltanschauung der indischen Denker, 9, 22, 2274-88, 2443(s),
    2501(s), 2590(s), 4455-71(s)
"Wer sagen die Leute dass ich sei?," 2857
"Wer sein Leben verliert. . . .," 2338
"Wie ich Urwaldarzt wurden," 216
"Wie lang had Jesu öffentlich gewirkt?," 2857
"Wie mein Lebenswerk entstand," 1398
"Wie sind J. S. Bachs Präludien und Fugen auf unseren modernen
    Orgeln zu registrieren," 3345
Wijsheid uit het oerwoud, 72
"Der Wille zur Wahrhaftigkeit," 2339
The Wit and Wisdom of AS, 73
"With regard to experiments carried out on animals," 2727
"Word from Dr. S," 1399
"Words to live by," 2340
"Words to live by--discover your true worth," 2341

"Worte des Anstosses," 2857
"Die Wunder Jesu," 2857

"Your second job," 2342

"Zum 28. Juli, dem Todestage Bachs," 3346
"Zum hundertsten Todestage des Philosophen Kant," 3967
"Zum Totensonntag," 2875
Zur Diskussion über Orgelbau, 3426
"Zur Geschichte der Kirchenchors zu St. Wilhelm," 3210, 3225
"Zur Reform des Orgelbaues," 3210
"Zur Reorganisation unserer Kirchenbehörde," 3968 ·
"Zwei Anekdoten aus Schweden," 3969
"Der zweite Iesaja, eine Adventsgestalt," 2876
Zwischen Wasser und Urwald, 1, 21, 31, 56, 63, 1218-1279, 4564-89(s)

2. Works by Others About Schweitzer

"A Árvore de S: Personalidade e obra," 455
"À 80 ans, S retourne pour le 21e fois chez las lépreux," 1505
"A figura de semana: AS," 852
"A focca das idéias--filósofa e idolo," 2495
A Lambarenei Doktor, 1474
"À l'hôpital de Lambaréné," 1779, 2072
"A l'intention de l'hôpital Dr. AS. Regard sur le travail et sa
     discipline," 1625
"A. P. über S erbost," 324
"À propos d'un recital d'orgue du Docteur S,"
"A revêrencia pela vida," 434
"A. Schweitzer dans les pays de l'est; un militant de l'humanisme,"
     2485
"A. Schweitzer et la Chine," 4170
"A significacão de AS," 921
Abend am Ogowe, 1480, 1999
Das Abendmahlsproblem in exegetischen Werk von AS. Ein methodolische
     Forschung, 4333
Aborra Oganga, Tesekkur Ederiz Beijaz Sihirbaz, 241
About AS, 74
"Abschied von Helene Schweitzer," 1017
"Abschnitt aus dem Leben ASs," 519
"Activité du comité de Paris," 4110
"L'activité médicale de l'hôpital Schweitzer en 1970," 2139
"Les activités du village de lumière," 2108
"Der ärztliche Weg der Humanität," 4200
"Ärztliches Wirken und ärztliche Ethik. Das Beispiel ASs," 2138
"The aesthetic foundation of S's ethics," 3241
"Aesthetische Reflexionen," 2626
"L'affrontement des complexes dans l'assistance au Tiers-Monde," 1596
Africa and S, 4349
The Africa of AS, 1463, 2023

"AS als Jesus- und Paulusforscher," 3024
"AS als Kulturphilosoph," 2473, 2663
"AS als Mensch und als Ethiker," 2527
"AS als Musiker," 3228, 3273, 3295, 3365
"AS als Musiker und Bach-kenner," 3391
"AS als Mystiker," 2617, 2660
"AS als Prediger," 3204
"AS als Prediker," 1738
"AS als religiöse wegweisende Persönlichkeit," 2987
AS als religiöser Charakter und als religionswissenschaftlicher
    Denker, 4318
"AS als Theologe," 2912, 2877, 2916, 3114, 3144
"AS als tuinman," 1713
"AS am Kongo," 1740
"AS: an anachronism," 1902
"AS an der Orgel," 3456
"AS--an evaluation at ninety," 345
"AS and America," 581
"AS and contemporary Africa," 1871
"AS and eschatology," 3161
"AS and existentialism," 2612
AS and Johann von Goethe: a comparative study of their contributions
    to the field of education, 4347
"AS and philosophy," 2466
"AS and Quakerism," 3129
"AS and the art of living," 429
"AS and the ethical ecology of life," 2753
"AS and the Munch family," 759
"AS and the New Testament," 2910
"AS and the New Testament in the perspective of today," 3157
"AS annonciateur du XXIe siècle," 2388
"AS: another apostle out of season," 3090
AS. Apologie eines Apostels der Humanität, 4336
"AS arbeidt eenzaam voort aan volbracht werk," 346
"Das AS Archiv in Frankfurt ist umgezogen," 4043
"AS, Arzt eines kranken Jahrhunderts," 2458
"AS--Arzt im Urwald," 4280
"AS, Arzt und Helfer," 822
"AS as a leader," 423
"AS as a man of medicine," 2168
"AS as a physician," 2100
"AS as critic of nineteenth century ethics," 2439
"AS as man and musician. Personal memories," 610
"AS at eighty," 525, 567
"AS at home," 864
"AS. Aus seinem Leben," 867
"AS, aus seinem Leben und Werk," 273
AS baut Lambarene, 1490, 4354
AS. Begegnungen, 273
"AS. Behind the legend," 958
AS. Beiträge zu Leben und Werk, 86

AS, great Humanitarian, 4236
AS, Grösse und Grenzen, 2357
"AS, guter Geist unserer Zeit," 604
"Das A-S-Haus in Günsbach," 4048
"AS. He lives by 3 words," 428
"AS, here, denies 36 African years are 'sacrifice,'" 678
"AS. His links with the teachings of Judaism," 3050
AS, his philosophy and influence on the century, 2367
"AS, his work and his philosophy," 2672
"AS, homme de coeur et de pensée," 2669
"AS, homme, et médecin généreux," 495
"The AS Hospital," 1601, 4261
"AS: humanism based on reverence for life," 2734
"AS, humaniste," 766
"AS, humaniste alsacien et citoyen du monde," 735
"AS, humanitarian," 2199
"AS--humanitarian. A Modern Hospital interview," 1984
"AS i forbindelse med hand besök i Norge," 3707
"AS; ich kreise um Jesus," 802
"AS im afrikanischer Urwald," 2022
AS im Emmenthal: vier Jahrzehnte Zusammenarbeit zwischen dem
    Urwalddoktor von Lambarene und der Lehrerin Anna Joss in
    Kröschenbrunner, 1070
"AS im engeren Kreise der Freunde des freien Christentums in
    Frankfurt am Main," 711
"AS im Religionsunterricht der höheren Schulen," 2960
"AS im Tübinger Stift, 1959," 876
"AS in Amerika," 771
"AS in Amerika: in de Californische Zephir," 694
"AS in Berner Oberland," 3267
"AS in de familiekring," 4891
"AS in den Augen von Afrikanern," 1496
"AS in der Nachfolge Goethes," 3597
"AS in der theologischen und philosophischer Lage der Gegenwart.
    Eine Würdigung zu sein Geburtstag," 2950
"AS in der UdSSR," 4189
"AS in Europe," 353, 685, 728
"AS in Frankfurt: das Orgelkonzert," 3475
"AS in Lambarene," 2601
"AS: in music, a new approach," 3287
"AS in Polen," 4193
AS in seinem Urwaldhospital, 4356
AS in Selbstzeugnissen und Bilddokumenten, 304
"AS in Stuttgart," 4945
"AS in theologisch-philosophischen Geistesleben," 2688
"AS in Tübingen am 12. Oktober 1951," 4946
"AS in Zürich," 868
"AS is moe," 354
"AS ist auf den Wege zur Menschheitshilfe," 2392
"AS Jako teolog i folozof," 559
"AS, Jesu-Livsforskaren, musikern och lakare-missionäre," 401

"AS no sekai," 599
AS: o, el respeto por la vida, 228
"AS, o homen do século," 453
"AS och J. S. Bach," 3399
"AS och ungdommen," 4943, 4944
"AS oder die Wiedergeburt der Kultur aus dem Denken," 2600
"AS oder eine Nussschale voll Frieden," 880
"AS og de gamle Norske orgler," 3466
"AS og hans Gerning i aekvatorialafrika," 1839
"AS og kristendommen," 2899, 3112
"AS og kristendommen. Svar til Sverre Riisøen fra Johan Hovstad,"
    3003
"AS og nordsk kulturdebatt," 3004
"AS og vi tale i Oslo rådhus 5 November," 3692
"AS--on and on!," 1915
"AS on Bach's motets," 3386
"AS on the right to life and happiness," 2779
"AS. Opvatting van 90-jarige botst tegen onbesuisde nationalistische
    staat. . . .," 1498
"AS, organist, physician and thinker," 3230
"AS, organiste," 426
"AS. Patriarch oder letzter Kolonialherr," 2000
AS. Persönlichkeit und Denken, 4337
"AS, physician," 1918
"AS: physician balances the biad," 687
"AS, physician, philosopher, and musician," 1583
AS: Pionier der Menschlichkeit, 254
"AS, PLC's newest alumnus," 1600, 3996
AS, pojken som inte kunde döda, 4239
"AS- Pontifex," 1910
"Der AS Preis," 4169
"AS, Premio Nobel," 3685
"AS prissonier à Saint-Remy-de-Provence," 716
"AS. Prix Nobel de la Paix," 704, 3697
"AS professeur de théologie à Strasbourg," 602
AS: prophet of freedom, 2366
AS: Prophet of Survival, 75
"AS protesta contra las provos atómicas," 3808
"AS--Queen's favorite," 3980
"AS resuscite au XXe siècle la haute figure de Goethe," 536
"AS . . . 'Reverence for Life,'" 2228
"AS: reverence for life," 2775
"AS, saint and scholar," 979
"AS se sentiu na verdade e na justica com a manifestacão de
    solidariedade de um menino," 361
"AS--Sebastian Kneipp," 572
AS. Sein Denken und sein Weg, 79, 3058
"AS, sein Grenzmarkschicksal und Geistesringen," 2500
"AS: sein Leben und sein Denken," 463
"AS. Sein Weg und sein Werk," 402
AS, sein Werk und seine Weltanschauung, 2362

"AS und seine Beziehung zu den Gefangenen," 2073
"AS und seine Legende. Heiliger oder Snob?," 450
"AS und seine Zeitzpiegel," 2685
AS und unsere Zeit, 2349
"AS und unsere Zukunft. . . .," 2398
"AS und Wang Yang-ming," 2679
"AS und wir," 656
"AS und wir. Beiträge zu seiner Pädagogik und Unterrichtsmethodik des
    gesunden Menschenverstands," 2696
"AS und Würtemmberger Orgeln," 3485
"AS, une vie exemplaire, une philosophie vie cue," 2658
"AS: universal man," 903
"AS: unveröffentliche Briefe an Margit Jacobi," 640
AS--Urwalddoktor und Christ der Tat, 4360
AS. Verzeichnis in der D.D.R. erschienenen Literatur, 4795
"A-S-Village," 4148
"AS: Von Reimarus zu Wrede," 2984
AS voor de kinderen verteld, 4247
"AS. Vor Tids Frans af Assissi," 552
"AS vor Ulbrichts Karren," 944
"AS: Vorbild im Wirken für Frieden und Humanität," 2486
"AS vu par les pays de l'Est," 2487
"AS waarschuwt de wereld. Oproep tot bezinning," 3810
"AS, wartime's greatest hero," 757
"AS was my teacher," 3268
"AS weer in Europe," 841
AS. Weg und Werk eines Menschenfreundes, 259
AS. Wegbereiter der ethischen Erneuerung, 260
AS. Wegweiser zu Büchern von ihm und über ihm, 4796
"AS weihte sein Leben den Menschen," 810
AS. Werden und Wirken., 288
"AS. Werk und Menschheit," 2455
AS; Wesen und Bedeutung, 290
"AS--wie ich ihn sehe," 328
AS: Wirklichkeit und Auftrag, 261
AS: Wirklichkeit und Legende, 267
"Eine A-S-Woche in Prag," 4923
"AS würde Ehrenbürger der Stadt Frankfurt," 4021
AS y la crisis moral de nuestra civilización, 2353
"AS y la tragedia moral de nuestra civilización," 2452
AS y su veneración por la vida; ensayo, 2731
"Das A-S-Zentral-Archiv in Günsbach," 4039
"AS zu Besuch in Tübingen. . . .," 3994
"AS. Zu seinem sechzigsten Geburtstag," 927
"AS zum 73. Geburtstag. Ein Radiogruss nach Lambarene," 4892
"AS zum Gedächtnis," 4863
"AS. Zur Charakterologie der ethischen Persönlichkeit und der
    philosophischen Mystik," 2540
"AS--zweiter Durchgang im Hinblick auf 'Protestantismus in
    Lebenskonfigurationen,'" 2538
"Albert Schweitzerhospital in Haiti," 4054

"Ein Heldenleben, der Charakterologie ASs," 2374
"Helene, ASs Gefährtin," 1021
"Helene Bresslau," 1050
"Helene Bresslau: Fürsorgarbeit in Strassburg," 1044
"Helene Bresslau-S," 1041
"Hélène Marianne Bresslau Schweitzer," 1022
"Helene S: am liebsten Inkognite," 1036
"Hélène S. Die Frau eines grossen Mannes," 1032, 1043
Helene S: Stationen ihres Lebens, 1016
"Helene S zum Gedächtnis," 1035
"Ein helles Band und ein Sonntag," 1518
"Hemma in Elsass. Minnen fran Strassburg och Gunsbach. . . .," 4924
"Herinnering aan Lambarene," 2074
"L'heritier de Jean-Sébastien. Une interview de Marcel Dupré," 3373
"Das hermeneutische in der Protestantischen Theologie der Gegenwart,"
    2953
Heroes of the Twentieth Century, 533
"Un héros d'humanité: AS," 383
"Das Herz befiehlt es," 1651
"Het Albertschweitzerhuis te Amsterdam," 4029
"Het Christendom en de wereldgodsdiensten," 2939
"Het Geheim van Ss Eenvoud," 972
"Het is mijn schuld," 633
"Het ordeel van een Doktor over het Ziekenhuis, en het werk in
    Lambarene," 2174
"Het problem: S," 2508
"Het spreekour van de kinderarts in Lambarene," 2156
"Het was een Passmorgen in Lambarene," 1736
"Het wetenschappelijk werk van AS. Culturphilosophie," 2430
"Het wetenschappelijk werk van AS. De betekenis van Paulus' visie
    op het evangelie," 2946
"Het wetenschappelijk werk van AS. Het christendom temidden der
    wereldgodsdiensten," 2947
"Heute Vortrag Prof. S. über der geschichtliche und geistige Jesus,"
    2995
"Die heutige Entwicklung der liberalen Theologie," 3153
"Hexenkessel Westafrika--im höchster Lebensgefahr," 1714
"Hier werkt S," 2066
Hikari to ai no Senshi, 313
"Hilaires Huhn," 1535
"Hilfe im Geist ASs. . . .," 4093
"Hiroshima 1945 and ASs Mahnung an die Welt," 3833
"His brother's keeper," 406
"His Gabon hospital is busy and growing," 1727
"His lasting contribution to the world of music," 3234
"Histoire philatélique d'AS," 4005
"The historical Jesus, an approach of faith?," 2967
The historical Jesus: S's quest and ours after fifty years, 2880
"The historical Jesus vs modern theology; ethics and eschatology,"
    2997
"History of the Friends of AS," 4124

"Hve kan met rette kalles Kristan?," 2931

"'I am the life that wills to live,' the inner meaning of AS's
    reverence for life," 2768
"I have found a living saint," 812
"I have one wish," 3831
"I know ten true Christians," 915
"I Lambarenes Urskovshospital," 2136
"I live at the S hospital," 4303
"I livets of Fredens tjeneste--AS: vi bygger opp," 2646
"I visited AS in Africa," 1699
"I worked for Dr. AS," 2064
"Die Ibo-Kinder in Lambarene und ihre Rückkehr nach Nigeria," 1958
"Ich besuchte des Menschenfreund AS," 1715
"'Ich bin den Wienern so dankbar.' Gespräch mit dem Nobelpreisträger
    Dr. AS," 594
"'Ich fahre nach Lambarene.' Die Milliardärin Olga Deterding
    arbeitet im Urwald-Hospital von AS," 1087
"Ich komme von AS," 1716
"The iconography of AS," 4935
"The idea of reverence for life and the problems of health care,
    with special emphasis on those of the developing world," 2769
"Ideal persönlichen Menschentums," 2630
"Der Idealismus," 2655
Igy élt AS, 226
Ik kom u helpen Doktor, 4258
"Ik sprak met doktor S," 2016
"Il est minuit, Docteur S," 4362, 4377(s), 4380(s), 4382(s),
    4384(s), 4392(s)
Il medico della giungla, 229
Ils vivent pour le paix, 3949
"Im A-S-Spital in Lambarene, 28. Juni bis 12. Juli 1958," 1586
"Im Dienst am Menschen," 609
"Im Dienste des 'Haussknechts Gottes,'" 1097
"Im dienstendes Friedens für alle Menschen. AS und unsere Zeit,"
    936
"Im Einbaum zu AS," 1786
"Im Geiste ASs," 1796
"Im Geiste wahren Menschentums," 2560
"Im Haus über der Strasse nach Münster," 1146
"Im Lande ASs," 1717
Im Lande ASs, ein Besuch in Lambarene, 1461
"Im Lichtbereich der Ethik AS," 2352
"Im Operationssaal von Lambarene," 2115
"Im Schussfeld der Reporter," 1641
"Im Urwaldspital," 1806
Im Urwaldspital von Lambarene, 4238
"Une image d'AS," 459
"Images et souvenirs de Lambarene," 1844
Immediate intuition in the new rationalism of AS, 4338
"The impasse of AS," 2583

"Living with a verity," 702
The living work of AS, 4364
Le Livre de la vie, 3940
"Die Lockungen der Welt. Olga Deterding verliess AS," 1092
"Lone doctor of Lambarene: AS's great work in Africa," 2013
"Looking back at S," 2227
"The Lord's Prayer--before and after S," 3089

"M. AS reçoit le Prix de la Paix fondé par l'Association des éditeurs
    allemande," 3649
M. et Mme. F. Dinner-Obrist ou 34 ans au service de Lambarene," 1101
"Ma recontre musicale avec le Docteur S," 3279
"Ma visite à Lambarene," 1829
"Die Macht des Aberglaubens," 2082
"Madame AS," 1024
"Madame S," 1033, 1034
"Madame S reports," 1956
"Människan AS. Minnen och intryck," 912
"Mästaren och hans Lärjunge," 3039
"Magyarországról jöttünk, Dr. S," 1812
"Malignancies at Lambaréné," 2106
"Malignancies at the hospital of Doctor AS, Lambarene, Gabon,
    1950-1965," 2105
Man discovers God, 518
"The man in the small back room," 976
"Man of compassion: a portrait of AS," 856
"A man of mercy," 1986
"Man of our century," 1784
"De man uit Lambarene: AS verjaart," 643
"'Man van Lambarene' komt orgels bespelen. AS besoekt Amerika," 924
"The manifold life of AS," 705
"Mann aus dem Urwald," 571
"Der Mann, der sich selbst gab," 801
"Ein Mann erklärt einer Fliege den Krieg. . . .," 4855
Der Mann in der Brandung, 3945
"Ein Manuskript 'AS' aus dem Jahr 1930," 2680
"Masern im Urwald Zentralafrikas. Aus dem Urwaldhospital ASs,
    Lambarene," 2159
"A master in darkest Africa," 715
"Matchet's Diary," 1813
"Max Caulet beheert ASs Erfenis: 'Lambarene is neiuw leven
    begonnen,'" 1669
"Max Caulet über seine Spitalsorgen," 1560
"The meaning and the future of ASs thought and work," 764
"The meaning of ASs life to medicine," 2112
"The measure of a man," 4284
"Med AS på Konsert- och Foredragarese," 526
"Le médecin AS," 2173
"Medecine e música: AS," 2099
"Medical care in developing countries, the contribution of Dr. AS,"
    2103

"Der Musiker AS. Ein Wort zu seinem 75. Geburtstag am 14. Januar,"
    3289
"Musterchen," 1994
"Muzykant v 84 goda," 648
"My father AS," 445, 732, 881
My friend in Africa, 4217
My monkey friends, 4245
"My mother: a remembrance," 1027
"My two years with AS," 1724
"My visit to Lambarene," 2070
"My visit with AS," 1587, 1165
"Mysticism and ethics: an examination of Radhakrishnan's reply to
    S's critique of Indian thought," 2489
"Mysticism and ethics in Hindu thought," 9, 2607
"Mysticism and ethics: Radhakrishnan and S," 2514
Mystiek en ethiek in S's geest; een anthropologische studie," 2358
"Mystik der Ehrfurcht vor dem Leben," 2784
"La mystique de l'apôtre Paul, rétrospective et prospective," 2392
"La mystique paulienne d'après AS," 2985
"The 'mythical Christ' and the 'historical' Jesus: a critical
    study," 3064
"Ein Mythos stirbt. Missbrauchter AS," 2426

Naar het land van Brazza en AS, 1489
"Nachrichten von AS," 1551, 1852
"Nachruf für Emma Haussknecht mit den Ansprachen von Pfarrer Mary,"
    1107
"Nachtgang in Lambarene," 1853
"Nachwort des Herausgebers--AS als Prediger," 3206
"Die Nähe der Urwaldes," 1725
"Ñagra intryck av AS," 645
Nam ül wihae sanun saram, 4250
"Natur, Mensch und Tier," 2179
"The natural and the spiritual," 2643
"Ein Nederlander in de Afrikaanse rimboe," 1718
"Nederlands AS Archief," 4050
"Negerspital 'Lambarene.' Mit AS in Afrikanischen Urwald," 1777
"Der neue Arzt von Lambarene," 1108
"Die neue Diskussion über die Frage nach dem historischen Jesus,"
    3068
"Neue Ehrung ASs. Verleihung des Goethepreises der Stadt Frankfurt
    A.M.," 3601
"Neue Helferinnen," 1109
Der neuen Mensch in einer neuen Welt, 2371
"Neue Verhältnisse--neue Aufgaben," 2018
"Ein neuer Weg," 2505
"Neues aus dem Urwaldspital von Lambarene," 1538
"Neues Entappe für das Urwaldspital ASs. . . .," 1944
"Ein neues Lambarene," 1846
"Neues von AS," 1528
"Das neueste von AS," 1552

"A new gallery of Karsh," 4920
"A new liberal theology: Fritz Buri of Basel," 2900
"Een nieuw Lambarene," 1847
"Nieuwbouw in Ss stijl," 1781
"De nieuwe cultuur," 2481
Ningen S, 281
"Nobel Prize to Dr. S," 3700
"Nobelman S," 3701
"De Nobelprijs toegekend," 3702
"Nobelpristagerin AS," 3703
"Noble erindringer om AS," 3233
"Noch ein Besuch bei AS," 1197
"A note on AS," 1008
"Notes sur la miséricorde," 420
"Notice, bio-bibliographique d'AS," 774
"Notre plus illustré voyageur de 3e classe, le docteur AS," 4911
"Nous avons besoin de lui," 1702
"Noveau cas de bilharzoise intestinale à schistosomo haematobium
    observé au Gabon," 2175
"Le noveau laboratoire d'analyses médicales," 2110
"Nouvelles confessions de Lambaréné," 1598
"Nouvelles de Paunat," 4157
"Nouvelles du Village AS, Paunat (Dordogne)," 4154, 4158
"Now it's AS, O.M., one of world's 24," 3984
"N'Touga, ein indelkind im Spital zu Lambarene," 1940
"Nursing at Lambarene," 2145

"O apóstolo das selvas," 2029
"O desengano do Dr. S," 713
"O Doutor S e o Brasil," 4807
"Objektive und subjektive Motivation--Bemerkungen zu Ss Ethik," 2578
"Obra de S--inspira construcão de hospital em Plena Selva Peruana,"
    4103
"Octogenarians--three abundant lives--Kreisler, Monteux, S," 779
"Odwie w Grunsbach," 2664
"L'oeuvre humanitaire et la pensée humaniste d'AS," 2462
"L'oeuvre inconnue d'AS," 370
"Une oeuvre médicale au Congo," 1974
L'oeuvre vivant du AS, 4365
Offrande au Docteur S, 4836
"Oganga: Capitulo XI, el viejo doctor," 1585
"Oganga. Den store medisinmannen," 4205
"Der Ogagna kommt zurück," 4842
"Oganga, the forest doctor," 4295
Oganga, wielki czarodziej, 1458
"Olga Deterding, die Milliarden-Erbin der 'Shell' als
    Krankenpflegerin bei Dr. AS," 1118
"Olga Deterdings Aufenhalt in Lambarene," 1127
Omoide no Rambarene, 1484
"On fait ce qu'on pout," 1946
"On the hill of Adalinanongo," 2061

"Rückkehr nach Lambarene," 2027
"Ein Rufer zu wahren Menschentum. Begegnung mit AS in seinem
    Briefen," 582
"'Rundbriefe' aus dem Spital," 1620
"Rundbriefe für den Freundeskreis von AS," 4128
"Rzecz o Albercie Schweitzerze," 4846

"Die säkulare Bedeutung Ss für die Leben-Jesu-Forschung," 3063
Safari of Discovery: the universe of AS, 289
"The saga of S's Bach edition," 3376
"A sage's reception," 3988
"Saiken no S bunken," 4831
"Saiken no S hakase," 950
"The saint of the forest," 906
"Saint of our century," 891
"Salute to S," 965
"Der Samariter, AS," 938
"Le scandale de Lambaréné," 1935
"Scenes in a great life," 4366
"Schöpferische Tat des Künstlers," 4930
"The scholar's dilemma," 2629
"Schonet die alten Orgeln!," 3450
"Die Schulschwester, Edmonde Gagnebin, berichtet," 1658
Schweitzer, 272
S, a biography, 275
"S à Gunsbach," 3281
"S admirer seeks aid for hospital in Peruvian jungle," 4089
The S Album, 224
"S als Arzt und Chirurg," 2165
"S als nieuwtestamenticus," 3124
"S and Bach," 3375, 4367
"S and humanity," 2114
"S and Indian philosophy," 2598
"S and Lambarene," 1508
"S and Marshall Nobel Prizemen," 3706
"S and Radhakrishnan; a comparison," 2479
"S and religious freedom," 3121
"S and the new Africa," 1647
"S as missionary," 1834
"S at Aspen," 627
"S at eighty," 624
"S at Günsbach," 825
"S at 77--no isms but humanism," 487
"S at the palace," 3981
"S awaits the great in a tea shop," 419
"S awards," 4204
"S calls U.S. aid spiritual. . . .," 3610
"S centennial today: a legacy eclipsed?," 857
"S Centers," 4047
"S cet inconnu," 966
"S convocation at Aspen," 4776

"S to gendai," 897
"S to visit America this summer," 888
"S über Bachs Ornamentik," 3378
"S und die Mühlhäuser Bachorgel," 3492
"S und Tolstoi," 2599
"S unit in Gabon begins $6-million hospital on founder's centennial,"
    1729
"S visits Sweden," 889
"S vs. Stalin," 916
"S wa indaina Christian de aru ka?," 3077
"S's aesthetics: an interpretation of Bach," 3411
"S's animal friends," 1731
"S's Bach: a study in symbols," 3410
"Ss Bachkonzert," 3495
"S's birthday at Lambarene," 1819
"S's birthplace revisited," 969
"Ss Blick auf die asiatischen Weltreligionen," 2929
"Ss bog om Bach," 3395
"S's character pervades hospital he left behind," 1697
"S's confessio fidei," 3123
"S's contribution to medicine," 2166
"S's debt to Goethe," 3604
"Ss eschatologische visie op het neiuwe Testament," 3140
"S's ethic," 2580
"Ss etikk og hans teologi," 3034
"S's extension of ethics to all life," 2751
"S's hospital imperiled by finances," 1964
"S's impact on philosophy: a positive existentialism," 2613
"S's influence: blessing or bane?," 2982
"S's Jesus: a psychology of the heroic will," 3074
"S's Jesus of history," 2980
"S's jungle hospital," 1566
"Ss kulturfilosofi," 2546
"S's moral theories," 2445
"S's new 'halt tests' call," 3843
"S's outlook on history," 2510
"S's philosophy of culture," 2499
"S's practical moral judgments and his ethical theory," 2632
"Ss preeken voor de negers," 1965
"S's radical Christianity and its impact today," 3009
"S's reverence for life," 490, 2785
"Ss revolutionäres Christentum. . . .," 3006
"Ss theologisches Erbe," 2977
"S's trial," 1966
"Ss Uhr geht anders," 1723
"Ss und unsere Sorge um den Frieden," 3635
"Ss Verdienst um die wahre Orgel," 3472
"S's wife honored with him," 1042
"The Schweitzerian Heresy," 3413
"Schweitzerverering?," 991
"Scientists in the news--AS," 3990

"Some corrections," 3449
"Some facts and figures," 2200
"Some sort of help to animals. . . .," 2754
"Sonntagsgaste aus aller Herren Länder bei Dr. AS," 404
"The sound of bells in a Christian country--in quest of the histor-
     ical S," 1631
"A South African visits Lambarene," 1517
"En souvenir de Adele Woytt-Schweitzer," 1110
"Souvenirs d'un musicien," 3277
"Souvenirs d'une infirmière," 2225
"Souvenirs sur AS," 2424
"Spabio, heroi ou santo?," 629
"Een spannende dag in Lambarene," 1874
"Spannung und Leben in Ss Persönlichkeit," 614
"A spark leaps the seas," 4078
"De sphinx van Lambarene," 1992
"La spiritualité d'AS," 3055
"Das Spital arbeitet weiter," 1612
"'Das Spital für uns noch einmal gebaut.' Ein Rückblick auf die
     Ära Kik," 1117
"Das Spital lebt weiter," 1849
"Spital setzt Tätigkeit fort," 1640
"Das Spital war ihr Leben--Nachruf für Mathilde Kottman," 1116
"Spørsmal til redaktør A. Berg," 3107
"Un stage médical à Lambaréné en été 1965," 2162
"Stamps--sale on the high seas--fight on leprosy," 4008
"Stamps--U.N. World Federation, Schweitzer," 4009
"Stand der Zahnärztliche Projekte zum 1.8.1971," 2133
"Stand und Fortführung der Arbeit an ASs philosophischem und
     theologischen Nachlass," 4835
"States' $50,000 stipend cut upsets 'superteachers,'" 4033
"The stature of a man," 4086
"Steht ASs Urwald-Hospital in Lambarene in einer Krise?," 1797
"Stimme des Gewissens," 2463
"Stimme des Weltgewissens. AS: Samariter der Barmherzigkeit," 3840
Den store doktorn, AS, 1487
The story of AS, 4212, 4231
"The strange case of Dives and Lazarus," 1564
"Strasbourg recollection of AS," 765
"Strassburg Speichergasse 2. Begegnung und Gespräch mit AS," 1132
"Strassburg und die Bach-Schütz-Pflege. . . .," 3387
"Streiter für Humanität und Frieden," 3627
"Strukturwandlungen der menschlichen Person: ein Vergleich der
     Anfassungen J. H. Pestalozzis und ASs," 2595
"Studies in S," 2381
A study of AS's precept of reverence for life with some implications
     for education, 4309
A study of AS's theory of religious experience: an analysis of the
     basic categories of a theory of religious experience of AS, 4314
"Eine Stunde mit AS," 1140

"La suite de la Philosophie de la Civilisation dans les Manuscrits
    Posthumes d'AS," 2587
"Sull'etica di AS," 2447
"Sundar Singh und AS. Zwei Missionare und zwei Missionsprogramme,"
    1891
"Sur AS," 460
"Surgery at the AS Hospital, Lambarene," 2124
"Surgery in the jungle," 2209
"Survey of cardio-vascular disease among Africans in the vicinity of
    the AS Hospital in 1960," 2167
Svaittsar: oru visvamanavante caritram, 316
"Svar til pastor Sverre Riisøen fra Johan Hovstad," 3005
"Svar til Ragnar Kvam," 3099
"Svedocanstva o Schweitzeru," 3265
"Svenska förbundet för stod till ASs Verksamhet," 4129
"Sverre Riisøens manglende kjennskap til Ss livssyn," 3035
"Sverre Riisøens retrett," 3036
"Sweet smell of success in air at S's jungle hospital," 1803
"Symbol der helfenden Liebe--das Beispiel ASs," 2476
"Szpital Alberta Schweitzera w Lambaréné," 1657

De taak van den arts in verband met de person en het werk van AS,
    2093
"Ein Tag im Urwaldspital," 1091
"Tage mit AS," 1744
"Taisen-chū no S," 770
"Takk til professor dr. med. G. Langfeldt," 3100
Täktar Alpart Svaitsar, 270
"Talk with AS," 431, 1141
"Taten, die das Wort authentisch Machen," 2911
The teaching of Jesus in Christian ethical theory as interpreted by
    New Testament scholarship, 4320
"Tecknik im Urwaldspital," 1525
"Teilhard, le miséricordieux," 465
"Tensions in S's ethics," 2420
"A tentative bibliography of AS," 4826
Terugblik op ASs orgelconcerten in Nederland, 3436
"Testament z Lambarene," 2014
"Das Thema der 'Kunst der Fuge,'" 3382
"Theodor Binder: Peru's AS," 4090
"Der Theologe, Musiker Arzt und Philosophe AS," 667
"La théologie et la musique d'AS," 3047
"Le théologien," 3048
They thought he was mad, 4226, 4276
"The thirteenth apostle," 3585
"The thirteenth disciple," 804
"This I believe," 2970
The thoughts of AS, 85
"Thoughts on revisiting Gunsbach," 520
"Three days with S at Lambarene," 1683
The three worlds of AS, 4240, 4294

"Um die Zukunft von Lambarene," 1701
"Uma vida dedicada ao próximo," 698
"Umweltsethik an der Wurzel: Fazit der ökumenischen Lenzburger
     Abende über AS," 2472
"Der unbekannte AS," 653
"Und Jesus kam niche wieder. . . .," 3120
An Understanding of AS, 274
"Unermüdlicher 'Urwalddoktor,'" 2021
"Unerwartete Begegnung im Elsass," 1201
"Unerwartete Begegnung in Günsbach," 1178
"Die Unitarier und Dr. AS," 3139
"Das Universale, das Menschliche, das Christliche im Wesen ASs," 913
"Ein universaler Denker und ganzer Mensch. AS," 2494
"Ein Universalgenie," 2530
"Universalgenies," 998
Die universalmenschen Goethe und S. Parallelen zwischen Weimar und
     Lambarene, 3574
"L'universel, l'humain, le chrétien chez AS," 2656
"Die universelle Erweiterung der Ethik im Denken ASs," 2737
"Die universelle Ethik der Ehrfurcht vor dem Leben," 2738
"Universität Tübingen zur Verleihung des Dr. theol. h.c.," 4003
"University hails S at 81," 4806
"The University of Copenhagen has awarded the Sonning Peace
     Prize. . . .," 3992
Unser grosser Freund, AS, 4254
"Unser Tag--Lambarene 1951," 1854
"Unter den Sonnenschirmbaum von Lambarene," 2196
"An unusual choice," 3705
"Unverfügarkeit des Lebens oder Freiheit zum Tode: Euthanasie als
     ethisches Problem," 2757
"Unvergessliches Erlebnis. Ein Tag bei AS," 1217
"Urchristentum und Religionsgeschichte," 2943
Der Ursprung des christlichen Dogmas; eine Auseinandersetzung mit
     AS und Martin Werner, 2879
"Ursprung und Wirking der Ehrfurcht vor dem Leben," 2742
"Urwald Arzt studiert Atome. Zwei Forscher besuchte AS," 3839
Der Urwalddoktor, 4253
Der Urwalddoktor AS, 4256, 4306
"Der Urwalddoktor. Das Leben des grossen Menschenfreundes AS," 722
"Der Urwalddoktor kehrt zurück," 1573
"Urwalddoktor von Lambarene--AS schreibt die Geschichte seines
     Lebens," 838
"Das Urwald-Hospital AS in Lambarene--ein Modelle für Hospitäler in
     Entwicklungsländer," 1880
"Das Urwaldspital von AS in Lambarene," 2084
"Urwaldtagebuch (9. April 1950)," 1990

Van en over AS; persoonlijkheid en humor, 319
"En vår hos AS," 1643
"Dem Vater der Bachpflege. Grusswort zum 80. Geburtstag von AS,"
     3401

"Vördnad for livet," 2794
"Voici le flambeau à Lambaréné et le docteur S," 2041
"Volgens dominee et wassenaar. Kritiek op S neit geheel terecht,"
    2048
"Vom alten zum neuen Spital in Lambarene," 2019
"Vom Saley: verzellt in Baseltitsch," 1838
"Vom Sinn des Lebens. Ein Gespräch aus Werk und Leben ASs gestaltet
    von Peter Lotar," 2558
"Vom urchristlichen Abendmahl," 3042
"Von ärztlichen Verrichtungen," 2193
"Von Andende nach adålinanongo. Aus Briefen," 1529
"Von der Selbstbedrohung des heutigen Menschen," 2639
"Von einem Besuch bei AS," 1212, 1213
"Von tragenden Grund. AS als Theolog und Philosoph," 2460
"Vorrang der Ethik. ASs Kulturphilosophie," 2566
"Ein Vortrag ASs in Zürich," 2624
"Vortrag über AS in Düsseldorf. 'AS, die geistige Position eines
    undogmatischen Christen unserer Tage,'" 3021
"Vortrag von Frl. Haussknecht im Missionskranz in Speyer. . . .,"
    1696
"Un voyage de Docteur AS en Grand-Bretagne," 4900
"Le vrai visage d'AS," 541
"Vue d' ensemble," 3049, 3272
Vzpominky na Dr. Alberta Schweitzera a na Lambaréné: 1875-1975, 266

"Waarheen gaat gij, mensheid? ASs Werk der naastenleifde," 973
"Waarheid en leugen over 'Lambarene,'" 2051
"Das wachsende Liebeswerk ASs," 2042
"Die Wahrhaftigkeit als Grundmotive in ASs Leben und Denken," 2554
"Die Wahrheit über Lambarene," 1549
"Waiting for Dr. S," 4909
"Eine Wallfahrt zu AS," 1174
"Walter Munz, M.D. medical director, AS Hospital, Lambarene," 1121
"War Jesus eschatologisch orientiert?," 3013
"Warum nach Afrika?," 1577
"Was hat AS uns heute zu sagen," 411
"Was hat uns AS für das Schwesternleben zu sagen," 2603
"Was ist mit AS los?," 1780
"Was ist uns S?," 2522
"Was S a mystic after all," 3010
"Was sollen wir heute tun?," 3634
"Was uns AS bedeutet," 2488
"Was uns nottut. Die Kultur setzt freie voraus. AS," 2682
"Was wird aus Lambarene," 1719
"The way to world peace," 3624
"We participate in a modern miracle," 4080
"We visited AS," 1166
"Weekend à Lambarene," 1567
"Der Weg zum Frieden ist ASs 'elementare Religion,'" 3636
"Der Weg zur Regeneration der Kultur," 2683
"Wegbereiter der Friedensgesinnung," 3628

"With S in Africa," 1721, 1957
"With S in Europe," 719
"With S in Lambarene," 1722
"With S in Lambarene. Noel Gillespie's letters from Africa," 1663
"With S in Oslo," 649
"Wolken übern Urwaldkrankenhaus. Lambarenes Zukunft is ungewiss-
    Sorgen um Ss Werk," 1572
"The women around Dr. S," 1083
De Wonderdokter van Lambarene, 1455
The world of AS. A book of photographs, 225
"A world-wide miracle!," 378
"Wort, Welt, und Gemeinde," 2979
"Wozu grösse Manner," 2644
"Wurzel für Ss Handeln," 2450
"Wurzel und Triebe," 4184, 4185
"Wurzel und Triebe. Bericht der Kommission für das geistige Werk,
    1972-73," 4186

"The youth of Thekla," 1928
"Youth should be served," 2593
"Your radiation diary," 3835

"Zeep voor Lambarene," 2081
"Zeitgemässe Theologie," 3119
"Zentralarchiv in Gunsbach," 4053
"Ein Zeugnis christlicher Humanität. ASs Predigt zum Gedächtnis der
    Toten des ersten Weltkrieges. . . .," 3209
"Zeugnis und Begegnung," 1153
"Ziekenhuis Dr. S. 75gebouwen met 1000 mensen--moderner en wat
    uitgebried," 2052
"Ein Zimmerman für Lambarene," 1530
"A zinc-lined piano," 4292
"Zu ASs Begegnung mit Goethe," 3599
"Zu Bachs Weihachts Oratorium. Teil 1 bis 3," 3416
"Zu Besuch bei Helene S-Bresslau in Königsfeld im Schwarzwald," 1038
"Zu Besuch in Lambarene," 1950
"Zu Ehren von AS," 3000
Zu Gast in Lambarene. Begegnung mit AS, 1460
"Die Zukunft der Ethik ASs," 2773
"Zukunft Lambarene," 1533
"Die Zukunft von Lambarene," 1532
"Zum 80. Geburtstag ASs," 3298
"Zum Boycott ASs," 3138
"Zum 50. Jahrestag der Gründung der Urwaldspitals in
    Lambarene. . . .," 4019
"Zum Gedächtnis an Helene S-Bresslau," 1039
"Zum Gedenken an Dr. René Kopp," 1090
"Zum Gedenken an Ulrich Neuenschwander," 1098
"Zum Gedenken: Dr. Paul Fischer--ein Freund ASs," 1128
"Zum Hinschied von Helene S-Bresslau," 1030
"Zum Persönlichkeitsbild ASs," 920